invitation to human communication

Cindy L. Griffin
Colorado State University

Jennifer Emerling Bone
Colorado State University

D1604684

WADSWORTH
CENGAGE Learning

Australia • Brazil • Japan • Korea • Mexico • Singapore • Spain • United Kingdom • United States

WADSWORTH
CENGAGE Learning

Invitation to Human Communication
Cindy L. Griffin, Jennifer Emerling Bone

Editor in Chief: Lyn Uhl

Publisher: Monica Eckman

Senior Development Editor:
Kathy Sands-Boehmer

Editorial Assistant: Colin Solan

Media Editor: Jessica Badiner

National Geographic Learning Associate
Manager: Leila Hishmeh

Senior Content Project Manager:
Michael Lepera

Senior Art Director: Linda May

Rights Acquisition Specialist:
Alexandra Ricciardi

Manufacturing Planner: Doug Bertke

Executive Brand Manager: Ben Rivera

Senior Market Development Manager:
Kara Kindstrom

Marketing Communications Manager:
Linda Yip

Marketing Coordinator: Brittany Blais

Production Service/Compositor:
MPS Limited

Text Designer: Joel Sadagursky

Cover Designer: Bruce Bond

Cover Image: ©OJO Images

For product information and technology assistance, contact us at
Cengage Learning Customer & Sales Support, 1-800-354-9706

For permission to use material from this text or product, submit all requests online at **www.cengage.com/permissions**
Further permissions questions can be emailed to
permissionrequest@cengage.com

Library of Congress Control Number: 2012945042

ISBN-13: 978-0-495-50196-1
ISBN-10: 0-495-50196-4

Wadsworth
20 Channel Center Street
Boston, MA 02210
USA

Cengage Learning is a leading provider of customized learning solutions with office locations around the globe, including Singapore, the United Kingdom, Australia, Mexico, Brazil, and Japan. Locate your local office at **international.cengage.com/region**

Cengage Learning products are represented in Canada by Nelson Education, Ltd.

For your course and learning solutions, visit **www.cengage.com**

Purchase any of our products at your local college store or at our preferred online store **www.cengagebrain.com**

Instructors: Please visit **login.cengage.com** and log in to access instructor-specific resources.

Printed in Canada
2 3 4 5 6 7 16 15 14 13

CONTENTS

4 | LANGUAGE 74

5 | LISTENING 98

PART II: INTERPERSONAL COMMUNICATION

6 | UNDERSTANDING INTERPERSONAL COMMUNICATION 118

7 | IMPROVING INTERPERSONAL COMMUNICATION AND RELATIONSHIPS 144

11 | GATHERING AND DEVELOPING SUPPORTING MATERIALS 262

12 | DELIVERING YOUR SPEECH 296

13 | INFORMATIVE SPEAKING 328

14 PERSUASIVE SPEAKING 352

15 INVITATIONAL SPEAKING 384

Acknowledgments

Invitation to Human Communication is the result of not only our own collaboration as coauthors but also the generous support, assistance, and guidance from a number of individuals. We wish to extend our sincere and heartfelt thanks to Monica Eckman, Publisher, who not only supported this project from its inception but had the vision to see the positive and productive link between *Invitation to Human Communication* and the National Geographic Society and the courage to help us develop and nurture that link. Many thanks go to Kathy Sands-Boehmer, senior development editor, for her work, patience, and flexibility as we negotiated this innovative partnership and brought the book to its first edition. To Lyn Uhl, senior publisher; Rebekah Matthews, assistant editor; Colin Solan; editorial assistant; Jessica Badiner, media editor; Kara Kindstrom, senior market development manager; Ben Rivera, executive brand manager; Michael Lepera, senior content project manager; Linda May, senior art director; Bruce Bond, design director; Edward Dionne, project manager; Anne Greenberg; and S. M. Summerlight, copy editor—we thank you from the bottom of our hearts for all the work you have done to support, develop, and market this fundamentals of communication book.

Many thanks are also in order to all the reviewers of this text: Shae Adkins, Lone Star College, North Harris; Todd Allen, Geneva College; Pete Bicak, Rockhurst College; John O. Burtis, University of Northern Iowa; Diane Carter, University of Idaho; Kathryn Coker, St. Charles Community College; Angela Gibson, Shelton State Community College; Cynthia Gordon, Syracuse University; Brent Kice, Frostburg State University; Darren Linvill, Clemson University; Yvette Lujan, Miami Dade College; Tami Olds, Northern Virginia Community College, Sandra Rath, Arizona State University; Adam Roth, University of Rhode Island; David K. Scott, Northeastern State University; Glynis Strause, Coastal Bend College; and Lisa Waite, Kent State University. We also wish to thank Kristin Slattery, Special Instructor at Colorado State University, for her invaluable research assistance in the early stages of this project; and Dr. Andy Merolla, now at Baldwin Wallace University, our "go-to expert" for random questions, source clarifications, and general great humor during the final stages of our writing.

To our National Geographic explorers and emerging explorers, and to those at National Geographic who saw the powerful link between the work that National Geographic does and communication principles and practices, we would like to extend our sincerest "Thank you." Thank you for reaching out to us; for sharing your innovative images, ideas, and practices with us; and for trusting us to showcase the important role communication plays in "inspiring people to care about the planet." The National Geographic stories told throughout the book, and the tips shared with our readers, illustrate the amazing potential each person has, working in teams and alone, to make a positive difference. We sincerely appreciate the time National Geographic explorers and emerging explorers T. H. Culhane, Aziz Abu Sarah, Mireya Mayor, and Alexandra Cousteau took to speak with us over the phone and to communicate with us via e-mail so they could share their important work and inspirational words and ideas with us. Each explorer's inspiring story demonstrates the importance of communication and civic engagement and the compassion of the human heart to help the environment, animal species, and humankind.

Jennifer would like to thank several people for their support throughout the process of writing this book. To Cindy, a special thank you for your academic support, mentorship, and confidence in partnering on this project. I appreciate the many conversations that reinforced the importance of collaboration, and respect for each other's ideas. I learned that friendship can be the foundation for amazing work. Your patience and honesty are admirable. Thank you! To Hilary Nye, thank you for your love and devotion to my family during the making of this book. I appreciate the hours spent in my home helping me to find the right words and examples and for always saying, "Yes," so that I could pursue this project. Thank you for being a friend and such an important person to Miles and Alex! And to my family, a heartfelt thank you for your continual support and encouragement. My parents, John and Betty Emerling; and my siblings, Becky King and Mike Emerling—you all inspire me in important and unique ways. Finally, the many hours of research, writing, and editing were accomplished with unwavering love from my husband, Ryan Bone, and children, Miles and Alex Bone. Their smiles, kind words, and warm gestures remind me daily how fortunate I am to have them in my life. They are my inspiration and the constant reminder of all things important.

From Cindy, a heartfelt thanks to Michael Harte and Joe Griffin-Harte, who offered me unending support, love, good humor, problem solving, and levity when it was most needed. To my family, John and Betty Griffin, Tracy, John, and Wendy, I offer my gratitude and deepest thanks. And to mom, I know you are up there watching and smiling. And finally to Jen, who had the courage to say, "Yes, I can do this with you," I say, "I couldn't have done this without you"—many, many thanks.

Cindy L. Griffin, Colorado State University
Jennifer Emerling Bone, Colorado State University

As professors of communication attempt to prepare their students for success in our increasingly complex, diverse, and interconnected world, materials that allow them to do so in meaningful, civil, and accessible ways become imperative. Because communication is central to the social, political, professional, and personal lives of our students, the Fundamentals of Communication course is poised to facilitate our students' success in these areas in important and powerful ways. *Invitation to Human Communication*, working in partnership with the National Geographic Society, acknowledges the complexity of today's world, the power of communication, and the necessity of teaching students the foundational skills they will need to both compete and succeed in this complex and exciting environment.

Because of our innovative alliance with National Geographic, *Invitation to Human Communication* is able to facilitate the teaching of foundational communication theories and skills in unique and groundbreaking ways. Our collaboration allows us not only to showcase the best of communication theories and practice but also to showcase and explore the ways that National Geographic explorers and researchers use communication to carry out their work, develop professional and personal relationships with others, and share their discoveries and research with the larger public. The addition of inspiring and thought-provoking photos and interesting videos enhance the connection between National Geographic and the *Invitation to Human Communication* program.

Invitation to Human Communication also incorporates practices and theories of civility, civic engagement, and ethical communication, which are central to a democratic society. This framing allows students to see that their own communication directly affects the quality of an interaction as well as the perpetuation of ethical and civil forms of interacting. Incorporating civic engagement and invitational styles of communication, also central to a democratic society, allows students to link concepts and practices to the world around them and to understand the various ways communication assists us in exploring, understanding, and even respecting our differences. The end result is not necessarily agreement, as many of our National Geographic explorers attest, but meaningful communication that assists us in making decisions that are informed and respectful of others.

The incorporation of case studies, research, and discussions related to the uses of technology, now a necessary aspect of our democratic society, provides an additional venue for students to think critically about the impact of technology on themselves, their styles of communication, and their approaches to others. Students' exposure to technology is framed as learning to communicate effectively through and with technology rather than simply "using" technology. And our National Geographic explorers help us teach our students about the important role of technology related to communication and effective and ethical communicative practices.

The framing of communication as foundational to our lives—and our partnership with National Geographic—runs consistently throughout the text. *Invitation to Human Communication* thus encourages students to make links between material read in the text, real-world examples and case studies, material presented by the instructor, and experiences they either have had or likely will have as they move beyond the fundamentals course and into their chosen professions.

Our approach and our National Geographic partnership also allows instructors to incorporate and discuss contemporary as well as historical events and issues, illustrate the ways communication is at work in those issues, and then link those events back to the material taught in the course. Thus, the complexities of communication, teaching and learning, and human interactions in a variety of venues and contexts are recognized and valued. In addition, links between the material students are asked to learn and their own lives are made relevant and honored. As such, the fundamentals course becomes clearly connected to their future goals and daily practices. And students are equipped to communicate more effectively in a variety of situations, some of them already familiar, that they will likely encounter in their futures outside the classroom.

Invitation to Human Communication is divided into four sections.

We begin with material that explores the foundations of communication principles and practices. In this section, we explore the process of communication, perception, nonverbal and verbal communication, and listening. In the second section, we address interpersonal communication, its nature, and its scope, as well as ways to improve communication in interpersonal relationships. Working with the voices and experiences of our National Geographic explorers, we frame these two sections to showcase the centrality of communication to our lives as well as the importance of civil and ethical communicative practices. We present not only the most recent and innovative research in these two sections but also to the foundational scholarship that lays the framework for the study of communication. *Invitation to Human Communication* also incorporates discussions of the effects of technology on our interpersonal relationships throughout the first two sections. With this integration, students are reminded that the theories and ideas they are learning are not arbitrary or found only in a text but are a part of their everyday interactions. In this way, the role of communication in helping them face communication dilemmas and interpersonal challenges is emphasized.

In the third and fourth sections of *Invitation to Human Communication*, we continue our partnership with National Geographic. Part III explores communication in groups, and Part IV examines public speaking. These components of communication are also presented through the lenses of civil and ethical communication and civic engagement, as well as invitational conversations and dialogues. The materials in these two sections are presented in a very skills-based manner, and this approach assists students in recognizing that they are learning skills that will help them attain success outside the classroom in their professional lives. We continue our partnership with National Geographic such that students can begin to see themselves as able to participate in both the larger public and professional dialogues that surround them. These dialogues are about complex issues that affect us all.

As a result of the framing of the text, students begin to recognize the importance of communication and to feel empowered to participate in contemporary conversations and dialogues. The impact of technology is also a key component of the final section of the book, and students are encouraged to understanding the benefits and dilemmas presented with the integration of technology into their speaking and work environments. The result of this coherent and real-world focus is that concepts that once seemed disconnected and linked only to the classroom become ideas and tools that help students succeed in both their personal and professional lives.

Features of *Invitation to Human Communication*

Features are an important part of any textbook, enticing students to read and learn the concepts. This text offers the following innovative pedagogical features.

National Geographic Partnership

Invitation to Human Communication is the only communication textbook to work collaboratively with National Geographic, highlighting the central role of communication in our work, social interactions, and personal lives. To this end, *Invitation to Human Communication* includes two very unique features:

- **National Geographic Explorer Tips from National Geographic Explorers** Alexandra Cousteau, Thomas Taha Rassam Culhane, Aziz Abu Sarah, Mireya Mayor, and Sylvia Earle. These tips are gathered through interviewing these nationally known researchers, explorers, and scientists and are included in every chapter of the book.

- **National Geographic Speaks** features Alexandra Cousteau, Thomas Taha Rassam Calhoun, Aziz Abu Sarah, Mireya Mayor, Sylvia Earle, Aydogan Ozcan, Dino Martins, and Albert Yu-Min Lin. These case studies, developed from interviews and research, showcase the importance and centrality of ethical and civil communication in the work of these nationally recognized explorers, scientists, researchers and activists. Questions at the end of each case study prompt students to reflect on the communication used by these explorers and the ways in which a particular communication strategy might also become a part of their own skill set.

Civic Engagement in Action

In addition to our partnership with National Geographic, *Invitation to Human Communication* continues to emphasize the role and importance of communication in civic engagement. To this end, we offer several Civic Engagement in Action feature boxes:

- The Listening Project: What Does the World Think of America?
- How to Respond to Cyberbullying
- Responding to Interpersonal Violence
- Group Communication That Supports Biodiversity and Human Diversity
- Protecting Human Rights
- I Had No Idea That Anyone Was Listening
- Alright, Hear This
- To the Rescue
- A Few Citizen Activists with Buckets
- Trespassers Welcome

Questions at the end of each Civic Engagement in Action box study prompt students to reflect on the communication used by these individuals and they ways a particular communication strategy might also become a part of their own communication skill set.

Ethical Moments

Recognizing the crucial role of ethics in communication, *Invitation to Human Communication* includes additional feature boxes that highlight moments of communication that raise ethical questions and dilemmas. In the foundations of communication and interpersonal communication sections, those ethical moments are:

- Global Graffiti: Whose Space Is It?
- Free Speech and "You're Going to Hell"
- Terminating a Relationship: Facebook or Face to Face?

In the group communication and public speaking sections, those ethical moments include

- Can Maneuvers for Power Be Avoided?
- When Must We Speak?

Questions are included at the end of each Ethical Moment box to prompt students to reflect on the ethical dilemma at play and the role of communication in addressing that dilemma.

Speaking Visually

Visual communication is an integral part of our student's lives and learning. To assist students in exploring the visual communication they are surrounded by, we include feature boxes that stress the importance of visual communication and its role in healthy relationships as well as public communication. Speaking Visually features include

- Media and Self-Concept
- What's in a Tattoo?
- Anti-Drug Campaigns Dissuade People from Trying Drugs—Even Once
- Social Commentary, YouTube Style
- Ribbon Campaigns and Awareness Bracelets

Questions are included at the end of each Speaking Visually box to prompt students to explore the communication theory they have been reading about and how it applies to speaking visually.

Communicating at Work

Understanding the role of communication in our workplaces is a necessary part of our students' education. As such, *Invitation to Human Communication* includes feature boxes that address contemporary dilemmas that relate to communication in the workplace. These include

- Leaders, Greetings, and Cultural Differences
- Seconds of Silence
- Employees of Different Generations Working Together
- The Consequences of Social-Media Blunders
- Do You Have a Bully at Work?

Questions are included at the end of each Communicating at Work box to prompt students to reflect on the role of communication in the workplace and strategies they might use to communicate effectively in the workplace.

Case Studies

To compliment our National Geographic case studies, we've included additional explorations of important moments of communication for students to discuss and explore. These include

- Artifacts, Ambiguity, and Arguments
- It Begins with the Phrase "That's So Gay"
- Food Not Bombs: Decision Making By Consensus

Questions are included at the end of most case studies so that students can explore the role of communication in these case studies and apply what they are reading to these important communication moments.

Practicing Human Communication

To learn effectively, students must go beyond reading and apply the concepts they are encountering for the first time. To assist with this learning, *Invitation to Human Communication* includes a hands-on feature that asks students to reflect on and apply the material they have just read. Practicing Human Communication boxes are included in every chapter and address such topics as ethnic and cultural backgrounds, stereotyping, flexibility, listening, stages of friendship, technology and conflict, reasoning, delivery, confidence during public speaking, and many more.

Writing Style

Invitation to Human Communication is written in an accessible and engaging writing style that draws students into the material and facilitates their exploration of ideas that may be familiar or new.

Practical Skills and Introduction to Theory

Invitation to Human Communication offers a skills-based approach and a careful introductory level framing of the research behind those skills. The text includes foundational and contemporary research so that the wide range of ideas and theories students explore are connected. Ideas build on or relate to one another throughout the text. This is done through the presentation of communication theory and skills in very pragmatic ways, highlighting the foundations and strengths of the communication discipline, as well as linking communication theory and skills to civility, civic engagement, invitational communication, and ethical practices.

Review and Reflect

Our end-of-chapter summaries, questions that ask students to apply what they have read, and list of key terms and definitions are helpful mechanisms for student review and self-testing. These are included at the end each chapter and serve as excellent reviews for studying for exams or reviewing chapters before class.

Technology

Invitation to Human Communication highlights and explores the power of technology and media and their relationship to communication throughout the text. We pay careful and comprehensive attention to technology, presenting the most up-to-date research and examples so that students can explore the role of technology and media in their lives, and their effects on communication.

Videos, Web Links, and Other Interactive Media

CourseMate Connection will link students to videos associated with National Geographic explorers and topics of interest related to chapter content.

Resources Designed to Streamline Teaching and Facilitate Learning

Resources for Students

Invitation to Human Communication features an outstanding array of supplements to assist in making this course as meaningful and effective as possible. **Note:** If you want your students to have access to the online resources for *Invitation to Human Communication,* please be sure to order them for your course. If you do not order them, your students will not have access to them on the first day of class. These resources can be bundled with every new copy of the text or ordered separately. Students whose instructors do not order these resources as a package with the text may purchase them or access them at **cengagebrain.com**. *Contact your local Wadsworth Cengage Learning sales representative for more details.*

SpeechStudio 2.0

This online video upload and grading program improves the learning comprehension of your public-speaking students. With **SpeechStudio 2.0**, students can upload video files of practice speeches or final performances, comment on their peers' speeches, and review their grades and instructor feedback. Instructors create courses and assignments, comment on and grade student speeches with a library of comments and grading rubrics, and allow peer review. Grades flow into a gradebook that allows instructors to easily manage their course from within **SpeechStudio**. Grades can also be exported for use in learning-management systems. **SpeechStudio**'s flexibility lends itself to use in traditional, hybrid, and online courses.

- See **CourseMate** for ISBNs.

Speech Builder Express™

This exclusive program guides students through every step of the speech-building process. Nine simple steps provide a series of critical-thinking questions that guide students to effective speech delivery. Links to video clips, InfoTrac® College Edition, and an online dictionary and thesaurus help students pull all aspects of their speeches together. Tutorial help is included for every aspect of the speech-building process. Any portion of the outline can be e-mailed to the instructor.

- See **CourseMate** for ISBNs.

Interactive Video Activities

Interactive Video Activities give your students a chance to watch videos of real speeches and communication scenarios that correspond to the topics in *Invitation to Human Communication*. Each scenario includes the transcript, note-taking tool, and more. Each speech activity provides a video of the speech; a full transcript so that viewers can read along; the speech outline—many in note card, keyword, and sentence form; evaluation questions so that students are guided through their assessment; and a note-taking tool. While viewing each clip, students evaluate the speech or scenario by completing short answer and multiple-choice questions or by embedding notes into the video and submitting their results directly to their instructor.

- See **CourseMate** for ISBNs.

CourseMate

Cengage Learning's **CourseMate** for *Invitation to Human Communication* brings course concepts to life with interactive learning, study, and exam-preparation tools that support the printed textbook. Watch student comprehension soar as your class works with the printed textbook and the textbook-specific Web site. **CourseMate** includes an integrated eBook; student workbook; interactive teaching and learning tools, including quizzes and flash cards; Interactive Video Activities; National Geographic resources; and Engagement Tracker—a first-of-its-kind tool that monitors student engagement in the course. Visit www.cengage.com/coursemate.

- Speech Communication **CourseMate** (with eBook, Speech Builder Express™, and InfoTrac®) for *Invitation to Human Communication* Printed Access Code: 9781285068916
- Speech Communication **CourseMate** (with eBook, Speech Builder Express™, and InfoTrac®) for *Invitation to Human Communication* Instant Access Code: 9781285068961

- Speech Communication **CourseMate** (with SpeechStudio 2.0, eBook, Speech Builder Express™, and InfoTrac®) for *Invitation to Human Communication* Printed Access Code: 9781285068954
- Speech Communication **CourseMate** (with SpeechStudio 2.0, eBook, Speech Builder Express™, and InfoTrac®) for *Invitation to Human Communication* Instant Access Code: 9781285068992

WebTutor

The WebTutor™ for WebCT® and Blackboard® provides access to all of the content of this text's rich CourseMate and eBook from within a professor's course-management system. CourseMate is ready to use as soon as you log on, and it offers a wide array of Web quizzes, activities, exercises, and Web links. Robust communication tools—such as a course calendar, asynchronous discussion, real-time chat, a whiteboard, and an integrated e-mail system—make it easy to stay connected to the course.

- Instant Access Code for WebTutor with eBook for WebCT® 9781285068619
- Instant Access Code for WebTutor with eBook for BlackBoard® 9781285068633
- Printed Access Card for WebTutor with eBook for WebCT® 9781285068824
- Printed Access Card for WebTutor with eBook for BlackBoard® 9781285068855
- **InfoTrac College Edition™.** This virtual library contains more than 18 million reliable, full-length articles from 5,000 academic and popular periodicals, and it allow students to retrieve results almost instantly.
- **CengageBrain Online Store.** CengageBrain.com is a single destination for more than 15,000 new print textbooks, textbook rentals, eBooks, single eChapters, and print, digital, and audio study tools. CengageBrain.com provides the freedom to purchase Cengage Learning products à la carte—exactly what you need when you need it. Visit **cengagebrain.com** for details.
- *A Guide to the Basic Course for ESL Students* by Esther Yook, Mary Washington College, is for nonnative speakers and includes strategies for accent management and overcoming speech apprehension, in addition to helpful Web addresses and answers to frequently asked questions.

Resources for Instructors

Invitation to Human Communication features a full suite of resources for instructors. These resources are available to qualified adopters, and ordering options for student supplements are flexible. Please consult your local Wadsworth Cengage Learning sales representative for more information, to evaluate examination copies of any of these instructor or student resources, or to request product demonstrations.

- The *Instructor' Resource Manual* by Jennifer Emerling Bone of Colorado State University provides a comprehensive teaching system. Included in the manual are sample syllabi, chapter outlines, in-class activities, and test questions for each chapter. All the Web Connect links and activities listed at the end of each chapter of the student edition are included in detail in the Instructor's Manual in the event that online access is unavailable or inconvenient.

- **The Teaching Assistant's Guide to the Basic Course** by Katherine G. Hendrix, University of Memphis, was prepared specifically for new instructors. Based on leading communication teacher training programs, this guide discusses some of the general issues that accompany a teaching role and offers specific strategies for managing the first week of classes, leading productive discussions, managing sensitive topics in the classroom, and grading students' written and oral work.
- **PowerLecture.** This one-stop lecture tool makes it easy for you to assemble, edit, publish, and present custom lectures for your course using Microsoft PowerPoint®. The PowerLecture lets you bring together text-specific lecture outlines and art, along with video and animations from the Web or your own materials—culminating in a powerful, personalized, media-enhanced presentation. In addition, the CD-ROM offers an electronic version of the Instructor Resource Manual, ExamView® software, videos, and JoinIn™ on Turning Point® lecture slides.
- **Instructor Workbooks: *Public Speaking: An Online Approach, Public Speaking: A Problem-Based Learning Approach,*** and ***Public Speaking: A Service-Learning Approach for Instructors*** were written by Deanna Sellnow, University of Kentucky. These instructor workbooks include a course syllabus and icebreakers; public speaking basics such as coping with anxiety, learning cycle and learning styles; outlining; ethics; and informative, persuasive, and ceremonial (special occasion) speeches.
- ***Teaching the Invitational Speech Resource Guide* and accompanying video and DVD** features an introduction by author Cindy L. Griffin and shows you how to effectively teach the invitational speech to your student.
- ***Guide to Teaching Public Speaking Online*** was written by Todd Brand of Meridian Community College. This helpful online guide provides instructors who teach public speaking online with tips for establishing "classroom" norms with students, utilizing course management software and other eResources, managing logistics such as delivering and submitting speeches and making up work, discussing how peer feedback is different online, strategies for assessment, and tools such as sample syllabi and critique and evaluation forms tailored to the online course.
- ***Service Learning in Communication Studies: A Handbook*** was written by Rick Isaacson and Jeff Saperstein. This invaluable resource for students in the basic course integrates or will soon integrate a service learning component. This handbook provides guidelines for connection service learning work with classroom concepts and advice for working effectively with agencies and organizations. It also provides model forms and reports and a directory of online resources.
- **CourseCare Training and Support:** Get trained, get connected, and get the support you need for the seamless integration of digital resources into your course. This unparalleled technology service and training program provides robust online resources, peer-to-peer instruction, personalized training, and a customizable program you can count on. Visit **cengage.com/coursecare/** to sign up for online seminars, first-day-of-class services, technical support, or personalized face-to-face

training. Our online and on-site trainings are frequently led by one of our Lead Teachers, faculty members who are experts in using Wadsworth Cengage Learning technology and who can provide best practices and teaching tips.

- The **Flex-Text Customization Program** allows you to create a text as unique as your course quickly, simply, and affordably. As part of our flex-text program, you can add your personal touch to *Invitation to Human Communication* with a course-specific cover and as many as thirty-two pages of your own content—at no additional cost. As part of the Custom program we also offer a variety of bonus chapters that you might consider in order to emphasize certain topics. Consult with your local representative to learn about options with Custom.

PART I   Foundations of Communication

THE COMMUNICATION PROCESS

IN THIS CHAPTER YOU WILL LEARN TO:

- Define communication and understand its relationship to civility and to ethics.
- Describe the process of communication.
- Understand the different types of communication and when they are best used.

- Recognize the three most common models of communication and how they help to explain this process.

1

Photomorphic Pte Ltd/iStockphoto.com

When we communicate civilly and ethically, we recognize the presence of others in our lives and around the world. How aware of other people are you when you communicate?

- Understand what it means to be a competent communicator.
- Appreciate the importance of communication in our lives and the benefits of studying it.

If I could have people do one thing to help save our world, it would be to keep learning. Keep that childlike enthusiasm for the new.

—*Ronald Beckett, professor, researcher, explorer, National Geographic Expeditions Council Grantee*

When we communicate, we connect with, learn from, influence, and even disagree with other people. With every communication encounter, we make choices about the kind of messages we will send and whether or not we will listen to someone else. We make choices about what feelings or ideas we will share, when to agree and disagree, when to explore and gather more information, and whether or not to pursue a relationship with another person. We even communicate with ourselves, talking to ourselves about jobs, friends and family, and how we want our futures to unfold. When we communicate, we bring our worldviews, ethics, and values to an exchange. And we expose ourselves to the worldviews, ethics, and values of other people.

bell hooks, a media scholar and cultural critic, explains that we need to practice understanding others. According to hooks, we need to practice listening to the logic of others (identifying the system, principles, and arguments that make up their worldviews) and practice interacting with other people. She says we need this "practice of interaction" because people in our fast-paced and media-driven society have forgotten how to slow down and really listen to others and how to communicate their views carefully. To hooks, in the "practice of interaction" there is "an opportunity for mutual recognition"—an opportunity to listen to other people and to think carefully about the impact of our words and gestures on others. This is the opportunity for ethical and civil communication. The practice of interaction does not mean we always agree with others. Instead, we recognize the "presence of one another" (hooks, 1994).

In this book, you will be invited to learn about the foundations of human communication from an ethical and civil perspective. You will learn

- the definition of communication;
- how communication shapes our identities and worldviews;
- how to use communication in personal relationships, professional lives, and groups;
- the different contexts for and models of communication; and
- strategies and tips you can use to be a competent, civil, and ethical communicator.

Definition of Communication

The word *communication* refers to an activity that occupies the very center of our lives. Communication is so central that this era has been titled the "Information Age," and communication scholars have found that college students spend 55 percent of their time listening, 17 percent reading, 16 percent speaking, and 11 percent writing (Emanuel et al., 2008) (see Figure 1.1). Outside the college setting, communication research suggests that people in the workplace spend between 50 percent and 80 percent of their day in communication-related activities (Klemmer & Snyder, 1972). Imagining a day without communication—no conversations with friends or family, no music or television, no internal dialogues—is quite difficult. In fact, communication is so central to our daily lives that we often take it for granted—we engage in communication constantly but rarely notice its presence. However, for psychologists and communication scholars alike, who we are and how we interpret the world around us are products and processes of communication.

Although communication has been defined in various ways, in its simplest form it is the human activity of creating and exchanging meaning. We can define **communication** as *the use of symbols by humans to create messages for other humans.* This definition involves several parts: it is symbolic, it is a process, it is human, and it is influenced by culture.

Civil and Ethical Communication

This book is not only about the choices we make as communicators but also about learning to communicate those choices ethically and civilly. When we make a choice to **communicate ethically**, we *consider the moral impact of our words, ideas, and views on other people.* When we choose to **communicate civilly**, we *make a decision to be open to hearing different views and perspectives, even though we may not agree with them.* Choosing civil and ethical communication does not require that we silence our own views or that we agree with everything another person says. Instead, ethical and civil communication means that we consider the impact of our words on other people before, during, and after we say them. It also means that we are willing to listen to other people and to consider what their words mean, even if we disagree with them.

When we choose to communicate civilly and ethically, we are choosing an interested, honest, and flexible approach to communication. Ethical and civil communication means that we listen to views that are different from our own, not to be persuaded of their rightness, but to try to *understand* those views. It also means that we communicate our views in the same spirit—so that others can try to understand us.

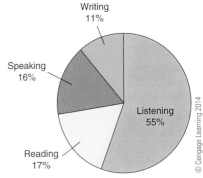

Figure 1.1 *Time college students spend communicating*

communication
use of symbols by humans to create messages for other humans.

Consider the amount of time you spend during a day communicating with others. How much of it is in person and how much is via phone or computer?

communicating ethically
considering the moral impact of our words, ideas, and views on other people when we communicate.

communicating civilly
making a decision to be open to hearing different views and perspectives, even though we may not agree with them.

understand
to gain knowledge of a view or an idea.

logic
system, principles, and arguments that make up a person's worldview.

symbol
word, gesture, sound, image, or object that stands in for or represents something else.

semantic triangle of meaning
ways people use or hear a symbol or word and attach a meaning to it.

referent
concept or thing the symbol represents.

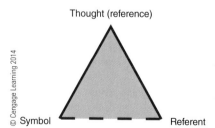

Figure 1.2 *Semantic triangle of meaning*

To **understand** a view or idea is *to gain knowledge of that view or idea.* It is to come to know it better and more fully and to recognize its logic. When we recognize the **logic** of someone else's views or ideas, then we are identifying the *system, principles, and arguments that make up that person's worldview.* This approach to communication will help us share our experiences, thoughts, and ideas with our families and friends, communities, and workplaces.

Communication Is Symbolic

When we communicate, we use symbols. A **symbol** is a *word, gesture, sound, image, or object that stands in for, or represents, something else.* We use symbols because without them we would have to act out— or *dramatize*—everything we wished to share with another person. This is because very few words literally replicate the thing we want to communicate. The closest we come to an actual replica of our meaning are words such as *bang*, *hiss*, and *woof*. These words are called *onomatopoeic* words because they are vocal imitations or representations of the thing they symbolize—that is, they actually sound like the thing they refer to. The majority of our words, however, are not imitations of something; instead, they are symbols of something else.

In 1923, C. K. Ogden and I. A. Richards created the **semantic triangle of meaning** to help us understand the symbolic nature of communication (Ogden & Richards, 1923). The semantic triangle of meaning illustrates the *ways people use or hear a symbol or word and attach a meaning to it.* It also illustrates the arbitrary or symbolic nature of this attachment. To understand this process, think of a triangle (see Figure 1.2). On the left corner of the triangle is the symbol—the word or phrase spoken by the speaker. For example, when a person says "Hope," as Barack Obama did during his campaign for the presidency, or when someone says, "It's all good," after a mistake or difficult moment, then those words are the *symbols.* They represent the idea being communicated.

On the right corner of the triangle is the **referent**, the *concept or thing that the symbol represents.* In the "Hope" example, the referent is the actual desire or wish that something good will happen. In an example that is included in the Urban Dictionary, "'It's all good," the referent could be twofold: either the 1999 album *It's All Good* by rapper M. C. Breed or the desire to rise above whatever problem a person faces or both (Urban Dictionary, 2009). Referents are the commonly held definitions of a word, phrase, or even object. This is sometimes called the *denotative definition* of a word. They are *denotative* because we could find the referents by looking in a dictionary or asking a large group of people what a word or phrase means. The symbolic nature of communication begins to emerge at this point because there is no direct connection between the word or phrase and the thing it represents. A wish for something good, or the desire to rise above a problem, could be called many other things. The word *hope* and the phrase "'It's all good" are human inventions. They are expressed by people to name emotions or desires and not the actual things they suggest. To help explain this referential or arbitrary aspect of communication, Ogden and Richards used a broken line between the two sides of the triangle. The broken line illustrates the indirect connection between the symbol and the referent.

Finally, at the top of the triangle is the **thought** or **reference** associated with a symbol. This is the *memory or past experiences people have with the words being communicated*. When we hear words or phrases, we recall our own experiences. The symbol *hope* and the phrase "It's all good" call to mind a variety of personalized and subjective interpretations, experiences, and memories for us. These may be successes or disappointments, or both, or even a like or dislike of a certain kind of music or commonly used phrase. These are called the *connotative* definitions of a word because they are the personal meanings we have for words or phrases. Our connotative definitions of words often are more powerful than the denotative definitions of words. When we hear words and phrases, we usually know "what they mean in the dictionary," but we also rely on our lived experiences to attach meaning beyond their denotative definitions.

The semantic triangle of meaning helps us understand that communication is symbolic because it helps us see that (1) we use symbols to represent things and to express ourselves, (2) although there may be common referents or meanings for those things (dictionary definitions), (3) there also are highly individual referents for those symbols (connotative definitions). This symbolic aspect of communication is part of what makes it so interesting to study and so challenging to use and sometimes understand.

Communication Is a Process

Although we sometimes make a single statement that fails to receive any reply, most often our statements are part of a larger and ongoing exchange. And even though we might utter a single word, sound, or gesture, we usually do so in response to something someone has said or done. We say that *communication is a process*, rather than an isolated act, because when we communicate civilly and ethically, we are part of an ongoing exchange of meaning. When we first meet another person, our communication unfolds: we consider what we want to say, we say that thing, and we listen to the other person's response. If the exchange goes well, then we continue the process, developing new messages and often new relationships or connections with the other person.

This process of communication also is present in larger familial, social, and professional contexts. This is because we often are part of a larger ongoing conversation when we communicate in these contexts. Kenneth Burke (1973) describes this process of communication as follows:

> Imagine that you enter a parlor. You come late. When you arrive, others have long preceded you, and they are engaged in a lively discussion, a discussion too passionate for them to pause and tell you exactly what it is about. In fact, the discussion had already begun long before any of them got there, so that no one present is qualified to retrace for you all the steps that had gone before. You listen

thought or **reference**
memory or past experiences people have with the words being communicated.

for a while, until you decide that you have caught the tenor of the argument; then you put in your oar. Someone answers; you answer them; another perspective is shared. The hour grows late; you must depart. And you do depart, with the discussion still vigorously in progress. (pp. 110–111)

As members of these larger family, professional, or social groups, we step into, contribute to, and build on this ongoing communication process.

For the process of communication to be civil and ethical, two things are important: *reciprocity* and *feedback*. **Reciprocity** is the *mutual exchange of symbols and meanings*, a process that represents our willingness to interact with other people and to not dominate a conversation. Although we sometimes may demand that someone do something or "give an order," most civil and ethical communication involves a mutual exchange between two or more people. **Feedback** refers to *the verbal and nonverbal signals we give to one another while we communicate with them*. When the people we are communicating with yawn, groan, look bored or angry, or laugh or smile, we are getting feedback—information that tells us a little bit about how our messages are being received.

When we say communication is a process, we are saying that it (1) involves an exchange of meaning, however short or long; (2) requires a mutual recognition of others; and (3) that we recognize the ongoing and influential nature of our communication.

reciprocity
the mutual exchange of symbols and meanings.

feedback
verbal and nonverbal signals we give to one another while we communicate.

When we give feedback to others, we send messages to them about how receptive we are to their communication. Positive feedback signals that we like their messages, and negative feedback communicates the opposite. How clear do you think your feedback is when you communicate with others?

Joe Corrigan/Getty Images

Communication Is Influenced by Culture

When he became the Anglican Archbishop of Cape Town, South Africa, in 1986, Desmond Mpilo Tutu, explained,

We Africans speak about a concept difficult to render in English. We speak of *ubuntu* or *botho*. You know when it is there, and it is obvious when it is absent. It has to do with what it means to be truly human; it refers to gentleness, to compassion, to hospitality, to openness to others, to vulnerability, to being available for others and to know that you are bound up with them in the bundle of life, for a person is only a person through other persons. And so we search for this ultimate attribute and reject ethnicity and other such qualities as irrelevancies. A person is a person because he recognizes others as persons. (1994, p. 125)

Archbishop Tutu captures the power of culture: it influences what we see as valuable, how we think, and the ways we interact with others.

Like the word *communication*, the word *culture* has been defined in many ways because it also is influenced and shaped by many factors.

Culture can be defined as the *learned patterns of perception, values, and behaviors, shared by a group of people* (Martin & Nakayama, 2008). These patterns are often called *dynamic,* meaning that *they change over time* and shape how we see ourselves in relation to the world around us. This, in turn, influences how we communicate with ourselves and other people. In some cultures (Asian and Native American, for example), communication is characterized by an indirect style that is designed to produce and maintain harmony. Communication scholar Deborah Tannen calls U.S. American culture an "argument culture," which is characterized by direct and open disagreement and "winning" or being right (Tannen, 1998).

Because cultures have unique ways of explaining and organizing the world, when we communicate ethically and civilly, we try to recognize these different worldviews and guard against **ethnocentrism**, or the *belief that our own cultural perspectives, norms, and ways of organizing society are superior to other cultures*. When we hold ethnocentric views, we see other cultures as odd, wrong, or deficient because they do not do things the way we do.

Cultural differences often cause people to argue with one another over their views of "right" and "wrong." These differences can make communication complex and difficult. Do you think either person will win this argument? Why or why not?

culture
learned patterns of perception, values, and behaviors shared by a group of people.

ethnocentrism
belief that our own cultural perspectives, norms, and ways of organizing society are superior to other cultures.

 ## Types of Communication

Because communication is such a central part of our lives, it can occur in a variety of contexts. In the course of any day, we might watch television, talk with other people briefly or at length, problem solve in groups at work or in our communities, or even share information in a formal setting such as giving a speech or Prezi presentation. Identifying the various contexts for communication helps us understand why and how we communicate, and it helps us study communication more effectively.

When people engage in **intrapersonal communication**, they are *communicating internally with their own selves*. Intrapersonal communication is the internal communication that goes on in our own heads, the mental processing of decisions we have to make, choices we have made, and even conversations we want to have or should have. Intrapersonal communication is sometimes called "self-talk," and it can be both positive and negative or even civil and uncivil.

Interpersonal communication is *communication with other people that ranges from the highly personal to the highly impersonal*. This type of communication usually takes place in a dyad (two people) or a small group (fewer than six people), but its defining characteristic is that it involves relationships. When we communicate interpersonally, we are establishing, maintaining, and disengaging from relationships with other people. We might communicate interpersonally in person or in a face-to-face setting, but we also communicate interpersonally via telephone, text message, e-mail, card or letter, or the like. In interpersonal communication, it often is easier to be civil to those we like and uncivil to those we do not because it is easier to listen to and communicate with people who

intrapersonal communication
when people communicate internally with their own selves.

interpersonal communication
communication with other people that ranges from the highly personal to the highly impersonal.

Aziz Abu Sarah,
Emerging Explorer and Cultural Educator

What types of communication do you enjoy most in your work and why? Are there cultural challenges that you have had to overcome as a communicator?

I talk about pretty tense things. I talk about being killed. I talk about war. I learned very early to use a little bit of humor. I spoke to a group in Northern Ireland, for example, and I remember coming in and seeing uneasiness, they're like, "Who is this guy?" Instead of starting my normal lecture, I started with a little bit of humor and slowly the same people who had their arms crossed were changed and much more open. I also use what I call *emotional communication*, which focuses on narratives and storytelling, and that's my favorite style. The bulk of the speaking that I do is persuasive. My goal is to persuade people. So when I tell a story, the goal is actually not just to tell the story, it's actually to move people from point A to B and try to show them a new alternative or a new narrative. In my case, we're talking about conflict. Many times I'm speaking to a group that disagrees with me. And the challenge I have to overcome is always to quickly turn that around and win that crowd back, which is very hard. So, that's where storytelling helps. When I think of our cultural divides, and the very different groups I speak with, I try to relate through listening to them and understanding their perspective, even when I personally have disagreements with them And, that's my own personal dilemma that I deal with. But I really believe that you can't make a change, and you can't have an effective conversation, if you're not willing to first listen and understand and show a respect to the person in front of you, regardless of how much you disagree. But you also have to make sure you are not losing your own values as you're doing that. And that's—that's the hardest dilemma I think I face on a personal level.

---

group communication
interacting with a small but organized collection of people.

are similar to us. However, in interpersonal communication we sometimes communicate uncivilly with those people we care deeply about, especially when we are angry or when ending a relationship. Interpersonal communication is explored more fully in Chapters 6 and 7.

Group communication, sometimes called *small-group communication,* occurs *when we interact with a small but organized collection of people.* When we engage in group communication, we usually have a focus or a goal. Group communication takes place when we communicate as part of a team, study or work group, collective or committee, or even hobby, club, or political organization. When we communicate in groups, we often are guided by rules or specific goals, and we may discuss strategies or plans that guide the interactions. Group communication may be formal or informal, and group members often assume certain roles such as team captain, recorder or note taker, or behind-the-scenes organizer. Group communication also occurs face to face or via technology. The most effective and successful groups make civil and ethical communication a priority. However, when groups engage in *group think* or when they turn against one or more members, uncivil and unethical communication can take over. Group communication is explored more fully in Chapters 8 and 9.

Mass communication is *communication designed to reach large audiences and that is generated by media organizations.* This type of communication is transmitted via television, the Internet, radio, print media, and even the entertainment industry. It is one of the most common and prevalent forms of communication today. Mass communication is one of the few types of communication that fits the linear model of communication discussed in the following sections. Mass communication fits the "linear model" because it flows one way and is one of the few forms of communication that involves limited immediate feedback and reciprocity. Although the invitation to write, "call or e-mail us," or "vote now" does offer some exchange, media messages tend to be highly scripted and slow to respond to viewer input. Mass communication ranges from highly civil and ethical to highly uncivil and unethical, and because people and cultures are so diverse, the interpretation of what is civil and uncivil varies across groups and over time.

Public or presentational communication is communication in which *one person gives a speech to other people, most often in a public setting.* Public communication differs from other forms of communication in many ways. First, in public speaking, our reasons for communicating are unique. Sometimes we are asked to give a speech because we have knowledge or expertise on a topic. At other times, we want to give a public presentation because an issue is very important to us. We may even be required to give a speech as part of our job or as a part of a formal ceremony. So public communication is characterized by particular reasons for speaking. Second, this form of communication occurs with a single person, a *speaker*, delivering a message to a group of people, an *audience*. In public communication, one person usually does more talking while others do more listening. Sometimes, however, a speaker acts as a facilitator, or listener, inviting other people to communicate so that the speaker can understand an issue more fully or gather information about a topic or problem. A third difference is that public speaking tends to be more formal than conversational, usually occurring on a stage or in a formal setting and sometimes making use of technology to support the ideas being presented. Finally, speeches have predetermined goals and are highly organized and practiced before they are given. Ethical and civil communication is important in public communication to ensure audience members get accurate and honest information that does not manipulate them or prey on their emotions. Public communication is discussed in Chapters 10 through 15.

Models for Communication

Linear Model of Communication

At times, we can view communication as a one-way transmission of meaning. Although rare, people sometimes engage in this one-way model of communication. The linear model of communication (see Figure 1.3) is in operation when your boss appears in your doorway and says "Finish the report by the end of the day," your manager sends an e-mail that announces "Tomorrow's meeting is at 3:00," or your professor writes on your paper, "Very nice, B+." In this model, there is a *sender* (your boss or professor) and a *receiver* (you). The sender **encodes** a

---

mass communication
communication designed and generated by media organizations to reach large audiences.

public or presentational communication
when one person gives a speech to other people, most often in a public setting.

encode
putting ideas, thoughts, and meanings into a message.

Figure 1.3 *Linear model of communication*

decode
interpreting or trying to understand what the sender is communicating.

channel
means by which ideas are communicated.

noise
things that interfere with the transmission and reception of a message.

external noises
things that keep you from sending or receiving a message clearly.

physiological noises
things that are going on in our bodies.

message—she or he *puts ideas, thoughts, and meanings into a message.* The receiver **decodes** that message, which is to say, you *interpret or try to understand what the sender is communicating.*

The way the message is transmitted is called the **channel**, or the *means by which the ideas are communicated.* A channel can be many things, such as your boss's spoken words, your manager's written words, or your professor's comments on your paper, but it can also be a telephone, text message, Web page, song, card or letter, or the like. The channel is important because how a message is sent affects the way it is received. In face-to-face communication, we can see the person's facial expression and hear his or her tone of voice. On a Web page, we are influenced by visual images and design features. When we know someone well, we can read the cues in their e-mails or text messages, but when we do not know them well, we sometimes misunderstand an electronic message.

In this linear model, noise also is present. **Noise** refers to *the things that interfere with the transmission and reception of a message.* There are three kinds of noise that disrupt communication: external or physical noise, physiological noise, and physiological or internal noise. **External noises** are *things that keep you from sending or receiving a message clearly.* These are such things as loud motors or large crowds, bad or disrupted phone connections, other people that pull your attention away from the message (a child, classmate or co-worker, for example), or even poor lighting or sound systems. **Physiological noises** are those *things that are going on in our bodies.* Hunger and fatigue are two common physiological noises, but illness and injuries also can create this type of noise. Physiological noise disrupts the sending or receiving of a message because we are distracted by our own physical needs or problems and are unable to send or receive a message effectively.

Finally, psychological or internal noise can influence our ability to understand and communicate. Psychological noises are traits such as shyness, which might cause us to communicate less, or the desire to be on "center stage," which might cause us to say more than we should. Psychological noises also are past relationships with someone that influence how and what we might communicate, as well as how easily we can listen to another person. Our mistrust of someone, for example, might change how we hear and interpret a message, but it might also affect the way we construct and send a message.

The last component of the linear model of communication is the **environment** or *cultural backgrounds and experiences people bring to the exchange*. This part of the model refers to the actual place where the communication occurs (office, home, coffee shop, car, etc.) as well as the worldviews of those communicating—their cultural norms and values, as well as individual experiences and expectations. In the linear model, environment and cultural backgrounds can influence communication in obvious or subtle ways. When your boss says in front of many of your co-workers, "Finish that project," you get a far different message than if he or she tells you the same thing in private. Similarly, if your cultural and familial background values humor, teasing, and verbal play but your receiver's cultural and familial background do not, then your message may be misunderstood as an insult rather than a sign of fondness and closeness.

Most communication does not fall into the linear model. This is because of the interactive nature of communication discussed previously. However, when we are in a hurry to get something done, when we want to send a quick message (meet me in front of the library at 9:00), and even when we are angry, we might find that this model best describes our communication. One-way communication can be civil or uncivil, but it is easy to interpret it as uncivil. When a sender makes no effort or opportunity to listen to the receiver's response to the sender's message, he or she ignores bell hooks's call for recognizing the presence of another person, and the result is an uncivil interaction. But when a quick text message saves a person time (meet me at the library) or a boss's "Finish that project" saves that person's job, then the linear model of communication might show us very civil communication.

Interactive Model of Communication

The interactive model of communication helps us understand communication interactions that are two-way (Figure 1.4). The model helps us understand how often communication is reciprocal and the role that feedback plays in communication. Recall that reciprocity is the *mutual exchange of symbols and meanings*. Feedback refers to the *verbal and nonverbal signals we give to one another while we communicate with them*. In the interactive model, symbols are exchanged between two people and feedback is present. When your friend sends a text message to meet at the library and you text back "I'm starving, can we meet at a coffee shop instead?" communication is reciprocal—you and your friend exchanged messages. When your boss stands in your doorway and says, "Finish that project by the end of the day," and you smile

environment
cultural backgrounds and experiences that people bring to the exchange.

PRACTICING HUMAN COMMUNICATION

What Are Your Ethnic and Cultural Backgrounds?

Can you name the ethnic and cultural identities of your family? Do you see ways in which those ethnic and cultural backgrounds are a part of your life today? Think of holidays, food, and traditions, for example. Do any of those reflect your ethnic and cultural heritages? Now consider the ethnic and cultural backgrounds of your friends or co-workers. Are there times when you have encountered different "environments" because of these different backgrounds? How have those differences affected the communication and relationship you have had with others?

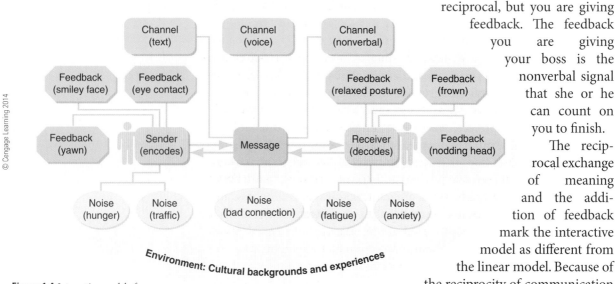

Figure 1.4 *Interactive model of communication*

and nod, not only is communication reciprocal, but you are giving feedback. The feedback you are giving your boss is the nonverbal signal that she or he can count on you to finish.

The reciprocal exchange of meaning and the addition of feedback mark the interactive model as different from the linear model. Because of the reciprocity of communication in this model, both the sender and receiver are engaged in feedback and are responsible for considering the ethical or moral impact of their messages. Each communicating person must consider how her or his communication is being received, how it is affecting the other person, the kinds of signals (feedback) the other person is giving, and the degree of honesty and integrity of the communication.

Both people also are responsible for thinking about the civility or incivility of their messages and their willingness to hear ideas they might not agree with. When we are exposed to information we disagree with, we may be inclined to fall back into the linear model of communication and not respond. Shutting down an exchange can be a sign of incivility. When we continue to communicate in the spirit of "interaction," as bell hooks suggests, we decide to remain civil, to listen to other people so that we can understand their messages, and to think carefully about the impact of our words and gestures on them. However, sometimes the message another person sends simply is too difficult or uncomfortable to listen to, and the civil and ethical response is to communicate that message to the other person. When it would be uncivil or unethical to continue a conversation, then it is appropriate to end it or change the topic.

Transactional Model of Communication

The transactional model of communication reflects the ongoing and collaborative nature of communication (Figure 1.5). This model helps us see that communication is more than a single act or a single event. In the transactional model, the relationships between the individuals communicating are highlighted. This model also emphasizes the ongoing and fluid nature of communication.

When we communicate with other people, we are in relationships with them. A relationship implies a connection. Sometimes that connection is brief and causal, but at other times it is long term and significant. When we are in a relationship with another person, we are involved with her or him. At work, this connection might take different forms. For example, we have bosses and co-workers, and we might be a manager or supervisor. Our connections to other people in our workplaces might be supportive and fun, but they might also be filled with power differences. You might be a manager, for example, and you want and need your staff to behave in certain ways for the business to be successful. Or you might be the dishwasher in a restaurant and want or need those who bus tables to help you do your job faster by clearing dishes in a certain way. At home, our connections and transactions also may be rewarding or difficult. Whether we greet our family with smiles and hugs, or repeatedly leave our shoes where others trip over them, our connections and power relationships are being communicated. These connections rely on transactions: on the ongoing exchange of communication. When people acknowledge the transactional nature of relationships, they also acknowledge the relationships they have with other people. When we see communication as a transaction, we recognize not only the power of communication to help us build healthy and positive relationships but also its power to affect other people's lives.

When we say communication is ongoing and fluid, we are saying that our relationships with other people usually are established and shaped over time. Although the length of a relationship can be a few moments (we assist a stranger with a door or a heavy box), they usually are developed over days, weeks, months, and years. In these long-term relationships, our communication shifts and changes because we are developing a history with that person, have a past with them, and are building a future. Thus, our communication is ongoing. When we first meet a person, for example, we have one style of communication. After we become familiar with that person, we know something of his or her background and preferences: our communication patterns and options change with this new information. When we know a person for years or even over the course of our lifetime, our communication choices continue to evolve and change. Through our communication, we develop a long history with this person. This history might be perhaps good or bad, but either way it shows us that our communication with other people is ongoing, changing, and always a transaction: an exchange that involves two people existing in relationship to one another.

Communication as an Act of Civility

Recall that when we choose to **communicate civilly**, *we make a decision to be open to hearing different views and*

PRACTICING HUMAN COMMUNICATION

What Kind of Interactions Have You Had Recently?

Identify different communication interactions in which you recently participated. Consider any conversations you have had with a roommate, a family member, or a professor. Think about your experiences working in a group to complete a class project or plan an extracurricular event or in using news media to gather information. Now choose one of these interactions. Write down what type of communication took place (e.g., interpersonal, group). Next, identify the sender, the receiver, the channel, and the environment where the communication act took place. Then list what noise might have interfered with the transmission or reception of the message. Finally, share your response with a partner and discuss ideas that would have helped the communication act be more effective.

Figure 1.5 *Transactional model of communication*

© Cengage Learning 2014

perspectives, even though we may not agree with them. When we make a choice to **communicate ethically**, *we consider the moral impact of our words, ideas, and views on other people.* When we choose to communicate civilly and ethically, we are choosing an interested, honest, and flexible approach to communication. The word *civility* comes from a root word meaning "to be a member of a household." In ancient Greece, *civility* referred to displays of temperance, justice, wisdom, and courage. Over time, the definition has changed only slightly; in the study of communication, **civility** has come to mean *expressing care and concern for others, the thoughtful use of words and language, and the flexibility to see the many sides of an issue.*

Choosing civil and ethical communication does not require that we silence our own views or that we agree with everything another person says. The models of communication share an additional component: communication is intertwined with civility. Law professor Stephen Carter explains civility in this way:

> The term *civility* is often translated as *politeness*, but it means something more. It suggests an approach to life, a way of carrying one's self and of relating to others—in short living in a way that is civilized. The word *civilité* shares with the words *civilized* and *civilization* (and the word *city*, for that matter) a common etymology, an Indo-European root meaning "member of the household." Of course: civility is what enables us to live together. To be civilized is to understand that we live in society as in a household, and that within that household, if we are to be moral people, our relationships with other people are governed by standards of behavior. (1998, p. 15)

civility

expressing care and concern for others, the thoughtful use of words and language, and the flexibility to see the many sides of an issue.

When we communicate with others, we are acknowledging that household, and we are acknowledging that we are members of it, as are other people. When we communicate with other people by e-mail, text message, or face-to-face interaction, we also acknowledge that we have a connection to other people. As Carter explains, in this increasingly interconnected and global world, it is important to recognize that we are "all passengers on the same train." Whether we are strangers or friends, we are traveling together.

Carter suggests that even when we do not agree with someone else, or perhaps do not even like them, we still have an obligation to practice civility in our communication. Interestingly, Carter says that sometimes this demands, even requires, "passionate disagreement." When we mask our differences in "politeness" or silence, we are not engaged in ethical communication with other people—instead, we are hiding our views from them. However, our "passionate disagreements" must be communicated civilly and ethically. Carter explains, "we must not encourage gratuitous insult simply to drive the point home" (p. 23). We must not let our anger and frustration push us into saying something rude or insulting. Instead, we must ethically express our disagreements and differences "for the sake of our common journey with others, and out of love and respect for the very idea that there are others. When we are civil, we are not pretending to like those we actually despise; we are not pretending to hold any attitude toward them, except that we accept and value them as our equals" (p. 23). We are, as hooks explains, recognizing the presence of others and communicating in ways that open up possibilities for listening and exchange rather than shutting others down.

Our attempts at communicating civilly with others have limits, however. Communication scholars Brian Spitzberg and William Cupach (2007) describe what is now called "the dark side of communication." In this "dark side," individuals communicate in ways that are "dysfunctional, distorted, distressing, and destructive." This kind of communication "dallies with deviance, betrayal, transgression, and violation" (Spitzberg & Cupach, 2007, p. 5). The dark side of communication is highly uncivil: it is mean spirited, dishonest, manipulative, and abusive or humiliating. Examples of the dark side of communication are bullying, name-calling, harassing or humiliating exchanges, stonewalling (refusing to communicate), and lies about one's self or others. Spitzberg and Cupach's research tells us that this dark side of communication is very common—and many people can easily recall dark communication encounters and relationships.

When we are faced with this negative and harmful communication, the role of civility is quite complex. Often the most civil thing we can do is to get out of or avoid the uncivil interaction. This is because allowing others to treat us poorly is not only harmful but also uncivil. Civility requires that we treat our own selves civilly and with respect. However, direct expressions of civility may have a role in our responses to communication from the dark side. To decide how to respond civilly, we have to ask ourselves several questions. What are the consequences of treating those who are very uncivil with civility? What options do we have to be civil? And what are the limits of our willingness to respect those who are uncivil?

ETHICAL MOMENT

Jon Reiss c. bombit-themovie.com 2006-2008

© Trevor Hunt/istockphoto

Global Graffiti: Whose Space Is It?

The film *Bomb It* (Reiss, 2007) is described as an "explosive new documentary" that "explores the most subversive and controversial art form currently shaping international youth culture: graffiti." Directed by Jon Reiss and filmed over several years, the award-winning documentary showcases the art of approximately two dozen street-graffiti artists from around the world, and it makes the argument that public space belongs to the public. In the film, artists argue that "Art is a weapon," that graffiti "represents life"—"It's energy, it's f—n' energy"—and that because it is on walls, in subways, and out in public, "It's alive, it's livin', it's communicatin' to you right now."

Reiss and those featured in *Bomb It* make the argument that graffiti artists are "not asking for the space" and are instead "taking the space." They suggest that "people believe that they live in a public space that's neutral," but that in reality we have become so numb to billboards and storefronts that we have become ignorant to what we really are "being assaulted with." Graffiti disrupts that numbness. Advocates of graffiti argue that what many people may not realize is presented as "neutral to them" actually is "excluding a lot of people." Beyond disrupting this supposedly neutral space, graffiti artists argue that their art takes ugly spaces and makes them beautiful. It goes beyond "Hello, world, I'm here," and adorns public property in ways that are aesthetic, accessible, and even political.

Other people, however, consider graffiti a nuisance, an eyesore, and a crime to be eradicated. Graffiti may be painted over hours or even moments after it is finished, and graffiti artists often land in jail if caught. Graffiti artists respond that their work is the marketing of an idea or an image, a way to participate in the larger conversations they and everyday people have been excluded from. Graffiti art transforms a public space, taking control of the communication disseminated there, and gives voice to those we normally would not hear from.

What Do You Think?

1. What do public space and free speech mean to you? Does graffiti fall into the category of communication? Is it uncivil to post graffiti on public buildings and spaces?

2. Do you think that graffiti artists are communicating important messages with their art? Why or why not?

3. Do you think that those who erase or paint over graffiti are ethical and civil in their actions? Why or why not?

Communication and Competence

To be competent is to do something well or to meet some required standard. When we say someone is "competent," we are saying that the person possesses a certain level of skill in an activity and understands and follows a particular set of rules or criteria for a task. A competent soccer player, for example, has a reasonable level of skill in running, kicking, passing, and the like and can follow the rules of the game. But what does it take to be considered a competent communicator? The answers to this question are varied, but communication research suggests the competence requires three different elements: flexibility, practice, and cognitive complexity.

Communication Competence Requires Flexibility

Most of us know from our own experiences that effective communication is different in different situations. What is appropriate with a child is ineffective with your instructor. How you communicate with your friends when you are relaxed is different from your communication on a job interview. In addition, at times, an outgoing and lively personality is as effective as a quiet and reserved style. Our language choices shift with various situations, as do our nonverbal manners. And what one person can "get away with" in an interaction may just be your biggest downfall. These examples tell us that to be competent in communication is to be flexible. In fact, flexibility is considered an essential part of communication competence.

With regard to communication, flexibility refers to three things: (1) a person's awareness that there are options in any communication situation, (2) a person's willingness to adapt to a situation, and (3) **self-efficacy**, or *a person's belief that she or he can be flexible*. Communication research also finds that confidence has a direct relationship to flexibility. Matthew Martin and Carolyn Anderson found that people who are flexible "have more confidence in their ability to communicate effectively, especially in new situations" (Martin & Anderson, 1998, pp. 1–9). So competent communicators adjust their styles to different people, situations, and forms of communication. They often blend a variety of styles to meet the environment and the feedback they receive. Competent communicators are able to adapt to different people, places, and needs, and they do so while staying ethical and civil to others and their own selves. And they possess a level of confidence that their communication efforts will be successful.

However, this notion of flexibility is one of the challenges of studying communication. The vast number of advice and self-help books for better leadership skills, sales techniques, relational advice, and even intrapersonal skills suggests that we are seeking "rules" for how to "best" communicate—formulas for communicating competently. However, the sheer number of such books indicates that no single rule applies. Competent communication changes from moment to moment, person to person, relationship to relationship, and situation to situation. The "first rule" of communication competency is to be flexible. And, although this need for flexibility may be one of the biggest challenges in the study of communication, it also is one of the most intriguing and exciting aspects.

Communication Competence Requires Practice

When we are babies, we listen to the communication going on around us. Even as infants, we try out sounds, putting them together in ways that do not make sense to those who hear us. At some point, we manage to utter something that makes sense. If English is our first language, we sometimes say "Ma ma," "Da da," or even "No no" or "Uh oh." We have practiced long enough to successfully send a message that someone understands. To be competent, however, we must continue practicing communication, regardless of how fluent we are in one or more languages. Research documents the ways we practice and learn to communicate as we mature. For example, our ability to successfully persuade others develops and improves over time. Susan Kline

self-efficacy
person's belief that she or he can be flexible.

and Barbara Clinton (1998) studied the persuasive abilities of young children and found that older children (sixth grade) were better able to construct persuasive messages than younger children (second and fourth grades). Kline and Clinton's research, and the research of those before them, found that younger children use fewer and more simple arguments as they attempt to persuade, and they employ "pleading, sulking, threats, and simple requests." Older children use more actual arguments in their persuasive attempts, and they appeal to "compromises, advantage arguments, appeals to social norms, and moral obligation and discussions of the advantages and disadvantages of competing alternatives" (Kline & Clinton, 1998, pp. 120–126).

Personal experience probably tells you that the more you practice something (a speech or an interview) the better your actual performance usually is. Studying communication in a class such as the one you are taking now is a good way to practice your skills. And the more you communicate with others, the more you are exposed to differences, similarities, and a wide range of communication styles. You can use these interactions as models or templates, and they will inform the decisions you make about what the best choices are for communicating with others.

Communication Competence Requires Cognitive Complexity

cognitive complexity
capacity to make sense of social behavior in a multidimensional way.

Competent communicators not only are flexible and willing to practice their skills but also possess what is called **cognitive complexity**. Joseph Bieri (1955) first introduced the concept as the *capacity to make sense of social behavior in a multidimensional way*. A person high in cognitive complexity is able to hold different and even competing definitions, perceptions, and explanations of an event comfortably together at one time. A person low in cognitive complexity has difficulty doing so and struggles with ambiguity and contradictions (Domangue, 1978). Competent communicators, in short, are able to offer different explanations for an encounter: your instructor is short with you because you were rude to him or her, she or he is rushed or just had an unpleasant encounter with another student or is worried about something, is in a bad mood, is hungry, or is generally unhappy, among a variety of other explanations.

empathy
ability to see the world through another person's eyes and to understand their feelings and perspectives.

sympathy
feeling sorry or pity for another.

Cognitive complexity involves more than the ability to manage ambiguity. It requires that we be both empathetic and able to monitor our own behaviors. **Empathy** is the *ability to see the world through another person's eyes and to understand their feelings and perspectives*. Empathy is sometimes confused with **sympathy**. When we feel sympathetic, we usually *feel sorry for or pity another*. When you are fired from a job, for example, some of your friends may feel sympathy for you—they feel sorrow or pity. Other friends feel empathy for you—they may have been fired before, too, and they know what it feels like to have that experience. They can "get into your shoes" and understand why and how you feel the way you do. We do not always have to share the same experiences to have empathy—in fact, it is almost impossible to have all of the same experiences as other people. Competent communicators make use of cognitive complexity, practice, and flexibility to take another's perspective and communicate with empathy.

Self-monitoring, or the *ability to observe your own behaviors and communication and to see how they are affecting others*, is a final component of cognitive complexity and competent communication (Snyder, 1974). People high in self-monitoring are very aware of social situations and watch themselves during an interaction. They give themselves feedback and make adjustments to their communication throughout the process in order to ensure the interaction goes well. Self-monitors say to themselves intrapersonally as they are talking, "I think my boss is receptive to my not coming in on Saturday," or "I think my boss is getting frustrated with me." Self-monitors say to themselves "This isn't going well" or "He seems to understand what I'm saying" and, where necessary and appropriate, change their communication styles to better fit a situation (Mill, 1984). High self-monitors are more skilled at communication—they are aware of their impact, the emotional states of others, and are better able to remember information. Low self-monitors, in contrast, overestimate their communication strengths and fail to recognize that communication may not be going well.

To determine whether or not you are a high- or low self-monitor, consider how much you pay attention to the feedback of others when you communicate with them. Are you aware of the signals they are giving you? Do you adjust your message accordingly? The answers to these questions also raise questions of civility and ethics. Communication competence involves not only the ability to be flexible and to self-monitor but also to practice civility—listening to others in respectful ways, regardless of differences and disagreements. It also requires our attention to ethics. Are we adjusting our communication so that we can communicate more clearly and effectively, or are we going against our principles and values to get what we want? Communication competence requires that we pay attention not only to what and how we say things but also to the ethical and civil impact of the things we do say.

Why Study Communication?

Communication Is All Around Us

Even if this era weren't called the Information Age, we can recognize the ever-present nature of communication. Communication is all around us; it helps us learn about the world, other people and cultures, and ourselves. We engage the world by talking, asking, watching, reading, and listening. Our identities are shaped by communication. We often find out what our choices are and how they will affect us and other people through communication. We make decisions, inform others of those decisions, and learn of theirs through communication. Indeed, communication is one of the most important and significant ways we

NATIONAL GEOGRAPHIC SPEAKS

Thomas Taha Rassam Culhane: The Great Conversation

"We're taught that garbage is garbage," states Thomas Taha Rassam (T.H.) Culhane, urban planner and explorer in residence for the National Geographic. But Cairo's Zabaleen people (literally, "garbage people") "view everything around them as useful for something." Culhane's work with the Zabaleen began when he watched mothers carry buckets back and forth and up and down stairs for seven hours just to secure water for their families. Wanting to understand firsthand what these families faced, Culhane and his wife moved into the poorest of neighborhoods in Cairo to experience the obstacles they faced. Culhane founded C.³I.T.I.E.S and worked with residents of the poorest neighborhoods in Cairo to install solar water heaters on the rooftops of their homes.

Culhane describes C.³I.T.I.E.S. as "not merely a solar power provider" but an organization that places group work and collaboration at its center. C.³I.T.I.E.S. is "an idea generator," Culhane explains. "We realize the value of collective intelligence. These neighborhoods are filled with welders, plumbers, carpenters, and glassworkers. We bring capital and plans; they bring talent and creativity. We build these systems together from scratch."

Promoting the value of working together, C.³I.T.I.E.S. also has reduced tensions between a primarily Coptic Christian community and an Islamic neighborhood. Culhane explains: "I knew if they could actually meet one another and connect on a project to solve common problems, they would overcome their differences. They immediately began sharing and building on each other's expertise. Now we're using the strengths of both Christianity and Islam to fight a common enemy: environmental degradation" (Culhane, 2011b).

Culhane is not satisfied with just developing options for solar power, however; he is also an advocate of what he refers to as "the Great Conversation." Our actions, Culhane explains, tell a story—but there is only one story, the story of "the Universe." This story "is a never-ending story, ever unfolding. When we learn to see our Earth . . . as a living thing, as a giant organism within that Universe, we can also learn to see our essential roles as parts of that planetary body. From an ecological point of view we can see that nobody is expendable." We all play different roles at different times, depending on our locations and our context, and what Culhane calls our "behavioral plasticity and flexibility." This plasticity and flexibility show us when to add our voice to the conversation, using the "appropriate voice at the appropriate time." When we tell our stories, Culhane explains, we become *interested* in our place in that story and *interesting* to others. What is more, according to Culhane, "today's globalized digital media platforms and technology have removed most of the barriers to entry! We can connect with each other across the globe via YouTube and Flickr and Facebook and MySpace and blogging and commenting and expand the great conversation to include our voices among the many" (Culhane, 2011a).

  CourseMate Connection: Go to cengagebrain.com to access your CourseMate for *Invitation to Human Communication* to view a video about T. H. Culhane.

1. Culhane talks about each of us having a story to tell and an important part in the Great Conversation. What actions might you share with others (as a story) that would help us understand your part in this Great Conversation?

2. Culhane also talks about behavioral plasticity and flexibility— knowing when and how to add our voices to this conversation. This chapter teaches you about communication flexibility and competency (see the following section). In what ways might Culhane be referring to communication flexibility and competency? How are these ideas similar?

3. How might today's technology help you add your voice to this Great Conversation in ways that are civil, ethical, and innovative?

move through the world. Because communication is all around us, it is easy to forget that we can study it and actually learn more about this complex and ever-present phenomenon.

Communication Is Irreversible

A second reason to study communication is that we cannot "take back" what we have said. Communication is irreversible. Because of this, knowing how to communicate effectively in a wide variety of contexts and with a wide variety of people becomes very important. Most of us can recall the moment we said something, followed by "I didn't mean it that way" because we confused, hurt, angered, or insulted someone. Once a message leaves our mouths, computers, phones, or the like, if someone receives that message, it is theirs—for better or worse. We can certainly backtrack, try to explain, apologize, or make amends, but the irreversible nature of communication is one very important reason for studying it.

Communication Is Always Evolving

Language and words are never static. Meanings shift and change over time, and new words are developed to name new events, processes, and ideas. In fact, the publisher Merriam-Webster recently announced the addition of more than 100 new entries to its *Collegiate Dictionary* (including such terms as *webinar*, which refers to an online, interactive, educational presentation) (Khodarahmi, 2008). Cultures, traditions, social norms, and people are in a constant state of change, as well, affecting the ways we interact with one another. In addition, mediums for communication are always evolving: technology adds new options and dimensions to communication—e-mail is barely twenty years old and smartphones, with all their communication options, are just now entering their second decade. People can communicate across continents in ways that were not possible just five years ago, thanks to computer and satellite technologies. The rapidly changing nature of our world and the ways we are able to interact with other people is a third reason to study communication.

Communication and Careers

Businesses report that competent communicators are among their most valued employees. The variety of situations, people, and tasks we must understand, work with, and accomplish, however, make communication competence feel almost impossible. People in the workplace must make sense of and generate communication in real time through virtual (i.e., electronic) means, as well as traditional face-to-face and written employment settings. As a result of information and communication technologies, people find themselves interacting with some individuals who are quite similar as well as those who are quite different from them. This "online mobility" creates opportunities for "networking instead of isolation," but it also requires that workers communicate their work, successes, dilemmas, and solutions across cultures and sometimes languages (Ferreira da Cruz, 2008). The importance of the information and ideas received and generated in our workplaces is a fourth reason to study communication.

Can you think of a time you hit "Send" and then wished you could take it back. Were you able to fix the exchange? Was your solution civil and ethical?

Communication and Family

Studying communication can also help us build and maintain healthy relationships with our families. It can assist us in understanding parent and child interactions, the reasons we are attracted to someone else, the evolution of our romantic relationships, power dynamics, and what makes someone a good listener, among many other things. In almost every relationship, we communicate at both the content level and the relational level. **Content messages** are *the actual things we say* while **relational messages** are *the parts of the communication that give us information about how we are connected (or not) to a person.* For example, if you say to a friend, with sincerity, "I'm happy to go with you to the doctor," you are communicating both content and connection or relationship. The content message is that you will go with your friend to the doctor. The relational message is that you value that person enough to assist them. When you change the tone or style of delivery, you may not change the content message, but you likely will change the relational message (you might feel pressured to help your friend, for example). Studying communication helps us learn how to communicate more clearly with our families and friends on both levels. And clearer communication helps us establish and maintain strong and rewarding relationships.

Communication and Self

Studying communication teaches us a great deal about ourselves. When we read about and practice different styles and techniques for communicating effectively, we learn about our own unique strengths and weaknesses. We can build on those strengths and try to eliminate or minimize our weaknesses. We also can learn where we are comfortable communicating—is it one on one? in groups? in front of large audiences? We can also find out where we might have some **communication apprehension** or *anxiety about communicating in any number of situations.* Almost everyone has some apprehension about communicating. Some people are anxious about job interviews or public speeches. Others become anxious when they need to ask for help or guidance. Many people get fearful when they decide to tell someone they like them and want to build a romantic relationship with them (or, conversely, do not like them and do not wish to see them again). So studying communication helps us understand not only what our own strengths and weaknesses are but also when we are likely to experience communication apprehension and how to work with that feeling (we will study communication apprehension more in Chapter 12).

Communication and Civic Engagement

A final reason to study communication is that we do not live in isolation from other people. We live, as Stephen Carter noted, as members of communities. Because of our relationships to other people, our need to communicate with people who are sometimes quite similar and sometimes quite different from us, and the nature of democracy in the United States, we must engage other people and ideas so that we can make informed and sustainable decisions. The term **globalization** has become a familiar part

content messages
the actual things we say.

relational messages
the parts of the communication that give us information about how we are or are not connected to another person.

communication apprehension
anxiety about speaking in any number of situations (interviews, speeches, etc.).

globalization
processes through which local and regional ideas, products, and practices are transformed into worldwide ideas, products, and practices.

of our everyday language and defines this increasingly interconnected way of life. It refers to the *processes through which local and regional ideas, products, and practices are transformed into worldwide ideas, products, and practices.* Globalization, a term more commonly used by economists in the 1980s, now has a lengthy entry in Wikipedia, and was used 1,000 times in major U.S. and world publications between 2006 and 2008.

Globalization helps us understand the importance of communication and civic engagement. **Civic engagement**, a term made popular by Thomas Ehrlich (2000), refers to *individual and collective actions designed to identify and address issues of public concern.* It does not refer to any particular political, religious, or social affiliation. It is a practice common to people around the world as they identify events and practices that benefit or harm (or both) their homes, workplaces, communities, states, countries, and continents. When we communicate about these issues, we are engaged civically: we recognize that what we do as individuals and collectives affects other people.

civic engagement
individual and collective actions designed to identify and address issues of public concern.

Chapter Summary

Communication Can Be Defined as the Use of Symbols by Humans to Create Messages for Other Humans

- Communication is the use of symbols by humans to create messages for other humans.
- When we communicate civilly we make a decision to be open to hearing different views and perspectives, even though we may not agree with them.
- When we communicate ethically we consider the moral impact of our words, ideas, and views on other people.
- Communication is symbolic process, which means that it consists of a symbol, a referent, and thought or reference, and reciprocal, a process that requires feedback.
- Communication is also influenced by culture.

The Five Types of Communication Are Intrapersonal, Interpersonal, Group, Mass, and Public Communication

- Three models describe the communication process: the linear model, the interactive model, and the transactional model.
- Each model contains the following components: sender, receiver, encoding, decoding, feedback, channel, noise, and environment.

Competent Communication Requires Flexibility, Practice and Cognitive Complexity; There Are Six Reasons to Study Communication

- Communication is inevitable, irreversible, and evolving. It influences careers, families, and self.
- In addition, it is important to recognize the effects of globalization and the importance of civic engagement as we communicate with others about issues that affect us all.

Key Concepts

group communication (10)

intrapersonal communication (9)

interpersonal communication (9)

logic (6)

mass communication (11)

noise (12)

physiological noises (12)

public or presentational communication (11)

reciprocity (8)

referent (6)

relational messages (25)

self-efficacy (19)

self-monitoring (21)

semantic triangle of meaning (6)

symbol (6)

sympathy (20)

thought or reference (7)

understand (6)

 # Invitation to Human Communication Online

Speech Communication CourseMate includes an interactive eBook and interactive learning tools, including National Geographic Explorer videos, student videos, quizzes, flashcards, and more. Speech Builder Express 3.0 and Speech Studio 2.0 are also available. Go to cengagebrain.com to access your CourseMate for *Invitation to Human Communication* where these resources can be found.

Further Reflection and Discussion

1. Consider what you want to get out of this course. Do you want to learn more effective ways to communicate at work? Do you hope to improve relationships with friends or family?

2. Think of a time when you expressed empathy as well as an experience in which you were sympathetic. What is the difference between the two?

3. This chapter presented Deborah Tannen's notion of an argument culture. What is your perception of this culture?

Have you been exposed to interpersonal communication as an argument? If the people engaged in this interaction were to communicate civilly, what specifically would change?

4. What does it mean to you to communicate ethically? Give an example of ethical communication.

5. Think about the African concept of *ubuntu* or *botho* and explain ways in which this concept might be communicated when talking with someone you have just met.

Activities and Web Links

Visit cengagebrain.com to access the CourseMate for *Invitation to Human Communication* where these activities and web links can be found.

1. Visit the Web site for the National Communication Association. Search for the list of publications related to one of the topics covered in this chapter. Which publications interest you? What would you like to know more about? Go to *Web link 1.1*.

2. Watch this video that shows a person who is a low self-monitor. What do you suggest he do differently to achieve his goal in this communication? Go to *Web link 1.2*.

3. Personal report of communication apprehension. Take this self-test and determine whether you have any communication apprehension. Score your results and note in which areas you have apprehension: group discussion, meetings, interpersonal communication, public speaking. Go to *Web link 1.3*.

COMMUNICATION, PERCEPTION, AND THE SELF

IN THIS CHAPTER YOU WILL LEARN TO:

- Define communication and understand its relationship to civility and to ethics.
- Define and understand what elements shape perceptions.
- Recognize the role standpoints play in shaping primary and secondary dimensions of our identities.

- Understand how family, culture, and communication influence self-concepts.
- Learn how to assess messages that influence self-esteem.
- Recognize the power that first impressions and stereotyping have in impacting perceptions of others.

2

Definition of Perception

Perceiving Our Self

Perceiving Others

Civility, Social Justice, and Perception

Self concept is the perception of who we are and how we are similar to and different from others. What are your perceptions of who you are?

Ming Thein/mingthein/Flickr/Getty Images

Whoever you are, whatever your interest or training, just step outside yourself and engage in some way.

—*Losang Rabgey, Tibetan Studies Expert, National Geographic Emerging Explorer*

No place to call home, people called me "A Lost Boy," meaning a child with no parents (Orphan). I live on my own in hardship, using only my tears. No father, no mother. I have never known the benefits of having parents. I don't know how good the world is. I was born in war, grew in fear, and remained in despair. My life has been useless, all useless. Suffering is my daily life. (Rose, 2004)

These are the words of Jacob Deng Ding, a child from the second civil war in southern Sudan (1983–2005), which claimed more than 2 million lives and left thousands of children, mostly boys between the ages of five and fifteen, orphaned or displaced. Known as the "Lost Boys," these courageous boys embarked on a terrifying journey across Africa to Ethiopia, back to Sudan, and finally to refugee camps in Kenya. These young men lived in thatched roof huts or tents, had never used electricity, and were accustomed to bathing in water drawn from a nearby river. As part of a resettlement program, approximately 3,800 Lost Boys came to the United States. Upon arriving to the United States, the Lost Boys claimed that everything was different—from living in their first apartment, trying different foods like potato chips and donuts, and seeing Santa Claus for the first time (National Geographic Video, n.d.). However, not all the differences were enjoyable. One Sudanese reminisces, "When we came [to the United States] it was very con-

Sudanese refugees and Lost Boys sit together on June 18, 1992, at a camp inside Kenya. Some 17,000 boys were lured away from home to receive military training in camps that held 300,000 refugees during a six-year period. After reading about their experiences, can you think of some of the ways your perception of the world might be different from theirs?

fusing; we were afraid to walk around because of our color and because we feared we would be abducted" (Muhindi & Nyakato, 2002). According to the documentary *God Grew Tired of Us: Cultural Differences* (National Geographic Video, n.d.), the Sudanese men were used to greeting people on the streets as they walked at home in Sudan, and they were confused when U.S. citizens ignored them. The resettled Sudanese young men claimed that "everything is different" in America.

Meanwhile, some Americans were also confused by practices of the young resettled Sudanese men. Another Sudanese man explained, "We went to church one Sunday, and we met people on the way who asked us why we were walking in a big group. They thought we were a gang. We answered by telling them that no, we are not a gang; to walk together is our nature. We are used to walking together from the time we lived in south Sudan, and we like to be with each other" (Muhindi & Nyakato, 2002). In addition, it made the group feel safe. The experiences of these Lost Boys illustrate the power of perception. How can the simple act of a group of men walking together lead to two very different perceptions? How can greeting strangers in one country be so different in another?

CourseMate Connection: Go to cengagebrain.com to access your CourseMate for *Invitation to Human Communication* to view the stories of these Lost Boys and to get a sense of how different our perceptions can be.

In this chapter, we will explore some of the reasons why different people interpret the same situation in different ways. First, we will discuss how our five senses can influence the way we understand ourselves and our experiences. Then we will examine how significant others in our lives and the surrounding environment can impact our self-concept and self-esteem. Finally, we will explore how our experiences shape the way we perceive others.

 ## Definition of Perception

When we interact with others, we focus on more than just the words being spoken: we focus on the occasion or context surrounding the interaction and the way things look, feel, smell, taste, and sound. The combination of these elements shapes our perceptions. **Perception** is *the process of acquiring and interpreting information from sensory data.* Perception is what we see, hear, smell, taste, and touch during any interaction. Every interaction contains sensory information or data; to understand our experiences, we must organize all the data collected by our senses. We may choose to focus on some senses (like the way something smells or tastes) and not on others (such as the way it looks). Because we receive a considerable amount of sensory input each day, we give attention to and remember only particular parts of each situation. This means we *select* (consciously or unconsciously) which sensory information to focus on. *The process of consciously or unconsciously selecting sensory data to maintain our focus* is called **selective attention**. Selective attention helps to explain the different perceptions between Americans and the Sudanese boys. Because perception is so important to understanding communication, we will examine several different factors that shape our perceptions.

Process of Perception

The processes of perception and selective attention, or focusing on particular sensory data, are influenced by a variety of conditions. Some of

perception
process of acquiring and interpreting information from sensory data.

selective attention
process of consciously or unconsciously selecting sensory data to maintain our focus.

Charles Gupton/Stone /Getty Images

Carnival mirrors intentionally distort our perception of ourselves by magnifying some parts of our appearance. When you selectively perceive events around you, you are engaged in a similar act, magnifying or reducing the attention you pay to that event.

the factors that help determine what we pay attention to include intensity and size, repetition, contrast, and personal motivations.

Intensity and Size The intensity and size of a stimulus will capture our attention. A loud noise or sound of a screaming child, a bright flashing light on an ambulance or police car, or seeing the bright lights and billboards of Las Vegas for the first time are intense stimuli that are immediately noticed.

Repetition When a noise or message is continuous, we are likely to pay attention to it. For example, we may focus on the ticktock of a clock, on a phone number repeated several times in an infomercial, or on teachers repeating information several times (we are hoping you will pay attention and remember the information).

Contrast We tend to notice objects, sounds, or behaviors that are different from our expectations: unanticipated storm clouds rolling in, an overly lethargic pet, or seeing food from another culture for the first time.

Personal Motivations Our feelings or intentions will also affect which sensory data get priority. If we are intending to purchase a car, then we will likely pay more attention to car advertisements than if we were not in the market for a vehicle. If we visit a new city, we may pay careful attention to street signs whereas we tend to ignore them when driving around familiar neighborhoods. If we want to do well on an upcoming exam, we may listen more carefully in class.

Understanding the process of perception helps explain why we notice and remember certain events and not others. But there are other factors that cause us to focus on some sensory data but not on others, including our families, cultures, and technology. We explore those influences next.

Influences on Perception

Our families, cultures, and even technology influence the process of perception in important ways, shaping who we are and how we see the world around us. We now take a look at each of these factors.

Self and Family Our perception of ourselves and the world around us is influenced by the roles we assume or are expected to take on in our families. A role is "the part an individual plays in a group" (DeVito, 1986, p. 269). In our families, roles include a variety of possibilities: sons and daughters, sisters and brothers, parents and children, youngest or oldest, responsible or forgetful, comedian or drama queen, and more. Perceptions about who we are get communicated through verbal and nonverbal feedback. A father might introduce one of his children this way—"This is my son, he's our risk taker"—but another by saying, "This is our youngest, the baby in the family." These roles are expressed verbally and communicate a set of expectations that the individual is expected to fulfill. A mother might reinforce these roles verbally and nonverbally by hesitating to let the younger one explore while encouraging the "risk taker" to do so, and even rewarding each one for fulfilling his or her role.

Although our roles evolve and change as we grow, our initial perceptions of who we are become defined early by the family unit. If your family continuously comments on your athletic ability, then you may begin to see yourself as having athletic talent. However, outside individuals may also influence your perception of yourself. If your teacher tells you that your academic work is not good enough to qualify you as "gifted and talented" or to progress to the next grade, then you may believe that you are not very intelligent. Researchers call this influence the **looking-glass self**, and it describes *the way other people's perceptions of us defines our own perceptions of ourselves* (Cooley, 1968). The looking-glass self begins at an early age and is primarily influenced by family members, but it also is affected by individuals such as our teachers, friends, coaches, and neighbors. And these messages influence how we see the world later on. So, in the preceding example, the risk taker might perceive new opportunities as an adventure, whereas the baby of the family might see them as challenges and obstacles to be avoided.

Self and Culture Culture also influences the way we perceive ourselves and the world around us. What we see, hear, smell, taste, and touch are often determined, influenced, or guided by the cultures in which we live (Singer, 1982). Cognitive psychologist Richard Nisbett has explored this influence, noting that people we describe as coming from an Eastern culture (Chinese, Koreans, and Japanese) and a Western culture (Europeans, Canadians, and U.S. Americans) differ in how they perceive objects and situations. He claims that people from Eastern cultures focus attention on backgrounds, group objects according to thematic relationships, and usually see both sides of an argument. People from Western cultures, on the other hand, focus directly on objects, group in taxonomies, and tend to reject one side of an argument (Nisbett, 2000). Hence, our culture shapes which sensory data are observed and how they are interpreted.

The speed at which tasks are accomplished is also bound by cultural influences. In many cultures, getting things done quickly is valued. Instant messaging and texting can produce immediate feedback, fast-food restaurants can produce meals in minutes, and overnight delivery services can have packages on doorsteps by the next (or even the same) day. However, fast service is not a priority in other cultures. In Central America, Mexico, and Spain, for example, people enjoy a more leisurely pace of life, and taking time to relax and enjoy life at a slower pace is a more typical cultural experience. So, although it is tempting to think that all humans organize their perceptions similarly, culture influences and helps explain differences in perceptions of time, appointments, and the overall pace by which tasks are completed.

looking-glass self
the way other people's perceptions of us define our own perceptions of ourselves.

Perception and Technology Technology and media also impact our perceptions. The sound from our computers indicating we have new e-mail, the vibration of our phones letting us know that someone is calling or texting, the bright letters flashing on our televisions with breaking news stories, and advertisements popping up on our PDAs—all of these show what some person or organization wants us to look at. The staggering number of advertisements an average person is exposed to each day (as many as 5,000 every day) means that there are plenty of requests and opportunities for us to pay attention to and organize certain sensory data (Story, 2007). These data, however, are already highly organized. Colors, images, words, and sounds are strategically placed in every advertisement to draw our attention to certain things and encourage us to accept a message or purchase an item. Beyond family or cultural influences, technology challenges us to sort through messages about who we are or can be, to consider what the looking-glass of technology is reflecting back to us, and to consider these influences more and more carefully and thoughtfully.

Our families, culture, and media, as well as the factors that influence perception, shape the way we experience and interpret situations. However, as individuals, we also bring an important component called a *standpoint* to the process of perception. We will explore standpoints and identity and their influence on perception next.

Perception, Identity, and Standpoint

Identity refers to the *social categories that we and others identify as important characteristics of who we are.* Although there are many social categories that exist, such as "Latina," "female," "college student," "middle child," "punk," "nerd," and "girly girl," they only become part of our identity if we accept or associate with them. Identities are what make us unique. Researchers Loden and Rosener (1991) explain that there are primary and secondary dimensions of our identities. **Primary dimensions** are *based on identity traits that we are born with and are a significant part of who we are.* Primary dimensions of our identity might include our race, gender, social class, sexual orientation, physical abilities, and ethnicity. **Secondary dimensions** are *identities that we acquire, develop, or discard throughout our lives.* Examples of secondary dimensions include educational level, career choice, and relationship status. Both dimensions of our identities shape our perceptions, but research suggests that our primary identities might hold more influence than the secondary dimensions because our primary identities tend to be more stable (Ting-Toomey, 1999).

As noted, both primary and secondary identities shape what is often called our standpoints. A **standpoint** is *the perspectives from which a person views and evaluates society.* Standpoints are influenced by the different aspects of our identities, or the complex combination of traits that make up our self. Each person's identity is unique and slightly different from others. One person may describe herself as "heterosexual, female, Asian American, adopted, and an only child." Another might offer the following description: "gay, male, Caucasian, youngest of six, and Texan."

identity

social categories that we and others identify as important characteristics of who we are.

primary dimensions

identity traits that we are born with and that are significant parts of who we are.

secondary dimensions

identities that we acquire, develop, or discard throughout our lives.

standpoint

the perspectives from which a person views and evaluates society.

zhu difeng/Shutterstock.com

We often have different standpoints, depending on our identities. What are your primary and secondary identities? How do they influence your standpoints?

SPEAKING VISUALLY

Media and Self-Concept

Intel's Museum of Me creates a visual archive of a person based on the images and content presented on the individual's Facebook account. Juxtaposing images, texts, and videos from a Facebook profile allows the user to travel through a virtual museum to explore who he or she really is.

Although the site itself has received hundreds of thousands "I like" reviews on Facebook, some users report feeling quite unsettled with the visual results displayed in the three-minute video. Ben Popper described the eerie feeling he had when he viewed an image of his sister directly next to a deceased friend followed by a co-worker in a goofy pose (Popper, 2011). Popper explains, "It was disturbing to look at the smiling face of a now-deceased college friend next to a dumb office joke. It was unpleasant to watch the deep important connections I recorded on the social network thrown in with weird corporate images I don't ever remember posting. My point is . . . the very personal nature of this information makes the context in which it sits extremely important" (Popper, 2011). Although some users find Museum of Me "creepy," not everyone agrees. One respondent to Popper's article stated he needed to "lighten up" and to "let the world have some fun" (Popper, 2011).

What Do You Think?

1. Do media have an impact on creating one's self-concept? Why or why not?

2. In what ways can an interactive media feature like Museum of Me both help and hurt the self-concept of Facebook participants?

3. Have you personally experienced a situation where something presented on a social media site affected your self-esteem?

4. What, if anything, should be done to monitor media content and images in order to protect adolescents and teenagers from the negative effects that media can have on self-perception?

A third might choose "young male from Sudan who lost his entire family when he was a small boy" as the best description of his complex identity. These identities, complex and different, influence not only how a person perceives events and experiences but also how others perceive them. The different parts of these identities make up a person's standpoint, or the perspective from which she or he sees and experiences the world.

Standpoints help to explain how the perception of who we are exists in relationship to others and how this relationship is based on social, political, cultural, and economic power systems (Hartstock, 1999). Standpoints help us see that different identities are weighted differently in our society. For example, although "heterosexual, white, college-educated male" may be ranked very high in U.S. culture, "gay" or even "Sudanese" affect rankings in ways that "heterosexual" or "white" do not. Similarly, although the identity of "heterosexual" holds a high ranking in the United States, "Asian American," "female," and even "relocated to the United States from Sudan" change that ranking slightly. And the identities of "only child," "adopted," or "youngest of six" affect how a person sees the world, as do "homeless" and "orphaned." Like the example of the Lost Boys that opened this chapter, the identities we find salient, the ones we describe as important to us, shape our perceptions. However, standpoint, as well as the primary and secondary dimensions of our identity, help explain our differences, our relationships to others, and the ways in which social, political, and economic systems affect our perceptions.

The process of perception is a complex one, and the ways we communicate are influenced by what we perceive and how others perceive us. Understanding these processes and influences helps us communicate more clearly with others and appreciate our uniqueness and similarities.

Perceiving Our Self

The perception of who we are influences the way we behave in our personal relationships, at work, and in society. The answers to the question "Who am I?" constitute our **self-concept**, or the *perception of who we are and what makes us unique as well as similar to others* (Hormouth, 1990). Our self-concept is based on many characteristics, such as our physical appearance, talents, intellect, popularity, age, starting a career, fears, and beliefs (Piers & Harris, 1996). Although some aspects remain stable, others change throughout our lives, and some characteristics may be more important or significant than others. Turning eighteen years of age and being eligible to join a political party and vote, graduating from college and obtaining employment, and committing to a relationship may help define our self-concept. In addition to these characteristics, our families, culture, and society affect our understanding of who we are. We will explore those influences now.

self-concept
perception of who we are and what makes us unique as well as similar to others.

labels
words used to describe ourselves and others.

What messages were communicated to you by family members that shaped your self-concept?

Self-Concept and Family

Family members help shape our self-concept, particularly as children. Parents, siblings, and relatives rely on verbal and nonverbal forms of communication to convey messages about who we are. **Labels**, or the *words used to describe ourselves and others*, are an important component of this influence. Andie, a five-year-old girl, may believe she is "shy, musically talented, and pretty" based on the way her family talks to and about her. Her sister, Georgia, however, sees herself as "outgoing, athletic, and a tomboy" based on the way her family labels her. Our self-concept also can be filled with positive or negative characteristics. A child growing up in a negative environment may be labeled a "problem child," whereas a child growing up in a positive environment with the same behaviors might be labeled "high spirited." Labels have a powerful influence on our self-concept. Positive labels can enhance our self-concept and self-esteem, and negative labels can be detrimental to our perceptions of who we are as a person.

Self-Concept and Culture

Culture also shapes our understanding of our self-concept. Particular cultural norms and social rules affect the way we think about ourselves, behave in public and private settings, and respond toward others. The United States is said to be an individualistic culture that values free enterprise and freedom of speech, religious freedom, and democracy. These cultural norms shape our perceptions of who we are; in the United States, our self-concepts are shaped by the belief that we should be independent and self-sufficient. Our self-concepts also are shaped by the U.S. view of religion and how religious practices are carried out. In addition, the United States' commitment to the freedom of speech shapes our views about our ability to speak out, write letters to public officials, and even tolerate hostile or hateful speech. Other cultures influence self-concepts differently. In some cultures, open conflict or speaking out publicly against the government is discouraged or even dangerous; the ways religions are practiced is quite different from the U.S. practices of Christianity, Catholicism, and Judaism; and even who can attend schools, what can be studied, and for how long varies from the views of the United States. These cultural factors affect a person's self-concept or response to "who am I?" in powerful and subtle ways.

Self-Concept and Communication

We receive all kinds of messages about who we are from family members, teachers, neighbors, friends, co-workers, and members of organizations or clubs in which we belong. **Symbolic interactionism** describes this influence and is the *process of understanding our sense of self based on other's observations, judgments, and evaluations of our behavior* (Mead, 1934). When similar messages about who we are get repeated by significant others in our lives, we begin to understand what makes us similar to and different from others. When friends, teachers, and neighbors comment on our artistic abilities, we are likely to believe we have a talent. When friends, co-workers, and significant others tell us we are generous, we may believe we are kind.

symbolic interactionism
process of understanding our sense of self based on other's observations, judgments, and evaluations of our behavior.

Our self-concept is shaped by the language used to define us as individuals. When we internalize labels or comments made about who we are and then *act in accordance to these expectations*, we are engaging in a **self-fulfilling prophecy**. When a child is labeled a "bad child," she may internalize this message and begin behaving badly at home and at school. If a child is labeled the "class clown," he may see himself as funny and continue to make jokes during class. Although some labels may be accurate for a particular time in our life, we often grow and develop in ways that reshape these expectations. If Erin is labeled as a "shy child," she may feel afraid in unfamiliar social settings. However, Erin may outgrow this fear and eventually become an outspoken and confident person later in life. Other labels may never be valid at all. If a child is told he will never succeed in college (even though he could), he may adopt a destructive self-fulfilling

self-fulfilling prophecy
to act in accordance to expectations.

Kimberly White/Reuters/Corbis

Stephen Hawking, internationally renowned physicist, was diagnosed with Lou Gehrig's disease and has now lost the use of his arms, legs, and voice. Still, his self-esteem remains high. When asked by BBC News (2007) how he feels about having the disease, he responded, "I try to lead as normal a life as possible and not think about my condition or regret the things it prevents me from doing, which are not that many."

self-esteem

how we feel about ourselves based on perceptions of our own strengths and weaknesses.

prophecy by choosing to not enroll in college classes. However, he may also overcome this label, avoiding the self-fulfilling prophecy, and find the self-esteem he needs to succeed. In the next section, we will look at how self-esteem can help us avoid the negative prophecies we hear from others.

Self-Esteem

Our **self-esteem** consists of *how we feel about ourselves based on perceptions of our own strengths and weaknesses.* Our self-esteem reflects our view of our own value or worth: it is the high or low regard we give to our selves. If we like ourselves and value who we are, then we are said to have high self-esteem. If we do not see ourselves as valued or worthy or if we do not like who are, then we are said to have low self-esteem. Self-esteem can and often does fluctuate over time. On days you are feeling good about yourself because things have gone well (you got that job offer you worked hard for) or when you feel good about what you accomplished throughout the day (you did well on an exam), you may have high self-esteem. On the other hand, if you receive a failing grade on an assignment that you spent a great deal of time on, or if you are the only one in a group who does not understand the rules or play a particular sport, then you may have a day of lower self-esteem. But how do you know what your self-esteem is? How can you be sure you have a healthy self-esteem rather than an overinflated one? The next sections discuss ways to assess and enhance your esteem as well as the role communication plays in both.

Assessing Our Self-Esteem We can assess our self-esteem in a few ways. One way is to listen to others' appraisals of who we are. Do other people praise us or criticize us? Do they label us positively or negatively? What kind of worth or value do they assign us? The influence of their communication is called **reflected appraisal**, *the process of developing an image of who we are based on the way others describe us.* Regardless of whether the appraisals are accurate or not, the impact is powerful. If we have received predominantly negative messages about ourselves, we might suffer from low self-esteem. However, if we have received predominantly positive messages, we might also suffer from an overinflated self-esteem.

As you consider the messages others have communicated to you and the value or worth assigned to those messages, keep in mind the concept of self-fulfilling prophecy and the impact it can have on our views of our self. You will also want to consider the effect of gender on self-esteem. Decades of research have determined that boys' and girls' self-esteem develops differently. Adolescent girls experience a significant drop in their self-esteem as they attend middle and high school. Adolescent boys may see a slight drop, but nothing as profound as lowering of self-esteem seen in girls at that same age (Kilbourne, 1999). The differences are attributed to many factors, including messages from media, teachers, and parents; athletic and extracurricular opportunities; social pressures; and even messages about physical appearance and development. In addition, even though girls fare far worse than boys during this time, research is beginning to suggest that boys' self-esteem regarding academic potential is lower than is girls' during this same period (Kimmell, 2008).

A second way to assess your self-esteem is through the process of social comparison. When we use **social comparison**, *we compare ourselves with others in order to determine our value or worth in relationship to that other person.* Although social comparisons can be helpful in assessing our own value or worth, they also can backfire and lower our self-esteem. Consider the following example.

Etine is a very good creative writer and poet. She likes to take long walks and loves quiet evenings, but she is not interested in or good at team sports such as soccer and basketball. She is tall (5'11") and has a very healthy body, fitting into the appropriate weight category for her height and bone structure.

Marlena is tall, like Etine, and has a very healthy body. She loves basketball and soccer and is quite good at both. She is not one to sit still, so writing is difficult for her. She would much rather watch a good movie with friends or go to a concert than read a book or take a walk.

Etine and Marlena can use social comparison positively or negatively. Used positively, Etine might say, "Marlena and I are both tall and healthy—and this is a good thing. Marlena is good at sports and in busy social settings, and I am better at quiet, creative activities. Together we

reflected appraisal
the process of developing an image of who we are based on the way others describe us.

social comparison
comparing ourselves with others in order to determine our value or worth in relationship to that other person.

make a great team." Used negatively, however, Marlena might say, "Etine and I are both too tall for women and not thin enough. I'm too much of a tomboy, and Etine is much better at the right sort of feminine activities than I am. I'm a failure at writing, and I'm too undisciplined—I waste my time with all these social activities."

Etine has used social comparison in a positive way, whereas Marlena has used it in a negative way. When we compare ourselves to others and find that we are lacking in all aspects, then we lower our self-esteem. If we compare ourselves to others and come away with a healthy balance, we are using social comparison more productively.

A final way to assess your self-esteem is to consider the role culture and society play in influencing the worth or value we place on our self. Psychologists suggest that individuals with strong ties to their racial or ethnic groups have higher self-esteem than do those who do not identify strongly with a group or are uncertain about their identification (Phinney, Cantu, & Kurtz, 1997; Umaña-Taylor, 2004). Individuals who have a negative view of their ethnic or racial membership also experience lower self-esteem. But these psychologists also discovered that even if the larger culture or society views the ethnic or racial category negatively, an individual who views it positively and identifies with it strongly maintains high self-esteem.

When people have high self-esteem, they have a positive appraisal of their worth and who they are as persons. Having high self-esteem can determine certain personality traits and even be an indicator of success. For example, people with high self-esteem tend to be extraverted, conscientious, emotionally stable, better at conflict resolution, and open to new experiences (Bechtoldt, Carsten, Dreu, Nijstad, & Zapf, 2010; Robins, Trzesniewski, Potter, & Gosling, 2001). In addition, one who possesses high self-esteem may be more independent, optimistic, and self-directed. By contrast, those who possess low self-esteem may be more pessimistic, insecure, lonely, and depressed (Mruk, 1999). If you have low self-esteem, then there are ways to begin to raise it. Similarly, if your self-esteem is too high, there might be ways to find a better balance.

Enhancing or Maintaining Our Self-Esteem Self-esteem is important for building healthy relationships, performing well in school and extracurricular activities, and for maintaining self-worth. The desire for high self-esteem begins at an early age. As children hear they are talented, smart, funny, or kind (and believe these things to be true), their self-esteem is likely to increase. If children are told the opposite—that they are not very talented or smart—then they may adopt low self-esteem. The desire for praise does not end with childhood. A recent study of college students found that receiving a compliment or earning a good grade to enhance self-esteem was more important than drinking alcohol, getting a paycheck, eating a favorite food, or seeing a best friend (Salamon, 2011). But we do not always receive compliments, and sometimes exams do not go well for us. There are ways we can improve or manage our self-esteem: get involved, move forward, make friends, exercise, and connect with our families.

Get Involved People who are involved in their families and communities, volunteer their time, and even attend social or community events (book clubs, fundraising events, etc.) report improved self-esteem. "'Engaged' individuals" report benefits to their "physical and psychological health," improved self-confidence and self-esteem, and a "sense of personal empowerment" and better social relationships. But do not overdo it: too much engagement can overtax us and leave us feeling fatigued (Attree, French, Milton, Poval, Whitehead, & Popay, 2011).

Move Forward In *Boost Your Self-Esteem*, John Caunt suggests that people need to sort out and then move past experiences that have damaged their self-esteem. Caunt suggests ten ways to "put yourself in the driver's seat" and move beyond emotional hurts and traumas that have brought a person lower self-esteem. Among his suggestions are identifying the excess baggage we carry around, moving beyond blaming others, finding positive outcomes from difficult experiences, and rewarding yourself for letting go of the negative experiences (Caunt, 2003). When we move beyond what is making us feel poorly about ourselves, we can begin to develop a positive view of ourselves.

Make Friends Sometimes a person's self-esteem may be low because of illness, injury, or loneliness. In "Cool Friends," Kath MacDonald and Alison Greggans discovered that individuals with health problems—in this case, cystic fibrosis—had improved self-esteem as a result of a "befriending" program. Those who were befriended felt more important and improved their social skills, and the befriending was described as a positive process by all parties involved. In addition, Jennifer Thomas and Kimberly Daubman report that for both boys and girls, friendship played an important role in achieving and maintaining positive self-esteem (MacDonald & Greggans, 2003; Thomas & Daubman, 2001). The role of friends is also important for lesbian, gay, bisexual, and transgendered individuals, who report that support networks other than family play a major role in the development of positive self-esteem (Wilson, Zeng, & Blackburn, 2011).

Exercise Decades of research suggest a positive correlation between healthy self-esteem and exercise (Holland & Andre, 1994; Taylor, 1995; Wilkins, Boland, & Albinson, 1991). Intuitively, we know that we often feel better about ourselves after we work out or engage in some form of exercise. However, Jo Barton and Jules Pretty suggest that "green" exercise—that is, exercise done outside in nature—goes even further in improving self-esteem. Barton and Pretty argue that "acute exposure to green exercise" positively affects the self-esteem of both women and men (Barton & Pretty, 2010).

Family Our families play a crucial role in our self-esteem. When individuals report receiving the guidance and positive support of one parent, their self-esteem tends to be strong; when they receive positive guidance and support from two parents, it is even higher (Bulanda & Majumdar, 2009). Studies also show that when our families are involved in our lives in positive ways, both males and females are less likely to engage

Our perceptions of the ideal male or female body change over time. The image of Batman in the 1980s is very different from his image today. Young men who do not meet our current ideal standard of the perfect male body may suffer from lower self-esteem.

in delinquent behaviors, take fewer risks sexually, and engage in less risky substance-abuse behaviors. For Latinas, who have higher rates of suicide attempts than their white and African American peers, *familism*, or the positive involvement of family, appears to reduce the risk of suicide attempts (Kuhlberg, Peña, & Zayas, 2011; Paterson, Buser, & Westburg, 2010).

Having a healthy self-esteem is important to leading a healthy life. However, individuals who have too much self-esteem—"big egos"—can be difficult to work or socialize with.

Self-Esteem and the Media

Messages communicated via the media affect our self-esteem, but this effect may not always be positive. In her video *Killing Us Softly IV*, Jean Kilbourne argues that the only image young girls see in the media today are images of tall, very slim, and very busty white or light-skinned women (Jhally & Kilbourne, 2010). Because many girls' self-esteem is directly related to body image, the pervasiveness of an unachievable ideal beauty standard and extreme thinness can prove deadly. Girls are constantly exposed to messages that communicate only thin girls are desirable, yet only 5 percent of the U.S. population genetically has the body type consistently depicted in popular media.

Young men also are susceptible to low self-esteem after viewing images of muscular men appearing in television, advertisements, and sporting events. Even action figures and superhero costumes now contain six-pack abs and large biceps. However, research suggests that men's perception of what women desire as the ideal chest size for men is larger than what women actually report as the desired size. And men experience lower self-esteem than women when they do not achieve their desired chest size (Tantleff-Dunn, 2001).

In addition, a 2008 study published in the *Journal of Social and Clinical Psychology* determined that

> both men and women are affected by exposure to idealized images in the mass media, which is often associated with negative feelings and thoughts about their bodies. This suggests that the use of muscular male models or skinny female models in the mass media is potentially damning to "everybody." (Barlett, Vowels, & Saucier, 2008, p. 306)

Media can and do affect our self-esteem positively, however. Independent films, documentaries, YouTube videos, blogs, Facebook posts, and a variety of organizational Web sites allow individuals to create their own images, narratives, and stories to poke fun at social norms and codes and

Women's Self-Esteem and the Media

Eating disorders are a growing epidemic in the United States. A recent study by Harris Interactive found the percentage of girls who believe they must be thin rose from 48 percent in 2000 to 60 percent in 2006 (Zaslow, 2009). *Wall Street Journal* reporter Jeffrey Zaslow has been tracking girls and dieting for more than three decades. He argues that "self-starvation in girls can be triggered by media images, including Internet sites promoting anorexia and bulimia as lifestyle choices" (Zaslow, 2009). He cites pitch lines used to lure in young women such as "Nothing tastes as good as thin feels" and "Thirty hours food-free sounds like heaven" promotes an unhealthy (and potentially deadly) fascination with starvation.

kentoh/Shutterstock.com

Finding support groups that encourage anorexia and bulimia are now just a click away. The new catchphrase for so-called pro-ana (pro-anorexia) Web sites is called "thinspiration," which means using very thin female models as role models and as inspiration to diet, binge, purge, or starve. Thinspiration videos, blogs, and tweets are available for young girls to encourage this distorted motivation to be thin. Borzekowski, Schenk, Wilson, and Peebles (2010), researchers at The Johns Hopkins Bloomberg School of Public Health, examined the content and messages of 180 Web sites that advocated for eating disorders and concluded the following:

- 91 percent of sites were open to the public;

- 85 percent of sites featured thinspiration material (e.g., photographs of extremely thin models and celebrities);

- 79 percent had interactive features such as calorie and body-mass-index (BMI) calculators;

- approximately 16 percent had a "creed" or "oath to Ana," such as the "Thin Commandments," or ten rules for eating disorders—"Thou shall not eat without feeling guilty," "Thou shall not eat fattening food without punishing oneself afterward," and "What the scale says is the most important thing";

- approximately 43 percent provided specific instructions on concealing eating disorders; and

- approximately 33 percent of sites did include information about recovery or treatment, though only 13 percent of sites contained an overt statement that eating disorders are a problem.

Many people are outraged at the availability of content that promotes eating disorders and online advice and images. Letters have been written to YouTube demanding that thinspiration videos be banned on the grounds that they promote eating disorders.

What Do You Think?

1. What influences the perception that self-starvation is a worthy goal for young women? Identify the cultural and individual influences as well as the role that media play in promoting self-starvation.

2. Do you believe regulations are necessary to limit or ban pro-anorexia Web sites and videos? Would regulations be civil or uncivil? Explain why.

3. What are some alternatives to these catchphrases and Web sites that draw young women in to the thinspiration craze? Create several catchphrases and locate online videos, blogs, and Web sites that create a healthy image and dialogue around weight and normal body sizes, altering the perception that unhealthy thinness is the desired goal.

challenge unhealthy standards, as well as share experiences. They provide venues to educate ourselves, communicate with others who are seeking to break out of constricting images of masculinity and femininity, and to try out new ways of being and living.

Self-concept and self-esteem play an important role in how we view ourselves and what makes us unique. The way we internalize labels, access our strengths and weaknesses, and respond to others' appraisals of us influence our feelings about who we and are reflected in our communication with ourselves and others. We have learned what influences our perceptions of ourselves, so now let us look at how we perceive others.

Perceiving Others

First impressions significantly affect how we perceive others. In this section, we look at how to check our first impressions to see if they are accurate. Note, too, that we are also influenced by stereotypes when we form perceptions of other people. These broad generalizations can be ill informed (all Asian students are good at mathematics, for example). This section examines first impressions and also takes a close look at stereotypes.

The Power of First Impressions

When meeting someone for the first time, we form an impression more quickly than we might think or believe. Some research suggests that initial opinions, or "first impressions," are formed within as few as three seconds of meeting someone (Sterling, 2006). Other research indicates that some impressions are made even faster than that. Princeton psychologists Janine Willis and Alexander Todorov (2006) claim that an impression of a stranger's trustworthiness and attractiveness is formed from her or his facial appearance in just one tenth of a second. Although these impressions may not be completely accurate, they are certainly powerful.

First impressions often determine the future success of the relationship and play an important role in how the relationship evolves. If two people determine an immediate liking for each other, then the relationship will likely continue over time. If the immediate impression is that one person is "cool toward the other," then it is unlikely the relationship will grow (Sunnafrank & Ramierz, 2004). Initial impressions can have a significant impact on long-term development of a relationship.

Unfortunately, first impressions can be determined by extraneous or atypical circumstances. Have you ever met someone while you were experiencing tremendous emotional, psychological, or physical stress? Perhaps you stayed up all night studying for a final, or maybe you learned that a grandparent had recently passed away. You likely exhibited behaviors that are not consistent with your usual demeanor. Yet meeting someone during stressful moments can create an

Lauren Nicole/Getty Images

To test the importance of first impressions, make a list of your initial reactions to the individuals in this photo. Now compare your list to that of a classmate. Are the lists similar or different?

impression of you as someone who is stressed out, requires high maintenance, is depressed, or is emotional. For these reasons, it is important to recognize that our first impression may be a perceptual error. To help avoid committing perceptual errors, we should engage in **perception checking**, which means that *we consider a series of statements or questions to confirm (or challenge) our perceptions of others and their behaviors.* Three types of statements or questions can help us determine the accuracy of our evaluations:

1. Describe the verbal and nonverbal behavior observed.

2. Provide two possible interpretations for the behavior.

3. Seek clarification of or an explanation for the behavior.

Here's how perception checking works. After your roommate failed to meet you after class, you approach her about the situation. You begin by saying, "When I noticed that you were not waiting for me after class" (the behavior), "I thought that you might have forgotten to do so" (first interpretation) "or perhaps you were mad at me" (second interpretation). "Why weren't you outside the building today?" (seek clarification).

When using perception checking to understand a person's behavior, try not to suggest interpretations that might make others feel defensive (e.g., "You always forget and you don't care about our friendship" will probably make your roommate defensive). Offering interpretations should not sound like accusations but as heartfelt attempts to understand the other person. Perception checking can be a valuable skill in maintaining healthy relationships with friends and romantic partners.

Understanding Stereotypes

When we make assumptions about others based on initial impressions, incomplete information, or oversimplified assumptions, we may resort to stereotyping. A **stereotype** is a *broad generalization about a group of people based on limited exposure to an individual or members of that particular group.* When we categorize people based on demographic characteristics such as age, sex, race, political or religious affiliation, occupation, socioeconomic backgrounds, or sexual orientation, we tend to rely on stereotypes. For instance, believing that all African Americans are good at sports, that employees on Wall Street do not care about those working on Main Street, that fraternity brothers only care about partying, or that all gay men are fashionable are all examples of stereotypes. In contrast to generalizations, stereotypes are the result of a limited and often incorrect assessment of a group. Although stereotypes can help predict certain actions or behaviors (employees on Wall Street do not work on Main Street), they also can lead to prejudice and discrimination (not all Wall Street employees are heartless).

When a stereotype consists of a negative evaluation of others (women are not intelligent enough to run a company, for example), then conscious or unconscious forms of discrimination may occur (a woman may not be promoted to the job of CEO). Therefore, it is important to

perception checking
when we consider a series of statements or questions to confirm (or challenge) our perceptions of others and their behaviors.

stereotype
broad generalization about a group of people based on limited exposure to an individual or members of that particular group.

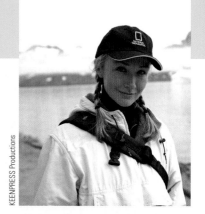

NATIONAL GEOGRAPHIC EXPLORER TIP ↗

Alexandra Cousteau
Emerging Explorer and Social Environment Advocate

Can you describe an experience in which perceptions of others played a significant role? For example, the impact of a first impression, or issues of stereotyping? How did this perception impact your effectiveness as a communicator?

I'm a young woman in a male-dominated legacy that includes my grandfather, my father, my brother, and my uncle and cousin, so it is always somewhat surprising when other people see a young blond girl who goes out at the field for seven months a year and does everything that the men of the family do. Sometimes when I go somewhere with my brother people think I'm his wife because we have same name.

On the other hand, I receive a lot of fan mail from women from all over the world. Women from places like Pakistan, India, and Bolivia write me letters saying, "You're such a role model for me." I realize that these women are watching and taking notes, and I hope that they feel empowered by the choices that I've made.

I tell young women, "Don't be afraid to have a big idea, and don't be afraid to go after it. If you fail, keep going because that failure will help you get up." I have had failures of my own, and I'm always happy in retrospect that I had these failures because they have taught me so much about how to get where I want to go. It is just a matter of knowing yourself, knowing what you want, and never giving up (Cousteau, 2012).

---

identity management
process of altering our own behaviors in order to shape others' impressions of who we are.

PRACTICING HUMAN COMMUNICATION

Experiencing Stereotyping

Think about a situation in which someone made a biased judgment about you or someone you know based on age, skin color, clothing, sex, sexuality, political affiliation, religious affiliation, ability or disability, socioeconomic status, or some other quality or attribute. Explain how you knew that stereotyping was occurring. What assumptions, words, or actions resulted from these stereotypes? How can communicating civilly help reduce stereotyping others?

remember that not all members of a group are alike. When we talk about a demographic trait or use language that indicates that an entire group "is" or "does" something—women *are*, lesbians *will*, Mormons *believe*, men *won't*, or politicians *don't*, for example—then we tend to assume that *all* members of the group are alike. Unfortunately, this viewpoint does not account for the differences and uniqueness of each individual person. To avoid stereotyping, we need to realize that members of a similar group or demographic category are still unique individuals with different life experiences and worldviews.

Managing Impressions

Sociologist Erving Goffman explains that people are actors who create an impression of who they are by behaving differently in different types of situations. According to Goffman, individuals attempt to manage others' impressions by modifying their behaviors, appearance, and manners (Trevino, 2003). He calls this **identity management**, which is *the process of altering our own behaviors*

KEENPRESS Productions

in order to shape others' impressions of who we are. Goffman uses the term *face* to describe each individual's socially approved and presenting self. The process of **facework** consists of the *verbal and nonverbal strategies used to present different faces to others.* Think of facework as similar to putting on different faces for different social situations. You may have one face or identity for communicating with family members, another face or identity for the workplace, a third face or identity for hanging out with friends, another face as a student attending class, and a final face for your romantic relationship. Although each face shares some common features with the others, there is something unique about each identity given the social situation. Putting on faces is part of identity management. We may continue to wear the faces that are rewarded and discard the ones that solicit negative reactions from others.

The ways we manage our identity—*self-monitoring*—may be conscious or unconscious. **High self-monitors** are *individuals who are acutely aware of their self-expressions and identity management behavior* (Snyder, 1979). High self-monitors adjust and respond to the social cues in the surrounding environment. They work at "behaving appropriately" for every situation and are good readers of nonverbal cues. You could say they wear many faces. Because of their desire to respond appropriately to each situation, high self-monitors may conceal true internal feelings (such as feeling ill or having opinions that strongly differ from those being expressed) by continuing to present themselves in the ways that are expected of them. High self-monitors may be referred to as "chameleons" because they "present the right image for the right audience."

Low self-monitors are more willing to respond the way they truly feel in most social situations. **Low self-monitors** *communicate without paying much attention to how others are responding to their messages.* Low self-monitors pay less attention to others' nonverbal cues and instead show more consistency between their own feelings and behaviors. Low self-monitors are more forthcoming about their true thoughts, feelings, and desires regardless of the social context surrounding the situation. Low self-monitors wear only a few faces, and you usually know their true feelings and where they stand on issues, regardless of who they are with.

High and low self-monitoring are simply different approaches to the way we interact with others. From a self-monitoring perspective, high self-monitors can adjust their behaviors to meet the demands of different situations. They may ask, "Who does this situation want me to be, and how can I be that person?" (Snyder, 1979). Low self-monitors are consistent in demonstrating behavior that is consistent with their inner feelings, attitudes, and beliefs (Mehra, Kilduff, & Brass, 2001). They may ask, "Who am

When we label someone "two-faced," we are making a negative assessment of that person. However, most of us do quite a bit of impression management and facework every day. What is the difference between being two-faced and engaging in impression management?

facework
verbal and nonverbal strategies used to present different faces to others.

high self-monitors
individuals who are acutely aware of their self-expressions and identity management behavior.

low self-monitors
people who communicate without paying much attention to how others are responding to their messages.

Paul Bradbury/The Image Bank/Getty Images

I, and how can I be me in this situation?" (Snyder, 1979). Martin Kilduff, a professor of management at the University of Cambridge, explains that high self-monitors may be better at managing conflict or difficult workplace circumstances (Toegel, Anand, & Kilduff, 2007). Because high self-monitors pay more attention to nonverbal cues and are sensitive toward others' needs, they are more likely to successfully mediate or manage difficult situations. Low self-monitors, however, may contribute positively to discussions of complex issues where a range of opinions are sought, because they are more willing to directly express who they are and how they feel.

 ## Civility, Social Justice, and Perception

The power of first impressions, stereotypes, limited exposure to diverse groups or individuals, and culture undoubtedly affect perception and civility. Consider the following examples.

University of California at Los Angeles (UCLA) student Alexandra Wallace received national attention and criticism after posting a three-minute video rant against Asians. In the video, Wallace complained about

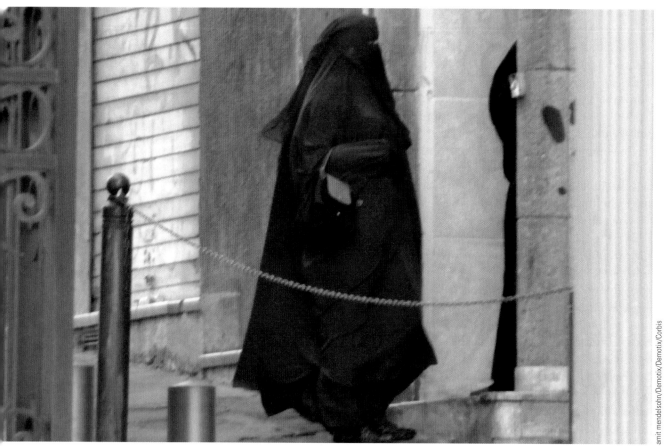

Burqas are the cultural norm for dress for women in several countries, yet they have been banned and critiqued but also worn and defended as acceptable dress for women. As a class, discuss what you think might be possible civil approaches to understanding the various perceptions of women wearing burqas.

Asian students sitting in the library talking on their cell phones to family members about the devastating tsunami that struck Japan. Sitting in front of her laptop camera, Wallace stated, "The problem is these hordes of Asian people that UCLA accepts into our school every single year, which is fine … but if you're going to come to UCLA, then use American manners" (Lovett, 2011). She then mimicked the people she spoke against. Wallace's video caused many debates about ethnocentrism, stereotyping, and racial discrimination. In fact, shortly after the video was viewed by more than 100,000 people, and after receiving death threats, Wallace withdrew from UCLA. Meanwhile, UCLA's chancellor posted a video response claiming Wallace's opinions were not the opinions of the UCLA community and called for more "civil discourse."

The state of Arizona passed immigration legislation that requires immigrants to carry identity documents that legitimize their presence in the United States. Authorities are free to consider anyone who looks "suspicious" as an immigrant and to ask for documentation. In addition, Arizona is considering laws that deny citizenship to children born in the United States with parents who are undocumented immigrants, require hospitals to ask for documentation of citizenship before treating individuals thought to be immigrants, and prevent children of undocumented individuals from attending school and their parents from purchasing vehicles (Rau, 2011). According to the American Civil Liberties Union (ACLU, 2011), Alabama has a similar law in place that allows police officers to ask for documents proving citizenship or immigration status during traffic stops as well as requiring school officials to verify children's immigration status. Civil rights attorney Thomas Saenz argues that these issues are federal issues, rather than decisions that can be made state by state, and that "we need a reform to ensure there is greater fairness, due process, and equal protection in our immigration system" (Skinner, 2010).

In Detroit, Michigan, a federal investigation followed allegations that Arab Americans and Muslims were inappropriately questioned about their religion, groped, and physically searched in "invasive and humiliating" ways at U.S. border crossings. Those who were searched described the events as "a form of sexual harassment." Chris Ortman, spokesperson for the Department of Homeland Security (DHS) said, "The DHS does not tolerate religious discrimination or abusive questioning—period" (Brand-Williams, 2011).

In France, a 2011 law banned women from wearing burqas in public and imposed fines if they do so. Police are to escort women wearing burqas to "a police station" and ask them "to remove the veil there for identification." According to one British newspaper, *The Guardian,* Rachid Nekkaz, a property dealer in France who is Muslim, is asking women to continue to wear the veil, "if they so desire," and states that "the street is the universal home of freedom and nobody should challenge that so long as these wom[e]n are not impinging on anyone else's freedom."

In each case, stereotypes, perceptions, and attitudes reduce civil discourse and potentially lead to acts of discrimination and violence.

Recall from Chapter 1 that when we decide to communicate civilly, we *make a decision to be open to hearing different views and perspectives, even though we may not agree with them.* Choosing civil communication does not require that we silence our own views or that we agree with everything another person says or does. Instead, civil communication means that we consider the impact of our perceptions, actions, and words on other people as we interact with them or even speak about them. Civil perception means that we understand stereotypes, engage in perception checking, and become aware of our first impressions. It means that we understand that our assumptions about others are shaped by our culture, our own experiences, and the media. To ensure our perceptions do not cause harm to others, we can monitor our tendency to stereotype, recognize ethnocentric acts (or the belief that one cultural perspective, norms, and ways of organizing are superior to others), and engage in perception checking to help increase civil discourse and action.

Chapter Summary

How Is Perception Defined?

- Perceptions are determined by what we see, hear, smell, taste, and touch.
- The intensity, size, repetition, contrast, and personal motivations that are part of many communication interactions help shape our perception of those interactions.

A Combination of Elements Shapes Our Perceptions of Our Self

- Families, culture, and technology affect the way we see ourselves—that is, our self-concept.
- Labels, cultural norms, and social rules have a powerful influence on our self-concept.
- Our self-esteem is influenced by reflected appraisals, social comparisons, and popular media.

Our Perceptions of Others Are Formed Quickly

- Perception checking can help ensure that we have formed appropriate evaluations of others.
- Categorizing people based on demographic characteristics may result in stereotyping.
- The process of identity management, including facework and self-monitoring, can shape other's impressions of who we are.

Civil Perception Means That We Make a Decision to Be Open to Hearing Different Views and Perceptions, Even Though We May Not Agree with Them

- First impressions, stereotypes, and limited exposure to diverse groups and cultures can negatively affect our perceptions.
- Civil perception means that we understand stereotypes, engage in perception checking, and become aware of our first impressions.

Key Concepts

facework (47)

high self-monitors (47)

identity (34)

identity management (46)

labels (36)

looking-glass self (33)

low self-monitors (47)

perception (31)

perception checking (45)

primary dimensions (34)

reflected appraisal (39)

secondary dimensions (34)

selective attention (31)

self-concept (36)

self-esteem (38)

self-fulfilling prophecy (37)   **standpoint** (34)   **symbolic interactionism** (37)

social comparison (39)   **stereotype** (45)

 Invitation to Human Communication Online

Speech Communication CourseMate includes an interactive eBook and interactive learning tools including National Geographic Explorer videos, student videos, quizzes, flashcards, and more. Speech Builder Express 3.0 and Speech Studio 2.0 are also available. Go to cengagebrain.com to access your CourseMate for *Invitation to Human Communication* to access these resources.

Further Reflection and Discussion

1. Who do you know personally who has high self-esteem? People with high self-esteem tend to be extraverted, conscientious, emotionally stable, better at conflict, and open to new experiences. Which of these attributes do you possess? Which ones do you want to develop?

2. Think about ways in which you may alter your behavior to management your identity. You may have one "face" or identity for communicating with family members, another for the workplace or for hanging out with friends, and one for a romantic relationship. What is unique about each of these identities in yourself? What are you

"managing" by changing your "face" for each type of communication?

3. Consider the information in this chapter about the French controversy in allowing women to wear burqas on the street. Is this civil and just? What is the reason France initiated this policy? Do you agree that "the street is the universal home of freedom"? If you agree, are there any exceptions? If you disagree, explain your viewpoint. How does perception play a role in this controversy? Is a fine or lessons in French citizenship a civil and just response to wearing a burqa? Explain the points of view of the French government and of those who oppose this.

Activities and Web Links

Visit cengagebrain.com to access the CourseMate for *Invitation to Human Communication* where these activities and web links can be found.

1. Read this brief *New York Times* article: "Anywhere an Eye Can See, It's Likely to See an Ad." Go to *Weblink 2.1.*

    Look at the photographs at the beginning of the article. Would you be influenced to buy the eggs with advertisements printed on them? Do you see yourself reflected in any advertisements? If not, what advertisements would you like to see that reflect your identity and values? How might these advertisements influence people's perceptions about the company that supplies the eggs or the doctor's office with the advertisement?

2. Read this article in *Business Week* online: "For College Students, Praise May Trump Sex and Money." What do you think about the five-year-old wearing the "I'm a winner!" sticker? Was it an effective way for the teacher to raise her students' self-esteem? What other methods may help to boost their self-esteem? What activities have boosted your self-esteem? Go to *Weblink 2.2.*

NONVERBAL COMMUNICATION

IN THIS CHAPTER YOU WILL LEARN TO:

- Identify the characteristics of nonverbal communication.

- Enhance your use of the different types of nonverbal communication.

Characteristics of Nonverbal
Communication

Types of Nonverbal Communication

Mark Read/National Geographic

*Different cultures assign different
meanings to nonverbal communication. What are some of the nonverbal
communication codes displayed in this
photograph?*

*I know photography can be a powerful tool, and
appreciation of our natural world is a good place to
start to get people thinking about the environment.*

—Jimmy Chin, climber, photographer, and National Geographic Emerging
Explorer

Starting at a young age, children quickly learn the basics of nonverbal communication (Boone & Sunningham, 1998). They learn to interpret the meaning of certain facial expressions such as smiling or frowning. They understand their parent's vocal cues that indicate whether they are excited, happy, or angry. Children also learn to follow hand signals that indicate which direction to move (a father points to the child's ball that has rolled behind a chair). All of us continue to use and interpret nonverbal communication throughout our lives. In fact, nonverbal communication tells us a great deal about the meaning of a message. In this chapter, we examine the characteristics of nonverbal communication and how gender, culture, verbal communication, and other factors affect nonverbal communication. Then we look at how to become more aware of nonverbal communication to be a more effective communicator.

Characteristics of Nonverbal Communication

We use nonverbal forms of communication every day. For example, when you raise your hand in class, your teacher recognizes that you want to ask a question. **Nonverbal communication** is *the process of conveying meaning without using the spoken word.* Nonverbal communication not only consists of nonword vocalizations such as "Shhh" and "Uh-huh" but also gestures, facial expressions, the movements of our body, and even the items with which we surround ourselves. We rely on nonverbal communication to help us understand the meaning of a message. In fact, studies indicate that between 65 percent and 93 percent of the total meaning of a message is determined by nonverbal signals (Birdwhistell, 1970).

This chapter explores the complex components of nonverbal communication. You will learn that your ability to understand nonverbal codes may be determined by your culture, gender, and even your age. We will also examine how relationships affect our nonverbal communication and the different forms, or codes, we use to communicate nonverbally. We also will explore the relationship between nonverbal and verbal communication. In the following sections, we examine each of these characteristics of nonverbal communication, as well as the influence of technology on our nonverbal messages.

nonverbal communication
the process of conveying meaning without using the spoken word.

COMMUNICATION AT WORK

Leaders, Greetings, and Cultural Differences

President Barack Obama has sparked controversy over his non-verbal greeting practices with several foreign leaders. Through-out his presidency, Obama has been photographed bowing to several foreign leaders, including Emperor Akihito of Japan, King Abdullah of Saudi Arabia, Queen Elizabeth of England, Ukrainian President Viktor Yushchenko, and more recently Chinese President Hu Jintao. Bowing is an expression of respect in many Asian and Middle Eastern cultures. Hence, some national and international viewers have interpreted President Obama's gesture as a sign of civility and respect for other cultures and customs. Supporters viewed the president's bows as acknowl-edging the worth of other world leaders and communicating respect for their traditional forms of greeting. Critics, however, were outraged at the sight of President Obama bowing to other leaders and believed that he displayed weakness and submis-sion to other cultures. In short, they argued that his bowing was an act of incivility to the American people—communicating that the United States was inferior to other countries.

Charles Dharapak/AP/Corbis

What Do You Think?

1. People in many Asian and Middle Eastern cultures bow their heads when greeting. Do you believe the president of the United States should follow traditional greeting practices of the country in which he is visiting, or should he always greet dignitaries and world leaders using the U.S. custom of a firm handshake?

2. If the U.S. president chooses to bow as a way to greet members of another culture, would you interpret this greeting as a sign of respect or of submission?

Nonverbal Communication Is Influenced by Culture

Have you ever felt uncomfortable when someone stood too close to you and occupied your personal space? Have you ever traveled and found it challenging to communicate with someone from a different culture because you were unfamiliar with their nonverbal customs? The meaning associated with different forms of nonverbal communication varies from one culture to another. For example, although many North Americans view "time as money" and expect things to start and finish "on time," other cultures have a more relaxed attitude about and a different sense of time than Americans. This can lead to a communication gap that is based in a nonverbal understanding of what it means to be on time. If you have plans to meet a friend for lunch at noon, it is common for North Americans to become fidgety if the friend has not arrived by 12:10 or 12:20. In other countries, it is customary and acceptable for there to be a timeframe of three or four hours.

The use and meaning of personal space and displays of emotions also vary between cultures. Many Americans converse with acquaintances or strangers while standing between four and twelve feet away from that person. People from the Middle East tend to stand much closer (Hall, 1969).

Although many emotions—happiness, anger, disgust, fear, surprise, and sadness—are considered "universal" (Ekman, Sorenson, & Friesen, 1969), there are differences in the rules for when it is appropriate to display these emotions. For example, open expressions of anger, disgust, and contempt are considered inappropriate in collectivistic cultures such as Japan because they are seen as threats to interpersonal harmony (Matsumoto, 1989; Safdar et al., 2009; Smith & Bond, 1994).

Cultural differences in nonverbal communication may be subtle or quite significant. It is likely that you already interact with people from a variety of cultural backgrounds and will continue to do so as you enter new work environments and social situations. You will read more about similarities and differences between cultures and nonverbal communication throughout this chapter.

Nonverbal Communication Is Influenced by Gender

There are real differences in the way men and women perform and interpret nonverbal communication. For example, women tend to be more responsive communicators than men. They tend to smile and gesture more often, maintain more eye contact, stand closer to others, and include more emotion in their facial expressions than their male counterparts. Men, on the other hand, tend to take up more space with their bodies, lean forward in conversations, speak louder, and hold onto the "talk stage" longer than women (Burgoon, Guerrero, & Floyd, 2010; Wood, 2013). The reasons for these differences are complex, and most scholars believe they come from our different gender socializations when people are boys and girls.

What types of nonverbal communication do you see being expressed as these women share a meal together? Are these nonverbal communication styles similar to your own or different? How so?

Multiple tests studying the ability to interpret nonverbal communication confirm that females typically score higher than males in decoding nonverbal cues (Hall, 1984; McClure, 2000). At a young age, girls begin decoding nonverbal cues at a higher success rate (an average of 2 percent better) than their male counterparts beginning in grade school and continuing through adulthood. Because these differences are important to communication, the influence of gender on nonverbal communication is discussed throughout this chapter.

Nonverbal Communication Is Relational

Nonverbal communication also conveys our view of ourselves and how we feel about others. We create a particular image about who we are based on our personal appearance, facial expressions, body language, and use of time and space. We can also reveal how we feel about others based on the way we greet another person, how closely we stand or sit by another person, and what forms of touch are used if any. Communication scholars studying nonverbal communication claim there are three dimensions of relationships that are expressed through our use of nonverbal messages: our liking and disliking of others, our positions of status and power in society, and our responsiveness toward others (Keeley & Hart, 1994; Mehrabian, 1971).

Nonverbal behaviors can communicate whether we feel positively or negatively about another person. **Liking** can be determined by *our body orientation, facial expression, use of touch,* and *proximity*. Standing or sitting face to face, leaning toward another person, being in close proximity, smiling, and making direct eye contact are all expressions of liking. Nonverbal behaviors that indicate liking also vary between genders and cultures.

An individual's status and power in society can also be determined through the use of nonverbal behaviors. Those in high-status positions tend to consume more space (have larger offices and houses), move into others' spaces more often, and use gestures and touch to exert control (Leathers, 1986). University presidents, company CEOs, and school principals tend to have the largest offices on campus and are more likely to enter the offices or spaces of teachers or subordinates than vice versa.

Finally, we communicate our interest or **responsiveness** to other people through nonverbal behaviors. *Displaying positive facial expressions, posture, and gestures* can indicate high levels of responsiveness. Remember that different cultures may express responsiveness in different ways. People in Western cultures tend to use eye contact to show interest, and they may look away, turn their body away, or physically move away to display disinterest. In other cultures such as Japan and some Native American cultures, direct eye contact is a sign of disrespect or even rudeness and can be seen as an invasion of another person's personal space.

Nonverbal Communication Is Ambiguous

Even though different cultures assign different meanings to nonverbal communication, different meanings also may be associated with the same display of nonverbal communication within a particular culture. This can make decoding nonverbal behavior challenging. For example, smiling and crying can have multiple meanings. You may smile to indicate happiness, because your workplace requires you to smile when greeting customers, or because you want to conceal a different, more private emotion. You may cry as a way to express an intense feeling of joy or to demonstrate feelings of pain, sadness, guilt, and even frustration. Paying attention to the context surrounding the nonverbal behavior can provide the information we need to help us interpret nonverbal messages.

liking
using our body orientation, facial expression, use of touch, or proximity to communicate our feelings about another person.

responsiveness
displaying positive facial expressions, posture, and gestures.

Because nonverbal messages are ambiguous, consider the many possible messages this man is communicating. Are there additional nonverbal cues he could use to clarify his intent?

Nomad_Soul/Shutterstock

In addition, our moods and age also influence our ability to understand nonverbal behavior. We often interpret how others are feeling based on our own mood. When we feel happy, we tend to see that same emotion in others' facial expressions; the converse is true as well. When we are feeling sad, frustrated, or angry, we tend to see that same emotion displayed by others (Niedenthal, Halberstadt, Margolin, & Innes-Ker, 2000). Our age also affects our success in decoding nonverbal cues. Our ability to decode non-verbal behavior improves as we grow older from age five and into our twenties and thirties (Harrigan, 1984; Markhan & Adams, 1992; Nowicki & Duke, 1994). As we continue to age, however, our ability to decode nonverbal communication declines. One study comparing women's ability to decode nonverbal communication reported that women in their sixties scored significantly lower than women in their twenties (Lieberman, Rigo, & Campain, 1988).

In summary, nonverbal communication is ambiguous, and many factors affect our ability to understand the meaning behind nonverbal behaviors. Our culture, gender, relationships, and age all influence how we interpret nonverbal messages. Although it can be a challenge to understand nonverbal communication, it is not impossible to interpret this form of communication accurately. Learning about cultural and gender differences, along with the different forms of nonverbal communication, can improve your ability to better understand the meaning behind the message.

Nonverbal Communication Is Related to Verbal Communication

Nonverbal and verbal forms of communication usually work together to send a message. There are six ways that nonverbal communication works in conjunction with verbal communication to create a message. Nonverbal communication can repeat, emphasize, complement, contradict, substitute, and regulate.

Repetition consists of *using the nonverbal signals that reproduce what is said verbally*. For example, when you turn your head from side to side while saying "No," you are using repetition. **Emblems** are *gestures that can be translated into words*, and they help to repeat spoken language. When you move your index finger side to side as you tell your friend "No," you repeat the "No" that is stated orally with an emblem.

Emphasis consists of *using nonverbal cues that strengthen what is stated verbally*. A person who yells "I'm so angry" while waving a fist in the air or hitting it against a table has added emphasis to the verbal statement.

Complementation occurs when *the nonverbal signal elaborates or expands the meaning of the verbal message*. An **illustrator** is a *nonverbal behavior that reinforces spoken words*. A child who says "I'm tired" while his eyes are beginning to close displays complementary forms of communication.

repetition
using the nonverbal signals that reproduce what is said verbally.

emblems
gestures that can be translated into words.

emphasis
using nonverbal cues that strengthen what is stated verbally.

complementation
when the nonverbal signal elaborates or expands the meaning of the verbal message.

illustrator
nonverbal behavior that reinforces spoken words.

Contradiction exists *when verbal and nonverbal forms of communication conflict with one another*. If a person's face begins to reveal signs of frustration or anger, but she indicates that "everything is okay" shows contradictory nonverbal cues and verbal messages. When contradiction exists, we typically believe the nonverbal cues over the verbal message.

Substitution occurs *when we rely on nonverbal codes instead of verbal ones*. When you give a "high-five" instead of saying "great job" or shrug your shoulders without speaking to indicate that you are unsure of something, you are using substitution.

Regulation is *the process of controlling conversations and interactions with others*. Looking at a clock or watch or grabbing your backpack or purse are examples of regulators that are used to control interaction with another and close a conversation. Making eye contact with a member of the group who has not contributed to the discussion may encourage that person to join the conversation.

Although these six components help explain how nonverbal and verbal communication relate to one another, there also are differences between the two modes of communication. As you have learned, nonverbal communication tends to be more ambiguous and have more options for communicating (e.g., posture, gestures, facial expressions, vocal cues) than verbal messages. Another important difference is that verbal communication is usually deliberate, whereas nonverbal communication is frequently unintentional. A yawning person probably is not intentionally revealing fatigue or boredom, but these are typical meanings associated with this nonverbal behavior.

Thus far, you have read how culture, gender, and relationships affect your ability to interpret nonverbal messages and that nonverbal cues are often ambiguous. You have also learned about the similarities and differences between verbal and nonverbal forms of communication. Now we will look at the different types, or codes, of nonverbal communication.

Types of Nonverbal Communication

Nonverbal codes of communication convey meaning through three interlocking systems: the visual, auditory, and invisible communication systems (Leathers, 1997). Communication scholar Dale Leathers offers the following scheme to explain these interlocking systems. The **visual communication system** includes *the codes of kinesics, proxemics, and artifacts*. The **auditory communication system** consists of *paralanguage*. The **invisible communication system** consists of *chronemics, olfactics, and haptics*. Although these codes intertwine and function together to create meaning, we will discuss each code individually.

Visual Codes of Nonverbal Communication

Visual codes of nonverbal communication include types of nonverbal communication that we can see: body movements (kinesics), the use of space (proxemics), and personal objects such as clothing or jewelry (artifacts).

Kinesics *The study of bodily movements such as gestures, posture, eye contact, and facial expressions* is called **kinesics**. Our bodily movements

---

contradiction
when verbal and nonverbal forms of communication conflict with one another.

substitution
when we rely on nonverbal codes instead of verbal ones.

regulation
the process of controlling conversations and interactions with others.

visual communication system
includes the codes of kinesics, proxemics, and artifacts.

auditory communication system
paralanguage.

invisible communication
chronemics, olfactics, and haptics.

kinesics
the study of bodily movements such as gestures, posture, eye contact, and facial expressions.

Mireya Mayor

Emerging Explorer, Primatologist, and Conservationist

In your work as an explorer, are there times when you are conscious of these various types of nonverbal communication? Do you adjust your nonverbal style in different situations and contexts? Can you give an example of how?

I've led many, many expeditions, and most of the teams are primarily, if not all, male. And so because I'm a woman, I have to communicate in a more authoritative manner at times. But also when I'm dealing with people in the local community or village, and even sometimes in particular the women, I have to change my nonverbal style in order to not seem intimidating. In some of the places that I have worked, for example, it is not appropriate for women's legs to be exposed. So if I'm in a place where one mode of dressing is inappropriate, then clearly I'm not going to choose that type because it is almost like you're immediately setting up a barricade for effective communication.

When I was in Mexico for a town meeting in a rural area, the women were not allowed inside the hall for the meeting. And the entire meeting was actually about me. There were all these discussions about whether or not I would be allowed inside, and I found myself being very conscious of the way that I was dressed and the way that I carried myself. Because in that situation the more gender neutral I appeared, the more comfortable the men were in allowing me in.

CourseMate Connection: Go to cengagebrain.com to access your CourseMate for *Invitation to Human Communication* and analyze the verbal and nonverbal communication of National Geographic Explorer-in-Residence Sylvia Earle as she talks about undersea exploration.

Our bodies often send powerful messages to others about how we are feeling. Consider your own body and your kinesic expressions. What messages are you communicating to others at this moment?

can communicate a great deal. In your classrooms, for example, notice students who sit upright and look directly at the professor. Others may be leaning back in their chairs and looking out the window. Others might be frowning as they take notes. Do you interpret these variations in posture, eye contact, and facial expression differently? Do you believe one student is more engaged in the lecture than the other? Of course, we cannot always make accurate interpretations based on bodily movements alone. Some students may look away from the professor while thinking about the course material, and others may learn better when seated in a more comfortable, relaxed position. The better you know a person, the better you can interpret her or his nonverbal communication.

Bodily movements such as posture, gestures, and eye contact also may indicate whether we are willing to interact with others. When we make direct eye contact and offer a smile, we tend to signal that we are open to interacting with another. If we have our arms crossed in front of our body and a stern expression on our face, we may signal disinterest or contempt. Kinesics also involve **affect displays**, which are *nonverbal movements that indicate how we feel.* Facial expressions reveal how someone is feeling, and body orientation indicates the intensity of those feelings (Ekman & Friesen, 1967). For example, facial expressions can indicate disappointment, confusion, hope, or happiness. Consider the actions of sports fans: jumping in the air while smiling and clapping sends a very different message than jumping up with a scowl and pointing fingers at the referee.

oliveromg/Shutterstock.com

People often use adaptors to control their feelings, especially when they do not want others to know they are hurt or upset. When you are hurt or upset, what sort of adaptors do you use to manage your emotions?

Finally, kinesics involves **adaptors**, which are *gestures we use to manage our emotions.* For example, when we feel nervous, we may use adaptors to control our nervousness. We may tap our feet, begin twirling our hair, biting our nails, or even holding on tightly to an object of security (Ekman & Friesen, 1969).

Gestures and body movements (whether intentional or unintentional) communicate our thoughts and feelings. In addition, we have to consider cultural meanings of different gestures. The thumbs-up gesture is often associated with something positive in the United States, but it is considered an obscene gesture in the Middle East. In the United States, the two-finger V sign can mean victory or peace, but it is considered a sexual insult in Great Britain if the palm faces the sender while the fingers form a V.

Gender also influences how frequently particular body movements are displayed. For example, you have read that women tend to smile more, but they also tilt their head when speaking or listening, and they take up less space than men do (e.g., they cross their legs when sitting, and they keep their arms close to their bodies). In addition, socioeconomic status, race, and ethnicity also influence how particular facial expressions are displayed. In the United States, Caucasian women, especially from middle-class families, tend to smile more than African American women (Eakins & Eakins, 1988; Halberstadt & Saitta,1987). Japanese women typically avoid smiling in formal settings because it often indicates a lack of seriousness (Dresser, 1996).

affect displays
nonverbal movements that indicate how we feel.

adaptors
gestures we use to manage our emotions.

PRACTICING HUMAN COMMUNICATION
Reading Between the Lines

Paul Ekman, former professor of psychology at the University of California at San Francisco, is well known for his research on nonverbal communication, facial expressions, emotions, and interpersonal deception. He has appeared on *48 Hours, Dateline NBC, Good Morning America, 20/20, Larry King Live, The Oprah Winfrey Show, The Tonight Show,* and many other TV programs. Government agencies, *Fortune* 500 companies, and educational and medical professionals have used Ekman's research and training tools to better "read" people and detect potential "lies." He was also heavily involved in the production of the TV show *Lie to Me.* Ekman teaches people how to read microexpressions, which are very brief facial expressions—1/15 to 1/25 of a second—that often reveal concealed emotions. How well do you think you read the microexpressions of other people? Watch your friends and family and see how accurate you are.

Proxemics **Proxemics** refers to *the use of space*: how much of it we take up, how it is arranged, and whose space it is. The way we use space may tell us something about the relationship we have with other people. According to Edward T. Hall, in the United States, four distinct spatial spheres communicate our relationship to others (Hall, 1959). Each sphere indicates the distance deemed most appropriate for various types of relationships existing in the United States.

- *Intimate distance* (0 to 18 inches) is usually reserved for close friends or romantic partners. This distance is often used for displaying physical and psychological intimacy.

- *Personal distance* (18 inches to 4 feet) is the space we use when conversing with friends and acquaintances. The range of personal distance can vary, depending on the relationship. Close friends are often allowed closer distances than acquaintances. You may feel uncomfortable when acquaintances violate your personal distance and stand too close to you.

- *Social distance* (4 to 12 feet) is the appropriate distance for many U.S. business interactions. Impersonal or informal business practices, such as purchasing a product (e.g., buying a car or articles of clothing), usually occur between 4 feet and 7 feet. Formal business situations, such as job interviews or performance evaluations, tend to take place closer to 12 feet.

- *Public distance* (12 to 25 feet) is appropriate for public ceremonies, lectures, concerts, and political rallies. When a large audience is present, a speaker may use public distance (and appear on a stage or platform) in order to be seen by all audience members (Hall, 1959).

The use of space also indicates power and status. For example, those who have power and status in society tend to enter the spaces of those with less power, but not vice versa. Because more men still have more power in this culture, this typically means that men enter the space of women more frequently. In addition, those with power and status also occupy larger spaces. Individuals who earn high salaries tend to live in larger houses, drive larger vehicles, and vacation at greater distances than those who earn lower salaries.

Finally, gender may influence who occupies particular spaces or rooms within the home. Did your father or stepfather occupy the same chair every night at the dinner table? Did your mother, sister, or grandmother use more closet and bathroom space? Did your mother refer to the kitchen as "my kitchen" or your father claim the basement or garage to be "his space"? Particular rooms such as kitchens, bathrooms, and closets are occupied

These business people are using social space to communicate their relationship to one another. Take a moment to look around you. What does your use of space communicate about your relationship to those near you?

Yuri Arcurs/Shutterstock.com

most often by mothers and daughters. Garages, recliners, and even the backyard barbeque may be considered men's spaces.

Artifacts **Artifacts** are the *personal objects we use to communicate something about ourselves.* Artifacts include clothing, jewelry, toys, and other personal accessories that reveal information about our identities and interests. For example, articles of clothing are considered an important factor in making a first impression. The way a person dresses communicates information about gender, age, socioeconomic status, mood, group affiliation, interests, and values. Positive first impressions are most often created when the person being judged has a similar clothing style to the person making the observation (Reid, Lancuba, & Murrow, 1997). In addition, one's occupation may be revealed through styles of dress. For example, police officers, firefighters, and military personnel have distinct uniforms worn on the job. An artifact such as a backpack may communicate that a person is a student.

Jose AS Reyes/Shutterstock.com

Consider what types of clothing you wear. What do they represent about you? Do you own T-shirts containing messages that express your attitudes, beliefs, political affiliation, or hobbies? Many artifacts reveal our likes and dislikes. Sports memorabilia signify our favorite sports teams. T-shirts, buttons, and bumper stickers disclose our political, religious, or cultural beliefs. In fact, because clothing and artifacts can reveal differences in socioeconomic status, group affiliation, and belief systems, many schools now enforce strict dress codes and school uniform policies.

Many people in the United States place enormous value on personal appearance and invest a great deal of time and money striving to achieve cultural standards of beauty. **Personal appearance** consists of *specific aspects of our appearance including facial features, skin color, hair color, length, and style, and body type.* Women and men invest in coloring their hair, tanning, dieting, exercise, and even plastic surgery to meet the ideal cultural standards for beauty and attractiveness. Studies support the belief that changes in hair color and makeup improve ratings for female's attractiveness and desired personality (Graham & Jauhar, 1981). Personal appearance and beauty standards, however, are not universal. Although the cultural ideal for American women is thinness, traditional African cultures equate full-figured bodies as being healthy, prosperous, and wealthy (Villaros, 1994).

The codes of kinesics, proxemics, and artifacts are visible forms of nonverbal communication that can convey information about one's thoughts, feelings, and identities. In addition to visual forms of nonverbal communication, we also learn information about people through auditory codes.

People often choose clothing, hair styles, and other accessories to communicate their identities or personal styles. Examine your own dress; what are you trying to communicate about yourself by the way you are dressed today?

artifacts
the personal objects we use to communicate something about ourselves.

personal appearance
specific aspects of our appearance including facial features; skin color; hair color, length, and style; and body type.

Artifacts, Ambiguity, and Arguments

Dearborn High School in Detroit, Michigan, received national attention when nine students of Arabic descent arrived at school wearing sweatshirts that referenced the September 11, 2001, attacks on the World Trade Center in New York City. The group of students from the class of 2011 wore sweatshirts with the number "11" representing the twin towers, the school's thunderbird mascot flying directly toward the numerals, and the slogan "You Can't Bring Us Down" at the bottom. Many teachers, staff members, and other students believed the image on the sweatshirt represented animosity toward Americans. Yet the nine students involved in the incident told school officials that they were simply showing pride for their class of 2011. Hiab Mussad, one of the students wearing the sweatshirt, stated that the public was overreacting. He claimed, "We just wanted to show our support (to our class)." Clearly, the image was ambiguous because multiple meanings were derived from the sweatshirt design. Although several angry parents called on school officials to suspend the group, school administrators eventually determined that the incident was a matter of "kids not thinking, not realizing the consequences of something they thought was pretty innocent." No disciplinary action was taken against the students (Lawrence, 2010).

The T-shirt worn by these students raises questions about the ambiguity of messages on articles of clothing.

What Do You Think?

1. Do you believe these students had the right to wear sweatshirts with a message pertaining to September 11? Why or why not?

2. What types of messages (or symbols) on clothing should be banned from public schools or the workplace?

3. Should students have the right to express their beliefs, group affiliations, or political and cultural views via artifacts brought to school?

Auditory Codes of Nonverbal Communication

Are you able to answer the phone and identify callers just by the way they say "Hello," even before they identify themselves (without checking caller ID first)? Can you hear several of your roommates or family members talking in the hallway and identify whose voice is speaking at any particular moment? If you answered "Yes" to either question, it is likely that you relied on paralinguistic cues. **Paralinguistics** refers to *the vocal aspects of nonverbal communication such as rate, volume, pitch, and emphasis.* Paralinguistics consists of language that is oral, but not verbal. We often determine the person on the other end of the phone or in the hallway because of the way they sound, not necessarily by the words they say. One study indicated that the utterance of a single sentence was enough for co-workers to identify between eight and ten of their colleagues with more than 97 percent accuracy (Van Lancker, Kreiman, & Emmorey, 1985). Accuracy rates, however, drop significantly when someone has not heard a particular voice for several months.

Vocal cues are *aspects of the human voice that create rhythm or musical flow.* Vocal cues consist of the following:

rate—the speed at which we speak;

volume—the loudness of the speaker's voice;

pitch—the highness or lowness of the speaker's voice;

paralinguistics

the vocal aspects of nonverbal communication, such as rate, volume, pitch, and emphasis.

vocal cues

aspects of the human voice that create rhythm or musical flow.

inflection—the manipulation of pitch to create certain meanings or moods;

pauses—hesitations and brief silences in speech conversation;

pronunciation—saying a word correctly according to accepted standards of a language;

articulation—the physical process of producing specific speech sounds in order to make language intelligible; and

dialect—the pattern of speech shared among ethnic groups or people from specific geographical locations.

These qualities also help us recognize particular voices. For example, consider the different vocal qualities of politicians. George W. Bush, Barack Obama, Hilary Clinton, and Sarah Palin have distinct vocal cues. In addition to the vocal cues listed, some speakers use **vocalized pauses** or include *filler words or sounds such as "er," "um,"* and *"uh"* in their speech. And some may speak in a **monotone** voice, which means they *lack variation in their rate, pitch, and volume* as they speak.

Vocal cues can also convey different feelings or emotions. Multiple studies indicate that most of us are highly accurate in determining another person's emotions simply by listening to their vocal expression (Chartrand & Bargh, 1999; Davitz, 1964; Pittman & Scherer, 1993). In addition, vocal cues often reveal information about a speaker such as age, gender, and height. High-pitched voices are often linked to someone who is younger, female, and shorter (Kramer, 1963). Women's voices tend to be more variable and expressive than men's. Advanced age also changes some speech patterns. Seniors tend to slow down their speech rate and incorporate more vocalized pauses (Hummert, Mazloff, & Henry, 1999).

Silence Silence, or *the lack of vocal sound*, is another powerful form of nonverbal communication. Silence is a lengthened pause and can convey a variety of meanings. To determine the meaning of silence, look carefully at the communicator, environment, timing of the silence, cultural norms, and other verbal and nonverbal messages surrounding the silence. For example, silence can indicate respect for an environment such as a church, library, hospital, or funeral. When a speaker includes silence in a speech, it may mean she wants to draw attention to the ideas previously conveyed, is thinking about what to discuss next, or has simply forgotten what she wanted to say. When a listener remains silent, it may indicate he is showing respect, empathy, agreement, or even disagreement with the speaker. Therefore, you must examine the context surrounding the silence in order to best interpret its meaning.

Using paralinguistics, we are able to identify voices, make assumptions about others' feelings and emotions, and determine a speaker's characteristics. In addition to these auditory nonverbal communications, invisible forms of communication—chronemics, olfactics, haptics, and environmental factors—also create meaning.

vocalized pauses
the use of filler words or sounds such as *"er," "um,"* and *"uh"*.

monotone
a lack of variation in a speaker's rate, pitch, and volume.

silence
the lack of vocal sound.

COMMUNICATION AT WORK

© photos.com

Seconds of Silence

When Arizona Governor Jan Brewer, The Republican nominee debated Democratic challenger, Attorney General Terry Goddard, on national television in September of 2010, it wasn't the harsh words they exchanged that caught people's attention. Rather, it was the 13 seconds of silence Brewer offered during her opening statement that caused people to take note. Journalists and Bloggers have called Brewer a "nutball" and as "skewered" by "Obama's mob" because of her silence. They also refer to her silence as the simple result of "stage fright or a brain freeze" Goldberg (2010).

Matt York/AP/Corbis

What Do You Think?

1. Do you believe that Governor Brewer's extended period of silence communicates a lack of knowledge or preparation for the debate or that she experienced a moment of stage fright or "brain freeze"?

2. How long should a pause or moment of silence be so that a speaker can collect her or his thoughts before speaking?

3. What types of speaking situations would it be considered appropriate or natural for a speaker to incorporate silence? What is an effective length of time for silence?

Invisible Codes of Nonverbal Communication

Invisible communication includes types of nonverbal communication that we cannot see: perceptions of time, the sense of smell, the use of touch, environmental factors, and technology.

Chronemics Temporal communication, or **chronemics**, refers to *how humans organize and structure time and the messages conveyed as a result of this organization.* Time dictates when we eat, sleep, go to school, or go to work. Many people in the United States view time as something tangible. North Americans tend to say phrases such as you should be "on time," that new technology will "save us time," or that you "need time to yourself." You may count the days until a favorite holiday arrives, or watch the clock to determine when class is over. Our watches, computers, and cell phones can be programmed to remind us when the time has arrived to be some place or meet a particular deadline. Individuals view the use of time differently, depending on whether they are from a monochronic or polychronic culture (Hall, 1959). People from **monochronic cultures** *carefully schedule tasks, complete them one by one, and follow strict agendas.* Monochronic individuals place tremendous value and priority on work-related objectives and view time as a rigid structure.

---

chronemics

how humans organize and structure time and the messages conveyed as a result of this organization.

---

monochronic cultures

cultures in which people carefully schedule tasks, complete them one by one, and follow strict agendas.

The United States and Germany are two examples of monochronic cultures. **Polychronic cultures** *work on several tasks at once and view time as flexible.* People from polychronic cultures value relationships with others over work-related tasks. Italy and Brazil are two cultures that are primarily polychronic.

Our personalities and status also help determine how we organize time. Individuals with relaxed attitudes may arrive late to events, whereas highly structured or task-oriented individuals may make it a priority to arrive on time. High-status professional positions, including physicians and politicians, may be granted the ability to arrive late to appointments, whereas patients and political aides are expected to show up at specific times.

Olfactics Olfactics is *the use of our sense of smell to gather information.* Although we have long understood that animals use smell to obtain information such as the presence of an enemy or to track other animals, the study of the human olfactory system began more recently. Like most other forms of nonverbal communication, the reliance on smell is cultural. Americans rely less on their sense of smell than they do on their senses of sight and hearing. But many Americans will rely primarily on their sense of smell when the smell is uncharacteristically strong or unique. This may help explain why Americans invest so much money in soaps, deodorants, perfumes, mouthwashes, breath mints, lotions, scented candles, and air fresheners that create pleasant but artificial scents.

Other cultures view odor differently, however. Kate Fox, the director of the Social Issues Research Center, reported how many non-Western cultures historically valued or had a heightened awareness of the sense of smell. Here are a few examples:

- In India, the traditional affectionate greeting—equivalent to the Western hug or kiss—was to smell someone's head. An ancient Indian text declares, "I will smell thee on the head; that is the greatest sign of tender love" (Fox, 2010, p. 28).

- In Arab countries, breathing on people as you speak to them signals friendship and goodwill—and to "deny" someone your breath smell conveys a shameful avoidance of involvement.

- Among the Amazonian Desana, all members of a tribal group were believed to share a similar odor. Marriage was only allowed between persons of different odors, which required that spouses be chosen from other tribal groups.

In addition to human odors, environmental odors may influence various bodily responses. Certain smells may trigger positive or negative memories. Certain scents may remind you of your grandparent's house, your first car, or a favorite vacation spot. On the other hand, the scent of a doctor's office or cologne of someone you do not like may elicit negative emotions.

polychronic cultures
cultures in which people take on several tasks at once and view time as flexible.

olfactics
the use of our sense of smell to gather information.

Can you recall being touched as a small child? How might this early touch have influenced your development or even your attitudes toward touch?

haptics
the study of communicating via touch.

functional or professional touch
the least intimate touch, including touch by others according to their professional position.

social or polite touch
part of an initial interaction, greeting, or informal ritual.

friendship or warmth touch
a sense of closeness and caring between individuals.

love or intimacy touch
touch between family members or romantic partners.

sexual arousal touch
the type of touching that conveys sexual meaning and stimulation.

Haptics **Haptics** refers to *the study of communicating via touch*. Research indicates the importance of touch in creating physically and psychologically healthy infants and children (Field, 2002). Infants and children who are given plenty of physical stimulation have higher IQs than those who receive less physical touch at a young age (Yarrow, 1963).

Touch is also important in maintaining relationships later in life. The amount of touch provided in a relationship may vary, depending on the stage of the relationship and sex of the initiator. Andersen and Guerro (1994) reported that married couples touch with the greatest frequency and casual daters touch the least. In more long-lasting and serious relationships, women tend to initiate touch more often than men, and they are more likely to initiate touch after marriage. Men, however, are more likely to initiate touch during the beginning stages of relationship development (Andersen & Guerrero, 1994).

Several categories of touch help distinguish relationships. Givens (2005) reports that most of the categories seem natural and are rarely noticed until a discrepancy occurs between the relationship type and form of touch (Givens, 2005). The following categories are listed in order from least intimate to most intimate (Heslin & Alper, 1983).

- **Functional or professional touch** is *the least intimate* and *includes touch by others according to their professional position*. This includes touch by physicians, hairstylists, tattoo artists, and other professions who require a certain degree of physical contact to do their jobs.

- **Social or polite touch** occurs as *part of an initial interaction, greeting, or informal ritual*. This includes the greeting of a handshake in the United States and hugging and kissing in many European countries when greeting acquaintances.

- **Friendship or warmth touch** conveys *a sense of closeness and caring between individuals*. Friends hugging, holding hands, or linking arms together are examples of friendship touch. A pat on the back or resting a hand on one's shoulder can convey warmth and support.

- **Love or intimacy touch** typically *occurs between family members or romantic partners*. Extended hugs between relatives, kissing between romantic partners, or a child sitting on a parent's lap are examples of love or intimacy touch.

- **Sexual arousal touch** describes *the type of touching that conveys sexual meaning and stimulation*. Some forms of kissing and stroking are examples of sexual arousal touching.

The form of touch considered most appropriate for a particular situation is often determined by the relationship level and type. The amount and kind of touch also varies between men and women. In the United States, women are expected to give gentle hugs, hold and comfort children, and reach out softly to someone in need. Men, by contrast, are expected to give vigorous pats on the back, shake a hand rather than gently hug someone, and engage in roughhousing with other men and even children (Derlega, Lewis, Harrison, Winstead, & Costanza, 1989).

Touch also conveys varied meanings across cultures. First Lady Michelle Obama sparked controversy for her use of haptics when greeting the queen of England. Mrs. Obama and Queen Elizabeth were standing side by side and having a casual conversation about their height difference. As the two women moved closer and continued their conversation, the queen put her hand on the back of the first lady. A moment later, Michelle Obama reciprocated by placing her own hand on the back of the queen. This gesture was immediately considered a breach of protocol ("Don't Touch," 2009). *Time* magazine reported, "The rules are set in stone. . . . 'Whatever you do, don't touch the Queen!'" (Chua-Eoan, 2009). In fact, previous visiting dignitaries and statesmen have been criticized for touching the queen. Some commentary on Mrs. Obama's gesture suggests there is room to debate the breach of protocol because she was reciprocating the queen's same gesture.

Environmental Factors Environmental factors consist of *surroundings that influence how we think, feel, and behave as we communicate with others.* In what is now a foundational study, Abraham Maslow and N. L. Mintz (1956) confirmed the important role environment plays in our reactions to a given situation. Maslow and Mintz asked people to rate photographs containing people with negative expressions in three different environments. One environment appeared "beautiful," the next "average," and the third "ugly." Participants in the study rated the photographs of the people in the beautiful room as having more positive energy and well-being than the same photographs of those people in the ugly room (Maslow & Mintz, 1956).

Colors also play an important role in creating certain moods. Within the first ninety seconds of meeting someone or seeing a product, a person has formed a judgment. Research suggests that approximately

environmental factors
surroundings that influence how we think, feel, and behave as we communicate with others.

Daniel Hambury/Reuters/Corbis

Do you believe First Lady Michelle Obama's use of touch as a sign of friendship and warmth was a reciprocal sign of support or a breach of England's protocol? Why do you think so?

62 percent to 90 percent of that assessment is based on colors (Singh, 2006). The influence of color and environment is so powerful that restaurants rely on environmental factors to influence customers' eating behavior. Restaurants may paint walls blue to ease stress and tension and create a calming atmosphere. The color blue may create an atmosphere in which customers linger and perhaps order dessert or after-dinner drinks. However, restaurants also are aware that the overuse of blue (too much relaxation and calmness) can act as an appetite suppressant, influencing their customers to order less (Kido, 2000). The color red, though, is believed to stimulate appetite and increase metabolism, so many restaurants, especially fast-food restaurants, choose red as their primary color.

In addition to color schemes, restaurants use music to create particular effects and restaurants that feature fast-paced music can actually speed up the eating process. So powerful is the effect of music that researchers have learned that, on average, customers spend 56 minutes eating when the background music is slow. But when the background music changes to fast-paced or rock music, customers tend to spend an average of 45 minutes eating (Prochnik, 2010, p. 100).

Technology Technology has become an important and familiar means for establishing and maintaining relationships, and communication scholars are now studying the communication patterns and styles of text-based messages. Because many interactions occur through the use of electronic devices, many of our familiar nonverbal cues are absent (tone, pitch, volume, pace, eye contact, expression, and the like), and text-based messages can easily be misunderstood. In fact, facial expressions are such an important part of understanding verbal messages that Internet and cell-phone users often rely on what are now called **emoticons,** or *typed characters used to convey feelings.* Emoticons may be used to emphasize or clarify one's feelings, regulate a communication interaction, or soften a negative tone—just as smiles and frowns do in face-to-face interactions (Derks, Bos, & von Grumbkow, 2008). Particular emotions such as happiness and sadness can be conveyed via smiling or frowning faces. Other emoticons are used to represent certain facial expressions such as a wink—;)—or vocal qualities such as getting LOUDER! Abbreviations can represent other nonverbal behaviors, including LOL (laughing out loud) or H&K (hugs and kisses). Using emoticons in text-based messages can help visually communicate the nonverbal messages that are absent when we communicate electronically.

However, it is important to consider the amount and appropriateness of using emoticons, especially in business and professional interactions. Currently, there is some disagreement over the use of emoticons in workplace communication. Bill Lancaster, a lecturer in communication at Northeastern University in Boston, blames emoticons in part for "the degradation of writing skills—grammar, syntax, sentence structure, even penmanship—that come with digital technology" (DiNardo, 2011).

emoticons
typed characters used to convey feelings.

He believes that "language, used properly, is clear on its own." British journalist Maria McErlane agrees. She is "deeply offended" by the use of the symbols and finds the use of emoticons "lazy." She states, "To use a little picture with sunglasses on it to let you know how you're feeling is beyond ridiculous" (DiNardo, 2011).

Martha Heller, president of Heller Search Associates, a search firm for technology executives for *Fortune* 500 companies, and Columbia professor Lisa M. Bates disagree. Heller likes to include a smiley or wink to signify that her previous comment was intended as a joke. Bates has also embraced the smiley, albeit "sparingly and strategically," because it "can take the edge off and avoid misunderstanding" (DiNardo, 2011). The differences in opinions over using emoticons in business and professional interactions is a clear indicator of the importance of understanding the perceptions in your own workplace before making the assumption that emoticons are appropriate, appreciated, and understood.

Each of these codes of nonverbal communication—the visual, auditory, and invisible codes—works with the others to contribute to the strength, clarity, and perception of our messages. Understanding their purpose and effects can help us communicate more effectively with others.

Chapter Summary

Nonverbal Communication Is the Process of Communicating Using Our Bodies, Faces, and Nonword Vocalizations

- A majority of what we understand about a message is determined by nonverbal forms of communicating.
- Culture, gender, and interpersonal relationships all influence how we communicate and interpret nonverbal behaviors.
- Nonverbal communication is ambiguous.
- Nonverbal communication works in conjunction with verbal communication in six ways: to repeat, to emphasize, to complement, to contradict, to substitute, and to regulate.
- Emblems, illustrators, and regulators are nonverbal behaviors that repeat or reinforce spoken words.

We Communicate Visually Through the Nonverbal Acts of Kinesics, Proxemics, and Artifacts

- Our posture, gestures, body movement, and eye contact all send messages about our willingness to interact with others.
- Affect displays help convey how we feel.
- The use of space provides signals about interpersonal relationships, gender, power, and status.

- Personal artifacts and appearance can reveal information about our identities and interests.
- Auditory communication consists of the way we communicate orally without uttering words.
- Vocal cues convey feelings and emotions.
- Paralinguistics affect our ability to identify voices, make inferences about others' feelings and emotions, and determine characteristics about a speaker.

We Can Communicate Without the Use of Sight and Sound

- The way we structure time differs between monochronic and polychronic cultures.
- Our sense of smell is viewed differently among different cultures.
- The form of touch considered most appropriate for a particular situation is often determined by the relationship level and type.
- Environmental factors can influence moods and reactions to particular events.
- When using technology to communicate with others, emoticons help reveal our emotions behind the message.

Key Concepts

adaptors (61)

affect displays (61)

artifacts (63)

auditory communication system (59)

chronemics (66)

complementation (58)

contradiction (59)

emblems (58)

emoticons (70)

emphasis (58)

environmental factors (69)

friendship or warmth touch (68)

functional or professional touch (68)

haptics (68)

illustrator (58)

invisible communication (59)

kinesics (59)

liking (57)

love or intimacy touch (68)

monochronic cultures (66)

monotone (65)

nonverbal communication (54)

olfactics (67)

paralinguistics (64)

personal appearance (63)

polychronic cultures (67)

proxemics (62)

regulation (59)

repetition (58)

responsiveness (57)

sexual arousal touch (68)

silence (65)

social or polite touch (68)

substitution (59)

visual communication system (59)

vocal cues (64)

vocalized pauses (65)

 ## Invitation to Human Communication Online

Speech Communication CourseMate includes an interactive eBook and interactive learning tools including National Geographic Explorer videos, student videos, quizzes, flashcards, and more. Speech Builder Express 3.0 and Speech Studio 2.0 are also available. Go to cengagebrain.com to access your CourseMate for *Invitation to Human Communication* for access to these resources.

Further Reflection and Discussion

1. What are some situations in which you might want to adapt your nonverbal skills to be less gender specific and to communicate more strength (if you are female) and more emotion (if you are male)?

2. Discuss the nonverbal communication that tells you when, for example, someone is the life of the party, someone is shy in social situations, or someone is trying to deceive you.

3. Based on the space in your school library, who has more power? less power? What aspects of the environment are giving you this information?

4. Discuss how you communicate emotions when chatting online or in a text message with a friend. Do you ever have trouble communicating your tone or feeling?

Activities and Web Links

Visit cengagebrain.com to access the CourseMate for *Invitation to Human Communication* where these activities and web links can be found.

1. Watch this video about the TV show *Lie to Me*. Ask a friend to guess what emotion your facial expression and body language are revealing. Include anger, sadness, contempt, joy, fear, excitement, fake happiness (fake smile), and other emotions. Go to *Weblink 3.1*.

2. **Exploring International Nonverbal Communication**. Test your ability to "read" samples of real nonverbal communication. Take the quiz "A World of Gestures" to see if you can identify the meaning of these gestures from around the world. Go to *Weblink 3.2*.

3. **Kismet: A Humanoid Robot with Emotions**. Kismet is a robot that can interact and cooperate with people. Kismet's goal is to enter into natural and intuitive social interaction with a human caregiver and to learn from the caregiver, a process that is reminiscent of parent–infant exchanges. Kismet perceives natural social cues from visual and auditory channels and delivers social signals to the human through gaze direction, facial expression, and body posture. Look at Kismet's expressions and see if you can figure out what changes in the face can be attributed to each emotion. Go to *Weblink 3.3*.

4. Discusses the differences in nonverbal communication between men and women in both the United States and Brazil. Go to *Weblink 3.4*.

5. See how well you can read facial expressions. Name the emotions shown by each face in the photograph. How good is your ability to decode facial expressions? Go to *Weblink 3.5*.

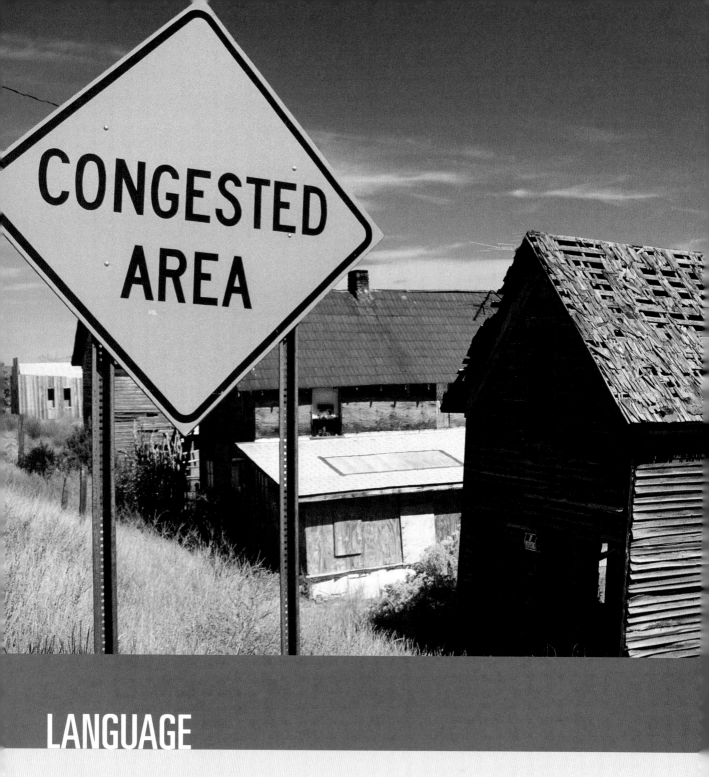

LANGUAGE

IN THIS CHAPTER YOU WILL LEARN TO:

- Recognize the rules of language.
- Describe how gender affects language.
- Use Internet communication more effectively.
- Make important language choices for interpersonal communication and small group communication.

- Avoid negative uses of language.
- Distinguish language skills useful in public speaking.
- Incorporate verbal skills necessary for civil communication.
- Consider the civil and uncivil aspects of language.

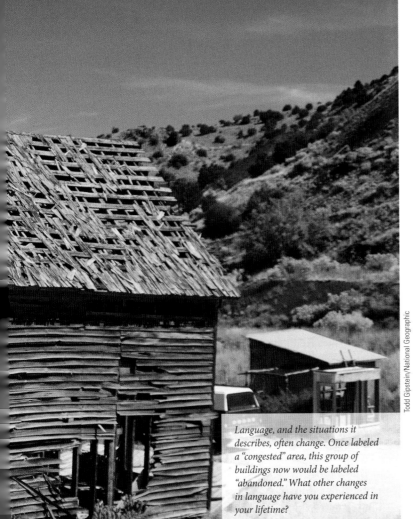

Language, and the situations it describes, often change. Once labeled a "congested" area, this group of buildings now would be labeled "abandoned." What other changes in language have you experienced in your lifetime?

Todd Gipstein/National Geographic

4

Clean water is a basic human right, yet so many don't have it. I'm using my music to be the voice of people who have no voice.

—Feliciano dos Santos, musician, activist, and National Geographic Emerging Explorer

How many people have you talked to in the past week? You probably talked to more people than you realize: family members, friends, teachers, bosses, co-workers, roommates, store clerks, and more. You probably communicated face to face, over the phone, via e-mail and texting, and maybe in a blog. Can you think of a time when you said something that was interpreted in a way you did not intend? Maybe your communication caused anger or confusion, made someone laugh, or even caused you extra work? Each day we rely on language to communicate with others. Sometimes our messages are understood exactly as we hope, and other times miscommunication is the result.

In this chapter, we will discuss the common characteristics of language. First, we discuss the nature of language. Then we turn our focus toward examples of how language affects our interpersonal relationships, group effectiveness, and public-speaking success. Finally, we focus on the connection between language, civility, and social justice.

 ## The Nature of Language: Rules, Culture, Gender, and Technology

In this section, we will learn three primary rules that govern language. Next we look at the ways in which language is ambiguous—that is, the way it causes potential confusion or misunderstanding between communicators. Then we will explore how language is influenced by gender, culture, and technology.

Language Is Governed by Rules

Language consists of the use of *a collection of symbols or words to communicate with others*. To communicate effectively, we must follow three primary rules of language use. First, we must learn the basics of **phonology**, which is *the study of how sounds are used to communicate meaning*. Each language has its own basic sound units, or *phonemes*, which include vowels, consonants, and diphthongs (the combination of letters that operate as one sound—e.g., "sh"). The English language has twenty-four consonant sounds, twelve vowel sounds, and eight diphthongs. To be competent in a language, speakers need to learn the phonological rules that govern that language because some words have different pronunciations

language
a collection of symbols or words used to communicate with others.

phonology
the study of how sounds are used to communicate meaning.

that will change the meaning of the word. For example, the word *content* has two different phonological rules. Are you content (satisfied) with the content (material) of the course? The first *content* is used as an adverb to ask how a person is feeling about something. The second *content* acts as a noun that refers to the topics covered in the course. Phonological rules (rules for pronunciation) help speakers communicate clearly and successfully—and these rules often prove challenging for someone who is just learning to speak a new language.

The second rule of language refers to *syntax*, or how symbols (words) are arranged to create meaning. **Syntax** refers to *the rules that govern word order*. The meaning of our communication often depends on the order in which our words appear. The following two examples illustrate how meaning is altered when the word order is rearranged:

syntax
the rules that govern word order.

The exam is tomorrow.

Is the exam tomorrow?

Understanding the correct order of words helps us communicate clearly and effectively. If you speak more than one language, then you know that each language has its own rules for syntax. The improper use of syntax can create confusion—and possibly a bit of humor for listeners or readers. For example, the *Spartanburg* (South Carolina) *Herald-Journal* newspaper created confusion and laughter after printing the following headline: "Sisters Reunite After 18 Years in Checkout Line" ("Sisters," 1983). Obviously the sisters were not standing in the checkout line for eighteen years, but the syntax made that a possibility! Now read the following two examples of syntax and see if you notice *what* is misleading in each statement.

Poor syntax: "For those of you who parked your car in the pay lot and don't know it, there's a free parking lot located a block away."

Poor syntax: "I was working on a group project and then it blew up."

The first example indicates the drivers did not know they parked their cars. The second example assumes the project exploded. Now look at how the following examples of proper syntax and how their meaning is much more clear.

Proper syntax: "For those of you who parked in the pay lot because you did not know there was free parking, the free lot is located a block away."

Proper syntax: "While we were working on a group project, we couldn't agree and began fighting with one another."

When we use proper syntax or sentence structure, we communicate more clearly.

The final rule that effective communicators understand about language relates to **semantics**, or *the meaning of specific words*. If a teacher asks the class to use a pencil on the exam, then the students know that a "pencil" is a particular type of writing utensil. However, if the teacher

semantics
the meaning of specific words.

Baghdad, Iraq—April 9, 2003. Iraqis celebrate the end of the Saddam Hussein regime while standing atop a huge statue of the dictator that was toppled by a U.S. Marine recovery tank in Baghdad's Firdos Square. Some citizens even vented their anger against the dictator. How might the word freedom differ in meaning for one of the Iraqis in this photo than it might for a U.S. citizen?

asks students to queue up for a pencil, then they might not know that a "queue" is a line we wait in to receive something. When we communicate successfully, we are using the "right" word to convey an idea. The word means the same, or something similar, for those who are involved in the act of communicating. However, it is easy to misunderstand someone based on multiple meanings of some words. Have you ever been told that your work is "fine" or that your ideas are "interesting"? Were you unsure how to interpret the feedback? We may be confused because these words are ambiguous and can be interrupted in different ways.

Language Is Ambiguous

Friends often argue over the meaning of a word. This is because words are symbols, and their meaning is determined by the people involved in the act of communicating. Remember from Chapter 1 that there are two different ways we can interpret the meaning of language:

denotative meanings

the literal or commonly accepted meaning of a word.

connotative meanings

the meanings we associate with particular words based on our experiences, understanding, or opinions of the word.

denotative meanings are *the literal, or commonly accepted, meanings of a word*, whereas **connotative meanings** are *the meanings we associate with particular words based on our experiences, understanding, or opinions of the word*. Understanding the difference between denotative and connotative meanings may help reduce confusion over the use of a term. For example, the word *freedom* is used frequently in the United States to mean our ability to act, think, or speak without external restraints (denotative definition). However, the term *freedom* may represent different meanings based on our cultural background, country of origin, sex, class, race, or occupation. Egypt and Iraq, for example, are countries now struggling for rights and opportunities. The word *freedom* means quite different things in those countries than it does here in the United States, a country with a long history of "freedoms" that are taken for granted: voting, religious expression, public protest, education, and the like. Because language can be ambiguous and meanings can differ between individuals, we communicate more effectively when we take time to clarify the meaning of ambiguous terms.

The idea that language is ambiguous is illustrated nicely by Ogden and Richards's semantic triangle of meaning (1923). This model illustrates the

PRACTICING HUMAN COMMUNICATION

Denotation and Connotation

On a sheet of paper, write down the following words: *space, mug, school, home, religion,* and *relationship.* Then write down both denotative and connotative definitions associated with each word. Share your definitions with a partner and identify similarities and differences in your denotative and connotative definitions. Discuss why it is likely that there were differences in the connotative understanding of the words.

Wesley Bocxe/Photo Researchers

Courtesy of Chris Rainier

T.H. Culhane
Emerging Explorer and Urban Planner

In your work as an explorer, have there been times where ambiguity or culture have affected clear communication? Can you give an example of when the ambiguous nature of language or cultural differences affected your communication and ability to understand others?

For the first week of what was a three-week expedition in Indonesia, we made little progress and couldn't understand why people were treating us civilly but not offering us any information. And some of the key scientists said, "You see what the problem is—they don't trust you. They believe that you're not here for knowledge of plants, but for gold or diamonds or oil or other minerals like the other people who have come in and lied to them in the past." And so there was tremendous mistrust. We did not know how we were going to get around this until one day sitting in the chief's hut trying very delicately to explain our motives and our backgrounds and establish our credentials which we thought we had done well enough up front. The chief saw me looking at a guitar that was at the far side of his hut. He said, "Play me a song." So he hands me the guitar and I sing the song "Burung Kakak Tua," which is a traditional Indonesian song, but I did it in sort of an Elvis hippy, hippy shake. The chief did not crack a smile at all; he just watched. And then when I finished it, I actually put down the guitar, and he pointed his finger at me and said, "Tomorrow you will perform in the village square celebration." Then he turned to the other scientists and he said, "You will perform with him." And one of the British scientists said, "I used to play drums in a high school band. I suppose I could play drums." One of the women said, "Well, I don't suppose you have a flute?" And he said, "Yes, there will be a reed flute."

The next day, they had a little stage built, and they had their own band playing and we got up and sang. The crowd went crazy and asked for more. Then we performed the next day at a village wedding. And then the chief said, "The next night there is another festival, and you will perform there." They still wouldn't speak about science at all. And finally the third day he invited us to his hut, and he said, "You have proven yourselves. Now we can trust you, so we are willing to take you anywhere, tell you anything, and get you everything you need to know."

And it dawned on me that you have to really insert yourself in the culture: celebrate together, eat together, honor each other's traditions—and then you can get to work. That is how I approach most of my work around the world. I find those cultural common points and work with them first. It is a give–give, win–win situation. For me, it turns into using music as one of the primary bridges to doing scientific research.

relationship between a word (*symbol*), the common definition it represents (*referent*), and the individual thoughts or reactions the symbol provokes (*reference*). Chapter 1 described how the semantic triangle helps us understand that language is symbolic—that is, beyond the dictionary definition, there often is no direct correlation between the word used to describe something and the thing itself. The word *bang* sounds like the

When you hear the word fraternity, *what do you think of? Does the photo match your connotative definition? Why or why not?*

equivocal words
words that have more than one meaning.

slang
informal nonstandard vocabulary used by members of a co-culture or group who have similar interests, goals, or life experiences.

thing it represents, but the word *door* has no direct connection to the solid wood slab "banging" in the wind. Moreover, our associations with words can be highly individual—like the example of *freedom* or even the example of *door*. Some may hear a banging door and think of freedom and escape, but others might think only of the irritating noise.

Because people associate their own experiences, emotions, or memories with particular words, speakers need to consider their audience's thoughts—their *references*—when communicating with others.

Equivocal Words Language is also ambiguous because words can have more than one commonly accepted or dictionary definition. **Equivocal words** are *words that have more than one meaning.* According to dictionary.com, the word *court* can mean a "place where justice is administered" or "an area open to the sky and mostly or entirely surrounded by buildings, walls, etc.," or "a smooth, level, quadrangle on which to play tennis, basketball, etc.," or "to seek another's love." The English language has numerous words with more than one meaning, and new words are created every year to represent new objects, experiences, and technologies. *Apple* is considered a piece of fruit or a brand of computers and other electronic devices. A *tweeter* has historically been defined as a type of loudspeaker that produces high-frequency sound. In 2009, though, *tweeter* emerged as one who uses the social Web site Twitter. As more equivocal terms enter our vocabularies, the greater the likelihood of confusion. But understanding the context surrounding the conversation or providing a quick definition can help reduce those misunderstandings.

Slang and Jargon Slang is *informal nonstandard vocabulary used by members of a co-culture or group who have similar interests, goals, or life experiences.* Members of sports teams and clubs often use slang to establish their membership. Skiers, for example, often use "powder days" to refer to skiing on fresh snow. Slang can also communicate an informal relationship between people. Addressing another person as "dude" is a form of slang often used between close friends. When people use slang, it usually indicates in-group membership. College students may use the phrase "hooking up" when describing an intimate encounter with another person, but decades ago the slang term was "making out." It may be appropriate for teenagers to say "peace out" when leaving a situation; however, they would likely find it strange, or embarrassing, if their parents used the same phrase.

Bob Krist/Corbis

Jargon refers to *technical language used by professional groups.* Scientists, technicians, educators, and physicians all incorporate jargon when communicating with other members of the same profession. Educators may discuss *tracking* systems where students are grouped according to ability. Members of online communities may describe people who post comments that are offensive or are designed to get readers upset as *trolls.* Jargon is also used in sports and hobbies. Skateboarders call a no-handed, aerial skateboarding trick an *ollie.* Like slang, jargon can create confusion for individuals who are not familiar with the language of particular professions, and sometimes people use jargon or even slang to signal their membership in a group.

digis/Shutterstock.com

Skateboarders use jargon to describe particular tricks. What jargon do you use when talking about particular hobbies or activities?

jargon
technical language used by professional groups.

Jargon can also consist of **acronyms**, or *the first letters or initials of terms that form a word.* Medical professionals often use the term "CAT scan" for *computerized axial tomography scan.* Groups and clubs may also use acronyms to describe their professional title or identity. The acronym EMT stands for "emergency medical technician," and LGBTQ stands for "lesbian, gay, bisexual, transgendered, and queer."

acronyms
the first letters or initials of terms that form a word.

Jargon is easily understood by members of the same group or profession; however, jargon is often confusing for those individuals who are external to the group. To avoid unnecessary confusion, provide a quick definition, demonstration, or explanation of the term or acronym you are using.

Euphemisms and Doublespeak Language also makes it possible for us to make something unpleasant sound pleasant or to disguise its actual meaning. **Euphemisms** are *polite terms or more socially acceptable ways to describe something that someone may find unpleasant.* To say you are going to the "ladies room" instead of the "bathroom" or that you are "in between jobs" instead of "unemployed" are examples of euphemisms. Even though euphemisms are often considered polite forms of language, they may be confusing for some listeners if the implied meaning is misunderstood. Being "in between jobs" may sound as if it is a choice rather than an undesirable decision made for us.

euphemism
polite terms or more socially acceptable ways to describe something that someone may find unpleasant.

Doublespeak is closely related to euphemisms. Whereas euphemisms attempt to make something sound more pleasant, **doublespeak** is *language used to purposefully disguise the actual meaning of something.* The phrase "friendly fire" is used by the military to describe the inadvertent firing toward one's own group or allies. When companies say they will be "outsourcing," they are using doublespeak for "laying off workers" or "taking business away from American cities and potentially American

doublespeak
language used to purposefully disguise the actual meaning of something.

Computers, the language used to describe them, and what they can do have changed dramatically and very quickly. What would the correct jargon be today to describe how computers work without phone cords?

THE PROBLEM IS YOUR ROUTER CAN'T INTERFACE WITH YOUR I.S.P. BECAUSE THE RJII LINK HAS INADEQUATE RANGE

WILL IT COST MUCH?

THAT DEPENDS ON WHETHER YOU KNOW I JUST SAID "YOU NEED A LONGER PHONE CORD"

workers." Doublespeak can be misleading because the new term disguises what is actually occurring, making it seem less harmful or more benign than it actually is.

Language Is Influenced by Cultures and Co-Cultures

Considering that language consists of a set of symbols used to represent human experiences, people with different life experiences define the world in different ways. As such, culture plays an important role in our ability to communicate with and understand one another. Some cultures use feminine and masculine nouns and pronouns to define words. For example, the word *bridge* in German is *brücke*, a feminine noun. When asked to provide three words that describe a bridge shown in a photograph, German speakers most often used words such as *elegant*, *fragile*, and *beautiful*. In Spanish, the word for *bridge* is *puente*, a masculine noun. When Spanish speakers were asked the same question, they responded that the bridge appeared "strong," "dangerous," and "big." A similar result was found for the word *key*. The German word for key (*keil*) is masculine, whereas the word for key in Spanish (*llave*) is feminine. When German speakers were asked to describe a key, they used words such as *hard*, *heavy*, and *useful*. On the other hand, Spanish speakers described a key as *little*, *intricate*, and *golden* (Krulwich, 2009). Because many languages define words as feminine or masculine, the meanings people assign to the word correspond to its perceived gender.

Individuals who live in the same country or share the same culture may also use language differently. In the United States, different regions use different words for the same concept. For example, do you ask for a *pop*, a *soda*, or a *coke* when asking for a carbonated soft drink? Typically, people from the upper Midwest use the term *pop*, people from the West say *soda*, and residents in the South say *coke*.

Regionalisms are *words or phrases common to particular geographical regions*. Residents of New York City often refer to *upstate* as the geographical region just north of the city (often referring to Westchester County), but this term can be confusing for nonnative New Yorkers. When looking at a map of New York state, it is clear that hundreds of miles exist between Westchester County and Clinton County, the most northerly county in the state, so *upstate* to nonnative New Yorkers often means something different than it does for those native to the state.

The geographical region in which we live can also dictate informal phrases used to relate to others. These differences are called **colloquialisms**, which are *words and phrases used in relaxed, informal conversations*. The different types of colloquialisms that exist between cultures can be quite prominent. Consider different greetings and salutations used throughout the United States and abroad. In the United States, the phrase "How y'all doin'?" is an informal greeting commonly used by those living in southern states. "G'day" is often used as an informal greeting in Australia, and "Cheerio" is a common way to say goodbye in English-speaking European countries. These phrases are considered colloquialisms because they are common, informal words used by members of a particular region; however, these words and phrases can easily be replaced by more formal language. Someone living in Texas may decide to not say "y'all" and use a more formal phrase when speaking to members of Congress or to a room full of CEOs.

Whether you are speaking to people from different cultures in your own hometown or online, traveling to another state, or heading abroad, it is important to consider cultural differences in language. Learning some of the colloquialisms common to different cultures shows respect and awareness for cultural differences. This **cultural competence** is *the ability to relate appropriately to members from a different culture*. In addition, it is important to be aware of your own use of colloquialisms, regionalisms, slang, jargon, euphemisms, and doublespeak. To avoid creating an awkward moment of confusion or misunderstanding, try to limit words and phrases that are ambiguous, difficult to interpret, or open to more than one definition. Understanding differences in cultural backgrounds and language is the first step to ensuring the successful transmission of information.

Language Is Influenced by Gender

Although we are more similar than different, our genders can and do influence the ways we use language and the word choices we prefer. In this section, we will explore some of the ways that gender influences language and the ways these influences affect our communication.

Games and Gender As young children, the games we played taught us how to communicate in important ways (Maltz & Borker, 1982). Games such as kickball, king of the hill, and four square taught us a communication style that is more competitive and instrumental. Playing house, playing school, or playing with dolls requires language that is cooperative and inclusive. Although both boys and girls engage in competitive

regionalism
words or phrases common to particular geographical regions.

colloquialism
words and phrases used in relaxed, informal conversations.

cultural competence
the ability to relate appropriately to members from a different culture.

Children play a variety of games as they grow up, and those games teach them certain communication skills. How do you think the games you played as a child have influenced your communication today?

games and imaginary play as children, there are notable differences in the frequency and type of games played by each sex (Leaper, 1996; Martin, Fabes, Evans, & Wyman, 2000). Different games teach different communicative skills. For example, highly competitive games have a clear objective: to win. These games typically require a larger group of children with limited discussion. When communicating, talk is instrumental: children negotiate their positions and strategize how to win. On the other hand, imaginary play such as house requires communication that is cooperative and inclusive. House roles are created, and a great deal of talk is needed to continue the play as children negotiate and define those roles and their relationship to others in the game. The lessons learned from communicating through play continue to be part of our language style as we grow older.

Communication Styles and Gender If we carry the lessons learned from childhood play forward, we bring a certain style of communicating with us. Communication scholars now agree that adult women's speech is often labeled as feminine. This feminine speech style tends to incorporate language that is supportive, expressive, personal, and disclosing (Mulac, Bradac, & Gibbons, 2001; Wood, 2011). Researchers sometimes call this *rapport talk* to refer to the bonds and relationships that are built and shared as a result of the communication (Tannen, 2007). Rapport talk consists of sharing personal information, asking questions about another's well-being, inviting others to participate in the conversation, and sharing information that help to build and maintain relationships—something that girls learned to do during their childhood play. According to linguist Deborah Tannen, "For women and girls, talk is the glue that holds a relationship together. Their best friend is the one they tell everything to. Spending an evening at home with a spouse is when this kind of talk comes into its own" (Tannen, 2007).

But men also bring the lessons learned from childhood play into adulthood. In contrast to women's styles of speech, men's verbal speech style is often labeled masculine and is characterized as instrumental, competitive, and assertive (Mulac et al., 2001; Wood, 2011). Also known as *report talk*, this style of speech is direct and used to accomplish

PRACTICING HUMAN COMMUNICATION

Practicing Human Communication: Gender

Make a list of games you played as a child. Identify the type of communication (cooperative or instrumental) associated with each game. Now create a class list of games played and tally how many men and women played each one. Discuss whether any games are divided along gender lines and what this teaches us about learning to communicate with others.

something such as giving instructions or solving a problem. For example, Carlos and Alex are working together on a class project and Carlos tells Alex, "Our project is due next Tuesday. You work on the written assignment and I will prepare the oral presentation. Meet me on Sunday night and we'll go over our assignment." Carlos is using report talk to communicate with Alex about the class project. Notice that Carlos did not ask Alex how he was feeling about the assignment expectations or what Alex's weekend plans involved outside of finishing the project. Carlos is using report talk, which is described as straight to the point to get things done.

Communication Topics and Gender Research also suggests that men and women often communicate about different topics and for different lengths of time (Holmes, 2006; Tannen, 2001; Wood, 2000). Female friends tend to discuss more personal topics such as family, friendships, and intimate relationships; health and reproductive matters; and issues related to personal appearance. Men are more likely to converse with other men about current events, sports, business, and dating. When the two get together, however, men and women both tend to discuss work-life issues and events occurring in popular culture.

Interruptions, Discussions, and Gender Who do you believe interrupts conversations more often—men or women? Some people may be surprised, but men interrupt conversations more often than women, especially when they are speaking with other men. In same-sex groups, men interrupt one another often and use more directives to begin their statements (Mulac, Wiemann, Widenmann, & Gibson, 1988). Studies also indicate that in mixed-sex dyads and large groups, men will speak for longer periods of time than will women. Linguist Marjorie Swacker observed an academic conference and studied conversational patterns. She concluded that women presented 40 percent of the papers and made up 42 percent of audiences, but they accounted for only 27 percent of the questions asked (as cited in Tannen, 2001). In addition, Swacker concluded that women's questions averaged half as long to ask as men's questions, twenty-seven to fifty-two seconds. Swacker determined that this is because men tended to preface their questions by making statements first, asked more than one question, and then responded to the speaker's comments with a follow-up question or an additional comment (Roth Walsh, 1997).

Conversation and Gender Studies also reveal that conversational length differs between members of large and small groups and when members are of the same sex. When groups are small, women typically talk more than their male counterparts. In addition, speech patterns are different in same-sex conversations. When women are speaking with other women, they tend to ask more questions, include more personal pronouns, and engage in what Leaper and Ayres call "affiliative speech," which includes agreeing with or acknowledging others' comments (Leaper & Ayres, 2007).

Mark Thiessen/National Geographic

Mireya Mayor, National Geographic Emerging Explorer, Primatologist, and Conservationist

Viktoriia Boliukh/Shutterstock.com

Mireya Mayor is a primatologist and National Geographic correspondent. One of Mayor's most notable accomplishments occurred in a remote part of Madagascar, where more than sixty species of lemurs live, but where at least fifteen lemur species have become extinct. In 2000, Mayor and her team discovered a new lemur species—microcebus, or mouse lemur. Fitting in the palm of her hand, this tiny and rare creature inspired Mayor to take her findings directly to the prime minister of Madagascar. Mayor was able to convince the prime minister to declare the region a national park in order to protect and conserve the remaining 10 percent of the island's original vast forests and ultimately protect the lemurs. Today, Mayor continues to travel to Madagascar and other regions around the world to study endangered species and to help preserve the forests (Mayor, 2011).

After her first two daughters were born, Mayor was invited by TV producer Mark Burnett to join the cast of *Expedition Africa*. She initially struggled with the decision of staying at home or venturing back out into the field. With the help of her mother, Mayor realized that being an explorer is not what she does—it is who she is—so she agreed to go on the expedition to Africa. While Mayor was away, her husband, Roland Wolff, and her mother cared for her children.

For Mayor, the toughest part of being in the field is not the mosquitoes or snakes or living in wet clothes or even the starving. The toughest part is being away from her family. Mayor's traveling is tough on her children, too. She tries to help them cope by making a countdown calendar with photos of her in the jungle, and she leaves behind scrapbooks of photos for her children to look at while she is away. Sometimes, Mayor says, she is lucky enough to have a satellite phone connection so she can talk to them from the jungle. Still, being away for weeks with little opportunity to communicate is challenging. Mayor's husband still leaves little notes in Mayor's backpack for her to find throughout her journey. In the end, Mayor knows that her work is important. Not only is she helping to save endangered plants and forests, but also "I want my children to know that as women, they can do whatever they dream as long as they believe in themselves. More than anything it is my responsibility to instill in my daughters the knowledge that they can have a family and everything else too" (Mayor, 2011, p. 297–298).

WHAT DO YOU THINK

1. In what ways does Mayor's communication conform to gender expectations? In what ways does her communication challenge those expectations?

2. Consider several of the possible professions you plan to enter. How might slang and jargon help you communicate? How might they confuse those you communicate with?

3. What cultural and co-cultural differences have you encountered in your education, work, or community? How have you used language to communicate more clearly across those differences?

Although there are distinct differences between men and women's communication styles, several studies suggest that men and women usually communicate in ways that are more alike than they are different (Canary & Hause, 1993; Pennebaker, Mehl, & Niederhoffer, 2003). Research shows that men and women are beginning to use both report and rapport speaking styles, and speaking styles may be influenced more by our occupations and social environments than by our gender. For example, preschool teachers, nurses, and social workers are often encouraged to use supportive and cooperative language. Politicians, lawyers, and executives are typically trained to speak in direct and assertive ways. As women continue to train for careers traditionally held by men and as men work in service-related positions and raise children, we will likely see more examples of individual's shifting between communication styles. This style of communication is called *androgynous*, and **androgynous communicators** are *individuals who are adept at using different speech styles, depending on the situation.* A father who uses rapport talk with his children and report talk at work and a college student who uses rapport talk when socializing with friends but report talk while working on a group project are examples of androgynous communicators.

androgynous communicators
individuals who are adept at using different speech styles, depending on the situation.

Language Is Influenced by Technology

Our increasing reliance and time spent using technology is shaping the way we use language to communicate. The Internet, cell phones, smartphones, iPods, and iPads have increased our ability to communicate with others while also altering the type of language we use to communicate. We now look at each type of technology.

The Internet   Because of the Internet, we have access to social-networking sites such as Facebook, LinkedIn, MySpace, Tumblr, and Google+ that allow people to communicate with family, friends, and even strangers. In addition, people can display their thoughts, stories, interests, and ideas on blogs, personal Web pages, and Twitter. Professional sites such as LinkedIn allow us to post our professional profiles and distribute them widely and quickly.

Before the widespread use of the Internet, communication researchers believed that personal information was disclosed only after trust was established in a relationship. We now know, however, that the Internet provides a space in which the intimate details of one's personal life often are disclosed quickly and to a large number of receivers—and people will disclose this information without the trust base that researchers thought was central to self-disclosure. Even our screen names and usernames create messages and carry meaning for the user. Consider what your screen name implies. Although some users may find usernames humorous, employers may be hesitant to hire someone with an e-mail address beginning with something like CrackBaby91.

What we communicate to others and how we use language also has changed as a result of new media. For example, Twitter limits messages to 140 characters. This limits the amount of space available in a tweet to communicate our thoughts and ideas. Therefore, users frequently use acronyms and fragments instead of spelling complete words, using complete sentences, and fully developing thoughts. Tweets and even texting, the result of advancements in media technology, create avenues for new words to enter the English language. For example, the *Oxford Dictionary of English* added thirty-nine new words or terms in 2010, eight of which pertained to new media. Among these were *social media*, *tweetup*, *microblogging*, and *defriend* ("New Words in the ODE," n.d.).

Advantages and Disadvantages In addition to creating language to represent new technology, rumors now circulate easily via new media and at a rapid speed. A hacker group calling itself Script Kiddies broke into several Twitter accounts to report false information. On the tenth anniversary of the September 11, 2001, terrorist attacks, the group hacked into NBC News's Twitter account and posted false information about a plane hijacking at Ground Zero. Hackers also gained access to foxnews.com Twitter feed and sent several false reports that President Obama had been shot. Tweeting false reports can certainly have serious implications. According to a Twitter study by pearanalytics (2009), most information posted on Twitter is considered "pointless babble" about oneself or one's relationship status with others. Although most of what we write may, in fact, be meaningless and trivial, it is important to carefully consider both the message and the intended receiver. Once sent, most messages cannot be retracted or deleted.

But technology is not all bad: it can also provide important relational outcomes. Communicating via technology can help maintain friendships and enhance perceptions of social value and belonging. As social networks keep track of how many "friends" we have and as instant messaging allows us to connect to others in real time, technology users often report high levels of satisfaction with using technology to communicate. In fact, when technology becomes unavailable (even momentarily), users can become frustrated, angry, and sometimes even panicky. BlackBerry has experienced several worldwide system shutdowns that have temporarily kept users from accessing e-mail and Internet services. The inability to access technology and communicate with others caused some users to later blog "Never Again Blackberry," illustrating their frustration over the temporary system glitch and the importance of this medium in their lives (Austin & Robins, 2009).

 ## Language and Interpersonal Communication

When we communicate in our interpersonal relationships, the meanings of the messages often are interpreted in two distinct ways. This is because every verbal statement has two dimensions: the content dimension and the relational dimension (Watzalwick, Beavin, & Jackson, 1967). Remember from Chapter 1 that content messages are the actual things we say and relational messages are the parts of the communication that give us information about how we are connected (or not) to a person. Usually,

Families often use Skype to communicate with one another across long distances and when they are separated for long periods of time. What do you think are some positive aspects to this type of connection? Can you identify any possible negative aspects?

Katherine Frey/The Washington Post/Getty Images

the type of interpersonal relationship we have with another person will help determine the relational meaning behind the message. With our close friends, a simple "Hey" as a greeting might signal familiarity and warmth, but with a supervisor that same "Hey" could signal disrespect or a lack of professionalism.

But what happens to the content and relational aspects of interpersonal messages when two people have been separated over an extended period of time? Because of long separations, military families have to find ways to maintain relationships while one (or both) partners are deployed. In *Relationship Maintenance During Military Deployment: Perspectives of Wives of Deployed US Soldiers* (see Web Links at the end of chapter for a link to the video), communication scholar Andy Merolla shows how couples communicated during deployment. After interviewing several dozen women with deployed husbands, Merolla discovered ten common communication strategies that helped couples maintain their relationships over long separations. Although each mode of communication had its own set of restrictions (e.g., time limits for telephone calls and lack of privacy when communicating via Webcams), women reported using similar strategies when communicating via different modes of communication. Four common strategies include debriefing talk, topic avoidance, affection and intimacy, and future planning.

Debriefing Talk

Reporting the events and news from the day (content messages) can create a sense of normalcy for a couple (relational messages). One interviewee reported that the first thing she and her husband discuss on the phone is "what's been going on since we last spoke—work, house, cars, bills, et cetera" (Merolla, 2010).

Topic Avoidance

Because of the limited time allowed for communication and concern for the deployed spouse's situation abroad (relational message), negative topics (content message) are often not discussed.

Affection and Intimacy

Verbally expressing affection by stating "I love you" or making kissing noises (content message) are two ways couples maintain their relationship (relational message).

Future Planning

Couples reported talking about future plans (content messages) that help create hopeful attitudes during periods of uncertainty, as well as increase relational commitment (relational messages).

What is talked about (or not talked about) is an important part in maintaining long-distance relationships, especially with military families. Understanding both content and relational messages can help mitigate some of the hardships experienced when one partner is deployed for a lengthy period of time. What we say and how we say it can make a difference in our interpersonal relationships.

Language and Small Group Communication

Language is an important part of successful group communication. Because groups form as a result of having a shared purpose or goal, it is important for group members to communicate effectively with one another. Have you ever been assigned a group project in which members preferred to communicate via e-mail instead of face to face? Did you feel that your communication was just as effective online as it would have been meeting in person? As our lives continue to be filled with a variety of responsibilities and commitments, and as our society continues to rely more and more on mediated communication, we need to understand how to use technology to enhance, not diminish, the productivity and quality of group communication.

In "E-Mail Is Easy to Write (and to Misread)," Daniel Goleman (2007) describes how easy it is for e-mail messages to be misinterpreted. He explains that face-to-face communication allows group members to interpret what others say from their tone, facial expressions, and body language. Because typed words do not convey the same emotional contexts provided by in-person communication, e-mail increases the likelihood of conflict and miscommunication. However, people who know each other well are less likely to misinterpret online communication because they are familiar with the communication context. But what happens when virtual groups have a task to complete and group members do not know one another? Clay Shirky, at New York University's interactive telecommunications program, believes that groups can be more successful if the members spend time meeting face to face. Once group members become familiar with one another and begin discussing ways to accomplish the intended goal, future e-mail correspondences are more effective (Goleman, 2007). With more options for conducting online virtual meetings via video-streaming programs, face-to-face communication is now a relatively easy and inexpensive way for groups to communicate. Companies like IBM, Cisco Systems, Hewlett-Packard, and Hilton Worldwide are increasingly relying on virtual events and get-togethers. In fact, approximately 60% of professional employees work in virtual teams (Kanawattanachai & Yoo, 2002). Yet, research indicates that groups report higher levels of work satisfaction when they relied on computer-mediated communication less than 90% of the time and supplemented face-to-face interaction at least 10% of the time (Johnson, Bettenhuasen, & Gibbons, 2009). Knowing this, it may be important for groups to spend some time meeting in person, or via a video-streaming program such as Skype or ooVoo.

Language and Public Speaking

Politicians, musicians, cartoonists, radio personalities, and pageant contestants all face similar situations in which their speeches, song lyrics, or print or video images are constantly scrutinized. What we communicate publicly may cost us our jobs or negatively affect our future goals, especially if our communication is copied, offensive, or unintelligible. We now look at three types of public mishaps and consider what went wrong in each.

Plagiarism

Plagiarism can occur in many mediums of communication, including public speeches, books, Web-site content, song lyrics, and cartoons. Senator Joe Biden's first presidential campaign only lasted three and a half months because of an allegation of plagiarism ("Offers Briton His Talks" 1998). Senator Scott Brown's welcome message on his Web site was allegedly taken verbatim from the welcome message on Senator Elizabeth Dole's former campaign Web site (Lee, 2011). Musician Usher was accused of plagiarizing the song "Burn" from songwriter Ernest Lee Straughter's song "Reasons." Rollingstone.com reports there are striking similarities between the two songs which share a "highly unusual 18-bar intro, strikingly similar arrangements, melodies and vocal phrasing" (Perpetua, 2011). Finally, cartoonist David Simpson was accused of copying a cartoon by the late Jeff MacNelly. The cartoon appears to be a replica "to the point of tracing and re-drawing it for publication in the *Urban Tulsa* weekly publication" (Spurgeon, 2011). Plagiarizing the words or images of another is highly unethical. It not only denies other people the recognition they deserve but also misrepresents the skills and talents of the person doing the plagiarizing.

Hate Speech

Some radio hosts and deejays have been known to make controversial statements on the air. Radio personalities Rush Limbaugh, Howard Stern, and Don Imus know just how powerful language can be, especially if their language is perceived to be hateful. DJ Cipha Sounds (whose real name is Luiz Diaz) found himself in the hot seat in for making insulting comments about Haitian women. While speaking on the air at Hot97, Sounds joked, "The reason I'm HIV negative is because I don't mess with Haitian girls." What Sounds claimed was meant to be a joke turned into an immediate suspension. After the station was flooded with phone calls from enraged listeners, the station's management announced that Sounds would undertake sensitivity training and that the station would work directly with the community to increase HIV awareness (Boyle, 2010). Still, many listeners called for Sounds to be fired. Hate speech often portrays others as inferior to the speaker or "joker" and is an extreme form of uncivil and unethical language.

Incoherent Speech

Pageant contestant Lauren Caitlin Upton represented South Carolina in the Miss Teen USA pageant in 2007. On stage, Upton also discovered just how difficult it can be to speak publicly. This time, however, it was not because she plagiarized her speech or chose to use offensive language.

ETHICAL MOMENT

Free Speech and "You're Going to Hell"

Minister Fred Phelps of the Westboro Baptist Church in Topeka, Kansas, has received quite a bit of attention for his recent public demonstrations. Beginning in the 1990s, members of Westboro Baptist publically demonstrated against what it considered to be American "sins" such as homosexuality and adultery. On March 10, 2006, Phelps led a protest at the military funeral of "Matthew Snyder, who had been killed by an improvised explosive device (IED) while serving in Iraq" (Congressional Digest Corp., 2010). The protestors held signs condemning the United States, the Catholic Church, and the U.S. military (Congressional Digest Corp., 2010, p. 30). The church's signs feature slogans such as "God Loves IED's" and "Thank God for Dead Troops." Shirley Phelps-Roper, a spokesperson for the church, which has no affiliation with mainstream Baptists, explains: "Our goal is to help the nation connect the dots. You turn this nation over to the fags, and our soldiers come home in body bags"(Harris, 2006, n.p.).

Snyder's father sued the church for defamation and was initially awarded millions of dollars in punitive damages. Westboro Baptist appealed, and the U.S. Fourth Circuit Court ruled that the protest speech was protected by the First Amendment. Since protesting at Snyder's funeral, Westboro Baptist members have picketed nearly 200 military funerals while carrying signs saying "Thank God for Dead Soldiers," "You're Going to Hell," and "God Hates Fags" (Burke, 2010). In addition, the church has expanded its activities to include protests at nonmilitary funerals and other public events such as theater productions and graduation ceremonies. Members of Westboro Baptist have visited more than 800 cities, picketed more than 44,000 events, and scheduled pickets for nearly every day of the week.

In addition to protesting in person at public events, the church's Web site contains derogatory comments about the deceased. After the death of Elizabeth Edwards, wife of former presidential candidate John Edwards, the Westboro Church's Web site stated that she "rode the talk show circuit spewing blasphemy" and "defied God, so she died, and went to hell. Suck it up!" (Westboro Baptist Church, 2010). Is this hate speech that should be stopped, or is the Westboro Baptist Church simply exercising its First Amendment rights? What constitutes hateful speech, personal opinion, or protected speech? Supreme Court Justice Stephen Breyer questions the lack of legal guidelines for posting personal attacks on the Internet. And the public also is at a loss not only about how to protect free speech but also about how to protect individuals.

Even without laws prohibiting such public protests and online personal attacks, several groups have formed to counterprotest Westboro's picketing. Two groups, the Patriot Riders and Line of Love, have attended funerals to protest in a different way. The Patriot Guard Riders attend funerals, but only at the request of the families of the deceased. This organization of approximately 10,000 members, both hawk and dove, form a protective shield with their motorcycles and American flags around grieving families, protecting the family from seeing and hearing the church protestors. When speaking of the group's presence at the funeral of a soldier killed by a roadside bomb in Iraq, Richard Wilbur, state captain of the group's Indiana chapter, summed up the Riders' purpose: to afford families some privacy and to honor what the soldiers died for—the right to protest. The Riders recognize the irony in the situation—that the members of the Westboro Baptist Church are also exercising their right to protest—but they feel their methods reflect respect and Westboro Baptists' do not. As Kurt Mayer, a founding member of the Patriot Guard Riders, explains, "We show families in grieving communities that America still cares" (Harper, 2006; Harris, 2006; Simmons, 2007).

Line of Love organized after learning of Westboro's planned protest at Elizabeth Edwards's funeral. The group appeared at her funeral to act as a human shield and provide a barrier between Westboro members and the funeral attendees. The Line of Love antiprotesters carried signs that read "Hope" and "Friend" while chanting "Love, not hate."

These examples illustrate the power of language, issues of social justice, and civility in both our content and relational messages to others. The Westboro members, the Patriot Guard Riders, and the Line of Love participants all believe there are specific rights and protections for public speech. Each group interprets these rights differently, however. Where do you stand on the issue?

What Do You Think?

1. What does free speech mean to you? Should speech that communicates uncivil ideas be protected as free speech or should it be restricted? Why do you think as you do?

2. Do you think the members of the Westboro Baptist Church are ethical and civil in their actions and words? Why or why not? Are there events in which protesting should be banned?

3. Do you think the Patriot Guard Riders and Line of Love are ethical and civil in their actions and words? Why or why not?

4. Social justice is about creating an egalitarian society in which human rights are valued. How might restrictions on free speech enhance or diminish aims toward social justice?

When she was asked why a fifth of Americans could not locate their own country on a world map, Miss Teen America contestant Lauren Caitlin Upton responded that a group of "U.S. Americans don't have maps" and the way to alleviate that would be to help the educational efforts in South Africa and "the Iraq."

Rather, her language choice was incoherent. Appearing in her first live television show, Lauren was doing well in the competition until it was time to answer the interview question. Lauren was asked her opinion on why twenty percent of Americans are unable to locate the United States on a world map. Lauren's response included a fragmented and rambling comment that referred to the absence of access to "maps" as well as mention of education, helping such countries as South Africa and Iraq, countries in Asia and "everywhere." In addition, Lauren used many vocalized pauses including three "uhs," two "likes," and two "such as" comments, making her response incoherent.

Speaking publicly can be challenging when we are just beginning to learn how to successfully respond to unplanned moments. It is even more challenging now that our mistakes can be widely disseminated.

Because of the increasingly public nature of spoken and written words, speakers need to consider carefully the impact of their messages on their audiences and be careful to maintain the highest of ethical standards. With planning and practice, we can become successful public speakers who are adept at choosing the right words for the audience and each public-speaking occasion. For more tips and information on creating an effective speech, see Part V (Chapters 10 through 15).

 ## Language and Civility

Throughout this text, you are asked to consider the role of civil communication in our interactions with other people. To be sure, most of us honor and respect our nation's commitment to free speech, and we recognize the value of hearing the widest range of views on various issues as possible. However, as students of communication, we also want to consider the civility and incivility that is a part of our language and the call for free speech. We want to be mindful of the language we use as we address others and to always consider whether our cultural commitment to saying whatever we want whenever we want also means that we must accept uncivil moments. As you have read in this chapter, our language is a powerful tool, and the ways we use language affects others, clarifies or confuses our messages, and communicates who we are and what we value. Consider the case study that follows and how civility and incivility plays a role in your own communication.

It Begins with the Phrase "That's So Gay"

Gay teenagers living in the United States face many challenges, especially during their middle and high school years. In 2010, news broke that five gay or suspected gay teenagers committed suicide within a three-week span after being taunted, harassed, and shamed for their sexual orientation. These deaths occurred across the United States: from the East Coast to California. Fourteen-year old Jamey Rodemeyer took his life after claiming he could not handle the verbal harassment he was facing at school and online. Moreover, many other teens were beaten because of assumptions about their sexuality. If we take closer look at the situations leading up to the tragic suicides and assaults, we can discover just how powerful language can be. Perhaps it begins with the phrase, "That's so gay." This common phrase is used by young and old alike to represent something as "silly," "tacky," "wrong," or "hideous"—in other words, unacceptable in some way.

Some people say "That's so gay" does not really mean anything, but others disagree. Freshman student Rebekah Rice discovered just how serious the phrase can be. After being teased for her Mormon background and asked if she had multiple moms, Rebekah replied, "That's so gay." She later found herself in the high school principal's office for using the phrase, and a note was placed in her permanent file. Rebekah's parents sued the school for violating her First Amendment rights. Rebekah herself claimed that she did not mean to intentionally insult gay people. Instead, she claims that she meant that asking her if she had multiple moms was "so stupid—that's so silly—that's so dumb" ("That's So Gay" 2007). Although Rebekah and her parents believe that she was unfairly punished for using a phrase that is widely used among youth, the school took a very different position. School officials argue that they are taking a strict stand against hurtful language after two boys were paid to beat up a gay student the previous year.

Teenagers are not the only ones to use the phrase. The movie *The Dilemma* received heavy criticism for using the phrase to make fun of an electric car. After Universal Pictures pulled the scene from the trailer and substituted a scene without the use of the term *gay*, director Ron Howard decided to keep the joke in the movie. When asked why he chose to keep the joke, Howard replied, "Our lead character . . . has a mouth that sometimes gets him into trouble, and he definitely flirts with the line of what's okay to say. He tried to do what's right but sometimes falls short. Who can't relate to that?" (Howard, 2010). Other celebrities have also faced public ridicule for making antigay remarks. Tracy Morgan, for example, claimed during his comedy routine that homosexuality is a choice and that he would kill his son if his son came out to him. Morgan later issued a public apology and claimed his humor was not meant to hurt anyone (Hughes, 2011).

Shannon Gilreath, a law professor at Wake Forest University, disagrees. "Physical violence begins with bullying, name-calling and homophobic remarks. When nothing happens to someone [for making slurs], it escalates to violence" (Petrow, 2009). Judy Shepard knows all too well the violence that can result from homophobia. Two men beat her son, Matthew, to death for being gay. Judy Shepard is now an advocate for LGBTQ people and makes the following plea:

> Our young people deserve better than to go to schools where they are treated this way. We have to make schools a safe place for our youth to prepare for their futures, not be confronted with threats, intimidation or routine disrespect. Quite simply, we are calling one more time for all Americans to stand up and speak out against taunting, invasion of privacy, violence and discrimination against these youth by their peers, and asking everyone in a position of authority in their schools and communities to step forward and provide safe spaces and support services for LGBT youth or those who are simply targeted for discrimination because others assume they are gay (Shepard, 2010).

Shepard is one of many public figures now educating audiences about the powerful impact of uncivil language. She and others like her argue that we have the power to shape and alter the meaning of words; we also have the ability to stop using language that can be considered hateful or derogatory.

What Do You Think?

1. Make a list of phrases such as "That's so gay" that have been banned from schools or workplaces or that cast people in negative, unflattering, or demeaning ways. What groups of individuals might be harmed by these phrases? How might they be harmed? If you think that these phrases have little meaning, explain why.

2. If language is as powerful as Judy Shepard and others argue, what are some other terms and phrases we might use to replace the derogatory ones we currently use?

3. Should director Ron Howard have removed the phrase "That's so gay" from the film instead of leaving it in? Why or why not? Is there some benefit from leaving it in, or would it be better to have taken it out completely? Why do you think so?

4. Should comedians such as Tracy Morgan have the right to make antigay comments in their comedy routines? Why or why not?

Chapter Summary

The Nature of Language

- Language is governed by rules.
- Phonological, syntactic, and semantic rules help us to communicate effectively.
- Slang, jargon, euphemisms, and doublespeak can create confusion for listeners who are unfamiliar with the terms.
- Differences in cultural and co-cultural language can create difficulty in communicating effectively with one another.
- Gender can affect the way we communicate. Men and women often talk about different topics and use different strategies to communicate.
- Technology also influences our language choices. The ease and accessibility of communicating via the Internet, cell phones, and personal digital assistants have affected the way we communicate.

Language and Interpersonal Communication

- The type of interpersonal relationship we have with another person will help determine the content and relational meanings of a message.

- Content and relational messages can be an important part in maintaining long-distance relationships.

Language and Small Group Communication

- Groups can be more successful when members spend some time meeting face to face.
- Virtual meetings via video-streaming programs now make face-to-face group communication relatively easy.

Language and Public Speaking

- Speakers need to carefully consider the effects of their messages on audiences.
- To maintain the highest ethical standards, speakers need to be cautious of plagiarism, hate speech, and incoherent speech.

Language and Civility

- Language can be used civilly and uncivilly to express our views. Competent communicators consider the civil and uncivil aspects of the language they use.

Key Concepts

acronyms (81)

androgynous communicators (88)

colloquialisms (83)

connotative meanings (78)

cultural competence (83)

denotative meanings (78)

doublespeak (81)

equivocal words (80)

euphemisms (81)

jargon (81)

language (76)

phonology (76)

regionalisms (83)

semantics (77)

slang (80)

syntax (77)

 # Invitation to Human Communication Online

Speech Communication CourseMate includes an interactive eBook and interactive learning tools including National Geographic Explorer videos, student videos, quizzes, flashcards, and more. Speech Builder Express 3.0 and Speech Studio 2.0 are also available. Go to cengagebrain.com to access your CourseMate for *Invitation to Human Communication* for access to these resources.

Further Reflection and Discussion

1. Give an example of an experience when you were talking with a friend or heard someone else speaking and the person said the words in the wrong order and therefore did not say what they meant to say.

2. Think of a word that has several definitions and share the word and its meanings with classmates.

3. What are some common slang words you and your friends use? Ask your parents what slang words they used when they were your age. Do you know what those words mean? Now make a list of euphemisms for something people do not like to talk about directly.

4. Give an example of a strategy you have noticed only a woman using to communicate. Now give an example of the reverse.

5. If you were preparing a speech about the damage that can be done by using hate language, what would be three major arguments and points you would make? If you were preparing a speech on the right to use hate speech, what arguments would you give?

Activities and Web Links

Visit cengagebrain.com to access the CourseMate for *Invitation to Human Communication* where these activities and web links can be found.

1. Watch this video clip from an episode of the television show *Friends*. What does it reveal about the difference in how men and women communicate? Are there things that the men in this clip should learn from how the women communicate? What might the women learn? Go to *Web link 4.1*.

2. Read this list of items for e-mail etiquette. Do you agree with all of the items on the list? Choose five that you feel are the most important and explain why. What does this list say about how technology has affected our communication? Go to *Web link 4.2*.

3. Boys and girls often learn what toys are "appropriate" for them based on the packaging, labels, and placement in stores. Listen to the girl in the video challenging the gender bias of toys. What toys do you believe are designed specifically for boys? What toys do you believe are designed for girls? How can manufacturers make gender-neutral toys? Go to *Web link 4.3*.

4. Watch this video and make a list of the communication strategies that you see being used in the film *Relationship Maintenance during Military Deployment: Perspectives of Wives of Deployed US Soldiers*. Go to *Web link 4.4*.

LISTENING

IN THIS CHAPTER YOU WILL LEARN TO:

- Explain how listening helps us learn and understand.
- Understand the difference between listening and hearing.
- Understand why sometimes we fail to listen.

- Describe a variety of listening styles.
- Explain the types of speaker interferences.
- Listen critically and civilly to new ideas and information.

Jason Edwards/National Geographic

When we listen, we have the opportunity to learn something new and express value for another. In what ways will you be listening to others today?

When you cover issues in faraway cultures, you arrive as a complete outsider. It's essential to find something in common with people, some way to connect.

—Bobby Model, photographer, climber, and National Geographic Emerging Explorer

Jason Edwards/National Geographic

The day after Thanksgiving is often referred to as Black Friday because retailers finally become profitable for the year by opening early, starting holiday promotional sales, and offering customers their best deals. However, thanks to Dave Isay, founder of National Public Radio's StoryCorps, people are now being encouraged to do something other than shop on Black Friday: they are encouraged to "listen." Isay asks Americans to take an hour out of their day to record an interview and listen to the stories of a loved one. In fact, Isay believes so strongly in the value of listening that he created the National Day of Listening. Tens of thousands of Americans have participated by listening to the stories of their families, friends, and community members. Although Isay asks Americans to spend one day per year supporting the National Day of Listening, research reveals that we actually spend a good portion of every day listening. During an average day of communicating, we spend 55 percent of the time listening followed by speaking (17 percent), reading (16 percent), and writing (11 percent) (Emanuel et al., 2008). You may be surprised to learn, however, that most people retain little of what they hear.

Why Listening Is Important

Until now, you may not have spent much time considering the importance of effective listening. However, there are five important reasons why being "good" at listening can benefit us and our communities: listening helps confirm others, helps us understand, helps us learn, promotes civic engagement, and promotes social justice.

Listening Helps Confirm Others

Communication is a central component of building and maintaining relationships with others. For communication to be successful, we must first be willing to truly listen to others. *Listening in order to recognize, acknowledge, and express value for another person* is the process of **confirming**. The process of confirming lets others know that you are paying attention and acknowledging their message.

confirming
listening in order to recognize, acknowledge, and express value for another person.

100 | CHAPTER 5 LISTENING

Aziz Abu Sarah
Emerging Explorer and Cultural Educator

Tell us about an experience where active listening made a difference in one of your speaking engagements. For example, did someone in the audience tell a story that you listened to that changed your thinking or how you made your next presentation?

When we speak to groups or individuals, the most important thing is to be able to listen—and not only to listen to the words. We have to listen to what is behind the words. We use active listening because there's an emotional component to what people are saying. So we listen to why they are upset, why they're angry, why they're ashamed, why they're sad or happy about what was just shared. And by doing that we avoid a lot of fights and unproductive conversations.

For example, when I was speaking in an Israeli classroom just a couple months after a suicide bombing had happened, I was speaking with an Israeli partner of mine. We told our stories and how we should try to overcome anger, bitterness, and hatred and begin to work together. But one of the students was very, very angry. And he interrupted us throughout the speech and was pretty verbally violent. And so we stopped, and we asked him to tell us what was bothering him. And eventually he shared that his uncle was in a suicide bombing just a couple months earlier, and he was very angry, and he had never met a Palestinian before. I was the first Palestinian he had met, and all his anger just came at me. He shared how he was just waiting to get a chance for revenge. But we started this conversation, and it ended up going on for a couple of hours, and we just listened. We listened to his position, and we learned where he was coming from, and we heard his pain. I think he needed somebody from the other side to yell at. And for me, that was fine. I think he needed to get all his emotions out, because after that we ended up having a very productive conversation. And at the end of our conversation, he said that he—although he was confused because he had a chance to say everything he wanted to say and because we listened—he was not as angry as he was earlier. And without us listening to the emotions and the pain, I think that would have been impossible to get to that point.

Listening Helps Us Understand

When we pay close attention to a message, we do so with the desire to *understand* what someone is attempting to communicate. The goal of understanding a message provides us the opportunity to ask questions to seek clarification or gather more information when necessary.

Listening Helps Us Learn

When we listen, we have the ability to learn important information. When we listen in order to learn, we may discover more about the likes and dislikes of our friends and family members, how to master a new skill, or the positions held by political candidates during an election campaign. In each of these situations, the process of listening to learn allows us to grow as individuals because we learn new things.

Listening Promotes Civic Engagement

Listening can provide us the information we need to identify and address issues of public concern. When we listen, we can make informed decisions about the positions we hold on contentious issues, candidates we support for public or political office, and practices that may benefit or harm our families, workplaces, communities, states, countries, and continents. Listening allows us to be more fully engaged with our communities, organizations, and political concerns.

Listening Promotes Social Justice

Listening can provide the means necessary to create social change. When we listen to stories of injustice such as cases of homelessness, poverty, hunger, discrimination, or bullying, we have the ability to recognize how we can act to improve the lives of those who are experiencing hardship or injustice. When we confirm, learn, understand, and engage with others, our listening helps us sort out complex ethical, moral, and social issues that affect the people we live and work with, as well as those we may not come in direct contact with.

After listening to a ten-minute oral presentation, the average person understands and retains only 50 percent of the information presented. Forty-eight hours after the presentation, those same listeners will only remember 25 percent of the information (Steil, Barker, & Watson 1993). Imagine that you could improve your listening skills. You would be able to participate in the public dialogue of your communities on topics you had learned about in school, work, and through news media. You would acknowledge value for another person's ideas by paying attention to their presentations. You might even improve your grades by recalling more information on exams. In this chapter, we will explore why listening is important, why our listening sometimes fails, and how to listen carefully, critically, and ethically. Learning the importance of listening effectively and communicating clearly can help improve our relationships with others and teach us about ourselves.

Facts about Listening

You may have heard that listening and hearing are not the same thing. Did you know that listening is not a natural process? It takes effort and understanding to listen effectively.

Listening Is Not the Same as Hearing

Although some people believe that hearing and listening are the same thing. The two processes are actually quite different. **Hearing** refers to the *vibrations of sound waves on our eardrums and the impulses that are then sent to the brain.* Hearing is a passive process. Assuming a person does not have a hearing impairment or an object blocking the eardrum, sound waves will automatically transmit to the brain. We hear many sounds and noises throughout the day without paying much attention to them. We may hear the sound of an air conditioner turning on, a car driving down the street, or people murmuring in the

hearing
vibrations of sound waves on our eardrums; the impulses are then sent to the brain.

distance. We typically pay little attention to these sounds. **Listening**, on the other hand, *is the process of giving thoughtful attention to another person's words and understanding what you hear*. This occurs when we focus on a teacher's presentation, pay attention to our friend confiding in us, or attempt to understand the messages delivered through the media.

Listening Is Not a Natural Process

Many people believe listening is a natural process, something that occurs without a great deal of effort. However, the process of listening is more complex than the act of physically receiving messages. The act of listening actually requires effort on behalf of the listener. Notice that the definition of listening contains the phrase "giving thoughtful attention" to another. The act of listening is an active but not necessarily natural process. When listening, we must focus, attempt to understand, and respond to what others are saying.

Why We Sometimes Fail to Listen

Think about recent situations in which you were expected to listen. Were you willing to confirm some people but not others? Similarly, were you able to understand some speakers but not able to follow others? Michael Nichols, a listening researcher, reveals that we sometimes fail to listen because "the simple art of listening isn't always so simple." Listening requires work, and "to listen well we must forget ourselves" and focus our attention on another (Nichols, 1995, p. 3).

We often fail at listening for many reasons. **Listening interference** is *anything that stops or hinders a listener from receiving a message*. Although interference can be external to the listener (such as noises that capture our attention or visual distractions), there are also many forms of internal interference (distracting thoughts or feelings) that hinder us from openly receiving a message. We will explore the most common of kinds of interference here.

Listening requires effort on the part of the listener. What signs are these two people giving that indicate they are actively listening to one another?

Pseudolistening

Pseudolistening occurs *when listeners act like they are listening or pretend to be paying close attention to the message*. Pseudolisteners appear to be focused on the speaker. They make eye contact, provide nonverbal feedback such as nodding in agreement or smiling at the appropriate times, and genuinely seem interested in the message; however, pseudolisteners are actually distracted by other thoughts. Internally, these listeners are thinking of other things (or not thinking much at all) instead of actually focusing on the speaker's message. Pseudolistening occurs when listeners are bored, disinterested, or preoccupied with other thoughts.

Golden Pixels LLC/Shutterstock.com

Employees of Different Generations Working Together

Generation Y (born in the 1980s and 1990s) consists of approximately 71 million young people who are tapped into technology and media, and are now entering the workforce. This is the first time in history that four generations—those who lived through World War II, baby boomers (born 1946–1964), Generation X (born 1965–1980), and Generation Y—are working together (Belkin, 2007). Generation Y, however, brings a new dynamic to the work environment. Its members rely heavily on technology to socialize, think, and work through tasks.

U.S. Army Colonel Lonnie G. Hibbard explains that members of Generation Y "are accustomed to immediate feedback and thrive in a rapidly changing environment because they have grown up with information at their fingertips due to computers and smartphones. This immersion in technology and being con- nected 24/7 has caused this generation to change the defini- tion of how interpersonal communication takes place as more people turn to social networking as a means to communicate" (Hibbard, 2011). Members of Generation Y are also accustomed to instant feedback and virtual problem solving, whereas older

generations continue to expect annual reviews and face-to-face meetings (Armour, 2011).

The reliance on technology and the expectation of constant and immediate feedback can cause some tension and confusion for employees of different generations working together. In fact, according to a report by Lee Hecht Harrison (2011), more than 60 percent of employers say they experience tension between employees of different generations, and 70 percent of older employees are dismissive of younger workers' ability. Although the differences in expectations are neither right nor wrong, it does illustrate some of the challenges that multiple generations face when working together.

What Do You Think?

1. How might listening practices help reduce conflict be- tween employees from different generations?

2. Can technology bridge rather than expand the gap between Generation X and Generation Y employees? In what ways?

---

selective listening
when listeners only pay attention to particular parts or sections of a message.

Selective Listening

Selective listening occurs *when listeners only pay attention to particular parts or sections of a message.* Selective listeners may tune out commercials or only pay attention to parts of a lengthy message that seem the most interesting to them. They may turn the radio on only to listen closely to the weather report or road conditions. In class, selective listeners may perk up and pay close attention after a teacher says, "Be sure to write this down," or, "This will likely be on the test," and then tune out again after they get the information. When listening to a lengthy speech such as the state-of-the-union address, selective listeners may only listen to the parts of the speech that directly and immediately affect their lives and selectively tune out other parts.

Defensive Listening

defensive listener
listener who perceives a message as a personal attack or a form of criticism.

Defensive listeners *perceive a message as a personal attack or form of criticism.* A person who listens defensively makes the judgment that the speaker does not like or respect him or her. Defensive listeners also as- sume there are negative motives behind the communication act. A stu- dent who is worried about his grade in class may listen defensively when a teacher asks about absences or reasons for late assignments. A teenager may listen defensively when parents ask questions about her day, hearing the questions as mistrust rather than curiosity or interest. Defensive listeners assume others are being mean spirited, even when that is not the intention of the speaker, and they hear comments and questions as challenges or as demonstrations of a lack of respect.

Ambushing

Ambushing is *listening carefully to information in order to attack what the speaker has to say.* When prosecutors cross-examine witnesses in court, they often use ambushes to attack what a witness has said. Politicians may ambush during a debate when they listen to their opponent and then attack their arguments. In our interpersonal relationships, we sometimes listen to those we are in a conflict with to find ways to attack their reasons or arguments rather than understand them.

Insulated Listening

Insulated listening is *purposefully avoiding listening to specific pieces of information.* Insulated listening is the opposite of selective listening: instead of listening to key parts of information, insulated listeners will choose to ignore any undesirable topic that arises. For example, when a parent explains the reasons a teenager needs to have a curfew or when a roommate provides a numbers of reasons why making a chore chart is important to help keep the apartment clean and the division of labor fair, the teenager or roommate may decide she or he does not want to listen to the explanations and insulates her- or himself by ignoring those reasons.

Insensitive Listening

Insensitive listeners *pay attention to the content or literal meaning of the message without attending to the relationship level of the meaning.* When listeners fail to acknowledge the relationship level or other subtle meanings in a message, they are insensitive to others' feelings on the topic. For example, Ivy tells her professor that she will be missing two weeks of class because her mother is having major surgery and needs additional help at home. Hoping for a sympathetic response, Ivy is surprised when her professor states that the absences will not be excused and she should plan to e-mail the assignments so they

What listening behaviors do these students exhibit? What type of listeners would you describe them as?

ambushing
listening carefully to information in order to attack what the speaker has to say.

insulated listener
listener who purposefully avoids listening to specific pieces of information.

insensitive listener
listener who pays attention to the content or literal meaning of the message without attending to the relationship level of the meaning.

will not be graded as late. Ivy feels the professor is insensitive by not showing concern for her new responsibility at home and her mother's well-being.

Stage Hogging

Stage hogging occurs *when people make the conversation about themselves instead of showing interest in the person who is talking.* Stage hogging can occur in two ways. First, it occurs when a person redirects the conversation back to him- or herself. For example, when you share with a friend your dismay at having your hours cut at work and are hoping for sympathy and even solutions to cope with your reduced income, your friend is stage hogging if she begins to lament the fact that she never has enough money to do the things she wants and never responds to your concerns. Stage hogging also happens when a person interrupts another to focus attention back on her- or himself. For example, Stan wants to share what happened at last night's hockey game with Omar. Stan begins his story only to find that Omar interrupts to tell him about all the outstanding hockey games he has been to, hogging the stage and never making time for Stan to finish his story. Stage hogging can have a negative impact on relationships because the person who began to share something feels his or her opinions are not being heard or validated.

Technology

Although technology can open up avenues for listening to others, when we are surrounded by technology we can easily fail to listen. Text messaging during class or at work, surfing the Internet with our laptops instead of listening to a spouse or co-worker, participating in multiple online chat discussions at the same time, or walking across campus with our earphones on can prevent us from listening to others. This often has serious negative consequences: we miss important information, fail to hear what others are saying to us, ignore friends who might be trying to get our attention, or even fail to hear important sounds, such as sirens, trains, or horns.

Differences in Listening Styles

Consider the following examples:

- Loretta loved her geology class. She was excited to spend class time touching and examining samples of rocks and minerals as her professor lectured. On field trips, she eagerly stood in front of the group, exploring the different soils and formations with her hands. When she studied for an exam, she could visualize the soil, rock, or mineral and remember its content and formation process.

- Phillip is a nutrition major. He enjoys learning about different nutrients that help the body grow and develop. Although Phillip's nutrition courses require him to read several textbooks on the subject, Phillip learns best when he hears his professor discuss the

stage hogging

when people make the conversation about themselves instead of showing interest in the person who is talking.

Corbis Flirt/Alamy

Do you believe cell phones create additional interference in the classroom? What message is this student sending about listening?

Many people "listen" best by seeing something in order to understand it. Others understand best when they hear something explained. What mode of listening suits you best?

information in detail. When Phillip tells his parents what he is learning at school, he often repeats much of the information he has heard in class.

- Sierra was an art history major. She enjoyed taking art history courses from the professors in the department who showed examples of the different artists' work. Sierra knew that without actually seeing the artwork, she would struggle understanding the different periods and artists. For Sierra, seeing was the easiest way for her to learn.

The students described here "listen" in different ways. Loretta is an **experiential listener**. She *learns best when she can touch, explore, and participate in what is being described.* She is the type of person who often says, "Let me try that," in order to learn the material. In the second example, Phillip is the "explain it to me" person. He is an **auditory listener** because he *needs to hear verbal descriptions and explanations.* Even if he reads the textbook, he understands the material better after hearing the professor talk about it. In the final example, Sierra *needs to see something to understand it* because she is a **visual listener**. Visual listeners often use the phrase "Show me" in order to fully comprehend new information (Kolb, 1984; Sims & Sims, 1995).

experiential listener
listener who learns best by touching, exploring, and participating in what is being described.

auditory listener
listener who needs to hear verbal descriptions and explanations.

visual listener
listener who needs to see something in order to understand it.

What styles of listening are these students displaying? Do they people-oriented, content-oriented, action-oriented, or time-oriented? What cues give you this sense?

Our senses can determine how we best listen and comprehend information: some of us prefer to touch, others to listen, and still others to see in order to listen best. In addition to learning and listening through stimulating our senses, we also may listen for specific types of information. These *listening styles* depend on the context surrounding the act of listening. There are four listening styles that influence how we listen and what we pay attention to.

Listening Styles

Each of us has an individual **listening style** or *preferred approach to understanding a message*. Some of us listen as a way to enhance the quality of a relationship, but others may listen to obtain as much information and detail as possible before making an informed decision. Researchers have identified four primary listening styles, which we will explore in the following paragraphs (Johnson, Weaver, Watson, & Barker, 2000).

People-oriented listeners are *concerned about other people's feelings and emotions as well as the quality of the interpersonal relationship*. Individuals using a people-oriented listening style can "read" others' emotions, so they focus on the emotional and relational aspects of the message. Listeners adopting this style tend to notice peoples' moods, understand the emotional meaning of a message, and display empathy toward other people. Although people-oriented listeners tend to be less apprehensive about communicating in groups and interpersonal situations, they may lose their ability to critically reflect on the information presented (Chesebro, 1999; Sargent, Weaver, & Kiewitz, 1997).

Content-oriented listeners *pay close attention to the facts and details of a message*. Content listeners obtain as much information about an issue as possible. They excel at understanding and analyzing various positions on a topic. They take time to collect as much information as possible, giving priority to expert opinions and other credible resources. They ask pointed questions, dismiss unreliable facts, and explore all perspectives and points of view. Content-oriented individuals often play the role of devil's advocate as a way to obtain information and explore different viewpoints, thus taking time before coming to a conclusion. There are many advantages to this approach, but it also can create an environment that seems disruptive, hostile, or even threatening to others if not used carefully.

Unlike content-oriented listeners who enjoy taking their time to learn about multiple perspectives on a topic, **action-oriented listeners** *want speakers to provide clear, detailed, and straight-to-the-point information.*

listening style
preferred approach to understanding a message.

people-oriented listener
listener who is concerned about the feelings and emotions of other people as well as the quality of interpersonal relationships.

content-oriented listener
listener who pays close attention to the facts and details of a message.

action-oriented listener
listener who wants speakers to provide clear, detailed, and straight-to-the-point information.

MIXA/Getty Images

Action-oriented listeners want to take care of business and are listening specifically for the information necessary to accomplish a task. They may grow impatient if a speaker includes nonessential information, digresses, or follows a tangent. Action-oriented listening can be an important part of getting a task completed, but these listeners may also avoid acknowledging important emotional concerns or cues of the message.

Time-oriented listeners *view time as a commodity and do not want to have it wasted.* These listeners, similar to action-oriented listeners, *want speakers to be clear, succinct, and to the point.* However, unlike action-oriented listeners, time-oriented listeners may set time guidelines for conversations or use particular behaviors to indicate their desire to end the interaction. Time-oriented listeners may verbalize that they only have "10 minutes to meet," may constantly check their watches, or even abruptly end conversations. This listening style can be quite effective in meeting deadlines, but it can also make speakers feel uncomfortable or insulted if they feel rushed to deliver their message.

Although most of us have a distinct listening style, or at least two strong listening preferences, it is important to consider which listening style is best suited for different types of interactions. Because each of the four listening styles has distinct advantages and disadvantages, one may be more appropriate than another for the context of a specific communication act. For example, you may be an active listener in class when an instructor is explaining a new assignment and then become a people-oriented listener when your roommate reveals that her romantic relationship just ended. If you were to approach the roommate's breakup with a time- or action-oriented approach, then you might unintentionally hurt her feelings. Similarly, if you approach your instructor's explanation from a people-oriented style, you may cause considerable confusion or even humor in the discussion.

Speaker Interference

As you have learned, there are many reasons why listeners have difficulty understanding and remembering information presented to them. Listener interference and listening styles are two important factors. However, there are times when listeners have difficulty listening to a

---

PRACTICING HUMAN COMMUNICATION

How Can You Listen More Effectively?

Take a few minutes to evaluate your listening skills.

1. Describe when you felt the most engaged with a face-to-face conversation this week. What was engaging about the conversation? Did you or the other person exhibit active listening?

2. At what point in the face-to-face communication did you feel most distant from what was happening? Explain what type of interference there was or other reasons why you felt distanced.

3. Consider what your responses indicate about your listening style and preferences. Also notice what types of interference may hinder your ability to listen. Now consider what you can do to listen more effectively in face-to-face communication (Brookfield, 1995).

---

time-oriented listener

listener who views time as a commodity and does not want to have it wasted and wants speakers to be clear, succinct, and to the point.

message because of speaker interference. To understand listening and how we might minimize speaker interference, whether we are listeners or speakers, we will explore the four most common types of speaker interference next.

Interference Caused by Information

Sometimes we simply stop paying attention to a message. Perhaps the speaker talked for a long period of time without taking a break, the information presented was too technical to understand, or you were bored with the simplicity of the message. Communication that is drawn out, overly complicated, or too simplistic can create interference. When we experience interference caused by information, we are likely to just give up on listening. There are three types of information interference: message overload, message complexity, and message simplicity.

Message Overload Klemmer and Snyder's classic study (1972) indicates that we spend an average of 70 percent of our day in some form of communication: attending meetings or class, talking or texting on the phone, reading or listening to the news. Today's college students spend a large portion of their day attending classes and listening to professors present information for fifty minutes, seventy-five minutes, or even two and a half hours. Yet research indicates that adult learners are unable to stay focused for more than fifteen to twenty minutes at a time—so we often are subjected to message overload (Johnstone & Percival, 1972; Middendork & Kalish, 1996).

In addition to listening to information presented in class, students are often required to conduct their own research to complete assignments. But sometimes our initial research into a subject yields more than 1,000 results for our keyword search, and we have to deal with yet another form of information overload. Then we consume many messages outside of our responsibilities as students. We communicate at work, likely have the television turned on while we are at home, listen to the radio in the car, surf the Web, or pay attention to our cell phones for incoming messages all day. Most of the time, we simply cannot absorb this much information throughout our day.

How much time do you spend communicating with others on an average day?

Yellow Dog Productions/Getty Images

Message Complexity When information is presented that is too complicated for us to understand, we likely give up on listening. Imagine the following scenario.

You walk into a biology class and hear the professor say, "Axonal signals transiently activate the expression of the transcription factor Oct6 in Schwann cells that will form myelin, and cyclic adenosine monophosphate can mimic axonal contact in vitro" ("Understanding Scientific Jargon," n.d.). Undoubtedly, you already feel behind on the material and consider dropping the class.

When messages are too complex for us to understand, we may decide to focus our attention elsewhere. When this happens, we may jeopardize our education, friendships, or ability to learn. On the other hand, speakers should take into account audience knowledge on the subject. At times, defining terms, providing examples, or showing visual representations of the information can help listeners stay focused.

Message Simplicity When information is too simple for the audience, listeners may become bored and stop listening. Consider the following examples:

- Martin was asked to deliver an informative speech in class, and he chose to present a speech titled "How to Make a Peanut Butter and Jelly Sandwich."

- Jacki delivered a speech at her high school graduation and read Dr. Seuss's *Oh, the Places You'll Go!* to her senior class.

- Jorge was invited to speak to a group of computer scientists and informed them about the history of computers.

In each of these situations, the messages presented were too simplistic for the audience. When listeners already possess the information provided to them, they can become bored or easily distracted. As speakers, we need to make sure our information is appropriate for our audience. We need to ensure that our information is neither too complex nor too simplistic.

Interference Caused by Language

Interference can also be caused by language that is unclear. Language that is too formal, too casual, too noninclusive, or too cluttered makes it easy for listening to fail.

Too Formal As discussed in Chapter 4, jargon refers to *technical language used by professional groups.* Jargon can be confusing for listeners who do not know what a particular word or acronym means. Imagine listening as your doctor tells you that "if you experience pain in your upper quadrant then you can take medicine PRN." When language is too formal, it becomes difficult to understand the message.

Too Casual Language can be difficult to listen to if it is too casual. It is easy to fall into our familiar, everyday language patterns, which may be too casual for our audience. One common way for language to be too casual is when it uses slang, or *informal nonstandard language.* A teenager telling her parents that the "band raised the roof with one totally sick song after another" and a student saying "she was hotting me up" as a way to describe someone interfering in his business are clear examples of slang that may be confusing to some people. When our language is too casual, people may not be able to follow the ideas we are communicating or may feel uncomfortable.

Noninclusive Language Listening can break down when you use *noninclusive* language or language that refers only to certain groups of people. When people hear language that excludes those who are not in the "in-group," they may be offended and tune out. Common examples of noninclusive language are *chairman*, *mailman*, and *policeman* (inclusive language would be *chair*, *mail carrier*, and *police officer*). **Spotlighting** or the *practice of highlighting a person's race, ethnicity, sex, sexual orientation, or physical disability* also can be a form of noninclusive language. When we spotlight, we describe a friend as an "Asian American friend," a professor as a "gay professor," or a neighbor as a "disabled neighbor." Spotlighting is often used by members of the dominant culture to mark differences as being atypical or unusual; most of the time, marking difference is intended to mean that something is surprising or abnormal.

However, there are times when including cultural differences is important. When talking about pay equity in the workplace, it is important to recognize that Asian American women earn approximately 88 percent of what a white man earns, whereas African American women earn approximately 70 percent of what a white man makes, and Latina women approximately 61 percent (Villeneuve, 2012; White House, 2012). In this example, spotlighting illustrates important racial and cultural differences.

When you avoid spotlighting while using culturally inclusive and gender-inclusive language, you communicate that you are aware of diversity. Use language that is respectful of the diverse people you are speaking with; this will make listening easier for everyone.

Verbal Clutter Sometimes we have difficulty listening when people use **verbal clutter** or *extra words in sentences that do not add meaning.* Although listeners can mentally process more words per minute than speakers can speak (on average a speaker speaks at a rate of 125 to 175 words per minute, but an active listener can process between 350 and 450 words per minute), verbal clutter impedes listening because listeners have to process words that are unnecessary or redundant (Wolvin & Coakly, 1996). Examples of verbal clutter include words and phrases such as *like*, *um*, *you know*, and *stuff like that.* These commonly used words and phrases distract listeners and add no useful meaning.

Similarly, verbal clutter also consists of loading our speech with adjectives and adverbs. Consider the following cluttered sentences and their uncluttered alternatives.

Cluttered: "Good, effective writers use carefully selected, well-planned, and detailed descriptions and stories to vividly portray images and ideas."

Uncluttered: "Effective writers use vivid stories to present their ideas."

spotlighting
practice of highlighting a person's race, ethnicity, sex, sexual orientation, or physical disability.

verbal clutter
extra words in sentences that do not add meaning.

The uncluttered example is much easier to listen to and understand. To help reduce clutter in our communication, we must ask ourselves, do the words we use help develop our ideas or make more work for the listener? How many of our words are redundant?

Interference Caused by Differences

Differences between a listener and a speaker can also cause interference with listening. Although we are all similar in many ways, no two people exactly match in appearance, mannerism, values, or background. When we confront differences, we may want to place value on or see those differences on a hierarchy. When we interpret differences as "right" or "wrong," "good" or "bad," we will have trouble focusing on the message. There are four types of differences that are common: speech style, appearance, values, and background and occupation.

Speech Style Accents, tonal and rhythmic qualities, stuttering, and speech patterns of nonnative speakers can affect our ability to listen. When we are unfamiliar with these styles, we may have a difficult time paying attention to the message.

Appearance Styles of dress, height, weight, hair color and style, body adornment, and even a person's mannerisms can affect listening behaviors. When a person's appearance captures our attention, we may not be closely listening to the message.

Values When a listener holds values that differ from the speaker, listening can be difficult. If listeners are convinced that their values are right or best, then they often have trouble listening to understand why someone holds a different position.

Background and Occupation Differences in race, ethnicity, religion, education, occupation, upbringing, and economic status can affect our listening. If we hold assumptions or make judgments about people based on their backgrounds and occupations, we may forget to be open to listening to their experiences.

As listeners, we need to remember that *difference* simply means *different*. When we refrain from focusing on differences and remember to be open enough to listen to others, we can overcome interference caused by differences.

Interference Caused by Technology

The amount of technology constantly available to us can create interference. When a cell phone rings during class; a sporting event is broadcast on television, radio, or the Internet; or a new message is posted to our social media accounts, our attention can quickly turn from the person we are talking with to the technology. Approximately 94 percent of today's college students and 75 percent of today's middle- and high-school students own cell phones (Burns & Lohenry, 2010; Reavy, 2008). With so many people carrying, talking, and texting on their phones, cell-phone etiquette has become an important topic of conversation. Shari Burns and Kevin Lohenry investigated cell-phone use in class and discovered that 73 percent of respondents admitted that their cell phones rang during class, and 84 percent of faculty claimed cell phones are a source of distraction during class time (Burns & Lohenry, 2010). Cell phones not only are distracting to us as listeners but also can distract others around us.

How to Listen Effectively

When we improve our listening skills, we increase the amount of information we comprehend and retain. To listen effectively, we must first overcome obstacles that interfere with our listening. A **careful listener** *overcomes listener interference in order to listen effectively to another person's message.* To reduce interference, try the following strategies.

- **Eliminate distractions**. Distractions may be external (auditory or visual distractions) or internal (distracting thoughts or feelings). Turn cell phones off and commit yourself to focusing your attention on the person communicating. Avoid thinking of thoughts outside of what the person is saying.

- **Use effective communication**. Although you may have the urge to interrupt and focus the conversation on yourself, avoid the tendency to dominate the discussion. Instead, ask questions that will help clarify information or demonstrate your understanding.

- **Offer feedback**. Providing appropriate and timely feedback is another important strategy for effective listening. Providing nonverbal feedback such as nodding your head in agreement, smiling at the right moment, and using direct body orientation (facing those who are speaking, maintaining a relaxed, alert, and open body position) can help ensure you are listening carefully to the speaker. In addition, offering verbal feedback can show others you are listening carefully to their message.

- **Ask for clarification**. When you do not understand someone because of language, style, message complexity, or the like, respectfully ask for clarification.

How to Listen Critically

To listen critically means that you assess the strengths and weaknesses of someone's information. Listening critically does not mean that you immediately judge the person or message or listen to find fault with a message. Rather, **critical listeners** *listen for the accuracy of content and the implications of a message.* This means that critical listeners remain open to new ideas, listen carefully to areas of disagreement, and consider how someone else's ideas affect oneself and one's community.

Guidelines for Critical Listening When we listen critically, we avoid making quick decisions about what is good or bad, right or wrong. Instead, we ask people appropriate questions about their ideas so we can more fully understand a message and explore areas of agreement or disagreement. First, we need to assess a person's credibility to decide if she or he has the authority to present information on the subject. Next, we

careful listener
listener who overcomes listener interference in order to listen effectively to another person's message.

critical listener
listener who listens for accuracy of content and the implications of a message.

CIVIC ENGAGEMENT

The Listening Project: What Does the World Think of America?

How well do you think you can listen to what others think of you? Asking the question, "What do you think of America?" four "listeners" traveled to fourteen different countries to hear the answers. Carrie Lennox (seventh-grade history teacher), Bob Roeglin (corrections), Bao Phe (spoken word artist and poet), and Han Shan (trainer of grassroots youth activists) traveled around the globe to ask common people "What's wrong" and "What's right with America?" They made a commitment to be curious and to listen to the answers, and the result is the documentary and award-winning film *The Listening Project*.

The producers of the film explain: "We had our own very strong feelings about the Unites States and its place in the world. How do you set that aside? How do you set aside your own personal views and really try to go out and very objectively talk to people and be able to really listen" to views you might not agree with? But the producers and the "listeners" made that commitment. Here is a little of what they heard, when they asked, "When I say 'America' or 'American,' what's the first thing that pops into your head?"

"There is a Japanese saying: To criticize is to help . . ."

"America really influences the world . . ."

"America is what gives to you with one hand and then takes away with both."

"I love America, and I hate America."

"Most Americans don't understand how we live where we live and what is going on. We are not a terrorist people."

"In America, there is a sense that if you've got drive and ambition, you can make it."

"America's role always been to try and make peace."

"You have always been so much involved with wars."

"The Greeks and the Romans—America should learn from history."

"The world is one, one, two, three: there we all are."

"Does it really make you so happy to drive home in your Beemer and go out again in your Lexis?"

"There is a saying: 'God has given you two ears and one mouth to listen more than speak.'"

Source: The Listening Project documentary (http://thelisteningprojectfilm.com/).

What Do You Think?

1. What listening skills do you think *The Listening Project* listeners might have used to really listen to the people they spoke with?

2. Have you been in a situation in which you listened to things you agreed with and did not agree with? What listening strategies did you use?

3. If you could go around and ask people a question with a commitment to hearing answers you might not agree with, what would that question be?

---

need to analyze whether arguments presented were supported by sound evidence. Finally, we need to determine what effect a message has on our own lives or the lives of others.

- Does the person have the experience, expertise, or ability to access accurate information on the subject? Does he or she have a personal stake in the outcome leading to possible bias on the topic?

- How fully has the person developed an idea? Is the information based mostly on fact or on opinion? Where did the information come from? Is the information recent?

- How does the information fit with what you know to be true? What information is new? What are the implications of the message for you and your community?

Listening critically means that we ask a series of questions to determine someone's credibility, the quality of the material provided, and the implications for the ideas presented. When we are committed to asking questions first, we are less likely to judge a person's ideas before we listen to the complete message.

How to Listen Civilly

Civil Listeners *are open to hearing different views and perspectives, even when there is disagreement.* Listening civilly does not mean that we have to agree with someone, be persuaded that she or he is correct, or remain silent about our own views. Instead, when we listen civilly we consider views that are different from our own and try to understand those views. When we understand a viewpoint more fully, we can engage in productive conversations about disagreements in our relationships, workplace differences, community challenges, or global concerns.

When we listen civilly, we compare and contrast our beliefs and values with others. By fully listening to other perspectives, we may gain a clearer sense of who we are and what we believe. We may be able to learn about and participate in the discussion of local, state, national, and international issues.

civil listener
listener who is open to hearing different views and perspectives, even when there is disagreement.

Chapter Summary

Listening Is Important for Several Reasons

- Listening allows us to confirm others, understand a message, and learn something new.
- Listening also provides us the opportunity to become engaged citizens and possibly work toward improving our communities, relationships, and workplaces.

It Is Important to Understand the Misconceptions about Listening

- The idea that listening is a natural process is not accurate; it takes effort to listen.
- The belief that listening and hearing are the same is also a misconception. Hearing is the physiological process that takes place when sound waves travel in our eardrums; listening is paying close attention to another's words.

We Sometimes Fail to Listen for Three Primary Reasons

- Differences in listening styles and preferences (experiential listeners, auditory listeners, visual listeners, people-oriented listeners, content-oriented listeners, action-oriented listeners, and time-oriented listeners) can impede our ability to understand others.
- There are many types of listener interference that hinder our ability to understand a message fully: pseudolistening, selective listening, defensive listening, ambushing, insulated listening, insensitive listening, stage hogging, and technology.
- Failing to listen can also be caused by speaker interference because of information, language, differences, and technology.

There Are Several Ways to Improve Our Listening

- To listen effectively, we must overcome obstacles that interfere with our ability to listen to others.
- To listen critically, we need to assess the strengths and weaknesses of a person's message.
- To listen civilly, we need to remain open to new ideas and information, even when we may disagree with those ideas.

Key Concepts

action-oriented listener (108)

ambushing (105)

auditory listener (107)

careful listener (114)

civil listener (116)

confirming (100)

content-oriented listener (108)

critical listener (114)

defensive listener (104)

experiential listener (107)

hearing (102)

insensitive listener (105)

insulated listener (105)

listening (103)

listening interference (103)

listening style (108)

people-oriented listener (108)

pseudolistening (103)

selective listening (104)

spotlighting (112)

stage hogging (106)

time-oriented listener (109)

verbal clutter (112)

visual listener (107)

Invitation to Human Communication Online

Speech Communication CourseMate includes an interactive eBook and interactive learning tools including National Geographic Explorer videos, student videos, quizzes, flashcards, and more. Speech Builder Express 3.0 and Speech Studio 2.0 are also available. Go to cengagebrain.com to access your CourseMate for *Invitation to Human Communication* where these resources can be found.

Further Reflection and Discussion

1. Do you ever hold more than one conversation at a time— for example, texting with a friend while also chatting online? Discuss experiences where you were able to listen well or not listen well in this situation. What is lost when holding two conversations at once? What might be gained?

2. Make a list of cell phone etiquette do's and don'ts. Compare them with others in your class and discuss the lists. Can you come to a consensus?

3. Think of a recent experience where your listening failed. What styles were you using? Was there speaker interference? How do you explain why your listening was ineffective?

Activities and Web Links

Visit cengagebrain.com to access the CourseMate for *Invitation to Human Communication* where these activities and web links can be found.

1. Watch this brief humorous video that depicts three people in a listening situation. What listening style does each person use? What types of interference do you notice? Go to *Web link 5.1*.

2. Watch this video clip demonstrating self-centered listening. Now write a brief paragraph explaining what the self-centered listener might have said to show she was a skilled listener and communicator. Go to *Web link 5.2*.

3. Make a list of all the jargon used in your workplace or in the discipline in which you are majoring in college. For examples of scientific jargon, go to *Web link 5.3*.

UNDERSTANDING INTERPERSONAL

IN THIS CHAPTER YOU WILL LEARN TO:

- Understand how relationships are unique, involve commitment, and are based on rules.
- Describe how relationships with family members, friends, and romantic partners evolve over time.
- Choose how much to self-disclose in a relationship.

- Explain the types of computer-mediated communication and how to use them wisely.
- Examine the effects of gender on relationships with family members, friends, romantic partners, and co-workers.
- Create successful relationships with people from different cultures.

6

Characteristics of Interpersonal Relationships

Types of Interpersonal Relationships

Understanding Self-Disclosure

Technology and Interpersonal Relationships

Gender and Interpersonal Relationships

Culture and Interpersonal Relationships

How to Listen Effectively

As we develop and maintain relationships with others, we often reveal personal information about ourselves. What personal information have you recently shared with another person?

Zane Gabriel Mercurio/National Geographic

COMMUNICATION

Only by being open and asking for help will we know that we are not alone. If you have someone who will walk the journey with you, it is always easier.

—Zinhle Thabethe, humanitarian and musician, National Geographic Emerging Explorer

The relationships we have with others are often the most rewarding parts of our lives. Because of the importance of relationships, this chapter will discuss various components that influence them. We will begin by defining the characteristics and types of interpersonal relationships. Next, we will explain how relationships develop and deteriorate. Finally, we will look at how technology, gender, and culture influence these relationships.

Characteristics of Interpersonal Relationships

Communication is the foundation for interpersonal relationships. When we communicate with friends, family members, colleagues, or romantic partners, we do so to build and maintain relationships. We ask questions, share personal information, solve problems, and engage in small talk to sustain relationships we consider to be significant in our lives. But just because we communicate with another person does not necessarily mean that we have a relationship with that person. **Interpersonal relationships** *involve a personal connection established with another person through the intentional use of communication.* These relationships are unique, require commitment, and are based on implicit or explicit rules. We will now look at what this actually means for people who want rich relationships in their lives.

Interpersonal Relationships Are Unique

Every human being is different. We look, talk, and behave in distinctive ways. And because of this, each interpersonal relationship is unique. You likely have friendships with many people, and each one of these friendships has particular patterns that make it unlike the others. You may share one kind of joke with one friend and a different kind with another. You may share one kind of information about yourself with your roommate but a different kind with your favorite classmate. The way we interact with others is often determined by the type of interpersonal relationship (e.g., friend, co-worker, family member, or significant other), the context surrounding the interactions, and the predetermined norms and routines created by those involved in the relationship. For these reasons, every interpersonal relationship is unique.

interpersonal relationship
relationship that involves the establishment of a personal connection with another person through the intentional use of communication.

Nga Nguyen/Flickr Select/Getty Images

Our relationships with family and friends can be very meaningful. If you have an older or younger person in your life who is important to you, what makes that person unique?

Interpersonal Relationships Require Commitment

Consider the different relationships that are important to you. Do you have a friend you socialize with on a daily or weekly basis? Do you regularly call a parent or sibling to check in? Do you have a co-worker you socialize with after work? Each of these relationships requires a degree of commitment, and these commitments are often (but not always) a choice. Some of us may choose to maintain a long-distance relationship with a friend or romantic partner. Some may choose to discuss an ongoing health issue with a close relative or friend. Others may choose to call a grandparent every Sunday or attend office hours regularly to chat with a favorite professor. On the other hand, you may decide to let a friendship dissipate or even not make friends with a neighbor. Although some commitments may be required by our families, professors, or supervisors (when they assign us to work in groups), most interpersonal relationships would not exist without a degree of voluntary commitment. Deciding to commit to a relationship in some small or large way is one characteristic that defines our interpersonal relationships.

Interpersonal Relationships Are Built Around Rules

Interpersonal relationships function by their own set of rules. These rules are typically implicit, meaning we do not always talk openly about them, but they are a necessary part of every interpersonal relationship. Many rules are established by cultural norms and practices: it is appropriate for a husband to kiss his wife goodbye; it is not appropriate for her physician to

COMMUNICATION AT WORK

The Consequences of Social-Media Blunders

Does what we say and how we say it matter in the workplace? Consider the following examples.

After calling her students "arrogant and snobby" and posting "I'm so not looking forward to another year at Cohasset School," Dr. June Talvitie-Siple, a supervisor of the high school's math and science program, lost her job ("H.S. Teacher Loses Job over Facebook Posting," 2010). Parents and students of this Massachusetts school found the postings, which Talvitie-Siple thought she had posted using her private setting on Facebook. The resulting furor led the teacher to resign. Students suggested that although she was a great teacher, she clearly did not understand the Internet and that "if you are in a professional position, maybe you shouldn't be putting what you really feel about your job or whatever on Facebook." Parents replied, "It's horrid. Who says that about children you are teaching; children you are raising that you are a role model for?" Talvitie-Siple said in an interview that she "is not apologizing for her comments, but that she is sorry that they went public" ("H.S. Teacher," 2010). She said she was referring to the political situation in the school, which she called 'very stressful,' and she said she thought she was only blowing off steam with friends in private" (Collins, 2010).

Three prison guards from Nebraska lost their jobs when Caleb Bartel's Facebook page said, "When you work in a prison, a good day is getting to smash an inmate's face into the ground. For me, today was a very good day" ("Facebook Post Prompts Prison Probe," 2010). The Nebraska Department of Corrections launched an investigation not only into Bartel but also into Shawn Paulson and Derek Dickey, two other guards who had replied favorably to the posting. All three guards lost their jobs. Former Nebraska State Senator Ernie Chambers described the posting as bringing "a cloud of negativity over the penitentiary." The state corrections department investigation "found that at least one of the guards used force on the day that the comment was posted, though there was no evidence of abuse." These findings were confirmed by a state patrol investigation as well as by prisons spokesperson Dawn-Renee Smith, who said "The inmate was not injured and the use of force in February was

justified." Because of the posting, however, Senator Chambers described the three former guards as not fit to hold employment. Bob Huston, director of state corrections, explained that the department does not abuse inmates: "We are not pleased any time we have any thoughts or beliefs or things that would indicate that there is suspected abuse of inmates. That concerns us deeply" ("Facebook Post," 2010).

Real situations such as these raise interesting questions about communication and its effects in the workplace. When individuals in positions of authority make claims, and those claims are aired or become publicly known, there can be serious consequences: people lose their jobs and their credibility, individuals are hurt and insulted, and supervisors, and bosses must respond to try to sort out facts, clarify details, and protect individuals from harm. Statements made in jest, without forethought, or even in what we think are private moments can reach a larger public and can be life altering; the individuals just described lost their jobs. Television, radio, and other media outlets such as Facebook make the mass distribution of our communication easy, fast, and accessible. Unlike previous generations, individuals today must monitor their public and private communication carefully; when they do not, they stand to lose a great deal.

What Do You Think?

1. What role, if any, do you believe companies have in monitoring what is written on social-media sites?

2. When an employee makes a comment using social media, and the comment is posted using privacy settings, should the communication be punishable by the loss of the person's job? Or should the employee receive a warning, something like a "two strikes" warning, before being fired or forced to resign. Why or why not?

3. Are there statements that should result in immediate firing or resignation? What are those statements, and why should an individual be fired for communicating them?

do so. Rules are also created by the context surrounding the relationship: your boss expects you to discuss your work with her; the server at the restaurant does not. Finally, rules are determined by those involved in the relationship: you expect your best friend to call every week, but you do not expect the same from your ex-boyfriend or -girlfriend. Relationships will continue to thrive as we follow the established relationship rules. Violating these rules can lead to a relationship deteriorating or ending. No longer calling a friend on a regular basis may lead to some deterioration in the friendship. Acting dishonestly in a relationship with a romantic partner could end the relationship entirely. The rules that are established in each relationship help make the relationship unique, and these are often rules that show one's commitment to the relationship.

Types of Interpersonal Relationships

Take a moment to consider who the most important interpersonal relationships are in your life. If they are your family, friends, co-workers, or romantic partners, then you fit the norm: our most significant interpersonal relationships come from these four major parts of our lives. Because they are so significant, we will discuss them in the following sections.

Family

In the past few decades we have seen family structures change, creating more diversity in today's families. Today, six out of every ten children live with both biological parents; every four of ten do not (Mondello, 2010). We'll consider those structures next.

Family Arrangements Although there are many ways to define a family, communication scholars Galvin and Brommel define **family** as "*a network of people who live together over long periods of time bound by ties of marriage, blood, or commitment, legal or otherwise who consider themselves as family and who share a significant history and anticipated future of functioning in a family relationship*" (Galvin, Bylund, & Brommel, 2003). Today, we see many different types of family living arrangements, so we will explore those here.

Communication scholar Mary Ann Fitzpatrick (2003) classified three primary types of relationships that exist for married or cohabiting couples: interdependent couples, independent couples, and separate couples.

Interdependent Couples. This traditional category consists of couples who are highly interdependent. The **interdependent couple** *shares traditional views of marriage and family life, activities, and interests.*

Independent Couples. **Independent couples** *hold less traditional views of family roles and expectations.* They are less dependent on one another and seek some autonomy in their activities.

Separate Couples. **Separate couples** *are extremely autonomous.* Each person in the relationship allows the other his or her own time and space to enjoy activities.

family
network of people who live together over long periods of time bound by ties of marriage, blood, or commitment, legal or otherwise, who consider themselves as family and share a significant history and anticipated future of functioning in a family relationship.

interdependent couple
couple who shares traditional views of marriage and family life, activities , and interests.

independent couple
couple who holds less traditional views of family roles and expectations.

separate couple
couple who is extremely autonomous.

There are three primary types of relationships for married and cohabiting couples. What type of relationship do you expect to have with a romantic partner? Will it be one of the three primary types, or will you blend styles?

Fitzpatrick realizes that not all married or cohabiting couples fit distinctly into one of these three categories and that some couples blend styles. Fitzpatrick claims that the most common form of blending styles is the separate-traditional style. In this type of relationship, one person, typically the wife or woman, holds a traditional view of marriage while the husband or man seeks more independence. Couples determine for themselves which type of relationship best suits their interpersonal and individual needs.

Marriage and family do not have universal meanings for all people. Currently, there is an ongoing debate in the United States, and other countries, over who has the right to marry. Because the U.S. government allows each state the right to decide which marriages get recognized under state law, it is difficult to determine the exact number of same-sex marriages in the United States. The U.S. Census Bureau (2011) estimates that approximately 130,000 same-sex couples identify themselves as being married and that more than 500,000 unmarried same-sex households also exist. In a story that aired on National Public Radio (2009), University of California demographer Gary Gates explained that same-sex couples often look a lot like opposite-sex married couples. They also are likely to have children and own their own homes.

The concept of family is also in transition, and many families consist of single parents raising children. According to the U.S. Census Bureau (2009), approximately 27 percent of children in the United States live with a single parent, and nearly 83 percent of those single parents are mothers. Children are raised not only by a single mother or father but also by grandparents. Whether consisting of a married or cohabiting couple with or without children or a single parent or grandparent raising a child, families tend to evolve as children grow and the makeup of a family changes. This is especially true for military families. For example, U.S. Army Major Daniel Kearney and his wife, Lauren, discuss the struggles that they and other military families have faced when a partner or parent is deployed for an extended length of time ("Military Life," n.d.). It can be difficult for the military families to reconnect with one another and adjust and readjust to day-to-day routines.

 CourseMate Connection: Go to cengagebrain.com to access your CourseMate for *Invitation to Human Communication* to view a video about military families. Family members who can adapt to the changes that occur in each stage of development are more likely to survive stressful times.

Friendships

Recall your first day as a college student. You arrived to campus, met your roommate, attended orientation, and began taking classes. You likely

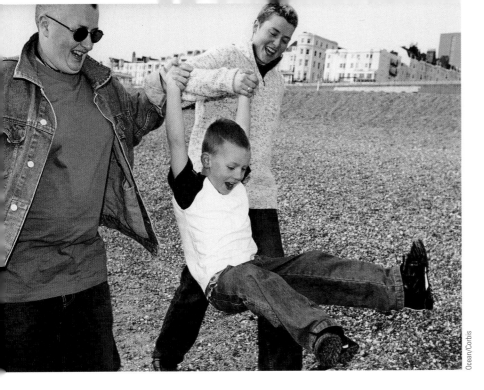

What is the makeup of your family and the families of your friends? With family demographics changing so rapidly, what do you imagine your family will look like in ten years?

Ocean/Corbis

interacted with a number of other students for the first time. Some of these individuals may have become close friends, but others have not. Have you ever wondered what makes a friendship grow and develop? Interpersonal communication scholar Bill Rawlins (1981) developed a six-stage model of friendship to help explain the stages of our friendships. These stages include:

1. role-limited interaction,
2. friendly relations,
3. moves toward friendship,
4. nascent friendship,
5. stabilized friendship, and
6. waning friendship.

Although not every friendship follows each developmental stage, you likely have friendships that have progressed according to the model. As you read about each stage in more depth, consider your own friendships and whether they followed the stages in sequence.

Stage One: Role-Limited Interaction   In this stage, we encounter people for the first time. We may greet a cashier at a store, interact with other students in a classroom, introduce ourselves to a new neighbor, or seek out new friendships online. Whether we choose to meet new acquaintances or are put into situations that require us to interact with others, we tend to limit the amount of personal information we share when we first meet someone. When we communicate in the **role-limited interaction** stage, we typically *engage in so-called small talk and share only minimal amounts of information*. This stage can feel awkward, especially for people who experience communication apprehension when meeting others for the first time.

role-limited interaction
engaging in small talk and sharing only minimal amounts of information.

friendly relations
situation that allows each person to determine whether common interests exist.

moves toward friendship
when people begin to self-disclose in small amounts.

nascent friendship
time when people interact on a personal level, choose to participate in a range of activities with another, and let down their guard in communication.

stabilized friendship
when trust has been established, allowing friends to communicate fully, share private information, and establish additional relationship rules.

waning friendship
friendship that experiences a breach in trust, less quality or quantity of time spent together, or a violation in relational expectations.

Stage Two: Friendly Relations The second stage of development focuses on the exchange of friendly conversation. The **friendly relations** stage *allows each person to determine whether common interests exist*. If enough interest and commonality are present, then the friendship moves forward. If not, the relationship remains limited to the constraints of the situation. For example, you may speak pleasantly to classmates or co-workers but not extend the friendship beyond the classroom or work environment.

Stage Three: Moves Toward Friendship When friendships reach the **moves toward friendship** stage, we *begin to self-disclose in small amounts*. Because we are continuing to discover common interests and whether we want to spend more time with another, we behave according to roles determined by our culture and social environment. We may choose to interact outside the original social context. This happens when students decide to meet outside of class for social purposes, or when co-workers get together before or after work hours. These gatherings often occur in public settings where others are present. Because friends enjoy interacting and can come and go as they please, many friendships remain in this stage.

Stage Four: Nascent Friendship Once people consider themselves as friends, they have reached the **nascent friendship** stage—the stage in which the friendship blossoms. This is the point at which *we interact on a personal level, choose to participate in a range of activities with another, and let down our guard when it comes to communicating*. Friends work out their own distinct communication and behavioral rules. Patterns and routines begin to emerge. Friends may meet to work out together regularly, have lunch several times a week or month, or hear new musicians at the local coffee shop on open mike nights.

Stage Five: Stabilized Friendship Trust is the characteristic that distinguishes the fifth stage of friendship development. Once friendships have reached the **stabilized friendship** stage, *trust has been established, allowing friends to communicate fully, share private information, and establish additional relationship rules*. Friends understand one another's personality and behavioral traits. Moreover, certain expectations for the friendship (often unspoken) exist. For example, friends may begin to expect a certain level of interaction and self-disclosure. The high level of interaction and amount of self-disclosure is what distinguishes this relationship as close and best friends.

Stage Six: Waning Friendship Friendships may wane slowly over time or end abruptly, depending on the reasons for the deterioration. **Waning friendships** *experience a breach in trust, decrease in quality or quantity of time spent together, or a violation in relational expectations*. Once friendships reach the waning stage, communication begins to be more strategic and less spontaneous. If we perceive the breach in trust or relational rules to be unintentional, then we may choose to continue the friendship with the hope that trust can be reestablished in the future. If we perceive the violation of trust or relational rules to be intentional, then we may choose to end the friendship. Many people have friendships that fall under all of these categories. This is because growing and developing friendships tend to shift categories, depending on the level of communication, self-disclosure, and trust that exists. But what about a friendship that has developed into a romantic relationship? Because romantic relationships are important parts of our interpersonal relationships, we will discuss those next.

Romantic Partners

Did you know that romantic relationships evolve much like friendships? This is because, like friendships, quality and quantity of interactions, relational rules and expectations, and trust are necessary parts of our romantic partnerships. However, just as there are different kinds of friendships, there are also different models for romantic relationships. One of the more popular models for explaining how relationships develop and deteriorate is explained by communication scholar Mark Knapp (Knapp, 1978, 1984; Knapp & Daly, 2010). Although not all romantic relationships develop or deteriorate following these stages, many do. Knapp's model uses a staircase metaphor to illustrate an upward climb toward commitment and a downward descent toward dissolution. Both staircases have five steps. Notice the similarities between the development of friendships as discussed by Rawlins and the development of romantic relationships as described by Knapp.

PRACTICING HUMAN COMMUNICATION

Can You Recognize the Stages of Friendship?

Next to each stage of friendship in the following list, give an example of communication when you were in that stage of friendship with someone who is currently a very close friend. For example, in a role-limited relationship, you may have first met your friend in one of your college classes and engaged in small talk about the teacher and the course. For the last stage, you might need to use an example of a different person, someone you are no longer in touch with.

Stage	Example of Communication
1. Role-limited, small talk	
2. Friendly relations, common interests determined	
3. Move toward friendship, begin to self-disclose, meet outside class or work	
4. Nascent, let down guard, interact more personally	
5. Stabilized, trust established communicate fully have relationship rules	
6. Waning, a breach of trust or someone who moved away and you see each other less	

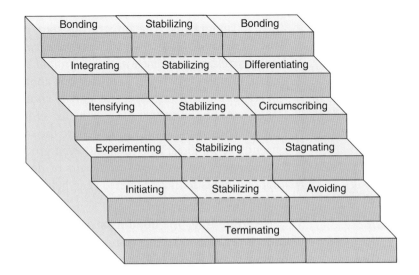

Figure 6.1 *Mark Knapp's relational stages model*
Source: Knapp, M.L., *Interpersonal Communication and Human Relation*, 1st Edition, © 1983. Reprinted by permission of Pearson Education, Inc., Upper Saddle River, NJ.

The Staircase Up: Climbing Toward Commitment The five steps leading toward commitment are initiating, experimenting, intensifying, integrating, and bonding.

Step 1 **Initiating.** The first step of initiating is similar to Rawlins's role-limited stage of friendship. The **initiation step** *involves the first set of interactions made between people.* Communication consists mostly of initial greetings and any additional information needed to fit the situation. For example, introducing ourselves to your best friend's new housemate or to a new co-worker initiates a relationship. At this time, our communication tends to be pleasant and provides little self-disclosure.

Step 2 **Experimenting.** In the **experimenting step**, *small talk is used to learn more about the other person and to help present a likable self-image.* Our communication continues to be polite, and we tend to discuss safe topics. We might discuss where we grew up, previous jobs, hobbies, musical interests, favorite television shows or movies, and the like. We are also concerned about showing our best selves to the other person, so we tend to present most of the information in a positive or safe light (so we might omit the recent family feud or that job we were fired from). Most relationships remain in the experimenting stage.

Step 3 **Intensifying.** We take the **intensifying step** when *there is an increase in communication, intimacy, and connectedness.* Verbal communication becomes more frequent and informal. The use of pronouns *we* and *us* signal that the relationship is developing. In the intensifying phase, we hear ourselves and our partner say things such as "We are going to Chicago this weekend," "We ate at Jay's last night," or "Do you think we should go to this party?" We may develop nicknames for one another or even shortened phrases that mean something to both people involved in the relationship but not outsiders.

Step 4 **Integrating.** The **integrating step**, *consists of two individuals merging their social circles and organizing their daily activities around each other.* Couples may begin to mirror one another in styles of dress, language, and activity choices. They may have a special place, song, or symbol that is "their own," and they may share the same friends, same social activities, and even grocery shop together or organize car repairs or doctor appointments so that one person can help out or support the other.

Step 5 **Bonding.** The **bonding step** occurs *when the couple commits to the relationship.* This commitment is usually conscious and intentional, and it may take the form of exchanging

initiation step
step involving the first set of interactions made between people.

experimenting step
step when small talk is used to learn more about the other person and to help present a likable self-image.

intensifying step
step when there is an increase in communication, intimacy, and connectedness.

integrating step
step consisting of two individuals merging their social circles and organizing their daily activities around each other.

bonding step
step that occurs when a couple commits to their relationship.

OLJ Studio/Shutterstock.com

What phase of the relationship might this couple be in? What do you think the next phase might be for this couple?

items that mark the relationship as official (rings or other jewelry and markers of togetherness, for example), cohabitation, or participating in a ceremony (e.g., civil union ceremony, marriage) to publicly or privately formalize the commitment.

Once a couple reaches the bonding stage, they usually engage in strategies to maintain the relationship. This is called **relational maintenance**; it is the *process of keeping a relationship together through the use of mundane activities*. These maintenance strategies are important; without routine maintenance, relationships often deteriorate. Of course, each relationship has its own unique maintenance strategies. However, scholars have studied relational maintenance strategies in both heterosexual and gay couples and found certain routine communicative behaviors that helped stabilize a relationship (Alberts, Yoshimura, Rabbi, & Loschiavo, 1995; Canary & Stafford, 1994; Haas & Stafford, 1998). Those common maintenance strategies are (1) dividing household tasks evenly, (2) spending time with the other's friends and family, (3) using humor and cheerful communication, and (4) being open through self-disclosure. All of these help to maintain the relationship.

relationship maintenance

process of keeping a relationship together through the use of mundane activities.

Although relational maintenance is a necessary part in continuing the relationship, not all relationships survive. When relationships come to an end, Knapp suggests that they follow a five-step descent down the ladder and toward deterioration.

The Staircase Down: Descending Toward Deterioration Knapp describes five phases that relationships go through when they begin to deteriorate: differentiating, circumscribing, stagnating, avoiding, and terminating.

Step 1 **Differentiating.** During the **differentiating** phase *couples begin to spend time on their own interests in order to express their individuality and separate from their partner.* Although spending time on one's own activities and interests is a healthy way to sustain self-identity, differentiating exists when couples consciously engage in separate activities or focus on separate interests in order distance themselves from the other person. In this early phase, couples might say, "I just need some time apart to get my head straight" or "I think I'll go to Chicago by myself this weekend."

differentiating

when individuals in a couple begin to spend time on their own interests in order to express their individuality and separate from their partner.

Step 2 **Circumscribing.** When couples enter the **circumscribing** phase, *they begin communicating less frequently, share less personal information, and spend shorter amounts of time together.* The couple may continue to appear in public or attend gatherings with friends, but private interactions and time spent together have decreased. The *we* and *us* language common in the intensifying stage changes back to *I* and *me* language, and couples begin to share fewer details of their days and how they feel about those details. As the relationship continues on its downward spiral toward dissolution, the couple may argue more or simply not want to share what is important with each other.

circumscribing

when couples begin communicating less frequently, share less personal information, and spend shorter amounts of time together.

This couple appears to be in the stagnating phase of their relationship. What advice could you give them as they work to rebuild their relationship or to continue to move toward its termination?

stagnating

when couples have minimal interaction or shared activities.

avoiding

when couples attempt to stay away from each other.

terminating

when individuals in a couple make their separation final.

Step 3 **Stagnating.** The **stagnating** step *consists of minimal interaction or shared activities.* The couple has now reached a point at which they anticipate time together and communication to be unpleasant. Because self-disclosure is minimal, couples likely have grown apart and feel distant from one another. Couples may begin revealing relationship details and struggles with close friends and admitting that the relationship has deteriorated.

Step 4 **Avoiding.** During the **avoiding** phase, *couples attempt to stay away from one another.* To accomplish this, couples may change their work schedules, sleep in separate bedrooms, or participate in more activities outside the home environment. Some couples may choose a temporary or trial separation. Communication often turns negative as each person blames the other for the relationship's problems and failures.

Step 5 **Terminating.** The final step in the dissolution of a romantic relationship is **terminating.** This occurs when *the couple makes their separation final.* One person may choose to move out or relocate to another city. If the couple is married, divorce proceedings begin. Friends and family are now aware the relationship has terminated. Important items are divided up, and the couple no longer exists as a romantic unit. Communication in this stage typically continues to place blame on the other person while also focusing on the future and exciting new possibilities.

Knapp explains that couples do not always progress through the deterioration steps in a linear way. Their behavior may indicate one phase (an individual moves out of the house for a trial separation, representing the avoiding stage) but the couple may continue to talk regularly and go on occasional dates together. Furthermore, not all relationships develop or decline as suggested previously. Many relationships decline before reaching the bonding stage. Other relationships dissolve in a more mutually pleasant way than described in the stagnating stage. And many relationships are able to stop the descent and climb back up the ladder of commitment and stay together. Because a relationship begins a descent does not mean it will ultimately end. Two people can rebuild their commitment to one another, especially if they are aware of Knapp's ladder metaphor and use their communication skills to establish and maintain the kind of relationship they want with one another.

ETHICAL MOMENT

© Trevor Hunt/istockphoto

Terminating a Relationship: Facebook or Face to Face?

Ilana Gershon, author of the book *The Breakup 2.0: Disconnecting over New Media*, explains that virtual breakups are becoming more common everyday. Gershon tells the story of a college student named Leslie who experienced an online breakup:

> Leslie checked her Facebook profile late one day and discovered that she was suddenly single. Her now ex-boyfriend had met someone new, and she learned this through the ubiquitous news feed that presented her personal rejection like a breaking news story. When he changed his Facebook profile, he also changed hers as well—they were no longer announced as a couple. Their friends received the news before she had.

Gershon claims that although most people believe people should break up face to face, social media and technology provide different options for ending relationships. Gershon explains that "texting, instant messaging, Facebook, e-mail, Twitter . . . [are] now widely seen as acceptable" for announcing the termination of a relationship (Gershon, 2010; Vlahakis, 2010). In addition, a study by the American Academy of Matrimonial Lawyers found that one of every five divorcing couples blame Facebook for the demise of their marriage. Couples now use Facebook to do their detective work: "A Facebook status update, a 140-character Twitter post, or a confessional entry on a blog all leave behind a pretty much permanent digital trail that can be used in court in case of a divorce" (Stevens, 2011). Author James Weaver is skeptical of the blame placed on Facebook as the *cause* of so many divorces. In a blog posting by Benjamin Stevens, Weaver says, "Sure, social media makes it easier to connect with old flames and strike up new relationships, but divorces and infidelity have been around for all of human history, whereas social media is less than a decade old. Truth is that people cause divorces, not social media" (Stevens, 2011).

What Do You Think?

1. What role if any do you believe social media should play in announcing the breakup of a relationship?

2. When might face-to-face interaction be more effective for communicating a breakup? When might social media be most effective?

3. Do you believe the accessibility of retrieving personal information from social media such as Facebook or Twitter is causing more relationships to terminate?

4. What rules or guidelines do you believe should be followed when using social media to end a relationship?

Understanding Self-Disclosure

As we sustain our families, forge friendships, become romantically involved, or converse with co-workers, we share information about ourselves with others. The more we trust another person, the more likely we are to reveal information that is personal. When we share information about ourselves, we are engaged in self-disclosure. **Self-disclosure** is *the intentional sharing of personal information that would not otherwise be known to others.* There are many ways to understand self-disclosure, but we will explore two models that help explain self-disclosure in our interpersonal relationships: self-disclosure as an onion and self-disclosure as a window.

Self-Disclosure Is Like an Onion

Self-disclosure varies in breadth and depth, depending on the relationship. For example, we may reveal limited information about ourselves with an acquaintance but a great deal of personal information with our close friends. We may talk about one or two topics while sitting next to someone on an airplane but an endless number of topics with our siblings. The **social-penetration theory** *describes the variation in breadth and depth of self-disclosure in relationships* (Altman & Taylor, 1973; Petronino, 2002). According to this theory, self-disclosure involves the degree of **breadth** or *the range of topics discussed* and **depth** or *how personal the information is.* For example, you may announce to your co-workers that you recently went on a date (little depth), but you may provide details about that date to close friends (more depth). In addition, we may only discuss work-related issues with our boss (little breadth) but talk about problems at work, family concerns, personal opinions on political issues, and our life goals with our romantic partner (more breadth). In the initial stages of building a relationship, the breadth may be high, but the depth is typically low until trust is established. This theory sees self-disclosure as similar to peeling an onion: as a relationship becomes more intimate, the depth of disclosure tends to increase, so we continually peel off the layers of the onion to reveal more and more of ourselves.

Self-Disclosure Is Like a Window

The Johari window is a model for self-disclosure that helps us understand ourselves and the reasons we might or might not disclose to others. This model shows us divided into four windows and labels them as *open, blind, hidden,* and *unknown* (Figure 6.2). Each window represents something personal about us. For example, the **open window** is *information about yourself that is already known by you and others.* The window may consist of your likes and dislikes, relationship or family status, hometown, occupation, or any other information you are aware of and have freely disclosed. The **blind window** is *information that others know about you but that you are unaware of.* The blind window may consist of some your personality traits (you are more picky than you realize, or more courageous than you thought) or talents (you are highly empathetic, an excellent artist, or a natural comedian) that others realize you possess but that you are unaware of. We can learn about this blind window by listening to and getting feedback from

---

self-disclosure
intentional sharing of personal information that would not otherwise be known to others.

social-penetration theory
describes the variation in breadth and depth of self-disclosure in a relationship.

breadth
the range of topics discussed in self-disclosure.

depth
how personal the information is in self-disclosure.

open window
information about yourself that is already known by you and others.

blind window
information that others know about you but that you are not aware of.

others. The **hidden window** consists of *information that you understand about yourself but are not willing to share with others.* The hidden window may consist of some of our past experiences, personal problems, or aspects of our identity (e.g, political affiliation, sexual orientation, religious affiliation, or age) that we choose for various reasons to not disclose. The **unknown window** is *information that is yet to be discovered by you and others.* The window may consist of hidden talents, passions, fears, or diseases we have yet to discover. Understanding self-disclosure as a window helps us see that the size of each window varies, depending on the relationship. In one relationship where we may not feel very safe, we likely will have a very large hidden window. In another relationship in which we are getting to know someone and coming to trust them, our open window may grow in size rapidly. And if we are resistant to feedback from others, our blind window might stay very large for some time. Remember, too, that the size of each window is rarely static: they shift as our relationships grow and develop.

Self-disclosure is very important to relationships for two reasons. First, when we disclose to others, we gain a deeper understanding of ourselves. When we share our opinions on community issues, our relationship triumphs and failures, our ambitions and fears, we gain a better sense of who we are as individuals. We learn what makes us unique and what commonalities we have with others. When that disclosure is reciprocal, we learn about the other person as well. Second, self-disclosure can improve the quality of our relationships. When we discuss our thoughts and feelings, difficult challenges, and even our successes and hopes, we learn about the ways we are similar and different—and that we are not the only ones to face adversity or to have hopes and dreams, that we can trust and respect others. But self-disclosure can be complicated, so we will discuss some of the guidelines for such disclosure next.

Guidelines for Self-Disclosure When we enter a relationship, we usually have expectations about self-disclosure. When we share information about ourselves, we expect others to share information in return. When self-disclosure is reciprocated, we view the relationship more favorably. On the other hand, we tend to feel uncomfortable in situations where someone self-discloses a lot of personal information early in the relationship or when someone self-discloses but we feel less favorable toward them. Several guidelines can help us understand these complex moments before we decide to share personal information with others.

Self-Disclosure Should Be Appropriate to the Relationship. You are already aware that there is a certain degree of breadth and depth to our self-disclosure. This helps us understand that there are levels of appropriateness associated with revealing personal information to others. With acquaintances or co-workers, sharing small amounts of personal information across a range of topics is appropriate. With our romantic partners or close friends, sharing more intimate details across this range of topics is expected. Generally speaking, begin with small amounts of self-disclosure and increase the levels of breadth and depth as the relationship progresses and trust is established.

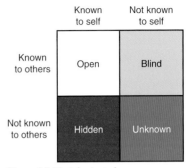

The Johari Window

Figure 6.2 *The Johari window*
Source: Adapted from Luft, Joseph, *Of Human Interaction,*
© 1969 The McGraw-Hill Companies, Inc. Reprinted with permission.

hidden window
information that you understand about yourself but are not willing to share with others.

unknown window
information about yourself that is yet to be discovered by you and others.

Match the Breadth and Depth of Disclosure Provided to You. This rule is known as the *norm of reciprocity,* and it governs the process of sharing personal information with others. Relationships that incorporate similar amounts of self-disclosure are preferred. When someone reveals too much personal information, we begin to feel uncomfortable. One sign of revealing too much personal information too soon occurs when one person begins sharing less information or reverting back to previous "safe" topics. Paying attention to the norm of reciprocity can indicate important information about the relationship.

Pay Attention to the Purpose of the Self-Disclosure. We have a great deal of private information we can choose to share or withhold from others. It is important to identify the reasons we choose to share particular information about ourselves. We may reveal our sexual history to our romantic partner as a way to establish trust in a sexual relationship. However, sharing this information in the locker room or with friends in a social setting serves a very different purpose. This self-disclosure often is intended as a boast of our experiences or past commitments. Self-disclosure is meant to enhance the quality of relationships rather than negatively affect them. Therefore, our most important and meaningful disclosures should be reserved for the relationships that are most important and special to us.

Relationships and our communication in them are affected by a variety of factors. The type of relationship we are experiencing, the level or developmental stage of the relationship, and degree of self-disclosure can shape the quality of and communication in the relationship. In the next section we will explore how technology, gender, and culture also affect our interpersonal relationships.

Technology and Interpersonal Relationships

For several decades, communication scholars have studied the association between technology and interpersonal relationships. At first, scholars believed the increased time spent using mediated channels led to an increase in individual isolation, decrease in relationship quality, and unwillingness to participate in one's community (Finholt & Sproull, 1990; Putnam, 1995; Shah, McLeod, & Yoon, 2001; Sproull & Kiesler, 1986). There was a growing concern that increasing amounts of time spent on the Internet negatively affected the time spent with family and friends (Nie & Hillygus, 2002). More recently, studies have indicated the opposite effect. The University of Southern California's Annenberg School of Communication and Journalism's annual study of Internet use reports that approximately 68 percent of Internet users between the ages of nineteen and thirty-five rank social media as "important and very important" for maintaining relationships, and more than 50 percent all other age groups agreed (USC Annenberg School, 2011). However, additional studies indicate that too many "friends" on social media can actually reduce the feelings of connection we have with others (Tom Tong, Van Der Heide, Langwell, & Waither, 2008).

We know that media have changed the way relationships form and evolve over time. Texting and tweeting make it possible to communicate in real time with others (and romantic partners prefer texting to

Courtesy of Chris Rainier

T.H. Culhane
Emerging Explorer Urban Planner

How does technology affect your ability to maintain long-distance working relationships?

I should just tell you that when I first joined Facebook back in, I guess it was 2007, I joined because I was a Harvard student and we knew about its potential. Then my lead professor at UCLA encouraged all his students to use it, and we were supposed to use it to further the research that we were doing. The people that I was communicating with on this tool became early adopters in Egypt and then in other parts of Africa and the Middle East. I have friends over in Indonesia and Guatemala who also saw Facebook as a tool for important things, which I think is why Egypt used it for a social revolution.

We now have Web 2.0 and social media to maintain our interpersonal connections. I use those tools to connect with friends in the Okavanga Delta or from Nigeria or Tanzania. We are all on our Facebook groups, and we are very active using Google Plus and YouTube. We make YouTube videos for each other, we've linked to other YouTube videos, and we've linked to Web sites. We sometimes chat. It doesn't matter whether they are in a small village or if they are in a slum or they are in a city, if they have access to a kiosk occasionally and the Internet, we can communicate. Integrating technologies can be an important part of maintaining relationships and continuing the work toward industrial ecology solutions for cooperative cities.

stay connected when they are apart) (Pettigrew, 2009), blogging helps us engage in political and civic discourse, and social-networking sites allow new friendships to form and old friendships to stay active. The rapid growth in technology leaves communication scholars scrambling to understand how new forms of technology affect our personal relationships. We will now look at ways that technology positively affects our relationships with others and the ways it might also have negative effects.

Relationships and Computer-Mediated Communication

Computer-mediated communication (CMC) is *the exchange of messages transmitted between two or more people using a digital electronic device.* Today's most popular CMC involves communicating online with others. According to the Pew Research Center's Internet and American Life Project, approximately 74 percent of adults over the age of 18 in the United States use the internet (Rainie, 2010). Two-thirds of Americans now use Facebook, Twitter, and other social-media sites, making it easy to connect with others throughout the day. In 2011, Facebook registered its 800 millionth user!

Most communication via the Internet is text based and either asynchronous or synchronous. **Asynchronous** means that the *messages are sent but not received at the same time.* This occurs when we post a message on our blog that is not immediately read, or when we send a text to

computer-mediated communication (CMC)
the exchange of messages transmitted between two or more people using a digital electronic device.

asynchronous
message that is sent but not received at the same time.

a cell phone that is turned off. E-mail, text messaging, blogs, and social-media postings are often asynchronous because the receiver typically does not receive the message immediately. **Synchronous** messages are *messages that are received in real time.* This happens when we communicate in chat rooms or send instant messages back and forth. Many forms of CMC can be asynchronous or synchronous, depending on whether the individuals are using the electronic device at the same time. Video sites such as Skype and WebEx are synchronous and becoming popular tools for maintaining long-distance working and romantic relationships. The one commonality between asynchronous and synchronous messages is that many CMC users engage in **hyperpersonal communication**—that is, *communication that occurs when individuals express themselves more freely in a mediated channel than in a face-to-face interaction.* As such, technology has become not only a way to stay connected to others but also a relational maintenance strategy for interpersonal relationships.

Although many people complain that too much time spent texting or on Facebook detracts from real-time interactions with peers, research suggests something quite different. In 2007, media studies scholars Nicole Ellison, Charles Steinfield, and Cliff Lampe studied students at Michigan State University (Ellison, Steinfield, & Lampe, 2007). These researchers wanted to know what the benefits of using Facebook might be for college students, and what they found was quite interesting. They discovered that new students use Facebook to stay connected with their friends from high school, which helped them feel less alone in their first year and minimized the "friendsickness" that came from missing their old friends. They also discovered that for those students who were shy, struggling with self-esteem, and feeling disconnected from the campus, Facebook helped them boost their self-esteem and confidence, make new friends, and feel more at home and involved in their school. Finally, they found that Facebook not only helped students at all grade levels maintain the friends they had before coming to college but also helped them make and strengthen new friendships with other students in their dorms and classes (Ellison et al., 2007).

Many individuals, bloggers, students, activists, and the like agree that social-networking sites are revolutionizing how we create and maintain friendships and also affecting politics, learning, work, and activism. Social networks make it possible for huge numbers of people to contact one another quickly and continuously. This means that information and ideas are shared and spread rapidly and immediately. Although this is a positive aspect of social networking, it also has a downside.

Studies show that teens between ages thirteen and seventeen are disclosing too much personal information and putting themselves at risk with these social networks: 69 percent share their addresses and physical location in their updates, 50 percent share their real first names with strangers, and 24 percent share their e-mail addresses. Tracy Mooney, one of the researchers who conducted the survey, explains that "Online, there's a sense of trust and anonymity, so kids let their guard down. . . . Kids would never hand out their name and address to a stranger in the real world, so it's alarming to see how many kids do that very thing online" (Schwartz, 2010). Young adults between ages eighteen and twenty-nine, however, seem to be more savvy about privacy. Research from the Internet and American Life Project found that 44 percent of young adult social-media users limit their personal information online, and 71 percent of the eighteen- to twenty-nine-year-old social-networking users have tightened their privacy settings (Elier, 2010). Still, many users need to continue monitoring their privacy settings and what they choose to display on their social-media sites.

CMC has had a major effect on our interpersonal relationships. From making new friends, meeting romantic partners, and staying in touch over long distances, CMC has provided the tools necessary to build and maintain strong relationships. Yet it also has the ability to negatively affect our professional and personal lives. The ever-increasing forms of CMC means there is a continuous need to understand its effect on human relationships.

CIVIC ENGAGEMENT

How to Respond to Cyberbullying

YURIKO NAKAO/Reuters/Corbis

Makoto, who requested that his last name not be used, poses for a photograph as he looks at his cell phone, which became an instrument of mental torture that nearly drove him to suicide when he was a high school student in Tokyo on October 22, 2007. Cyberbullying is a global problem, but in Japan it is almost endemic because of rampant bullying in schools.

> She kept texting me so many mean things that I wanted to throw my phone against the wall. I told my mom and she called her. After that the mean girls texted me, "Wow, you can't fight your own battles!"
>
> —Eleven-year-old from Michigan

Although bullying has been around for a long time, cyberbullying takes this uncivil form of communication to new levels of hostility. Cyberbullying is defined as children or teens using mobile phones, interactive technologies, and the Internet to repeatedly, willfully, and intentionally torment, threaten, harass, humiliate, and embarrass another child or teen. According to the Cyberbullying Research Center, cyberbullying teens have "created Web pages, videos, [and] profiles on social-networking sites making fun of others. With cell phones, adolescents have taken pictures in a bedroom, a bathroom, or another location where privacy is expected and posted or distributed them online. More recently, some have recorded unauthorized videos of other kids and uploaded them for the world to see, rate, tag, and discuss." More than harmful, cyberbullying can have deadly consequences. Megan Meier, Phoebe Prince, Tyler Clemente, and Jamey Rodemeyer were all young people who committed suicide in response to cyberbullying.

Victims of cyberbullying report feeling "depressed, sad, angry, and frustrated." They fear going to school, and cyberbullying lowers their self-esteem and increases conflicts in their families and even violent or delinquent behaviors. "As one teenager stated: 'It makes me hurt both physically and mentally. It scares me and takes away all my confidence. It makes me feel sick and worthless'" (Hinduja & Patchin, 2010, p. 1). Approximately 20 percent of teens report being victims of cyberbullying—and, surprisingly, 20 percent of teens admitted to being cyberbullies.

When an adult gets involved in the cyberactivity, authorities call the harmful actions *cyberharassment* and *cyberstalking* and take their investigation to new levels of criminal seriousness out of concern about sexual predation and harassment.

What role does technology play in cyberbullying? How does it increase the severity of this hostile communication? First, victims often do not know the identity of their bullies because technology helps the bullies stay anonymous. Second, the bullying communication can be spread more widely and more quickly because of technology, making the uncivil communication more public. Third, research suggests that it may be easier to be more cruel because technology distances the bully from the person being targeted and allows the bullies to post hostile messages and images that invade another person's privacy from a distance; in other words, bullies can do damage without even being in the same room as their victims.

Who does the cyberbullying? This is also an important question to answer. Studies indicate that more than 50 percent of cyberbullies are students from the same school as the victims, and 36 percent are so-called friends. Siblings also cyberbully (13 percent), but it should be no surprise that 48 percent of cyberbullies are unknown to the person being bullied. Beyond this sketchy profile, however, we still know little about the personalities of cyberbullies except that they also engage in "traditional" forms of bullying (Hinduja & Patchin, 2010; "STOP cyberbullying," n.d.).

What Do You Think?

1. What do you think causes or encourages uncivil cyberbullying communication? Is cyberbullying communication the result of individual actions and communication styles? Is it related to school climates? Does it reflect broader styles of communication we see in media and politics? Or is it perhaps be a combination of all or several of these factors?

2. Reports of cyberbullying often focus on the victims rather than on the bullies. What kinds of communication might we use to discuss the bullies rather than the victims? Should we do so (discuss the bullies), and should our communication be civil toward the bullies? Why or why not?

3. If you have been a bully or watched others bully someone, describe the style of communication used and explain why your think you or they used this particular style.

4. If you find yourself being cyberbullied or cyberharassed (or have been in that situation already) how will you communicate? Will you speak to the bully or to a person in a position of authority? What will you say and why?

 ## Gender and Interpersonal Relationships

Have you ever wondered why women are expected to talk more openly about their relationships than men, or why men are expected to fix things around the house? Our sex and gender affect the way we experience our relationships. **Sex** refers to *our biological and genetic characteristics*. This consists of the chromosomal pattern that distinguishes whether we are male or female. **Gender**, on the other hand, is socially constructed and *refers to society's use of verbal and nonverbal symbols to express masculinity and femininity*. Communication scholar Julia Wood explains that gender "is neither innate nor necessarily stable. It is defined by society and expressed by individuals as they interact with others and media in their society" (Wood, 2013, pp. 20–21). In the United States, we consider masculine men to be strong, ambitious, successful, and rational thinkers who are emotionally controlled (Wood, 2013). On the other hand, to be feminine typically means that someone is physically attractive, emotionally expressive, nurturing, and caring (Spence & Buckner, 2000). Gender, however, is a fluid concept and varies across cultures and co-cultures, over time and between relationships. Today, many of these traditional definitions of masculinity and femininity are being challenged, even though families, society, and media emphasize traditional understandings of gender. We will explore those factors next.

sex
biological and genetic characteristics.

gender
society's use of verbal and nonverbal symbols to express masculinity and femininity.

Gender and Family

Family is one relationship that has an enormous influence in teaching us how to perform gender. The family is usually the first group of people that teaches us about gender roles and expectations. The term **gender role** is "commonly *used to refer to feminine and masculine social expectations in a family based on a person's sex*" (DeFrancisco & Palczewski, 2007, p. 154). According to Allen and Walker (2007), "there is no better predictor of the division of household labor than gender" (p. 7).

Think back to how work was divided in your household. Who was responsible for house-work and child care? Who was more likely to be responsible for fixing broken items, doing vehicle maintenance, and doing yard work? (Canary & Wahba, 2006). Did your family designate certain spaces in the house as "belonging to" a mother or father? Mothers tend to occupy the kitchen, closet, and bathroom spaces, whereas fathers tend to claim the basement, the easy chair, and the garage as their space. Same-sex couples often reject these gendered divisions of labor and space (Peplau & Beals, 2004). Instead, same-sex couples divide labor based on ability, interest, and the common goal of sharing responsibility for household labor and child care.

The roles we are socialized into or that we take on consciously affect how we communicate with others. If we have a very fluid view of gender roles, we likely will adopt the same-sex-couple approach, and our communication will center on discussing who is best at and likes a task. If we subscribe to more rigid or traditional views of gender roles, however, then some of our communication will likely focus on keeping those roles in place and not stepping into someone else's "role."

Gender and Friendships

Gender also affects the type and quality of our friendships. Research indicates that women's friendships are often based on their ability to communicate and to self-disclose. Many women are socialized when very young to engage in expressive and supportive communication. They typically talk about their feelings, daily lives, and personal struggles. This type of communication allows women to feel closely connected with one another. Men also create and maintain close friendships with others. However, instead of building friendships via communication as many women do, men tend to build friendships around shared activities such as playing or watching sports or video games or working on projects (Wright, 1982). These gendered differences in friendship formation are also carried into cross-sexed friendships. Although both men and women enjoy cross-sexed friendships, they do so for different reasons. Men

Radius Images/Getty Images

Many fathers are taking a more active role in the lives of their children than ever before. What roles did your parents and caregivers take during your child hood and what roles do you expect to take on as you begin a family of your own?

gender role

used to refer to feminine and masculine social expectations in a family based on a person's sex.

Floresco Productions/OJO Images/Getty Images

Some of the traditional roles expected of each person in a romantic relationship are changing. What roles are expected of you in your romantic relationships?

typically receive more social and emotional support from their female friends and feel more comfortable expressing themselves emotionally without being criticized for violating perceived societal expectations for masculine behavior. Women tend to engage in more competitive activities with male friends and value men's instrumental behavior. In addition, women report that men offer a more "objective viewpoint" than their same-sex friendships (Monsour, 2002).

Gender and Romantic Relationships

If you want to date someone, who is responsible for making the first move? Once you manage to get that date, who pays? And when problems happen in a relationship, who is in charge of handling the emotional aspects of that problem? Although traditional norms for dating and relationships are changing, research shows that men still are expected to initiate dates and physical intimacy and women are expected to perform relationship maintenance (Laner & Ventrone, 2000). Men continue to be the primary breadwinners whereas women assume responsibility for domestic labor and child care (only 22 percent of women earn more money than their husbands) (Fry & Cohn, 2010). However, these tendencies are beginning to shift. Studies show that both women and men appreciate partners who not only have professional lives but also assume domestic responsibilities, engage in expressive communication, and do things for and with their partners (Cancian & Oliker, 2000). Meanwhile, more and more men want to and are becoming more involved in raising their children.

Gender influences how we experience and communicate in our interpersonal relationships. The ways we negotiate our first meetings, our dates, our time together—in short, our romantic relationships—are often determined by society's expectations for gender. Sexuality plays into these scripts as well: heterosexual couples tend to follow more traditional roles and expectations, gay men tend to be more emotionally expressive than straight men (but less than heterosexual and lesbian women), and lesbian couples tend to rank the highest of all groups for emotional expressiveness and relationship maintenance (Biblarz & Savci, 2010; Downing & Goldberg, 2010; Goldberg & Perry-Jenkins, 2007). In addition to learning how we perform gender based on our interpersonal relationships, our culture also affects the way we experience our relationships.

Culture and Interpersonal Relationships

culture

the learned patterns of perception, values, and behaviors, shared by a group of people.

Interpersonal relationships are influenced by the culture in which they reside. **Culture** is defined as *the learned patterns of perception, values, and behaviors, shared by a group of people* (Martin & Nakayama, 2004). Perhaps you have traveled to another country and noticed differences in communication styles, dress, behaviors, or lifestyles. Some of these differences may be based on the type of culture you were visiting. **Individualistic cultures** such as those in North America and northern Europe believe individual autonomy and independence is important. Individuals are expected to *make their own decisions, take responsibility for their actions, and be self-sufficient.* **Collectivist cultures** such as those in Latin America and Asia emphasize the needs of the group. *Collectivist cultures value relationships and harmony with others; therefore, the individual's needs are subordinate to the group's needs.*

When different cultures perceive different goals for relationships, it is not surprising that there are also differences in how members of a given culture communicate with one another. **Low-context cultures** *emphasize direct and literal communication.* For example, in the United States, straightforward, honest, and detailed information is valued. People tend to say what they mean and mean what they say. By contrast, **high-context cultures** often avoid confrontation and use the context surrounding the communicative act and nonverbal cues to determine the meaning of the message. High-context cultures, which are common in many Eastern cultures, may use *less straightforward and more indirect communication.* Therefore, people must "read between the lines" to understand what another is actually saying. For example, instead of answering a question using "yes" or "no," members of high-context cultural groups may respond by saying, "Let me get back to you." Cultures are not necessarily high context or low context in an isolated and absolute way; rather, contexts exist on a continuum with some cultures being higher or lower than others.

To maintain a successful relationship with members of different cultures, it is important that we understand the differences in communication styles and behavioral practices. Learning about the history, values, and practices from other cultures is the first step toward building and maintaining our intercultural relationships. You will read more about how culture affects working in groups and teams in Chapter 8.

individualistic culture
culture in which individuals make their own decisions, take responsibility for their actions, and are self-sufficient.

collectivist culture
culture that values relationships and harmony with others.

low-context culture
culture in which people emphasize direct and literal communication.

high-context culture
culture in which people use less straightforward and more indirect communication.

Chapter Summary

Interpersonal Relationships Consist of Personal Connections Made with Others Through the Intentional Use of Communication

- The way we interact with others is often determined by the type of interpersonal relationship, therefore making every interpersonal relationship unique.
- Relationships require a certain degree of commitment.
- Interpersonal relationships function by their own set of rules as determined by those involved in the relationship.

- There are different types of interpersonal relationships, including families, friendships, and romantic partners.

Families Consist of a Network of People Who Are Bound Together by Ties of Marriage or Blood or Through Commitment to Another

- Married or cohabiting couples may have relationships that are interdependent, independent, separate, or a combination of relationship types.
- There is no universal definition of family in the United States.
- Family relationships tend to evolve and shift over time.

Friendships Tend to Go Through Stages as They Develop Over Time

- Friendships go through six stages as they form, develop, and dissolve: (1) role-limited interaction, (2) friendly relations, (3) moves toward friendship, (4) nascent friendship, (5) stabilized friendship, and (6) waning friendship.
- Friendships grow and develop depending on the level of communication, self-disclosure, and trust that exists.

Romantic Relationships May Develop Similarly to Friendships

- The five steps that occur as the romantic relationship develops toward commitment include initiating, experimenting, intensifying, integrating, and bonding.
- Relational maintenance, or everyday mundane activities, can help keep a relationship together.
- Relationships go through five stages when they begin to deteriorate: differentiating, circumscribing, stagnating, avoiding, and terminating.

Self-Disclosure Can Be an Important Part of Relationship Development and Maintenance

- Self-disclosure involves the degree of breadth and depth of oneself as shared with another person.
- Self-disclosure allows us to gain a better understanding of our thoughts and opinions, improve the quality of our relationships, and provide us the opportunity to discover new things about ourselves.
- It is important to carefully consider the appropriateness and purpose of self-disclosure before sharing personal information with others.

Technology Has Changed the Way Relationships form and Evolve Over Time

- Most communication via the Internet is text based and is either asynchronous or synchronous.

- Internet users often use hyperpersonal communication to maintain interpersonal relationships.
- Computer-mediated communication has the potential to negatively affect personal and professional lives, so users should be cautious about posting personal information, photos, and videos.

Sex and Gender Affect the Way We View Relationships

- The family is usually the first source of information to teach us about gender roles and expectations.
- Women's friendships are often based on their ability to communicate and self-disclose, whereas men tend to build friendships around shared activities.
- Gender may affect women and men differently in the workplace. For example, women continue to earn less than their male counterparts.
- Heterosexual romantic relationships continue to uphold many traditional gender roles. For example, many men are still expected to initiate dates and physical intimacy, whereas women are expected to perform relationship maintenance.

Culture Influences Interpersonal Relationships

- Individualistic and collectivist cultures approach relationship goals differently.
- Low-context cultures emphasize direct communication and tend to mean what they say.
- High-context cultures use less direct communication and rely more on nonverbal communication and context surrounding the communication act.
- Successful relationships between members of different cultures requires an understanding of each culture's difference in communication styles and behavioral practices.

Key Concepts

asynchronous (135)

avoiding (130)

blind window (132)

bonding step (128)

breadth (132)

circumscribing (129)

collectivist culture (141)

computer-mediated communication (CMC) (135)

culture (140)

depth (132)

differentiating (129)

experimenting step (128)

family (123)

friendly relations (126)

gender (138)

gender role (139)

hidden window (133)

high-context culture (141)

hyperpersonal communication (136)

independent couple (123)

individualistic culture (141)

initiation step (128)

integrating step (128)

intensifying step (128)

interdependent couple (123)

interpersonal relationship (120)

low-context culture (141)

moves toward friendship (126)

nascent friendship (126)

open window (132)

relationship maintenance (129)

role-limited interaction (125)

self-disclosure (132)

separate couple (123)

sex (138)

social-penetration theory (132)

stabilized friendship (126)

stagnating (130)

synchronous (136)

terminating (130)

unknown window (133)

waning friendship (126)

Invitation to Human Communication Online

Speech Communication CourseMate includes an interactive eBook and interactive learning tools, including National Geographic Explorer videos, student videos, quizzes, flash cards, and more. Speech Builder Express 3.0 and Speech Studio 2.0 are also available. Go to cengagebrain.com to access your CourseMate for *Invitation to Human Communication* where these resources can be found.

Further Reflection and Discussion

1. Think about married couples in your family: parents, aunts and uncles, cousins. Which couples have interdependent relationships? Independent? Separate? A combined type? Explain how each couple exhibits that type of relationship.

2. What are some activities or actions that indicate a relationship is in the initiating stage? What are some activities that indicate the experimenting, intensifying, integrating, and bonding stages?

3. Discuss how you know when it is appropriate to disclose personal information about yourself in a relationship with a friend, family member, or romantic partner.

4. In romantic relationships, who is expected to initiate dates? Who is expected to maintain the relationship? Discuss how these roles may be between same-sex and heterosexual relationships and what advantages or disadvantages there might be.

5. What is your experience with gender roles in the home? Discuss this with one or more of your parents or grandparents. Do they represent gender equity? Are gender roles generational?

6. What personal information do you share about yourself in a friendship with a same-sex friend? How do you make this decision?

Activities and Web Links

Visit cengagebrain.com to access the CourseMate for *Invitation to Human Communication* where these activities and web links can be found.

1. Read the article and watch the video about Zach Wahls defending the right to same-sex marriage. Does this change your opinion on the issue? What is your definition of a family? Think critically about the arguments on the other side of the issue—that is, those who disagree with you. What are their arguments? How do you respond civilly? Find a credible online newspaper or magazine article that supports each side of the debate. What arguments are given? Are they presented civilly? Go to *Weblink 6.1*.

2. Read this article on how social-media blunders can affect interpersonal relationships at work, at home, and even in the government. Search the Internet for other Twitter or Facebook blunders and devise a policy to present your supervisor at work on how employees can avoid making blunders and what actions to take if they make such a mistake. Go to *Weblink 6.2*.

IMPROVING INTERPERSONAL COMMUNICATION

IN THIS CHAPTER YOU WILL LEARN TO:

- Recognize how you respond to conflict.
- Understand how gender affects conflict styles.
- Monitor how you manage conflict.
- Explain how computer-mediated communication affects conflict.
- Create a positive communication climate to manage conflict.
- Examine external pressures that create challenges in interpersonal relationships.

ok®

7

Armin Weigel/dpa/Corbis

*Computer-mediated communication
(CMC) allows us the ability to maintain
relationships over periods of geographic
separation. How many relationships are
you maintaining via the use of CMC?*

AND RELATIONSHIPS

*Walls that separate people are often built on
ignorance, hatred, and fear. I try to put cracks in those
walls. When people realize they feel the same pain,
they begin to see how much we all have in common.*

—*Aziz Abu Sarah, Cultural Educator, National Geographic Emerging Explorer*

Conflict. Very few people like it, but it is a common occurrence in interpersonal relationships. Did you have a recent disagreement with someone in your family or a friend or a co-worker? How did you react? Did your heart beat faster as you raised your voice toward the other person? Did you walk away from the situation? Or did you respond using a calm voice? When people are in close relationships with family members, roommates, friends, or romantic partners, there is an increased opportunity to disagree (Lloyd & Cate, 1985). According to researchers Ritu Kaushal and Catherine Kwantes (2006), whether conflict "occurs in the form of a difference of opinion, harsh words, or a form of direct action taken to resolve competing goals, it has the potential to exist in the many domains of our lives" (p. 580). Kaushal and Kwantes contend that our increasingly busy lifestyles have translated into less time for ourselves and the people around us, leaving a precarious balance between work, family, and everything in between. This increased sense of time urgency has left many of us scrambling and without the time we need to speak with family members, friends, and co-workers. We often do not have time to communicate our needs, to clarify the motivations and intentions behind our behaviors, or to understand the needs and motivations of others. This increases the potential for misperception and miscommunication, two of the negative aspects of conflict (Kaushal & Kwantes, 2006).

Understanding the reasons for interpersonal conflict and appropriate ways to handle conflict improves our interpersonal relationships. In this chapter, we will discuss the nature of conflict, reasons for interpersonal conflict, and strategies for successfully managing conflict situations.

Interpersonal Relationships and Conflict

Although some people try to avoid engaging in conflict because they believe conflict signals the end of a relationship, having an honest discussion about differences can actually be quite healthy for relationships. In fact, healthy conflict is a natural part of most interpersonal relationships. Conflict acknowledges that those involved are in close relationships, are connected to one another, and have feelings for another person. Those feelings might be love, friendship, or even jealousy or anger. **Interpersonal conflict** occurs *when two interdependent parties express different opinions, goals, or interests.* When those goals or interests clash, they come into conflict and a struggle or battle occurs. Because there are many ways people react to conflict, we will explore the nature of conflict next.

 ## The Nature of Conflict

When people are in conflict, incompatibility (e.g., two people wanting different things) or perceived scarcity of rewards (e.g., time and money) is often the root cause. Friends may disagree over personal needs. Romantic partners may disagree about where to purchase a home. Parents may disagree on the best approach to raising a child. Roommates may disagree about who is responsible for certain chores around the apartment. Co-workers may disagree about how to complete a project. Although some people choose to ignore the conflict in hopes that the conflict will go away, other people may rush in to engage in a heated argument with the goal of "winning" or achieving their goals.

Our responses to conflict can be distinguished by two dimensions: (1) concern for self and (2) concern for others. When someone expresses **concern for self**, *they seek to satisfy their own desires and needs through direct and assertive communication.* In contrast, *when we attempt to get along with and satisfy the other's needs using cooperative communication,* we are said to be showing **concern for others**. Consider the following two scenarios:

Concern for self: Marissa and Manuel (sister and brother) are in conflict over who gets how much space and time in their shared bathroom. Marissa, expressing concern for herself, wants one uninterrupted hour every morning and to leave her "stuff" on the counters, floors, and so on. Manuel also wants an hour of uninterrupted time at the same hour that Marissa wants, and he also does not feel the need to clean up after himself. Both are expressing concern for self; as you can imagine, the conflict remains heated and unresolved.

Concern for others: Marissa and Manuel (sister and brother) share a bathroom, and both have jobs that require professional dress and appearance. Both have to be at work at the same time, and they have to travel an equal distance to their jobs. They also do not want to take time every morning to clean up their messes. After conversation, they agree on the following compromise. They will alternate mornings, so that one person gets the bathroom from 5:30 to 6:30 and the other from 6:30 to 7:30. To help keep their messes contained, they set up shelves and baskets so that they each can "dump" their stuff in the assigned spots. They show concern for one another in deciding to alternate "early mornings," and they agree to try out the solution for one month and then check back with each other to see how the arrangement is working.

interpersonal conflict
when two interdependent parties express different opinions, goals, or interests.

Although most people do not like conflict, it can be an important part of a relationship. Think of the last conflict you had with someone. Were you more concerned for yourself or for the other person?

concern for self
when individuals seek to satisfy their own desires and needs through direct and assertive communication.

concern for others
when individuals attempt to get along with and satisfy another's needs using cooperative communication.

Research suggests that beyond our concerns for self and others are five conflict styles that depend on our perceived goals and help to explain the different ways we handle conflict (Thomas & Kilmann, 2007): competing, accommodating, avoiding, compromising, and collaborating.

1. **Competing.** People who use a competing style seek to control the interaction. They are more concerned with their own goals than the goals of the other person. People who compete want to "win" any argument.

2. **Accommodating.** People who use an accommodating style are more concerned for others than they are for themselves, so they will yield to others, passively accepting others' decisions, and neglect to make their own needs a priority.

3. **Avoiding.** The avoiding style occurs when someone chooses to physically or psychologically withdraw from conflict. People who use the avoiding style tend to believe that "if we don't talk about it, maybe the problem will go away." Other behaviors include denying a conflict exists, avoiding particular topics, or remaining silent about a conflict.

4. **Compromising.** The compromising style emphasizes cooperation. When people compromise, each person is willing to give up something to reach an agreement. This is often referred to as "meeting someone halfway."

5. **Collaborating.** The collaborating style focuses on cooperative problem solving in order to satisfy everyone's goals and needs. People who use a collaborative style are concerned not only for themselves but also for others. Establishing open lines of communication and seeking and sharing information will help those involved reach a solution in which everyone "wins."

How we choose to respond to conflict may also depend on our family of origin—or what we learned from those who took care of us when we were growing up. Recent studies suggest that people use styles of managing conflict that were learned in their family of origin (Taylor & Segrin, 2010). If our caregivers avoided conflict, then we might model that same strategy. If they fought heatedly or showed concern for one another, we are likely to adopt those styles as adults. In addition to the relationship type, our reactions to conflict may also be determined by gender and culture.

Gender and Conflict

In Chapter 4, you learned that language is influenced by gender; in Chapters 8 and 9 you will read about gender in group communication and how it can affect leadership. But how might our gender play a role in interpersonal conflict? We know that from a young age, boys and girls are encouraged to use language differently and strategically. On the one hand, girls typically learn to communicate in order to be cooperative and inclusive. They may be encouraged to "play nice." This can result in girls using avoiding or accommodating conflict styles that minimize

ERproductions Ltd/Blend Images/Corbis

Conflict can be affected by our gender roles. What types of communication would you expect from these two women engaged in conflict? Does your style of conflict conform to gender expectations?

conflict and help maintain relationships. On the other hand, boys may be encouraged to use competitive language. When boys assert themselves to establish the rules of a game or achieve some desired result, they may resort to using a competing style to manage conflict. We carry these language styles and practices into adulthood, and these styles as well as our learned gender roles influence how we manage conflict. Remember, though, that gender influences (not determines) our language styles, and our other master statuses also shape our communication.

Gender roles, *the social expectations for how males and females should behave*, have also been linked to conflict styles. Strongly sex-typed individuals (those who strongly identify as masculine or feminine) may be constrained by stereotypical behaviors associated with their gender. This means that these individuals may manage conflict in ways that are perceived as appropriate for their gender (Bern & Lenney, 1976). For example, masculine gender roles often are associated with competing styles (so highly gender-identified males might use the win–lose approach to conflict) while avoiding behaviors are more consistent with feminine gender roles (so highly gender-identified females might use accommodating or

gender roles
the social expectations for how males and females should behave.

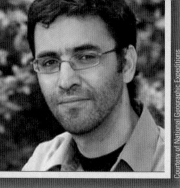
Courtesy of National Geographic Expeditions

Aziz Abu Sarah, National Geographic Explorer and Cultural Educator: Throwing Stones

Have you ever felt animosity toward someone or even a group of people that you had little or no actual interaction with? Have you ever had a neighbor you rarely spoke to yet did not particularly care for? Did your high school have a rival school? Did you or any of your classmates pull pranks against students at this rival school? If you answered yes to any of these questions, you have something in common with Aziz Abu Sarah.

Aziz Abu Sarah was born in Jerusalem. He was only nine years old when he watched Israeli soldiers storm into his home and arrest his eighteen-year-old brother, Tayseer, for allegedly throwing stones at Israeli cars. Tayseer was kept without a trial, interrogated, and beaten for fifteen days until he was finally coerced into admitting he had thrown the stones. Tayseer was held for eleven months, beaten repeatedly, and finally died within weeks of being released from prison. Aziz describes the pain he felt for losing his closest brother and how angry and bitter he felt toward Israelis. He wanted someone to be held responsible for his brother's death. He wanted revenge.

Aziz spent his adolescence and teenage years writing angry articles for a youth magazine. He describes how he used his "pain to spread hatred against the other side." Aziz refused to learn Hebrew because it was considered the "enemy's language." However, he knew that to attend college or obtain a good job, he would have to put his anger aside and study Hebrew. So he attended an institute that taught Hebrew to Jewish newcomers to Israel. Aziz recalls, "It was the first time I had sat in a room of Jews who were not superior to me. It was the first time I had seen faces different from the soldiers at checkpoints. Those soldiers had taken my brother; these students were the same as me. My understanding of the Jewish people started to collapse after just a few weeks of the Ulpan. I found myself confused, thinking 'How can they be normal human beings just like me?'"

Aziz soon discovered that he had a few things in common with his Jewish classmates, and he eventually formed friendships with them. Aziz believes, "As humans, we try to rationalize our hatred. In our minds we demonize the enemy, and discredit their humanity. This is the lie that fires the conflict between Israel and Palestine." Aziz now works as a lecturer and speaks in churches, synagogues, and mosques on the subject of Israeli-Palestinian conflict, peace, reconciliation, and interfaith dialogue. Aziz has won numerous awards for his work in the Israeli–Palestinian peace movement. Sarah, 2009.

 CourseMate Connection: Go to cengagebrain.com to access your CourseMate for *Invitation to Human Communication* to view a video about Aziz Abu Sarah.

Rostislav Glinsky/Shutterstock.com

1. In what ways does Aziz's story illustrate concern for self and concern for others?

2. How does a civil approach to handling conflict help explain Aziz's ability to resolve his feelings toward the Israeli people?

3. How do cultural differences influence conflict between two cultural groups such as the Palestinians and Israelis? In what ways can understanding different cultural (and religious) norms begin the process toward conflict resolution?

4. Consider a conflict you have had. What conflict strategies discussed in this chapter would work to resolve this conflict?

?

avoiding styles of conflict) (Brower, Mitchell, & Weber, 2002). Individuals perceived as **androgynous**, meaning they *display both masculine and feminine behaviors,* are more likely to adopt compromising styles. So, the communication styles and gender-role behaviors we learn as children for managing conflict often are carried into adulthood.

Culture and Conflict

Our conflict-management styles also are influenced by culture. As we become more aware and connected to individuals from other countries, scholars are working to understand how cultural norms and practices influence conflict. Social psychologist Geert Hofstede explains that in Asian cultures, which are predominately collective in nature, people tend to value harmony and relationships with others (Hofstede, 1986). Many people from Asian cultures believe in the importance of studying and working hard to prepare for their future. On the other hand, many Western cultures (including the United States) value independence and autonomy. Rather than focusing on the future, individuals from these cultures tend to be more focused on immediate gratification. The differences between collectivist and individualist can influence communication patterns and conflict-resolution strategies. For example, people residing in collectivist cultures may tend to avoid expressing direct opinions about their own motivations and personal goals. In contrast, individualist cultures often use more direct and explicit language to convey personal thoughts and motivations and to handle conflict (Hall & Hall, 1989). Leung and Lind (1986) examined how American and Chinese people responded to conflict and concluded that Americans had a stronger preference for using adversarial resolution strategies, and Chinese individuals preferred nonadversarial or cooperative strategies. More recently, Holt and DeVore (2005) concluded that members of collectivist cultures tend to rely on more passive strategies to manage conflict such as the avoiding strategy.

But a person's cultural background influences more than just how conflict is managed. Culture influences which goals are considered incompatible, why such goals are seen as incompatible, how one responds to incompatible goals, and whether the outcome is perceived as satisfactory or not. Therefore, the nature of conflict itself varies across cultures. What one culture may address as an incompatible goal may not be acknowledged at all in another culture (Kaushal & Kwantes, 2006).

Conflict occurs for many social and personal reasons, and this means that the same conflict scenario may be handled differently across different cultures. For example, "disagreeing with a parent may be entirely acceptable in Canada and not at all condoned in Africa" (Kaushal & Kwantes, 2006, p. 581). Psychologists Kwantes and Kaushal also remind us that it is important to acknowledge both cultural and personality factors when trying to predict how someone will respond to conflict situations (2006, p. 581). For example, self-monitoring, regardless of the culture an individual is from, can affect the way conflict is managed. High self-monitors, those who emphasize "concern for others," are more likely to resolve conflict by using collaborative and compromising strategies. In contrast, low self-monitors often display less concern for others' needs and will likely resort to using the competing or avoiding resolution strategies (Warech, Smither, Reilly, Millsap, & Reilly, 1998). (For additional information on self-monitoring, see Chapter 2.) Although cultural practices and norms do affect how conflict is managed, they are just some of many factors in how disputes get resolved. Technology, which is explored next, also affects conflicts and their resolution.

Technology and Conflict

Today, many of us are continuously connected to our family, friends, and co-workers using some form of technology or electronic device. Computers, cell phones, and smartphones allow us to communicate constantly with others. As more time is spent using technology to interact, complete group projects, solicit feedback, and comment on our daily lives, it is no surprise that technology provides us the means by which conflict can be created and resolved. Let us look at three ways technology and conflict are intertwined: technology as a source of conflict, culture and technology, and technology and international conflict.

Technology as a Source of Conflict Information and communication technology (ICT) actually may be a source of conflict. This is because a "digital generation gap" often exists between children and their parents and grandparents. For many young, savvy ICT users, conflict occurs with parents or grandparents, who know little about more advanced forms of technology. A study examining U.S. teenagers and their parents' interactions over technology use revealed that when parents or grandparents lacked technology awareness, they would encourage older siblings or relatives to monitor technology use. This often spurs conflict between family members. Lynn Schofield Clark explains that "extended families were often a source of additional supervision and advice, especially when the young person's parents were less savvy about MySpace and cell-phone use than their teen children" (p. 397). One young woman reported that her aunt had a MySpace page and would often tell her grandparents about her activities. Other teenagers believe their parents were "snooping" into their private lives by checking their social-networking sites (Clark, 2009).

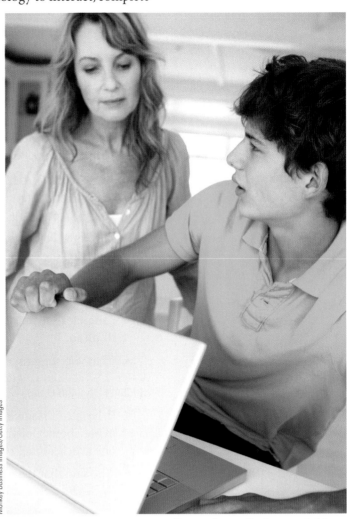

Parents often monitor the amount of time their children spend on their computers, as well as the sites they are visiting. Even though it can create conflict, do you think this is an effective way to parent? Why or why not?

Monkey Business Images/Getty Images

Regardless of which family members were responsible for monitoring teenagers' online activity, conflict took place regarding how much privacy teenagers should have online from their parents. Schofield Clark concluded that teenagers and their parents used different strategies to address the knowledge gap. Although some parents used a competing strategy by imposing authoritarian practices to determine the amount of time spent and content posted on Internet sites, other parents took a different approach by talking to their children and asking questions about their online participation. Regardless of how knowledgeable parents are about digital technology, they can "retain a positive relationship with, and even an authoritative role in, their teens' lives, when they expressed trust and respect for their teenage children and the ways in which they chose to engage in practices in the digital realm" (Clark, 2009, p. 403).

Technology and Culture Cultural influences also affect the ways technology contributes to conflict. Research examining how students from collectivist and individualist cultures engaged in potential conflict in their online discussion forums illustrated a few of these cultural differences. When comparing students from Hong Kong with students from the United States participating in threaded discussion forums, the amount of disagreement as well as the way in which students disagreed was different. Take a look at some of the responses to the topic of global warming:

Students from Hong Kong

- "I can see your point, but I think global warming is the most important thing that we have to pay attention to."

- "Someone expressed that the factories need to control their pollutants, but I wanted to point out that without many of the factories and their way of production we would lack many resources."

- "Therefore, ozone depletion is a serious problem, too. Do you think so?"

- "Can you suggest other methods to protect our world?"

Students from the United States

- "I have to disagree with some of the assumptions that you have made about global warming, which you clearly based off of this one article alone."

- "She said that the air quality is improving. I was wondering where she learned this. It is completely wrong."

- "It helps out the wildlife, plant life, and us. Anyway those are my feelings on this discussion."

- "I strongly doubt that anyone is willing to give up their cars. End of story" (Seo, Miller, Schmidt, & Sowa, 2008).

Notice that the students from Hong Kong avoided using the words *disagree* or *wrong* and encouraged participation by inviting others to respond. On the other hand, the students from the United States were more direct and straightforward when they disagreed, and they rarely encouraged further discussion. The Hong Kong students' posts indicated little explicit disagreement. Meanwhile, the U.S. students' posts often directly confronted one another when disagreeing. So, although technology is present for students from both countries, disagreements are handled differently.

Technology and International Conflict Finally, computer-mediated communication (CMC) can provide support and outlets for those living in regions that experience war. For example, blogs create a safe space for people who are experiencing conflict to interact with people from around the world. Blogs allow people to share their perspectives and experiences, provide advice and support, create online communities, and reach a new understanding of different cultures and traditions. University of California professors Ban al-Ani, Gloria Mark, and Bryan Semaan (2010) studied blogs created from Iraqi citizens after the Iraq war began in 2003. They concluded that when it was unsafe for Iraqi citizens living in conflict zones to travel or express ideas publicly, they would share their stories, opinions, grief, or support in a virtual environment. Al-Ani et al. (2010) explain that an Iraqi doctor presented his social and political views on his blog using an alias because his opinions were not appropriate given his occupation.

In addition, in 2008, news of an Iraqi journalist throwing a shoe at then president George W. Bush received global media attention. In response to the shoe-throwing incident, bloggers explained why they supported or condoned the action. In many posts, bloggers explained that the significance of throwing a shoe at a person in Iraq is not to harm a person but to disgrace or shame him or her. A blog written by a female student living in Iraq tried to clarify this issue and set the record straight regarding Iraqi cultural practices and norms:

> And no, Iraqis DO NOT go around throwing shoes everywhere. What outraged me on the Internet today, [were] the statements of "in Iraqi culture" and "in Arab culture" shoe throwing is apparently common. It's ridiculous exactly how the media portrays the East. First, we are always the bad guys in movies, and now our welcome to foreigners is shoe throwing! (Al-Ani et al., 2010)

Used during times of international conflict, blogs can help people understand different views of the conflict and people's actions, and they can assist in understanding customs and cultures (Al-Ani et al., 2010).

Even though it is a way of life, computer-mediated communication can create challenges for families when a "digital generational gap" exists, when group members are attempting to accomplish a task,

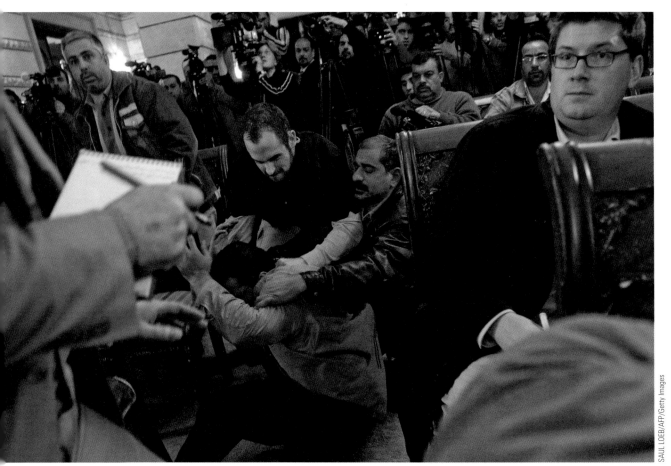

SAUL LOEB/AFP/Getty Images

Press conferences generate news about events that are timely and relevant. What types of situations are most appropriate for holding a press conference? How might press conferences be used to increase cultural awareness and understanding?

flaming

uninhibited expression of hostility such as swearing, name-calling, ridicule, and insults directed toward another person, his or her character, religion, race, intelligence, and physical or mental ability.

or when friends post hurtful messages to their social-media accounts that ultimately foster interpersonal conflict. Hurtful messages known as *flames* are used to verbally attack others online. **Flaming** is *the uninhibited expression of hostility such as swearing, name-calling, ridicule, and insults toward another person, his or her character, religion, race, intelligence, and physical or mental ability* (Kayany, 1998). It may be tempting for the recipient of a flame to respond using similarly hurtful language, but it is best to try to establish a dialogue by asking for information that led to the sender's assumptions or conclusions, using appropriate humor, or acknowledging the claim and then stating an alternative perspective.

However, CMC can also be used to help increase cultural awareness, understanding, and appreciation. As our world continues to become more interconnected, we will continue to see the effects that CMC has on our ability to communicate effectively and to resolve differences across the globe. In the next section, we will explore some of the most common and most effective ways to manage conflict in our interpersonal relationships.

Managing Conflict

Managing conflict can be difficult, especially when the individuals involved are determined to have their goals met. We will look at four possible outcomes for conflict: win–lose, lose–lose, compromise, and win–win.

Win–Lose The win–lose conflict-resolution outcome occurs when one person succeeds at accomplishing the desired goal at the expense of the other person. This means that one person essentially "wins" and the other "loses." Typically, this outcome is based on positions of power, access to resources, or even voting. Take a look at the following win–lose scenarios.

Charlene learns from her supervisor that her work hours will be cut in half and that she will lose her company's health-insurance benefits. Charlene speaks to human resources and asks to be kept at forty hours per week so she can retain her health-care benefits. She is told that her hours and her benefits will be cut. The supervisor won; Charlene lost.

Nine-year-old Timmy wants to stay up past his usual bedtime, but his mother disagrees and forces him to go to bed at his usual time. Timmy's mother achieves her goal of getting Timmy to bed on time, and Timmy loses his attempt to stay up late.

Jassim runs for public office in his hometown. He campaigns for several months and learns on election night that he lost the election to his rival. Jassim's opponent won, and Jassim lost.

The first two examples illustrate how positions of authority can determine the outcome of a conflict situation. The third example reveals how a democratic process, or competition decided by a vote, can create a *win–lose* situation. At times, the win–lose scenario is unavoidable. For example, sporting events and elections are designed to have clear winners. At other times, the winner may not actually gain much; this is called a *lose–lose* strategy.

Lose–Lose In a lose–lose conflict-managing strategy, neither party is content with the outcome. Take, for example, Charlene's work situation. The company Charlene works for is facing a financial crisis, making it difficult to pay Charlene a full-time salary and benefits; however, the workload for the company has remained the same. Charlene's supervisor now has to assume more responsibility; therefore, both Charlene and her supervisor lose something in the resolution. Charlene is now being paid less, and her supervisor is now expected to work more. Moreover, the company still is having a difficult time paying their expenses. In this situation, no one is likely to feel content with the outcome. In situations in which both parties are unsatisfied with the outcome, it is important to consider whether another resolution such as compromise is possible.

This mother and daughter have achieved a win–win. By agreeing to share computer time, the mother is confident that her daughter uses her online time more productively and safely. The daughter wins because she is allowed more time on the computer. Think of a recent conflict that ended in a win–win. What strategies were used to achieve that result?

Compromise When two parties compromise, each party is willing to give up part of its desired goal. Consider Timmy's request to stay up past his bedtime. Timmy's bedtime is at 8 P.M. On Friday night, he asks to stay up until 9 P.M. Although Timmy's mother wants him to go to bed at his usual time to prepare for a busy Saturday filled with activities and errands, she decides to allow him to stay up until 8:30 P.M. In this situation, Timmy and his mother both achieved part of their initial goals.

If Charlene is able to compromise with her company to cut her hours to part-time but allow her to keep her benefits, then Charlene and her company each gain part of their desired goal. Charlene promises to not leave (forcing the company to bear the burden of finding another part-time employee or making other employees take on additional responsibilities), and Charlene keeps her health insurance.

Sometimes compromise can make those involved feel satisfied that part of their desired goal was accomplished. However, sometimes compromise can produce a sense of uneasiness, especially if a person's compromises are on important values and beliefs. For instance, if Jassim adjusts his political platform so that he will be more appealing to voters but those changes go against his values, he may win but he has created a very uneasy and perhaps unethical path for himself in office.

Win–Win Ideally, everyone involved in a conflict will be satisfied with the solution. However, it can be extremely difficult to find a solution that everyone believes accomplishes their desired goals. Communication and conflict-management scholar Linda Putnam describes important steps that can be taken to help successfully resolve conflict situations and lead to win–win outcomes. Although we use framing in many types of situations, Putnam explains that **framing**, *the way people use language to define the conflict situation* (Putnam, 2010), can help create a productive communication climate that allows parties to find an agreeable solution. When we frame a conflict, we describe it in a particular way, and this causes us to see it in a particular light. Framing consists of three features that will shape the conflict-resolution process:

1. *Naming the conflict*. Those involved in the conflict need to give it a name and agree on the labels and language choices used to describe the conflict. This might include introducing a new label, term, or description for the conflict situation. For example, are two

framing
the way people use language to define the conflict situation.

people "at war," "at each other's throats," or "struggling to understand different perspectives"? Using different labels to name the conflict can help move the conflict toward resolution.

2. *Next, consider ways to redefine and shift the blame in the dispute.* Putnam describes this as "shifting the level of abstraction, or location, of the conflict." When the blame or cause of a conflict moves away from a person and becomes about a policy, institutional decision, or some other external force, individuals will likely feel less defensive and more focused on a solution. Although this is often hard to do when we are in an argument with a friend or someone close to us, Putnam urges us to consider how the issue can be moved from "specific to general, part to whole, individual to system level, or vice versa" (Putnam, 2010, p. 329). So, in an interpersonal conflict, rather than accuse the other person of always being late and not caring about you, this strategy would suggest that you talk about how showing up on time communicates respect and value for you.

3. *Employ the use of systematic questioning.* The third step in this win–win approach is to ask critical questions that can help each party understand the other's needs and goals. Avoid using loaded or leading questions. Leading questions might be "Don't you think that it would be better for you to help out with the chores?" and "Isn't it true that I am the one who always completes the month-end reports for work?" Instead, Putnam suggests that individuals use *story questions* or *systematic questioning*. Story questions provide some background to the concern or complaint and allow parties to expand the conflict definition and discuss other details involved in the conflict situation. For example, saying "I am feeling overwhelmed with my responsibilities at work and at home. I feel as though I can't keep up with it all. Do you think you could help with some of the chores this week?" shares the story behind the request. Providing information (the story) for how you are feeling and why you may be feeling a certain way gives context to the other person and helps her or him feel less attacked by the request.

Systematic questioning, which involves asking for the reasons something might be happening, is a second approach. In this next example, the systematic question helps the individuals in the conflict determine the motivation behind the issue that is causing the conflict: "I seem to be the one who turns in the month-end reports each month. Is there a reason you haven't attempted to complete one of these reports?" Using systematic questioning (rather than leading questions) helps two people explore the history and background related to the conflict and can provide additional context for the conflict. "I'm so glad you asked, I don't understand these forms at all and was embarrassed to ask for help" and "I didn't realize we had to do these monthly—no one told me that" are two possible win–win responses to the systematic question previously asked.

Asking questions can sometimes cause additional frustration for those involved in the conflict; therefore, timing is important in this step. Asking questions is ideal when both parties are feeling defensive and losing hope that an amenable solution will be reached. Used correctly, story or systematic questions rather than leading or attacking questions can move a conflict toward helping, rather than inhibiting, the process of reaching an agreeable resolution.

 ## Creating a Positive Interpersonal Communication Climate

communication climates
climates that set the tone for interpersonal relationships.

disconfirming statement
statement that rejects or invalidates another person's statements.

confirming statements
statements that validate other people by recognizing them, acknowledging their ideas and feelings, and approving or supporting their ideas.

Communication climates *set the tone for interpersonal relationships.* Communication climates can either create a conflict situation or help to resolve conflict. When disconfirming statements are used, a negative climate is established. A **disconfirming statement** is one that *rejects or invalidates another person's statements.* For example, telling someone that her ideas are dumb or that he would never be able to make the team, pass a class, or get a job creates a negative communication climate. Disconfirming statements often use "you" language: "Your idea is terrible." "You never take responsibility for your schoolwork." "You aren't very good at basketball." These and similar examples use disconfirming statements. We can also disconfirm others by ignoring them. When Marcos says, "I'm going out for a while, do you need anything at the store?" and gets no response from his partner, he is being disconfirmed. His partner is creating a negative environment by his lack of acknowledgement of Marcos.

Confirming statements can help us build healthy communication climates and manage conflict productively. **Confirming statements** *validate another person by recognizing other people, acknowledging their ideas and feelings, and approving or supporting their ideas.* One way to initiate confirming statements is by using "I" language: "I really like that idea" or "I think you have a chance at making the team." These confirming statements recognize the ideas and talents of another person and show support for him or her. Confirming statements, however, may not always be appropriate. For example, if someone has chosen to do something harmful, unethical, or unlawful, then it would be inappropriate to agree with those choices. Talking about why you choose to not go along with such decisions is a better option. And lying to another person is also inappropriate. When your roommate says, "I really like this shirt for the job interview—what do you think?" and it actually looks unprofessional, you can ask what the roommate likes about it and offer some other, more professional options rather than support the original choice.

Although managing conflict can be challenging for most of us, conflict can be resolved with practice and effort, open and respectful communication, and a desire to understand the needs of others. We now turn our attention to some of the external challenges individuals face as they manage their interpersonal relationships.

Civility in Interpersonal Conflict

Civility, as you read in earlier chapters, calls to mind not simply "good manners" but the reality of the "common journey" we share with others. When we participate in interpersonal relationships, we are, as law professor Stephen Carter states, "traveling on the same train" with other people. According to Carter, civility—which involves being willing to listen to others and to give them the chance to explain their reasons, ideas, views, and goals—makes "the ride tolerable" (Carter, 1998, p. 15). Although U. S. American culture is often known for its many incivilities (road rage, cyberbullying, domestic abuse, interpersonal violence, and even marital infidelity), we do not have to bring these models into our interpersonal relationships. But how do we behave "civilly" in a conflict, especially one in which there are profound disagreements? Consider the scenario of Grace and Lisbeth and the steps that follow.

Grace and Lisbeth, friends for ten years, are furious with one another. Grace just broke up with her partner of three years, and Lisbeth shares with Grace that she now is dating that person. Grace feels a strong desire to lash out at Lisbeth in order to make her feel badly about her decision. Lisbeth feels defensive and confused—she really likes this person, but she also values Grace's friendship enormously. How might these two work through the conflict civilly?

> Step 1 Grace and Lisbeth find a neutral and safe place to communicate with one another. This might include help from a third party such as a counselor or therapist to help them talk though the issues. Although both are feeling angry and uncertain, they decide to meet at a quiet and neutral place like a coffee shop.
>
> Step 2 They agree on several civil ground rules. They agree to not interrupt or accuse one another, to be honest, to use "story" and "systematic" questions, and to listen and try to understand the other person even though they both really want to defend themselves.
>
> Step 3 After Grace explains how hurt and betrayed she feels, she tells Lisbeth, "I thought our friendship was one of trust and value, but I feel really hurt and betrayed. I don't understand how you could date my ex, when you know how devastated I was when we broke up." Lisbeth listens without interrupting, even though she wants to defend herself as Grace talks, and she honestly tries to understand her friend.
>
> Step 4 Lisbeth explains her actions. She shares that she has been attracted to Grace's ex for a long time, and she explains how difficult it was to see the two of them together. Because she listened to Grace in step 3 and tried to understand Grace's position (rather than defend herself), she has a better idea of how hurt Grace is. She says, "I didn't really think about how hurt you would be; I only thought about my feelings. I should have talked with you about my attraction, right?" Because Grace felt like Lisbeth really listened to her when she shared her feelings and anger, she is more able to put down her defensive side and try to understand Lisbeth's own feelings.

Step 5 Although hurt feelings remain and the conflict is not yet resolved, Grace and Lisbeth are now able to talk about their long friendship, some of the competitive and jealous feelings they have had, and some of the ways they have taken each other for granted. They give one another the opportunity to explain, without interruption, and they create feelings of reciprocity and that each person is valued and listened to.

Step 6 Neither really knows how to resolve the conflict yet. Grace still feels upset, and Lisbeth still really cares for Grace as well as her ex-partner. Lisbeth is able to apologize for not talking to Grace first, and Grace is able to apologize for making it hard for Lisbeth to do so. They agree to meet again in a week and to try to talk more about a possible resolution to the conflict that will work for both of them.

Although the conflict is not resolved, this civil approach lets the two continue to work out issues—as opposed to Grace saying, "I hate you! How could you betray me like this? You're a lying, cheating little #%*!!!" and Lisbeth saying, "I'm a #%*!!!/ You #*@&!!—you only think about yourself and what you want! I introduced the two of you, and look what I get for it!? I'm out of here and good riddance."

In summary, a civil approach to conflict involves six steps:

1. Find a neutral place to talk.

2. Establish ground rules that promote civil communication.

3. Share feelings and experiences using story questions and sequential questions and without interrupting.

4. Listen to understand the other person rather than defend yourself.

5. Create new awareness and understandings of one another.

6. Agree to continue the conversation after some time has passed rather than force a resolution immediately (Bone, Griffin, & Scholz, 2008; Ratcliff, 2005).

Although not always successful, this approach to conflict can and does prevent unnecessary hurt and the selfish expression of anger. When both parties are willing, working through conflict civilly can be a powerful and productive communication tool.

Challenges in Interpersonal Relationships

Many pressures can create challenges in our interpersonal relationships. Three types of external challenges that interpersonal relationships face are distance, difference, and interpersonal violence. We will discuss each in the following sections.

Distance

The number of interpersonal relationships facing a geographic separation has been steadily increasing over the past few years. Although there are different understandings of what constitutes a long-distance relationship, such as the actual distance and duration of the separation, it is important to recognize how relationships can continue to thrive in times of physical separation. Friends, family members, and spouses live apart from one another for many reasons. Attending college, military deployment, occupational needs, and dual-career marriages all attribute to geographic separation or distance in a relationship. Traditional understandings of long-distance relationships suggested that geographical distance would eventually result in a deterioration of the relationship; however, more recent research suggests that long-distance relationships can and often do thrive during times of separation.

Research on long-distance relationships has focused heavily on the importance of the face-to-face communication used to maintain long-distance relationships (Dainton & Aylor, 2001; Gerstel & Gross, 1984). For this reason, it is easy to understand how previous scholarship on long-distance relationships concluded that many relationships do not survive over long periods of separation. However, the ability to communicate with friends (and maintain friendships) over long distances is now easier than ever. Advancements in computer-mediated communication such as Webcams allow long-distance partners to communicate face to face. In addition, texting, blogging, and communicating via social-media sites can provide daily updates on the happenings and whereabouts of friends, family members, and romantic partners that were not possible until recently. Happily, the use of CMC helps relationships stay strong through times of geographic separation.

Most people have at least one close long-distance friendship. How do you deal with long-distance relationships with family and friends? What role does CMC have in maintaining those relationships?

homestudio/bigstock.com

MARK THIESSEN/National Geographic

Mireya Mayor
Emerging Explorer, Primatologist, and Conservationist

What strategies do you use to help maintain the relationship with your kids, particularly when you're gone for long periods of separation?

I have four girls, and in many situations, I don't have a way of communicating with them because I don't have access to the Internet or a phone. And in many cases, I can't even send a letter. So I make a poster with a calendar on it, and I put a picture of me at home with them at the beginning of the calendar. The calendar tracks each day and tells them where I'll be—in the jungle, or flying, that sort of thing. Then at the end I have a picture of me at home with them. So they get a sense of time and place because sometimes I'm gone for six weeks at a time without any sort of communication whatsoever. I'll also create a little photo album and leave that with them to open up when they miss me.

As far as with the adults in my life, there are times where I do have access to a satellite phone, so the communication is infrequent but possible. And then, of course, there's letters, but also the journals that I keep. My journals are open access. I write in them at the end of every day, so that when I get home, the adults in my life can read them and "catch up" with me and where I've been. In fact, I wrote my book based on the journals that I kept while I was on these expeditions.

You know, we take for granted the fact that we have endless options for communicating, whether it is text or Twitter or Facebook or the telephone, or e-mail. There are just so many ways in which you can communicate with somebody. But in the line of work that I'm in, those are all completely removed. And so you do have to think of other ways, and while they're not as instantaneous as we are used to, they still tell your story.

Research also reports that approximately 90 percent of individuals have at least one close long-distance friendship (Rohlfing, 1995), and 82 percent of college students report keeping in contact with a long-distance friend at least once per week (Johnson et al., 2004). Whereas distance was once believed to cause friends to be less committed to the friendship, a recent study revealed that 81 percent of long-distance friends report an increasing level of commitment to their friendship (Johnson, Becker, Craig, Gilchrist, & Haigh, 2009).

An increasing number of intimate relationships also face the potential challenges of geographic separation. Nearly half of all college students are in long-distance dating relationships, and as many as 3 million American spouses are residing in different locations (Aylor, 2003). But how do these relationships stay healthy and productive? Interpersonal communication scholars suggests that long-distance romantic relationships thrive when those involved do three things: (1) engage in positive self-presentation, (2) avoid conflict during face-to-face interactions, and

(3) engage in romantic idealization of the partner and the relationship (Merolla, 2010; Stafford & Merolla, 2007).

The not so good news is that long-distance relationships may experience additional conflict and tension when both partners reunite and move to the same location. In fact, one-third of reunited relationships will terminate within three months of becoming geographically close (Stafford, Merolla, & Castle, 2006). Regardless of whether those involved in an interpersonal relationship are geographically separated or close in proximity, communication, face to face or otherwise, is an important component in maintaining such relationships.

Difference

Sex, gendered norms, and cultural differences all play a role in our ability to successfully maintain interpersonal relationships. Communication scholars have investigated differences that exist between same-sex and cross-sex friendships and report that female friends are often preferred over male friends (by both males and females) when people need emotional support. This is because females tend to provide more social and emotional support than do men (Kunkel & Burleson, 1998). Men and women rate affective, supportive communication skills as more important than instrumental communication skills—and these are the skills women tend to have. Women are socialized to attend to others' emotions to a greater extent than men are, and this helps to explain why both men and women report greater satisfaction with friends who communicate more affectively. However, cross-sex friendships do provide unique benefits for women: women report appreciation for men's instrumentally oriented skills (Holstrom, 2009), and men's friendships with other men are highly valued, providing them with friends to go and do things with.

Cultural differences also present challenges for interpersonal relationships. For example, the cultural distinction of individualism and collectivism helps to explain potential challenges for cross-cultural interpersonal relationships. Recall that although individualistic cultures rely on direct communication, many collectivist cultures place value on indirect and polite forms of communication. As such, tensions may result from different communication styles used in cross-cultural relationships. When a culture relies more on "indirect and nonverbal information to reduce uncertainty in personal relationships . . . direct communication" can put people "in awkward situations and hurt the existing relationship and harmony" (Zhang, Merolla, & Lin, 2009). If someone from one culture is less likely to self-disclose information, then building a sense of trust and openness can be difficult for the person whose culture values disclosure (Zhang et al., 2009). Understanding cultural variations can help reduce potential conflict, and learning about differences in cultural norms can help minimize conflict in cross-cultural relationships.

Interpersonal Violence

According to the National Coalition Against Domestic Violence (NCADV; n.d.) domestic violence, now known as **intimate partner**

intimate partner violence
willful intimidation, physical assault, battery, sexual assault, or other abusive behavior perpetrated by an intimate partner against another.

violence, is *"the willful intimidation, physical assault, battery, sexual assault, . . . or other abusive behavior perpetrated by an intimate partner against another"* (p. 1).

The NCADV states that domestic violence occurs in all cultures regardless of age, economic status, race, religion, nationality, or educational background (n.d., p. 1). However, the prevalence of interpersonal violence against women is astounding. The coalition has estimated that 85 percent of all domestic violence victims are women. In the United States alone,

- a woman is assaulted every nine seconds,

- females who are twenty to twenty-four years of age are at the greatest risk of nonfatal intimate partner violence, and

- more than three women are murdered by their husbands or boyfriends every single day. (Domestic Violence Statistics, n. d.)

Figure 7.1 *Domestic violence*
Source: Original figure created by Domestic Abuse Intervention Project, Duluth, MN, from http://www.ncadv.org/files/DomesticViolence FactSheet(National).pdf

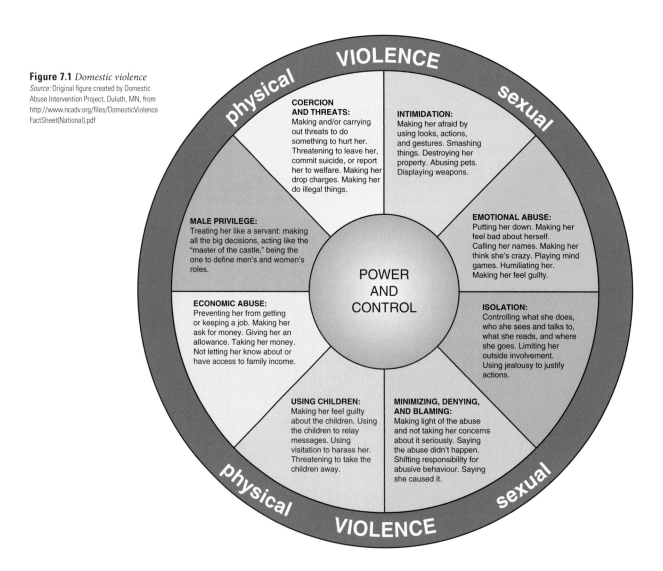

CIVIC ENGAGEMENT IN ACTION

Responding to Interpersonal Violence

There are many organizations working to end intimate partner violence. And, one way to get involved is to be aware of them and to share what you know about them with friends and family. Campaigns such as the Domestic Violence Awareness Project encourage the display of purple ribbons to demonstrate support for victims and families. The RESPECT! campaign aims to increase positive relationships by coaching boys into becoming nonviolent men. The National Domestic Violence hotline is open 24 hours a day that provides resources and help for callers to stay safe. The White Ribbon Campaign, an international organization founded in 1991 to protest and call attention to the violence against women, is the largest men's anti-violence group in the world (White Ribbon Campaign, 2011). Mentors in Violence, founded by Jackson Katz, educates men about the socialization men receive that encourages men to think of masculinity as linked to violence. And, shelters and support groups are available in many cities.

Beyond these important organizations, communication scholar Julia Wood (2013) advocates the following approaches to reducing interpersonal violence:

1. Make a conscious choice to not be violent or to accept violence in your life.

2. Become aware of the violent terms and phrases you use and eliminate them from your speech.

3. Educate yourself about the issue and become knowledgeable about the many faces of interpersonal violence.

4. Speak out against violence—make others aware of its prevalence and the harm it does to women and men.

5. Share that knowledge with others civilly and respectfully.

Although speaking out is an important way to generate awareness and help stop the pattern of intimate partner violence,

it can be difficult—especially for women. The act of speaking out itself can lead to more abuse. Others may not know who to speak out to. FrontlineSMS, a software program that allows users to send, receive, and manage text messages without an Internet connection, is now being used to report incidents of domestic violence (and other forms of abuse such as human trafficking). One organization in Oklahoma that uses FrontlineSMS to assist victims of domestic violence received more than 4,000 text messages within the first three months of service from women in abusive situations. The text messages provided enough evidence from women that several men were jailed and convicted for their abuse (Thornton, 2010).

You can speak out against interpersonal violence, seek help for yourself or others, and participate in national, community, and campus organizations and events that raise awareness of interpersonal violence. Supporting and being aware of these antiviolence organizations can provide you, or the people you care about, with invaluable resources to stop interpersonal violence.

But scholars are also beginning to question the "real numbers" related to interpersonal violence inflicted on men: bell hooks (2004); Abby Ferber, Christina Jimenez, Andrea Herrera, and Dena Samuels (2008); and Michael Kimmel (2011) are beginning to suspect that the rate of male-on-male interpersonal violence (in the workplace, friendships, athletic teams, and social settings like bars and parties) may be underreported and understudied, and they are beginning to turn their attention to this aspect of violence as well.

The causes of interpersonal violence are complex and can be difficult to understand. Experts agree that interpersonal violence occurs because of some combination of cultural values, gender socialization, a family's approach to conflict, the prevalence of violent images and stories in our media, and an individual's unique approach to conflict and relationships. There are no direct causal links, but we do know that hypermasculine individuals are more likely to inflict violence on their partners and even their children and pets; furthermore, threats of death or harm as well as few economic resources or options often keep individuals in violent relationships.

Chapter Summary

Conflict Is a Natural Part of Interpersonal Relationships

- Conflict occurs because of incompatibility or the perceived scarcity of rewards.
- Our response to conflict is often determined by our concern for self and concern for others.

Gender Shapes the Way Conflict Is Handled

- Because boys and girls are encouraged to use language differently for strategic purposes, they often handle conflict differently.
- Gender roles have also been linked to conflict styles.
- Androgynous individuals are more likely to adopt flexible and compromising conflict-resolution styles.

Conflict-Management Styles Are Also Influenced by Culture

- The differences between collectivist and individualistic can influence communication patterns and conflict-resolution strategies.
- Collectivist cultures tend to avoid expressing direct opinions and personal goals.
- Individualist cultures tend to use more direct and explicit language to convey personal thoughts and motivations.
- Because conflict occurs for many social and personal reasons, the same conflict scenario may be handled differently across different cultures.
- Self-monitoring can affect the way conflict is managed.

Technology Provides a Means by Which Conflict Can Be Created and Resolved

- Technology may be a source of conflict because of a digital generation gap.
- Collectivist and individualistic cultures may handle on-line conflict differently.
- Computer-mediated conflict (CMC) may provide a support and outlets for those living in areas of conflict or separated from families and friends.

Managing Conflict

- There are four possible outcomes for resolving conflict: win–win, lose–lose, win–lose, and compromise.
- Framing the conflict is an important step in finding a suitable solution.
- Creating a positive communication climate by using confirming statements can help manage conflict.
- Approaching conflict civilly can be a productive communication tool to resolving it.

Several External Pressures Can Create Challenges for Interpersonal Relationships

- Geographic separation can be challenging for interpersonal relationships.
- Sex, gendered norms, cultural differences, and interpersonal violence all play a role in our ability to successfully maintain interpersonal relationships

Key Concepts

androgynous (152)

communication climates (160)

concern for others (147)

concern for self (147)

confirming statements (160)

disconfirming statement (160)

flaming (156)

framing (158)

gender roles (149)

interpersonal conflict (147)

intimate partner violence (165)

 ## Invitation to Human Communication Online

Speech Communication CourseMate includes an interactive eBook and interactive learning tools including National Geographic Explorer videos, student videos, quizzes, flash cards, and more. Speech Builder Express 3.0 and Speech Studio 2.0 are also available. Go to cengagebrain.com to access your CourseMate for *Invitation to Human Communication* where these resources are located.

Further Reflection and Discussion

1. What is your style for managing conflict? Why do you think this style is constructive? Are there changes you want to make? Using the information in this chapter, identify one way you could change your approach to conflict management.

2. What are some ways to maintain a positive relationship (romance, family, or friend) over a long distance? Are there actions you can take to improve the relationship that go beyond using computer-mediated communication?

3. What are examples of flaming that you have observed on social-media sites? Were these justified statements? What strategies can a recipient of a flame use to turn a hostile statement into a civil conversation?

Activities and Web Links

Visit cengagebrain.com to access the CourseMate for *Invitation to Human Communication* where these activities and web links can be found.

1. Search online for National Geographic explorer Ken Banks and how he helped provide cell phones to solve conflicts in other parts of the world. How can technology help resolve conflicts? Think globally. Go to *Weblink 7.1*.

2. Visit the Web site for the National Coalition Against Domestic Violence. Click on "Resources" and choose an article or fact sheet to read. What did you find out that you did not know before? How would you advise a friend in trouble to approach this interpersonal conflict? Go to *Weblink 7.2*.

UNDERSTANDING COMMUNICATION IN

IN THIS CHAPTER YOU WILL LEARN TO:

- Explain the features and types of groups and teams.
- Describe the variety of roles for members of groups and teams.
- Implement the steps of a decision making in groups.
- Discuss the impact of culture on group communication.
- Define the types of group presentations.

Definition of Groups and Teams

Roles in Groups and Teams

Decision Making in Groups

Culture and Communication in Groups

Types of Group Presentations

Groups and teams come together for both work and play. How many groups and teams are you a part of and what do you and the other members accomplish when you are together?

Tyrone Turner/National Geographic

GROUPS AND TEAMS

A sustainable society will only come about through the accumulated actions of billions of individuals, and that's an enormous challenge.

—Alexandra Cousteau, social environment advocate and National Geographic Emerging Explorer

Tyrone Turner/National Geographic

Our workplaces, classrooms, and social lives remind us that we regularly find ourselves working collaboratively with others. In this chapter, we will explore the different features of small groups and teams as well as the ways these groups and teams work together. We will discuss the kinds of work that gets accomplished in groups and teams of individuals. By the end of the chapter, you will have a better understanding of the benefits of group work as well as some of the reasons why individuals find working in groups frustrating or difficult.

Definition of Groups and Teams

A **group** can be defined as a *small number of people who belong together, share something in common, or are assigned a similar task*. Groups are distinct in that the people in a group have a shared purpose or goal that brings them together. That shared purpose or goal keeps them together as they work to accomplish a common task. Groups might last only a few moments (a group of individuals who help move a stalled car from an intersection, for example) or they can last for years (a group of cancer survivors, for example). Although they share similarities, groups are slightly different than teams, which have a competitive element to them. **Teams** are *collections of individuals who come together to attempt to win something, to set a record, or to be the best at some task or event*. Both groups and teams share similar features, however, so let us look at what those might be.

Features of Groups and Teams

Size Small groups usually consist of a minimum of three and a maximum of fifteen people. Teams can be as small as three individuals but often are larger than fifteen people. Athletic teams, for example, can consist of dozens of members, whereas a research team that might be focused on winning a contract or developing a product might have twenty or more individuals helping to achieve those goals. When a group or team is small, its members are more visible and usually have more responsibility. When a group or team is larger, some of its members may be less visible or have more limited responsibilities. Athletic or research teams, for instance, usually have their "first-string" members, those

group
small number of people who belong together, share something in common, or are assigned to a similar task.

team
collections of individuals who come together to attempt to win something, to set a record, or be the best at some task or event.

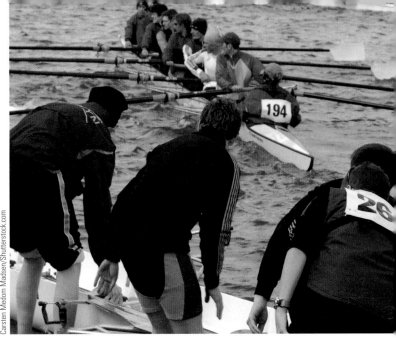

individuals who get more attention and have more responsibility, and their "second-" or "third-string" members, or those people who contribute important work but do not get the attention or recognition that the first-string members do. When groups and teams are small, communication often is faster and more immediate. When a team or group is large, communication may take more time as dozens of members respond to requests or weigh in on various issues and conversations.

Cohesion Cohesiveness is "the *degree of mutual interest among members*" of a group (Littlejohn & Foss, 2007). A cohesive group or team is one in which members are unified and have a shared identification with the group's purpose. Group cohesion can be a good thing because "it brings the members together and enhances" the interpersonal relationships within the group. However, Irving Janis and his associates identified a phenomenon they labeled *groupthink* to describe the negative aspects of group cohesion. According to Janis, **groupthink** is a "*mode of thinking that people engage in when they are deeply involved in a cohesive in-group, when the members' strivings for unanimity override their motivation to realistically appraise alternative courses of action*" (1972, p. 9). Groupthink occurs when members begin to think too much alike and avoid or silence disagreements. It also takes place when a group focuses more on cohesiveness and goodwill among its members than on fully exploring issues or raising questions that might lead to conflict or differences of opinion.

Although it is tempting to think that a small group of people will be highly cohesive and a larger group will be less likely to fall into groupthink, that is not always the case. When a group, no matter its size, follows the "Don't rock the boat" mentality of groupthink, it is placing cohesion and agreement over critically evaluating a situation and exploring many different approaches to that solution. When working in groups and teams, remember that a degree of cohesion is important—members need to feel like they are working toward a common goal—but too much can be dangerous and cause a group to fall into groupthink.

Power Most communication scholars today would agree that when you have a collection of individuals and they are communicating with one another, you also have relationships of power (Foucault, 1972). Researchers also agree that power can be defined in various ways. When individuals work together in groups or teams, looking at two types of power can be useful. First, **power over** can be defined as *the ability to control others and dictate the course of events* (as in police officers or judges, controlling bosses, or even demanding coaches or parents).

Small teams and groups often have incredible cohesion. If you are a member of a small team such as this crewing team, what unifies you?

cohesiveness
degree of mutual interest among members of a group.

groupthink
mode of thinking that people engage in when they are deeply involved in a cohesive in-group, when the members' striving for unanimity override their motivation to realistically appraise alternative courses of action.

power over
ability to control others and dictate the course of events.

CIVIC ENGAGEMENT IN ACTION

The Everest Peace Project: International Teamwork

For sixty days, people who were supposed to hate each other actually worked together "under incredibly difficult circumstances (rain, sleet, snow, hurricane force winds—at an elevation that passenger jets fly!)." The diverse members of Our Everest Climb for Peace literally put themselves and their lives in one another's hands, as well as their tents, and made history doing so. The climbers came from five major religious traditions—Hinduism, Islam, Judaism, Christianity, and Buddhism—as well as atheism and consisted of individuals from two countries at war for decades: Palestine and Israel. Their mission was to work together as a team to climb one of the world's most spectacular and difficult mountains—Mt. Everest—and to inspire others. Working as a team, the climbers wanted to show that "people from diverse cultural backgrounds and faiths can unite together as friends and accomplish incredible things."

The climb received the endorsement of the Dalai Lama, who wrote that the project not only documents "a spectacular climb of the world's tallest mountain" but also shows how "people from different faiths and cultures" can work "successfully as a team to accomplish their goal. It reinforces my strong belief that if we adopt the right approach and make a determined effort, cooperation, trust, and understanding can always be established for a true and worthy cause."

But members of the Everest Peace Project did not put their commitment to teamwork to rest once they reached the top of the world. At the summit, one of the Israeli climbers, Dudu Yifrah, raised a "sewn together Israeli–Palestinian flag" and "dedicated his climb to his newfound brother and climbing partner, Ali Bushnaq" from Palestine. Lance Trumbull, the founder of Our Everest Climb for Peace, described it as "a magical moment, perhaps the greatest moment" of his life. After descending, the two climbers from Israel and Palestine kept their historical friendship and efforts at teamwork alive. Despite how difficult it is to cross borders or even to communicate via telephone, they "meet at least once a year to climb" and "now consider themselves lifelong friends" (Everest Peace Project, 2009; Mesterhazy, 2009).

What Do You Think?

1. What kinds of group communication do you think members of this climbing group used to bridge their vast cultural and religious differences as they climbed Mt. Everest?

2. How do you think culture affected their communication styles and practices? How might they have worked across these differences?

3. What group roles do you think were necessary to fill in order for this international group to reach the top of the world?

4. The Everest Peace Project has continued its efforts to promote international teamwork. Can you think of other types of international teamwork efforts that could be as successful as this one? What kinds of communication would need to be emphasized to facilitate their success?

This type of power is usually referred to as *power over* someone or thing. When individuals have this type of power in a group or team, they often control resources and even the ability to punish or reward others in the team or group.

Communication scholars have explored some of the different bases of this authoritative form of power. People draw from five foundations or sources of power when they interact with others.

legitimate power
ability to control or influence others because of the formal position one holds in the group.

coercive power
ability to punish those who do not meet demands or follow the rules set by the group.

Legitimate power: the ability to control or influence others because of the formal position one holds in the group.

Coercive power: the ability to punish those who do not meet demands or follow the rules set by the group.

Reward power: the ability to give others what they seek or will benefit from for meeting the demands of the group or following the rules set by the group.

Referent power: the ability to influence others because of an association with or respect for the people who hold power in the group.

Expert power: the ability to influence others because of some skill, knowledge base, or set of experiences (French & Raven, 1968).

When someone has power over others, communication usually flows from the person on top down to those lower on the hierarchy. This type of communication can be quite linear: those with power give directions, and those without power follow those directions. Although too much power over others can be a negative thing, this type of communication is not always bad. In some groups and teams, military and emergency service workers, athletic teams involved in strenuous and serious competition, and even those dealing with crisis situations in the workplace or community, we often respect and need "powerful leaders who act decisively" and with clarity (Castells, 2009; Johnson, 2009, p. 8). We sometimes need individuals to take charge and lead others through a challenging or difficulty situation. However, too much power over others can "have a corrosive effect on those who possess it," causing those with power over others to use that power unethically and irresponsibly (Johnson, 2009, p. 8).

reward power
ability to give others what they seek or will benefit from for meeting the demands of the group or following the rules set by the group.

referent power
ability to influence others because of an association with or respect for the people who hold power in the group.

expert power
ability to influence others because of some skill, knowledge base, or set of experience.

Firefighters use a combination of "power over" and "power with" in their jobs. The chief takes charge of a scene and is in command, whereas the firefighters always work together to carry out the chief's orders.

Bill Stormont/Surf/Corbis

power with
power of a strong individual in a group of equals, the power not to command, but to suggest and be listened to, to begin something and see it happen.

Another type of power can also be present in teams and groups. In many groups and teams we find a form of power called **power with**, *reciprocal power*, or *dialogic power* (Bakhtin, 1993; Darlington & Mulvaney, 2002; Starhawk, 1990). Power with is "*the power of a strong individual in a group of equals, the power not to command, but to suggest and be listened to, to begin something and see it happen*" (Albrecht & Brewer, 1990; Starhawk, 1990, p. 10). Famous individuals who model power with are Mohandas Gandhi, Jane Goodall, Mother Teresa, and Nelson Mandela. These individuals worked with others, listening carefully to them, inspiring them, and treating other people in respectful and egalitarian ways as they led movements and worked for particular causes. Less-famous individuals working in teams or groups display power with when they model these same respectful and inspiring behaviors. These people often are the captains of teams, community leaders, and heads of projects at work. Using power with, their communication takes on a reciprocal, back-and-forth, and interactive pattern, with ideas being shared freely and openly as people work toward a common goal.

Interaction To be considered a group or team, members must also interact with one another for a period of time. These interactions are both verbal and nonverbal, and they can take place in person or electronically. Although we sometimes work independently within a group or team, gathering information or perfecting a skill, for example, our independent work becomes a part of the team when we share it with other members. We can interact with other group and team members verbally, sharing our message in person or via Internet or text message. And we can interact with them nonverbally, using gestures and expressions and even showcasing our skills on the playing field or during a workout.

virtual group
group of individuals who have never met one another in person, but communicate regularly through electronic means.

In today's workplace and in our social networks, it is common to be a part of a **virtual group**, a *group of individuals who have never met one another in person but communicate regularly through electronic means*. Although early research on virtual communication in groups expressed hope that many of the power dynamics present in face-to-face teams and groups would be eliminated, we now know that this is not so—group members find ways to assert their power and negotiate status electronically as well as in person (O'Sullivan & Flanagin, n.d.; Reid & Hammersley, 2000).

norms
patterns of behavior that are expected of individuals and seen as correct or even necessary in specific situations.

Norms Groups and teams also conform to certain group norms. **Norms** are *patterns of behavior that are expected of individuals and seen as correct or even necessary in specific situations*. In groups and teams, norms can be as simple as setting an "away" message on your e-mail when you will be out of the office for several days or scheduling a vacation during the off-season if you are a member of an athletic team. Norms also can be very complicated, though, and can involve who to invite to a work-related function, how to dress for particular occasions, whom to ask first for assistance with a problem, and even how and when to share a problem or dilemma with others in the group. Group norms are learned, and newcomers to a group try to learn those norms quickly in order to become productive members of a group. When group norms are violated, a group or team either must revisit those norms to determine whether they still are committed to that norm or try to instruct the person who violated that norm in the "expected" and "correct" behavior (Reid & Hammersley, 2000).

Types of Groups

Groups can take on a variety of purposes or functions, depending on their goals. The most common types of groups are social, learning, task, and growth or therapy groups.

Social Groups Social groups are *formal or informal groups of individuals who gather to meet the personal, communal, and collective needs of people.* As you read in Chapter 6, today's social groups and networks can be established online via Facebook, LinkedIn, Twitter, and other social media, as well as face to face through our churches, clubs, and neighborhoods. Facebook is the most popular source of online social networking. Because it is so new, research about the users of Facebook (and other forms of social media) still is developing. However, we do know the following about the demographics of Facebook users (Corbett, 2010):

Ages 13–17	10.4%	Males	42.6%
Ages 18–24	25.3%	Females	54.3%
Ages 25–34	24.9%	Unknown	3.03%
Ages 35–54	29.0%		
Ages 55+	9.5%		

Twitter is another widely used social-media platform for social groups. Twitter accounts that contain links to Web pages and include discussions rather than updates of personal information are becoming very popular. Thousands of people now obtain and share information on legal, technical, or other workplace topics. Professionals share reliable information on their area of expertise. Lawyers such as Andrew Sharpe (@TMT_lawyer) are contacted by those seeking law advice, and Emily Goodhand of Reading University (@CopyrightGirl) provides advice on her Twitter account for those who have copyright questions (Green, 2011). Twitter is not just for use in the workplace, however; many colleges classes now incorporate Twitter as a way to get students to involved. University of Texas at Dallas professors Monica Rankin and David Perry use Twitter to promote student engagement. Professor Rankin, who teaches a class with more than ninety students, provides the opportunity to become more involved in class discussion by setting up a class Twitter account. Rankin invites students to post messages and ask questions during class, which are then displayed on a large screen. Rankin discovered the practice encourages more student participation. Professor Perry uses Twitter to keep students engaged in the course outside of class time. Perry reports that students stay engaged in course material by including on their Twitter account about world events that relate to the course. Business Professor Elaine Young believes Twitter is about creating connection with others and building professional networks (Minors, 2010).

KEENPRESS Productions

NATIONAL GEOGRAPHIC SPEAKS

Alexandra Cousteau: The Internet and Water

Take a sip of water—what do you taste and see? To Alexandra Cousteau, daughter of Philippe and Jan Cousteau, and granddaughter of the legendary Jacques Cousteau, "Water is life." We must redefine our relationships to it and our decisions around it. Cousteau established the Blue Legacy initiative, and she and her team are in the process working with people around the world to "help shape society's dialogue to include water as one of the defining issues of our century." Cousteau and her team are also combining the technologies developed in her grandfather's era with new media opportunities to create platforms for individuals concerned about the environment to speak out about water. And she is undertaking an exploration of many of the world's most precious water ecosystems to chronicle their connectivity and link to our own survival.

Cousteau and her team travel around the world telling the story of our water systems and their centrality to sustaining life on this planet. This story includes the Ganges River in India, "the cultural and spiritual lifeblood" of a nation. The Ganges provides water and spiritual cleansing to more than 400 million people, yet it is literally toxic. More than 400 tannery factories along the river pump more than 20 million liters of waste every day, not to mention raw sewage, into this most sacred of rivers. The story continues in Botswana, where, in a land that is mostly desert, she continues to explore the interconnected nature of water. In an interview with Onkokame Kitso Mokaila, Botswanian minister of the environment, wildlife, and tourism, Cousteau asks how Botswana, a land-locked country, views water as its most precious commodity. Mokaila responds: "All living things require water, whether you are in agriculture, tourism, or wildlife. . . . You have to treat it as gold." Cousteau and her team continue their work and their story as they travel to the Middle East, Mississippi, and Cambodia (forty-five major water sources in all) chronicling "the interconnectivity of water . . . what it means to live in a world where water is our most precious resource" (Boyes, 2011).

To tell her story, Cousteau relies on the most recent Internet technologies. And even though her father and grandfather were pushing the edge of technological advances, Cousteau explains that where the *Calypso* carried a crew of thirty people in the field for months and sent film back to Los Angeles for development, today she is able to work for three months in the field with a crew of only seven and post her stories immediately. She sees this as truly engaging people and as a truly interactive experience. Working with others and media in this way is very exciting for Cousteau. "From a communication standpoint, to be able to engage people through their networks and give them stories to talk about and start conversations around is one of our greatest opportunities" for change. Where 50,000 people see a movie in a theater, "I can reach 50,000 people in a day and maybe in an hour with this next expedition" (Cousteau, 2009, 2011, 2012).

Cousteau works as a member of a team, yet she presents information on panels and at symposiums and even narrates videos and interviews individuals who are working in environmental preservation.

 CourseMate Connection: Go to cengagebrain.com to access your CourseMate for *Invitation to Human Communication* to view a video about Alexandra Cousteau.

Steve Mcculloch/National Geographic

1. Alexandra Cousteau's family has a legacy of credibility from her grandfather's work as well as the work her mother and father did in oceanography. What kinds of power do you think this gives Alexandra Cousteau? What kinds of power do you think she is most comfortable using as she works with her team of explorers?

2. Although technology can be used for uncivil and unethical ends, Cousteau uses technology to capture and disseminate her story. What are the civil aspects of her use of technology? What might be some potential uncivil aspects that her team would want to consider?

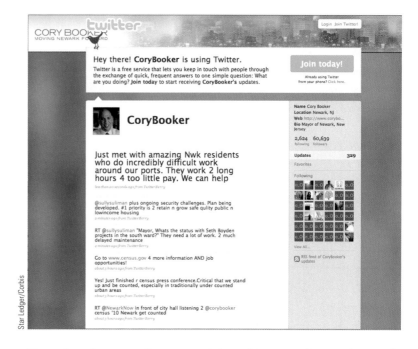

If your college instructor started a class discussion on Twitter, would you be more likely to engage with the class?

Star Ledger/Corbis

Even though many of us use social-media networking online and it is a powerful way to maintain a social group, research also reminds us that "face-to-face time makes us happier than relying solely on social media to communicate." Researchers surveyed between 500 and 1,000 people in sixteen different countries and discovered that 40 percent reported "catching up with loved ones after work was the happiest time of their day." Only 5 percent said "they were happiest when connecting online with friends," and only 2 percent said "the first text message of the day made them joyful" (Fahmy, 2010).

Task Groups Sometimes called *problem-solving groups,* **task groups** *are formed when individuals want to take on a job or solve an issue that is affecting them or those around them.* Missionary groups, Mothers Against Drunk Driving (MADD), and People for the Ethical Treatment of Animals (PETA) are examples of task groups. When task groups form to address an issue, the issue or problem can be close to home or something taking place in another city, state, or even country. When task or problem-solving groups are working at their best, they usually follow several stages or steps:

identifying the problem,

gathering information about the problem,

analyzing the information and the problem,

suggesting possible solutions,

considering the implications of those solutions,

reaching a decision about the best solution, and

implementing that solution. (Dewey, 1910)

Task groups also must consider the **ethics** of their problem-solving efforts, which can be defined as the *moral standards behind the decisions*

task groups
problem-solving groups formed when individuals want to take on a job or solve an issue that is affecting them or those around them.

ethics
moral standards behind the decisions and how they affect others.

ETHICAL MOMENT

© Trevor Hunt/istockphoto

Can Maneuvers for Power Be Avoided?

Ethical communication is an "explicit system" of individual and group "responsibilities and rights." According to organizational communication scholar Karen Ashcraft, ethical communication "mandates authentic expression, declaring the group's right to know individual agendas. It asserts the group's duty to make room for all voices, affirming the individual's right to be heard." It also addresses conflict promptly, directly, and with "mutual accountability" (Ashcraft, 2001). Ethical communication is grounded in *open communication* that recognizes that hostility, hidden agendas, and misinformation block progress for a group and can inhibit change. Seven principles follow this commitment to open communication. Read these principles and then consider the questions at the end of the list.

1. *Different perspectives enrich the group process, and every member's views are important.* Rather than supporting conformity or the superiority of one or two voices over others, the goal of the group's communication is to find a mutual and acceptable balance among equal voices.

2. *Silencing others is a power-over maneuver.* Silencing others discourages true consensus and decreases long-term commitment to the group's goals and decisions. Communication within the group should promote individual expression and a feeling of being heard.

3. *Communication should create a climate in which opposing views can be raised.* Group members should feel free to express and negotiate their positions openly. Even though an individual might hold a very different view, she or he should not feel alone.

4. *Group members should address each situation as directly as possible.* Individuals in the group are responsible for

communicating clearly and directly with one another. Members of the group will not "tell tales" or spread rumors about others, and they will address issues directly with the person or people involved.

5. *Conflict does not always have to be engaged, but it has to be named openly and clearly.* Hiding or avoiding conflict creates negative environments and encourages negative communication, which can damage individuals. Each member of a group is responsible for "naming what is going on" when conflict arises.

6. *Personal relationships affect the whole group.* Individual relationships have an effect on the whole group. They are sources of affiliation, power, and conflict.

7. *The means are the ends.* How we communicate with others defines the product or outcome of the communication. How we communicate with others expresses our values, commitments, and relationship to the group and its goals.

What Do You Think?

1. Do you think you could practice ethical communication as it was just described? Why or why not?

2. Can you think of times when you or someone you know practiced ethical communication? Describe those situations.

3. Do you agree with principle five—that conflict does not always have to be engaged but it does have to be named openly? Why or why not?

4. What do you think Ashcraft means by principle seven—"the means are the ends"? Are there times when this principle might not matter to a communication situation? Offer examples.

---

and how they affect others. In considering the ethical component of a problem, a task group must take into account the diversity of perspectives it actually has considered, whether or not the actual voices of those affected by the problem and the possible solutions have been solicited and listened to, and any hidden or unintended consequences of the solution to the group. Without this kind of ethical consideration, task groups may be creating more problems than they solve or causing harms they did not intend to cause as they implement a solution.

Learning Groups **Learning groups** function to *teach members a new skill or to provide them with new information.* Study groups and classes are common examples of this type of group. Learning groups often have explicit agendas, and when you join or start a learning group you will want to learn or state that agenda clearly. This will help you decide if the learning group is right for you to join, and it helps those who might be thinking about joining the group in making that same decision. Although an agenda may be stated explicitly, sometimes learning groups also have **hidden agendas** or *unspoken goals and visions for the group that a can get in the way of progress or take a group in a direction other than the one it has explicitly stated.* When hidden agendas take over, they can detract "from the real work at hand. Even a discussion that seems to be centered on substantial issues may, at a deeper level, concern issues of power, prestige, and other personal needs" (Kets de Vires, 2001, p. 189). You can sometimes spot a hidden agenda when your efforts to raise an issue or solve a problem are met with resistance, or when the issue is tabled or reframed so that it does not address the original issue you raised.

hidden agendas
unspoken goals and visions for the group that a can get in the way of progress or take a group in a direction other than the one it has explicitly stated.

Growth and Therapy Groups **Growth groups** are *groups whose goals are to help individuals cope with issues, recover from a crisis or trauma, or resolve personal concerns.* The group's common goal is to assist others in healing or resolving issues. In growth and therapy groups, self-expression, support, analysis, exploration, and conversation about the issues being addressed are the primary focus. Growth and therapy groups often are led by an experienced counselor or therapist, and they can bring different individuals together who are facing a similar crisis (cancer, for example) or an entire family or several families struggling with a common problem (such as alcoholism). Growth and therapy groups can last for years, or they can form for a shorter time and disband once the situation is resolved or even when it becomes apparent that group support is no longer productive or helpful (Davison, Pennebaker, & Dickerson, 2000; Goodwin et al., 2001; Kelly et al., 1993).

growth group
group whose goals are to help individuals cope with issues, recover from a crisis or trauma, or resolve personal concerns.

PRACTICING HUMAN COMMUNICATION

Speaking Up

Imagine you are working with a group of students to complete a class project. At the first meeting, the other students quickly decide on a project idea and begin dividing up the work. You are concerned that the other members rushed into a decision without discussing other ideas. Consider how you will respond. Now discuss as a class ways to handle and respond to groupthink.

Strengths of Groups and Teams
Working in a team or group can have many advantages. Let us look at a list of the strengths of working in groups and teams. Working as a team, individuals

- share different knowledge bases and experiences;
- contribute different skill sets and expertise;
- work collaboratively to create new ideas, products, and solutions;
- praise and reward one another;

identify and troubleshoot problems together;

help one another accomplish a task; and

develop an identity and a sense of belonging.

When groups are working well together, these strengths and advantages provide individuals a sense of well-being and a collective purpose. With many people working together productively on a task, a group often can accomplish a good deal more than a single individual working alone. In short, when groups and teams function well, there can be considerable positive payoffs for the individuals involved as well as the solutions and ideas they develop.

Animal rights activists often use public protests to advocate for the rights of animals and against using them to test products. Use Ashcraft's ideas for ethical communication to access the effectiveness of this approach to resolve differences.

Limitations of Groups and Teams

Working in groups and teams can have limitations, though, and it is important to recognize not only the strengths of group work but also the limitations. Let us look at a list of the disadvantages of group work. Working as a team, individuals must

make time to communicate with one another,

make the time to process information together,

support those individuals who need more time to develop a skill or idea,

focus on group goals rather than individual advancement and promotion, and

be willing to resolve conflicts civilly and ethically.

Although these limitations are not insurmountable, taking the time to work with others in a busy world can sometimes feel like a burden. Sometimes we do not want to put aside our differences for the good of the group goal, or we simply do not support a direction the group is moving in. Being patient with others as they develop a new skill or explore an idea also can be frustrating when we are in a rush to move forward. When you find yourself working in a group, it is important to consider the strengths and weaknesses of group work. Regardless of whether the group is functioning well or struggling, recognizing that there are both strengths and limitations of working in a group will help you remain a productive member of the group.

Students often are assigned group projects. Can you recall one experience where the group worked well together and one where it did not? What were the strengths and limitations of those groups?

Technology in Groups and Teams

In *Digital Freedom: How Much Can You Handle?* (2008), Narian Batra asks two questions: "How much freedom do you need?" "How much privacy do you need?" Batra suggests that the explosion of technology that has occurred over the past several decades means that individuals must consider questions and issues of surveillance, intellectual property, and the ways in which technologies shape each moment of our working (and social) lives. Batra calls attention to what he calls the "boundlessness of the Internet" and "its impact upon human expression, privacy, and social controls" (Batra, 2008, p. 1). But what does this mean for our work as members of groups and teams?

Technology and Time

No one can dispute the fact that the infusion of technology into the workplace has saved us considerable time. We can retrieve and transmit information quickly and efficiently, and we can connect instantly with individuals who are not physically present. Because of technology, we can do many parts of our work faster than ever before. Indeed, we have saved others and ourselves considerable time. Yet with so much information available to us, the ability to connect with so many people so quickly, and the fact that we can take technology with us wherever we are, we sometimes find ourselves spending inordinate amounts of time working through technology. We research and retrieve, communicate constantly with others, write and rewrite documents and reports, compile images and graphs, and create our own videos and Web sites—and we can do all this from our offices, homes, cars, bus stops, taxis, waiting rooms, coffee shops, restaurants, grocery stores, health clubs, sporting events, and the like. It is no wonder that we sometimes feel that technology is all that there is or that we do.

In groups, technology can present many of the following time-related dilemmas (Kiesler & Sproull, 1992):

Too much time is spent responding to inquiries by others.

Too much time is spent sending inquiries to others.

Missed messages cause delays or misunderstandings.

Time is spent avoiding sending responses to messages sent by others.

Repetitive information comes with the "Reply All" or "Forward" functions on e-mail.

Overly lengthy conversations are held on listservs and in chat rooms.

Virtual meetings may leave us feeling dissatisfied with or disconnected from other members of a group.

Virtual meetings must be scheduled with people working in different time zones.

Mountains of information available on the Internet must be sorted through.

Mountains of documents sent to us by others must be worked through and sorted.

So although technology can be a tremendous benefit, it can also demand many hours of our days and weeks as we communicate with other members of our groups and teams. As Batra suggests, the tremendous freedom we gain with technology also comes at a price: our time.

Technology and Civility

Similar to technology and its effects on our time in groups and teams, technology also has affected our level of civility with others. Technology helps us reach out and connect professionally, positively, and respectfully with others. We can receive a message from someone and take time to sort out what and why that person might be asking us to take on a new job or solve a problem for them. We can acknowledge the speed with which a person responds to our questions and concerns, and we sometimes communicate more effectively when we are using e-mail, offering more detail or context in a difficult or complex situation or checking and verifying facts and opinions before we reply to others. However, the technology coin also has its uncivil side. With technology, we can engage in the following uncivil behaviors. We may, for instance,

expect immediate replies to our inquiries,

forward messages and texts that make others look bad,

distribute photos that cast others in an unprofessional light,

misrepresent others by using images and e-mail messages inappropriately,

engage in cyberbullying,

gain access to other peoples' private information via hacking or surveillance,

take credit for the ideas generated by members of the group, and

plagiarize information from the Internet.

As groups work together via technology, conversations about protocols, boundaries, and respect can help them practice civility rather than incivility. Although accidents do happen—for example, we might mistakenly forward a message we were not supposed to or expect a quick reply when a slow one is coming—there are several guidelines groups can implement to help them manage time and civility with regard to technology. Because electronic communication does not allow for the cues we get when we are communicating with group members face to face, guidelines such as these can help a group work together productively and avoid unnecessary conflict or misunderstandings (Table 8.1).

TABLE 8.1   TECHNOLOGY GUIDES

Discuss how much interaction will take place via technology:
Identify whether the group is a virtual work group or the members will also meet face to face.
Determine how much and what kind of communication will take place electronically and in person (meetings in person or information shared electronically).

Discuss timelines for working electronically:
Establish reasonable timelines for responding to electronic inquiries (2 hours, 24 hours, 2 days).
Establish exemptions for these timelines (emergencies that delay a response or increase the need for an urgent response).
Establish protocols for listservs and chat rooms (how many, how many postings are expected, how often they should be read).

Discuss protocols for sharing information:
Establish guidelines for forwarding messages (never; only when given permission; all messages sent can be forwarded to others).
Establish guidelines for length and number of attachments (different projects will require different kinds of information, so be clear about reasonable workload management).

Establish frameworks for giving people credit for the work they do:
Determine whether reports will be written and authored collaboratively or by one person (the contact person, first author, or responsible party or parties).
Identify ways to give all those involved credit for their contributions (list names by amount of work done alphabetically, by seniority, or by some other format).
Discuss plagiarism and how to avoid it (define what the group means by plagiarism; establish practices that record who and where information and ideas come from).

Establish guidelines for civility:
Define civility and share examples of what it is and is not (acknowledging others for their good work would be civil; discrediting individuals or damaging their reputation would be uncivil).
Identify what kinds of information are private and what information can be made public (determine whether you can share good news and bad news with other members of the group, for example).
Set standards for electronic styles of communication (how formal and informal messages can be and when formality or informality is expected).
Rotate meetings when different time zones are a part of the group (alternating early mornings and late afternoon or evenings).

© Cengage Learning 2014

---

role
expected and defined pattern of behavior carried out by an individual or individuals.

formal role
role that is clearly defined and assigned.

informal role
role that is not formally assigned to individuals in the group.

 Roles in Groups and Teams

Every group and team has formal and informal roles. A **role** is *an expected and defined pattern of behavior carried out by an individual or individuals.* **Formal roles** are those that are *clearly defined and assigned*—team captain, meeting facilitator, and note taker, for example. Formal roles help a group function smoothly, and they provide order and predictability for the members of a group. **Informal roles** are those *roles that are not formally assigned to individuals in the group*, and they usually are not talked about directly or even acknowledged by the group. These informal roles, sometimes called *functional roles*, are as important as the formal ones, but they also can be a source of group conflict. This is because they can remain unrecognized and unappreciated, even though people are doing important work, or because individuals compete for these informal roles in order to receive rewards or praise. Table 8.2 shows the most common informal or functional roles in groups:

TABLE 8.2   INFORMAL ROLES

TASK ROLES

Information giver	Provides information to the group
Information seeker	Requests information be provided
Opinion giver	States preferences about what group should do or think
Opinion seeker	Seeks the preferences and thoughts of others in the group
Starter	Gets the group going on tasks, discussions, brainstorming, etc.
Direction giver	Tells others how and when a task should be done
Summarizer	Reviews the discussion and sums up ideas and issues
Diagnoser	Identifies potential and real problems
Energizer	Gets the group excited and moving forward
Gatekeeper	Monitors and controls the process and individual input
Reality tester	Checks to see if the tasks and goals are realistic and feasible

RELATIONAL ROLES

Participation encourager	Makes sure all voices are heard and recognized
Harmonizer	Works to reduce conflicts and disagreements
Tension reliever	Provides humor to relax and lighten the mood
Evaluator of emotional climate	Assesses how others might be feeling; shares own feelings with group
Praise giver	Encourages others and expresses approval
Empathic listener	Listens to others for clarification and without evaluation

DYSFUNCTIONAL ROLES

Blocker	Rejects ideas, refuses to cooperate, takes a negative stand on all issues
Attacker	Aggressive toward others, challenges and attacks people and ideas
Recognition seeker	Seeks acknowledgment and praise, exaggerates accomplishments
Joker	Uses humor to avoid productive conversation and participation
Withdrawer	Remains aloof, daydreams, engages in side conversations
Cynic	Skeptical of all options; voices inevitable failure of group efforts

Source: Adapted from Frey (1999, 2003), Putnam and Stohl (1990), and Wilson and Hanna (1986).

Emergence of Roles

Although formal roles in groups are usually assigned (note taker or facilitator, for example), the informal roles listed in Table 8.2 usually develop without direct communication among group members. Instead of assigning these roles, people tend to gravitate toward them. In most groups, you will notice that certain people regularly ask for additional information, others look out for the emotional tone of meetings or offer praise, and still others remain aloof or are jokers with each project assigned to the group. In groups that are functioning well, individuals will rotate in and out of both formal and informal roles. Different individuals will take on the role of facilitator, note taker, energizer, starter, opinion giver, or information seeker, for example, at various stages in a project or even as the group works on different projects together.

Role-Related Problems and Solutions

Most groups experience minor struggles and problems related to the roles individuals adopt in the group. This might happen when there is a bid for a role and one person feels it is necessary to compete for a role at the expense of others. For example, a member of the group might want to be the sole evaluator or diagnoser and will not allow anyone else to occupy that role. Occasionally, role-related problems are severe enough for the group to disband, but usually these problems can be overcome. In this section, we will look at three of the most common role-related problems groups face and the ways in which groups can successfully overcome those problems and work together productively.

One of the first problems that groups might face is individuals competing for both formal and informal roles. This happens when several people see themselves as the formal leader of the group or when more than one person competes for an informal role such as the direction giver. A second problem can arise when there is a shortage of people to fill roles. In this situation, no one wants to be the note taker, for example, or none of the group members takes on the informal role of analyzer. Finally, problems can arise when individuals become too attached to their roles and insist on performing them when they are unnecessary. This can happen when the emotional evaluator continually shares emotions or constantly checks in on the emotions of others or when the joker insists on cracking jokes at every opportunity. Although these problems can disrupt the work of the group, Table 8.3 illustrates several ways to solve them.

Decision Making in Groups

One of the most widely used methods to solve problems and come to a decision is the **reflective-thinking method**, which was developed by philosopher John Dewey. This *six-step method is used to structure a problem-solving and decision-making discussion.* The name of this method highlights the importance of using a thoughtful and reflective process that involves taking a careful, systematic approach to a problem. The following are the six steps of this model:

1. Identify the problem.
2. Analyze the problem.
3. Suggest possible solutions.

reflective-thinking method

six-step method for structuring a problem-solving and decision-making discussion.

TABLE 8.3   SOLUTIONS TO ROLE-RELATED PROBLEMS

Identify the roles that people are competing for.	If they are formal roles, dialogue with the group to determine who should fill each role. If they are informal roles, communicate as a group about those roles as well, naming the function and contributions of each role, as well as the dysfunction of some of them. Identify the group norms for productive and professional behaviors as members take on different formal and informal roles.
Identify the roles that no one is filling.	If they are formal roles, develop a plan for filling the important ones and talk about those that might not be necessary for that particular task and eliminate them. If they are informal roles, dialogue as a group about those and decide whether to move some of the informal roles to the status of formal. The group might decide, for example, that the gatekeeper role is particular important if there is considerable disagreement or energy around a project. Turn those important informal roles into formal ones.
Check to be sure that roles are being rotated.	Discuss with the group the importance of rotating both formal and informal group roles. Communicate about the value of each role, as well as the problems caused by the dysfunctional roles. Pay attention to who typically assumes a role; perhaps assign someone to monitor roles and ensure their rotation.
Discuss with the group strategies for avoiding the dysfunctional roles.	If the group is just forming, talk about strategies for identifying dysfunctional roles and for stopping them if they happen. If the group has been together for some time, hold a meeting to discuss productive roles, unproductive roles, and how to manage them so that the group can work effectively. Make sure all of the members of the group share their perspectives and are heard during this conversation. This will help the group identify and understand why the dysfunctional roles are happening and how to minimize them.

© Cengage Learning 2014

4. Consider the implications of the solutions.

5. Reach a decision about the best solution.

6. Implement the solution.

We now look at these steps in more detail.

Identify the Problem

The first step of the reflective-thinking model is problem identification. In this stage of the decision-making process, group participants identify the nature of the problem, the extent of the problem, who is affected by

Alexandra Cousteau,
Emerging Explorer Social Environment Advocate

Are there specific decision-making strategies that you employ in your work? Can you tell us why they are effective?

My team and I are very strict with regard to personal integrity. We are always very courteous to the local community and respectful— we don't leave behind a mess. That's incredibly important to me. When it comes to how we tackle problems or projects, we listen to each other's ideas and work things out collaboratively. And I think the most important thing that I've learned is to be strategic rather than opportunistic. I have a strategy for what we want to accomplish. The projects that are meaningful and part of the strategy, that are helping us move forward with how we shape the conversation, are ones we take on. If they don't match up to those requirements, then we send our regrets.

the problem, and the impact on those affected. Groups often do considerable research and may use an invitational approach at this stage to be sure that they have identified all aspects of the problem they have been asked to solve. Once the group identifies the problem, it moves on to the next step of the model—problem analysis.

Analyze the Problem

It might be natural to jump to a discussion of solutions to the problems that have been identified. Instead, effective group communication starts by discussing why the problem exists. Much like a physician who must diagnose a patient's illness, the reflective thinker must understand the causes of the problem before moving on to discussing solutions. Besides helping the group arrive at a more reasoned solution, this step helps the group present its findings more successfully. At this stage, you will want to continue to use an open, invitational approach to ensure as full an understanding of the problem as possible. After group members have thought carefully about the reasons the problem exists, they can move on to suggesting solutions.

Suggest Possible Solutions

A popular method used by groups at this stage of the problem-analysis process is **brainstorming**, the *process of generating ideas randomly and uncritically without attention to logic, connections, or relevance.* When groups brainstorm, they suggest as many ideas as they can think of without judging those ideas. After the group has listed as many ideas as possible, they can do two things. They can go through the list and eliminate those ideas that are not suitable until just a few options remain. Or the group may rank a longer list of options and then choose the solution that has the most support.

brainstorming
process of generating ideas randomly and uncritically without attention to logic, connections, or relevance.

A potential pitfall for groups as they generate solutions is *groupthink* (discussed previously), which occurs when the group conforms to a single frame of mind and chooses a solution without fully and objectively examining other possible solutions. Groups that fall victim to groupthink often are under a tight timeline, are pressured by a leader, or are afraid to question each other's ideas. They also tend to get along well and favor consensus over conflict. Groupthink can be avoided by having a group member play the role of devil's advocate who questions the decisions made or ideas offered, removing the group's leader from discussions, or taking time to fully evaluate each solution.

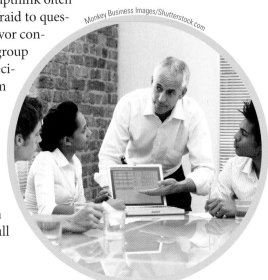

Monkey Business Images/Shutterstock.com

Consider the Implications of the Solutions

After a group has arrived at potential solutions, it studies the implications of those solutions. The discussion in the group should avoid immediately enacting a single solution and instead take time to fully examine its disadvantages or impact on others. This requires a good deal of discussion about cause and effect to allow the group to explore the full implications of each solution that is identified as feasible.

Reach a Decision about the Best Solution

Groups may use several methods to reach a decision about the best solution. For example, if the group has time and resources to implement a pilot study, it can study the effects of the decision over a period of time. Groups can also use reasoning to choose the solution that has the fewest detrimental effects. Groups can also use a consensus model for deciding on the solution, which requires all members to agree on a single best solution. Or it can use a simple voting process, with the majority of group members supporting a single solution over others.

Groups often brainstorm ideas as they consider the impact of the solutions to a problem. Computers can help groups identify potential affects. Can you recall a time when you used your computer to help your group solve a problem?

Implement the Solution

Although Dewey's reflective-thinking model originally had five steps, researchers now often include a sixth step: implementing the solution. In this stage, the group determines how to carry out what it has decided. It is important for the group to consider who will be responsible for the different parts of the solution and when the solution should be implemented. Although it is not a part of Dewey's model, groups often return to step one to assess whether or not there are any new problems they need to address as a result of the process they have just completed.

When you work in groups, you will be faced with a variety of problems to solve and issues to sort through. When you use six steps for solving problems, you can help your group arrive at a solution that will actually solve the problem and should benefit all involved.

Culture and Communication in Groups

As our teams and groups become more international and diverse, they consist of individuals with different backgrounds, cultures, and ways of working with one another. Scholars agree that there are five major ways that a culture affects its individuals, and by culture they refer not only to national and ethnic cultures but also to regional and even community or business cultures. The five ways in which cultures can present challenges are discussed in the following sections as well as how those differences might affect us as we communicate in groups and teams (Hofstede, 2010; Stohl, 2001).

Collectivism and Individualism

A culture values collectivism when it promotes interdependence, community, and loyalty to the group, family, or community. A culture values individualism when it promotes independence, self-reliance, and looking out for one's own self (recall that you learned about collectivistic and individualistic cultures in Chapter 6).

How This Affects Groups and Teams Individualistic members of a group will be more likely to look out for their own needs, whereas collectivist members will look out for the needs of the whole group. Individualistic members work well independently; collectivistic members work well collaboratively.

Equality and Inequality

A culture that values equality will work to ensure that all members are cared for and treated equally, whereas a culture that sees inequalities as an accepted part of life will be comfortable with some of its members having more than others. This is sometimes referred to as *power distance*, or the degree to which members of a culture are comfortable with differences in power.

How This Affects Groups and Teams Individuals from cultures that value equality and sameness will be less likely to be comfortable with power hierarchies and the benefits given to those higher up in the hierarchy. They also may be less comfortable following a decision made by authority and more likely to be comfortable with consensus forms of decision making. Individuals from cultures that accept or see inequality as inevitable will follow leaders and authorities with more ease. They also will work to earn authority so that they can be higher on the hierarchy.

Uncertainty and Change

Cultures that value uncertainty and change are comfortable with risk, ambiguity, and even indecision. Cultures that value certainty and stability are more comfortable with strong convictions, clear expectations, and firm protocols for working together.

How This Affects Groups and Teams Individuals from cultures that value uncertainty will be more comfortable with flexible norms and rules and fluid processes for working together and solving problems. Individuals from cultures that value certainty will be happier with clear rules and norms and clearly defined rules for working together, making decisions, and solving problems.

Task and Social Orientation

Cultures that value task orientation are cultures that focus on training, learning the latest methods and technologies, and on "getting the job done." Task-oriented cultures value efficiency and saving time by doing a job well or accomplishing a task quickly. Cultures that value social orientation are cultures that put relationships before tasks and will work to avoid hurting people just to finish a job quickly.

How This Affects Groups and Teams Socially oriented members of a group or team will focus on creating a welcoming and friendly atmosphere, and they will monitor the feelings and undercurrents of group members and dynamics. They may slow down a group decision to ensure that the relationships in the group stay healthy. Task-oriented members of a group will push to get a job done and seek efficiency in making decisions. They may push a decision forward at the expense of group satisfaction.

Short- and Long-Term Orientation

Cultures with a short-term orientation look for immediate benefits or payoffs from a group's efforts and work. Short-term orientations encourage members to focus on the most pressing issue or the most obvious and direct advantage to a process or decision. Cultures that have a long-term orientation are willing to put off immediate gratification for rewards that come much later down the road. Long-term orientations encourage group members to consider what may happen later or what the consequences of a decision may be weeks or years from the time the decision is made.

How This Affects Groups and Teams Individuals from cultures with long-term orientations encourage a group to focus beyond the immediate and take a more visionary, interconnected, or even sustainable view of a process or decision. Individuals from cultures with a short-term orientation are quick to get a job done, and they encourage a group to focus on narrower goals and actions that lead to immediate decisions and solutions to issues.

Types of Group Presentations

Members of a group often have to report on the decisions they have made, make recommendations, or share the information they have gathered and compiled with other entities. These presentations can take several forms, and the most common are oral reports, panel discussions, symposiums, team presentations, and online forums.

Oral Reports

Oral reports are *presentations given by one or two of the group members who present a group's findings, conclusions, or proposals to other members of the group or to a larger audience.* When you present an oral report, use the skills you will learn in Chapters 10 to 15 for giving a speech. Remember to prepare your general purpose, specific purpose, and thesis statement. Outline your main points and select your pattern of organization. Be sure to prepare an introduction that catches your audience's attention, reveals the topic of your report, establishes your credibility, and previews your main points. Include connectives between the major sections of your report and write a conclusion that reinforces your thesis statement and brings your presentation to a close.

oral reports
presentations given by one or two of the group members who present a group's findings, conclusions, or proposals to other members of the group or to a larger audience.

When you give an oral report, remember that you either are speaking to other members of your group who may be familiar with the issues under consideration or to outside audiences who may be less familiar but are highly invested in the issue. Be sure to consider your audience carefully, the amount of time you have for the presentation, and whether or not you will have technology to help you present your information. Carefully considering these factors will help you design and deliver a successful oral report.

Panel Discussions

A **panel discussion** is a *structured discussion among group members and facilitated by a moderator that takes place in front of an audience.* When you are part of a panel discussion, you not only share your ideas with the other members of your group but also share them with a larger audience. A panel discussion typically begins with brief opening statements by each panelist followed by an informal discussion among panelists about their ideas. A moderator, who may be a member of the panel, facilitates the discussion. Usually, the discussion becomes more focused as group members learn from each other and the audience. Occasionally, the moderator or panel members may wrap up the discussion and summarize what has been said, but just as often the discussion ends without resolution or summary. Because the goal of the panel discussion is to react to the ideas of another person, it is an ideal setting for invitational communication (Chapter 15). Group members can present their current thinking on a topic, learn from each other and the audience, and refine their ideas for future decision making.

When you are part of a panel discussion, prepare your opening remarks beforehand, thinking of your speech as a short informative speech that previews what you hope to discuss during the session. Then view your participation in the discussion as a series of short speeches in which you develop a particular idea, invite others to understand your perspective, explore an issue with the other panel members, or encourage others to adopt your views. If you can, work closely with other members of your group to be sure that you are not duplicating information and that you are presenting the full spectrum of information your group has gathered.

Symposiums

A **symposium** is a *public discussion in which several people each give speeches on different aspects of the same topic.* Unlike panel discussions, which usually feature short opening statements by the participants, symposium speakers usually have fully prepared speeches that are formally presented. At a symposium, either the speakers are experts in a particular subject area or a topic may be divided into different areas so the audience can learn about many aspects of a single topic. If you are part of a symposium, a moderator usually introduces each speaker and his or her topic and facilitates audience questions and comments if appropriate. Symposiums usually feature three to five speakers, with each person speaking for ten to fifteen minutes. Typically, a symposium session lasts anywhere from one to two hours, with the time divided between the participants and audience questions.

panel discussion

structured discussion among group members and facilitated by a moderator that takes place in front of an audience.

symposium

public discussion in which several people each give speeches on different aspects of the same topic.

If you are part of a symposium, follow the procedures for giving your speech outlined in Chapters 10 to 15. You probably will find that you use a manuscript for this presentation or that your speaking outline is quite detailed. Remember to stay within your time limits so other speakers can present their speeches and to ensure time for the question-and-answer session. Typically, a moderator will time the speeches and give signals to the speakers as their time reaches the end. Be sure to practice your presentations before you give the speech and anticipate questions from the audience so you can formulate your answers. Again, work with your group before the symposium to ensure a fair and comprehensive presentation of information.

Team Presentations

A **team presentation** consists of *several individual members of a group, with each presenting a different speech on a single topic.* For instance, you might make a team presentation with other members of your group so you can present a proposal for a new program or product you have developed as a team. Each speech is formal, with speakers addressing different parts of the proposal or product and each speaker using similar delivery styles. The individual speeches in team presentations follow each other without interruption. To make sure the presentation flows smoothly, team presentations usually have one group member acting as the moderator.

team presentation
when several individual members of a group each present a different speech on a single topic.

If you give a team presentation, it should be well organized using one of the organizational patterns that will be discussed in Chapter 10. Ask each group member to give a speech on a single main point, with one member presenting the introduction and conclusion. This person usually is the moderator, who may introduce each speaker and his or her topic. Team presentations are common in groups that work in businesses, as well as grassroots or community organizations that want to present proposals to city councils or other government entities. Team presentations are very collaborative projects, so make sure that your group has given itself enough time to work together to develop the presentation and then for each member to practice those presentations before you deliver them.

Online Forums

Today's workplace also lends itself to online group presentations and discussions. **Forums** *occur when messages or topics are posted online and individuals have an opportunity to post their individual responses and ideas to those original messages.* Forums are an excellent way for members of a group to present their ideas to a select audience and then receive feedback and input from that audience about those ideas. Typically, online forums have a moderator who is in charge of posting the original information, organizing the categories or topics to be discussed (which become known as *threads*), and setting the time constraints for the discussion. Group members will be in charge of setting rules for the discussion, determining if and when individuals might be asked to leave the discussion, and compiling a summary of the various threads and subthreads from the forum (Bulletin Community Forum FAQ, n.d.; Cong, Wang, Lin, Song, & Sun, 2008; Internet and Environmental Education, 2010; Jansenn & Kies, 2005; "What Is an 'Internet Forum'?" n.d.).

forums
occur when messages or topics are posted online and individuals have an opportunity to post their individual responses and ideas to those original messages.

Chapter Summary

A Group Is a Small Number of People Who Belong Together, Share Something in Common, or Are Assigned a Similar Task

- Teams come together to attempt to win something, to set a record, or to be the best at a task or event.
- The features of groups and teams include size, cohesion, and several types of power (legitimate, coercive, reward, referent, and expert power). Reciprocal power dynamics are called *power with*.
- The most common types of groups are social, learning, task, and growth or therapy groups.
- Working in a team or group has advantages that include but are not limited to sharing knowledge and skills, creating new products or solutions, troubleshooting problems, and accomplishing a task. Disadvantages include difficulty making time to communicate or process information together, focusing on group goals, and being willing to resolve conflicts civilly and ethically.
- Groups and teams use technology to communicate efficiently and with civility. Deadlines and protocols are important for success, as well as giving credit to people for their work and establishing guidelines for civility.

In Every Group and Team, the Members Take on Formal or Informal Roles

- Formal roles are clearly defined and assigned. Informal roles usually are not talked about directly and include a variety of task, relational, and dysfunctional roles.
- Most groups and teams experience role-related problems such as competition for certain roles, not enough members to fill the roles, or becoming overly attached to a role. Strategies to solve these problems include identifying certain roles, rotating roles, and avoiding dysfunctional roles.

The Reflective-Thinking Method Is a Method for Solving Problems and Decision Making in Groups

- This method includes identifying and analyzing the problem, suggesting and considering solutions, reaching a decision, and implementing the solution.

Culture Affects the Members of a Group

- Members from individualistic cultures may work independently and look out for their needs; members from collectivistic cultures may look out for the needs of the group.
- Members from cultures that value equity may be less comfortable with power hierarchies; members from cultures that accept inequities may be more comfortable with hierarchy and authority .
- Members from cultures that value uncertainty and change may be comfortable with flexible norms and rules and fluid processes; members from cultures that value stability may be happier with clear rules and norms for working together.
- Members from cultures that value social orientation may focus on creating a welcoming atmosphere and may take more time making a decision; members from a culture that values task orientation may make a decision quickly at the expense of group satisfaction.
- Members from cultures that value long-term orientations may take a more visionary focus; members from cultures that value short-term orientations may encourage a more immediate decision and action.

There Are Five Common Types of Group Presentations: Oral Reports, Panel Discussions, Symposiums, Team Presentations, and Online Forums

- Oral reports are presentations given by one or two of the group members who present a group's findings, conclusions, or proposals to other members of the group or to a larger audience.
- A panel discussion is a structured discussion among group members facilitated by a moderator that takes place in front of an audience.
- A symposium is a public discussion in which several people each give speeches on different aspects of the same topic.
- A team presentation consists of several individual members of a group, with each one presenting a different speech on a single topic.
- Online forums occur when messages or topics are posted online and individuals have an opportunity to post their individual responses and ideas to those original messages.

Key Concepts

brainstorming (190)	groupthink (173)	panel discussion (194)	social groups (177)
coercive power (174)	growth/therapy group (182)	power over (173)	symposium (194)
cohesiveness (173)	hidden agendas (182)	power with (176)	task groups (180)
ethics (180)	informal role (186)	referent power (175)	team (172)
expert power (175)	learning groups (182)	reflective-thinking method (188)	team presentation (195)
formal role (186)	legitimate power (174)	reward power (175)	virtual group (176)
forums (195)	norms (176)	role (186)	
group (172)	oral reports (193)		

 ## Invitation to Human Communication Online

Speech Communication CourseMate includes an interactive eBook and interactive learning tools including National Geographic Explorer videos, student videos, quizzes, flash cards, and more. Speech Builder Express 3.0 and Speech Studio 2.0 are also available. Go to cengagebrain.com to access your CourseMate for *Invitation to Human Communication* where these resources are located.

Further Reflection and Discussion

1. Have you ever experienced groupthink? What was the group? How would you describe the cohesive in-group and the drive to be united? What alternative actions may have benefited the group if the groupthink attitude had not been present? Who was silenced in the group? What differing opinions did not come to light?

2. Think about different historical figures (presidents, civil rights leaders, and so on) who have each of these kinds of power: coercive power, reward power, referent power, and expert power. Explain how each historical figure exhibited the characteristics of that type of power.

3. Batra's book *Digital Freedom: How Much Can You Handle?* asks two questions: "How much freedom do you need?" and "How much privacy do you need?" Discuss these questions with classmates. Think about social media as well as other freedoms and rights to privacy.

Activities and Web Links

Visit cengagebrain.com to access the CourseMate for *Invitation to Human Communication* where these activities and web links can be found.

1. Read the article "Face-to-Face Time Makes Us Happier than Facebook" (Fahmy, 2010). Do you agree with this article? Explain your viewpoint. Go to *Web link 8.1.*

2. Watch this video clip from the movie *Twelve Angry Men.* How does it exhibit groupthink? What pressures are being used in the group to change the mind of the group member who disagrees with the majority of the group? Go to *Web link 8.2.*

3. Read "Eight Tips for Better Brainstorming." Which suggestions might work well for individualistic cultures? Which ones would work for collectivist cultures? Are there tips in the article that both types of cultures could learn to use to come up with effective ideas for solving a problem? Go to *Web link 8.3.*

LEADERSHIP AND IMPROVING COMMUNICATION

IN THIS CHAPTER YOU WILL LEARN TO:

- Recognize a variety of leadership styles.
- Explain the traits of effective group membership.
- Solve problems in a group or team.
- Organize meetings and group discussions.
- Explain the importance of civility and social justice in group and team meetings.

9

Leadership Defined
Leadership Styles
Gender and Leadership
Culture and Leadership
Civility and Leadership
Working Productively in Groups and Teams

nicole waring/iStockphoto

Consider the leadership roles you have held in groups and teams. What kind of power have you had as a leader and how have you communicated that power?

IN GROUPS AND TEAMS

Environmental issues have the power to unify groups with seemingly irreconcilable differences. Shared concerns about resources and conservation can help resolve even bitter conflicts.

—Saleem H. Al, environmental scientist and National Geographic Emerging Explorer

nicole waring/iStockphoto

How important are leadership skills? What makes an effective group member? How do we solve problems as we work together in groups and teams? What makes an effective meeting? These questions come up for most of us, regardless of where we work or volunteer our time. In this chapter, we explore the answers to these questions, the communication skills individuals need to function effectively as leaders and members of groups and teams, and the ways we can model civility and respect as we work together with others.

Leadership Defined

Although we are familiar with the term *leader,* and most of us can easily recognize a "good leader" or have studied "great leaders," we seldom take time to explore the definition of this term or the specific communication practices that go with leadership. Some scholars say leadership is in the eye of the beholder or that "I know a good leader when I see one," but others have spent decades systematically outlining the aspects of leadership and the differences between leading, ruling, and managing (Western, 2008). Most research suggests that to lead is to "guide others"; to "be the head of an organization," event, or activity; and to possess "charisma" and "vision." In addition, leaders believe that they are capable of changing things. They tend to be optimistic and positive thinkers, and they are responsive and caring toward others. Because leadership is somewhat subjective, it does require that the "followers" perceive the individual to be a leader and to have "exceptional qualities" (Fairhurst, 2001; Popper, 2005). So, a **leader** can be defined as *someone who guides or directs a group or activity with vision, charisma, and care.* This person is perceived to do these things—that is, to be a leader—by those in the group.

Leaders, rulers, and managers play different roles. Rulers often "force people to act" because they hold power or control over people and resources. Managers organize or control processes and people in order to make sure things run smoothly, and they do so usually because they are hired or asked to coordinate and oversee things. In contrast, leaders help construct and carry out the larger vision of the organization. They also work with individuals, and this causes them to "want to act" because

leader
someone who guides or directs a group or activity with vision, charisma, and care.

Steve Jobs was known as a visionary and inspiring leader who turned an idea and a small computer company into a market leader. As you read about the various leadership styles in this section, identify those you think he likely used to inspire his employees and build his company.

people feel involved in the decisions and respected by or important to the process (Popper, 2005; Western, 2008). Leaders operate without force or coercion, and they develop relationships of respect and mutual support with the people they communicate with.

Not all leaders produce positive outcomes, and we can think of individuals such as Adolph Hitler or religious cult leaders who lead individuals in ways that caused them to harm others and themselves. Because leaders can cause individuals to "want to act" in negative as well as positive ways, we will explore four of the most common styles of leadership and the ways they can produce positive outcomes: authoritarian, democratic, laissez-faire, and transformative.

Leadership Styles

Authoritarian Leadership

An authoritarian leader is a leader who functions a little like the stern parent or person in charge. Although **authoritarian leaders** often possess vision and charisma, they *tell others what to do, give orders, and make the final decisions regarding how to act or what to do next*. Authoritarian leaders can sometimes act like rulers, failing to listen to others or to take them into consideration. They sometimes bark out orders and demand that others do what they want. However, the best authoritarian leaders do have the larger vision of the organization or event in mind, and they

authoritarian leaders
leaders who tell others what to do, give orders, and make the final decisions regarding how to act or what to do next.

function well in highly structured organizations such as the military and police and fire services or for short periods of time when decisions must be made quickly and without extensive discussion.

The late Raymond Downey, deputy chief of New York City's fire department, is remembered as an effective leader who, because of the emergency circumstances he often found himself and his firefighters in, exemplified the best of authoritarian leadership. Downey is remembered as "one of the world's leading authorities on specialized rescue," and he lost his life on September 11, 2001, attempting to save others after the attacks on the World Trade Center. Even though he led others in an environment in which decisions must be made quickly and by the person in command, Downey always kept the larger mission or vision of the fire service in mind, and he possessed incredible charisma (Halverson, Murphy, & Riggio, 2004). He worked actively as a mentor and teacher to his staff and is described as "incredibly humble yet incredibly knowledgeable. Chief Downey never missed an opportunity to pass on what he knew to the younger members of the service and exercised a magnificent understanding of human character and soul" (Sargent, 2006, pp. xv–xvii).

Authoritarian leadership can spiral out of control, with individuals attempting to rule or dictate rather than lead. But, as the example of Chief Downey suggests, individuals can lead effectively with this style during periods of stress or when decisions must be made quickly and orders must be delivered clearly and carried out safely.

Democratic Leadership

Democratic leaders favor dialogue, discussion, and deliberation with members of the group before making decisions or issuing plans of action. **Democratic leaders** embrace three principles: *the distribution of responsibility among the group members, a desire to empower all members of the group, and a willingness to assist in decision making.* Democratic leaders spread responsibilities, tasks, and opportunities across the membership, giving those involved a sense of involvement and personal "buy in." They empower group members by giving them the opportunity to develop skills, learn new things, and challenge themselves. The result is an increase in self-esteem for members of the group. Finally, democratic leaders facilitate the decision-making process by describing procedures and processes, encouraging discussion and participation, and monitoring the process to be certain individuals are involved, engaged, and establishing and maintaining positive and healthy relationships (Gastil, 1994).

Democratic leadership is very effective when a group has ample time to discuss an issue and gather additional information and when individuals can learn to trust and respect one another (or when they already hold one another in high regard). It also is effective when no clear course of action is obvious or when issues are highly complex and affect many individuals or entities. Democratic leadership can fail, however, when a group is unwilling to openly discuss or deliberate, when there is a high

democratic leaders

leadership type characterized by the distribution of responsibility among the group members, a desire to empower all members of the group, and a willingness to assist in decision making.

Group Communication That Supports Biodiversity and Human Diversity

Communication among expert groups of scientists is essential to solving problems that affect wildlife, biodiversity, and the lives of people who depend on these resources. Four rivers in different parts of the world have caused diverse scientists to communicate with one another about how to retain these important resources. Governments in each of the countries that house these rivers want to dam them for power, but the damming would greatly affect the biodiversity in the rivers and therefore the lives of the people dependent on these rivers for their livelihoods and food. The rivers in the center of this crisis are Asia's Mekong River, Ethiopia's Omo River, Honduras' Patuca River, and the United States' Klamath River. Teams of scientists are working together to understand these unique rivers, the ways they sustain and support important bio and human diversity, and the impact on that diversity if the rivers are dammed.

The Mekong River, home to scores of giant fish, is known as one of the top three rivers in the world in terms of its biological diversity and the numbers of species it supports. The Omo River supports more than 200,000 people, as well as their ancient and traditional ways of life, and the food they need to sustain that life. If dammed, Honduras's Patuka River would destroy the largest wilderness area in Central America as well as the home of thousands of indigenous people who live near and depend on the river for their survival. The Klamath River, winding through southern Oregon and northern California, supports the largest run of salmon and steelhead fish on the West Coast, as well as an important fishing industry and people from three different Native American Indian nations. Teams of scientists, working closely with the people who live on the banks of these rivers and depend on them for their very existence, are communicating their findings to one another across borders, cultures, and languages in order to understand the role, importance, and complexities of these sources of water. Without this intricate web of communication, these groups and teams would not be able to share their findings and insights with one another, the governments that are proposing dams, and the world at large (National Geographic, n.d.).

What Do You Think?

1. What styles of leadership do you think would be effective as scientists work with local people in their efforts to study and save these rivers?

2. What cultural factors do you think the scientists had to consider as they communicate with people living near these rivers or whose livelihoods depend on the rivers?

3. What communication strategies might these teams of scientists use to avoid groupthink as they work with one another, local people, and government officials?

---

level of mistrust or animosity among group members, or when group members do not understand the process of or value in discussing ideas and sharing information. In the right settings, democratic leadership can be extremely successful, but it does take a skilled and confident leader to manage lively discussion, share responsibilities, and empower all members of a group.

Laissez-Faire Leadership

Usually described as a "hands-off" leader, a **laissez-faire leader** can be described as one who *offers little or no guidance and allows individuals to make all decisions themselves, giving them as much freedom as possible* (Lewin, Lippitt, & White, 1939). The laissez-faire leader is available for brainstorming, troubleshooting, resources, and conversation, but under this style of leadership, group members are given total freedom

laissez-faire leader
leader who offers little or no guidance and allows individuals to make all decisions themselves, giving them as much freedom as possible.

to make decisions and plan courses of action on their own. This style of leadership can be very effective "in situations where group members are highly skilled, motivated, and capable of working on their own" (Cherry, n.d.). It can be ineffective, however, when members of a group are less experienced or have trouble setting and achieving deadlines, because communication can become competitive, deadlines overlooked or postponed, and team members fail to receive clear guidance or leaders (Eagly, Johannesen-Schmidt, & van Engen, 2003; Skogstad, Ståle, Torsheim, Aasland, & Hetland, 2007).

Transformative Leadership

A **transformative leader** can be defined as one who exhibits leadership that *creates significant change in the life of people and organizations.* Transformative leadership depends on a person leading by example and modeling behaviors, values, and ideas that inspire others to accomplish great things. In the 1970s and 1980s, James MacGregor Burns and Barnard M. Bass determined that transformational leaders are characterized by the following traits:

- their influence on others;

- the level of trust, admiration, loyalty, and respect the group feels for the leader;

- the display of charisma, intellectual stimulation, and consideration for each individual from the leader; and

- the willingness of group members to work harder than expected for something greater than their own self-gain (Bass, 1985; Burns, 1978; Popper, 2005).

Nelson Mandela is often described as an example of a transformational leader. After spending almost three decades in a South African prison, many of those years in isolation or hard labor, people admired and idolized Mandela when he was released at age 71. He rarely used the word "I" in his speeches and presentations, and he stated repeatedly that he "was simply the servant of the public": someone who sought a greater good from his years in prison instead of personal revenge or benefit. Mandela inspired generations of people to work for a cause larger than themselves—the righting of a terrible imbalance of power—and his leadership modeled the kind of transformation that South Africa eventually accomplished (Popper, 2005). Table 9.1 summarizes the four types of leadership discussed, as well as the effectiveness and ineffectiveness of each.

transformative leader
leader who creates significant change in the life of people and organizations.

Nelson Mandela is recognized across the globe as a transformational leader, inspiring a nation of people to work toward ending apartheid. Can you think of other transformational leaders, well known or lesser known, who inspired individuals and transformed lives? What communication traits did they display?

Neftali/Shutterstock.com

TABLE 9.1 EFFECTIVE AND INEFFECTIVE TRAITS OF LEADERSHIP

LEADERSHIP STYLE	EFFECTIVE	INEFFECTIVE
Authoritarian leadership tells others what to do, gives orders, and makes the final decisions regarding how to act or what to do next.	When decisions must be made quickly; when leader holds a vision of the greater good; in highly structured situations.	When leader becomes too dogmatic and authoritarian; fails to listen to others; fails to consider needs of others.
Democratic leadership is characterized by the distribution of responsibility among the group members, a desire to empower all members of the group, and a willingness to assist in decision making.	When ample time to discuss issues; when issues are complex; when procedures and trust for discussion issues can be established.	When a high level of mistrust exists; when members do not understand procedures; when members do not see value in discussion ideas.
Laissez-faire leadership offers little or no guidance and allows individuals to make all decisions themselves, giving them as much freedom as possible.	When group members are highly skilled; when individuals do not need guidance and are good at setting and meeting deadlines.	When group members are inexperienced; when members have trouble setting and meeting deadlines.
Transformative leadership creates significant change in the lives of people and organizations by inspiring and motivating others to work harder than expected for a cause bigger than themselves.	When the leader can put aside own needs or desires; when issues are larger than individual group members; when leader displays consideration for individuals.	When leader puts own needs above others; when leader fails to inspire; when no intellectual stimulation exists; when leader fails to consider the needs of individuals.

© Cengage Learning 2014

 ## Gender and Leadership

Decades of research supports the idea that the gender of an individual significantly influences a group's perception of that leader. Studies show that when women and men display the same leadership traits with regard to authoritarian, democratic, and laissez-faire styles, they are perceived differently. For those styles, men are seen as focused and competent (authoritarian); confident, flexible, and in touch with the process (democratic); and willing to trust others to get the job done (laissez-faire). When women display authoritarian, democratic, or laissez-faire leadership styles, groups are more likely to evaluate them as bossy and demanding (authoritarian), too ineffective and wishy-washy (democratic), and as too soft or incompetent (laissez-faire) (Barbuto, Fritz, Matkin, & Mark, 2007; Druskat, 1994; Eagly et al., 2003; Jamieson, 1995). In addition, men are more likely to assume the role of leader, whereas women are more likely to emerge as the "social leader" who "contributes to morale and good interpersonal relations" (Barbuto et al., 2007, p. 72).

With regard to transformational leadership styles, research indicates that both women and men are perceived as competent leaders and

Aziz Abu Sarah
Emerging Explorer and Cultural Educator

Have you ever faced issues of gender or culture when leading a group? How did you respond? In other words, how did the group respond to your gender or culture or that of the group's leader?

I often find myself in situations where I am put in a team or even put in a leadership position because of my ethnicity. And I have been in situations where I was taken out because of ethnicity. So if it's one of those situations where [if] there is a need for an Arab and I have the qualifications, then it's "Oh, you're an Arab, okay well we'll put you in." Sometimes they'll exclude because of your ethnicity: I have applied for something where I was told that I didn't get it because of my ethnicity.

In my work now, I think the trick is learning different cultural styles of communication. I come from a culture where interrupting is normal and everybody says what they think at the moment. Well, in the United States, for example, you can't do that, so I have to adjust and remember what is correct in other cultures. I have to adjust my communication style for each country. And I have to ask questions about what is appropriate. For example, in Spain I had to ask what certain hand gestures meant because I know there are differences internationally, and I don't want to use those gestures that could be offensive. I have to understand cultural differences.

But even with gender, for example, handshakes are important. Sometimes I can shake a woman's hand, and sometimes I can't. And if I did shake a woman's hand in a country where that is not acceptable, I could really offend people. So, although it's acceptable for your own culture and maybe you disagree with the fact that a woman isn't allowed to shake your hand, you still have to respect that cultural practice if you're going to communicate effectively. It takes time to learn and to understand important cultural difference—but you have to if you want to be effective.

groups perceive that competence as a balancing of both masculine and feminine traits. So, as transformational leaders, both women and men display a balance of gender traits: the masculine traits of authoritative-ness and confidence and the feminine traits of being friendly, kind, and considerate toward others (Barbuto et al., 2007). In fact, Eagly et al.'s (2003) research identified women as using a transformational leader-ship style more often than men. They believe this is because the transfor-mational leadership style may give women "a means of overcoming the dilemma of role incongruity—namely, that conforming to their gender role can impede their ability to meet the requirements of their leader role" (Eagly et al., 2003, p. 573). In addition, psychology professor Vanessa Urch Druskat at Boston University argues that this transformational style of leadership likely will become increasingly common and important as "unstable social and economic times and rapidly changing organizational environments increase the need for able, transformational leaders" (Druskat, 1994, p. 99).

CourseMate Connection: Go to cengagebrain.com to access the CourseMate for *Invitation to Human Communication* to view a video about the rising world population.

Culture and Leadership

The Internet, travel and tourism, foreign industry, and the internationalization of banking and investment all contribute to what scholars are labeling the "globalization of business." According to Robert J. House, professor of management at the University of Pennsylvania, "the increasing connection among countries and the globalization of corporations does not mean that cultural differences are disappearing or diminishing. On the contrary, as economic borders come down, cultural barriers could go up" (House, Hanges, Javidan, Dorfman, & Gupta, 2004, p. 4). Professor House is one of the founding members of Global Leadership and Organizational Effectiveness (GLOBE), which is comprised of "170 social scientists and management scholars from sixty-one cultures throughout the world." Since the late 1990s, GLOBE has been working to understand the relationships between culture and leadership. GLOBE researchers have found that "selected cultural differences strongly influence" the ways in which people think about leaders and the norms they have "concerning the status, influence, and privileges granted to leaders" (House, R. J., et al., n.d., p.2). The traits that are influenced by cultural differences are uncertainty avoidance, power and assertiveness, collectivism, gender egalitarianism, and humane orientation.

- **Uncertainty avoidance** is the *extent to which members of an organization or society strive to avoid uncertainty by relying on social norms, rituals, and bureaucratic practices to alleviate the unpredictability of future events.*

- **Power and assertiveness** measure the *degree to which members of an organization or society expect and agree that power should be unequally shared or that individual assertiveness is valued.*

- **Collectivism** is the *degree to which organizational, societal, and family practices encourage and reward collective distribution of resources and collective action as well as the degree to which they express pride and loyalty.*

- **Gender egalitarianism** is the *extent to which an organization or a society minimizes gender-role differences.*

uncertainty avoidance
extent to which members of an organization or society strive to avoid uncertainty by relying on social norms, rituals, and bureaucratic practices to alleviate the unpredictability of future events.

power and assertiveness
degree to which members of an organization or society expect and agree that power should be unequally shared or that individual assertiveness is valued.

collectivism
degree to which organizational, societal, and family practices encourage and reward collective distribution of resources and collective action as well as the degree to which they express pride and loyalty.

gender egalitarianism
extent to which an organization or a society minimizes gender-role differences.

humane orientation
degree to which individuals in organizations or societies encourage and reward individuals for being fair, altruistic, friendly, generous, caring, and kind to others.

- **Humane orientation** is the *degree to which individuals in organizations or societies encourage and reward individuals for being fair, altruistic, friendly, generous, caring, and kind to others* (House et al., n.d., pp. 24–26).

GLOBE scholars also have explored such individual leadership traits as charisma, self-protection, other and team orientation, ability and willingness to delegate, decisiveness, and modesty. It is no surprise that cultural influences on leadership are profound and a culture's values are highly interconnected with the culture's view of effective and ineffective leadership. For example, Americans, Arabs, Asians, Britons, Eastern Europeans, French, Germans, Latin Americans, and Russians tend to romanticize the concept of leadership and consider leadership in both political and organizational arenas to be important. In these cultures, leaders are commemorated with statues, names of major avenues or boulevards, and names of buildings. Many people of the Netherlands, Scandinavia, and the German-speaking areas of Switzerland are skeptical about leaders and the concept of leadership out of fear they will accumulate and abuse power. In these countries, it is difficult to find leaders who have been publicly commemorated (House, 2004, p. 5).

How do we communicate effectively as leaders interacting with other cultures given the complexity of cultures, language differences, and the range of value systems and religious beliefs we will encounter? GLOBE researchers acknowledge that more studies are necessary to help us understand how to communicate effectively across cultures, and they urge the following:

- acknowledge and appreciate cultural differences,

- stay flexible as you respond to those differences,

- respond positively to values that may be drastically different from your own,

- be open to the ideals and opinions of others, and

- recognize that what your culture values (directness and frankness, for example) may be offensive to members of another culture.

 ## Civility and Leadership

We all are familiar with media reports that tell us that incivility is rampant in our society. Reports of cyberbullying, school shootings, road rage, and single individuals acting out in hostile ways toward others remind us that there are uncivil people in too many aspects of our lives. Unfortunately, those in positions of leadership can be among this group of uncivil people. Called "mobbing" in the United Kingdom, U.S. workers recognize this leadership incivility as "bullying" and "workplace hostility" (Davenport, Schwartz, & Elliot, 2005). The Workplace Bullying Institute (2011) defines bullying as a systematic campaign of interpersonal destruction that jeopardizes someone's health, career, and the job (Namie & Namie, 2011). The Washington State Department of Labor and Industries (2011) defines **bullying** as "*repeated, unreasonable actions of individuals (or a group) directed towards an employee (or a group of employees), which are intended to intimidate, degrade, humiliate, or undermine; or which create a risk to the health or safety of the employee(s).*"

bullying
repeated unreasonable actions of individuals (or a group) directed toward an employee (or a group of employees) that are intended to intimidate, degrade, humiliate, or undermine—or actions that create a risk to the health or safety of the employee(s).

COMMUNICATION AT WORK

© photos.com

Do You Have a Bully at Work?

In "How to Handle a Workplace Bully," Jennifer Alsever (2008) argues that if you run a company, no matter how large or small, you have employed at least one bully. Alsever identifies the signs of a bully in the office:

- complaints of screaming, tantrums, public humiliation, sabotage, and verbal abuse;

- subtle signs such as a person always taking credit for the accomplishments of others;

- someone dominating meetings with sarcasm, insults, and interruptions;

- people refusing to speak at meetings or displaying signs of stress and tension; and

- inappropriate nonverbal behaviors when others are talking such as doodling, rolling eyes, squeaking chairs, and sighing heavily or obviously shifting in a seat.

Also watch out for mobbing, or a group of people ganging up on a single individual. This might take the form of hostile humor that is explained away as "just teasing," ostracizing an employee by repeatedly "forgetting" to put someone on the e-mail list or on a listserv, or repeatedly "forgetting" to extend invitations to a social gathering.

What do we do about bullies? Jennifer Alsever and Gary Namie and Ruth Namie of the Workplace Bullying Institute (2011) suggest the following:

- Do not ignore the bullying because it will only get worse.

- When an employee complains, talk directly to the bully.

- Communicate specific facts and details to the bully: "Saying 'You're an idiot,' even as a joke, is uncivil and not tolerated here." Or "When Joe speaks at meetings,

you roll your eyes. It's rude and needs to stop." And "Claire has asked many times to be added to the listserv. Leaving her off is unprofessional. Add her name to the list now."

- Target the behavior and not the person. Tell the bully the behavior must stop rather than attack the person.

- Create a policy for civility in the workplace and make employment contingent on following that policy.

However uncivil workplace bullying is, it is also expensive and toxic to the workplace environment. Although employers often fear that a bully might retaliate by filing a grievance or lawsuit, as Gary Namie and Ruth Namie observe, "The truth is that it is costlier to fail to act than it is to pursue solutions. Bullies are undermining legitimate business processes and harming people in secret. It's time to examine the real costs of unwanted turnover, absenteeism, lawsuit or complaint settlements, workers comp, and disability claims. The bully is expensive" (Alsever, 2008; Namie & Namie, n.d.).

What Do You Think?

1. What kinds of bullying behaviors have you seen in your workplace? Make a list and compare them with other students' lists.

2. Alserver and Namie & Namie advocate talking to the bully about the hostile behaviors. How might it help to communicate specific facts and details to a bully? What communication strategies or choices would you use to talk to a bully and why?

3. What would you include in a policy for civility in the workplace?

Since the 1970s, organizations have been asked to recognize and respond to incidences of sexual harassment and discrimination based on sexual orientation, health, physical ability, and racism in our workplaces. Fortunately, there are laws in place designed to prevent these uncivil acts from occurring or to prevent them from happening repeatedly. Workplace bullying, however, has yet to be identified as a legal category. According to the Washington State Department of Labor and Industries, studies show that bullying is present in almost 35 percent of workplaces, 41 percent of workers reported being bullied in 2010, and somewhere between 13 and 53 million U.S. employees have experienced such hostility.

Bullying is different from aggression in that it is a repeated and systematic action. Examples of workplace bullying include repeated

unwarranted or invalid criticism,

blame without factual justification,

being treated differently than the rest of your work group,

being sworn at,

exclusion or social isolation,

being shouted at or humiliated,

excessive monitoring or micromanaging,

being given unrealistic work or deadlines, and

being denied work you are qualified to accomplish (Davenport et al., 2005).

This ongoing pattern of incivility usually occurs between a superior and a subordinate (a boss bullying an employee, for example), but it can also occur between peers. And, bullying is slightly gendered: Sixty percent of all bullies are men, yet, if a woman is doing the bullying, she likely will target another woman (71% of women-bullies targets are women as compared to 46% of women-bully targets being male).

Stopping this kind of leadership incivility is complex because most businesses have yet to recognize its severity in terms of loss of worker productivity, worker morale, and even loss of income from absences, stress-related illnesses, and hiring and training new employees when the bullied worker quits. In addition, bullies tend to be "close to powerful people in the organization and carefully target less powerful" people. However, New York and at least sixteen other states are considering so-called healthy workplace bills (one version of this bill passed the New York state senate in 2010) that would make it possible for workers to "sue for physical, psychological, or economic harm due to abusive treatment on the job" (Cohen, 2010). And some organizations are adopting policies to address workplace bullying. The Commission of Occupational Safety and Health in Western Australia is taking the lead in this effort, and the state of Washington recommended version of this policy appears in Table 9.2.

TABLE 9.2   WASHINGTON'S HEALTHY WORKPLACE POLICY

Company X considers workplace bullying unacceptable and will not tolerate it under any circumstances. Workplace bullying is behavior that harms, intimidates, offends, degrades, or humiliates an employee, possibly in front of other employees, clients, or customers.

Workplace bullying may cause the loss of trained and talented employees, reduce productivity and morale and create legal risks.

Company X believes all employees should be able to work in an environment free of bullying. Managers and supervisors must ensure employees are not bullied.

Company X has grievance and investigation procedures to deal with workplace bullying. Any reports of workplace bullying will be treated seriously and investigated promptly, confidentially, and impartially.

Company X encourages all employees to report workplace bullying. Managers and supervisors must ensure that employees who make complaints or witnesses are not victimized.

Disciplinary action will be taken against anyone who bullies a co-employee. Discipline may involve a warning, transfer, counseling, demotion, or dismissal, depending on the circumstances.

The contact person for bullying at this workplace is:

Name: _____

Phone Number: _____

Source: http://www.lni.wa.gov/Safety/Research/Files/Bully.pdf.

 ## Working Productively in Groups and Teams

In Chapter 8 you read about the different types of groups and teams, the roles members can take on in a group or team, and the process of making decisions. But what makes groups and teams function well? Why does one group seem to achieve its goals with ease and even pleasure, whereas another group takes forever to reach a decision and only after a great deal of disagreement and even hostility? Some groups and teams work well together, and we will explore some of the reasons for this positive interaction.

How Groups Function

A group or team works well together when the members understand how they are to operate, what they are to do, and the job they are to perform. Communication scholars Hirokawa, Gouran, Julian, Leatham, Propp, and Salazar explored the kinds of mistakes groups often make

Large groups often break into smaller groups to brainstorm solutions to problems. Can you identify the strengths and weaknesses of this step in problem solving?

and concluded that problems and breakdowns occurred largely as a result of faulty communication (Hirokawa & Salazar, 1999; Salazar, Hirokawa, Propp, Julian, & Leatham, 1994). These scholars take a functional approach to group communication, suggesting that communication functions in particular ways: to share information, explore issues, identify errors and problems, clarify thinking, and even persuade. Hirokawa and his colleagues suggest that groups that work effectively take several things into account as they try to solve problems or reach their goals: identify group goals, identify appropriate group structure, identify ways to gather and evaluate information, identify ways to consider options, and maintain a civil approach.

Identify Group Goals Determine the reason the group is a group, the tasks it hopes to or is expected to accomplish, and the timelines for doing so. Is the goal realistic and can it be accomplished, or is it too ambitious and something that cannot be achieved in the time allowed? Does the group have the resources it needs to accomplish the goal? Is everyone clear about the goal and the timelines?

Identify Appropriate Group Structure Determine what role each member will assume (Chapter 8). Determine how the group will operate: Will it meet via e-mail? in person? How often will it meet? How will discussions be managed? Will there be subcommittees, and how will information be shared (in writing, orally, or in Google documents?) How often are updates expected? How much time are people given to respond to e-mails and message boards? Is everyone clear about the structure? Does the structure need to be put in writing?

Identify Ways to Gather and Evaluate Information Identify the best sources of information and begin collecting it. Share information with group members. Assess and evaluate that information. Does the group need additional information? Are more questions raised than answered? If answers and solutions

For centuries, families and communities have worked together to run farms as well as other businesses. Are you part of a family- or community-run business? How well does each member work with others?

begin to emerge, then make sure you have enough information to adequately evaluate their strengths and weaknesses. Follow the group structure or establish a new structure for evaluating information. Is everyone satisfied with the amount of information gathered and the evaluation process?

Identify Ways to Consider Options Develop and formulate answers and plans of action that will satisfy the group's goals. Determine the pros and cons of each solution or option. Identify who is affected by the option. Select or identify the best option or solution.

Maintain a Civil Approach Recall that civility is "giving the world a chance to explain itself" and that decisions that are made affect individuals outside the group and the organization. Take stock of whose voices and perspectives were and were not included in the group's process. Can everyone's voices be included? Have different and even dissenting voices been listened to? Even if a decision or option is selected that goes against these voices, can the decision take into account the different views—is there a way to minimize the harm or damage a decision might cause to others?

Using the six steps for decision making explained in Chapter 8 and the aspects of effective group communication should help groups work together productively and positively. One additional facet of working in groups and teams is important to consider as you attempt to work productively with other people: the stages most teams and groups go through.

Stages in Group Work and Teamwork

Groups and teams evolve through several stages as they meet to discuss and work through tasks and dilemmas. Understanding the evolution or stages of group processes can help you communicate more effectively, so we will explore those stages here (Fisher, 1970; Forsyth, 1990; Miller, 2006; Reid & Hammersley, 2000).

Orientation Stage

Members of a group get to know one another. They are hesitant to share their views on the issue or problem, and they offer ideas and suggestions tentatively and cautiously. There is little disagreement.

Conflict Stage

Members express their views openly and often with a great deal of investment, and they defend their views strongly. Disagreements may become personal, but conflict, although at times intense, helps sort out stronger and weaker ideas and solutions.

Emergence Stage

Some ideas begin to emerge as better solutions to the problem than others. Disagreements lessen, and consensus begins to form. Communication becomes more respectful, polite, and cooperative.

Reinforcement Stage

A decision is made and members of the group support that decision; disagreements and concerns are not voiced; group members work toward harmony and consensus.

Dissolution Stage

The group's job is accomplished, and members part ways. They may feel a sense of loss, even if they knew the group's work would end. Sometimes a group ends abruptly (funding is pulled or resources dissolve, for example, or the members just cannot get along). Members might also leave suddenly (illness, anger, or unworkable disagreements) or with planning and notice (retirements or a change of jobs, for example).

Most groups pass through these five stages, and if a group exists over a long period of time, accomplishing many jobs or tasks, it will cycle through these stages again and again. Groups and teams must also manage specific kinds of relationships to work together effectively, so we will look at those relationships and how they might be managed productively next.

Managing Relationships in Groups and Teams

Working with other people can be both rewarding and challenging. To help groups get the most out of their time together, pay attention to how discussions are managed, pressures to conform to "what the group wants," and information overload.

Manage Participation Groups and teams work most effectively when everyone feels comfortable participating. Many groups find a structure that satisfies the styles of its members, allowing individuals to participate equally and comfortably. This may be Robert's Rules of Order or some other structure (every one speaks once before someone can speak again, for example). But sometimes, even with the best of efforts, some individuals "take over" and participate far more than is equitable or productive. When that happens, try the following:

1. Determine who is speaking most often or for the longest. Is this based on rank, expertise, investment in the issue, or the like? Set up a structure for discussion to make the discussion more equitable. This might

include setting time limits for speaking or requiring that ideas be submitted in writing before the discussion begins.

2. Pay attention to groupthink. To avoid groupthink, set up a structure that disrupts this process. This might include asking one or two people to voice disagreements or play devil's advocate. Or ask everyone to present one idea or solution not yet mentioned, even if they do not support that idea or solution.

Avoid Pressures to Conform When people work in groups, they often feel a good deal of pressure to "go along with the crowd." Occasionally, one person's personality is so charismatic and strong that group members feel compelled to follow that person's lead. At other times, a group of individuals might gain control of resources or might begin bullying behaviors. This, too, can cause individuals to go along even if they do not agree or support the ideas or solutions. To avoid this pressure, try the following:

1. Rotate group tasks, assignments, and roles. Distribute work evenly and do not assume that the person with the "most personality" is the best leader or that the quietest member is the best note taker. Rotate these tasks and others among the group to help prevent some individuals from taking over and others being silenced.

2. Develop a healthy workplace bill or an antibullying policy. Ideally, the group would work together to develop the policy, but it may be necessary to bring in someone from the outside to help.

Prevent Information Overload As groups gather information, individuals may feel as though they must understand every bit of data they find. This can cause members to do any of several things such as withdraw, become resentful, or even decide there is no workable solution. To prevent information overload, try the following:

1. Divide the gathered information among group members and ask individuals to study and then present that information to the group. This helps members feel invested in the solution, and it shares the workload of understanding the problem and its possible solutions evenly.

2. Bring in an expert or resource from outside the group to help explain complex or emotionally charged ideas or arguments. This prevents one person from within the group from becoming the "know-it-all" or the target of hostility. It also creates a safe place for group members to ask questions and explore ideas without threatening or insulting one another.

Managing Technology Technology can contribute positively to group work, but it also can contribute to difficult group dynamics. When

Wavebreak Media Ltd./Corbis

When groups work together for a period of time, they can fall prey to groupthink or one person may continually take charge. How might groups and teams avoid this groupthink or takeover when it happens? How might they civilly respond to it if it does happen?

Courtesy of the Ozcan Research Group at UCLA

photobank.kiev.ua/Shutterstock.com

Aydogan Ozcan, Emerging Explorer and Electrical Engineer: What Can Your Cell Phone Communicate?

Just how important is a cell phone? Most of us use one to call our friends and families, but for Aydogan Ozcan, electrical engineer and emerging explorer for National Geographic, it is far more than a simple device to stay in touch. A cell phone can be a matter of life and death. Ozcan and his UCLA research team are turning "common cell phones . . . into imaging tools that will bring accurate medical diagnoses to the most remote, resource-poor corners of the planet." In a remote village, Ozcan explains, you cannot depend on electricity, let alone advanced medical technology. Although the technology in many countries is already state of the art so that any advancements will be incremental, in "developing nations, even basic technology can be transformative." Enter the cell phone—more than a device used to communicate "Hello, how are you?" Ozcan and his colleagues are "creating digital technologies that can replace microscopes and enable cell phones to make diagnostic decisions, even in a distant desert village."

Ozcan explains that microscopes are expensive and heavy, not to mention delicate, and many misdiagnoses occur in remote parts of the world because of lack of training. So, Ozcan and his team are modifying the common cell phone with a "special light source," and using the "phone's camera to capture an image of a blood sample, essentially turning the phone into a lens-free microscope. It's lightweight, instantly shows us huge numbers of cells, and fits into the palm of your hand." Working with his team of engineers, Ozcan has turned our familiar "call me" technology into a lifesaving device.

Source: http://www.nationalgeographic.com/explorers/bios/aydogan-ozcan/

1. Ozcan and his team use cell phones to communicate across the globe, helping people to live more healthy lives. How might you use your cell phone to move beyond social networking and to assist others?

2. Identify one team you now are a part of. In what ways could you use cell phones to increase the effectiveness of your team's work?

3. What are the biggest ethical considerations and dilemmas created by the use of cell phones? How might groups and teams minimize the potential negative affects of cell phone use?

relational stress

stress that occurs when there are interpersonal incompatibilities among group members based on differences in their personalities, communication styles, attitudes, and preferences

task stress

stress that consists of contrasting views and opinions among group members regarding the tasks at hand.

avoidance

a conflict style in which individuals will not address or acknowledge its existence.

accomodation

a conflict style in which individuals do what they are asked in order to "resolve" the conflict.

reciprocity

actions of interdependence or mutual respect; when people who help you later need help, you return the favor.

competition

a style of managing conflict in which one individual makes sure his or her needs are met, with disregard for the needs of others.

working together, groups tend to experience two types of stresses that can be magnified by technology: relational and task. **Relational stress** *occurs when there are interpersonal incompatibilities among group members based on differences in their personalities, communication styles, attitudes, and preferences.* **Task stress**, on the other hand, *consists of contrasting views and opinions among group members regarding the tasks at hand.*

To manage these pressures as you work via electronically mediated communication (EMC), try the following:

1. Because nonverbal cues cannot be read via EMC, make sure group members add them to their messages and take time to clarify if a message seems to be leading to conflict.

2. Using technology rather than face-to-face communication often increases the number of ideas and suggestions, and the ideas generated must be sorted, organized, and read by all the members of the group. So try setting a limit to the number of messages, the length of messages, and even guidelines for the content of messages.

Conflict in Groups and Teams

At some point, conflict will be a part of almost every group or team. However uncomfortable conflict makes most of us, when handled productively, conflict can result in a positive outcome. But when conflict is handled poorly, it can lead to a group's demise. As discussed in Chapter 7, there are negative and positive approaches to handling conflict. Possible outcomes are avoidance, accommodation, competition, compromise, and workplace democracy.

Avoidance Usually unproductive, the avoidance style *occurs when individuals will not address the conflict or acknowledge its existence.* "It's all good," "Not now," and "I'm not talking about this with you" are examples of the avoidance style. Although an individual may have good reasons for avoiding conflict (possible job loss or becoming the target of bullying, for example), this style rarely leads to productive resolution.

Accommodation With this style, *an individual "resolves" the conflict by doing what she or he is asked.* At times, the style is successful—for example, "I'll go with your idea this time, and you'll support mine next time." Too often, however, it leaves one individual feeling used and unappreciated. When Franklin agrees to meet at a time that is inconvenient for him to avoid conflict, the other group members feel great about the decision, but Franklin's needs must be accommodated in other ways to prevent his feeling alienated and used. This requires the practice of **reciprocity**, or *actions that demonstrate interdependence or mutual respect*—for example, *when people who help you later need help, you return the favor* (Forsyth, 1990).

Competition The competition style of conflict management is present *when one individual makes sure that her or his needs are met*—but *with complete disregard for the needs of the other members of a group.* This is a win–lose style of conflict: in a group, one member (or a small group of individuals) walks away happy, but others are frustrated, angry, and feel as if their own needs have been sacrificed or ignored. Although competition is appropriate in many parts of life, in groups or teams, internal competition can cause a group to fall apart or become unproductive and unhealthy.

Compromise   Commonly referred to as a *win–win approach*, when conflict is handled in the spirit of compromise, all parties involved should feel respected and valued. In a compromise, *the needs of every group member are considered and met*—at least some of the time in the life of the group. In the spirit of compromise, meeting times are rotated so that they are convenient (or inconvenient) for all members of the group, the "best" assignments are shared among all group members (as are the tasks that are less fun), and individuals check in with one another regularly to be sure that the compromises made continue to be win–win and not lose–lose for some.

Workplace Democracy   Many communication scholars now advocate and study *workplace democracy*, a concept that describes ways in which groups work together productively and positively and thus avoid many of the pitfalls previously described. **Workplace democracy** is described as a *system of governance that truly values individuals' goals and feelings*. This system also values the objectives of the organization, but it brings the individual and the organization together "by encouraging individual contributions to important organizational choices" (Miller, 2006, p. 184). According to the National Coalition for Dialogue and Deliberation, workplace democracy requires deliberation:

> The ancient Greeks called deliberation the talk we use to teach ourselves before we act. Deliberation is the kind of reasoning and talking we do when a difficult decision has to be made, a great deal is at stake, and there are competing options or approaches we might take. At the heart of deliberation is weighing possible actions and decisions carefully by examining their costs and consequences in light of what is most valuable to us. Deliberation can take place in any kind of conversation—including dialogue, debate, and discussion (National Coalition for Dialogue and Deliberation, n.d.).

In the context of groups within organizations, workplace democracy and deliberation rely on three things: (1) shared values among the members of a group, (2) organizational structures that support cooperation and encourage individual participation, and (3) fostering the development of individual talents and resources, as well as making appropriate use of those talents and resources. Although complex, workplace democracy can be a successful approach to working within a group when the members

- take time to identify the values they share as well as the values of the organization,

- establish structures and practices that welcome and encourage participation and cooperation, and

- identify the talents of each member of the group and then use those talents positively and productively.

compromise
a style of managing conflict in which the needs of every member of the group are considered and met.

workplace democracy
system of governance that truly values individuals' goals and feelings.

Problem Solving in Groups and Teams

One of the most important functions of a group is to make a decision about an issue, project, or course of action. This usually happens after conversation, careful exploration and analysis, and looking at the implications of the final choices as discussed in Chapter 8. Here we will explore three of the most common ways groups make decisions: consensus, voting, and authority rule.

Consensus A **consensus** is a *general or widespread agreement among all the members of a group*. When groups reach a decision by consensus, they have determined that all members agree on a particular course of action. To reach a consensus, groups usually spend considerable time exploring an issue as well as the possible alternatives that could solve or address the issue. When an issue or problem is complex or when the impact of a decision is quite profound, consensus can be a perfect method of making a decision because some decisions can have enormous impact. Pay cuts, reductions or increases in services, protocols for granting awards or privileges, and job qualifications, for example, all profoundly affect individuals. When decisions are of this magnitude and a group wants to be sure that all members agree with the decision, then consensus is a way to do so.

Consensus can be hard to reach, however, and groups will want to be sure that they are not falling prey to two potential problems: groupthink and ultimatums. When groups are fairly cohesive or when there is pressure to conform, a group may think that it has consensus, when in fact it has failed to fully explore issues, differences of opinion, and varying perspectives; in reality, it has engaged in groupthink. Although a decision is made, a group usually discovers later that there is dissension and dissatisfaction among its members, or that members made a poor decision because they failed to fully explore all the options. When this happens, the group either has to revisit the decision or attempt to function with considerable disharmony and a poorly made decision.

Attempts at consensus also can lead to ultimatums. These occur when a member tries to block a decision by delivering a threat or demand. Ultimatums usually are communicated in a quid pro quo fashion: "If you do X, then I'll do Y." A group member may threaten to quit, to never agree to another decision again, to expose sensitive information, or to breach confidentiality. When members of a group feel isolated and backed into a corner by the overall group's attempts at consensus, they may resort to ultimatums to try to get their way. To preempt ultimatums if your group has decided to make a decision by consensus, set clear ground rules for discussion that do not allow any member to use ultimatums (Alderton & Frey, 1986; Frey, 2003; Keyton & Stalworth, 2003; Oetzel & Ting-Toomey, 2006; Poole & Garner, 2006; Seibold & Myers, 1986).

Voting Groups can also come to a decision through voting. When a group makes a decision by vote, it can decide to go with a simple majority, which means that more than 50 percent of its members must vote in favor of the decision, or it can select a vote by two-thirds majority. A

consensus
general or widespread agreement among all the members of a group.

Food Not Bombs: Decision Making by Consensus

Committed to the equal distribution of food worldwide, consensus, and self-empowerment, the first Food Not Bombs chapter began in Cambridge, Massachusetts, in 1980. Currently, groups of individuals are working in hundreds of autonomous Food Not Bombs chapters "sharing free vegetarian food with hungry people and protesting war and poverty" (Food Not Bombs, n.d.). As the group's Web site explains, "Food Not Bombs is not a charity. This energetic grassroots movement is active throughout the Americas, Europe, Africa, the Middle East, Asia, and Australia. Food Not Bombs is organizing for peace" and . . . for "thirty years the movement has worked to end hunger and has supported actions to stop the globalization of the economy, restrictions to the movements of people, end exploitation and the destruction of the Earth" (Food Not Bombs, n.d.).

With so many members, why would a group like this want to reach decisions by consensus? According to Food Not Bombs, "Voting is a win or lose model in which people are more concerned about the numbers it takes to win a majority than they are in the issue itself. Consensus, on the other hand, is a process of synthesis, bringing together diverse elements and blending them into a decision which is acceptable to the entire group. . . . Each person's ideas are valued and become part of the decision." Working with a consensus model of decision making allows everyone to participate in a discussion, and this creates an environment in which trust and the valuing of all group members are of utmost importance. In addition, Food Not Bombs believes that when a consensus model is used, people are more committed to the final decision and its outcome.

Food Not Bombs suggests that a proposal is stronger when everyone works together to create the best possible decision for the group. The group explains that any "idea can be considered, but only those ideas which everyone thinks are in the best interests of the group are adopted." Although there are many models for reaching a decision by consensus, for Food Not Bombs, "It is most important . . . that whatever process you use is clear, consistent, and able to be easily taught and learned so that all can participate fully." Groups also want to recognize that leaders are important, but we can avoid having power "concentrated in the hands of a few entrenched

Food Not Bombs

leaders" by developing leadership skills in every member of the group. "This can be accomplished by holding skill-building trainings and by encouraging and supporting people to be self-empowered, especially those who are generally reserved." The benefits are many, according to Food Not Bombs: cultivating leadership skills in all group members "helps the group become more democratic and helps individuals feel more satisfied and, therefore, less likely to burn out or fade away" (Food Not Bombs, n.d.).

What Do You Think?

1. Explain what you think is meant by, "Voting is a win or lose model in which people are more concerned about the numbers it takes to win a majority than they are in the issue itself." Could consensus be used instead of voting for local matters such as voting to give more tax money to the schools, or voting to reduce levels of pollutants from local factories?

2. Have you ever tried to reach consensus in a group? What difficulties arose? What communication strategies worked well to address those difficulties?

3. Describe a problem you currently face in a group. What models for reaching a decision could you use to solve this problem? Given the makeup of the group, which models do you think would be most effective? Why?

two-thirds majority vote means that at least two thirds of the members must cast their vote in favor of the decision. Sometimes, groups simply need to know that more than half of their members support a decision (to postpone the vote until the group can gather more information on an issue, for example). But there are other times a group needs to know that a significant majority of its members support a decision (for example, to elect someone as the spokesperson for the group), so it will rely on a two-thirds majority vote. If a group decides to use the simple majority vote, it needs to remember that if it gets only 51 percent of its members to support a decision, then 49 percent do not—and those members may be very unhappy with a decision. Similarly, if it requires a two-thirds majority, the group also needs to consider that one third of its members do not support the decision. In both cases, it is inaccurate and even uncivil to act as if the full group is 100 percent in support of a decision.

Authority Rule When a group makes a decision by **authority rule**, it is *allowing the leader or head of the group to make the final choice.* When decisions are made this way, three things usually are happening. First, a group may not have time to meet, gather information, and then discuss a decision, so it will turn the choice over to a selected leader or authority. Second, a group may not need to meet and gather and then process information. This happens when the choice being made is a simple one that does not involve extensive work or deliberation. Third, the group trusts its leader to have the expertise and best interests of the group at heart to make a credible and ethical decision. Under this third condition, the person in authority needs to be certain she or he actually has the full support and trust of the group and should check in with other group members regularly to share decisions made, to gather information before making new decisions, and to stay connected and in touch with the members of the group.

Reaching decisions by consensus, voting, and authority rule all have a legitimate place in groups and teams. When you find yourself working in a group or team, take time to decide which option might work best for different situations. Be sure to communicate with other members of the group about the decision making model that will work best for a situation, and recognize that all models have their strengths and weaknesses.

Asking Questions

Effective group work relies on asking good questions. Although asking questions feels intuitive and something that we should not have to learn, research shows the following:

- The most important part of a question is listening to the answers.
- You should understand your reasons for asking the question.
- Do not ask too many questions.
- Rather than think about the next question you will ask, be sure to listen to the answers to the ones you already have asked (Reid & Hammersley, 2000).

Members of a group can ask several types of questions: closed, open, affective, probing, and leading. These questions are discussed as follows and each type can be use for both positive and negative reasons.

Closed Questions Often *described as "Yes or no" questions, closed questions limit the kind of answers a person can give.* "Are we ready to begin?" "Did you ask him for more information?" "Do we need more time to

authority rule
allowing the leader or head of a group to make the final choice.

closed questions
yes or no questions that limit the kind of answers a person can give.

think about this?" and "Do you think we should meet again?" are examples of closed questions. Closed questions can be useful when a group needs a quick answer, must take a poll of where the group is at on an issue, or needs to determine the next course of action. Too many closed questions can be awkward, however, so try to mix closed questions with open questions.

Open Questions Open questions *give people freedom to answer in a range of ways.* In groups, open questions help with brainstorming, evaluating ideas and solutions, and avoiding groupthink. Open questions are framed so that individuals can share what they think about an issue or problem: "What do we think about David's idea?" "What haven't we discussed?" "Who has other ideas about this problem that we need to hear?" and "Who is affected by this decision?" Open questions generate ideas and help people share what they are worried or excited about. Too many open questions, however, can lead a group to go offtrack, so try to balance open questions with closed questions as you sort through issues and solutions.

Affective Questions Affective questions *acknowledge that people have feelings as well as ideas—and that those feelings are important to share.* Affective questions can be both closed and open: "Are we happy about this choice?" "How do we feel about this decision?" and "I'm hearing some frustration with this discussion—can anyone elaborate on why?" are examples. A group can get too tied up with emotions, however, or focus on a single person's emotional state, so affective questions should be a part of the group discussion but not dominate the process.

Probing Questions Probing *questions help people talk more about an idea or a feeling.* They open up a space for more discussion on a topic. Examples of probing questions are "We seem stuck on this one issue—why is that so?" "I'm hearing only the positive aspects of this solution—are there negative outcomes we need to consider?" "Lisa, you've been very quiet during the conversation—is there something you want to add?" Probing questions can put people on the spot, asking them to become involved in a discussion when they might have good reasons not to, so use them carefully. If a person responds with "No, nothing to add," it is probably best to double-check that response privately rather than publicly.

Leading Questions Leading questions *urge people to respond in a particular way.* They set the stage for agreement or disagreement and do not always result in an honest answer or encourage productive conversation. A leading question that seeks agreement might be "She's an amazing resource and an expert in this area. Don't you agree?" or "I think that's a wonderful solution—who wouldn't?" Examples of leading questions that seek disagreement are "That feels unethical to me, but I guess that's the approach you want to take, right?" or "I think we are making a huge mistake, but when have my ideas ever mattered?" Leading questions force a response, but they also might not add productively to the discussion, so use them carefully, if at all.

open questions
questions that give people the freedom to answer in a range of ways.

affective questions
questions that acknowledge that people have feelings as well as ideas that are important to share.

probing questions
questions that help people talk more about an idea or feeling.

leading questions
questions that urge people to respond in a particular way.

real time

when people in a room together can speak and hear one another in the moment without needing computers, phones, or the like.

virtual meetings

meetings that take place via electronic means such as Skype or teleconferencing or other electronic media that can bring people together across distances.

Organizing Meetings and Group Discussions

One of the most time-consuming aspects of group work is meeting with other members of the group. Because members of a group usually have busy schedules and responsibilities outside their group tasks, organizing and planning for meetings is important. There are two venues for meetings: real time and virtual. When groups meet in **real time**, they are *in a room together and can speak in the moment with one another without needing computers, phones, or the like.* **Virtual meetings** *take place via electronic means such as Skype, teleconferencing, or other electronic media that can bring people together across distances.* Real-time meetings offer group members the advantage of being able to clearly see all individuals who are attending and monitoring nonverbal cues. Virtual meetings eliminate the need for long days of travel to get to meetings, and they are easier to schedule when people work off-site or in different time zones, or when they simply have demanding and full work schedules.

Facilitating Group and Team Meetings

Regardless of the venue, productive meetings take planning and structure. Let us look at some of the components of planning meetings.

Determine the Goals for the Meeting Groups need a reason to gather, and depending on where the group is in its process, the reasons for meeting will vary. If the group is newly formed, it might set an initial meeting with a goal of getting to know one another and understanding the job or reason for coming together. If the group is beyond the orienting stage, it might meet to share information, assess or evaluate information or options, come to a final decision, or even bring a project to its conclusion. If the group is in the middle of intense conflict,

Virtual meetings are common in today's online and global working environment. What are some of the advantages of this type of meeting? Can you identify any disadvantages, and how you might minimize them as you meet virtually?

AVAVA/iStockphoto.com

it might meet with a facilitator to help work through the conflict. If it needs more information, the group might meet with an outside resource. Whatever the reason, it is important to clearly answer the question, "Why are we going to meet?" Because it is important not to waste people's time, determine the reason you are bringing the group together before you set a meeting.

agenda

formal and organized outline of items to address in order to meet the goals of a meeting.

Organize the Agenda Your next step is to develop the agenda for the meeting. An **agenda** is a *formal and organized outline of the items you want to cover in order to meet the goals of the meeting.* To run effectively, meetings need a plan or structure, so take time to set out the agenda and assign time limits to each item on that agenda. Computer programs such as those at Office.com can provide templates for agendas.

Most agendas include the time, place, phone-in number and access code, and a list of business items to be covered. Depending on the goals for the meeting, you will want to organize your items accordingly. You may have one lengthy issue to cover, for example, but several small items that can be handled quickly. If so, take care of those small items first and then turn to the bigger item. However, you may have a series of small items that need discussion and delegation, and you might want to discuss each of them and then decide who will take responsibility for them after all tasks have been explained. Or you may be calling a meeting to vote on several matters, hear reports from members of the group, or set forth a plan of action for the next several weeks.

Once you determine the goals for the meeting, carefully map out how the group will accomplish those goals the most productively. You might have headings such as "Old Business," "Reports," "Action Items," and "Discussion Items" on the agenda. Carefully think about assigning a time frame for each item so that those who are attending the meeting can plan their reports and comments to match the agenda. Finally, distribute the agenda before the meeting whenever possible. This will give everyone in the group time to prepare and think about the goals for the meeting and how they can best help the group meet those goals.

Manage the Meeting Meetings run most effectively when one person is in charge. That person usually is the group leader or the person who establishes the agenda for the meeting, but you also can appoint someone or even rotate the job of facilitator. Before you begin the meeting, make sure the rules for conducting the meeting are clear—this might require rules for governing who may speak, for how long, and how often; how decisions will be made; and how votes will be taken. Many groups have an established procedure for conducting meetings that is easy for new group members to pick up as they attend a few meetings. The following is a general procedure for conducting a meeting.

- Begin the meeting by establishing the facilitator and appointing someone to take the minutes or notes of the meeting or asking a volunteer to do so.

- Open the meeting by stating what is to be discussed and what the group should try to accomplish by the end of the meeting.

- Begin with the first agenda item. If any group members have been asked to present information to the group, ask them to do so now.

- Open up the meeting to discussion, facilitating the conversation so that the group stays focused.

- Use the skills you have learned in this chapter to help you communicate effectively, manage the discussion, work with conflict, avoid groupthink, and gather information.

- When the group has concluded its discussion, summarize the main points that were raised.

- Specify how the group should follow up on the meeting, assign any tasks that need to be accomplished, and set a time for the next meeting.

Follow-Up Communication After the meeting, provide copies of the minutes to group members. The minutes of a meeting should clearly identify what the group discussed and any action taken by the group. Be sure to identify group members who are responsible for certain tasks and assignments. Remind the group of timelines and the date for the next meeting.

Your communication skills as a leader and as a member of a group or team will help you work productively with others. Understanding the roles that culture, gender, and civility play in our workplaces and our social settings will enhance our communication with others and assist us in leading meetings and in solving problems.

Chapter Summary

A Leader Guides or Directs a Group or Activity with Vision, Charisma, and Care

- There are four types of leaders authoritarian, democratic, laissez-faire, and transformative.
- Women and men are perceived differently even when they display the same leadership styles.
- When women display authoritarian, democratic, or laissez-faire leadership styles, they are perceived as bossy and demanding (authoritarian), too ineffective and wishy-washy (democratic), and too soft or incompetent (laissez-faire).
- Although both women and men are effective leaders, men are more likely to assume the role of leader, and women are more likely to emerge as the social leader who contributes to higher morale and good interpersonal relations.

Certain Cultural Differences Strongly Influence the Ways People Think About Leaders

- Influential factors include uncertainty avoidance, power and assertiveness, collectivism, gender, and a humane orientation.
- Bullying is the repeated, unreasonable actions of individuals that are directed toward an employee and are intended to intimidate, degrade, humiliate, or undermine a person.
- Bullying creates a hostile environment and presents a risk to the health or safety of the employee being bullied.

To Work Effectively in Groups, Begin by Identifying Group Goals, Determining Appropriate Group Structure, Gathering and Evaluating Information, Providing Options, and Maintaining a Civil Approach

- To work effectively, understand the stages through which groups typically go: orientation, conflict, emergence, reinforcement, and dissolution.
- Effective group work and teamwork also involve managing participation, avoiding pressures to conform, and preventing information overload.
- All groups experience conflict as their members work together. The communication styles that contribute to conflict productively and unproductively are avoidance, accommodation, competition, compromise, and workplace democracy.

When You Solve Problems in Groups and Teams, Use Consensus, Voting, or Authority Rule

- To solve problems or manage discussions in groups, use closed questions, open questions, affective questions, probing questions, and leading questions.

Meetings Can Occur in Both Real Time and Virtual Time

- To facilitate meetings, determine the goals for the meeting, organize the meeting, manage the meeting, and provide follow-up communication.

Key Concepts

accommodation (218)	**avoidance** (218)	**bullying** (209)
affective questions (223)	**authoritarian leaders** (201)	**closed questions** (222)
agenda (224)	**authority rule** (222)	**collectivism** (207)

competition (218)

compromise (219)

consensus (220)

democratic leaders (202)

gender egalitarianism (207)

humane orientation (208)

laissez-faire leader (203)

leader (200)

leading questions (223)

open questions (223)

power and assertiveness (207)

probing questions (223)

real time (224)

reciprocity (218)

relational stress (218)

task stress (218)

transformative leader (204)

uncertainty avoidance (207)

virtual meetings (224)

workplace democracy (219)

Invitation to Human Communication Online

Speech Communication CourseMate includes an interactive eBook and interactive learning tools including National Geographic Explorer videos, student videos, quizzes, flash cards, and more. Speech Builder Express 3.0 and Speech Studio 2.0 are also available. Go to cengagebrain.com to access your CourseMate for *Invitation to Human Communication* where these resources can be found.

Further Reflection and Discussion

1. Think of a former and current work supervisor. What type of leadership style did each one have? Were they effective? What conflicts or complications might each supervisor have faced? How would you have handled the leadership roles differently?

2. Do you know of any countries that have women leaders? Are there women leaders in the United Nations? Research to find out the answers to these questions and discuss the types of leadership styles these women might have and what types of problems they are faced with solving.

Activities and Web Links

Visit cengagebrain.com to access the CourseMate for *Invitation to Human Communication* where these activities and web links can be found.

1. Read this National Coalition for Dialogue and Deliberation article on consensus, "Top Ten Most Common Mistakes in Consensus Process and How To Avoid Them." Now think of a disagreement in your family or at your workplace. How would you build consensus about the disagreement? How can you avoid the common mistakes? Be specific. Go to *Web link 9.1*.

2. Watch this brief video clip, "Think Different." How many of the transformative leaders do you recognize? Write down their names. Choose one and explain how this person led by example and modeled and created significant change in the life of people and organizations (do some research if you need more information). Go to *Web link 9.2*.

3. Visit this Web site and read about the three women who won the Nobel Peace Prize in 2011. What leadership qualities do these women share? Go to *Web link 9.3*.

DEVELOPING YOUR SPEECH TOPIC AND PURPOSE

IN THIS CHAPTER YOU WILL LEARN TO:

- Understand public dialogue is an ethical and civil exchange of ideas.
- Examine how your audience affects speaking goals.
- Select your speech topic.
- Identify the general purpose and specific purpose of your speech.

- Develop a thesis statement and main points for your speech.
- Identify the parts of an introduction and ways to conclude your speech.

10

Why Enter the Public Dialogue?

Your Audience

Choosing Your Speech Topic

Stating Your Speaking Goals

Organizing Your Speech

Introductions and Conclusions

Jung Yeon-Je/AFP/Getty Images

*More than any other time in our
history, the issues facing us are global
and central to the lives of each one of
us. What issues do you feel concerned or
even passionate about? Consider using
these as a topic for your first speech.*

*The way we, as a global community, respond to the
intertwined problems of hunger and climate change
will define the legacy of our generation.*

—*Jennifer Burney, environmental scientist and National Geographic
Emerging Explorer*

dialogue

civil exchange of ideas and opinions between two people or a small group of people.

public dialogue

ethical and civil exchange of ideas and opinions among communities about topics that affect the public.

When you speak publicly, you participate in a dialogue that can influence others. With every speech you give, you make choices about the kind of influence your part in the dialogue will have. We are all familiar with the combative exchanges popular media present to us, but you may also be familiar with the call for more civility in these public exchanges. Recall from Chapter 1 that the word *civility* comes from a root word meaning "to be a member of a household." Approaching public speaking as an act of civility means that we can think of the speeches we give as adding our views and voices to that household by way of a public dialogue or conversation. A **dialogue** is a *civil exchange of ideas and opinions between two people or a small group of people.* The **public dialogue** is the *ethical and civil exchange of ideas and opinions among communities about topics that affect the public.* To participate in the public dialogue is to offer perspectives, share facts, raise questions, and engage others publicly in stimulating discussions. When we enter the public dialogue, we become active and ethical citizens who participate in our nation's democratic process and consider the needs of others in our communities as well as our own needs.

In this section of this book, you will learn about the power of public speaking and the ways it helps us enter this larger, sometimes global, dialogue. As you engage with this power yourself, strive to give speeches that help clarify issues and stimulate thinking as you inform, persuade, or invite others to consider a perspective. Although you may have strong views on issues, a civil and ethical approach to public speaking can be the most powerful way to present those views.

Why Enter the Public Dialogue?

People decide to participate in the public dialogue for three main reasons: they decide to speak, they are asked to speak, or they are required to speak.

Deciding to Speak

The most common reason to speak is because we find an issue so important or relevant that we decide to speak about it. Before the advent of television and radio, people used a variety of platforms to share their opinions and ideas. They spoke in churches and town halls, at street corners, and in town squares or centers. Today, people often view mass media as the voice of the public, forgetting we still can and do insert our own voices into public discussions. New technologies make it possible for us to record our views via Web sites, blogs, and other Internet formats. And people still give real-time speeches so that they can express their views. We give class presentations and participate in student government and student organizations debating issues and proposing solutions. In business and professional meetings, we discuss ideas, give presentations, and create new plans or programs. In community forums, we speak about issues that are important to us such as the environment, education, and social services.

Individuals often feel so strongly about an issue that they decide to speak out publicly. When you have listened to people speak out, what makes them effective or ineffective speakers?

Being Asked to Speak

When we are asked to speak, we are asked to share a part of ourselves with others. When we are asked to speak, we can share our knowledge, skills, experiences, and perspectives with others. In this setting, we are recognized as experts or at least as someone who has information others want. It can be exciting to think about sharing our experiences and knowledge with other people. As you move through life, you might find you are asked to speak in educational settings, at service clubs, or at formal or professional gatherings. If you are asked to speak publicly, it is because people want to hear your views and ideas. But remember that expertise in a particular subject area does not always guarantee you are an expert at giving speeches. Although you may be considered an expert, you will be a more successful speaker if you follow the principles of speech preparation discussed in this book.

Being Required to Speak

Being required to speak can be a regular part of our lives. For example, you are now taking a communication course that requires you to give speeches. But outside your class, you may have a job that requires public speaking, such as in marketing or as a tour guide. Occasionally, you may have to fulfill a civic obligation such as speaking in front of a town council, at a public hearing, or even in a courtroom or for a legal investigation.

Although we may not like required public speaking, learning to give speeches in a communication course can be invaluable. If you view a classroom speaking requirement as an opportunity to prepare for other speaking contexts, then you can make the most of the time you spend in class.

Understanding how you become a public speaker is the first step in preparing a successful presentation. Once you recognize why you are speaking, you can turn your attention to who is in your audience, selecting and narrowing your speech topic, and deciding on your purpose for speaking.

CourseMate Connection: Go to cengagebrain.com to access the CourseMate for *Invitation to Human Communication* to view a video about UNHRC.

CIVIC ENGAGEMENT IN ACTION

Asianet-Pakistan/Shutterstock.com

Protecting Human Rights

If you conduct a Google search for award-winning actor Angelina Jolie, you will get literally millions of hits, almost all highlighting her many children, her relationships, her sexy image, and her movies. However, many people outside the reaches of Hollywood know her primarily for her humanitarian work. Through her efforts as a goodwill ambassador for the United Nations High Commissioner for Refugees (UNHRC), she has assisted the United Nations in providing relief to more than 20 million refugees displaced by violence, war, and poverty around the world. She not only engages directly with the men, women, and children who are affected but also assists in building shelters for refugees, has released many of her journals that document her travel experiences, and visits U.S. detention centers so she can

more effectively advocate for the reunion of families separated while escaping their home countries.

Jolie became interested in the plight of refugees after visiting Cambodia to film *Lara Croft: Tomb Raider.* "I started to travel and realized there was so much I was unaware of," she explains. "There were many things I hadn't been taught in school and daily global events I was not hearing about in the news. So I wanted to understand." Her belief in what the United Nations has always stood for—equality and the protection of human rights for all people—has resulted in her commitment to use her status as an A-list celebrity to learn as much as she can and speak out about the refugee crisis. For example, she says, "When I read about the 20 million people under the care of UNHCR, I wanted to understand how in this day and age that many people could be displaced."

Jolie's focus is on the humanity and heroism of those who have been forced to leave their homes and live in overcrowded and dangerous refugee camps. "What was really shocking was that every individual person you meet will tell you that their immediate family was [affected]. Somebody's child was killed, somebody's husband. Someone was beaten. . . . You go to these places and you realize what life's really about and what people are really going through. . . . These people are my heroes" (Braun, 2009; UNHCR, n.d.).

What Do You Think?

1. Are there issues you want to learn more about, like Jolie did? What are those issues and could you use them as possible speech topics?

2. Jolie is a powerful example of one person's voice and actions making a difference in the lives of others. Can you think of other people who are using their time and energy to learn about issues and then speak out about them?

💬 Your Audience

Your Audience Is a Group of Diverse People
People are unique for a variety of reasons that relate to some combination of culture, upbringing, experiences, personality, and even genetics (Wood, 2011). These differences are part of what causes speakers to want to be **audience centered**. An audience-centered speaker is one who *considers the positions, beliefs, values and needs of an audience.* As public

audience-centered speaker
speaker who considers the positions, beliefs, values, and needs of an audience.

speakers, how can we give a speech that considers audience members' differences as well as their similarities? To stay audience centered, review the material presented in Chapter 2 and try to consider how the members of your audience might view the world by analyzing their master statuses and their standpoints.

Master Statuses

Groups of people share common experiences, perspectives, and attitudes because they occupy certain master statuses. **Master statuses** are *significant positions a person occupies within society that affect that person's identity in almost all social situations* (Marshall, 1994). A person's master statuses might include race or ethnicity, gender, physical ability, sexual orientation, age, economic standing, religion or spirituality, and educational level. They could include positions in society such as being a parent, child, or sibling; being employed or unemployed; and so on if those positions affect someone's identity in almost every social situation. Here's how one public-speaking student, Miranda, described her master statuses and how they influenced her life and speaking experiences:

> I have many master statuses. I am a daughter dedicated to her family and her family values. I am forever a student, always craving new knowledge. I am a first-generation student, boldly going where no one else in my family has gone before—college. I am a Mexican-American living life for my ancestors. Last but not least, I am curious, always searching for new adventures in life. All of this makes up who I am and affects every decision I make each day, from what clothes I choose to wear to the books I choose to read. It also affects what topics I choose to speak about and how effectively I listen to other speakers.

A status is a *master* status when it profoundly influences a person's identity and the way in which he or she is perceived by others. Whether we intend to or not, we often respond to other people based on one or more master statuses. For example, teenagers with rumpled and baggy clothes are often treated differently in a grocery store than neatly dressed adult mothers with children. Whether or not our assumptions about these people are correct (teenagers will cause problems; mothers are responsible and will manage their children), we categorize and respond to people based on the positions they hold in society.

Master statuses affect our view of the world because we make judgments based on them, and hence we see some as more valuable than others. For example, whether we are comfortable acknowledging such differences or not, American culture tends to rank whiteness, heterosexuality, and masculinity higher than color, homosexuality, and femininity. Because the first three statuses are considered more valuable, they are generally rewarded with higher salaries, more acceptance and protections, and more personal freedoms, whereas the last three, on average, receive lower salaries, less

master statuses
significant positions a person occupies within society that affect that person's identity in almost all social situations.

Will Gray/Passage/Corbis

Master statuses affect our identity in most social situations. What are the master statuses of this young girl? What are your master statuses?

acceptance and fewer protections, and greater threats to physical safety (Bennett & Ellison, 2010; Browne & Williams, 1993; Buzawa, Austin, & Buzawa, 1995; Dobash, Dobash, Cavanagh, & Lewis, 1998; "Facts About Violence," 2010; Federal Bureau of Investigation, 1989, 1995; Lackie & de Man, 1997; National Coalition Against Domestic Violence, n.d.; National Organization for Women, n.d.; U.S. Bureau of Labor Statistics, 2010).

Standpoints, Attitudes, Beliefs, and Values The impact of different treatment because of master statuses can affect an individual's standpoint, the perspective from which a person views and evaluates society. Members of your audiences will have different standpoints. This is because they will have different master statuses and thus different experiences. For example, teenagers often see life as unfairly biased against them, and mothers often see the world as expecting them and their children to behave perfectly in all situations.

Note that although master statuses can have a powerful influence on a person's view of the world, master statuses do not *determine* a person's standpoint (see Chapter 2). For example, not all women believe they need to have children to fully experience womanhood, just as not all men believe their masculinity is weakened if they are not the primary breadwinners for their families. In addition, we all occupy numerous master statuses throughout our lives, and each influences us in different ways. For example, although we maintain our ethnicity throughout our lives, if we move to a new country, adapt to a new culture, and learn a different language, our experience of our ethnic identity can evolve. Moreover, we all move from young to old and experience changing family and job roles, shifting from child to parent, unemployed to employed, and so on.

Our standpoints influence our attitudes, beliefs, and values. An **attitude** is *a general positive or negative feeling a person has about something*. Attitudes reflect our likes and dislikes and our approval or disapproval of events, people, or ideas (Eagly & Chaiken, 1998; Olson & Zanna, 1993). A **belief** is *a person's idea of what is real or true or not*. Beliefs are more conceptual than attitudes and reflect what we think we know about the world. A **value** is *a person's idea of what is good, worthy, or important*. Our values reflect what we think is an ideal world or state of being. Values help us determine whether we think a person, idea, or thing is acceptable in our worldview (Kidder, 1994; Rokeach, 1970, 1973; Schwartz & Blisky, 1990).

Conversations, debates, and arguments held as part of the public dialogue are heavily influenced by the different attitudes, beliefs, and values that result from our different standpoints and master statuses. In particular, attitudes, beliefs, and values are often influenced by our cultural backgrounds. All cultures have unique ways of explaining and organizing the world. Audience-centered speakers recognize these different worldviews and guard against ethnocentrism. Recall from Chapter 1 that **ethnocentrism** is the *belief that our own cultural perspectives, norms, and ways of organizing society are superior to others*. Speakers who let ethnocentric views come through in their speeches run the risk of alienating audience members who do not hold similar views.

attitude
general positive or negative feeling a person has about something.

belief
a person's idea of what is real or true or not.

value
a person's idea of what is good, worthy, or important.

ethnocentrism
belief that our own cultural perspectives, norms, and ways of organizing society are superior to others.

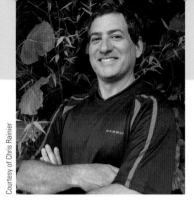

T. H. Culhane

Emerging Explorer and Urban Planner

What beliefs or values are important to consider about your audience before you speak to them?

Well, I try to find out the expectations of the target audience. And some are really tough, so I do get very nervous. And I've had some failures. We were flown in after a very successful Cairo speech and asked to give one to some people in Abu Dhabi. The slides that I showed and the music that I played and experiences I related—they didn't resonate with the audience at all. And I could feel a misunderstanding and tension in the room, and it turned out it was because seeing slums and poverty, even though my messages are always hopeful and always about where we are going and how we are climbing up together, they didn't resonate. These very wealthy people, who were philanthropists, they didn't feel very motivated seeing what the other 90 percent go through and how they live. Many people actually felt threatened. So, I always try to get the message out that we human beings are part of something my dad introduced me to—part of the Great Conversation. We have been sharing stories for centuries that have helped us to progress, and because of that great conversation, I always say no human beings should be excluded from it. But that doesn't always work. I thought the idea that you can turn your waste into energy and fertilizer, and produce your own electricity from the available sunlight—doing it yourself—I thought it would have universal appeal, but it doesn't always.

To be audience centered, speakers must consider the significant influence of master statuses, standpoints, attitudes, beliefs, and values on audiences. When speakers take these factors into consideration, they increase their chances of giving effective speeches.

Choosing Your Speech Topic

Your **speech topic** is the *subject of your speech*. Selecting a topic for a speech can be a highly creative and energizing part of putting a speech together. The steps described in this section will help you find interesting and relevant speech topics for your required speeches, articulate your purpose, and narrow your topic.

speech topic
subject of your speech.

The Classroom Setting
Before you can select an appropriate and interesting topic for your assigned speech, you must consider the requirements of your assignment.

- *Preselected purpose.* An instructor usually tells you to give a particular type of speech such as a speech to inform or persuade. You do not have the freedom to select your speech purpose, and you must select a topic that is compatible with the purpose.

- *Highly structured assignment.* You are usually asked to incorporate several specific speech components such as a specific number of outside sources, visual aids, or a specific style of language. And you will usually have strict time limits, so the structure of an assigned speech often influences topic selection.

- *Your audience.* You give your classroom speeches to an instructor, who is already a skilled public speaker, and your classmates. You must select a stimulating topic that both will appreciate and that is not commonly used.

So how do you select a manageable, interesting, and dynamic topic for your required speeches? The process takes a bit of planning and effort, but you will discover that you have a wealth of usable ideas once you organize your thoughts about who you are, what you know, and what issues and events capture your own attention.

Outline the Requirements for the Assignment The first step to selecting a topic is to outline the requirements of the speech assignment. Your assignment might look like this:

Informative purpose; four minutes long; three to four sources; one statistic; one of the following: metaphor, analogy, narrative, or alliteration; inclusive language.

The second step is to match your interests or expertise to these requirements.

Matching Your Interests to the Speaking Assignment Before you can match your interests to a particular assignment, you must determine what they are. Divide your interests into the following categories: what you like to do, what you like to talk about, and what you would like to know more about.

Most people can identify many activities they like to participate in. Make a list of them, including those that seem serious as well as playful or silly. Try to be as detailed as possible. Krista, a twenty-three-year-old college senior, likes to do the following:

swim, run, cycle	spend time with friends
play soccer, volleyball, tennis, and Frisbee golf	coach children in sports during the summer
snowboard, skateboard, and hike	get good grades
watch television and movies	stay up late
Facebook	eat pizza, hamburgers, anything barbecued, and some vegetables

With a little adjustment and creativity, any of these interests could be turned into an interesting and engaging topic. Krista could inform her audience about any of the following:

the top ten medal-earning swimmers in the world

the history of marathon running

how to play Frisbee golf

who invented skateboards

the longest-running television sitcom

the first chat room on the Web

gender differences in friendship styles

the relationship between grades and annual income

medical research on optimal sleeping patterns

the origins of pizza

These are just a few of the many informative topics Krista could speak about, all relevant to her instructor, her classmates, and the public dialogue.

Issues, events, people, and ideas you are curious about also often make excellent speech topics. You could give a speech that informs others of a particular event, or you could persuade them to participate in that event. If you are intrigued by a famous person, you could give a commemorative or informative speech about that person's life and accomplishments. If you are curious about a place, an idea, an object, or an animal, you could explore it with others in an informative or invitational speech. If you participate in an activity or have always wanted to do so, you could give a persuasive, informative, or invitational speech about it. Speeches that grow out of a speaker's curiosity often capture the attention, interest, and curiosity of an audience as well.

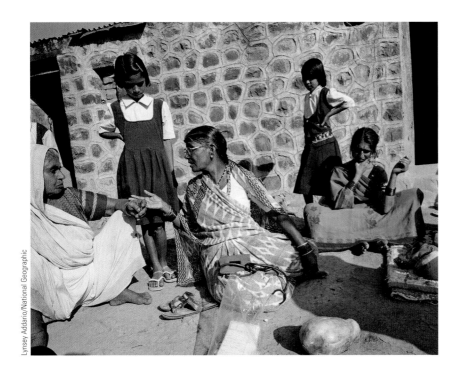

Lynsey Addario/National Geographic

This traveling midwife is speaking to women in Afghanistan about health and hygiene. What are your areas of expertise? What topics could you teach your audience?

Matching Your Expertise to a Speech Assignment Whether we realize it or not, almost everyone is an expert in some area of life. Some people are experts in obvious ways, such as playing a musical instrument, painting, or computer programming. Other people are experts in less obvious ways. They may have an unfailing sense of direction, know the right gift to buy for any occasion, or tell jokes that make people laugh. Dynamic speech topics can come from your own skills and talents. Consider the following examples:

- Tomás is an excellent cook. He decides to give an informative speech on the differences between traditional Bolivian and Spanish foods.

- April is fluent in American Sign Language. She decides to give a speech persuading her audience to learn a second language.

- Gardner is a mechanic. He decides to give a commemorative speech on nineteenth-century French inventor Gustave Trouvé, the creator of the first automobile powered by electricity.

These are interesting speech topics about activities or skills that may seem mundane to the person who has them. You can identify areas in which you may be considered an expert by asking yourself the questions in Practicing Human Communication. Your answers may reveal expertise that you have not thought much about.

brainstorming
process of generating ideas randomly and uncritically without attention to logic, connections, or relevance.

PRACTICING HUMAN COMMUNICATION

How Am I an Expert?

Answer the following questions to help you identify areas in which you may be considered an expert.

- What comes naturally to me?
- What runs in my family?
- Do I often get compliments when I do a particular thing?
- Do others repeatedly ask me to take the lead, take care of some situation, or solve a problem for them?
- Have I ever had special training or lessons?
- Have I spent years studying, practicing, or doing something?
- Do I have degrees, certifications, licenses, or other markers of my accomplishments?

If you answered yes to any of these questions, you may be an expert in some area that would make an interesting topic for a required speech. A few final tips: As you translate your experiences into speech topics, be certain you can talk about them easily without getting upset or revealing more than you are comfortable with. And note that although you might know a lot about a topic, you should still research it to discover interesting aspects about which you might be unaware.

Brainstorm Possible Topics Brainstorming is *the process of generating ideas randomly and uncritically, without attention to logic, connections, or relevance.* This process requires you to free associate rather than plan, and it is often used as a problem-solving strategy in business settings. Brainstorming can be an effective tool for coming up with speech topics in required speaking situations, and you can use this technique by yourself, in pairs, or in groups. Here are some tips for successful brainstorming:

- Let your thoughts go where they will. Do not censor yourself or others. Allow all ideas, even those that seem trivial or odd.

- Write down your ideas quickly. Do not worry about spelling or punctuation, and abbreviate whenever you can.

- Keep your list handy over the course of several days, and add to it as new thoughts come to you.

You can approach brainstorming in several ways: by free association, by clustering, by categories, and by technology.

When you brainstorm using free association, you use a pencil and paper or your computer with a blank screen, and record all ideas that come to your mind (Rosa & Escholz, 1996). After only a minute, a typical free-association list might look like this:

> hands, keyboard, letters, movement, running, wind, kites, children, play, laughter, skinned knees, Band-Aids, nurses, hospitals, sterile, feral cats, tiger, cougars, wilderness, encroachment, farming, ranching, cows, cowboys, rodeos, circus, clowns, entertainment, containment, buckets, garage, car, war, peace, hostility, conflict, harm, warm, cold, snow skiing, skis, lifts, chairs, dining rooms, meals, holidays, families, celebration, gifts

When you are trying to come up with a speech topic, try to spend at least several minutes brainstorming by free association to generate as many ideas as possible. Once you have compiled your list, explore it to determine if one of your ideas might be an appropriate speech topic. The free association list here could generate the following interesting speech topics:

- the inventor of the Band-Aid

- what to do when you encounter a feral cat

- different kinds of clowns

- how different countries celebrate holidays or the starts of new seasons

You can also brainstorm by clustering. Using this method, you write down an idea in the center of a piece of paper and then draw four or five lines extending from it. At the ends of these lines, write down other ideas that relate to your first idea. Then extend lines from these new ideas to even more ideas.

Take a look at Jeret's clustering diagram. He began scuba diving at a very young age, so he used this as his general idea and developed the cluster of ideas shown in Figure 10.1.

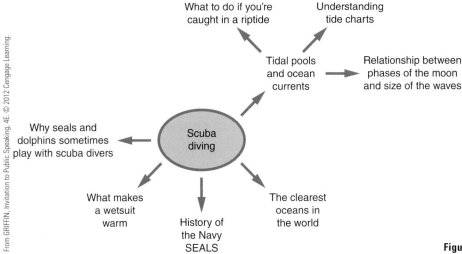

Figure 10.1 *Cluster diagram*

The figure shows that from his general idea of scuba diving, Jeret was able to branch out to many additional ideas. Brainstorming by clustering is a good way to generate speech topics because it gives some structure to the brainstorming process without limiting your possibilities too much.

You can also brainstorm by listing items in various categories. Most speeches given in public-speaking classrooms are about concepts, events, natural phenomena, objects, people, places, plans and policies, problems, and processes. As you have probably noticed, these topics represent different categories. Brainstorming by generating ideas in these categories is an excellent way to select a speech topic, and it provides more structure than free association or clustering. To brainstorm using categories, list the following nine categories on your computer screen or a piece of paper. Then list five or six different words under each heading that fit into the indicated categories. Two students working together came up with the list shown in Table 10.1.

If none of the words you write down immediately strikes you as a good speech topic, then select one or two and use free association or clustering to narrow your scope, generate new ideas, or frame the topic in a way that is interesting and fits the requirements of your assignment.

TABLE 10.1 BRAINSTORMING BY CATEGORY

CONCEPTS	EVENTS	NATURAL PHENOMENA
Socialism	Haitian earthquake-relief efforts	Tornadoes
Tourism	Political elections	Eclipses
Sustainability	Walk for the Cure	Monsoons
Astrophysics	Mardi Gras	Geysers
Dieting	Inti Raymi	Mudslides
Relationships	Oktoberfest	Glaciers
OBJECTS	**PEOPLE**	**PLACES**
Cell phones	Barack Obama	My hometown
Guitars	Sarah Palin	Machu Picchu
Soda fountains	Tiger Woods	Germany
Books	Ellen Degeneres	China
Teapots	Kanye West	Tanzania
Mountains	Apollo Ohno	Stonehenge
PLANS AND POLICIES	**PROBLEMS**	**PROCESSES**
Universal health care	Terrorism	Brewing beer
Stimulus plan	Sexism	Building a house
No Child Left Behind	Racism	Preparing a meal
Sex education	Cancer	Debating, dialoguing
Censorship laws	Obesity	Making jewelry

© Cengage Learning 2014

Similarly, if none of your brainstormed topics catches your interest, link several of them together. Can you find a connection among Mexico, India, and political elections? What about these locations and tsunamis or earthquakes? How about laptops, espresso machines, and theme dining? Linking any of these topics, randomly or with purpose, gives you additional opportunities to develop interesting speech topics.

Finally, you can brainstorm by using technology. If you have access to the Internet, you can discover possible topics by browsing a search engine's subject indexes. Using technology, you can explore an array of topics, click a general subject, and link to more and more specific Web sites until you find a topic that interests you and fits the requirements of your speech assignment.

Libraries also provide many online indexes for journals, newspapers, magazines, and the like. Browse through the *Reader's Guide to Periodical Literature,* InfoTrac College Edition, *The New York Times Index,* or subject-specific indexes about medicine, physics, science, or women's studies.

Stating Your Speaking Goals

Articulating Your Purpose

Once you have selected the topic of your speech, you will want to consider your *speaking goals,* which can be explained in terms of general purposes and specific purposes. The **general purpose** of a speech *is its broad goal: to inform, invite, or persuade.* The **specific purpose** is *a focused statement that identifies exactly what a speaker wants to accomplish with a speech.* Take a look at how you use each of these purposes to organize your thoughts about your speeches.

general purpose
The broad goal of a speech—to inform, invite, or persuade.

specific purpose
focused statement that identifies exactly what a speaker wants to accomplish with a speech.

General Speaking Purposes Suppose you have decided to speak about organic farming. You could speak about many aspects of this topic. Without knowing your purpose for your speech, it can be difficult to know where to begin. Do you describe organic farming, what it is, and who practices it (informative)? Do you invite your audience to explore the impact of organic farming on the environment and the average family's grocery bills (invitational)? Do you attempt to convince your classmates that organic farming is the most efficient type of farming (persuasive)? Your first step toward answering these questions is to determine the overall goal for your speech or your general purpose:

to inform—describe, clarify, explain, define;

to invite—explore, discuss, exchange, understand; or

to persuade—change, shape, influence, motivate.

Notice that each of these overall goals is quite different from the others. For example, the goal of describing is different from the goal of exploring, which is different from the goal of influencing. So by determining your general purpose, you begin to find a focus for your speech.

Specific Speaking Purposes Specific speaking purposes help you narrow the focus of your speech. A specific purpose states exactly what you

Objects such as this automobile often make interesting subjects for a speech. Brainstorm as many different ways as you can to give a speech related to this image of a car.

Rob Wilson/Shutterstock.com

behavioral objectives
actions speaker wants audience to take at the end of a speech.

want to accomplish in the speech. To understand the importance of a speech's specific purpose, consider Ashley's speaking situation.

Ashley tutored fourth graders in an after-school math homework program. This experience prompted her interest in several topics related to the public school system in her state, including possible gender bias in math education and the pledge of allegiance. She decided that she wanted to talk about the pledge and that her general speaking purpose was to persuade. But what did she want to persuade them to do or think? If she had not figured this out, she would have found herself going in circles as she prepared her speech. She would have researched supporting material she did not need, and she would have gotten frustrated as she lost sight of what she wanted to accomplish with her speech.

Ashley needed to develop a specific-purpose statement. How did she do this? First, she identified her **behavioral objectives**, *the actions she wanted her audience to take at the end of her speech.* After some thought, she decided that she wanted her classmates to change their view of the pledge. She wrote on a piece of paper, "I want my classmates to believe a certain way about the Pledge of Allegiance." This speech purpose was still fairly broad, but it was more focused than her general purpose of persuading her classmates to change.

Ashley's next step was to narrow the focus of her behavioral objective even further. She defined what she meant by "believe a certain way." Based on her experiences in the public school and her research, she gained increased understanding of what the pledge means and why she thought it should be recited with the phrase "under God" by children in school. After some thought, Ashley realized that more specifically than wanting her classmates to believe a certain way, she wanted them to adopt her views about the pledge.

So even though Ashley generally wanted to persuade her audience to believe something, she specifically wanted to persuade them to support the pledge. Thus, her specific-purpose statement was, "I want to persuade my audience that the pledge, with the phrase 'under God,' should be recited in schools." At this point, she had a focused idea of what she wanted to communicate to her audience. She then found it much easier to prepare a speech with a specific purpose than if she had stopped at her general purpose of wanting her audience to change.

Table 10.2 shows more examples of general and specific purposes. Notice the differences between the general purposes and the specific purposes. From the three general purposes, you could generate specific purposes for at least twelve very different speeches.

When you state your specific speaking purpose, state it clearly and remain audience centered. Consider the following tips.

TABLE 10.2 GENERAL AND SPECIFIC SPEAKING PURPOSES

GENERAL PURPOSE	SPECIFIC PURPOSE
To inform	To inform my audience of the services offered by our campus counseling center.
	To inform my audience of the process of planting, harvesting, and preparing organic produce.
To invite	To invite my audience to explore the benefits of individual and group counseling.
	To invite my audience to explore the implications of turning part of our community park into organic gardening space.
To persuade	To persuade my audience to use the services offered by our campus counseling center.
	To persuade my audience to buy organic produce.

© Cengage Learning 2014

State your specific speaking purpose clearly. Begin your specific-purpose statements with the infinitive phrases *to inform, to invite, or to persuade.* These phrases clearly indicate what your general purpose is and what you hope to accomplish with your speech. Compare the following correct and incorrect statements of purpose.

Correct	Incorrect
To inform my audience of the history of martial arts in the United States.	I'm going to talk about martial arts.
To invite my co-workers to explore ways we could support local community organic gardens.	Supporting community gardening.
To persuade my audience to participate in Walk for the Cure.	Walk for the Cure is a good event.

Notice that the incorrect statements are unfocused and do not indicate the overall goal of the speech. Although it may seem that the incorrect statements leave greater room for a speaker's creativity, they are too vague to be of much help when you prepare your speech.

Keep your audience in the forefront of your mind. Remember, you are speaking to and for a particular audience, and you research and organize your speech with this fact in mind. Your specific purpose should clearly reflect the presence of your audience. To this end, be sure your specific-purpose statement includes the words *my audience* or a more specific synonym.

Notice how the correct examples encourage you to reflect on the makeup of your audience in ways that the incorrect examples do not.

James A. Sugar/National Geographic

Sylvia Earle, National Geographic Explorer-in-Residence and Oceanographer: Ocean Hero

Sylvia Earle, an oceanographer for more than fifty years, has written more than 175 publications, lectured in more than seventy countries, and led more than sixty diving expeditions worldwide. She is affectionately known as "Her Deepness" because she holds several world records for depth of diving. Earle has a profound commitment to civic engagement and communicating her insights and passions in as many ways as she can.

An explorer in residence for National Geographic, Earle received the coveted TED Prize (TED stands for Technology, Entertainment, and Design) in 2009 for her proposal to establish Mission Blue, a global network of marine protected areas she dubbed "hope spots." Recipients of the TED Prize are known for their effective communication, commitment to civic engagement, and passion for the work they do. The prize includes $100,000, and the recipient is granted a "wish to change the world." Earle explained her wish as nothing short of saving our oceans. In her book *The World Is Blue: How Our Fate and the Ocean's Are One,* she explains, "My wish is a big wish, but if we can make it happen, it truly can change the world and help ensure the survival of what is actually my favorite species, human beings." She explains,

> Fifty years ago, when I began exploring the ocean, no one—not Jacques Perrin, not Jacques Cousteau, or Rachel Carson—imagined that we could do anything to harm the ocean by what we put into it or by what we took out of it. It seemed, at that time, to be a sea of Eden, but now we know, and now we are facing paradise lost. In fifty years, we've lost—actually, we've taken, we've eaten—more than 90 percent of the big fish in the sea; nearly half of the coral reefs have disappeared; and there has been a mysterious depletion of oxygen in large areas of the Pacific. It really should concern you. It does concern you.

When asked, "if you could have people do one thing to help the ocean, what would it be?" Earle replied,

> Hold up a mirror and ask yourself what you are capable of doing, and what you really care about. Then take the initiative—don't wait for someone else to ask you to act. . . . Everyone has power. But it doesn't help if you don't use it. Knowing is the key. Become informed! With knowing comes caring, and with caring there is hope that we will find an enduring place for ourselves within the natural—mostly blue—systems that sustain us.

Earle believes that becoming informed is the most important contribution to saving the ocean. And she has made it her mission to help inform people around from around the world (Earle, 2011; National Geographic. com, 2009; National Geographic.com, n.d.).

Logon to http://www.ted.com/talks to watch Earl's TED Talks speech. As you listen, consider her speaking goals, how audience centered she is, and her introduction and conclusion.

Imagedj/Shutterstock.com

1. Sylvia Earle was *asked to speak* at the TED2009 conference. What experiences or expertise does Earle possess that make her a good candidate to speak on changing the world? What are Earle's master statuses?

2. What are Earle's attitudes, beliefs, and values that influence her understanding of the ocean?

3. Based on the information presented in Earle's speech introduction, what would her specific purpose and thesis statement be?

4. How does Earle attempt to satisfy the four objectives to a speech introduction? Do you believe the introduction is effective? Why or why not?

The phrases "my audience" and "my co-workers" encourage the speaker to focus not on some unspecified entity but on a specific group of people with particular traits and characteristics.

As you begin to organize your materials about your speech, write your general and specific statements of purpose at the top of all your research notes. Like any good road map, clear statements of purpose will help you select and navigate the path toward putting the final touches on your presentation.

Stating Your Thesis

So far in this chapter, you have explored how context affects your speaking goals, how to stay audience centered, how to select a speech topic, and what your general and specific purposes are. Now you are ready to take the final step to complete this initial part of the speech preparation process. Every successful speech has a *thesis statement,* sometimes called a *central idea.* A **thesis statement** summarizes *in a single declarative sentence the main ideas, assumptions, or arguments you want to express in your speech.* It adds focus to your specific purpose because you state the exact content of your speech in a single sentence.

Note that the thesis statement is closely related to the specific purpose. Recall that the specific-purpose statement indicates what you want your audience to understand or do as a result of your speech. The thesis statement helps you identify the main ideas of your speech; these will become the main points for your speech.

Look again at some specific-purpose statements to see how they relate to thesis statements.

Specific purpose: To inform my audience of the different belts in the martial arts

With this statement, Oscar claims it is useful to understand the different belt levels in the martial arts. To focus his speech on a manageable aspect of this topic, he must determine exactly what he wants the audience to know about the martial arts belt systems. He considers what he is asked most often about this topic. Thus, his thesis statement looks like this:

Thesis statement: In the three most common schools of martial arts in the United States—judo, karate, and tae kwon do—the black belt is the most esteemed belt level among the slightly differing belt systems.

With his thesis statement, Oscar considers how much common knowledge there is about the martial arts as well as what people are most curious about. In addition, his thesis statement summarizes and previews two main points:

1. Judo, karate, and tae kwon do are the most common schools of martial arts in the United States.

2. Each school has a slightly different belt system, but the black belt is the most esteemed belt level in all the schools.

Table 10.3 shows the three different speech types as they evolve from the general purpose to the specific purpose and then into a thesis statement.

thesis statement

single declarative sentence that summarizes the main ideas, assumptions, or arguments you want to express in your speech.

TABLE 10.3   GENERAL AND SPECIFIC PURPOSE AND THESIS STATEMENT

INFORMATIVE SPEECH

General purpose	To inform.
Specific purpose	To inform my audience about where to seek shelter during a tornado.
Thesis statement	When a tornado strikes, seek shelter in a storm cellar, a fortified storm closet, or your bathtub.

INVITATIONAL SPEECH

General purpose	To invite.
Specific purpose	To invite my audience to explore the pros and cons of retaining the death penalty in the United States.
Thesis statement	I'd like to describe the benefits and drawbacks of retaining the death penalty in the United States and then explore with my audience whether this punishment is still appropriate for serious crimes.

PERSUASIVE SPEECH

General purpose	To persuade.
Specific purpose	To persuade my audience to learn a second language.
Thesis statement	When we learn a second language, not only do we learn to appreciate the culture of the people who speak that language, but we also increase our understanding of our own culture.

© Cengage Learning 2014

 ## Organizing Your Speech

You now are ready to begin organizing a speech. Start this process by identifying your **main points**, which are *the most important and comprehensive ideas you address in your speech*. They give your speech focus and help you decide which information to include and which to leave out.

main points
most important and comprehensive ideas you address in your speech.

Identify Your Main Points

If you have already written your thesis statement, then you should be able to find your main points within it. Notice in the following example about folding a flag that Cindy's thesis statement defines her main points: (1) the symbolism in the U.S. flag, (2) how a flag should be hung, (3) how it should be handled, and (4) how it should be folded. Without a thesis statement, a speaker's ideas are simply a random collection of points.

PRACTICING HUMAN COMMUNICATION

Generating Purpose Statements

Look over the list of topics that you generated in the previous Practicing Human Communication boxes. Select one or two topics and write a specific purpose and thesis statement for each. Consider which topics work best for informative, invitational, or persuasive speeches.

Specific purpose:	To inform my audience about the rules and regulations for handling the U.S. flag.
Thesis statement:	The flag, a symbol of much that is great about this nation, should be hung, handled, and folded in a specific manner.
Main points:	I. Each part of the flag has a specific meaning or purpose dedicated to symbolizing patriotic ideas. II. Because of the symbolism of each of these parts, the flag should be hung in a specific manner. III. Flag etiquette, more than just stories told from generation to generation, tells us how to handle a flag properly. IV. Flags also should be folded in a specific way, with each fold representing important qualities of our country.

 CourseMate Connection: Go to cengagebrain.com to access the CourseMate for *Invitation to Human Communication* to view a video about the process of folding a flag. You can watch the video, respond to the analysis questions, and compare your answers to those provided by the authors.

There are three keys to developing your main points. First, keep each main point separate and distinct—do not combine points. Second, word your points consistently. Finally, devote appropriate coverage to each main point. We will take a look at each key.

Tips for Preparing Main Points

Keep Each Main Point Separate and Distinct. Each main point should be a separate idea. Once you have identified your likely main points, double-check them to be sure you have not combined two ideas into one main point. We may be tempted to combine two ideas to cover as much information as we can. But notice what happened when Aaron combined two ideas into a single point.

Ineffective Main Points	**More Effective Main Points**
I. Electronic music is produced from a variety of machines that make noise electronically.	I. Electronic music is produced from a variety of machines that make noise electronically.
II. Electronic music has become more popular in recent years and is performed by many well-known artists.	II. Electronic music has become more popular in recent years. III. Electronic music is performed by many well-known artists.

Although both columns cover the same ground, the points in the right column are clearer because each addresses only one idea. By separating the two points, Aaron can avoid confusing or overwhelming his audience.

Word Your Main Points Consistently. Try to word your main points as consistently as possible. A parallel structure is easier to organize and remember. In the next example, Michael presented an informative speech on the reasons for stop signs. Notice how the parallel main points in the right column are clearer and more memorable than those in the left column.

Ineffective Main Points	More Effective Main Points
I. Drivers need to know who has the right of way, and a stop sign tells us that.	I. Stop signs assign the right of way to vehicles using an intersection.
II. Stop signs slow down drivers who are traveling at unsafe speeds.	II. Stop signs reduce the problem of speeding in certain areas.
III. Sometimes pedestrians need protection from vehicles, and stop signs give them that protection.	III. Stop signs protect pedestrians in busy intersections or near schools.

With a simple reworking of phrasing, Michael made his main points parallel: stop signs assign, stop signs reduce, stop signs protect. Although this kind of parallel structure is not always possible, your ideas will be clearer and more memorable when you can use it.

Devote the Appropriate Coverage to Each Main Point. Remember that your main points are your most important ideas. Therefore, each point should receive the same level of development and attention in your speech. On the one hand, if you find yourself spending little time developing a particular point, then ask yourself whether it really is as important as you thought and whether it should be a main point in your speech. On the other hand, you find yourself putting a lot of development into one point, then consider whether you should divide it into two points. In preparing a speech on the art of batik, Martha discovered the following imbalance.

Specific purpose: To inform my audience about batik, a beautiful and diverse art form that has been practiced for centuries.

Thesis statement: The art of batik has an intriguing history as well as methods of production and designs that reflect the skill and politics of the artisan.

Main points:
    I. The history of batik (65 percent of the speech)
    II. The production of batik (15 percent of the speech)
    III. The designs of batik (15 percent of the speech)
    IV. Where to purchase batik (5 percent of the speech)

    Martha realized she had spent so much time on her first point that she did not have time to cover her remaining points. Although the history of batik is important, it was not the only information she wanted to share with her audience. She also wanted to show them the production process and some of the designs she loved. After some consideration, Martha reduced the scope of her speech by dropping her fourth point (which was not really a part of her thesis statement), and she condensed

Batik is a complex process that results in beautiful designs and patterns. Can you think of other processes that are complex, but still would make an interesting speech?

the details of her first point. She reworked her speech as follows, saving 20 percent of her time for her introduction and conclusion:

Specific purpose: To inform my audience about batik, a beautiful and diverse art form that has been practiced for centuries.

Thesis statement: The art of batik has an intriguing history as well as methods of production and designs that reflect the skill and politics of the artisan.

Main points:
  I. The history of batik (30 percent)
  II. The production of batik (25 percent)
  III. The designs of batik (25 percent)

Your goal, as Martha's revised main points suggest, is not necessarily to spend exactly the same amount of time on each point but to offer a balanced presentation of your ideas.

Connectives

Your main points are the heart of your speech. Once you have them on paper and supported with your research, you must find ways to connect them to enhance the audience's understanding. The *words and phrases we use to link ideas in a speech* are called **connectives**. They show audiences the relationship between ideas.

Before you read the descriptions of the four types of connectives, consider some of the connectives that speakers use unconsciously: "all right," "next," "now," "um," "and," "so," "so then," and "ah." These words are often called *fillers* because they are words or sounds that tell the audience almost nothing about the relationship between ideas. Fillers can be annoying, especially when the same one is repeated often in a speech.

connectives
words and phrases used to link ideas in a speech.

The following section offers four useful alternatives to these fillers: transitions, internal previews, internal summaries, and signposts. These will add meaning and help your audience remember your ideas.

Transitions

Transitions are *phrases that indicate you are finished with one idea and are moving to a new one*. Effective transitions restate the idea you are finishing and introduce your next one. In the following examples, the transitions are underlined:

> Now that you understand how our childhood memories influence our relationship to money, let's explore the relationship we have to money as adults.

> Once you've visited Manarola, you're ready to move to the final village, Riomaggiore, also known as "the village of love."

You can consciously insert transitions such as "let's turn to," "now that you understand," "in addition to," and "that brings me to my next point." But many will come naturally as you close one point or idea and begin a new one. Use transitions to link ideas within your main points and to guide your audience from point to point as you deliver your speech.

transitions
phrases that indicate you are finished with one idea and are moving to a new one.

Internal Previews

An **internal preview** is *a statement in the body of your speech that details what you plan to discuss next*. Internal previews are used to introduce a new point in your speech. Internal previews focus on what comes next in the speech rather than linking two points as transitions do. In the next example, Martha introduces her second point, batik production, with an internal preview:

> In discussing the production of batik, I'll explain the four steps: the preparation of the cloth, the mixing of the dyes, the application of the dye, and the setting of the image in the cloth.

After hearing this preview, the audience is ready for four steps and begins to appreciate the intricacies of the batik process. Internal previews are often combined with transitions, as in Robert's discussion of theatrical lighting:

> As you can see, (*transition*) with the invention of the lightbulb came exciting and safer possibilities for theatrical lighting. And the now familiar lightbulb takes me to my third point, (*internal preview*) the invention of three instruments that revolutionized lighting in the theater: the ellipsoidal, the fresnel, and the intelabeam.

Not every main point requires an internal preview, but the unfamiliar terminology in Robert's third point lends itself to a preview. Introducing new concepts or terminology before offering the details enhances your audience's understanding of your topic.

internal preview
statement in the body of your speech that details what you plan to discuss next.

Internal Summaries

An **internal summary** is *a statement in the body of your speech that summarizes a point you have already discussed*. If you have just finished an important or complicated point, add an internal summary to remind your audience of its highlights. In Jeremy's speech on sibling rivalry, he used an internal summary at the end of the first point:

internal summary
statement in the body of your speech that summarizes a point you have already discussed.

To summarize, the causes of sibling rivalry—birth order, sex, parental attitudes, and individual personality traits—can cause children to compete for their parents' affection and attention.

Like internal previews, internal summaries can be combined with transitions so you can move efficiently into your next point. Here's an example from Brandon's speech:

> In short, (*internal summary*) the lack of funding for before- and after-school meal programs leads to poor academic performance, increased absences, and behavioral problems. But let's see (*transition*) what this bond issue will do to remedy many of these problems.

Internal summaries are excellent tools to use when you want your audience to remember key points before you move on to a new idea. When combined with transitions, internal summaries can help audiences move smoothly from one idea to the next.

Signposts

A **signpost** is *a simple word or statement that indicates where you are in your speech or highlights an important idea*. Signposts tell your audience where you are in the presentation of your main points and help your listeners keep track of a detailed discussion or list of items. These tools add clarity to a speech and can make it flow. Signposts can be numbers ("first," "second," "third"), phrases ("the most important thing to remember is," "you'll want to make note of this"), or questions you ask and then answer ("so how do we solve this dilemma?"). In Alex's speech on women in extreme sports, she asked questions to introduce each of her main points. For her first main point, she asked,

> How many of you know who Layne Beachley is?

For her second, Alex asked,

> So, you didn't know Layne Beachley. How about Cara Beth Burnside? Can anyone tell me her accomplishments?

And for her third, Alex asked,

> Okay, I'll give you one more try. Who knows Tara Dakides's contributions to the world of extreme sports?

Although you do not want to overuse these kinds of questions, they can be effective in getting an audience involved in your speech because audience members will try to answer the questions in their own heads before you do.

The final use of signposts is to mark the most important ideas in your speech. When you hear or use any of the following phrases, they are signposts that ask the audience to pay close attention:

The most important thing to remember is . . .
If you hear nothing else from today's speech, hear this . . .
Let me repeat that last figure for you . . .
This next point is crucial to understanding my arguments . . .

signpost
simple word or statement that indicates where you are in your speech or highlights an important idea.

FloridaStock/Shutterstock.com

Signposts give us important information about where we are in a speech. Be sure to include them in your main points.

You should use this kind of signpost only once in a speech. If you use it more often, the audience quickly loses confidence that what you are about to say is really "the most important thing."

Now that you have explored how to link your main ideas together, we will turn to techniques for introducing your speech as well as concluding it.

SPEAKING VISUALLY

What's in a Tattoo?

According to the Smithsonian Institution's Web site, "Humans have marked their bodies with tattoos for thousands of years. These permanent designs—sometimes plain, sometimes elaborate, always personal—have served as amulets, status symbols, declarations of love, signs of religious beliefs, adornments and even forms of punishment" (Lineberry, 2007a, 2007b). The earliest examples of tattoos are found on the 5,200-year-old "Iceman" found along the Italian–Austrian border in 1991, and 4,000-year-old Egyptian female mummies. The Iceman's tattoos are thought to be the result of an effort to release pain, as they are found in random spots along his joints. The tattoos on the Egyptian mummies are believed to be artistic markers of status or permanent amulets designed to protect women during pregnancy. Ancient tattoos are thought to have marked status (high or low, depending on the era), and other tattoos were used to identify someone as a slave.

Facial tattoos—most commonly associated with the Maori of New Zealand and some Native American people such as the Cree—were also found on the mummified bodies of six Greenland Inuit women who lived around 1475 A.D. In the Maori culture,

> the head was considered the most important part of the body, with the face embellished by incredibly elaborate tattoos or "moko," which were regarded as marks of high status. Each tattoo design was unique to that individual and since it conveyed specific information about their status, rank, ancestry, and abilities, it has accurately been described as a form of ID card or passport, a kind of aesthetic bar code for the face (Lineberry, 2007a).

However, tattoos as markers or conveyors of information have also been used by sailors so that they could be easily identified should they drown, to identify prisoners of Nazi concentration camps, and as symbols of gang membership or activities.

A 2006 telephone survey conducted by the Pew Research Center for People and the Press (2007) found that 36 percent of Americans ages eighteen to twenty-five, 40 percent of those twenty-six to forty, and 10 percent of those forty-one to sixty-four had a tattoo. Today, the ten most popular tattoo designs are flowers, lettering, symbols, religious signs, skulls, Japanese designs, portraits, symbols of love, birds, and wildlife. Although the excessively tattooed body was once seen as deviant or lower class and was displayed at fairs and circuses, according to communication scholar Mindy Fenske, today's tattoos are a form of "writing on the body" that communicates a challenge to notions of class, acceptability, and even what a body is for and can do. Today's tattooed bodies, Fenske argues, are a "performance of resistance" and often serve as visual statements about someone's identity and the body's ability to speak out about or for something (Fenske, 2004).

What Do You Think?

1. As a class, discuss what you think tattoos communicate and why. How much agreement is there among your class?

2. If you were to give a speech about tattoos, what kind of speech would you give, and why?

Introductions and Conclusions

Introductions, even short ones, make an audience more willing to listen to a speech, think more highly of the speaker, and understand the speech better (Andeweg, de Jong, & Hoeken, 1998). Similarly, conclusions reinforce thesis statements, remind listeners of main points, and frame the speaker's ideas and arguments in just the way he or she wants. As you read the following discussion, keep in mind that your introduction and conclusion frame the way you enter and exit the public dialogue.

The Introduction

In your introduction, you set the stage for what is to come, connect your audience to your topic, and establish your purpose for speaking. Introductions are like first impressions—they are important and lasting. We will now look at the four parts of an introduction.

1. Catch the Audience's Attention As a speaker, you want your audience to listen to you and to be intrigued and curious about your topic. When you catch audience members' attention, you not only pique their curiosity but also show them how the topic relates to them. As you catch your audience's attention, remember to act ethically: you must be honest, respectful, and behave in a manner consistent with the principles of an open and healthy public dialogue.

2. Reveal the Topic of Your Speech In your introduction, you also want to let the audience know the subject of your speech. Although guessing games can be fun, your audience wants to know what you will be discussing. Keeping the audience in suspense for a moment or two is fine, but your introduction should reveal your topic before you begin your first main point.

3. Establish Your Credibility To be **credible** is *to gain the trust of your audience and to communicate that you have considerable knowledge of your topic*. If your audience members regard you as credible and competent, then they will believe they have good reasons to listen to your ideas. Establishing credibility also contains an ethical dimension. Audiences do not like to be lied to or misled. If you distort your credibility on a subject, your audience is less likely to believe you or be influenced by your speech.

4. Preview Your Speech In your **preview**, you share with your audience *a brief overview of each of the main points in your speech*. Previews communicate to your audience that you are organized and competent. Previews also help your audience organize their thoughts about your topic and mentally prepare for what you are going to say next.

There are several creative ways to gain your audience's attention, reveal your topic, establish your credibility, and preview your speech. The following techniques will help you prepare compelling, memorable introductions.

Preparing a Compelling Introduction

Ask a Question. A question can arouse your listeners' curiosity and capture their attention. A question can also reveal the topic of your speech—the answer should relate to your topic. Sometimes, speakers use

credible
to gain the trust of your audience and to communicate that you have considerable knowledge of your topic.

preview
brief overview of each of the main points in your speech.

a **rhetorical question**, a *question used for effect that audience members are not supposed to answer out loud but rather in their own minds*. At other times, speakers may ask questions to solicit answers directly from the audience. Notice how Nathan asks rhetorical questions and supplies his own answers as he begins his speech:

> Do you think you could walk from New York to just beyond Chicago? How about from Georgia to Maine? If you're up for such a hike, take the route from Georgia to Maine—that will put you on the Appalachian National Scenic Trail, a trail that stretches more than 2,000 miles and traverses fourteen states. This trail is also the topic of my speech today.

Tell a Story. A second way to capture your audience's attention and reveal your topic is to tell a story. Stories can draw people into a speech and personalize topics that might seem remote or disconnected to some members of an audience. Notice how Brandi uses language creatively to draw her audience into her story.

> It seemed like such a harmless thing to do. What could be wrong with putting out a little food to help the foxes and deer make it through a hard winter? Besides, seeing wildlife in your backyard is one of the many benefits of living in Colorado. Or so thought a family who set out dog food, hamburger, and grains for foxes and deer near their home in the wooded foothills just outside Denver. But guess who also came to dinner? Tasty treats left in the family's backyard lured hungry mountain lions into the neighborhood. The wild cats not only liked the hamburger but also had their eyes on one of their favorite prey—the deer.
>
> It didn't take long for the real trouble to start. Residents' cats and dogs began disappearing from their yards. Fear and anger set in, and people began calling officials to do something about the mountain lions. What started as a well-meaning effort for deer and foxes ended in the death of one of Colorado's favorite wild animals. The mountain lion was killed in a trap set out to make the neighborhood safe again.
>
> Hi, my name is Brandi Lafferty, and today I'd like to describe some of the negative consequences associated with feeding big game wildlife and encourage you to help keep our wildlife wild.

Recite a Quotation or a Poem. You also can catch your audience's interest and reveal your topic through a quotation or poem. Quotations lend your speech the credibility of someone more famous or knowledgeable than you are. They also can teach lessons or illustrate perspectives that are relevant to your speech. Quotations can be quite simple or fairly complex. In a speech on adoption, Chad began with a simple quotation:

> Dennis Rainey, author of the book *One Home at a Time,* states, "I have a wife and six children, two of which are adopted—but I can't remember which ones."

In the next example, Jessica begins her speech with a poem to set the tone and reveal her topic:

rhetorical question
question used for effect that audience members are not supposed to answer out loud but rather in their own minds.

Andersen Ross/Blend Images/Getty Images

Poems and quotations can be creative ways to begin a speech and reveal your topic. As you do your research for your speech, consider including something from a book, movie, song, or poem that matches your topic.

May your thoughts be as glad as the shamrocks.
May your heart be as light as the song.
May each day bring you bright happy hours,
That stay with you all year long.
For each petal on the shamrock,
This brings a wish your way—
Good health, good luck, and happiness
For today and every day.

My family has its roots in Ireland, and the shamrock has a long history of meaning . . .

When you use a quotation or poem, be sure it relates directly to your topic or illustrates the importance of your subject. Like stories, there are many great quotations and poems, but you should only use one that sums up your topic and grabs your audience's attention.

Give a Demonstration. When you demonstrate some aspect of your topic, you can capture your audience's interest and make them want to see or hear more. In the following example, Megan began by singing. After she had captured her audience's attention, she revealed the topic of her speech, the author of her song. In the second paragraph, she previewed her speech so her audience knew exactly what she was going to cover.

(Begin by singing "Amazing Grace.") Comfort is what I feel when I hear this song. No matter if I am at a funeral service or singing it in a choir, this song overwhelms me with a sense of peace. I know it has the same effect on others as well. But who was the man behind this song? And isn't it, as some say, a bit overdone? Dr. Ralph F. Wilson states that he used to think "Amazing Grace" was just that—overdone. Wilson says, "'saved a wretch like me,' come on, really now. But the author really was a wretch, a moral pariah." Wilson is the author of *The Story of John Newton,* and John Newton is the author of America's most popular hymn, "Amazing Grace."

But what happened to John Newton that made him a "moral pariah"? What happened in this man's life that it was only the "grace of God" that could save him? Well, today I'm going to share with you just how a "wretch" like John Newton wrote such a well-known hymn. I'll begin by telling you a little bit about his early life. Then, I'll tell you how he came to write "Amazing Grace." Finally, I'll conclude by discussing this hymn's legacy.

Make an Intriguing or Startling Statement. An intriguing or startling statement is an excellent way to draw your audience in with the unknown or the curious. As you read the following example, see if you can identify all four of the criteria for a strong introduction. Notice how Katy takes a little extra time in her introduction to relate the topic to her audience and to establish her credibility:

3.14159265358979323846264433832795. Most of you know the name of the number I just recited. It's a number found in rainbows, pupils of eyes, sound waves, ripples in the water, and DNA—a ratio that both nature and music understand but that the human mind cannot quite comprehend.

This number has sparked curiosity in many minds over the past 4,000 years. I'm talking about pi—not the dessert, but the circle ratio.

Now, a class of speech majors is probably wondering if they can survive a six-minute speech about math. My own interest came about when I was challenged to memorize more digits than a friend of mine could. As a result of that challenge, I have researched this topic, finding information not only technical and historical but also fanatical. Today, I plan to inform you of what pi is, the history of pi, and how pi has created an obsession in people's lives.

When you choose to introduce your speech with a startling statement, be careful. You want to startle rather than offend your audience. If you are thinking about using a statement that may be too graphic or inappropriate, find an acceptable alternative. Your startling statement should invite the audience to listen, not shut down communication.

State the Importance of the Topic. When you state the importance of the topic, you tell the audience why they should listen. Tina used this technique to introduce a speech on a topic that seemed fairly ordinary but was actually quite relevant to her audience:

Okay. Everyone look down at your feet. How many of you have shoes on? Just as I thought. Each of us has a pair of shoes or sandals on our feet. But how many know where those shoes come from? And let's be honest. How many women in the audience have shoes with heels of an inch or more? Um-hmm. Don't answer. And for the men, do you steer the women in your lives toward the heels in the shoe stores? Maybe even some of you men own a pair of heels? Well, when I look in my closet, I see one pair of sneakers, two pairs of boots, and a dozen high-heeled shoes. But do I know where these shoes come from or how heels were invented? No. At least not until I did some research into my shoe fetish.

Today, I'd like to share the story of shoes with you. I'd like to discuss the origination of shoes, the changes they've gone through, the invention of high heels (which originally were made for men, by the way), and the troubles those heels have caused.

Share Your Expertise. Although you know your qualifications for speaking on a subject, your audience may not. Establishing credibility does not mean boasting and bragging. Instead, it means you share your expertise with your audience. Recall how Jessica, Katy, and Tina stated their credibility in their introductions:

Shamrocks. My family has its roots in Ireland.

Why Pi? As a result of that challenge, I have researched this topic, finding information not only technical and historical but also fanatical.

History of Shoes. Well, when I look in my closet, I see one pair of sneakers, two pairs of boots, and a dozen high-heeled shoes. But do I know where these shoes come from or how heels were invented? No. At least not until I did some research into my shoe fetish.

State What's to Come. Previewing your speech is a necessary component of your introduction. When you preview your speech, you give your audience an overview of your main points. The best previews are brief; they set the audience up for what's to come but do not go into too much detail. Here's how Nathan previewed his speech:

> *Appalachian Trail.* First, I'll give you a brief history of the trail's formation. Then, I'll share some facts with you about the trail itself and how it's maintained. Finally, I'll tell you the stories from some of those who have hiked the trail.

The Conclusion

Your conclusion is your final contact with your audience. Just as the introduction represents the first impression you make on your audience, the conclusion represents your last impression. Take time to prepare and practice your conclusion, so you end your speech with as much care as you began it. When you deliver your conclusion, you have two primary goals: bring your speech to an end and reinforce your thesis statement.

End Your Speech When you end a speech, you are signaling to the audience that your presentation is over. This signal comes through your words as well as your style of delivery (Knapp, Hart, Friedrick, & Shulman, 1973). You can use simple words and phrases such as "in closing," "in summary," "in conclusion," "let me close by saying," and "my purpose today has been" to signal that you are finishing your speech. Although these transitions seem obvious, they alert your listeners that you are moving from the body of your speech to your conclusion.

Reinforce Your Thesis Statement The second function of your conclusion is to reinforce the thesis statement of your speech. When you restate or rephrase your thesis statement in your conclusion, you remind your audience of the core idea of your speech. Notice how this reinforcement can be very succinct as in Chad's speech on adoption or more elaborate as in Katy's on pi:

> In my family, I have two parents, an older sister, and two younger brothers. One of them is adopted, but in my heart I could not tell you which one.

> In conclusion, no one knows why pi has caused such a craze or why several books, movies, and fanatical Web pages have been produced on this subject. What inspired the Chudnovsky brothers to devote their lives to the search for pi? What inspired me to write a speech on a silly number? The answer lies in the mystery. Exploring pi is an adventure, which is why people do it. I want you to remember pi not only as the circle ratio, not only as the biggest influence on math over the course of history, but as a number that has an influence on everything we do.

Restating your thesis statement reinforces your arguments and encourages your audience to remember your speech.

Preparing a Compelling Conclusion There are several techniques for signaling the end of a speech and reinforcing your thesis statement.

As you develop your conclusion, ask yourself, "What final ideas do I want to leave my audience with?"

Summarize Your Main Points An effective tool for ending your speech and restating your thesis statement is a summary of your main points. A **summary** is a *concise restatement of your main points at the end of your speech.* You use it to review your ideas and remind your audience of what's important in your speech. Review Katy's conclusion presented earlier and notice how she summarized each main point as she drew her speech to a close.

Answer Your Introductory Question If your speech begins with questions, answer them in the conclusion. This technique reminds the audience of what they have learned in the speech. Nathan began with questions about hiking the Appalachian Trail, so he now returns to those questions in his conclusion:

> So, now do you think you could walk from New York to Chicago or from Georgia to Maine? Well, even if you're not up for the hike, many others have been. As a result of the efforts to maintain the Appalachian Trail, individuals have hiked the 2,200-mile-long footpath to raise funds, overcome disabilities, and seek out spiritual insights. The next time someone asks you if you want to "take a hike," perhaps you'll say, "Why not?"

Refer Back to the Introduction Occasionally, a speaker opens with a word, phrase, or idea and then returns to it in the conclusion. Like answering introductory questions, this technique brings the speech full circle and provides a sense of completeness. This technique usually is combined with others such as summarizing the main points.

Reggie, who opened his speech with a story of a boy's battles with chronic health problems, finished the story in his conclusion. After restating his thesis, he said,

> And that boy I told you about in the opening of my speech? Well, I'm that boy, I'm now nineteen, doing fine, and in fact, I haven't set foot in a hospital for more than four years now.

Recite a Quotation When you conclude with a quotation, you rely on someone else's words to reinforce your thesis statement. A concluding quotation should come from someone you cited in your speech or from a famous person the audience will recognize. In the following example, Tina not only summarizes her main points but also returns to a source she had cited earlier in her speech:

> As we've heard today, shoes have gone through great changes over time. What started with animal skins and then lace transformed itself into the twenty-four-inch heels worn by both men and women and on to the modern look we know today. But as Dr. Rene Cailet says, "Shoes should protect the foot and not disturb it. Having sore feet is not normal. As in any body part, pain is a signal that something is wrong."

summary
concise restatement of your main points at the end of your speech.

Chapter Summary

When We Give a Speech, We Enter the Public Dialogue with Civility

- The word *civility* comes from a root word meaning "to be a member of a household."
- A dialogue is a civil exchange of ideas and opinions between two people or a small group of people.
- The public dialogue is the ethical and civil exchange of ideas and opinions among communities about topics that affect the public.
- People decide to participate in the public dialogue for three main reasons: they decide to speak, they are asked to speak, or they are required to speak.

To Be Audience Centered Is to Consider the Positions, Beliefs, Values and Needs of an Audience

- Master statuses are significant positions a person occupies within society that affect that person's identity in almost all social situations and can affect an individual's standpoint, or the perspective from which a person views and evaluates society.
- Our standpoints influence our attitudes, beliefs, and values.
- An attitude is a general positive or negative feeling a person has about something.
- A belief is a person's idea of what is real or true or not. A value is a person's idea of what is good, worthy, or important.
- Ethnocentrism is the belief that our own cultural perspectives, norms, and ways of organizing society are superior to others.

Your Speech Topic Is the Subject of Your Speech

- To select your topic, match your interests to the assignment, consider your expertise, and brainstorm.
- When you brainstorm, you generate ideas randomly and uncritically without attention to logic, connections, or relevance.

Keep in Mind the Goals of Your Speech

- The general purpose of a speech is its broad goal: to inform, invite, or persuade. The specific purpose is a focused statement that identifies exactly what a speaker wants to accomplish with a speech.
- To narrow your specific purpose, consider your behavioral objectives, which are the actions you want your audience to take at the end of your speech.

A Speech Is Organized Around the Thesis Statement, Which Is Sometimes Called a *Central Idea*

- A thesis statement summarizes in a single declarative sentence the main ideas, assumptions, or arguments you want to express in your speech.
- Main points are the most important, comprehensive ideas you address in your speech.
- Keep each main point separate and distinct, use parallel word structure, and devote appropriate coverage to each main point.
- The words and phrases we use to link ideas in a speech are called *connectives*.
- Connectives consist of transitions, internal previews, internal summaries, and signposts.

The Introduction of a Speech Has Four Parts: Catching the Audience's Attention, Revealing the Topic, Establishing Credibility, and Previewing the Speech

- Your conclusion signals the end of the speech and reinforces your thesis statement.
- Your conclusion should offer a summary, which is a concise restatement of your main points at the end of your speech.
- You can conclude your speech by answering your introductory question, referring back to your introduction, or reciting a quotation.

Key Concepts

attitude (234)

audience-centered speaker (232)

behavioral objectives (242)

belief (234)

brainstorming (238)

connectives (250)

credible (254)

dialogue (230)

ethnocentrism (234)

general purpose (241)

internal preview (251)

internal summary (251)

main points (247)

master statuses (233)

preview (254)

public dialogue (230)

rhetorical question (255)

signpost (252)

Invitation to Human Communication Online

Speech Communication CourseMate includes an interactive eBook and interactive learning tools including National Geographic Explorer videos, student videos, quizzes, flash cards, and more. Speech Builder Express 3.0 and Speech Studio 2.0 are also available. Go to cengagebrain.com to access your CourseMate for *Invitation to Human Communication* where these resources can be found.

Further Reflection and Discussion

1. Discuss how you might state a specific purpose for a speech on these topics: Olympic gold medals, natural disasters, giving 10 percent of your income to charity, and hybrid cars.

2. Think about the specific purpose of the topics listed in question 1. For each topic, discuss how your audience affects what you say about the topic.

3. Imagine that you have been asked to give a speech on the history of bubble gum. Brainstorm some intriguing or startling introductions.

4. In class, write a possible speech topic on a slip of paper and trade that paper with another student. Now write an introduction and a conclusion for a speech on that topic using the techniques discussed in the chapter. Present your introduction and conclusion to the class for feedback on each of their components.

Activities and Web Links

Visit cengagebrain.com to access the CourseMate for *Invitation to Human Communication* where these activities and web links can be found.

1. Choose one of the facts listed on this Web page about violence as an introduction to your speech. How would you need to consider your audience? What type of audience would respond well? What might you need to add or say to increase your credibility with the audience? Go to *Web link 10.1.*

2. Read the article "Tracking the Wage Gap: In Honor of Equal Pay Day; 12 Sobering Figures about Men, Women, and Work." Consider the issue of equal pay as a speech topic. Create a thesis statement and three main points you would cover in your speech. Go to *Web link 10.2.*

3. Watch this short video of Ken Banks talking about how an innovative idea for communication occurred to him while he was watching a soccer match on television. How does he establish credibility? Is his conclusion effective? Explain. Go to *Web link 10.3.*

4. Listen to the introduction to this speech by Robert Ballard on oceanography. What approach does he use in the introduction to his speech? How does he effectively engage the audience with his introduction? Go to *Web link 10.4.*

5. Watch emerging explorer Jimmy Chin tell his story about being trapped in an avalanche. How effective do you think climber and photographer Chin's story is? Why? Go to *Web link 10.5.*

GATHERING AND DEVELOPING SUPPORTING

IN THIS CHAPTER YOU WILL LEARN TO:

- Use your knowledge and experience to gather effective materials for your speech.
- Search for materials on the Internet and in the library.
- Conduct research interviews.

- Develop examples, statistics, definitions, and other information for your speech.
- Organize your speech using a pattern of reasoning.
- Explain common types of fallacies in logical reasoning.

Use Your Personal Knowledge and Experience

Search for Materials

Conduct Research Interviews

Develop your Supporting Materials

Understand the Patterns of Reasoning

Be Aware of Fallacies in Reasoning

Bloomberg/Getty Images

Speakers often use the words of credible people as testimony, giving strength and credibility to the ideas being developed. If you could interview the President and use his testimony for your next speech, what questions might you ask him? What other supporting materials might you also include?

MATERIALS

I don't believe in setting boundaries or firm expectations—those are just limitations. That's why I find both underwater cave exploration and interdisciplinary research so engaging.

—Kenny Broad, ecological anthropologist and National Geographic Emerging Explorer

One of our primary responsibilities as public speakers is to provide audiences with accurate information. In addition to expressing our opinions on the topics we speak about, we must also provide facts, examples, and evidence. We can find this type of information, called *supporting material*, by consulting our own experiences and knowledge, by doing research over the Internet and at the library, and by interviewing the right people. This chapter will help you collect the supporting materials you need and then develop them ethically and confidently in order to enter the public dialogue successfully.

Use Your Personal Knowledge and Experience

One excellent way to gather materials for your speech is from your personal, firsthand knowledge about a subject. After you have selected a topic, use your personal experience as a starting point for your research. Take a moment to consider what knowledge you already have about your topic. This knowledge can come from your own experiences and training, your family background, hobbies, job or profession, and even things you have read or observed.

Before you decide to use your own experiences as material for your speech, you will want to be sure it is appropriate and ethical to use that information. Ask yourself several questions:

- How much do I actually know about this topic?
- Does my knowledge fit with the purpose of the speech and the assignment?
- Would sharing my experiences harm others or violate their privacy?
- Will sharing my experiences help me build my arguments or develop a point?

If you have a solid background (you have ridden horses since you were four years old, for example) and sharing that background is both ethical and appropriate, then you might consider ways that knowledge and those experiences can help you develop your ideas.

Search for Materials

For public speaking students, the Internet and the library offer information on local, regional, national, and international events and issues and provide a truly staggering range of ideas to pick from in selecting your supporting materials.

Find Materials on the Internet

Certain search techniques such as Google Scholar will help you with your research, taking you to the most recent scholarship on your topic. Using the Internet, you can also find government documents. Government documents can help you find statistics; information on social, political, and historical issues; what Congress has been discussing or debating; what kind of research the government is sponsoring; and maps, charts, and other images you can download and use as visual aids for your speech. Most government information now is available on the Internet, and you can search by subject or by agency.

The Ethics of Internet Research Because the Internet is easy to access and is open to anyone, information from a variety of sources is posted on the Internet that may not be accurate. Many Web sites are maintained and regularly updated by reputable people, companies, and institutions, but just as many others are not. Websites are regularly abandoned, and thus never updated, by operators who lose funding or simply lose interest. As a result, Web sites range dramatically in accuracy, complexity, and usefulness. Many sites include information that is old, incomplete, or based on personal opinions and biases. In addition, identifying credible Internet sites can be difficult because many sites are well designed and look professional even if they are not.

Challenges like these place particular ethical responsibilities on you when you use the Internet to find supporting materials. To act in good faith with your audience, use only reliable and relevant information from the Internet and accurately credit the sources for this information in your speech. Knowing how to evaluate the quality of information you find on the Internet is crucial and ensures that you develop your speech ideas ethically and responsibly.

Evaluating Internet Information How do you know whether a source found on the Internet is one you can use in your speech? As you would with any other source of information, evaluate your data according to the criteria in Table 11.1

If you keep the five criteria in Table 11.1 in mind as you research your speech topic on the Internet, you will be more likely to use supporting materials that are credible, reliable, authoritative, current, complete, relevant, and consistent. The Internet is certainly a source of much credible material, but it should be only one of many tools you use to gather materials for your speech.

Research Materials at the Library

The library gives you access to resources and materials you will not find on the Internet: librarians (to help you find materials); the most recent (or historical) copies of journals, magazines, and newspapers; books (old as well as new); databases and indexes; and hard copies of documents.

TABLE 11.1   HOW TO EVALUATE INFORMATION FROM THE INTERNET

Is the information reliable?	Check the domain in the uniform resource locator (URL). Is it *.com* (a commercial enterprise that might be trying to sell something), *.org* (a nonprofit organization that may be more interested in services and issues than in commerce), *.edu* (an educational institution), or *.gov* (a government agency)? What bias might those operating the site have about your topic?
Is the information authoritative?	URLs that include a tilde (~) often indicate that a single individual is responsible for the information on a Web site. Can you find the person's credentials posted on the site? Can you contact the person and ask for credentials? Can you find the person's credentials in any print sources, such as a *Who's Who* reference? And is the author an expert on the subject of the site?
How current is the information?	Many Web pages include a date that tells you when it was posted or last updated. If you do not see such a date, you may be able to find it in your browser's View or Document menu. If you determine that the Web site is current, is the time frame relevant to your subject or arguments?
Is the information consistent and unbiased?	Is the information you find consistent with information you find on other sites, from printed sources, or from interviews? Can you find other sources to support the statements, claims, and facts provided by a Web site? To guarantee a comprehensive picture of your topic, search several sites and be wary of outrageous or controversial claims that cannot be checked for accuracy or are not grounded in reasonable arguments or sources (Bolner & Poirier, 2002; Hult, 1996; Kennedy, 1998).

Bolner and Poirier, 2002; Kennedy, 1998

So much information is available on the Web that it can be difficult to determine which material and sources are the most ethical to use. How will you assess the ethical aspects of the research you find for your next speech?

Angela Waye/Shutterstock.com

Your librarian can help you with materials you might not be familiar with: databases, indexes, and reference works.

Databases Databases store large collections of information electronically so they are easy to find and retrieve. You can search databases and indexes using keywords and subjects, and you can refine your search by indicating the time frame you want to limit your search to. Databases provide two types of information:

1. **full-text databases** give you the complete text of newspapers, periodicals, encyclopedias, research reports, court cases, books, and the like (an example of a full-text database is InfoTrac College Edition, which is included in the online resources for this book);

2. **abstracts** summarize the text in an article or publication and help you decide if the research is relevant to your speech.

Indexes Indexes are alphabetical listings of the topics discussed in a specific publication, along with the corresponding year, volume, and page numbers. You can find indexes from almost every academic discipline and area of interest. Table 11.2 presents a list of commonly used indexes.

It is always a good idea to cross-check information you find on the Internet (e.g., information found on Wikipedia), track down someone's credentials (something you read in a popular magazine), or find specific details of

TABLE 11.2 LIST OF COMMONLY USED INDEXES

InfoTrac and InfoTrac College Edition	Citations, abstracts, and full-text articles from thousands of magazines, journals, and newspapers.
LexisNexis	Full-text database for legal, business, and current issues. Includes U.S. Supreme Court and lower court cases.
Academic Search Premier	Scholarly academic multidisciplinary database. Covers a broad range of disciplines, including general academic, business, social sciences, humanities, general sciences, education, and multicultural topics.
IngentaConnect	Indexes scholarly journals and delivers documents. A fee is charged for document delivery.
Readers' Guide to Periodical Literature	Indexes almost 300 popular and general-interest magazines, including *The New Yorker, Newsweek,* and *National Geographic Traveler.*
DataTimes	Online newspaper database, including *Washington Post, Dallas Morning News*, and *San Francisco Chronicle.*
Christian Science Monitor	Indexes the *Christian Science Monitor* International Daily Newspaper.
New York Times Index	Indexes the *The New York Times* newspaper.
NewsBank	Microfiche collection covering current events from newspapers in more than 100 cities.
The Times Index (London)	Index to *The Times* (daily), *The Sunday Times, The Times Literary Supplement, The Times Educational Supplement,* and *The Times Higher Education Supplement.*
Wall Street Journal Index	Emphasizes financial news from the Journal. Includes *Barron's Index*, a subject and corporate index to *Barron's Business and Financial Weekly.*
Washington Post Newspaper	Index of the newspaper from our nation's capital.

© Cengage Learning 2014

SPEAKING VISUALLY

Anti-Drug Campaigns Dissuade People from Trying Drugs—Even Once

In 2007, the U.S. Office of National Drug Policy Control (ONDCP) joined with news media and several states in a campaign to prevent methamphetamine use and raise awareness about the treatment of meth addiction. Two years later, the ONDCP launched an aggressive advertising campaign targeted at people ages eighteen to thirty-four in the sixteen states with the highest levels of reported meth use and lab seizures: Alaska, Washington, Oregon, Nevada, Wyoming, Arizona, New Mexico, Oklahoma, Arkansas, Missouri, Iowa, Minnesota, Illinois, Indiana, Kentucky, and Nebraska (Buddy T., 2009; Methresources.gov, 2009). The ads for this campaign—created in conjunction with various state campaigns such as the Montana Meth Project's "Not Even Once" campaign and Alabama's "Zero Meth" campaign—are described as graphic and disturbing. They also seem to be effective in reducing meth use among young users (Life or Meth, 2002). To see many of the most disturbing ads, log on to blogger Brian Lovin's Web site "40+ Most Powerful Anti-Meth Advertisements." The ONCDP also designed a second campaign, *Above the Influence,* to target youth between the ages of twelve and seventeen. The campaign includes broad media messages at the national level and promotes active engagement at the local community level. The campaign's in-market survey indicates that teens who are aware of the Above the Influence campaign "held significantly stronger anti-drug beliefs than those who were unaware of the campaign" (see chart above).

Much research suggests that if fear appeals are too graphic and cause an audience to feel immobilized, then speakers lose the support of the audience (Casey, Timmermann, Allen, Krahn, & Turkiewicz, 2009; Jessop & Wade, 2008; Nabi, Roskos-Ewoldsen, & Carpentier, 2008; Rippetoe & Rogers, 1987; Roser & Thompson, 1995; Schmitt & Blass, 2008; Wong & Capella, 2009). However, compared with appeals that cause an audience to shut down and dismiss the speaker, something unusual and effective

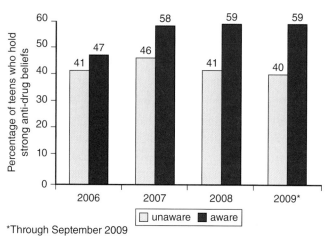

*Through September 2009

Source: National Youth Anti-Drug Media Campaign Tracking Study from "Fact Sheet: Office of National Drug Control Policy" www .WhiteHouseDrugPolicy.gov, http://www.whitehouse.gov/sites /default/files/ondcp/prevention/national_youth_anti_drug_page _media_campaign_fact_sheet_7-16-10.pdf

is happening with the antimeth ads. The ads are appealing to fear by using fairly graphic and disturbing images with success.

What Do You Think?

1. Log on to Lovin's Web site and explore the images there. Do you find the images too graphic or effective? Why?

2. What sources will you use to search for visual images to support or clarify the claims you want to make in your speeches? How will you evaluate their credibility?

3. How might you model the success of the antimeth visual and the *Above the Influence* campaigns in your own speeches?"

a person's life (something you heard on the news, for example). Your local library includes reference works such as almanacs, atlases, and encyclopedias to help you focus on a specific time frame (the worst storms in 2011), and they can give you ideas for other places to look for the materials you need.

Evaluate library sources by using the same strategies you use to assess Internet sources: check that the source is reliable, authoritative, current, complete, relevant, and consistent.

Conduct Research Interviews

An **interview** is a *planned interaction with another person that is organized around inquiry and response, with one person asking questions while the other person answers them* (Steward & Cash, 2006). Interviews require planning, so to make the most of an interview, decide whom you will interview and what questions to ask, and then schedule and conduct the interview in a professional and ethical manner. Remember to follow up with a thank-you letter.

Determine Whom to Interview

To determine whom you will interview for your speech, ask the following questions:

- Who are the experts on my speech topic?
- Who has personal experience with the topic?
- Who will my audience find interesting and credible?
- Who has time to speak with me?
- Who do I have the time to contact?

A good interview subject might be a well-known expert or scholar, a head of an agency or company, someone on staff or in a support position, or a member of a community group, club, or organization.

Design the Interview Questions

Even seasoned interviewers plan their questions carefully, so take time with your interview questions because they are your guide for an interview (King, 1995). The goal of your interview questions is to obtain information that you could not find through your Internet and library research. Three kinds of questions are commonly used in interviews: open-ended questions, closed-ended questions, and probes.

- Open-ended questions invite a wide range of possible responses. They can be as broad as "How did you become an environmental activist?" and "What are your thoughts on this most recent form of legislation?" Open-ended questions are useful for several reasons. They are usually nonthreatening and so prompt interviewees to do most of the talking. They do not restrict the form or content of an answer, and they allow interviewees to offer information voluntarily. Finally, they encourage interviewees to pull together ideas, knowledge, and experiences in interesting ways.

- A closed-ended question invites a brief, focused answer and allows the interviewer to keep tighter control of the direction of the conversation. A closed-ended question might be "How long have you taught elementary school?" or "Do many of your students think about going to college?" Closed-ended questions are useful because they can be answered easily and quickly, encourage interviewees to give you specific information, and result in shorter answers for you to process.

Most research on interviewing suggests that a combination of open-ended and closed-ended questions yields the best results in an interview. Open-ended

interview

planned interaction with another person that is organized around inquiry and response, with one person asking questions while the other person answers them.

questions give you more stories and details than closed-ended questions, but when you just need facts, there is nothing like a closed-ended question to prompt the specific answer you need (Killenberg & Anderson, 1989).

Schedule and Conduct the Interview

Many people are flattered to be asked for an interview. Take a moment to prepare your request and work through the following steps when you contact someone for an interview.

- Identify who you are, providing your full name, where you are from (school, place of business), the course you are in, and your instructor's name.

- Specify the requirements of your assignment including its purpose, length, and topic.

- Describe why you have chosen to contact the person (for example, she is an expert in the field; he is the head of an agency).

- Request the interview, letting the person know how much time it will take and what kinds of questions you will ask. You might even share two or three of your most important or engaging questions so your interviewee can prepare.

 You can find a sample interview request by going to cengagebrain.com to access your CourseMate for *Invitation to Human Communication*.

The guidelines for conducting interviews are essentially grounded in the rules of common courtesy, so they are not difficult to follow.

- Dress appropriately, show up (or phone in if it will be a telephone interview) on time for your interview, and begin by introducing yourself to your interviewee.

- Restate the purpose of the interview and your assignment, and request permission to record the interview.

- Start with questions that will put the interviewee at ease and then follow those with your most important questions.

- At the end of your interview, ask your interviewee if she or he would like to add any information. (You may get a piece of information or a story you did not think to ask for directly but that fits into your speech perfectly.)

Research interviews are an excellent way to gather materials for speeches. Consider the people you might interview for your next speech. What questions could you ask them?

- Finally, thank the interviewee orally for his or her time, and be sure you have recorded names, professional titles, and addresses correctly so you can cite them accurately and send a letter of thanks.

Ethical Interviews

Ethical interviewing means preparing, using quotations and information honestly, including only what was said and staying true to the intention of the speaker, and giving credit to interviewees for the words and ideas you include in your speech. If an interviewee provides information that seems inconsistent with what your other research supports, take the time to double-check your own research and the credentials of your

"I Had No Idea Anyone Was Listening"

Wangari Maathai (1940–2011), the daughter of a sharecropper father and a farmer mother, was often considered something of a first lady. She is the first woman from eastern and central Africa to earn a PhD (in biological sciences); the first woman to become a department chair of the University of Nairobi; the first president of the African Union's Economic, Social, and Cultural Council; and the first African woman to earn a Nobel Peace Prize. Maathi certainly earned the respect a first lady deserves.

Maathai began her impressive career as an environmental and political activist in the 1970s. As part of her work with the National Council of Women of Kenya, Maathai established the Green Belt Movement in response to her conversations with rural women about their concerns over water, energy, and nutrition. Seeing the connections between the clear-cutting of forests and the diminished quality of life for many in Kenya, she began to lead high-profile campaigns to save Kenya's forests and protect its green spaces. Working with thousands of other women, she planted trees to replenish the soil, protect the watersheds, provide fuel, and enhance nutrition. "If you understand and you are disturbed," she said, "then you are moved to action. That's exactly what happened to me."

The government responded to the movement by harassing Maathai and many other women, holding them in jail and sending them death threats. At one point, Maathai was labeled a "mad woman" and beaten almost to death. However, these setbacks did not stop her. By the late 1990s, the government had abandoned its illegal deforestation and development plans, and more than 30 million trees have now been planted throughout Kenya. However, when Maathai received the Nobel Peace Prize in 2004 for her work with the Green Belt Movement, she was surprised. She said, "I had no idea that anyone was listening."

Wangari Maathai

As the Green Belt Movement's official Web site notes, the movement has evolved into "one of the most prominent women's civil society organizations, . . . advocating for human rights and supporting good governance and peaceful democratic change through the protection of the environment." Maathai explained this evolution by saying, "When you start working with the environment seriously, the whole arena comes: human rights, women's rights, environmental rights, children's rights—you know, everybody's rights. Once you start making these linkages, you can no longer do just tree-planting" (Maathai, n.d., 2003, 2006).

What Do You Think?

1. If you were to give a speech on the Green Belt Movement, and the work its members have done since Maathai's death, where would you go for supporting materials? How would you make certain that your research is credible and comprehensive?

2. What issues do you spend time learning about and listening to? Would any of these make a good topic for a speech? Why?

interview subject. Ask your interviewee for documentation or sources that support unusual claims. If an individual shares something with you "off the record," that information should stay out of your speech and out of your conversations with others. In addition, if an interviewee provides information that is highly personal or would compromise the integrity or reputation of others, do not use that information in your speech.

Now that you have explored what type of supporting material you need for your speeches and how to go about obtaining it, we can explore some of the kinds of supporting materials you will want to use in your speech.

Develop your Supporting Materials

The materials we gather from our research must be turned into **evidence**, the *information speakers use to develop and support their ideas.* Strong evidence helps you build your credibility. In this section, you will learn about five of the most common types of evidence: examples, narratives, statistics, testimony, and definitions.

Examples

Examples are *specific instances used to illustrate a concept, experience, issue, or problem.* Examples can be brief, only a word or a sentence or two, or they can be longer and more richly detailed. Examples can also be real or hypothetical. A **real example** is *an instance that has actually taken place.* A **hypothetical example** is *an instance that did not take place but could have.* Generally, real examples are more credible and convey a sense of immediacy. In her speech on binge drinking on college campuses nationwide, Eileen used a powerful example of a binge drinker by describing her friend who "consumed twelve to fifteen beers combined with shots of hard liquor, and stopped only because she ran out of alcohol, time, and money."

Occasionally, you can clarify a point with a hypothetical example. A hypothetical example usually begins with words and phrases such as *imagine, suppose,* or *let's say that.* For example, when Clara addressed a group of teenagers in an after-school program on proper eating for her service learning

---

evidence
information speakers use to develop and support their ideas.

examples
specific instances used to illustrate a concept, experience, issue, or problem.

real example
an instance that has actually taken place.

hypothetical example
an instance that did not take place but could have.

When you give a speech to your classmates, you are speaking to a room of your peers. What kinds of examples do you think your classmates will find relevant and credible?

Mireya Mayor,
Emerging Explorer, Primatologist, and Conservationist

How do you gather your supporting materials for your public speaking appearances? What is your process for gathering materials—where do you locate materials, how to you choose the best materials, how do you decide what not to use?

There are some audiences that lend themselves to more serious topics. For example, during my lectures I talk about the poaching that goes on in Congo with the gorillas, and I have some extremely graphic and powerful images of, well, slaughtered gorillas. They are very graphic, and I clearly wouldn't show that to an audience that's going to have kids or an audience where the venue is a more light-hearted. However, if I'm speaking to scientific audiences, or if I'm speaking to a more mature audience, and I feel that it is appropriate, then I would insert those pictures. If I feel that there is any question that somebody there might be offended, I won't use that kind of supporting material. I have to be very careful and I have learned to gauge who my audience is and who I am talking to.

project, she could have simply said, "Skipping breakfast isn't good for you." Instead, she supported her claim with a hypothetical example:

> Suppose you skipped breakfast this morning. Let's see what that would do to your energy level by about 9 or 10 o'clock—that's during second period, right? If you haven't eaten by then, you'll probably feel bored or restless, and maybe sad or unmotivated. You might also feel angry or irritable, kind of grouchy and crabby. And maybe you'll feel a little light-headed or dizzy if you stand up fast. You might have a headache. You'll definitely have trouble concentrating on your schoolwork because your blood sugar is low or because all you can think about is how hungry you are. Sound familiar to any of you?

Clara's hypothetical example, although not real, grew out of research that was grounded in real experience and helped her audience understand more clearly why skipping meals is not good for them.

Narratives

A **narrative** is *a story that recounts or foretells real or hypothetical events.* Narratives help us explain, interpret, and understand events in our lives or the lives of others (Fisher, 1987; Jamieson, 1988). Speakers can use *brief narratives*, sometimes called *vignettes*, to illustrate a specific point or *extended narratives* to make an evolving connection with a broader point. Josiah used this brief story, which he found as he gathered materials for his speech on the history of battles portrayed in theatrical productions:

> Planned stage combat reduces the level of danger that is part of any battle scene in a play. According to William Hobbs in *Fight Direction for the Stage and Screen*, in early sixteenth-century Stockholm, the actor

narrative
a story that recounts or foretells real or hypothetical events; narratives can be brief or extended.

who played the part of Longinus in *The Mystery of the Passion*, and who had to pierce the crucified Christ, was so carried away with the spirit of the action that he actually killed the other actor. The king, who was present, was so angry that he leapt onto the stage and cut off the head of Longinus. And the audience, who had been pleased with the actor's zeal, were so infuriated with the king that they turned upon him and slew him.

When used in speeches, stories can give historical context to events, make strong connections between ideas and experiences, add emotional depth to characterizations, and describe subjects, settings, and actions with sensory details that can captivate an audience.

Statistics

statistics
numerical summaries of facts, figures, and research findings.

Statistics are *numerical summaries of facts, figures, and research findings.* They help audiences understand amounts ("100 individuals participated"), proportions ("that's almost half the people in this organization"), and percentages ("fully 50 percent said they'd participate again"). Numbers summarize and help audiences make sense of large chunks of information ("eight glasses of water a day, every day of the year, is the equivalent of almost 3,000 glasses of water a year"), and they help people see where something is in relation to other things ("he's the third fastest runner in the world"). See Figure 11.1 for a visual representation of statistics that could help an audience understand how the U.S. government classifies people who immigrate to the United States.

Figure 11.1 *Visual representation of statistics*

Visual representations of statistics help an audience understand complex or abstract information. This graph shows the numbers of immigrants to the United States who became permanent residents in 2007 and 2008 by class of admission.

Source: U.S. Department of Homeland Security, Office of Immigration Statistics, *2008 Yearbook of Immigration Statistics.* See also http://www.dhs.gov/ximgtn/statistics/publications/yearbook.shtm.

Numbers and statistics may seem less glamorous than a story or a clever example, but relevant, surprising, or little-known statistics can grab an audience's attention (Best, 2001, 2008; Taylor, Rice, & Wilson 2000). In fact, according to Cynthia Crossen, author of *Tainted Truth: The Manipulation of Fact in America*, 82 percent of people surveyed said statistics increase a story's credibility (Crossen, 1994).

Common statistics include totals and amounts, costs, scales and ranges, ratios, rates, dates and times, measurements, and percentages. Other more technical statistics are the *mean, median,* and *mode.* The mean, median, and mode are numbers that summarize sets of numbers. The descriptions that follow will help you determine the type of statistics you need in your speech. Also see Figure 11.2 for a visual representation of the differences between mean, median, and mode. The figure shows the mean, median, and mode of the range of rents for fifteen one-bedroom apartments in the Boston area in September 2011.

The **mean** tells you *the average of a group of numbers.* Find it by adding all the numbers in your data set and then dividing by the total number of items. Use the mean when you want to describe averages, patterns, tendencies, generalizations, and trends, especially for large groups of data. For example, the mean is what you need if you want to find the average weight of a group of teenagers, as Clara did in her speech to the after-school youth in our previous example. To find her mean, Clara added together the weight in pounds of each of the teens in her audience (115, 121, 126, 132, 154, 159, 163, 167, and 170) and then divided that number by the total number of teens she had weighed (nine). This gave her the mean, 145 pounds, the average weight in her audience. She used that average, or mean, to compare her audience's average to the average weight of teenagers fifty years ago and then to teen athletes and nonathletes. She and her audience then entered into a discussion about average weights of teenagers in general.

When your data sets include extreme values, or what are called *outliers,* using the mean to generalize about the data is misleading (Fadei, 2000). A group of students speaking to county commissioners about affordable housing illustrates why this is so. The students presented information about the average cost of housing in their area. Most of the houses rented for $900 to $1,500 a month, but one particular home rented for $2,250 a month. In this case, the students could not have used the mean because the outlier in this set of data ($2,250) would have distorted the picture of housing costs in their area. To provide a more accurate statistic, the students need to use the median or the mode or leave out the $2,250 rental and explain why.

The **median** is *the middle number in a series or set of numbers arranged in a ranked order.* A median tells you where the midpoint is in your set of data. It shows you that one-half of your observations will be smaller and one-half larger than that midpoint. Use the median when you want to identify the midpoint and make claims about its significance or about the items that fall above or below it. For example, the median weight of Clara's teens is 154 pounds. This means that half the teens weighed more

mean
the average of a group of numbers

median
the middle number in a series or set of numbers arranged in a ranked order.

NATIONAL GEOGRAPHIC SPEAKS

Albert Yu-Min Lin, Emerging Explorer, Research Scientist, and Engineer : Extreme Engineering in the "Forbidden Zone"

Albert Yu-Min Lin, research scientist, engineer, and emerging explorer for National Geographic, has a passion for finding and preserving stories, especially as they help us understand our "collective cultural heritage." Lin and his team of explorers believe they may have found the tomb and last resting place of Genghis Khan, a leader the world knows little about but whose influence has been profound. Many Mongolians consider the tomb an extremely sacred place and believe any desecration could trigger a curse that would end the world. According to Lin, the world does not know the full story of Khan's life or contributions.

The tomb, located in Mongolia's "Forbidden Zone," represents a discovery that has eluded historians and scientists for centuries. Yet Lin and his team are not going about this potential discovery with the traditional excavation methods, because, Lin explains, "using traditional archeological methods would be disrespectful to believers." Instead, Lin's team is using advanced technology that "leverages photographs taken firsthand on the ground, images gathered from satellites and unmanned aircraft, GPS tracks from expeditions, and geophysical instruments." Although finding the tomb represents years of attempting to communicate to others that he could indeed find it, honoring cultural beliefs and traditions is also paramount to Lin. As he explains, "there are many ways to look under the ground without having to touch it." Communicating respect for the beliefs and practices of cultures is central, and now

the ability to explore in a noninvasive way lets us try to solve this ancient secret without overstepping cultural barriers. It also allows us to empower Mongolian researchers with tools they might not have access to otherwise. Today's world still benefits from Genghis Kahn's ability to connect East with West. He forged international relations that have never been broken. By locating his tomb, we hope to emphasize how important it is for the world to protect such cultural heritage treasures.

A few years ago, Lin shares, he thought he was destined to be stuck in an office in a job he did not love. Following his family's heritage and his grandfather's words, he left the United States for Mongolia, finding "a world that had changed little in a millennium. And at its core [was] Genghis Khan." Lin states, "Engineers are really just explorers, pushing the limits of what we think we can do." He realized he could be a scientist and still do "crazy extreme things, and that's what I wanted to do" (Lin, 2012a, 2012b, 2012c).

 CourseMate Connection: Go to cengagebrain.com to access the CourseMate for *Invitation to Human Communication* to view a video about Albert Yu-Min Lin.

WHAT DO YOU THINK

1. Lin uses a different approach to collecting supporting material. Can you identify how his research methods differ from traditional data collection?

2. Lin and his team are not sure, but they believe they could have found a tomb in the "Forbidden Zone" that might be Genghis Khan's tomb. What type of reasoning is Lin using to support this belief that the site might be the actual tomb?

?

Figure 11.2 *Visual representation of mean, median, and mode*

The mean, median, and mode are numbers that summarize other groups of numbers. This figure shows that mean, median, and mode of the range of rents for fifteen one-bedroom apartments in the Boston area in September 2011.

Source: From GRIFFIN, *Invitation to Public Speaking*, 4E. © 2012 Cengage Learning.

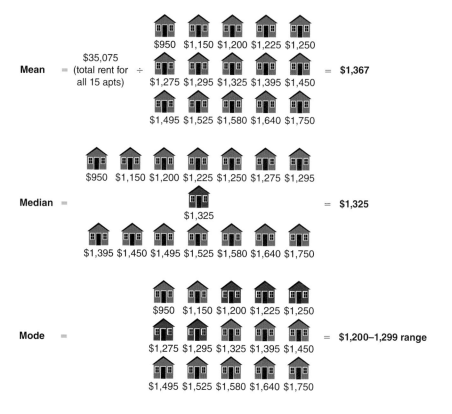

Mean = $35,075 (total rent for all 15 apts) ÷ = **$1,367**

Median = = **$1,325**

Mode = = **$1,200–1,299 range**

than 154 and half weighed less. Both Clara and her audience now have more information than simply the average weight of teens (145 pounds) and, for example, can begin to explain weight in relation to body type or height (those below the median ranged in height from four feet eleven inches to five feet eight inches and those above the median ranged from five feet six inches to six feet one inch).

The **mode** is *the number that occurs most often in a set of numbers.* Use the mode when you want to illustrate the most frequent or typical item in your data set to establish the occurrence, availability, demand, or need for something. For example, if the students showed that the most common monthly income for people looking for rental homes was $1,500, they could use the mode to show that most of the homes for rent in their area were priced too high for these people. Thus, they could argue that Habitat for Humanity homes were crucial.

Testimony

When speakers use the *opinions or observations of others*, they are using **testimony** as a source of evidence. We usually think of testimony as coming from an authority, an expert, or a person who has professional knowledge about a subject. This is often true, but testimony can also come from average people who have relevant experience with your topic. Speakers sometimes also provide their own testimony—their own words and experiences as sources of evidence.

mode
the number that occurs most often in a set of numbers.

testimony
opinions or observations of others.

Testimony often takes the form of a **direct quotation**, *an exact word-for-word presentation of another's testimony*. At other times, speakers **paraphrase** the words or *provide a summary of another's testimony in the speaker's own words*. Direct quotations often are seen as more credible than paraphrasing, but sometimes a person's words or stories are too long, too complex, or contain inappropriate language for a particular audience, making paraphrasing a better option. When you use the *testimony of someone considered an authority in a particular field*, you are using **expert testimony**. When you use the *testimony of someone who has firsthand knowledge of a topic*, you are using **peer testimony**, which is sometimes called *lay testimony*. You also can *use your own testimony to convey your point*. This is called **personal testimony**. To use each type of testimony ethically, always give credit to the person you are quoting or paraphrasing, including his or her name and credentials.

Definitions

A **definition** is a *statement of the exact meaning of a word or phrase*. Definitions can make terms, whether simple or complex, clear and meaningful for your audiences. Every word has both a denotative and a connotative definition. Recall from Chapter 4 that the **denotative definition** is the *objective meaning you find in a dictionary*, the definition of a word on which most everyone can agree. In contrast, a **connotative definition** is the *subjective meaning of a word or a phrase based on personal experiences and beliefs*. Be aware that providing the dictionary definition of a word may not always be enough to get your point across—definitions come from personal experiences as well as from the dictionary.

> **CourseMate Connection:** Go to cengagebrain.com to access the CourseMate for *Invitation to Human Communication* to view a video of Sylvia Earle discussing the need to take care of our oceans. Earle's speech includes real and hypothetical examples, narratives, statistics, and testimony to add support to her main points.

 ## Understand the Patterns of Reasoning

After you decide on the kinds of evidence to use in your speech, you must put that evidence into a pattern of reasoning. Although scholars have developed more than twenty-five different patterns of reasoning, we limit the discussion here to five of the most useful for beginning public speakers: reasoning by induction, deduction, cause, analogy, and sign (Gleason, 1999; Perelman & Tyteca, 1969; Toulmin, 1950; Toulmin, Rieke, & Januk, 1979; Walton, 1996). These patterns can help you develop logical arguments in all of your speeches. You probably are already familiar with most of these patterns because we use them commonly every day without giving them much thought. What makes them unique in public speaking is that speakers consciously employ the patterns to arrange their evidence and develop the logic of their main points and subpoints.

direct quotation
an exact word-for-word presentation of another's testimony.

paraphrase
to provide a summary of another's testimony in the speaker's own words.

expert testimony
the testimony of someone considered an authority in a particular field.

peer testimony (lay testimony)
testimony of someone who has firsthand knowledge of a topic.

personal testimony
one's own testimony used to convey a point.

definition
statement of the exact meaning of a word or phrase.

denotative definition
objective meaning of a word found in a dictionary.

connotative definition
subjective meaning of a word or a phrase based on personal experiences and beliefs.

Inductive Reasoning

inductive reasoning

a process of reasoning that uses specific instances, or examples, to make a claim about a general conclusion.

Inductive reasoning is *a process of reasoning that uses specific instances, or examples, to make a claim about a general conclusion* (Faigley & Selzer, 2000; Kahane & Cavender, 1998; Toulmin, 1969). When we observe patterns or trends and then make a claim about something we expect to happen based on them, we are reasoning inductively. Inductive reasoning looks like this:

- James is an excellent basketball player.
- His brother Jeff is an excellent swimmer.
- Their sister Julia is the star of the track team.
- Therefore, Jenny, the youngest of the family, will be a fine athlete, too.

Inductive reasoning, sometimes called *argument by example*, is best used when you can identify patterns in evidence that indicate something is expected to happen again or should hold true based on previous experience (Vancil, 1993; Zarefsky, 2002). Look at how inductive reasoning is used in the following speech. Ruby states her claim first and then provides specific instances:

> The amount of privacy we are allowed to keep is under siege every day (*claim*). Beverly Dennis, an Ohio grandmother, completed a questionnaire to get free product samples. Instead, she got a sexually graphic and threatening letter from a convict in Texas who was assigned the task of entering product data into computers for the company [*specific instance*]. Similarly, the dean of the Harvard Divinity School was forced to resign after downloading pornography to his home computer. He asked a Harvard technician to install more memory to his computer at home, and in the process of transferring files, the technician discovered, and reported, the pornography [*specific instance*].

When you reason from specific instances, you can state your claim (general observation) first and then offer your supporting instances, or you can present the instances first and then make your claim.

Expressed as a formula, an inductive argument looks like this:

Specific instance A	or	Claim you want to establish
Specific instance B		Specific instance A
Specific instance C		Specific instance B
Specific instance D		Specific instance C
Claim based on the specific instances		Specific instance D

Guidelines for Inductive Reasoning There are three guidelines for reasoning from specific instances:

1. Make sure you have enough examples to make your claim.
2. Make sure your generalizations are accurate.
3. Support your inductive arguments with statistics or testimony.

Ethical Inductive Reasoning

There are three ways to be sure your reasoning is ethical. First, avoid **anomalies,** which are *exceptions to a rule and unique instances that do not represent the norm.* When a speaker relies on anomalies or uses too few examples to make a claim, she or he may be guilty of making a **hasty generalization** or *reaching a conclusion without enough evidence to support it.* To support your claim, find more than three instances before you make any inferences about larger patterns. However, your audience probably needs no more than four specific instances, even if you have identified many more.

Second, make sure your generalizations are accurate. Although it can be tempting to make a claim about something you see happening in one place, be careful not to overgeneralize. For example, if more and more people in your community are "going green" it is tempting to label this a "national trend." However, you cannot extend that prediction to other parts of the country unless you have specific examples to support your claim. Do not be too hasty in extending examples from one area or group to another unless your data support that claim.

Third, support your inductive arguments with statistics or testimony. For example, if you want to explain that organic farms produce competitively priced, high-quality crops, then offer examples of two or three farms that do so. Then strengthen your inductive process with statistics showing that organic farmers are successfully competing with nonorganic farms at a county, state, or national level. You also could support your examples with testimony from the head of the U.S. Department of Agriculture, validating the profitability of organic farming. Statistics and testimony help your audience better understand the validity of the larger trend you are describing.

Deductive Reasoning

When speakers reason from general principles to specific instances (the opposite of inductive reasoning), they reason deductively. **Deductive reasoning** is *a process of reasoning that uses a familiar and commonly accepted claim to establish the truth of a very specific claim.* Deductive reasoning looks like this:

- All college students need to take an oral communication course.
- Jody is a college student.
- Jody needs to take an oral communication course.

The first statement, "All college students need to take an oral communication course," is called the **major premise** or the *general principle that states a familiar, commonly accepted belief.* The combination of the major premise with the second statement, "Jody is a college student," is called the **minor premise,** the *specific instance that helps establish the truth of the third statement,* "Jody needs to take an oral communication course," which is called the **conclusion,** or *the claim you are attempting to prove as true.*

anomalies
exceptions to a rule and unique instances that do not represent the norm.

hasty generalization
reaching a conclusion without enough evidence to support it.

deductive reasoning
a process of reasoning that uses a familiar and commonly accepted claim to establish the truth of a very specific claim.

major premise
the general principle that states a familiar and commonly accepted belief.

minor premise
specific instance that helps establish the truth of the conclusion.

conclusion
the claim you are attempting to prove as true.

Expressed as a formula, a deductive argument looks as follows:

- major premise, or general principle;
- minor premise, or specific instance of the general principle; and
- conclusion based on the combination of the major and minor premises.

Guidelines for Deductive Reasoning Reasoning from general principles to specific instances is an effective way to build a case for your claims. When your general principle is firmly established or commonly accepted, your reasoning should unfold smoothly. For example, some general principles that are clearly established and commonly accepted are that asbestos causes lung cancer, driving drunk is dangerous, and elected officials should act with integrity.

Sometimes, audiences will not accept your general principle. When they do not, you will need to strengthen it with additional evidence or reasoning. This process is called *establishing the validity of the major premise*. We often enter the public dialogue precisely *because* we want to establish the truth of a general principle. Consider how one very famous speaker, Susan B. Anthony, worked from a controversial general principle. In the 1870s, Anthony spoke in favor of women's right to vote. She built her reasoning for women's right to vote on the premise that the U.S. Constitution guarantees all citizens the right to vote. Her full line of reasoning looked as follows:

Major premise:	The U.S. Constitution guarantees every citizen the right to vote.
Minor premise:	Women are U.S. citizens.
Conclusion:	The U.S. Constitution guarantees women the right to vote.

Although this deductive argument makes sense to us today, Anthony's major and minor premises were open to dispute more than 140 years ago. People did not agree that the Constitution guaranteed all citizens the right to vote, nor did they agree about who was a citizen. Anthony and many other suffragists devoted much of their speeches to trying to convince their audiences of their major and minor premises. Despite their well-reasoned efforts, women did not get the right to vote in the United States until 1920 (Campbell, 1989; Fitch & Mandzuick, 1997).

Causal Reasoning

Causal reasoning is *a process of reasoning that supports a claim by establishing a cause-and-effect relationship*. Causal reasoning identifies an "if–then" relationship that suggests "if" one factor is present, "then" another is sure to follow (Faigley & Selzer, 2000; Inch & Warnick, 1998; Kahane & Cavender, 1998; Toulmin, 1969). Consider the following claims:

- If I don't study, then I'll do poorly on my exam.
- If I use recreational drugs, then I'll eventually turn to more addictive ones.

causal reasoning
a process of reasoning that supports a claim by establishing a cause-and-effect relationship.

- If I study self-defense, then I'm less likely to be hurt if someone attacks me.

These statements are examples of causal relationships. Each establishes a cause-and-effect relationship: lack of preparation (the cause) results in poor grades (the effect); use of recreational drugs (the cause) leads to the use of addictive ones (the effect); and learning self-defense (the cause) lessens the risk of harm in the event of an attack (the effect).

Speakers often use causal reasoning to develop their ideas with great success. In the following example, Kameron uses causal reasoning to develop his argument that zebra mussels, native to the Caspian Sea in Europe but not to the waters of the United States, are seriously damaging the aquatic environment:

> Zebra mussels cause damage to every aspect of any aquatic ecosystem they encounter. They destroy the natural balance of the ecosystem by filtering the food from water at an insane rate of one liter of water each day. Not much you think? Well, these mollusks can live in colonies of up to 70,000 mussels. That's 70,000 liters of water cleared of all food each day. This means the zebra mussels consume all the food usually eaten by animals lower in the food chain. The result is catastrophic repercussions on down the line. For example, a body of water whose food is filtered away cannot support any kind of life. The larger fish then have nothing to eat, resulting in fewer fish for anglers.

Kameron's causal reasoning allows him to argue compellingly that zebra mussels (the cause) lead to aquatic devastation (the effect).

Guidelines for Causal Reasoning Causal reasoning is an effective form of reasoning because it allows you to link two events together. But because causal relationships are sometimes difficult to prove, consider the following three guidelines.

First, avoid false causes. A **false cause** is *an error in reasoning in which a speaker assumes that one event caused another simply because the first event happened before the second*. It can be easy to assume a false cause. You pick up your "lucky" pen from your desk and five minutes later you get a creative brainstorm for the project you are working on. Did the lucky pen cause the creative brainstorm? Perhaps, but it is hard to tell. Although it is tempting to assume direct causes when one event happens shortly after another, the two events may not be directly related. When one event happens immediately after another, there may be a link, but to stay ethical you would have to investigate further to be sure.

Second, avoid assuming that an event has only one cause. Events often have many causes, especially those that become topics in the public dialogue. For example, it is unrealistic to try to pin the cause of teen suicide on one factor. It is far more appropriate to address the multiple factors that contribute to teen suicide: the home and school environment, social pressures, individual personality traits, and the teen's support system and friendships.

Third, strengthen your cause-and-effect relationships by citing strong supporting evidence. For example, in his informative speech about zebra

false cause
an error in reasoning in which a speaker assumes that one event caused another simply because the first event happened before the second.

mussels, Kameron identified a very strong connection between the over-population of zebra mussels and the damage done to boats, buoys, docks, and anchors. He supported his connection by providing testimony from local fishers who had seen buoys sink from the weight of too many mussels.

Analogical Reasoning

When we compare two similar things and suggest that what is true for the first will be true for the second, we are reasoning analogically. In their article about Michelle Obama's campaign against childhood obesity, *Newsweek* writers made the following analogy:

> Public-health advocates are taking on Big Food just as their predecessors took on Big Tobacco. Dr. David Kessler, the former head of the FDA, argues that the fattening of America has happened by design as food companies intentionally manufactured irresistible cocktails of sugar, fat, and salt. Manufacturers' efforts to do better don't assuage Kelly Brownell, head of Yale's Rudd Center for Food Policy and Obesity. "The country defaults to giving industry the benefit of the doubt," he says. "Industry says you don't need to regulate us; we'll police ourselves." The tobacco industry abused that with [who knows] how many lives as a consequence. To expect the food industry to be different may be wishful thinking (Kalb, 2010; Obama, 2010).

analogical reasoning
reasoning by way of comparison and similarity.

Analogical reasoning, or *reasoning by way of comparison and similarity*, implies that because two things resemble each other in one respect, they also share similarities in another respect. So when *Newsweek* writers compare the U.S. food industry to the so-called Big Tobacco corporations, the writers argue that the food industry, like major tobacco companies before they began to be regulated in the late 1990s, cannot be trusted to put the health of consumers before its own profits.

Although they can be detailed, as in the previous example, analogies also can be very simple. For example, when speaking to her audience about the importance of more than direct care, physician Deborah Prothrow-Stith used this simple and effective analogy: "We were just stitching them up and sending them back out on the streets, back to the domestic equivalent of a war zone" (Rogat Loeb, 1999).

Guidelines for Analogical Reasoning To increase the effectiveness of analogical reasoning, be sure the items or ideas you are comparing are truly alike. When you compare two things that do not share characteristics, your analogy is invalid and will seem illogical to your audience. Most of us have heard invalid analogies and thought to ourselves, "That's like comparing apples to oranges." For example, it is invalid to suggest that proposed nonsmoking ordinances will succeed in Kentucky, Tennessee, and North Carolina because they succeeded in California, Oregon, and Washington. This analogy is invalid because the public attitudes toward smoking in the three tobacco-growing southern states are different from those in the three western states whose economies do not depend on tobacco. If you make an analogy between two things, they must share true similarities for the analogy to be valid.

Reasoning by Sign

A **sign** is *something that represents something else*. It is one of the most common forms of reasoning we use in our daily lives: Dark clouds are a sign of a storm rolling in; a decrease in the number of applications for a certain academic program is a sign of declining interest; the bailiff's command "All rise" is a sign that the judge is about to enter the courtroom. Signs have an important function in the reasoning process because they prompt us to infer what is *likely* to be. They help speakers establish relationships and draw conclusions for their audiences based on those relationships.

Reasoning by sign assumes something exists or will happen based on something else that exists or has happened. Signs, like causal relationships, can have strong or weak relationships. Reasoning by sign is strengthened when you can point to the repetition of one example to build a case. For example, when the Richter scale registers above a certain level for an undersea earthquake, it is a sign that a tsunami can occur. Scientists have accurately predicted all five of the significant ocean-spanning tsunamis since 1950. But they also predicted fifteen that turned out to be false alarms, so note that few signs are infallible, and most are open to question (Alder & Carmichael, 2005).

Guidelines for Reasoning by Sign Because signs are fallible, consider three guidelines for using them:

- Think about whether an alternative explanation is more credible.
- Make sure a sign is not just an isolated instance.
- If you can find instances in which a sign does not indicate a particular event, you do not have a solid argument.

The first guideline asks whether an alternative explanation is more credible. In a speech on the standards for licensing teachers, Seogwan suggested that the low test scores in the nation's public schools were a sign of poorly trained teachers. He reasoned that low scores represented, or signaled, poor teaching. However, when his audience questioned him, they raised a number of equally credible explanations. Could the lower scores be a sign of outdated or biased tests? of overcrowded classrooms? of the need to restructure our classrooms? of poor testing skills? Each explanation is as likely as the one Seogwan offered, and much evidence supports each one. As a result, his audience thought Seogwan's reasoning was flawed. To avoid this pitfall, be sure that when you claim one thing is a sign of another, an alternative explanation is not equally valid or better.

Second, when you reason by sign, make sure the sign is not just an isolated instance. Speaking against the new no smoking ordinance in his town, Mark argued that all of his friends, even nonsmokers, had no problems with designated areas for smokers in public places. This, he claimed, was a sign that most people do not think a no-smoking ordinance is necessary. He ignored the many local and nationwide campaigns in favor of establishing no-smoking ordinances in public places. He mistakenly

sign
something that represents something else.

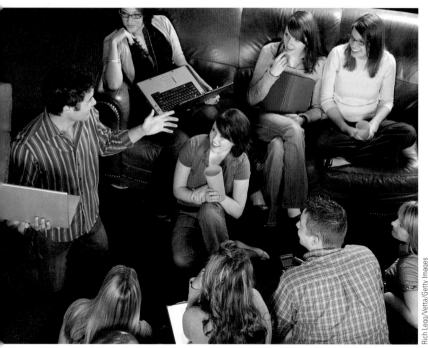

Consider the reasoning you plan to use in your speech. If you share that reasoning with your friends or classmates, do you think they will find it credible? Why or why not?

Rich Legg/Vetta/Getty Images

assumed that one instance (his friends' support of smokers in public places) represented a larger pattern.

Third, when you reason by sign, you are suggesting the sign almost always indicates a particular event. If you can find instances in which the sign does not indicate that event, then you do not have a solid argument. In his speech on our ability to predict natural disasters, Tim offered the evidence that not every undersea earthquake of a certain magnitude results in a tsunami, nor does every hurricane result in massive damage. Thus, he argued, blaming scientists for not notifying authorities before such natural disasters occur is unreasonable. However, Tim argued, the occurrence of the Sri Lanka tsunami and Hurricane Katrina, and the tragedies left in their wake are signs that warning systems, regardless of their overprediction rates, are imperative.

Reasoning and Emotion

Now that you have learned about the five most common patterns of reasoning used in speeches, we will consider appeals to emotion and how they can affect your reasoning. The use of emotional appeals can be one of the most challenging aspects of public speaking. On the one hand, research suggests that effective speakers appeal to emotions because they encourage the audience to relate to an issue on an internal personal level. On the other hand, because emotions are so personal and powerful, research also suggests that an inappropriate appeal to emotions can cause an audience to shut down in an instant (Perloff, 1993; Stiff, 1994). Appeals to emotions can be complicated, so it is useful to understand what emotions are and which emotions people most commonly experience.

Emotions are *internal mental states that focus primarily on feelings* (Stiff, 1994). Communication research has identified six primary emotions that tend to be expressed similarly across cultures and four secondary emotions that are expressed differently depending on age, gender, and culture (Perloff, 1993). The primary emotions are

- *fear*, or an unpleasant feeling of apprehension or distress, the anticipation of danger or threat;

- *anger*, or a feeling of annoyance, irritation, or rage;

- *surprise*, or a feeling of sudden wonder or amazement, especially because of something unexpected;

emotions
internal mental states that focus primarily on feelings.

- *sadness*, or a feeling of unhappiness, grief, or sorrow;
- *disgust*, or a feeling of horrified or sickened distaste for something; and
- *happiness*, or a feeling of pleasure, contentment, or joy.

The secondary emotions are

- *pride*, or an appropriate level of respect for a person, character trait, accomplishment, experience, or value; feeling pleased or delighted;
- *guilt*, or an awareness of having done wrong accompanied by feelings of shame and regret;
- *shame*, or a feeling of dishonor, unworthiness, and embarrassment; and
- *reverence*, or a feeling of deep respect, awe, or devotion.

In public speaking, you make appeals to emotions to accomplish the following goals: gain attention and motivate listening, reinforce points, express personal commitment, and call to action or conclude memorably.

Gaining Attention and Motivating Listening You often catch an audience's attention and motivate them to listen by appealing to their emotions with a compelling short story, testimony, or examples.

Reinforcing Points You can use emotional appeals to reinforce main points or subpoints. For example, when you support a point with a statistic and then reinforce the statistic with an example of how some aspect of the statistic has affected a specific person, an audience can understand your point on a more personal level.

Expressing Personal Commitment When you care deeply about an issue and want your audiences to recognize this depth of commitment, you may appeal to emotions by shifting your delivery to a more passionate or intense tone, or you may personalize your claims and arguments.

Calling to Action or Concluding Memorably You can often move an audience to action by asking them to envision the result of that action and how it could affect them personally. You might end your speech with a compelling story or quote and so conclude memorably.

Because emotional appeals engage an audience personally, you will want to consider three things to help you use them effectively: balancing emotion with reason, staying audience centered, and and using vivid language carefully.

Balancing Emotion and Reason Overly emotional speeches may stimulate your audience, but without sound reasoning they are less likely to be effective. Balance emotional appeals with sound reasoning and your audience will see more than one dimension of your ideas and arguments.

Staying Audience Centered Consider your audience very carefully before you decide what kinds of emotional appeals to use. Before you incorporate emotional appeals, ask yourself the following questions:

- *Is my appeal to emotion overly graphic or violent?* When a speaker's use of emotion provides extensive details about the horrors or injuries of a person or situation, the audience may shut down or feel overwhelming revulsion.

- *Is my appeal to emotion overly frightening or threatening?* When a speaker describes something so frightening or threatening that the audience feels helpless or panicked, members may stop listening or feel immobilized.

- *Is my appeal to emotion overly manipulative?* When a speaker relies on theatrics, melodrama, and sensation rather than on fact and research, the audience can feel manipulated or reject the message or argument.

Using Vivid Language Vivid language helps an audience recall some of their most profound experiences and create images that are rich with feeling. Use vivid descriptions and examples that are not overly graphic or manipulative to help your audience connect with those experiences.

PRACTICING HUMAN COMMUNICATION

Test the Reasoning of Your Arguments

Bring one of your main arguments to your speech to class. Present this argument and determine which pattern of reasoning will help you develop this argument most fully (inductive, deductive, causal, analogical, or by sign). After each person has presented her or his argument and selected a pattern of reasoning to support it, discuss the strengths and weaknesses of each person's approach.

 Be Aware of Fallacies in Reasoning

Whether or not it is intentional, speakers sometimes make inaccurate arguments called fallacies. A **fallacy** is *an argument that seems valid but is flawed because of unsound evidence or reasoning.* Fallacies are a problem in speeches not only because they undermine speakers' arguments but also because, despite their factual or logical errors, they can be quite persuasive. Fallacies can seem reasonable and acceptable on the surface, but when we analyze them, we see that their logic is flawed. Although there are more than 125 different fallacies, we will discuss the most common types for beginning public speakers: ad hominem, bandwagon, either–or, red herring, slippery slope, false cause, and hasty generalization (Kahane & Cavender, 1998; Van Eemeren & Gootendorst, 1992).

Ad Hominem: Against the Person

Ad hominem is a Latin term that means "against the person." Perhaps one of the most familiar fallacies, an **ad hominem fallacy** is *an argument in which a speaker attacks a person rather than that person's arguments.* By portraying someone with an opposing position as incompetent,

---

fallacy
an argument that seems valid but is flawed because of unsound evidence or reasoning.

---

ad hominem fallacy
an argument in which a speaker attacks a person rather than challenge that person's arguments.

unreliable, or even stupid, you effectively silence that person and discredit her or his arguments or ideas. Here are two examples of an ad hominem fallacy:

1. Certainly, Obama worked so hard to pass the health-care bill—he's a liberal democrat who only wants to make our country socialist.

2. Of course the commissioner would argue for cuts in social services; she's been an insensitive, money-grubbing Republican all her life.

Ad hominem fallacies turn the audience's attention away from the content of an argument and toward the character and credibility of the person offering that argument. They cloud an issue, making it hard for an audience to evaluate the ideas the speaker challenges.

Bandwagon: Everyone Else Agrees

When you fall prey to the **bandwagon fallacy**, you are *suggesting that something is correct or good because everyone else agrees with it or is doing it*. In public speaking, this translates to making statements like these:

- Many other communities are adopting this nonsmoking ordinance in restaurants. It is a perfect solution for us as well.

- How can we allow gays and lesbians in our organization? They have not been allowed in the military or scouting organizations, so why should we accept them in ours?

The bandwagon fallacy works a little like group pressure: It is hard to say no to something everyone else is doing. But the logic of the bandwagon is flawed for two reasons. First, even though a solution or a plan might work well for some, it might not be the best solution for your audience. You need to do more than argue "it will work for you because it worked for others." You need to explain exactly why a plan might work for a particular group of people, community, or organization. Second, just because "lots of others agree" does not make something "good." Large groups of people agree about many things, but those things are not necessarily appropriate for everyone. When you hear the bandwagon fallacy, ask yourself two questions: If it is good for them, is it good for *me* or *us*? Even if many others are doing something, is it something I or we support?

Either–Or: A False Dilemma

A dilemma is a situation that requires you to choose from options that are all unpleasant or mutually exclusive. When we are facing a dilemma, we feel we must make a choice even if it is not to our liking. In persuasive speeches, an **either–or fallacy**, sometimes called a "false dilemma," is *an argument in which a speaker claims our options are "either A or B," when actually more than two options exist*. To identify a false dilemma, listen

bandwagon fallacy
a suggestion that something is correct or good because everyone else agrees with it or is doing it.

either–or fallacy (false dilemma)
an argument in which a speaker claims our options are "either A or B," when actually more than two options exist.

ETHICAL MOMENT

Are We Free to Say Anything We Want?

Conservative political commentator Rush Limbaugh is known for speaking his mind and criticizing liberal politicians and policies. On his radio show that aired October 20, 2009, Rush Limbaugh criticized a blog written by Andrew Revkin, a journalist for *The New York Times*. In his blog post "Are Condoms the Ultimate Green Technology?" Revkin claimed that an increase in the human population correlates directly with an increase in carbon dioxide emissions. He wrote that "recent research has resulted in renewed coverage of the notion that one of the cheapest ways to curb emission in coming decades would be to provide access to birth control for tens of millions of women around the world who say they desire it." He raised the question of implementing a "baby-avoidance carbon credit," similar to selling "CO_2 credits for avoiding deforestation," and stated that this idea was "purely a thought experiment, not a proposal" (Revkin, 2009a).

After learning of Revkin's thought experiment, Rush Limbaugh called Revkin and others who believe humans are ultimately to blame for climate change "environmental wackos." Limbaugh lamented, "This guy from *The New York Times*—if he really thinks that humanity is destroying the planet, humanity is destroying the climate, that human beings in their natural existence are going to cause the extinction of life on Earth—Andrew Revkin, Mr. Revkin, why don't you just go kill yourself and help the planet by dying?" After ten days of media stories questioning

Limbaugh's integrity for making the comments, Limbaugh (re) framed his position. On his show, he stated, "Mr. Revkin, for crying out loud, I'm making a point. I'm not advocating death. I do not advocate death on this program. I do not advocate control over anybody else's life" ("Limbaugh to NY Times", 2009; Revkin, 2009a, 2009b; New York Times, September 15. 2009; Media Matters for America, 2009; New York Times, October 20, 2009).

What Do You Think?

1. What is the definition of free speech? What does free speech mean to you?

2. Were Rush Limbaugh's original comments regarding Andrew Revkin in the realm of free speech? Why or why not.

3. If you or others found either Limbaugh's or Revkin's remarks offensive, do you still think they should be protected by free speech principles?

4. What are the ethical implications of Limbaugh's statement that Revkin should "just go kill" himself?

5. Do you think Revkin was ethical in expressing his thought experiment on using birth control as a means to reduce carbon emissions? Why or why not?

---

for the words *either* and *or* as a speaker presents an argument. Consider these two examples:

> Either we increase access to our before- and after-school meal programs or our students will continue to fail.

> Either we increase our candidate's appeal to women or we don't get elected.

In both examples, the audience is presented with a false dilemma. Intuitively, we know there must be other options. In the first example, there are other ways to respond to poor student performance—better nutrition is only one part of the solution. In the second, there likely are other ways to increase a candidate's appeal and chances of success. Sometimes, it is hard to see the other options immediately, but they are usually there.

Either–or arguments are fallacious because they oversimplify complex issues. Usually, the speaker has created an atmosphere in which the audience feels pressured to select one of the two options presented. Even if those options may be good choices, an either–or argument prevents us from considering others that may be even better.

Red Herring: Raising an Irrelevant Issue

The term *red herring* comes from the fox-hunting tradition in England. Before a hunt began, farmers often dragged a smoked herring around the perimeter of their fields. The strong odor from the fish masked the scent of the fox and threw the hounds off its trail, keeping the hounds from trampling the farmers' crops. Although this worked well for the farmers, trailing the equivalent of a red herring around an argument is not such a good idea. When we make use of the **red herring fallacy**, we *introduce irrelevant information into an argument to distract an audience from the real issue.* The following example illustrates the red herring fallacy:

> How can we worry about the few cases of AIDS in our town of only 50,000 when thousands and thousands of children are dying of AIDS and AIDS-related illnesses in other countries?

In this example, the speaker turns the argument away from her own community and toward the international problem of AIDS. The audience then becomes more concerned about AIDS in other countries. Undoubtedly, this is an important issue, but it is not the one under discussion, which is equally important. Because of the red herring, the audience is less inclined to move toward a solution for the local situation. This type of fallacy can be hard to spot because both issues usually are important, but the audience feels pulled toward the most recently raised issue. As an audience member, listen carefully when a speaker introduces a new and important topic in a persuasive speech; you might be hearing a red herring fallacy.

Slippery Slope: The Second Step Is Inevitable

A **slippery slope fallacy** is *an argument in which a speaker claims that taking a first step in one direction will inevitably lead to undesirable further steps.* Like a skier speeding down a hill without being able to stop, a slippery slope fallacy suggests the momentum of one decision or action will cause others to follow. Here is an example of a slippery slope fallacy:

> If we allow our children to dress in any way they want at school, they soon will be wearing more and more outrageous clothing. They'll start trying to outdress one another. Then it'll be increasingly outrageous behaviors inside and outside the classrooms. Soon they'll turn to violence as they try to top one another.

The speaker is making a slippery slope argument by suggesting that if one unwanted thing happens, others certainly will follow. The audience gets caught up in the momentum of this "snowball" argument. Slippery slope arguments can be persuasive because the speaker relates the first claim (for example, the dress codes) to a larger issue (violence) when the

red herring fallacy
irrelevant information inserted into an argument to distract an audience from the real issue.

slippery slope fallacy
an argument in which a speaker claims that taking a first step in one direction will inevitably lead to undesirable further steps.

two may not even be linked. Before you accept the full claim made with a slippery slope argument, stop and consider whether the chain of events really is inevitable.

False Cause: Mistaking a Chronological Relationship

A **false cause fallacy** is *an argument mistaking a chronological relationship with a causal relationship.* There are two types of false cause fallacies. The first type occurs when a speaker assumes that one event *caused* the second to occur. Notice how the speaker in the following example mistakenly assumes that the first event caused the second:

> After the state passed legislation in favor of the death penalty, violent crimes decreased. The new legislation has deterred criminal activity.

Criminal activity may have declined after the state implemented a new pro-death penalty policy; however, it does not prove that the legislation caused the decline. Other factors may have influenced the decline, such as methods of reporting violent crimes, rehabilitation programs in prisons, and even educational opportunities for individuals at risk to commit violent crimes.

The second type of false cause fallacy is known as a **single cause fallacy**. This occurs *when speakers assume a particular effect only has one cause.* Many public problems are complex, resulting from multiple causes. Speakers want to avoid oversimplifying an effect to a single cause. Notice how the following example blames only one cause on childhood obesity

> The number of obese children in the United States has significantly increased over the past decade. According to pediatric experts, approximately 30 percent of children under the age of thirteen are obese. This is because of the unhealthy school lunches being served in schools across the nation. We need legislation mandating more nutritious lunches in order to solve the obesity epidemic.

This example assumes that there is only one cause to the problem of childhood obesity—unhealthy school lunches. In fact, there are a number of reasons American children are obese: fast food, junk food, and trans fats consumed outside of school; lack of physical exercise inside and outside of school; and possibly genetic factors. Assuming only one cause exists for a complex problem is committing a false cause fallacy.

Hasty Generalization: Too Few Examples

A **hasty generalization fallacy** is *an argument based on too few cases or examples to support a conclusion.* When speakers rely only on personal experiences to draw conclusions, for example, they may fall into the trap of a hasty generalization because personal experiences often are not enough to prove a claim true. Notice how the following student relies only on her personal experience to support a larger claim:

> The school of business and finance is the hardest program to be accepted into at our university. I have applied three times and still have not been admitted.

This student uses her personal experience of being rejected multiple times to support her argument on the overall difficulty of getting into the school of business and finance. Although this student may have been denied admission into the program, this does not prove that the program is the toughest one to enter for all students.

As you listen to speeches, and as you put your own arguments together, keep in mind that a fallacy is an error in logic. When we reason, we want to be sure our logic is sound and not based on error or deception.

Tips for Reasoning Ethically

Evidence, reasoning, logic, and arguments are powerful tools in the public dialogue. With them, we can share information, express our perspective, and invite dialogue on an issue. However, we also can manipulate, confuse, and misrepresent with our reasoning. To ensure you reason ethically and effectively, follow these two tips: use accurate evidence and verify the structure of your reasoning.

Using Accurate Evidence As a speaker, you are ethically obligated to use accurate evidence in all of your reasoning. Although you may be able to present a fully developed argument based on fabricated evidence, that would be deceiving your audience and counterproductive to the public dialogue. To avoid this, use only evidence you are sure is from accurate and reliable sources.

Verifying the Structure of Your Reasoning When you give a speech, watch out for any fallacies that creep into your arguments and reasoning. Take time to assess each claim you make and be sure it is based on strong and credible inductive and deductive reasoning. When you spot a fallacy, take time to figure out what kind you are using and replace that fallacy with a sound example, bit of evidence, or statistic.

Chapter Summary

Gathering a Range of Materials for Your Speech Will Help You Enter the Public Dialogue Responsibly and Ethically and Deliver an Effective Speech

- Gather information from personal experiences and knowledge, the Internet, the library, and research interviews.
- Evaluate the strength of the materials you find on the Internet or in the library: Is the information reliable? authoritative? current? consistent and unbiased?

When You Conduct a Research Interview, Determine Whom to Interview, Design the Interview Questions Using Open or Closed Ended Questions, and Schedule and Conduct the Interview

The Material You Gather From Your Research Becomes the Evidence You Use to Develop and Support Your Ideas

- The five most common types of evidence are: examples, narratives, statistics, testimony and definitions.
- Examples can be real or hypothetical. Narratives can by brief or extended.
- Statistics can present the mean, median, and mode. Testimony consists of direct quotations or paraphrasing, as well as expert, peer, and personal testimony.
- Definitions can be either denotative or connotative.

Put the Evidence Into One of the Five Most Common Patterns of Reasoning: Induction, Deduction, Cause, Analogy, and Sign

- Inductive reasoning uses specific examples to make a claim about a general conclusion.
- To ensure your reasoning is ethical, avoid anomalies and hasty generalizations; make sure your generalizations are accurate; support your inductive arguments with statistics or testimony.

- Deductive reasoning includes the major premise (the general principle), a minor premise (the specific instance that helps establish the truth of the third statement), and a conclusion (the claim you are attempting to prove as true).
- Causal reasoning supports a claim by establishing a cause-and-effect relationship. Avoid false causes, avoid assuming an event has only one cause, and strengthen your causal reasoning by offering supporting evidence.
- Analogical reasoning compares two similar things and suggests that what is true for the first will be true for the second. To increase the effectiveness of analogical reasoning, be sure what you are comparing is truly alike.
- Reasoning by sign assumes something exists or will happen based on something else that exists or has happened. Because signs are fallible, consider whether an alternative explanation is more credible. Make sure a sign is not just an isolated instance; if a sign does not indicate a particular event, then you do not have a solid argument.

- In public speaking, emotional appeals accomplish the following goals: gain attention and motivate listening, reinforce points, express personal commitment, and make a call to action or conclude memorably. When you use appeals to emotion, be sure to balance emotion with reason, stay audience centered, and use vivid but appropriate language.

Common Types of Fallacies for Beginning Public Speakers Are Ad Hominem, Bandwagon, Either–or, Red Herring, Slippery Slope, False Cause, and Hasty Generalization

- Keep in mind that a fallacy is an error in logic. When we reason, we want to be sure our logic is sound and not based on error or deception.
- To be certain you are reasoning ethically, make sure your evidence is accurate and your reasoning does not rely on any fallacies.

Key Concepts

ad hominem fallacy (288)

analogical reasoning (284)

anomalies (281)

bandwagon fallacy (289)

causal reasoning (282)

conclusion (281)

connotative definition (279)

deductive reasoning (281)

definition (279)

denotative definition (279)

direct quotation (279)

either–or fallacy (false dilemma) (289)

emotions (286)

evidence (272)

examples (272)

expert testimony (279)

fallacy (288)

false cause (283)

false cause fallacy (292)

hasty generalization (281)

hasty generalization fallacy (292)

hypothetical example (272)

inductive reasoning (280)

interview (269)

major premise (281)

mean (275)

median (275)

minor premise (281)

mode (278)

narrative (273)

paraphrase (279)

peer testimony (lay testimony) (279)

personal testimony (279)

real example (272)

red herring fallacy (291)

sign (285)

single cause fallacy (292)

slippery slope fallacy (291)

statistics (274)

testimony (278)

 Invitation to Human Communication Online

Speech Communication CourseMate includes an interactive eBook and interactive learning tools including National Geographic Explorer videos, student videos, quizzes, flash cards, and more. Speech Builder Express 3.0 and Speech Studio 2.0 are also available. Go to cengagebrain.com to access your CourseMate for *Invitation to Human Communication* where these resources can be found.

Further Reflection and Discussion

1. Bring a newspaper to class. In groups, identify as many different types of reasoning as you can find in the text, photographs, and advertisements. Label each item you find as inductive reasoning, deductive reasoning, causal reasoning, analogical reasoning, or reasoning by sign and evaluate the strength of each type of reasoning according to the guidelines discussed in this chapter.

2. Evaluate the strengths and weaknesses of the information you have gathered for your speech. Is it reliable, authoritative, current, complete, relevant, and consistent? Based on your assessment, identify information you might discard and consider whether you need to do more research for your speech.

3. Draft a list of questions you would like to ask a personal contact for your next speech. Keep in mind your speech goals, time limitations, and audience. Now organize that list so the most important questions are first and the least important ones are last. Next consider how you will begin your interview. Will you start with your most important questions or some warm-up questions? What questions will you use to close the interview?

4. Consider the sources that you gathered your research from. Did you use a wide range of materials? Did you consider the credibility of those sources? Did you evaluate the ethical nature of the sources and the information you plan to use in your speech? Are there any changes you might make to ensure your research is unbiased, appropriate, and ethical?

Activity and Web Link

Visit cengagebrain.com to access the CourseMate for *Invitation to Human Communication* where these activities and web links can be found.

1. Visit the following databases and indexes and write brief notes about what type of information and sources you find there that could be helpful in gathering information for your speech: *New York Times* Index, *Wall Street Journal* Index, DataTimes, Academic Search Premier, IngentaConnect. Go to *Web link 11.1*.

DELIVERING YOUR SPEECH

IN THIS CHAPTER YOU WILL LEARN TO:

- Use different types of delivery methods for a speech.
- Examine the verbal and nonverbal components of your speech.
- Develop skills for speaking at question-and-answer sessions.

- Identify ways to address feelings of nervousness that may accompany delivering a speech.
- Review the speeches of others to help you identify strengths and weaknesses in delivery.

12

Methods of Delivery

Verbal Components of Delivery

Nonverbal Components of Delivery

Question-and-Answer Sessions

Building Your Confidence as a Public Speaker

Sample Speeches

Stephen Morton/Getty Images

Many celebrities are quite comfortable when they stand in front of an audience. What skills do you think most "every day" people need to deliver effective speeches?

People must first become aware of a situation and then must recognize their connection to it before they are likely to become involved.

—*Joshua Howard, photojournalist/filmmaker, National Geographic Young Explorers Grantee*

When you deliver your speech, you connect with and share your ideas with an audience. Because of the importance of delivery, this chapter covers the methods of delivery and the verbal and nonverbal components that will help you present your ideas in the most effective way. It also addresses question-and-answer sessions and ways to control the nervousness many of us feel when we give speeches. In the first section below, you will learn about four methods of delivery, the verbal and nonverbal components of delivery, and some strategies for rehearsing your speech.

Methods of Delivery

The four types of delivery we can use for public speaking are extemporaneous, impromptu, manuscript, and memorized. We now look at each method of delivery and the reasons for using it.

> **CourseMate Connection:** Go to cengagebrain.com to access your CourseMate for *Invitation to Human Communication* to compare the differences between a speech delivered in a conversational style and one that is read. Watch the video of student speakers Shelley Weibel and Eric Daley. Which style of delivery do you think is more effective?

Extemporaneous Delivery

Most of your speeches will be extemporaneous. When you give an **extemporaneous speech**, you present a *carefully prepared and practiced speech from brief notes rather than from memory or a written manuscript.* Because an extemporaneous delivery tends to be more natural than other deliveries, it is one of the more common methods. The advantages of extemporaneous deliveries are many. Your speaking outline or speaking notes prompt your ideas but do not allow you to read every word to your audience. Your eye contact and gestures are natural, and your tone is conversational. Finally, because extemporaneous deliveries encourage direct communication between the speaker and audience, it is easier to stay audience centered.

Delivery Tips Many beginning speakers worry they might forget their speeches if they use an extemporaneous delivery. However, the way to overcome this fear is not to write out every word of your speech but instead to add more keywords and phrases—not full sentences—to

extemporaneous speech
carefully prepared and practiced speech from brief notes rather than from memory or a written manuscript.

your outline. This way you will have more cues to aid your memory. Next, practice your speech often before you give it so you will feel more confident about what you will remember and want to say. Your goal is not necessarily to eliminate your fear by reading your speech but to give yourself tools so you can "talk" your speech.

The differences between an extemporaneous delivery and a speech read aloud to an audience are striking. An extemporaneous delivery follows a **conversational style**, which is *more formal than everyday conversation but remains spontaneous and relaxed*. In addition, with a conversational style, your posture and gestures are relaxed, and you make frequent eye contact with your audience (Branham & Pearce, 1996).

conversational style
more formal than everyday conversation but it remains spontaneous and relaxed.

Impromptu Delivery

When you give an **impromptu speech**, you present a *speech that you have not planned or prepared in advance*. Although you may be wondering why anyone would do this—especially in light of the previous discussions

impromptu speech
speech that you have not planned or prepared in advance.

© Geoffrey Holman/istockphoto

CIVIC ENGAGEMENT IN ACTION

Alright, Hear This

Founded in 2001 by former Def Jam head Russell Simmons, the Hip-Hop Summit Action Network (HSAN) is dedicated to using hip-hop as a catalyst for education and advocacy related to the well-being of at-risk youth. HSAN focuses on issues of community development, access to high-quality public education and literacy, freedom of speech, voter education, economic advancement, and youth leadership development. Since its beginnings, HSAN has sponsored several civic events such as its Smackdown Your Vote! campaign, which sought to register 2 million additional voters in 2004; its 2008 get-out-the-vote campaign to register "50K in one day" (with the Hip-Hop Caucus); and the 2009 national Hip-Hop Summit on Financial Empowerment titled "Get Your Money Right." HSAN also works with the Recording Industry Association of America in support of the advisory labels that alert parents to explicit content in music. It has defended hip-hop culture before members of the U.S. Congress and such federal regulatory agencies as the Federal Trade Commission and the Federal Communications Commission.

HSAN also seeks to harness the immense popularity of hip-hop to educate others about hip-hop music and culture. "Once an underground, controversial style characterized by gangsta mythology and all-too-real turf wars," says Nelson George, author of *Hip-Hop America*, "rap music is now embraced across the radio dial and across the nation by a diverse, multiracial fan base. . . . Rappers are pop stars, pop stars rap, and the sound is as integral to the cultural landscape as country music or rock." HSAN's goal is to use this mainstream success to encourage the recording

industry to establish mentoring programs and forums that will stimulate dialogue between artists, hip-hop fans, and industry leaders and promote understanding and positive change.

Recently, HSAN has been involved in a dialogue with the recording and broadcast industries about forming a coalition to recommend guidelines for lyrical and visual standards. In particular, it recommends that these industries "voluntarily remove/bleep/delete the misogynistic words *bitch* and *ho* and the racially offensive word *nigger*." They maintain that these words are utterly derogatory and show a complete lack of respect for the history of suffering and oppression that women, African Americans, and other people of color have experienced in the United States. They are not advocating censorship. Rather, "we are consistent in our strong affirmation, defense, and protection of the First Amendment right of free speech and artistic expression. . . . Our discussions are about the corporate social responsibility of the industry to voluntarily show respect to [African Americans, other people of color, and to all women]" (Bode, 2007; Gamboa, 2007; " Hip-Hop Setting the Beat," 2003; Smiley Group, 2006).

What Do You Think?

1. HSAN is recommending guidelines for the use of images and words in the entertainment industry. How useful do you think these guidelines will be?

2. How will you monitor your language and the images you use in your speeches? How do you think this will affect your audience?

Dr. Benjamin Chavis, president and CEO of HSAN during the Miami Hip-Hop Summit on Financial Empowerment.

American writer and speaker Mark Twain joked, "It usually takes more than three weeks to prepare a good impromptu speech." This is not true, of course, but with a few minutes of thoughtful organization, you can make it seem as if you took three weeks to prepare.

about the importance of preparation, planning, and practice—impromptu speaking is quite common. It occurs in meetings or public gatherings when someone is asked to speak or feels the need to share her or his perspective. When you decide to speak, you have the advantage of having a moment or two to organize your ideas. If you suddenly are asked to speak, you may not be able to jot down notes, but you still can organize your ideas. Consider the following scenario.

As a senior at the university, José was having trouble registering for the courses he needed to graduate. Enrollment on his campus was at an all-time high, and the number of majors in his own department had grown enormously. As a result, classes filled early. He expressed his frustration to his adviser, who suggested José attend a campus open forum on graduation requirements. José's adviser facilitated the discussion, and during the question-and-answer session, the adviser asked José if he would share his frustrating experiences with the audience. José paused and quickly organized his thoughts about his frustrations and how they related to the discussion. His speech was a success not only because it addressed the discussion directly but also because he was candid about his experiences.

José entered the public dialogue through impromptu speaking. He took a few seconds to organize his thoughts and then began. That quick organization gave him confidence and helped him deliver an audience-centered speech that was easy to follow. If you decide to give an impromptu speech, you may have time to make a quick speaking outline and jot down key ideas and points before you begin. However, if you have no time to make even a few notes as in José's case, you can quickly organize your ideas in your head before you begin to speak.

Delivery Tips Although you never have much time to prepare an impromptu speech, you can practice impromptu deliveries. In fact, your speech instructor likely will ask you to give several impromptu speeches. When you deliver an impromptu speech, use the following guidelines:

1. Quickly and calmly decide on the main points you want to make.

2. Introduce your main points as you would in a speech you had prepared in advance. Offer a preview such as "the three things I'd like to cover are" and use signposts such as "first."

3. Support your main points with subpoints and sub-subpoints.

4. Summarize your main points in a brief conclusion.

If you find yourself in an impromptu situation, stay calm. The skills you learn in your public-speaking course are invaluable for such situations. Even though you may be nervous, you have learned to organize ideas, relate them to the audience, and deliver various types of speeches. Remember, too, that when you give an impromptu speech, your audience does not expect elaborate source citations, fancy visual aids, or creative introductions. Members are looking for immediate clarity or guidance.

If you rely on the fundamental skills you have learned in your public-speaking course, then you can handle impromptu speeches successfully.

Manuscript Delivery

When you give a **manuscript speech**, you *read to an audience from a written text*. Although most speeches are best delivered extemporaneously, some speeches require a manuscript delivery such as the following occasions:

- when detailed and exact information must be reported carefully, such as to a professional board or a formal committee;

- when your speech will be scrutinized word by word, archived, and referred to later (for example, the president's address to the nation); and

- when your speech text will be used later for some other purpose (for example, a keynote address at a conference, which often is published).

A manuscript speech is one of the most challenging forms of delivery. Contrary to what most beginning public speakers think, speaking effectively from a manuscript requires more preparation and skill than extemporaneous or impromptu speaking (Hildebrandt & Stephens, 1963). Two problems are likely when a speaker reads from the full text. First, the speech often sounds like a written text and not an oral text, or a speech that "reads" well but doesn't "talk" well. Second, the speaker may be inclined to read to the audience rather than talk with them. There are some solutions to these problems, and we will explore those now.

Delivery Tips First, when you write your speech in manuscript format, the best way to avoid a written style is to talk the speech aloud as you write it. Working from your preparation outline, sit at your desk and speak the words as you write them on your computer or paper. If you find yourself thinking the speech rather than saying it aloud, go back and speak the part you have just written. You usually will notice that you have slipped into a writer's style instead of a speaker's style. Change the language in these sections to reflect spoken ideas rather than written ideas. Remember, your goal is to write a speech, not an essay.

The second problem with using a manuscript is the temptation to read the manuscript to the audience. This reduces your eye contact, and your words may sound wooden because you are reading. Finally, your delivery may be too fast because you are reading to rather than speaking with your audience.

The way to overcome the challenges associated with reading a speech is to practice speaking from the manuscript many times. If you become familiar with your manuscript during practice, you will find your natural

PRACTICING HUMAN COMMUNICATION

Comparing Delivery Methods

In class, take an item out of your backpack or from your pocket. Turn to the person next to you and give an impromptu speech about this item. Now find an example of something written—a paragraph in this textbook, the newspaper, or something online. Give another sixty-second "speech" reading the written material. With your partner, discuss the differences between the delivery styles. Which did you prefer to deliver? Which did you prefer to listen to?

manuscript speech
speech that is read to an audience from a written text.

Consider the type of delivery you will use for your next speech. What steps will you take to ensure this is the most effective delivery you can use? Use the following tips to help you prepare for your speech.

rhythm and conversational style. You will figure out where you can make eye contact with your audience easily for extended periods. Like your extemporaneous speeches, you will be able to deliver full ideas or subpoints without reading. You also will discover that you will want to slow down because, even though the words are in front of you, you feel comfortable enough to speak the words with feeling rather than rush through them.

Table 12.1 reviews the advantages and disadvantages of the three delivery methods.

TABLE 12.1   ADVANTAGES AND DISADVANTAGES OF THE THREE DELIVERY METHODS

	EXTEMPORANEOUS	IMPROMPTU	MANUSCRIPT
Definition	A speech that is carefully prepared and practiced from brief notes rather than from memory or a written manuscript.	A speech that is not planned or prepared in advance and uses few or no notes.	A speech that is completely written out and read word for word to an audience.
Advantages	Combines a conversational style with a speaking outline. Encourages careful organization.	Allows for a conversational style with few or no notes.	Helps present very detailed or specific information exactly as the speaker intends.
Disadvantages	Requires practice time. Speaker may be tempted to memorize the speech.	Requires thinking and organizing ideas quickly. No time for preparation.	Requires a conversational style that can be hard to achieve because the speaker reads from a full text.

© Cengage Learning 2014

Verbal Components of Delivery

A speech's success comes not only from its words but also from how they are delivered. Speakers known for their delivery—for example, John F. Kennedy, Barack Obama, Ann Richards, and Martin Luther King Jr.—use **vocal variety**, or *changes in the volume, rate, and pitch of a speaker's voice that affect the meaning of the words delivered*. We achieve vocal variety by consciously using certain verbal components of delivery: volume, rate, pitch and inflection, and pauses. The proper articulation and pronunciation of words and a consideration of dialect are also important components of delivery.

Volume

Volume is *the loudness of a speaker's voice*. Common sense tells us that we want to speak loudly enough for our audiences to hear us but not so loudly that we make our listeners uncomfortable. Knowing just how loud to speak can be difficult because our own voice sounds louder to us than to the audience and because the appropriate volume varies with each situation. Culture also affects perceptions about appropriate speaking volume. For example, in some Mediterranean cultures, a loud voice signals sincerity and strength, whereas in some parts of the United States, it may signal aggression or anger. In some Native American and Asian cultures, a soft voice signals education and good manners. However, in some European cultures, a soft voice may signal femininity, secrecy, or even fear (Andersen, Hecht, & Hoebler, 2002; Samovar & Porter, 1991).

Pay attention to nonverbal cues from your audience to help you adjust your volume. If you are speaking without a microphone, watch people in the back of the room as you begin to speak. If they are giving you cues that they cannot hear, that is a signal to increase your volume. When you use a microphone, you still need to pay attention to your volume. Before you begin your speech, test your voice with the microphone and make sure you are the proper distance from it (neither too far nor too close) so the audience can listen comfortably.

Rate

Rate is the *speed at which we speak*. There is no formula for the proper rate at which to deliver a speech. For example, Dr. Martin Luther King, Jr., began his "I Have a Dream" speech at a rate of 92 words per minute and finished at a rate of 145 (Lucas, 2001). The rate at which we speak conveys different feelings. When we speak quickly, we project a sense of urgency, excitement, or even haste. When we speak slowly, we convey seriousness, heaviness, or even uncertainty. Both rapid and slow rates have their place in a speech. However, too much of one or the other strains audience members' attention and may cause them to stop listening. To check your rate, record yourself for several minutes. Play back the recording

The late Ann Richards, then governor of Texas, gave the keynote address at the 1988 Democratic National Convention. This speech and many others she delivered were almost always direct, humorous, gutsy, and memorable.

vocal variety
changes in the volume, rate, and pitch of a speaker's voice that affect the meaning of the words delivered.

volume
loudness of a speaker's voice.

rate
speed at which we speak.

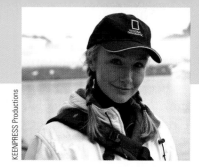

KEENPRESS Productions

Alexandra Cousteau
Emerging Explorer and Social Environment Advocate

Do you vary the tone and complexity of each talk geared toward your audience?

Absolutely. Sometimes I'm speaking to audiences that are already knowledgeable about environmental problems, so it's a matter of shaping the conversation on water issues and issuing a call to action. Sometimes, though, the audience is not as engaged on the environment or may have opposing views to mine. Those audiences need a softer approach. So, yes, I think knowing your audience is really important because it helps you choose the right stories. I find that picking my stories wisely gives me a little door into their heart or into their mind—that they open up more easily to what I have to say if my stories ones they can relate to.

and assess your speed. Remember, rate is an audience-centered concern. We want to engage our audience, and our rate of speaking helps us in this effort by communicating certain emotions or energies.

Pitch and Inflection

Pitch refers not only to the position of tones on a musical scale but also in public speaking as the *highness or lowness of a speaker's voice.* **Inflection** is the *manipulation of pitch to create certain meanings or moods.* Together, pitch and inflection help us communicate more effectively with our audience. Consider the word *well* and its different meanings when used in spoken language. The control of pitch and inflection allows us to say "well" in ways that suggest joyful surprise or indecision or indignation or caution. All speakers manipulate their pitch to create meaning during their speeches. All of us alter our pitch to ask a question, express satisfaction or displeasure, convey confidence or confusion, or even communicate threats or aggression. Variations in pitch clarify meaning and help catch and maintain our audience's attention.

Speakers who do not pay attention to their pitch and inflection risk losing their audience. *Speakers who do not alter their pitch* speak in a **monotone**. Other speakers may say everything in too low or too high a pitch. When a speaker says everything in a monotone or a low pitch, the audience senses a lack of interest or energy. When the pitch is too high for too long, every word is communicated with equal enthusiasm, or "excessive zeal," and the audience begins to wonder which points are the most important (Soper, 1956).

You can monitor your voice by recording yourself so you can hear your pitch. If your pitch is too high, practice breathing more deeply (from the abdomen rather than the throat) and relaxing your throat muscles as you

pitch
highness or lowness of a speaker's voice.

inflection
manipulation of pitch to create certain meanings or moods.

monotone
speaking without any change in pitch.

Jose Gil/Shutterstock.com

President Obama is an example of a speaker who varies his pitch and inflection to keep his audience engaged. Practice your delivery with someone you trust, and ask her or him to evaluate your pitch and inflection before the day of your speech.

speak. Speak from your diaphragm rather than your throat, and read aloud regularly to practice this technique until you can get your pitch to drop naturally. (Note that proper breathing also helps you increase the volume of your voice and project your voice farther.) If you speak in a monotone or in too low a pitch, practice delivering your speech (or reading something aloud) in an overly dramatic way, using inflection, exclamations, and vocal variation as much as possible. With practice, vocal variation will come naturally and carry over into public-speaking situations.

Pauses

Pauses are *hesitations and brief silences in speech or conversation.* In speeches, they often are planned and serve several useful functions. Pauses give us time to breathe fully and collect our thoughts during a speech or before we answer an audience question. Pauses also give audiences time to absorb and process information—they are like rest stops, giving the audience a breather before continuing. Finally, pauses before or after a climactic word or an important point reinforce that word or point.

Pauses can also add clarity. Read the passage here without stopping to pause after any of the words.

> The back of the eye on which an image of the outside world is thrown and which corresponds to the eye of a camera is composed of a mosaic of rods and cones whose diameter is little more than the length of an average light wave.

pauses
hesitations and brief silences in speech or conversation.

Without pauses, it is hard to understand what's being said here. Now read the passage again and note where you would naturally pause. Does the meaning of the passage become clearer?

The back of the eye
on which an image of the outside world is thrown
and which corresponds to the eye of a camera
is composed of a mosaic of rods and cones
whose diameter is little more than the length of an average light wave

The four pauses that make this passage easier to understand are after *eye, thrown, camera,* and *cones* (Soper, 1956). These are places in written text where we would add commas to indicate meaning. In written text, pauses often are indicated by punctuation, but an audience cannot see punctuation in a speech. Pause to punctuate your words, as well as to establish mood, indicate a transition, take time to reflect, or emphasize a point. For example, in his speech on the pollution caused by using fossil fuels, Preston used a pause to make a particular impact: "In fact," Preston argued, "according to the Southern California Edison Electric Transportation Web site, updated only last month, running for half an hour in urban air pollution introduces as much carbon monoxide into your lungs as [pause] smoking a pack of cigarettes."

Learning the art of the pause takes time and practice. Before you become comfortable with the brief moments of silence necessary in a speech, you may have the urge to fill the silence. Avoid **vocalized pauses**, or *pauses that speakers fill with words or sounds like "um," "er," and "uh."* Vocalized pauses not only are irritating but also can create a negative impression of the speaker. When a speaker uses so many vocalized pauses that they intrude into an audience's awareness, listeners may begin to question the speaker's knowledge and speaking capabilities (Christenfeld, 1995). If you have a habit of vocalizing pauses, try the following process to eliminate them:

1. Listen for vocalized pauses in your daily speech.

2. When you hear one, anticipate the next one.

3. When you feel the urge to say "um" or "er" to fill space, gently bite your tongue and do not let the word escape.

4. Wait until your next word of substance is ready to come out and say that word instead.

It may take time to eliminate vocalized pauses from your speech, and you may feel awkward with the silence, but the results are worth the effort.

Articulation

Articulation is the *physical process of producing specific speech sounds to make language intelligible to our audiences.* Our clarity depends on our articulation—whether we say words distinctly or mumble and slur. Articulation depends on the accuracy of movement of our tongue, lips,

Najlah Feanny/Corbis News/Corbis

Senator Edward Kennedy was an inspiring speaker who was also known for a tendency to overuse pauses. If you are prone to using a lot of vocalized pauses, consider the four strategies noted in the text to help you eliminate some of them.

vocalized pauses
pauses that speakers fill with words or sounds such as "um," "er," and "uh."

articulation
physical process of producing specific speech sounds to make language intelligible to our audiences.

jaws, and teeth. This movement produces either "Didjago?" or "Did you go?" In fact, scholars of performance and delivery argue that poor articulation is a trend across all sectors of U.S. culture (Dowis, 2000; Gates, 2000; Martin & Darnley, 1996; Rodenburg, 2001).

Audiences expect public speaking to be more clearly articulated than private conversation. Speakers with an audience-centered focus care about clear articulation. Clearly articulated words communicate that you want your audience to understand you, which can add to your credibility. For your audience to understand your ideas, they must be able to decipher your words. To improve your articulation skills, try the following exercise:

1. Several days before your speech, select a part of your speech or a short written text you can read aloud.

2. Practice saying each word of your speech excerpt or text as slowly and clearly as possible, exaggerating the clarity of each word.

3. Repeat this exercise once or twice each day before you give your speech.

This exercise will help you recognize how much you slur or mumble and teach you to speak more clearly when you give your speech. Do not worry—you will not speak in this exaggerated way when you finally deliver your speech, but your words will be much clearer.

Pronunciation

Just as you would not turn in an essay you knew was filled with spelling errors, never deliver a speech filled with pronunciation errors. **Pronunciation** is the *act of saying words correctly according to the accepted standards of a language*. Pronunciation and articulation may seem similar, but pronunciation refers to how *correctly* a word is said, whereas articulation refers to how *clearly* a word is said. For example, saying the word *nuclear* as "nu-cle-ar" (correct) rather than "nu-cu-lar" (incorrect) has to do with pronunciation, and mumbling either pronunciation rather than speaking it clearly has to do with articulation.

Pronouncing words correctly communicates to your audience that you have listened carefully to the public dialogue going on around you. You have taken care to learn the common language and pronounce it correctly. In addition, correct pronunciation of terms and names in a language other than your native one communicates your respect for that culture and enhances your credibility.

Dialect

A **dialect** is a *pattern of speech shared by an ethnic group or people from specific geographical locations*. Dialects include specific vocabulary that is unique to a group as well as styles of pronunciation shared by members of that group. All people have a dialect, and your own dialect comes from your ethnic heritage as well as the place you grew up. For example, do you say "wash" or "warsh" when you want something clean? How about "soda," "pop," or "coke" when you want a soft drink? Your choices reflect your dialect.

pronunciation
act of saying words correctly according to the accepted standards of a language.

dialect
pattern of speech shared by an ethnic group or people from specific geographical locations.

People who use a standard American dialect (the dialect newscasters use when they are on the air) often forget that they, too, have a dialect, and they sometimes view the dialect of others as inferior. For public speaking, dialect is important because speakers need to consider the effect their dialect has on those who are unfamiliar with it. Speakers may use words that are not familiar to their audience or may pronounce words in ways that sound odd or different.

If you know your dialect will be unfamiliar to your audience, try the following:

1. Acknowledge your region of birth or ethnic heritage.

2. Talk about how that shapes your use of language by giving examples of some of the differences you have encountered between your dialect and those of your audience.

3. Define terms that are unfamiliar to your audience.

4. Soften the accent associated with your dialect if that accent is fairly strong and might hinder understanding.

Nonverbal Components of Delivery

The nonverbal components of delivery are those aspects communicated through our bodies and faces. For public speakers, these include personal appearance, eye contact, facial expression, posture, gestures, and proxemics.

Scholars of interpersonal communication recognize that nonverbal communication has a powerful effect on the meanings exchanged between people. Researchers suggest that between sixty-five percent and ninety-three percent of the total meaning of a message comes to us through nonverbal signals (Birdwhistell, 1970; Mehrabian, 1981). In addition, when nonverbal signals contradict verbal signals (for example, you say you are glad to see someone but your facial expression and physical posture suggest you are not), people tend to believe the nonverbal signals over the verbal ones (McCroskey, Sallinen, Fayer, Richmond, & Barraclough, 1996; Mino, 1996; Trees & Manusov, 1998; Wood, 1999).

For public speakers, nonverbal communication is especially important because it conveys meaning and can either enhance or detract from the overall message. We now look at how the components of nonverbal communication affect a speech.

Personal Appearance

Personal appearance, or *the way you dress, groom, and present yourself physically*, is an important part of delivery. But how important? Consider the following sayings:

You can't judge a book by its cover.

Beauty is in the eye of the beholder.

Looks are everything.

personal appearance
the way someone dresses, grooms, and presents her- or himself physically.

Beauty is as beauty does.

You can never be too rich or too thin.

You can dress him up, but you still can't take him out.

Good-looking lawyers make more money.

Which statements are true? Does physical appearance matter, or is it irrelevant? Studies show that personal appearance actually does matter quite a bit. People deemed "more attractive" earn more money than their "less attractive" peers, and personal grooming plays a large part in our perception of a person's attractiveness for both men and women (Morris, Gorham, Cohen, & Huffman, 1996; Rozell, Kennedy, & Grabb, 1989; Weiss, 2008). Attractive characteristics are defined as "those characteristics that make one person appear pleasing to another" (Hartz, 1996, p. 683; Morrow, 1990). Even though we may say we should not judge people by their looks, we actually do just that.

Without a doubt, standards for attractiveness and beauty change with generations, as well as with cultures and subcultures. Despite these differences, though, there is a basic standard for acceptable personal grooming in public-speaking situations. That standard is that the speaker's dress should be appropriate to the occasion (Herman, Zanna, & Higgins, 1986; Rubinstein, 2001). If the occasion is formal, then the speaker is expected to dress formally. If the occasion is casual, the speaker's clothing should be less formal. A speaker who shows up at a formal occasion in a T-shirt and shorts not only displays a lack of audience awareness but also is likely to lose credibility. Similarly, wearing formal business attire to speak at a casual gathering is also inappropriate. In short, be sure your clothing matches the style and tone of the occasion.

Personal appearance is a complex combination of social norms, cultural and generational influences, and personal style. Your personal appearance should match your objective as a speaker, which is to have your words and ideas taken seriously in the public dialogue. Delivery begins the moment the audience sees you, so pay careful attention to your personal appearance and present yourself appropriately for the occasion at which you are speaking.

Eye Contact

The second essential component of nonverbal delivery is **eye contact**, or *visual contact with another person's eyes*. Like personal appearance, appropriate eye contact is affected by culture and gender. Most North Americans and Western Europeans expect a speaker to make extensive eye contact. However, in Native American cultures, in Japan, and in parts of Africa, extensive eye contact is considered invasive and disrespectful (Gudykunst & Moody, 2002). Gender, too, affects the meaning of eye contact. For men, direct and extended eye contact with another man may be perceived as a challenge or threat. For women, direct and extended eye contact with a man may be interpreted as an invitation to flirt. So knowing what to do with our eyes as we deliver a speech depends on knowing who is in our audience.

eye contact
visual contact with another person's eyes.

Even though the nuances of eye contact are complex, most cultures expect at least some eye contact during a speech. Eye contact has three functions. First, it is a way to greet and acknowledge the audience before the speech begins. Second, it is a way to gauge and keep our audience's interest. We use eye contact to monitor feedback from our audience and adjust our volume, rate, and pitch accordingly. Third, it is a way to communicate sincerity and honesty.

Audiences rate speakers who make eye contact for less than half their speech as tentative, uncomfortable, and even as insincere and dishonest (Palmer & Simmons, 1995). In contrast, speakers who make eye contact for more than half their speech are viewed as more credible and trustworthy (Beebe, 1974, 1979–1980; Cobin, 1963).

For eye contact to be effective, try to do two things as you look out at your audience. First, make eye contact with many people in the audience rather than a few friendly faces. Make eye contact with people in all parts of the room, not just those immediately in front of you. Gather information about level of comprehension, interest, and agreement from as many people as you can.

Second, look with interest. Rather than scanning faces in the audience or looking over listeners' heads to the back of the room, really look at individual people in the audience. Slow down the movement of your eyes so you actually make a connection with people through your eye contact. Looking with interest communicates that you are pleased to be speaking to your audience and are interested in members' responses.

Facial Expression

Your face plays a central role in communicating with audience members, letting them know your attitudes, emotional states, and sometimes even your inner thoughts. Your **facial expression** is the *movement of your eyes, eyebrows, and mouth to convey reactions and emotions*. Actors are highly skilled at using their faces to communicate, and audiences appreciate this talent. Although you do not need to be as skilled as an actor, you do need to consider your facial expressions as you deliver your speech. A poker face, although useful in a card game, will not help you communicate your ideas.

You can use your facial expressions to communicate your own interest in your topic, your agreement or disagreement with a point, your openness to an idea, and even your feelings about an issue. Take some time to decide which facial expressions might be useful to include in your speech. If these expressions do not come naturally to you, then practice them until you are comfortable delivering them.

Posture

Posture is *the way we position and carry our bodies*, and people assign meaning to our posture whether we realize it or not. We are perceived as confident and relaxed or tense and insecure based, in part, on our posture. A confident speaker is often called "poised," possessing assurance, dignity, and a sense of calm. Nervousness can affect our posture,

facial expression
movement of eyes, eyebrows, and mouth to convey reactions and emotions.

posture
how speakers position and carry their bodies.

making us feel awkward and act in ways we would never do in other situations: gripping the podium with both hands, slouching over our speaking notes, pacing back and forth, or standing stuck in one spot. These nervous reactions detract from our delivery and communicate a message we probably do not want to send (Bull, 1987).

But by paying attention during practice to the way we carry our bodies, we can eliminate some nervous postures. To become aware of your posture during a speech, practice your speech in the way you actually will give it. If you will deliver your speech standing, then practice it while standing. Consider devising a makeshift podium. If you are to sit while giving the speech, then practice while sitting, with chairs beside you and your notes on a table in front of you. Similarly, if you will use a handheld or attachable microphone, practice with something resembling it so you get the feel of speaking with a microphone.

By practicing the speech in the way you will actually give it, you can correct your nervous habits before you deliver the speech. For example, if you find that you pace or grip the podium tightly, you can replace the bad habit with a better one. If you discover you stand immobilized when you practice, then you can add cues to your speaking outline to remind you to move during your speech. If you slouch, you can practice sitting up straight and looking out at your audience. In sum, your posture during your speech should improve if you pay attention to your body during practice.

One final word about posture and delivery: Pay attention to the way you begin and end your speech. Wait until you are at the podium or have the microphone in your hand before you begin talking. Do not start speaking until you are facing your audience and have made eye contact. Similarly, do not walk off the stage until you have finished the last word of your conclusion. Finishing your conclusion or your final answer before you leave the spotlight communicates confidence and a willingness to give every word the attention it deserves. These guidelines will help you remain audience centered.

Gestures

Gestures are *movements, usually of the hands but sometimes of the entire body, that express meaning and emotion or offer clarity to a message.* Students of rhetoric in ancient Greece and Rome spent hours learning specific gestures to accompany specific parts of their speeches. For example, certain gestures were used with transitions, and others signaled specific kinds of main points or ideas. These choreographed gestures were used until the eighteenth century (Austin, 1966; Bulwer, 1974). Today, research on gestures in public speaking indicates that gestures should be as natural as possible rather than memorized.

However, beginning public speakers do not always know what gestures will appear natural in a speech. With only minor variations, natural gestures in a speech are the same as those you normally use in personal conversations to complement your ideas and bring your words to life. The same is true for public speeches. Gestures make our delivery lively,

gestures
movements, usually of the hands but sometimes of the entire body, that express meaning and emotion or offer clarity to a message.

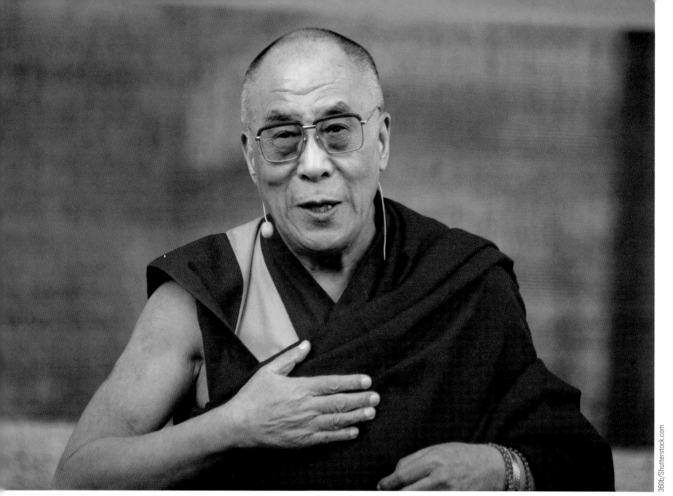

The Dali Lama is known for his engaging and genuine delivery. Watch a video clip of him speaking and assess whether his gestures contribute to his appeal as a speaker.

offer emphasis and clarity, and convey our passion and interest. Use the following tips to help you with gestures.

1. **Vary your gestures.** Try to use different kinds of gestures rather than repeating only one gesture. Some gestures emphasize (a fist on the podium), clarify (counting first, second, third on your fingers), or illustrate (drawing a shape with your hands in the air). Try to incorporate a variety of these gestures into your speech.

2. **Use gestures that fit your message.** Sometimes, a point needs an extravagant gesture; at other times, a more subtle gesture is much more effective. For example, use a relaxed pattern of hand movement as you explain a point but a larger more vigorous movement when you are emphasizing something quite important.

3. **Stay relaxed.** Your gestures should flow with your words. Try to keep your movements comfortable and effortless. If you find a gesture makes you tense, drop it from the speech and replace it with something more casual and familiar.

You will find that as you relax and gain experience speaking, you will stop thinking about your gestures and simply use them as you normally do in conversation.

Proxemics

Effective speakers pay close attention to **proxemics**, the *use of space during communication*. Be mindful of how far away you are from your audience as well as how elevated you are from it (for example, on a platform or a podium). The farther away you are, the stronger the idea of separation. The higher up you are, the more the idea of power is communicated.

You can work with proxemics in your delivery. One of the strengths of skilled speakers is their ability to move close to their audiences at key points during their speeches. Although you do not want to remain too close to your audience throughout your speech, getting close to them at key points allows for greater connection and communicates a desire to be perceived as more of an equal. Try stepping from behind the lectern or down from the podium and moving closer to your audience. If you cannot do this because you need a microphone or a place to put your notes, then you might be able to move closer during a question-and-answer session. Doing so will help you communicate openness and a willingness to engage in conversation with your audience.

Technology and Delivery

Technology refers to the tools speakers use to help them deliver their message. Technology can be as elaborate as a computer and a liquid crystal display (LCD) panel or as simple as a pen and a flip chart. Table 12.2 presents a list of technologies that speakers typically use. When you are thinking of using technology for your speech, stay audience centered by asking yourself the following questions:

- Have I asked what types of technology will be available for me to use?

- Do I have time to prepare the materials I need to use that technology?

- Do I have the time to practice using the technology? Have I worked out any glitches?

- Am I prepared to speak if the technology fails?

- Does the technology help me communicate my messages clearly? Does it enhance my speech or detract from it?

proxemics
use of space during communication.

TABLE 12.2   TECHNOLOGIES FOR SPEAKERS

TRADITIONAL TECHNOLOGIES	ELECTRONIC TECHNOLOGIES
Podiums for notes	Microphones
Tables or easels for displays	Laptop computers and LCD projectors
Presentational aids such as posters	Overhead projectors and screens
Handouts	Slide projectors and screens
Chalk, chalkboards, and erasers	Presentational aids such as PowerPoint or Prezi slides
Ink markers, whiteboards, and erasers	Televisions, DVD players, and Smart Boards
Markers, pens, and flip charts	CD-ROM players
Tacks, pins, or tape	Audiocassette players

© Cengage Learning 2014

When you decide to use technology, you want to be sure you can use that technology competently. Consider the importance of this competence in the following example.

Mike wanted to include several YouTube clips into his speech. He identified the ones he wanted a day or two before he spoke, and he figured he could pull them up during his speech. When he set up his computer on the day of his speech, he had trouble getting Internet access, because the system was not running smoothly that day. After several tries, he was finally able to log on, but he could not locate his YouTube sites easily because he had searched for them by subject and failed to record the YouTube address. Then, because he was not familiar with the technology in the room, when he played his first clip, he discovered the volume on the projector had been turned off and no one could hear the clip.

SPEAKING VISUALLY

Social Commentary, YouTube Style

Providing a forum for people to connect, inform, and inspire others across the globe, YouTube acts as a distribution platform for original content creators and advertisers large and small ("YouTube Fact Sheet," 2010). YouTube allows its users to create their own videos and upload and manipulate their favorite movie clips, TV clips, and music videos. Created in 2005 by former PayPal employees Chad Hurley, Steen Chen, and Jawed Karim, YouTube is now immensely popular. Every day, people watch 2 billion videos and upload hundreds of thousands more to the site ("YouTube Fact Sheet," 2010). In 2009, *Entertainment Weekly* magazine put YouTube on its end-of-the-decade best-of list, summing up its appeal by describing the site as "providing a safe home for piano-playing cats, celeb goof-ups, and overzealous lip-synchers since 2005" (Geier, Jensen, Jordan, Lyons, & Markovitz, 2009). According to the *Boston Globe*, YouTube is also influencing a growing number of activists who use video imagery to speak their minds online. For example, when 23-year-old Elisa Kreisinger wanted to protest the lack of gay characters and story lines on television, she did not petition people to boycott HBO or write an angry letter to *The New York Times*. Instead, she remixed scenes from the TV and movie versions of *Sex and the City* into two pro-gay narratives and uploaded them to her blog, drawing 21,000 hits. "I wouldn't have done it if it was text-based," says Kreisinger. "Things are more easily communicated through video . . . . And there can be more powerful statements" (Aucion, 2010, p. A1). The trend to use video to speak out about political and social issues has exploded recently, facilitated by Web 2.0 technology and inspired by the entertaining and informative videos created by video bloggers and *The*

Daily Show. "Making media now is a powerful way of participating in all kinds of life, including civic and political life," says Lee Rainie, director of the Pew Research Center's Internet and American Life Project. People in their teens and twenties "are now deeply connected to the political process in a way that their parents, at their age, could never be" (Aucion, 2010, p. A12).

What Do You Think?

1. Explore several YouTube clips that might help you communicate your message in your next speech. How might you incorporate them as you deliver your speech?

2. What issues might you begin to comment on via YouTube? Would those make good topics for your next speech?

Mike did what he could to recover, but after his speech, he felt he had not really created the kind of environment he wanted. He wanted people to get excited by his material, but he felt they simply were patient with him instead.

Remember, although technology is a tool that can help you give a more effective speech, it has its drawbacks. If your speech relies on technology to be effective but the technology you need is not available when you arrive to speak, your presentation will be negatively affected. That is why you need to take the time to consider how to present your speech without technology. Putting this time into your speech before you give it will help you stay audience centered by keeping your attention focused on delivering your message to your audience in a way that they appreciate.

 ## Question-and-Answer Sessions

Speeches often involve question-and-answer sessions. These sessions provide an opportunity for audience members to explore an idea or proposal in more detail, ask for clarity, and share their own perspectives. Even though you will not know for sure what to expect during question-and-answer sessions, there are ways you can prepare for them, and advanced preparation can make the difference between a mediocre question-and-answer session and a stimulating one. Ensuring a good question-and-answer session has two steps: preparing for potential questions beforehand and managing the discussion during the session.

Public figures such as firefighters often get interviewed for information about a scene. What sorts of questions might you ask a firefighter after a fire that would give you interesting information for a speech?

Karin Hildebrand Lau/Shutterstock.com

Preparing for Questions

You can do several things to prepare for the question-and-answer session. First, take time to identify the questions you think might be asked. Then prepare your answers to the questions.

Identify Potential Questions As you think about the topic under discussion, keep a log of the questions your audience might ask. Pay attention to the controversies or disagreements raised by the issue you are discussing to help you identify potential questions. If you can discuss the topic with others before the session, they can help you identify likely questions. Add these to your log of questions.

Formulate and Practice Answers After you have identified the questions you might be asked, prepare your answers as thoroughly as you can. Write out your answers, outline them, and record pertinent quotes, statistics, examples, or other data that support each answer. Although this may seem like a lot of extra work, it can give you the confidence you need to respond to your audience in respectful and audience-centered ways.

Although you cannot always anticipate the exact questions you will receive, you often can come close. You should be able to answer a question that is similar to one you anticipated by making minor adjustments to the answer you formulated. If some of the questions are likely to be controversial, then practice your answers in front of other people. They can help you with wording and organization as well as with adding and subtracting details.

As a rule, your answers to simple questions should be brief—between ten and sixty seconds in length. Answers to complex questions may take longer, but remember that you are answering questions, not giving a speech. Remember, too, that others are waiting to ask questions. If you spend all your time on one question, then you will prevent others from raising important issues.

Managing the Question-and-Answer Session

Several techniques will help ensure a productive question-and-answer session. They can help you manage the flow of conversation as well as keep an audience-centered perspective.

Explain the Format It is a good idea to establish the format of the question-and-answer session during the introduction to the session. You might want to establish a few rules, such as time limits for each question, the number of questions a person may ask, or rules to ensure that as many sides of an issue as possible are raised and discussed. Setting the rules will help all involved know what to expect and help you manage the flow of discussion ethically and effectively. Selecting a "process person," someone who monitors the session and the rules you have established, can help ensure that the group follows the format you have set.

Listen and Clarify One of your most important tasks when managing a question-and-answer session is to listen thoughtfully to each question before answering in a respectful manner. This can be a difficult task if the question is unclear or hostile. When an audience member asks you an

Alexandra Cousteau
Emerging Explorer and Social Environment Advocate

Do you have any tips for managing nervousness before and during a public presentation?

Practice, practice. practice! I'll tell you, the first time I did a talk, I almost died of shame. I was just fifteen years old when my grandfather sent me to East Berlin to attend the inauguration of a high school that had been named after my father, Philippe Cousteau. I arrived and was taken on a tour of the school, and then they led me to the auditorium for a schoolwide inaugural event. Little did I know that they planned for me to get up on stage and give a short speech of appreciation. To this day, I have no recollection of what I said. I just remember feeling like I was going to pass out from extreme embarassment. I had never spoken in public before, and it was a brutal introduction. My voice was trembling; my legs felt like spaghetti; the room started spinning. It felt like an eternity until I was back in my chair. But I survived it, and now public speaking is something I really enjoy.

It's very rare for someone not to have stage fright on their first attempt. The important thing is to know you want to say before you get up to say it. And you get better and more relaxed with practice.

unclear question, try to listen carefully for the keywords and important points. Then restate the question using this information so it is clear to you and ask the person if this is what she or he meant. Use such language as, "If I understand the question, you are asking me . . . Is that correct?" or "I think what you're asking is . . . Am I right?" If you simply cannot make sense of the question, then you can always ask the person to repeat it for you.

When you are faced with a hostile question, it can be hard to understand what the person is asking. Hostile questions usually come from someone who feels threatened or believes you have not addressed his or her needs and concerns. Sometimes you can respond to the content of the question as well as acknowledge the emotion. This takes practice. The following tips may help.

1. Do not take the hostility personally. If you can, establish goodwill and common ground by identifying points of agreement, shared experiences, or common background with the members of your group.

2. Display an audience-centered perspective and communicate with civility as you respond. Responding civilly is more likely to decrease the hostility than an uncivil response.

3. Listen to the content as well as the emotional components of the questions being asked. Separate out the emotions and determine the facts or information you are being asked to provide.

4. Address your answer to the content of the question, not the emotion. Offer information that will clarify your ideas or position. In responding, also strive to reinforce an invitational environment (see Chapter 15) so you can explore an issue and get as many perspectives on it that you can. Try to explain rather than argue.

5. Offer evidence for your position. Use the skills you learned in Chapter 11 to present your ideas logically and reinforce your own credibility. Sometimes, the hostility can be reduced when you respond with strong evidence that supports your claims.

After you have tried these strategies, if you feel confident enough to do so, you can acknowledge the emotion attached to the issue. You want to be careful here, though, because many people do not like to be told how they feel. If you say something like "I understand the anger attached to this issue," the person may either appreciate the recognition or snap back with a retort about not being angry. As a rule, use caution when answering emotionally charged questions.

Keep a Positive Mind-Set Some beginning speakers are uneasy about question-and-answer sessions. One way to feel more confident about this part of a speech is to frame it positively. Most questions are signs of interest and curiosity—your listeners genuinely want to know more about a subject. A question-and-answer session gives people a chance to ask for additional information and allows you the opportunity to provide it.

Address the Entire Group Even though a specific person in the group has asked a question, keep your answer audience centered. First, restate the question so that everyone in the room can hear it. Second, deliver the answer to the entire group, not just to the person asking the question. These two actions bring the full audience into the conversation and help keep everyone interested. Usually, a question asked by one audience member is a question that others have, too. However, you occasionally receive a question whose answer applies only to the person asking it. When this happens, respond that the question seems to address the needs of only one person, and you will be glad to speak with him or her after the presentation. In doing so, you acknowledge the importance of the person, but not at the expense of the larger audience.

Answer with Honesty At some point in your speaking career, you will be asked a question for which you do not have an answer. Rather than trying to fake an answer or justify why you do not have one, be honest. Admit you do not know the answer. Then acknowledge the importance of the question, refer it to someone who may know the answer, or offer to try to find the answer after the session if it seems appropriate to do so.

Stay Focused Unlike a speech, which has a specific purpose and thesis statement, question-and-answer sessions can cover a wide range of ideas and perspectives, some of them only remotely related to the topic at hand. In addition, with many people asking questions, keeping track of time and the flow of ideas can be difficult. However, you can do several things to keep the dialogue focused.

1. State how much time you have for the question-and-answer session. This will help your audience gauge the number of questions that members can ask and the amount of detail you can provide in your answers.

2. You occasionally will get a few people who try to dominate the session. They either ask repeated questions or use their question to engage in an extended monologue. When you can regain the floor, thank those people for their interest and ideas, and explain that it is important to hear from a variety of audience members. Then turn to other people with questions to keep the discussion moving.

3. Keep track of time, alerting the audience when the question-and-answer session has reached its midpoint as well as when the session is nearing its end. At these points, refocus the discussion, stating, "We've had a number of questions related to [this aspect of the topic]. Do we have any questions on topics we haven't covered yet?" In this way, you can make a space for people who have not yet been able to ask their questions.

Building Your Confidence as a Public Speaker

Even the most experienced speakers get a little nervous before they give a speech, so it is normal that you might feel a bit nervous, too. One reason we become anxious is that we care about our topic and our performance. We want to perform well and deliver a successful speech. Another reason we might be nervous before a speech is because we fear the unknown; we anticipate the speaking event and imagine that it will be stressful long before we actually give the speech. These are also normal, and it is helpful to know that there are ways to build your confidence as a speaker and reduce some of the nervousness your might feel.

Our nervousness before a speech is often called **communication apprehension**; it is *the level of fear or anxiety associated with either real or anticipated communication with another person or persons* (Finn, Sawyer, & Schrodt, 2009; McCroskey, 1977; Winters et al., 2007; Witt, Roberts, & Behnke, 2008).

communication apprehension
the level of fear or anxiety associated with either real or anticipated communication with another person or persons.

trait anxiety
apprehension about communicating with others in any situation.

state, or situational, anxiety
apprehension about communicating with others in a particular situation

Our confidence as speakers increases the more we give speeches. Consider the reasons you might be nervous about your speech and try to develop a plan to minimize some of your anxiety.

Communication apprehension can take two forms. People who are *apprehensive about communicating with others in any situation* are said to have **trait anxiety**. People who are *apprehensive about communicating with others in a particular situation* are said to have **state, or situational, anxiety**.

To help reduce your nervousness, take a moment to consider whether you are trait anxious or state anxious in communication situations. Do you fear all kinds of interactions or only certain kinds? Most of us experience some level of state anxiety about some communication events, such as asking a boss for a raise, verbally evaluating another's performance, or introducing ourselves to a group of strangers. This is quite normal.

Most people also experience some level of state anxiety about public speaking. This is called *public-speaking anxiety* (PSA), the anxiety we feel when we learn we have to give a speech or take a public-speaking course (Behnke & Sawyer, 1999; Bippus & Daly, 1999; Robinson, 1997). You can build your confidence and reduce some of your PSA by following the tips provided in this section. However, if you are extraordinarily nervous about giving speeches, see your instructor for special assistance with your fears.

Knowing why we become nervous before a speech can help us build our confidence. Research suggests that most people's state anxiety about public speaking exists for six reasons. Many people are state anxious because public speaking is

1. **novel**—we do not do it regularly and thus lack necessary skills;

2. **done in formal settings**—our behaviors when giving a speech are more prescribed and rigid than usual;

3. **often done from a subordinate position**—an instructor or boss sets the rules for giving a speech and the audience acts as a critic;

4. **conspicuous or obvious**—the speaker stands apart from the audience;

5. **done in front of an audience that is unfamiliar**—most people are more comfortable talking with people they know, and we also fear that an audience will not be interested in what we have to say; and

6. **a unique situation in which the degree of attention paid to the speaker is quite noticeable**—audience members either stare at us or ignore us, so we become unusually self-focused (Beatty, 1988; Bippus & Daly, 1999).

It helps to know that research also suggests people are usually nervous only about specific aspects of public speaking. When people ranked what they fear while giving a speech, they said the following (McCullough, Russell, Behnke, Sawyer, & Witt, 2006; Stein, Walker, & Forde, 1996; Witt & Behnke, 2006):

Trembling or shaking	80%
Mind going blank	74%
Doing or saying something embarrassing	64%
Being unable to continue talking	63%
Not making sense	59%
Sounding foolish	59%

When we combine this research, a pattern emerges that helps us understand our nervousness. Because public speaking is novel and usually done in a formal setting, our nervousness can make us shake or tremble. Then when the spotlight is on us as the speaker, we fear our minds will go blank, we will say something embarrassing, or we will be unable to continue talking. Finally, we often do not know our audience well, which can make us fear evaluation, not making sense, or sounding foolish more than we ordinarily would. As you can see, some of our nervousness is legitimate. Even so, we can get past it and build our confidence as speakers.

The suggestions offered here should help you build your confidence and turn your nervous energy to your advantage.

PRACTICING HUMAN COMMUNICATION

Building Your Confidence

With another member of your class, make a list of what makes each of your feel nervous about public speaking. Now sort this list into categories that reflect your view of yourselves as speakers, your audience, the process of developing your speech and presentational aids, and delivering your speeches. Identify which aspect or aspects of the public-speaking process generate the most anxiety for each of you. Discuss which techniques for easing public-speaking anxiety presented in this chapter might work best for you.

Do Your Research

One way to build your confidence before giving a speech is to prepare as well as you can (Daly, Vangelisti, & Webber, 1995). Careful preparation will help you feel more confident about what you will say (and what others will think) and ease fears about drawing a blank or not being able to answer a question. Speakers who research their topics thoroughly before they speak feel prepared. As a result, they tend to be much more relaxed and effective during their presentations.

Practice Your Speech

You can build your confidence and reduce the nervousness associated with the formality of a speech by practicing. And the more times you practice, the more confident you can become. The following example shows how this can be done.

Randy was terrified to give his first speech. His instructor suggested a solution he reluctantly agreed to try. When no one else was home, Randy began to present his speech out loud and alone in his room. He then stood in front of a mirror and delivered his speech to his own reflection. After several horrifying attempts, he began to feel more comfortable. Soon after, he began to trust his speaking ability enough to deliver his speech to his older sister, whom he trusted to be kind and constructive. After doing this a few times, he asked her to give him honest feedback. Finally, he practiced once more in the clothing he planned to wear and delivered his speech in his kitchen, which he arranged so it resembled his classroom as much as possible.

When speakers practice their speeches before they give them, they become more familiar with the process of speaking and the formality of the situation. As they gain comfort by practicing alone, they can move to rehearsals before an audience. They also have time to make changes in their presentation and smooth out the rough spots before they actually speak. This practice is part of a process known as **systematic desensitization**, a *technique for reducing anxiety that involves teaching your body to feel calm and relaxed rather than fearful during your speeches*. This technique can help you give successful speeches and build your confidence, thus breaking the cycle of fear associated with public speaking. Talk to your instructor if you would like to learn more about this technique (Kangas Dwyer, 1998, 2000; McCroskey, 1972; Smith & Frymier, 2006).

Have Realistic Expectations

A third way to build your confidence is to set realistic expectations about your delivery. Few speakers sound or look like professional performers. When real people give real speeches, they sound like real people who are invested in their topic and speech. So rather than worry about delivering a flawless performance, adjust your expectations to a more realistic level.

Remember, speakers pause, cough, rely on their notes for prompts, occasionally say "um," and even exhibit physical signs of nervousness, such as blushing or sweating. As we give more speeches, these "flaws" either go away or become less noticeable or we learn to manage them effectively. Here are a few realistic expectations for beginning speakers:

- Take a calming breath before you begin your speech.
- Remember your introduction.
- Strike a balance between using your notes and making eye contact with your audience.
- Make eye contact with more than one person.
- Gesture naturally rather than hold on to the podium.
- Deliver your conclusion the way you practiced it.

Practice Visualization and Affirmations

Sometimes, we increase our nervousness by imagining a worst-case scenario for the speech, and these images often stay in our minds. We have set up what is called a *self-fulfilling prophecy*: if you see yourself doing poorly in your mind before your speech, you set yourself up to do so in the speech. There are two ways to turn this negative dynamic around and build your confidence as a speaker: visualization and affirmations.

Visualization Visualization is *a process in which you construct a mental image of yourself giving a successful speech*. Research on the benefits of visualization suggests that one session of visualization (about fifteen minutes) has a significant positive effect on communication apprehension (Ayres & Hopf, 1985, 1989, 1990; Ayres, Hopf, & Ayres, 1994; McGarvey, 1990). The techniques of visualization are used by a wide range of people—athletes, performers, and executives—and can range from elaborate to quite simple processes. For public speakers, the most effective process works like this.

Find a quiet, comfortable place where you can sit in a relaxed position for approximately fifteen minutes. Close your eyes and breathe slowly and deeply through your nose, feeling relaxation flow through your body. In great detail, visualize the morning of the day you are to give your speech.

You become filled with confidence and energy, and you wear the perfect clothing for your speech. You drive, walk, or ride to campus filled with this same positive and confident energy. As you enter the classroom, you see yourself relaxed, interacting with your classmates, full of confidence because you have thoroughly prepared for your speech. Your classmates are friendly and cordial in their greetings and conversations with you. You are *absolutely* sure of your material and your ability to present that material in the way you would like.

Next, visualize yourself beginning your speech. You see yourself approaching the place in your classroom from which you will speak. You are sure of yourself, eager to begin, and positive in your abilities as a speaker. You know you are organized and ready to use all your visual aids with ease. Now you see yourself presenting your speech. Your introduction is wonderful. Your transitions are smooth and interesting. Your main points are articulated brilliantly. Your evidence is presented elegantly. Your organization is perfect. Take as much time as you can in visualizing this part of your process. Be as specific and positive as you can.

Visualize the end of the speech: it could not have gone better. You are relaxed and confident, the audience is eager to ask questions, and you respond with the same talent as you gave your speech. As you return to your seat, you are filled with energy and appreciation for the job well done. You are ready for the next events of your day, and you accomplish them with success and confidence.

Now take a deep breath and return to the present. Breathe in, hold it—and release. Do this several times as you return to the present. Take as much time as you need to make this transition (Ayres & Hopf, 1989).

Research on visualization for public speakers suggests that the more detail we give to our visualizations (what shoes we wear, exactly how we feel as we see ourselves, imagining the specifics of our speech), the more effective the technique is in building our confidence and reducing apprehension. Visualization has a significant effect on building our confidence because it systematically replaces negative images with positive images.

Affirmations Speakers sometimes undermine their confidence through negative self-talk; they listen to the harsh judgments that many of us carry within ourselves. When we think "I'm no good at this," "I know I'll embarrass myself," or "Other people are far more talented than I am," we engage in negative self-talk. We judge ourselves as inferior or less competent than others. Although it is natural to evaluate our own performances critically (that is how we motivate ourselves to improve), negative self-talk in public-speaking situations often is unhelpful. When our internal voices tell us we cannot succeed, our communication apprehension only increases (Ayres, 1988).

To build your confidence, however, and counter the negative self-talk that might be going on in your head before a speech, use **affirmations**, *positive statements that assert that what we wish to be true is already happening*. To replace the negative self-talk with affirmations, try the following technique. For every negative assessment you hear yourself give, replace it with an honest assessment that you reframe to be positive. This technique, sometimes called **cognitive restructuring**, is *a process that builds confidence because it replaces negative thoughts with positive thoughts called affirmations* (Fremouw & Scott, 1979). Affirmation**s** are positive, motivating statements. They are very helpful in turning our immobilizing self-doubts into realistic assessments and options. Consider the following examples.

Negative	Positive
I don't know how to organize this material.	I can find a way to present this effectively. I have a good sense of organization. I can get help if I need it.
I know I'll get up there and make a fool of myself.	I am capable of giving a wonderful speech. I know lots of strategies to do so.
I'll forget what I want to say.	I'll remember what I want to say, and I'll have notes to help me.
I'm too scared to look at my audience.	I'll make eye contact with at least five people in the audience.
I'm scared to death!	I care about my performance and will do very well.
I'll be the worst in the class!	I'll give my speech well and am looking forward to a fine presentation. We are all learning how to do this.

Positive affirmations build confidence because they reframe negative energy and evaluations and shed light on your anxieties. To say you are terrified is immobilizing, but to say you care about your performance gives you room to continue to develop your speech. It is also a more accurate description of what is going on inside. Affirmations can assist you in minimizing the effects of your internal judgments and, along with visualization, can help build your confidence about public speaking.

Connect with Your Audience

A final way to build your confidence is to connect with your audience—getting to know them in class or gathering information about them before a more formal speaking situation. As you prepare your speech, identify what you know about them, the ways you are similar to audience members, and the ways you might be different. The similarities may be as general as living in the same town or working for the same company or as specific as sharing the same views on issues. Whatever the level of comparison, finding out about your audience reminds you that we all share many aspects of our daily lives. This helps you see that, despite differences, we do share similar views and experiences.

You can also build your confidence by being a good member of the audience when others are speaking. Although this might seem unusual, ask yourself the following questions: When you are listening to a speech, do you make eye contact with the speaker? Do you sit with an attentive and alert posture, taking notes or showing interest in the presentation? Do you ask relevant questions of the speaker when the speech is over or offer constructive comments if you have the opportunity to evaluate his or her performance? Speakers who fail to behave as engaged and interested audience members often fear the very same response to their speeches.

One way to overcome this fear of disrespectful audiences is to behave as an audience member as you would want others to behave when you speak. Doing so helps establish rapport (if you are kind to a speaker, she or he likely will respond similarly to you). It also helps you learn about how to put together and deliver an effective speech.

The solutions offered in this section may help you reduce some of the speech anxiety so common to beginning public speakers. Preparing, practicing, being realistic, visualizing and affirming, finding connections, and modeling appropriate audience behavior are options that even experienced public speakers use to build their confidence. Learning to relax while giving speeches enhances your ability to contribute to the public dialogue.

PRACTICING HUMAN COMMUNICATION

Building Your Confidence

In a column, write down a list of negative statements that you typically think or feel about giving a speech. Next, create a second column and change each negative statement into a positive statement. Now identify which statements pertain to aspects of speech preparation, delivery, and audience feedback. Discuss as a class how speakers can build their confidence and how listeners can help assist the speaker in building confidence.

Sample Speeches

CourseMate Connection: Go to cengagebrain.com to access your CourseMate for *Invitation to Human Communication*. To view a speech about self-introduction, watch Tiffany Brisco's speech. To view an informative speech, watch Cindy Gardner's "U.S. Flag Etiquette." To view an introduction using a narrative, watch Brandi Lafferty's opening story in her speech "Feeding the Wildlife: Don't Do It!"

Chapter Summary

The Four Methods of Delivery Used by Public Speakers Are Extemporaneous, Impromptu, Manuscript, and Memorized

- Effective speakers use vocal variety in their delivery—changes in the volume, rate, and pitch of a speaker's voice that affect the meaning of the words delivered.
- Vocal variety is achieved when speakers adjust the volume, rate, pitch and inflection, pauses, articulation, pronunciation, and dialect throughout their speeches.

The Nonverbal Components of Delivery Are Those Aspects Communicated Through Our Bodies and Faces

- For public speakers, these include personal appearance, eye contact, facial expression, posture, gestures, and proxemics.
- *Technology* refers to the tools speakers use to help them deliver their message. Speakers use both traditional and electronic technologies in their speeches.

Speeches Often Involve Question-and-Answer Sessions

- Ensuring a good question-and-answer session has two steps: preparing for potential questions beforehand and managing the discussion during the session.

- When you prepare for the question-and-answer session, you do two things: identify potential questions and formulate and practice answers to those questions.
- When you manage the discussion, you explain the format before the session begins, listen thoughtfully and clarify any potential misunderstandings, keep a positive mind-set, address the full audience when you offer answers, answer with honesty, and keep the session focused.

Our Nervousness Before a Speech Is Often Called *Communication Apprehension*, and Speakers Can Have Trait Anxiety or Situational Anxiety

- Tips for managing speech apprehension are do your research, practice your speech, have realistic expectations, practice visualization and affirmations, and connect with your audience.
- Speakers sometimes undermine their confidence through negative self-talk. To replace the negative self-talk, use affirmations—positive statements that assert that what we wish to be true is already happening.

Key Concepts

affirmations (324)

articulation (306)

cognitive restructuring (324)

communication apprehension (319)

conversational style (299)

dialect (307)

extemporaneous speech (298)

eye contact (309)

facial expression (310)

gestures (311)

impromptu speech (299)

inflection (304)

manuscript speech (301)

monotone (304)

pauses (305)

personal appearance (308)

pitch (304)

posture (310)

pronunciation (307)

proxemics (313)

rate (303)

state, or situational, anxiety (319)

systematic desensitization (322)

trait anxiety (319)

visualization (322)

vocalized pauses (306)

vocal variety (303)

volume (303)

Invitation to Human Communication Online

Speech Communication CourseMate includes an interactive eBook and interactive learning tools including National Geographic Explorer videos, student videos, quizzes, flash cards, and more. Speech Builder Express 3.0 and Speech Studio 2.0 are also available. Go to cengagebrain.com to access your CourseMate for *Invitation to Human Communication* where these resources can be found.

Further Reflection and Discussion

1. Identify speakers you consider to have good delivery. What characteristics make their delivery strong? How many of these characteristics might you incorporate into your style of delivery?

2. Identify the differences among extemporaneous, impromptu, manuscript, and memorized deliveries. What are the strengths and weaknesses of each type of delivery?

3. Write a quick speech and exchange the speeches among classmates. In groups, give that speech as though it were a tragedy, a surprise, or a hilarious story—or choose some other approach that will allow you to work on vocal variety. How well are you able to match the verbal aspects of your delivery to the mood you have selected?

Activities and Web Links

Visit cengagebrain.com to access the CourseMate for *Invitation to Human Communication* where these activities and web links can be found.

1. Listen to this brief portion of Randy Pausch's famous last lecture. How would you describe his delivery? What is most compelling about his delivery? Go to *Web link 12.1.*

2. Read or listen to Ann Richards's speech at the Democratic National Convention in 1988. What makes her delivery unique? How does she maintain her audience's attention? Go to *Web link 12.2.*

3. Read this article about Senator Edward Kennedy's speeches and delivery. Did his delivery hinder the effectiveness of his speeches? Why or why not? Go to *Web link 12.3.*

4. Read this article about Chicano dialect. What advice would you give to a classmate about what to tell the audience about his or her dialect? Go to *Web link 12.4.*

INFORMATIVE SPEAKING

IN THIS CHAPTER YOU WILL LEARN TO:

- Describe the five types of informative speeches.
- Apply the four most common patterns of organization for informative speeches.

- Identify three tips for giving effective informative speeches.
- Identify three principles for giving ethical informative speeches.

13

Types of Informative Speeches

Organizational Patterns for Informative Speeches

Tips for Giving Effective Informative Speeches

Ethical Informative Speaking

Neustockimages/iStockphoto

As you read in an earlier chapter, most of our days are spent listening to others. If you could select three informative speech topics you would like to listen to, what would those topics be? Why would you select those topics?

People have a lot to learn about ecology—but first you have to get their attention.

—*David de Rothschild, Environmental Storyteller and National Geographic Emerging Explorer*

informative speech

speech that communicates knowledge and understanding about a process, an event, a place or person, an object, or a concept.

informative speaking environments

environments in which a speaker has expertise or knowledge that an audience needs but does not already have.

When we need information on what a new health-care plan will mean, how to fix a flat tire, or which bottled water is the highest quality, we need complete and accurate information. To meet that need, speakers in the workplace, in the classroom, and in our communities often speak informatively. An **informative speech** *communicates knowledge and understanding about a process, an event, a place or person, an object, or a concept.* Informative speakers share what they know or have researched to familiarize an audience with a topic its members want or need to understand.

Informative speakers create **informative speaking environments**, *environments in which a speaker has expertise or knowledge that an audience needs but does not already have.* Informative speakers attempt to enhance an audience's understanding of how some part of the world works.

As you enter the public dialogue, you will give many informative speeches (Johnson & Szczupakiewicz, 1987). In fact, across professions, demand is growing for employees with strong public communication skills and an ability to share information with others in a wide range of settings (Dannels, 2001; Morreal, Osborn, & Pearson, 2000; National Association of Colleges and Employers, 2012; Wolvin, 1989). We emphasize informative speaking because we need information every day—for example, to understand how a new medication will affect us, to learn how to parallel park, to deliberate over the governor's proposal for spending a budget surplus, or to complete the complex assignment our boss just gave us.

 ## Types of Informative Speeches

The five types of informative speeches most common in classes that teach public speaking and in the workplace are speeches about processes, events, places and people, objects, and concepts. Each type of speech has a different focus, and each is suited to a different occasion.

Speeches about Processes

Commonly called a how-to or a demonstration speech, **speeches about processes** *describe how something is done, how something comes to be*

speeches about processes

informative speech that describes how something is done, how something comes to be what it is, or how something works.

what it is, or how something works. Process speeches help an audience learn how to complete a task, understand how something develops over time, or comprehend how a process unfolds. The fundamental goal of a process speech is to show your audience how to *perform* a process or how to better *understand* a process. Sample topics for process speeches include the following:

How to get a passport

How coal is mined in the United States

How a solar panel converts the sun's heat into our energy

How to protect yourself from harmful sunburns

How to decide how much to tip a server in a restaurant

Process speeches are common because people are constantly learning how to perform new tasks. For example, your boss may ask you to explain to a colleague how to fill out and submit an expense report. Or you may be asked to explain to new staff how an employee incentive program came to be implemented, especially if you have a history with that particular program. In the classroom, you may be required to speak about a process that your classmates will benefit from learning more about.

The following two examples illustrate process speeches about a very familiar topic: coffee. In the first example, Tracee describes how coffee came to be a popular drink in North America.

Specific purpose:	To inform my audience how coffee became one of the most popular drinks in North America.
Thesis statement:	Through a series of historical events beginning in the 1500s, coffee replaced tea as one of the most popular drinks in North America.
Main points:	I. Coffee found its way to North America in the 1500s when trade routes opened between coffee-growing countries and Europe, then expanded to North America.
	II. Coffee began to gain in popularity as tensions with England accelerated in the 1700s and imports of tea decreased.
	III. By the 1900s, international commerce, marketing techniques, and individual lifestyles made coffee one of the most popular drinks in North America.

In the second example, Wynton describes how the process of growing and harvesting a particular kind of coffee works.

MARK THIESSEN/National Geographic

Mireya Mayor

Emerging Explorer, Primatologist, and Conservationist

When giving an informative speech, what types of visual aids have you used and which have been most effective?

My most popular presentation is based on my life, so the materials come from me and my experiences. What I really like to bring to those presentations are visuals. I start telling stories about my childhood and being an NFL cheerleader and going to these wild and remote places and the animals there. I try to support that with visuals.

I think it's really important to use visual aids to connect people to what I'm talking about. They might not be able to visualize what a tropical rainforest in Madagascar looks like, so I show them, or the amazing array of species there, so I show them. I also try to find timely references that relate to, say, the science that I'm talking about or things that have inspired me. For example, there was an article in *Time* magazine entitled "Death Row," and it showed these critically endangered primates. And that's what really captured my attention and was actually the motivating factor in me going into this field. And years later I dug that article up, scanned it, and I use that as one of the pictures in my PowerPoint. It's so important to show them, to really show them what you are talking about.

Specific purpose:	To inform my audience how shade-grown coffee is grown and harvested.
Thesis statement:	The process of growing and harvesting shade-grown coffee differs from the process used by coffee plantations in three significant ways.
Main points:	I. Shade-grown coffee is grown in small plots, quite unlike the more familiar coffee plantation method. II. As the plants grow, these plots provide non-chemical forms of fertilizer and pest control. III. When the coffee beans are mature, they are harvested and stored in ecologically friendly ways.

Notice how each speech follows a progression of steps from first to second to third. Because process speeches describe step-by-step progressions, they are almost always organized chronologically A chronological pattern of organization allows you to develop your speech from the first step to the last or from the earliest signs to the most recent examples. (Later in this chapter, you will explore organizational patterns for informative speeches more fully.)

Speeches about Events

Speeches about events *describe or explain significant, interesting, or unusual occurrences.* These speeches help an audience understand what happened, why it happened, and what effect the event had. Just as we

speeches about events

informative speeches that describe or explain significant, interesting, or unusual occurrences.

often describe what happens in our personal lives so we can better understand how events influence our lives, public speakers share what happens with audiences to help them understand a significant event in the context of history or society or community. In some ways, speeches about events are mini history lessons that educate audiences about key moments. Sample topics for speeches about events would be

the resignation of Egyptian President Hosni Mubarak,

the radioactive leaks at Japan's Fukushima nuclear power plant,

the origins of the Occupy movement, and

large-scale food recalls.

Speakers are often asked to speak about events, usually in professional settings. Consider Sophia, whose boss asked her to speak to her fellow employees about the latest recall of beef in their region.

Specific purpose:	To inform our staff of the most recent recall of beef and products that contain beef.
Thesis statement:	This most recent recall of beef from our stores requires that we identify all beef purchased within the last three months, identify all products containing beef purchased within the last three months, and remove and dispose of these products in very specific ways.

In a community setting, people may decide to speak about local events as a way to inform councils, planning boards, or community service agencies and perhaps assist them with the decisions they make.

Specific purpose:	To inform the city council about the high rate of accidents at the corner of College and Elm Streets.
Thesis statement:	The intersection of College and Elm is the site of an unusually high rate of accidents during certain hours of the day.

When you are required to speak about an event, select a topic your audience will find interesting and relevant. For example, inform your classmates of an event that affects your own campus (a public hearing to improve public transportation to the campus), the community that houses your campus (an annual jazz festival that showcases successful musicians from the community), or your state or region (a recognition ceremony for local volunteers who helped elect a candidate to Congress).

Most speeches about events, especially historical events, are arranged chronologically. However, if the way an event unfolds is not the focus of your speech, then you can organize your speech topically. Or if you want to analyze why an event occurred and what effect it had, you can use a causal pattern. (These and other patterns of organization are examined later in the chapter.)

Speeches about Places and People

Speeches about places and people *describe significant, interesting, or unusual places or people.* These speeches can be fun to give in a classroom because you can share your experiences with places and people you have visited or have found fascinating. In the workplace or the community, speeches about places and people help audiences understand the importance, nature, appeal, charm, or integrity of a particular place or person or the contributions a particular person has made to an organization or a community. Sample topics for speeches about places and people might be

service agencies in the community,

Lady Gaga,

New Orleans,

Nelson Mandela,

Haiti, or

Jane Goodall.

Because you will not have time in a speech to discuss all there is to know about a place or a person, the goal of this type of speech is to capture the *spirit* of that place or person. You want audience members to understand why this place or person is important or useful to them or their community, important historically, or just interesting and worth learning about. Look at this example of a speech that Adrianna gave in her public-speaking course.

Specific purpose: To inform my audience about the history and features of the Freedom Trail in Boston, Massachusetts.

Thesis statement: The Freedom Trail, which originated in the late 1950s, is a pedestrian path through downtown Boston that links sites of historical importance to the United States, such as our first public school and the site of the Boston Massacre.

In the next example, Garrett informs his classmates about Captain Nicole Malachowski, the first woman selected to join the Thunderbirds, the Air Force's most elite team of pilots.

Specific purpose: To inform my classmates of Lieutenant Colonel Nicole Malachowski, the first woman selected to fly with the Thunderbirds.

Thesis statement: In 2005, the Thunderbirds, a small elite team of the best pilots in the Air Force, selected its first woman pilot, Nicole Malachowski, to join them, opening the doors for other talented female pilots to fly the most advanced aircraft in the world.

Speeches about places or people can be organized topically (how the Freedom Trail was conceived, the importance of the historical sites to

CIVIC ENGAGEMENT IN ACTION

© Geoffrey Holman/istockphoto

Downtown Dog Rescue

To the Rescue!

Often people join the public dialogue to speak for those who cannot speak for themselves. Sometimes these unheard voices belong to other people, such as children, or to entities such as the environment. Many times, these voices belong to animals (LeBeau, 2008; Weise, 2009).

Dog owner Lori Weise, a manager at a furniture store in Los Angeles, crossed paths one day with a homeless man named Benny Josephs and his pit bull, Iron Head. The bond between this man and his dog had a profound impact on Weise. "I was so impressed with how the two were really one," she says. "Iron

Head was never on a leash and never strayed too far from Benny's sight." Her interactions with Josephs and Iron Head inspired her to found Downtown Dog Rescue in 1996. Since then, this organization has rescued and adopted out more than 3,000 dogs, provided resources for homeless people and their pets, and raised awareness in the Los Angeles area about animal cruelty. Lori is a tireless advocate for healthy and responsible pet ownership, using many channels to get the word out, including community events, letter-writing campaigns, speeches at conferences, and Twitter.

Luigi "Shorty" Rossi, also from Los Angeles, credits pit bulls with saving his life when he was young and providing loyal companionship during the hardest times of his life, including a stint in prison for gang-related activity. In 2001, after having made a successful career for himself as an entertainer and talent manager, he founded Shorty's Pit Bull Rescue. Just as Downtown Dog Rescue does, Shorty's Rescue rescues, rehabilitates, and adopts out neglected and abused pit bulls. The organization also promotes a positive view of this misunderstood breed, using education and activism to help prevent animal cruelty. Shorty's forums for speaking out include short films, public service commercials, and *Pit Boss*, Animal Planet's reality show about his endeavors ("Meet Shorty Rossi," 2010).

What Do You Think?

1. If you could give an informative speech about "unheard voices" which group would you speak about and why? How would you capture the spirit of that group?

---

which the trail leads), chronologically (events in Captain Malachowski's life that led to her selection), or spatially (Big Bend National Park in Texas features recreational areas in the mountains, in the desert, and along the Rio Grande River).

Speeches about Objects

Speeches about objects are about *anything that is tangible—that is, can be perceived by the senses.* When we speak informatively about objects, we describe the components or characteristics of something so an audience can better understand it and why it might be important or valued. Sample topics for speeches about objects include

    credit cards,

    honeybees,

speeches about objects
informative speeches about anything that is tangible—that is, can be perceived by the senses.

Art often makes an interesting topic for a speech. Make a list of your favorite photos, paintings, music, or other art forms. Could you give a speech on one of these topics?

hybrid automobiles, and

poisonous frogs.

Speeches about objects are common in the working world. For example, a product-development coordinator might speak regularly to her colleagues about new products that come across her desk, describing their qualities, uses, and appeal. Similarly, tour guides often speak about local objects of importance or interest, describing buildings, sculptures, and pieces of art. For a required classroom speech about an object, you might describe something useful, rare, or interesting to a speech class audience. For example, Jun Lee gave a speech about *Mona Lisa*'s mysterious smile.

Specific purpose:	To inform my audience about the *Mona Lisa* and the many theories about her famous smile.
Thesis statement:	One of the most famous paintings of all time, the *Mona Lisa* has inspired several theories about why she has such a mysterious smile.

A very popular topic for speeches about *animate* objects is animals and their behaviors, habitats, and ways of interacting with humans and other animals. Here is a sample specific purpose and a thesis statement for Shana's speech about the African serval.

Specific purpose:	To inform my audience about keeping the African serval as a house pet.
Thesis statement:	Although the African serval's legs, ears, and coloration aid in its survival in the wild, these same adaptations have a whole new meaning in the context of keeping a serval as an exotic house pet.

Many speeches about objects are organized topically (the characteristics of the poisonous frog). Others are organized using a causal pattern (possible causes of the colony collapse disorder plaguing our honeybees) and sometimes, a speech about an object can be organized chronologically (hybrid automobile, from the first to the latest model) or spatially (the different features of a hybrid car). Be sure to select the pattern that helps you express your ideas clearly and efficiently.

Speeches about Concepts

Speeches about concepts are *about abstractions, things you cannot perceive with your senses—such as ideas, theories, principles, worldviews, or beliefs.* The goal of a speech about a concept is to help your audience understand your subject, its history, its characteristics, and its effect on society or individuals. Some sample topics for speeches about concepts are

the new frugality,

sustainability,

adult literacy,

theories of adolescent development,

health-care reform, and

global citizenship.

When you give speeches about concepts, you help audiences more fully understand or appreciate issues, principles, systems, and the like. Consider Tory's speech about the new frugality, sometimes described as "less is more."

Specific purpose:	To inform my audience about the new frugality, which is sometimes called "less is more."
Thesis statement:	Because of our country's economic crisis, many people are embracing the values of frugality, which involve owning fewer material possessions, being less "possession-identified" and more "self-identified," and, of course, spending less money.

speeches about concepts
informative speeches about abstractions, things you cannot perceive with your senses—such as ideas, theories, principles, worldviews, or beliefs.

Speeches about concepts can be challenging because it might be difficult to explain an abstraction clearly. However, this type of speech is also very helpful because sometimes audiences need to understand concepts before they can understand how something works or why a person is significant. Speeches about concepts are often organized topically (the principles behind health-care reform) or chronologically (early theories of adolescent development to the most recent theories). Sometimes, a speech about a concept can be organized causally (the causes of the idea of global citizenship).

 ## Organizational Patterns for Informative Speeches

Informative speeches can be organized in a variety of ways, and you will probably use a wide range of organizational patterns as you become a proficient public speaker. These organizational patterns are chronological, spatial, causal, and topical. Using these patterns, you can organize your main points logically.

Chronological Pattern

chronological pattern
a pattern of organization in which you illustrate how a topic has developed over time or what sequential steps an audience must take to complete a task.

With a **chronological pattern**, you can *organize your main points to illustrate how a topic has developed over time or what sequential steps an audience must take to complete a task*. Most of us are familiar with the chronological pattern because most stories we tell or hear progress from start to finish chronologically. Chronological patterns are especially effective for process speeches, but as you learned earlier in this chapter, they also are well suited for other kinds of informative speeches. In the following example, Alan gives a speech to explain to his audience how the Ford Mustang set the standard for the so-called muscle cars of the 1960s.

Specific purpose:	To inform my audience of the history of the Ford Mustang.
Thesis statement:	The Ford Mustang, which quickly became the muscle car to beat in 1964 with its combination of high performance and low cost, continues to be the most popular car of that decade.

Main points:	I. Pontiac's GTO—which stands for "gas, tires, oil"—is credited as the first of the muscle cars of the 1960s.
	II. Ford quickly took the top spot among muscle cars, releasing the high-performance, low-cost Mustang to the public on April 17, 1964.
	III. Ford then added new makes with increasingly attractive features and options to maintain its popularity—among them the Fastback, the Grande, the Mach I, the Boss 302, and the Boss 429.
	IV. The muscle cars of the 1960s remain some of the most popular cars of that decade, and the newer Mustangs give us a glimpse into why this is so.

Alan takes his audience through the evolution of muscle cars in the 1960s, beginning with the Pontiac GTO; moving on to Ford's first Mustangs and the company's release of newer makes, features, and options; and then showing the current influence of those features on today's cars. By using this pattern, Alan provides his listeners with basic information they can build on as he progresses through his speech.

Spatial Pattern

The **spatial pattern** allows you to *address topics logically in terms of location or direction.* With this pattern, you can arrange your main points by the position they represent within a physical space. You also can use this pattern to inform your audience of the places that relate to your topic, the activities that occur in those places, or the activities that are necessary to the functioning of your topic. In the following example, Scott uses a spatial pattern to describe the different parts of a guitar and how each part works to produce sound.

spatial pattern
a pattern of organization that allows you to address topics logically in terms of location or direction.

Specific purpose:	To inform my audience of how the different parts of the guitar work together to produce sound.
Thesis statement:	The guitar has three main parts—the head, neck, and body—and each works with the others in intricate ways to produce the sounds we call music.
Main points:	I. The top of the guitar is the head, which houses the nut and the tuning pegs.
	II. The next part is the neck, which contains three essential parts: the frets, the truss rod, and the fingerboard.
	III. The bottom part is the body, which is made of a reinforced front, back and side panels, a sound hole, and the bridge and saddle.

The spatial pattern is a clear and effective way to describe the different parts of an object.

Causal Pattern

Causal patterns *highlight cause-and-effect relationships.* A cause is an event that makes something happen, and an effect is the response, impression, or change that results from that cause. When you use causal patterns, you inform your audience about what causes certain events, places, objects, or concepts to come into being.

In the following example, Kelsey describes the causes of the onion's tearful effect as well as methods to prevent tears when cutting an onion.

Specific purpose:	To inform my audience about the cause of an onion's tearful effect and methods used to prevent tears when cutting an onion.
Thesis statement:	The internal chemistry of the onion is the cause of its tearful effect when being chopped, but various methods may be used to prevent this occurrence.
Main points:	I. The onion's chemical makeup combines with the physiology of the human eye to induce tears.
	II. The first method to prevent tears is chilling the onion.
	III. The second method involves using an open flame during onion preparation
	IV. Using water around the onion is a helpful technique to reduce tears as well.
	V. The last method involves cutting the core from an onion, where most tear-producing compounds—lachrymators—are thought to be stored.

Kelsey's use of the causal pattern helped her explain what caused the tears, and then show certain ways of cutting an onion to reduce tear production.

Topical Pattern

The **topical organizational pattern** *allows a speaker to address different aspects of a topic.* For example, in Shana's speech on the African serval, she organized her ideas topically to address the physical characteristics that make the animal so suited to life in the wild and then the consequences of bringing it into a domestic setting.

causal patterns
a pattern of organization that allows you to highlight cause-and-effect relationships.

topical organizational pattern
a pattern of organization that allows a speaker to address different aspects of a topic.

PRACTICING HUMAN COMMUNICATION

Select an Organizational Pattern for Your Informative Speech

Return to the list of possible informative speech topics you prepared in Practicing Human Communication earlier in this chapter. In groups, select a single topic and see if you can create a rough thesis statement and main points for four different informative speeches on this topic, using each of the organizational patterns you have just read about. As a class, discuss which of these speeches you would find most interesting and why. As you discuss your favorite topic and organizational pattern, consider the tips for giving effective informative speeches in the next section.

Topical patterns work well in informative speeches with topics that can be easily and logically divided into subtopics. Using a topical pattern, you can highlight the aspects of a topic that are most useful and important for an audience to understand. In Lauren's speech about the nursery rhyme, she used a topical pattern to discuss their dark history.

Specific purpose: To inform the audience about the dark history of the origin of nursery rhymes.

Thesis statement: Nursery rhymes are seen as innocent and lighthearted tales because they are always associated with children, but the truth is that stories such as "Ring Around the Rosie," "Peter Peter Pumpkin Eater," and "Mary, Mary, Quite Contrary" may have dark and often gruesome origins that would seem anything but appropriate for children.

Main points:
    I. The rhyme "Ring Around the Rosie" goes all the way back to the year 1350 Europe when the Black Plague was at its peak.
    II. The rhyme "Peter, Peter Pumpkin Eater" is actually a rhyme about a man who forced his mistress to wear a chastity belt.
    III. "Mary, Mary, Quite Contrary" is actually the most gruesome rhyme of the three.

By using this organizational pattern, Lauren was able to inform her audience of the dark origins of many of their favorite childhood nursery rhymes.

Tips for Giving Effective Informative Speeches

In an informative speaking environment, you contribute to the public dialogue by sharing your knowledge with your audience, illustrating with clarity and detail the relevance of that knowledge to your listeners. Three tips that will help you create informative speaking environments and give effective informative speeches are (1) bring your topic to life, (2) tailor your information to your audience, and (3) use language that is clear and unbiased.

Bring Your Topic to Life

When you give an informative speech, you want your audience to understand your topic in a detailed and dynamic way. Effective informative speakers bring a subject to life for an audience, engaging their listeners so they appreciate the information they receive. Take careful stock of your topic and your audience so you can be sure to share information that is both *engaging* and *relevant*. Engaging material draws audience members in and excites or interests them. Listeners find material

Demonstration speeches are often very engaging because they provide audiences with especially relevant and useful information. Whether you give this type of speech, remember to avoid overwhelming your audience with too much information. Consider a demonstration speech you might like to give. What is the most important information you think your audience would need?

relevant if it is useful or something they must know to do their jobs, live in a community, or make informed decisions.

One way to bring a topic to life is to stay audience centered. As you craft your speech, continually ask yourself how your overall topic, main points, and subpoints relate to your audience.

What do audience members need to know?

How will they use the information you present?

How can you make the information clear?

If you keep these questions in mind throughout your preparation process, you will be more likely to present your material in an engaging and relevant way. For example, in the speech about school violence, Erin brought her second point—manipulation by other students—to life by asking her audience a rhetorical question: "Think back to high school. How many examples of manipulative behavior can you think of? Probably too many. In my junior year, I remember one group of students who constantly picked on my friends and me. It felt like no matter what we did, we were the brunt of their jokes and the focus of their hostility." By sharing her own experience of manipulation, she touched on an experience common to many members of her audience.

Another way to bring your topic to life is to share the human side of your topic. If you are presenting technical information, explaining intricate details, or carefully outlining a process, try to use examples, images, and descriptions that help your audience connect to your topic personally. If you are presenting numbers or statistics, give the figures a human face. As one student asked after hearing an informative speech about how to avoid the kinds of sunburns that lead to skin cancer, "What do all those SPF factors and fancy names mean for me and my skin tone personally?" As you prepare your speech, anticipate this kind of question and look for opportunities to relate your information to the human experience. For example, in a speech on modern art, you might personalize different techniques and styles by drawing parallels to skills learned in art classes or by asking your audience to attempt the techniques on their own as you describe them.

Tailor Your Information to Your Audience

Just as you can feel overwhelmed by the abundance of information you find in your research, your audiences can be equally overwhelmed by the information you share with them in your speech—no matter how engaging and relevant you make that information. As an informative speaker, one of your most challenging tasks is to decide how much information to include in a speech and how much to leave out. Here are reasons why:

- When you present too much information, you run the risk of over-whelming an audience.

- When you present too little information, you run the risk of leaving them unclear or confused about your topic.

- If you present material that is too technical, detailed, and complicated, your audience will have a hard time following it.

- If the information in your speech is too simple, audience members will become bored or feel that you are talking down to them.

Given these dilemmas, the best way to tailor your information to your audience is to *stay audience centered* throughout the speech process. As you develop and present your speech, continually reflect on the needs and interests of your audience. Include information that you think would be of the greatest educational value for your audience, and then adjust your presentation of this information so that it matches your audience's level of knowledge, expertise, and experience.

Use Language That Is Clear and Unbiased

Because informative speeches focus on describing, defining, and explaining, use language that is descriptive and instructive. To ensure your audience can follow you, define all new terminology, break complicated processes into steps, and explain language specific to a particular field or activity. For example, when Wynton spoke about shade-grown coffee, he explained what the terms *shade grown, fair trade, organic,* and *sustainable* mean. Similarly, when Sophia spoke to her colleagues about the beef recall affecting their company, she made sure her audience understood the specific dates and the exact methods of disposal. You can also make a point of explaining familiar words you use in new ways. For example, Lauren took time to link what her audience thought were lighthearted phrases and words from the nursery rhymes to their darker historical origins.

Informative language should be as objective as you can make it. Focus on presenting your information as clearly and accurately as you can and avoid expressing your own views (as in invitational speaking) or trying to sway your audience (as in persuasive speaking). Remember that the goal of informative speaking is to pass along information your audience needs or wants. Make sure the language of your speech is fair and unbiased. Use phrases like "My research indicates that" or "According to the experts" rather than "I hope I've convinced you that this is the best way."

Similarly, when you incorporate personal knowledge into an informative speech, which is common when you describe or explain something you have experience with, make sure the language you use reflects your *experience,* not your biases or preferences. For example, phrases like "After seven years with these machines, I'd recommend the following steps" and "I've been involved in four food recalls since I began in this industry, so I can give you some background and details" are more informative than persuasive.

Ethical Informative Speaking

Ethical informative speakers make sure their speeches are based on careful research, unbiased information, and the honest presentation of information. Take a look at each of these components of ethical informative speaking.

First, our audiences expect that we have taken the time to find information that is accurate and complete, so we must carefully research the details of our topic and share the full story with our audiences. If we have not done this, then we may wind up giving our audiences inaccurate or incomplete information.

Second, as an informative speaker, you want to present unbiased information to your audience. Although we all hold biases, we can take steps to minimize them. You can minimize your biases by presenting examples, statistics, testimony, and other materials as fairly and as neutrally as possible, regardless of your personal positions. Save your preferences for your persuasive speeches; use your informative speeches to help your audiences gain a full understanding of your topic.

Finally, present your information honestly. Do not distort your evidence or make up supporting material as you need it. A healthy public dialogue depends on accuracy. If you misrepresent your speech topic, your audience will come away with an inaccurate view of important issues and situations. Ethical informative speaking relies on the honest and accurate distribution of information, which can happen only if speakers present that information truthfully.

Robert, Kyncl, vice president of global content partnerships at YouTube, delivered the keynote speech at the Entertainment Matters 2012 International Consumer Electronics Show. What would you listen for to evaluate whether this speech was an ethical informative speech?

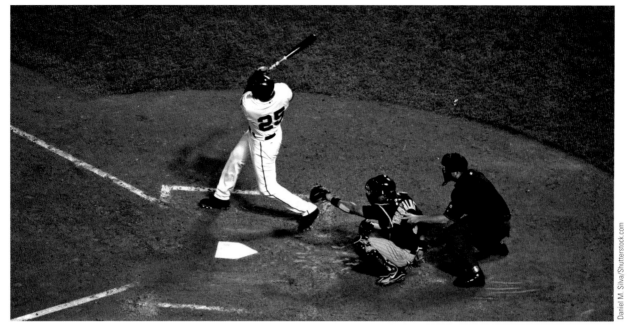

Barry Bonds of the San Francisco Giants hits career home-run number 723 in a game against the Colorado Rockies on August 4, 2006, in San Francisco.

ETHICAL MOMENT

When Must We Speak?

In 2003, as part of a federal case against the Bay Area Laboratory Co-Operative (BALCO) for distributing illegal "designer steroids" to professional athletes, baseball great Barry Bonds told a grand jury that he had not taken steroids during his career. Bonds provided this information because he and other athletes were offered immunity if they testified in the case, which targeted Victor Conte, the founder of BALCO, and Greg Anderson, Bond's trainer and longtime friend. Bonds explained that he trusted Anderson and used the creams and gels Anderson supplied because he thought they were simply flax seed oil and arthritis pain relievers. His testimony, which was supposed to be secret, was leaked to outside sources. Believing that Bonds had lied under oath, prosecutors began a perjury investigation. Bond's attorney, Mike Raines, responded by claiming that the federal government was persecuting Bonds and "going after his client because of his name and notoriety, not the allegations leveled against him." He said, "You offer immunity and you get him in there and then you ask them questions and you get them on lying to federal officers. That's the trap. That's exactly what they got Martha [Stewart] for." In 2011, however, "a federal court jury found [Bonds] guilty of obstruction of justice," for "giving an evasive answer under oath"

in 2003. Although Bonds was acquitted on three other charges of making false statements, he was convicted on the obstruction of justice charges, and he received a sentence of two years of probation and 30 days of house arrest (Martinez and Simon, 2011; Quinn, 2007; Rosynsky, 2007; Rowlands, 2006; Williams and Fainaru-Wada, 2004).

What Do You Think?

1. Both Barry Bonds and Martha Stewart were required to speak in a court of law about cases that were not about them specifically. Do you think people should be required to speak in this way? Why or why not?

2. Whether Bonds was telling the truth or not, do you think that people should always be completely forthcoming about what they are required to speak about? Should some information be kept private and immune from punishment? Why or why not?

3. When potentially damaging information that is supposed to be private is leaked, as in Bonds's case, is it ethical to use that information against the person? Why or why not?

Preparation Outline with Commentary: Tap by Rachel Rota

Specific Purpose: To inform my audience about the art of tap dancing.

Thesis Statement: Tap dancing, one of the oldest forms of dance, is based on just a few basic steps and was popularized in modern times in part by the great tap dancer and choreographer Gregory Hines.

You may have already given an informative speech in your class. Whether you have or whether this is the first time you have spoken informatively, you can use the following outline as a model.

> **CourseMate Connection:** Go to cengagebrain.com to access your CourseMate for *Invitation to Human Communication* to view a video about Rachel Roto giving this speech and see her transcript and speaking outline.

Rachel gave this speech in an introductory public-speaking class in 2006. The assignment was to give a four- to six-minute speech, citing a minimum of four sources. Students were also asked to create a preparation outline that included a Works Cited section and to use at least one visual aid in their speech. (Remember that you can go to your CourseMate to access videos of several other informative speeches, including Chungyan Man's "Chinese Fortune Telling," Elizabeth Lopez's "The Three C's of Down Syndrome," and Josh Valentine's "The Dun Dun Drum.")

Planet5D LLC/Shutterstock.com

INTRODUCTION

(Begin by doing a short tap routine) (*catch attention*)

I. Tap dancing is a vibrant art that is popular around the world and continues to appeal to people. (*reveal topic*)
   A. According to performingarts.net, tap artist Gregory Hines once said, "Tap is here, now."
   B. The art of tap dancing can be found all around our nation, with style variations around the world.
   C. Public interest in tap is growing, and tap can be seen in many forms of entertainment, such as films and theatrical Broadway shows.
II. Still alive today, tap is one of the oldest styles of dance.
   A. Many may think tap went out with performers like Gene Kelly and Fred Astaire, but it is still thriving.
   B. Have you encountered tap dancing? (*connect to the audience*)
III. I am interested in this topic because I have been dancing since the age of four and have found tap quite enjoyable. (*establish credibility*)
   A. Not only have I been a student of tap, but I have also taught tap to young dancers.
   B. I also enjoy watching entertainment that includes tap dancing.
IV. Today I will tell you about the beginnings of tap dancing, some basic techniques of tap, and I will also discuss a tap great, the late Gregory Hines. (*reveal thesis statement and preview main points*)

BODY

I. According to performingarts.net, tap is a combination of elements of African drumming and dancing and European clog and step dancing.
   A. The core of all forms of tap is percussive footwork, but the unique rhythms of jazz distinguish American tap dance from other types of tap.
   B. From the 1600s to the early 1800s, tap evolved from European step dances (for example, clog and jig) and African religious dances (for example, juba and ring shout).
   C. These dances were performed mostly by African slaves.
      1. Around 1828 the juba and the jig evolved to dances performed on the minstrel stage.
      2. Later these dances were polished into what is now American tap dance.
   D. The article "The History of Tap" from performingarts.net outlines the evolution of modern tap.
      1. Vaudeville talents like Bill "Bojangles" Robinson and John Bubbles helped define the rhythm of tap dance.
      2. Hollywood popularized tap in films starring Fred Astaire and the Nicholas Brothers.
      3. According to offjazz.com, Gene Kelly became a star in the 1950s and created his own style of tap by adding movements from ballet and modern dance.

Commentary

Rachel begins her speech with a demonstration and a quotation pertaining to her speech topic, and she cites the source of the quotation.

After Rachel reveals the topic of her speech, she proceeds by asking her audience to think about their experiences with her speech topic. Notice how Rachel uses this strategy to connect the audience to her topic.

Rachel clearly establishes her credibility as a speaker by revealing her personal experience as both a student and teacher of tap.

Rachel briefly previews the main points of her speech, revealing her topical organizational pattern. Notice how she will elaborate on each main point in the same order provided in this internal preview statement.

Rachel's first main point discusses the evolution of tap to provide her audience a brief overview of the history of her topic. Within her explanation of how tap evolved, Rachel cites the Web sites that contain the information provided in her speech. Notice that she cites them in her speech as well as in her outline.

4. Although tap lost some popularity in the 1950s, it became known as an art form as well as a form of entertainment in the 1960s.
5. In the 1970s tap returned to film, the concert stage, and the theater in the United States, Europe, and Japan.
6. Tap still flourishes in the entertainment industry today and can be seen on stage, TV, and in the movies.

Transition: In light of the early beginnings of tap, the steps that created the history are just as important.

II. Tapdance.org lists a few basic movements and steps in tap dance.
   A. The shuffle, flap, heel drop, brush, tip, step, stomp, and stamp create the basis of all the steps and sounds of tap.
   B. These basics create steps like the cramp role, time steps, Maxi-ford, and the rolling pullback.
   C. To successfully create these sounds, tap shoes have hard leather soles with metal "taps" screwed into them.
   D. Although there are many variations of tap shoes, the sounds and steps of American tap dancing remain the same.

Transition: We've heard about the history and the basics of tap. Now, let's take a deeper look into the life of a tap dancing great.

III. According to an article at the Web site cigaraficionado.com, one famous modern tap dancer, Gregory Hines, led an interesting life and became a highly acclaimed dancer and choreographer.
   A. When he was five years old, he was in a tap group called the Hines Kids with his older brother, Jake.
      1. When the boys reached adolescence, they were called the Hines Brothers, and they spent much of their time performing at the Apollo Theatre.
      2. In 1954, Gregory debuted on Broadway at the age of eight in the musical *The Girl in Pink Tights.*
      3. In 1963, the family group became Hines, Hines, and Dad, and they performed in New York nightclubs and on television.
      4. In 1992, Gregory was awarded a Tony for his role in *Jelly's Last Jam.*
      5. He showcased his dancing talent in movies such as *The History of the World, The Cotton Club,* and *White Nights.*
   B. Gregory has left his mark on the world of tap, and his technique and style continue to be studied.
   C. His untimely death in August 2003 from liver cancer has been a great loss not only for the tap community but also for the entire entertainment industry.

CONCLUSION

I. As we have seen today, tap is a very old form of dance, and the steps and sounds of tap have been performed by many talented people throughout its history. (*reinforce thesis and summarize main points*)

Rachel provides a clear transition from her first to her second main point to signal that she has finished discussing the history of tap and will move on to discuss tap steps. She also performs the steps she describes in her first subpoint. This demonstration adds clarity to her speech.

Again, between Rachel's second and third main points, she provides a short internal summary and transitions to her third point.

Notice how her three main points are fairly balanced, providing approximately the same amount of information in each. Also notice how each of her points, subpoints, and sub-subpoints includes only one complete sentence.

Rachel signals that she is concluding her speech by saying, "As we have seen today." She provides a clear internal

A. The basic steps of tap remain about the same as they have throughout tap's history.
B. The work of Gregory Hines contributed greatly to tap.
II. If any of you desire to be a tap dancer, I hope I have equipped you with enough information to get you started.
III. Just go and screw some metal taps into the bottom of your shoes and start tapping! (*end memorably*)

WORKS CITED

"The History of Tap." Accessed April 30, 2005. http://www.performingarts.net.

Rothstein, Mervyn. "The Man in the Dancing Shoes: Gregory Hines Scores Big on Broadway with *Jelly's Last Jam*." *Cigar Aficionado*. Autumn 1992. Accessed April 30, 2005. http://www.cigaraficionado.com/Cigar/CA_Archives/CA_Show_Article/0,2322,863,00.html.

"Tap Steps." Accessed April 30, 2005. http://www.tapdance.org/tap/steps/index.html.

"Top of the Taps." Accessed March 19, 2005. http://www.offjazz.com/tap-stars.htm.

summary, briefly recapping her three main points. Her conclusion is short, and she ends memorably.

Chapter Summary

To Speak Informatively Is to Share Knowledge with an Audience to Increase Their Understanding of a Particular Topic

- To create an informative speaking environment is to bring a topic to life for an audience and to illustrate its relevance so audience members better understand its impact on their world.

The Five Types of Informative Speeches Are about Processes, Events, Places and People, Objects, and Concepts

- Process speeches describe how something is done, how something comes to be what it is, or how something works.
- Speeches about events describe or explain a significant, interesting, or unusual occurrence.
- Speeches about places and people describe something significant, interesting, or unusual about places and people.
- Speeches about objects inform your audiences about anything that can be perceived by the senses.
- Speeches about concepts describe or explain abstractions, or things you cannot perceive with your senses, such as ideas, theories, principles, worldviews, or beliefs.

The Five Different Types of Informative Speeches Can Be Organized Chronologically, Spatially, Causally, or Topically

- Chronological patterns illustrate the development of an event or a concept or describe the steps necessary for completing a task.
- Spatial patterns reveal how various locations relate to a topic or how activities related to a topic occur in specific locations.
- Causal patterns are useful when you want to show important cause-and-effect relationships or clarify how ideas or behaviors relate to one another.
- Topical patterns allow you to highlight the different facets or characteristics of a topic for an audience.
- Three tips that can help you give an effective a speech are
  - bring your topic to life,
  - tailor your information to your audience, and
  - use language that is clear and unbiased.

When You Bring Your Subjects to Life, You Relate Your Topic to Your Audience by Sharing the Human Side of That Topic with Engaging and Relevant Details

- When you tailor your information to your audience, you remain audience centered so you can determine how much an audience knows about a topic and thus how much information to present.

- Use language that focuses on descriptions, definitions, and explanations so audiences can more easily learn new information.
- The principles of ethical public speaking include careful research and presenting unbiased and honest information.

Key Concepts

causal pattern (340)

chronological pattern (338)

informative speaking environments (330)

informative speech (330)

spatial pattern (339)

speeches about concepts (337)

speeches about events (332)

speeches about objects (335)

speeches about places and people (334)

speeches about processes (330)

topical organizational pattern (340)

Invitation to Human Communication Online

Speech Communication CourseMate includes an interactive eBook and interactive learning tools, including National Geographic Explorer videos, student videos, quizzes, flash cards, and more. Speech Builder Express 3.0 and Speech Studio 2.0 are also available. Go to cengagebrain.com to access your CourseMate for *Invitation to Human Communication* where these resources can be found.

Further Reflection and Discussion

1. Consider the following subjects as possible informative speaking topics for your next assigned speech:

   carpets
   making pizza
   graffiti
   religion
   Eminem
   subways

   How many different kinds of informative speeches could you give on each topic? What would be the strengths or advantages of choosing one type of speech over another for these topics? How would your speech be relevant to the public dialogue?

2. Create a preparation outline for an informative speech on the topic of the U.S. response to natural disasters. How

   many different organizational patterns could you use for this topic? How would each pattern highlight a different aspect of this topic? How would you reduce the scope of your speech to make it manageable for your public-speaking course?

3. In groups or as a class, identify five or six of the most commonly used but poorly defined terms you hear regularly. Use informative language to define those terms for your classmates. Some terms to define might be include the following:

   democracy
   socialism
   free speech
   hate speech
   gun control
   conservation

4 Select one of the topics from question 3 and write a specific purpose and thesis statement for a speech about that topic. Next, choose your organizational pattern and develop the main points for this speech. How might you bring this topic to life and manage the information you have about this topic so it is relevant to the audience?

Activities and Web Links

Visit cengagebrain.com to access the CourseMate for *Invitation to Human Communication* where these activities and web links can be found.

1. Choose one of the speeches from the list at this Web site. As you listen to the speech, write down which pattern of organization is used for this speech, which parts of the speech are information, and which parts might be persuasive. Go to *Web link 13.1*.

2. Look online for resources that will provide information on organic farming, laser surgery, or alternative fuels for automobiles. Create a speech outline for a process speech on one of these topics.

PERSUASIVE SPEAKING

IN THIS CHAPTER YOU WILL LEARN TO:

- Describe the three types of persuasive speeches.
- Apply the most common patterns of organization for persuasive speeches.
- Understand the importance of the elaboration likelihood model (ELM).

- Identify three tips for giving effective persuasive speeches.
- Identify the principles for giving ethical persuasive speeches.

14

Types of Persuasive Speeches

Organization of Speeches on Questions of Fact

Organization of Speeches on Questions of Value

Organization of Speeches on Questions of Policy

Connecting with Your Audience

Tips for Giving Effective Persuasive Speeches

Ethical Persuasive Speaking

Dr. Martin Luther King, Jr. is known as one of the most effective persuasive speakers of the last century. What combination of factors do you think made him so successful at persuasive speaking?

James P. Blair/National Geographic

It is impossible to convince tribal people to be part of wildlife conservation without first understanding and having empathy for their own fundamental needs.

—*Aparajita Datta, wildlife biologist and National Geographic Emerging Explorer*

Throughout history, people have given persuasive speeches in political arenas, courtrooms, workplaces, community settings, social gatherings, and classrooms. Today, just as our ancestors did, we use persuasive speech in the public dialogue to influence and alter the perspectives, the positions, and even the lives of others. When you understand the principles of persuasive speaking, you too can add your voice to the public dialogue as a persuasive speaker whether you decide to speak, are asked to speak, or are required to speak.

A **persuasive speech** is one *whose message attempts to change or reinforce an audience's thoughts, feelings, or actions.* When we speak to persuade, we ask an audience to think as we do about a topic, to adopt our position, or to support our actions and beliefs. In that sense, we act as advocates for a particular issue, belief, or course of action.

This chapter examines several aspects of speaking that are central to persuasion. You will explore the three major types of persuasive speeches, the organizational patterns best suited to persuasive speeches, some strategies for gaining audience support, and some of the common challenges and ethical considerations that persuasive speaking presents.

Types of Persuasive Speeches

Attempts at persuasion generally address questions of fact, questions of value, or questions of policy. Each category concerns a different type of change sought from an audience. Knowing which type of change you want to request from your audience helps you develop a listenable message for them.

Questions of Fact

When we want to persuade an audience about debatable points, we are speaking about questions of fact. A **question of fact** addresses *whether something is verifiably true or not.* For example, we can determine with certainty who won last summer's Boston marathon by consulting a yearbook or looking up marathon records online, and so the facts concerning this topic are not open to debate. But we cannot absolutely determine the training schedule that will produce the fastest marathon runners in the future. Any claim to such knowledge is speculative and therefore open to dispute. An audience, however, can be persuaded to accept one

persuasive speech
speech whose message attempts to change or reinforce an audience's thoughts, feelings, or actions.

question of fact
question that addresses whether something is verifiably true or not.

opinion or another about the best training method by a speaker's use of arguments, evidence, and reasoning.

Our understanding of many topics today derives from theories that have not yet been conclusively proven. Whether it is the reason dinosaurs became extinct, the original purpose of Stonehenge, the techniques used to construct the Egyptian pyramids, the way to end hunger and poverty, or the most effective methods to improve student reading skills, the facts about these issues are not absolute and leave room for competing theories. Therefore, they make excellent topics for speeches in which you try to persuade audiences that you have the correct answers.

Questions of Value

When we want to persuade an audience about what is good or bad, right or wrong, we are speaking about questions of value. A **question of value** *addresses the merit or morality of an object, action, or belief.* Is it right to continue offshore drilling or to support nuclear power, even though both present risks to the environment and to humans? Is it moral to punish certain crimes with death? Is it ethical to require all children to say the pledge of allegiance in school or to pause for a moment of prayer? These

question of value
question that addresses the merit or morality of an object, action, or belief.

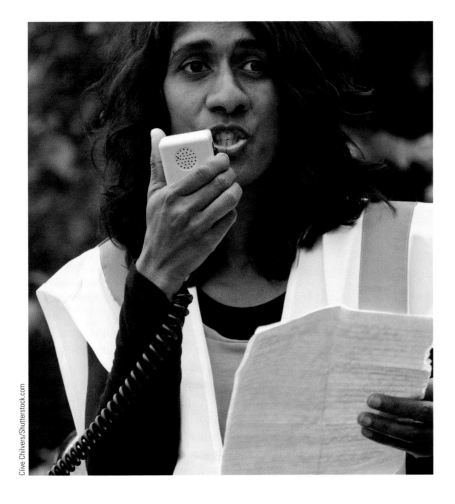

Clive Chilvers/Shutterstock.com

Questions of value are often complex yet very important to discuss. Here a woman is speaking as part of a British May Day demonstration against the government's spending cuts.

are questions of value, as are debates over what constitutes "good" and "bad" art, music, poetry, and theater.

When you attempt to persuade your audiences about questions of value, you move from asserting that something is true or false to advocating that one thing is better or worse than another. Questions of value cannot be answered simply by analyzing facts. Rather, they are grounded in what people believe is right, good, appropriate, worthy, and ethically sound. Thus, it can be difficult to persuade audiences about questions of value. This is because when we speak on questions of value, we must *justify* our claims. We must provide suitable reasons for accepting a particular action or view. When we justify a claim, we set *standards*, and we argue that our view satisfies certain principles or values generally regarded as correct and valid by most people. So when we try to persuade an audience that drilling for oil is worth the risk to the environment, we justify that claim by arguing that the oil from offshore drilling meets a certain standard of necessity that warrants risks to the environment. Or when we attempt to persuade our audience that it is moral to punish certain crimes with death, we try to justify our claim on the basis of a particular standard: that certain actions fall into a specific category that warrants this kind of punishment.

Questions of Policy

When we want to persuade an audience about the best way to act or solve a problem, we are speaking about questions of policy. A **question of policy** *addresses the best course of action or solution to a problem.* What form of support should employers provide for veterans with disabilities? How should the federal government implement mandatory drug testing? How many credits for graduation should the university require? At what age should people be allowed to legally drink alcoholic beverages? Each of these questions focuses on an issue that cannot be resolved solely by answering a question of absolute fact or debating the morality of an issue.

Although questions of policy might address the facts about the contributions veterans make in the workplace or the morality of mandatory drug testing, they go beyond these questions to offer solutions and plans of action. In sum, speeches about questions of policy present audience members with a specific solution or plan to a problem and try to persuade them that the solution or plan will eliminate the problem satisfactorily.

Because each type of persuasive speech—questions of fact, value, or policy—focuses on different issues and

question of policy
question that addresses the best course of action or solution to a problem.

CIVIC ENGAGEMENT IN ACTION

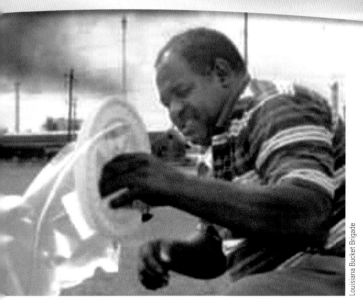

Louisiana Bucket Brigade

A Few Citizen Activists with Buckets

When activist Erin Brockovich and attorney Edward Masry—both made famous by the movie *Erin Brockovich*—became ill in 1995 from fumes emitted by an oil refinery that Masry was suing, the bucket brigade movement was born. Bucket brigades are community-based groups that use specially designed buckets, commissioned by Masry, to gather and test air samples in neighborhoods near oil refineries, chemical plants, and similar facilities that emit toxins into the environment. When people in these neighborhoods experience health problems they suspect are caused by pollution, they form bucket brigades to help crack down on facilities that are violating environmental laws.

The bucket brigade movement achieved one of its most important successes in 1999 when a Louisiana brigade successfully monitored emissions from more than fifty industrial facilities around Mossville, Louisiana, including vinyl plastic manufacturers, chemical-production facilities, oil refineries, and a coal-fired power plant. Mossville residents had long complained of numer-

ous illnesses but were repeatedly told by industry representatives that the facilities' emissions were not harmful. "I've asked [the refinery officials] to solve their problems, but they deny, deny, deny," explained Ken Ford, president of St. Bernard Citizens for Environmental Quality.

Fed up with the companies' total lack of response to their complaints, the community decided to make its problem a "national issue," says Anne Rolfes, director of the Louisiana Bucket Brigade. Mossville residents formed their own bucket brigade and began taking samples of air around the facilities, which revealed extraordinarily high levels of contaminants. Those levels were verified by the federal Environmental Protection Agency, and offending companies were forced to pay fines and upgrade to state-of-the-art monitoring equipment. In addition, other towns in Louisiana's "cancer alley" took Mossville's cue and formed their own bucket brigades, leading to the establishment of the Louisiana Bucket Brigade. As a result, reports the Louisiana Bucket Brigade's Web site, "Pollution has been significantly reduced, all of which stemmed from a few citizen activists with their buckets."

The brigade now is partnered with Grassroots Mapping, a group of Gulf Coast residents and activist mappers who are documenting the effects of the BP oil spill in the Gulf Coast. Their goal is to collect data that will assist in the federal government's assessment and response to the disaster, as well as in the coming litigation over the spill (Cannizaro, 2003, 2004; Louisiana Bucket Brigade, n.d.; Sine, 2000; Smiley, 2006; Swerczek, 2002; "Watchdog Group to Protest Refinery," 2005).

What Do You Think?

1. Is there an event or issue in your community that could be addressed at the local level, by citizens like those in the Bucket Brigade? What might that issue or event be?

2. Could you give a persuasive speech about the issue or event you identified in the first question? What might you try to persuade your audience to do or think?

goals for change, each requires a different type of organizational pattern to be most effective. Many persuasive speeches can be organized according to the patterns discussed in Chapter 13, particularly speeches about questions of fact and value. However, because speeches about questions of policy often call on an audience to take a specific action, they sometimes require unique organizational patterns.

Organization of Speeches on Questions of Fact

Speeches on questions of fact can be organized chronologically, spatially, and topically. To help you decide which organizational pattern is best, ask yourself the following questions: can you achieve your goals best by describing the issue as it developed over time, by describing a spatial arrangement, or by covering distinct topics?

Thomas used the spatial pattern to organize his speech about the lack of sufficient lighting at night on the college campus. He traced the layout of the campus from its center to its perimeter to make the case that it is not adequately lit for safety.

Specific purpose: To persuade my audience that the lighting on campus is not adequate.

Thesis statement: From the library to the farthest parking lot, the lighting on campus is not adequate to ensure safety after dark.

Main points:
   I. Lighting near the center of the campus casts many shadows in which someone can hide.
   II. Around the perimeter of this center, the lighting is spaced too far apart to offer adequate protection.
   III. The lighting in the parking lots that border the campus should be much brighter than it currently is.

This spatial pattern of organization helped Thomas highlight the key spots on his campus where lighting was inadequate.

 ## Organization of Speeches on Questions of Value

Like speeches on questions of fact, speeches on questions of value can be organized chronologically, spatially, or topically. In the following example, Eiji used the chronological pattern to develop her speech about the value of encouraging girls to participate in the sciences.

Specific purpose: To persuade my audience that encouraging girls to participate in the sciences is of value to us all.

Thesis statement: Throughout history, when women have been encouraged to participate in the traditionally male-dominated world of science, they have made significant contributions that have benefited all of us.

Main points:
   I. In the late 1700s, Caroline Lucretia Hershel's father and brother encouraged her interest in astronomy, and she developed the modern mathematical approach to astronomy.

II. In the late 1800s, with the support of her husband and colleagues, botanist Elizabeth Knight Britton built impressive botanical collections and is said to be the first person to suggest the establishment of the New York Botanical Gardens.

III. In the early 1900s, Maria Goeppert-Mayer was encouraged by her university professors to pursue her interest in science, which led to her winning the 1963 Nobel Prize in physics for her groundbreaking work in modeling the nuclei of atoms.

When we give persuasive speeches on questions of fact or value, we may ask our audience to change their view or agree on what is right or wrong, but we do not ask them to do anything. Therefore, the chronological, spatial, and topical patterns work well for these types of speeches. However, for persuasive speeches about questions of policy, we also ask our audience to agree on what must be done to solve a problem. Thus, we must rely on different types of organizational patterns.

Organization of Speeches on Questions of Policy

Persuasive speeches about questions of policy usually require organizational patterns that clearly define a problem and then offer a well-developed solution. Determining the best pattern for your speech depends on the kind of change you are hoping to get from your audience: *immediate action or passive agreement.* The differences between the two are simple, yet the effects they have on a speech are significant.

When you attempt to gain **immediate action**, *your goal is to encourage an audience to engage in a specific behavior or take a specific action.* You want to move beyond simply asking your audience to alter a belief. When you seek immediate action, you want to be as specific as possible in stating what you want your audience to do. You need a clear **call to action**, *an explicit request that an audience engage in some clearly stated behavior.* For example, rather than asking audience members to simply agree with you that the lighting on campus is inadequate, you ask them to contact the school administration and urge its staff to provide the funds needed to improve campus lighting in next year's budget.

In contrast, when you want to gain **passive agreement**, *your goal is to ask audience members to adopt a new position without asking them to act in support of that position.* When you seek passive agreement, you still advocate a solution to a problem, but you do not call your audience to action. Instead, you simply encourage listeners to adopt a new position or perspective. Consider the differences between requesting immediate action and passive agreement in the following specific purpose statements.

immediate action
when the speaker's goal is to encourage an audience to engage in a specific behavior or take a specific action.

call to action
an explicit request that an audience engage in some clearly stated behavior.

passive agreement
when the speaker's goal is to ask audience members to adopt a new position without asking them to act in support of that position.

Cecilia Lewis

Dino Martins. Emerging Explorer and Entomologist: Working Behind the Scenes with Insects

Dino Martins is a Kenyan entomologist who loves insects. His passion is studying threatened insect habitats in East Africa. Martins explains that two foods we love, chocolate and coffee, are among the hundreds of foods that are made possible by pollinating insects. Martins explains, "Every single person on our planet has a diet that includes food made possible by pollinating insects. When this connection is threatened, all of humanity is threatened." He continues, "Insects are the invisible, behind-the-scenes workers that keep the planet going." However, many people do not realize that deforestation, charcoal burning, and high pesticide use threaten the insects that are responsible for pollinating the crops needed to feed entire nations. Africa is especially vulnerable because some of the last remaining African violets and other wildflower species on which bees depend are fighting for survival as the forest shrinks. Martins claims, "If these species vanish, so could the bees, and ultimately acres of crops would be negatively affected." Unfortunately, farmers sometimes see carpenter bees as the enemy or farm in ways that negatively impact wild pollinators. Martins helps educate farmers to recognize and protect the major pollinators in their areas. He says, "Farmers look at the big scary carpenter bees swarming around their trees and rush to kill them. . . . They need more bees, not fewer." Therefore, Martins tries to convince farmers that leaving a space for nature and pollinating insects is necessary for productive agriculture. This task is not always easy. Martins relies on persuasive arguments to convince farmers to save a space to protect pollinators. He knows that he must demonstrate new farming practices and prove these techniques work. "When others see the proof, they all want to try it." However, it is not only farmers that are the solution to saving pollinating insects. Martin encourages everyone to "look at your next plate of food and ask where it came from, how it got to you. Every time you eat you can choose to support farming that's shown to be good, rather than abusive, to nature and people. You vote with your wallet, your feet, and your mouth" (Martins, 2012).

 CourseMate Connection: Go to cengagebrain.com to access your CourseMate for *Invitation to Human Communication* to view a video of a persuasive speech about his work with insects.

Lilkar/Shutterstock.com

1. Log on to your CourseMate Connection and view Martins's speech. What are questions of fact, value, and policy that Martins uses to create persuasive arguments?

2. What organizational pattern do you think works best for Martins to convince farmers in Africa to reserve a space for pollinating insects? Why?

3. What types of visual aids could Martins use to help support his arguments?

?

Courtesy of National Geographic Expeditions

NATIONAL GEOGRAPHIC **EXPLORER TIP** ↗

Aziz Abu Sarah
Emerging Explorer and Cultural Educator

Tell us about a persuasive speech you gave and how you used evidence fairly and ethically without compromising the power of persuasion. Was the speech about a statement of "fact" that you questioned, proved, or disproved; a speech based on a question of value(s); or an issue of policy?

I always start with the personal level; then I move to a value that people agree on. The main thing is to understand who you're speaking to and to understand your crowd and what statistics and what facts would speak to them. In every situation, it's not always useful to just recount multiple facts. I try to show many studies to prove a point. And even if you are successful, sometimes facts alone don't always move people and their ideals. There are also values. Let me give you an example. If I'm speaking to a religious Jewish group, what I try to do is to understand that their values have a lot to do with the Torah and their Holy Bible. So I try to relate to that as much as possible. I try to use stories from the Torah as much as possible. I will share with them the story of the burning tree, for example, one of the things that I happen to know, and I'll share the scripture that they relate to. Then the fact becomes related to their value. That's my strategy for connecting these two—fact and value—together.

Immediate Action

To persuade my audience to vote against placing vending machines in our public schools.

To persuade my audience to adopt my aerobics training program.

Passive Agreement

To persuade my audience that open space in a city benefits that city and its residents by making it more attractive and livable.

To persuade my audience that childhood obesity is a serious problem.

Notice how the requests for immediate action focus on asking an audience to do something specific, whereas the requests for passive agreement simply ask an audience to alter a belief. We now look at some organizational patterns that will help you meet your speech goals whether you request immediate action or passive agreement.

Problem–Solution Organization

Speeches that follow a **problem–solution organization** *focus on persuading an audience that a specific problem exists and can be solved or minimized by a specific solution.* These types of persuasive speeches are generally organized into two main points. The first point specifies

problem–solution organization
pattern of organization that focuses on persuading an audience that a specific problem exists and can be solved or minimized by a specific solution.

a problem, and the second proposes a solution to that problem. In the problem component of your speech, you must define a problem clearly, and the problem must be relevant to your audience. In the solution component, you must offer a solution that really does help solve the problem and that an audience can reasonably support and implement.

Consider the following example of a problem–solution speech given by Sheri. Notice how she used her thesis statement to state a problem clearly and then how she communicated that problem to her audience in her first main points. Also notice how she related the problem to her audience directly and personally.

Specific purpose:	To persuade my audience that although light pollution is a problem that increasingly affects us every day, we can implement simple solutions to reduce the effects of this pollution.
Thesis statement:	Light pollution disrupts ground-based astronomy, is a costly energy waste, and affects our health and safety, but there are simple solutions to the problem of light pollution.
Main points:	I. Light pollution poses three significant problems.
	A. In cities, light pollution causes urban sky glow, which disrupts ground-based telescopes.
	B. Light pollution represents an extreme waste of energy, and that waste is costly to all of us.
	C. Light pollution causes mild to severe medical conditions and so is unsafe for our communities.
	II. The problem of light pollution can be alleviated in two ways.
	A. Light pollution can be controlled through government regulations, such as light codes, which are similar to noise codes.
	B. Light pollution can be reduced through personal actions, such as using less unnecessary light and purchasing equipment that reduces light directed toward the sky.

Notice how Sheri's first main point clearly defines the specific problems created by light pollution and how her second main point offers reasonable solutions. Also note that she requests both passive agreement and immediate action. She asks for passive agreement when she states that supporting government regulations is a good idea, and she asks for immediate action when she suggests her audience modify the lights in their homes.

Because problem–solution speeches pose a problem while simultaneously offering a solution, they are excellent vehicles for persuading an audience to support a cause or take an action.

> **CourseMate Connection:** Go to cengagebrain.com to access your CourseMate for *Invitation to Human Communication* to view video of persuasive speeches that urge immediate action from an audience.

Problem–Cause–Solution Organization

The problem–cause–solution pattern of organization is a slight variation of the problem–solution pattern. Speeches that follow a **problem–cause–solution organization** *focus on identifying a specific problem, the causes of that problem, and a solution to the problem.* This type of speech is especially effective when you think you will be more persuasive if you explain how a problem came about. Explaining the causes of a problem can help your audience better see the merits of a proposed solution. Describing causes also allows you to explain how an audience came to believe what they do and to clarify any misconceptions they may have about a topic. In either case, you are sometimes more persuasive if you provide an audience with more information about a problem.

Problem–cause–solution speeches generally have three main points. The first identifies a clear and relevant problem, the second identifies the relevant causes of that problem, and the third details a clear and appropriate solution to the problem. The next example illustrates this pattern of organization.

Specific purpose:	To persuade my audience that the problems caused by feeding big-game wildlife can be easily solved.
Thesis statement:	The problems of wildlife overpopulation, the spread of disease, and other negative consequences caused by feeding big-game wildlife can be solved by keeping food away from wild animals.
Main points:	I. In many areas where people and big-game wildlife live near each other, there is overpopulation in certain species, outbreaks of disease, and a decrease in our acceptance of hunters and hunting.
	II. These problems are caused by well-meaning people leaving food out for wildlife in the winter and by campers who are not careful about keeping their food and food smells away from wild animals.
	III. These problems can be solved by simply not feeding wildlife; by protecting our food, washing our dishes, and washing our faces and hands when camping; and by putting our garbage in sealed containers.

Notice how Brandi was able to make a stronger case for her solution by identifying the specific causes of wildlife overpopulation, the spread of disease, and other wildlife-related problems. Once her listeners knew the reasons for the problems, they could see the merits of a solution that might have seemed too simple to be effective.

Problem–cause–solution organizational patterns are useful when you think that providing information about the cause of a problem will help persuade audience members to change their views or beliefs.

Causal Organization

When *a problem is based on a cause-and-effect relationship,* a **causal organization** will work well to persuade an audience. There are two possible ways to arrange a speech using a causal pattern: moving from cause to effect or from effect to cause. For example, Eli wanted to discuss the effects of reintroducing wolves in several western states. He first described the process of reintroducing the wolves (cause) and then focused on the decline in wildlife population (effect).

causal organization
pattern of organization used when a problem is based on a cause-and-effect relationship.

Specific purpose:	To persuade my audience that the reintroduction of the gray wolf has significantly decreased the elk population in Idaho, Montana, and Wyoming.
Thesis statement:	Since the reintroduction of wolves in Western regions, the elk population has declined dramatically, and farmers' cattle, sheep, and dogs have been killed.
Main points:	I. In 1995, gray wolves were reintroduced to Yellowstone National Park and the surrounding states of Montana and Idaho.
	II. Since the reintroduction of wolves in Western regions, the elk population has declined dramatically, forcing some regions to ban elk hunting.
	III. Other animals, including cattle, sheep, and dogs, have also been affected by the reintroduction of wolves.

A cause-to-effect pattern worked well for Eli's topic because it emphasized that the wolves were the main reason for the decline in elk populations. In contrast, Rupa chose to arrange her speech using a contrasting pattern of organization: effect to cause. She wanted to make her point by first capturing her audience's attention with a real story of five girls who died in a car accident (effect) and then explaining the events leading to the horrific accident (cause).

Specific purpose:	To persuade my audience that texting while driving can lead to fatal accidents.
Thesis statement:	When drivers text while driving, they are putting their lives, and their passengers' lives, in danger.

| Main points: | I. In 2007, five high school graduates from Rochester, New York, died when their vehicle swerved into oncoming traffic and hit a tractor trailer. |
| | II. Authorities believe the driver became distracted while she was sending text messages, which caused the head-on collision. |

In this speaking situation, Rupa's audience were members of the western New York community and had heard about the accident (the effect) weeks before learning of the cause. Rupa believed that reminding the audience members of the deadly outcome of the accident before revealing its cause would help persuade them that texting while driving is a serious issue.

Narrative Organization

Speeches can also be organized using a **narrative organizational** pattern, or *one or more stories to construct an argument.* Depending on the topic, a speaker may share an extended narrative to help personalize an argument that may seem difficult for some audience members to fully comprehend. In the example that follows, Razz implemented this strategy in his speech on the problem of children being abducted and forced to work as child soldiers in countries such as Sierra Leone in western Africa. Razz wanted to share Ishmael Beah's story as an extended narrative to reveal the thoughts, reactions, and experiences of one boy's journey from abduction to rehabilitation.

Specific purpose:	To convince my audience that rehabilitation programs work to change child soldiers' lives for the better.
Thesis statement:	Ishmael Beah is a former child soldier from Sierra Leone in western Africa, and his story teaches us that rehabilitation programs can work to give child soldiers a new life.
Main points:	I. Ishmael Beah was a young boy when his village was attacked and burned, forcing him and several other children to wander from place to place to survive.
	II. At the age of twelve, Beah was captured by the Revolutionary United Front and forced to become a child soldier.
	III. Beah was rescued by UNICEF, was given counseling and rehabilitation services, and received the opportunity to start a new life in the United States.

By using Beah's story to personalize the problem of child soldiers, Razz made his topic more accessible for his audience. This strategy

narrative organization
organizational pattern that uses one or more stories to construct an argument.

Noah Addis/Star Ledger/Corbis News/Corbis

Ishmael Beah speaks to students at Montclair Kimberley Academy in Montclair, New Jersey. Beah has written about being forced to serve as a child soldier in his native Sierra Leone. He is the author of A Long Way Gone: Memoirs of a Boy Soldier.

helped him convince his audience that rehabilitation programs sponsored by UNICEF can work to provide these young children with a better life.

Comparative Advantages Organization

When your audience agrees with you about a problem but feels the solution is up for debate, a comparative advantages speech is often an excellent choice. Speeches that follow a **comparative advantages organization** illustrate *the advantages of one solution over others*. In this type of speech, use each main point to explain why your solution is preferable to other possible solutions. If you must criticize alternative solutions to strengthen your explanations, then simply explain why the alternatives will not work, taking care not to degrade or belittle them.

Consider Angela's situation. Her co-workers and bosses already knew a problem existed: sales were down, and they were beginning to lose what had once been faithful customers. Therefore, Angela chose to give a comparative advantages speech so she could focus on illustrating the strengths of her proposed training program.

comparative advantages organization

an organizational pattern in which the speaker illustrates the advantages of one solution over others.

Specific purpose:	To persuade my co-workers that my new training program will increase our sales and enhance our public profile.
Thesis statement:	My proposed training program—which includes a longer initial training period, a more detailed assessment and understanding of the strengths of our products, and a stronger mentoring component than our current program—will turn our sales around.
Main points:	I. A longer initial training program will give our staff more time than our current program allows to develop a working knowledge and appreciation of the company and its mission.
	II. A more detailed knowledge of our products and their value will enable our staff to work with our clientele more expertly than our current training allows.
	III. A stronger mentoring program will improve the communication style of our new sales staff and help them respond to unfamiliar situations more effectively than our current mentoring program does.

Angela did not spend time outlining the problem because her audience already knew the training program needed improvement. Instead, she compared the advantages of her program to the weaknesses of the company's current program. She was careful to avoid criticizing the current program too heavily because her boss had been instrumental in bringing that model to the company. Rather, she simply said, "Our current program no longer is meeting our needs. If we make these changes, we'll be back on top."

Monroe's Motivated Sequence

Monroe's motivated sequence is an organizational pattern that helps you address an audience's motives and how those motives could translate into action. Developed in 1935 by Alan Monroe, **Monroe's motivated sequence** is a *step-by-step process used to persuade audiences by gaining attention, demonstrating a need, satisfying that need, visualizing beneficial results and calling for action.* Monroe maintained that this pattern satisfies an audience's desire for order and helps a speaker focus on what motivates an audience to action. Monroe's motivated sequence organizes the entire speech, not just the body, and takes listeners through a step-by-step process of identifying a problem and resolving to help solve that problem (Gronbeck, McKerrow, Ehninger, & Monroe, 1990).

1. **Attention.** In this step, you catch audience members' interest so they take notice of an issue. Your goal is to motivate the audience members to listen and see the personal connection they have to a topic. Using statistics or a story can accomplish this task. For example, Sierra began her speech by telling a story to capture her audience's attention. She began, "I was only ten years old when I found my mother sitting on her bed crying. Not knowing how to react, I sat down beside her and grabbed her hand. When I asked her what was wrong, she replied, 'I am sick and hope that I can hold your hand for many, many more years.' I soon learned my mother had breast cancer and that she would not be able to hold my hand much longer."

2. **Need.** In this step, you identify the need for a change—that is, the problem can be solved. You define the problem and how it directly or indirectly affects the audience. Your goal is to encourage your audience to become invested in the problem, feel affected by it, and want to find a solution. Sierra began the need section by proving the severity of the problem. She stated, "The latest study on breast cancer indicates that one in eight women will be diagnosed with breast cancer in her lifetime! That means two of you in this room will be directly affected, and almost everyone else will likely know someone affected by breast cancer."

3. **Satisfaction.** In this step, you define what the specific solution is and why it solves the problem. In doing so, you show audience members how their "need" is "satisfied." Sierra argued in her speech that the Susan G. Komen Breast Cancer Foundation was making important strides in finding a cure for breast cancer and needed more national, state, and local funding to support its research efforts.

Monroe's motivated sequence

step-by-step process used to persuade audiences by gaining attention, demonstrating a need, satisfying that need, visualizing beneficial results, and calling for action.

4. **Visualization.** In this step, you describe the benefits that will result from the audience's need being satisfied. You can describe what life will be like once the solution is in place, or you can remind the audience what it would be like if the solution were not implemented. Either way, you help audience members visualize how the solution will benefit them. Sierra achieved the visualization step by asking her audience to imagine life without the fear of breast cancer. She described, "Imagine one day you're standing in your bedroom and your daughter walks in and takes your hand. Now imagine being able to tell her that you want to be able to hold her hand for many years in the future, and this time, you can. Reducing the rates of breast cancer will ensure longer, healthier lives for women."

5. **Action.** In this final step, you outline exactly what the audience should do. This is your call to action, the plea for the audience to take immediate action or make a personal commitment to support the changes you are advocating. Sierra asked her class to join her for a breast cancer walk being held in the community. She concluded, "This Saturday at 9 A.M., a walk to raise money for breast cancer research will take place right here on campus. I ask that you join me in this fight and join me on the walk."

Connecting with Your Audience

Petty and Cacioppo's (1986) **elaboration likelihood model (ELM)** explains that *receivers process persuasive messages in either a central processing or a peripheral processing* route, depending on how motivated the audience is to think critically about a message. The more a speaker encourages listeners to become consciously engaged to think about a persuasive message, the more likely they are processing information in the central route. This means listeners are evaluating the overall quality of the argument, evidence and supporting material included, and any call for action presented in the speech. In this situation, listeners may research additional information on the topic after they listen to the speech because they want more details before deciding if they will support the speaker's argument.

When listeners lack motivation to think critically about a topic, they move toward using the peripheral route. In this situation, listeners

elaboration likelihood model (ELM) model that explains an audience's motivation for processing persuasive messages in either a central processing or a peripheral processing route.

consume messages passively. They may focus on parts of the speech without thinking critically about the message in its entirety. In addition, listeners may be influenced by the speaker's style of dress or delivery, not the quality of speech structure and content.

To encourage listeners to process information in the central route, speakers should connect their topic to their audience, explain the reasons that the audience should be concerned about the speech topic, and continually work toward keeping the audience actively and critically thinking about the speech information. Listeners using the central processing route tend to be more heavily influenced by a speaker than those using the peripheral route.

Visual Aids and Persuasive Speeches

Research suggests that visual aids may increase your persuasiveness and enhance your credibility (Seiler, 1971). Visual aids

- clarify your message,
- organize information,
- identify key points, and
- facilitate the reasoning process.

In addition, images encourage audiences to make associations, so you can use both text and images to move your audiences toward a particular position.

Visual aids also can add to your credibility by bringing a nonverbal dimension to your speech. Professional-looking and creative visual aids can energize your speech, making you appear more prepared, engaging, and lively. For example, a graph that displays a trend in people's attitudes is an excellent way to display the evidence you are using to back up a claim. It also helps you organize and clarify information, communicating an audience-centered perspective that contributes to your credibility.

Like your informative speeches, you can use objects, models, demonstrations, DVD or Internet clips, and even drawings, paintings, and photographs to increase your persuasiveness. You might also want to use charts and graphs in your persuasive speeches.

Charts

Charts show steps in a process or parts of a concept. They can help speakers illustrate the relationship between the steps or parts and how each relates to the whole process or concept. The two most common charts used as visual aids are the flow chart and the organizational chart. A **flow chart** illustrates *direction or motion*—for example, the unfolding of a process or the steps to a goal. An **organizational chart** illustrates *the structure of groups*, such as organizations, businesses, or departments. Use a chart as a visual aid when you want to represent the parts of a whole or to simplify a complex process. Because charts are usually drawn in advance, the types of visual media best suited to them are handouts, poster boards, and PowerPoint slides.

flow chart
chart that shows direction or motion.

organizational chart
chart that illustrates the structure of groups.

Graphs

When you want to compare numbers, quantities, or statistics, graphs are excellent visual aids. A **graph** is a *visual comparison of amounts or quantities.* Graphs help audiences see growth, size, proportions, or relationships. You can use different kinds of graphs for different purposes. **Bar graphs** compare *quantities at a specific moment in time.* **Line graphs** show *trends over time.* **Pie graphs** show *the relative proportions of parts of a whole.* **Picture graphs** present *information in pictures or images.* Figure 14.1 shows how data from the U.S. Census Bureau could be represented.

Like charts, graphs are most effective when prepared in advance and used for handouts, poster boards, flip charts, and computer-generated presentations. When you decide to display the figures you present in a chart or graph, consider the following guidelines: emphasize the visual image; use lines, arrows, shading, and color to show relationships and direction; use clear and consistent labels; or use a computer to design your chart or graph.

Emphasizing the Visual Image When you create a chart or graph, use single words or short labels for titles and positions and as few words as possible to describe the steps of a process or progression of data. Help your audience visualize the process and its parts quickly and clearly by keeping it simple. Figures 14.2 and 14.3 are examples of a bar graph and pie chart that emphasize the visual aspect of the message.

Using Lines, Arrows, Shading, and Color to Show Relationships and Direction To keep audience members' attention moving in the direction you want, use lines, arrows, shading, and color to help them follow your

Total U.S. Population: 1960 to 2040

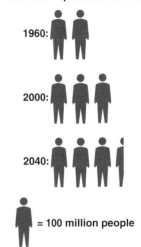

Figure 14.1 *Picture graph*
Source: U.S. Census Bureau. Census 2000.

graph
a visual comparison of amounts or quantities.

bar graph
a graph that shows quantities at a specific moment in time.

line graph
a graph that show trends over time.

pie graph
a graph that shows the relative proportions of parts of a whole.

picture graph
a graph that shows information in pictures or images.

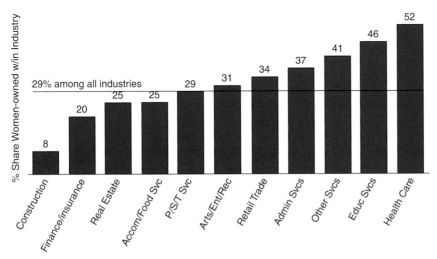

Figure 14.2 *Sample of a bar graph*
Source: American Express OPEN/Women estimates as of 2011, 1997–2007 data from US Census Bureau.

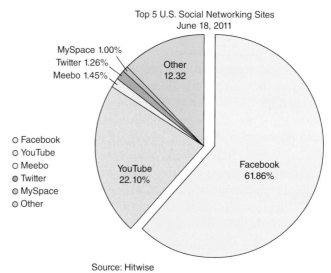

Top 5 U.S. Social Networking Sites
June 18, 2011

MySpace 1.00%
Twitter 1.26%
Meebo 1.45%

Other
12.32

○ Facebook
○ YouTube
○ Meebo
◉ Twitter
◎ MySpace
○ Other

YouTube
22.10%

Facebook
61.86%

Source: Hitwise

Figure 14.3 *Sample of a pie chart.*

Source: r-rwebdesign.com. Reprinted with permission.

points as you explain the steps in a process or the structure of an organization. Notice how Figure 14.3 uses color to emphasize size and percentages.

Using Clear and Consistent Labels Use descriptive headings for graphs that contain horizontal and vertical axes—for example, "Year" and "Percentage." For line graphs, mark equal intervals in the graph's grid—for example, numbers by tens, hundreds, or thousands and dates by decades or centuries. Show the numbers of those intervals on the horizontal and vertical axes. Notice how Figure 14.2 uses clear and consistent labels to help the audience track complex information.

Using a Computer to Design Your Chart or Graph Because charts and graphs display amounts, relationships, and proportions, presenting this information accurately is important. A computer can help you represent this information cleanly and precisely, drawing images to scale and clearly marking points on a graph. Using software such as Microsoft Excel (or an equivalent), simply enter the numbers and labels into the program's data table and select the type of graph you want to depict. You can even experiment with different kinds of graphs to see how each one shows your information.

 Tips for Giving Effective Persuasive Speeches

Consider the many times you wanted to convince others to join with you, think like you, or support you. You may have wanted them to do something as simple as go to a movie or eat a new kind of food or to do something as complicated as join a particular organization or share your passionate social views. Most people are deeply committed to certain things in life such as spiritual or political beliefs. Or because of deeply

SPEAKING VISUALLY

A woman walks past a work of art by Athina Robie depicting AIDS awareness ribbons at an exhibition inside an Athens metro station marking World AIDS Day.

Yiorgos Karahalis/Corbis Wire/Corbis

Ribbon Campaigns and Awareness Bracelets

Are you wearing a ribbon or bracelet to show your support for a cause you believe in? This trend has been popular with military families who display yellow ribbons to communicate support for military troops and their families. However, the meaning of this visual symbol has changed over time. Four hundred years ago, the reference to the ribbon originated in a song about a woman wearing a yellow ribbon to signal that she was waiting for the return of her beloved. In the late 1800s and early 1900s, the yellow ribbon became associated with waiting for the return of a soldier. And in the 1970s, Irwin Levine and L. Russell Brown wrote "Tie a Yellow Ribbon Round the Ole Oak Tree," a song about a convict returning home. In the song, if the convict's lover tied a yellow ribbon around the oak tree near a certain bus stop, she communicated that he was welcome to come home.

In addition to communicating support for our soldiers, today's yellow ribbons also communicate our awareness of and desire to prevent teen suicide. Other ribbon colors communicate a commitment to different causes: red symbolizes AIDS awareness as well as a drug-free lifestyle; pink expresses breast cancer awareness; white symbolizes ending men's violence against women; blue supports free speech; and green supports open adoption records.

Similar to ribbons, gel bracelets also speak to us visually. A well-known example is the yellow Livestrong band established by Lance Armstrong to promote support for cancer research. Other examples include a white gel bracelet that speaks out against poverty and a half-blue and half-red gel bracelet that speaks for epilepsy awareness.

Gel bracelets also make statements. Popularized by Madonna in the 1980s, they were once just an inexpensive form of teen fashion. But in recent years, "some teens and pre-adolescents, including elementary school students, know gel bracelets as sex bracelets. Sex bracelets are a coded form of communication among teens and young people where wearing different colored jelly bracelets indicate what sexual acts the teen is supposedly willing to perform" (Gargaro, n.d.; Livestrong, n.d.; Martell, n.d.; TeenHelp.com, n.d.; Yellow Ribbon America, n.d.).

When people convey their messages through ribbons and bracelets, they expect their audiences to respond on different levels (Lester, 2004). First, the audience must respond personally to the object. For example, they might be curious ("What is it about?") or annoyed ("I don't like all these useless ribbons and bracelets!"). Second, the audience places the object into a historical framework, responding with "I know (or don't know) the history of this cause or issue." At this level, the audience relies on mythos and a cultural memory of the issues the object supports and the circumstances that prompted its creation. Finally, the audience responds ethically, assessing the "rightness" of the object's visual communication and the wearer's explanation of it. As a result of the audience's own ethical framework and the arguments and evidence that back up the meaning of the object, the audience responds with, "I support (or don't support) this cause" (Lester, 2004).

What Do You Think?

1. Are you or someone near you wearing a gel bracelet or ribbon? What persuasive argument are you or they attempting to make with that ribbon or bracelet?

2. With a partner, discuss whether these visual arguments are seeking active or passive agreement. Why do you think so?

3. Discuss the strengths of these visual arguments. How do they compare to their verbal equivalent (for example, wearing a pink bracelet as compared to speaking out in support of breast cancer research)?

held convictions, they feel a strong sense of right and wrong about certain issues, such as whether women should participate in active military combat. It is natural to want others to share our commitments and beliefs, and most of us can think of many times we wanted to convince others to think, feel, and act as we do.

To help you give persuasive speeches, remember the following tips to increase your chances for successful persuasion:

- Be realistic about changing your audience's views.

- Use your evidence fairly and strategically for the best results.

- Use language that respectfully motivates your audience to change.

Be Realistic about Changing Your Audience's Views

Researchers generally agree that for persuasion to succeed, an audience must be open to change. If an audience is not open to change, then even your best persuasive efforts are likely to fail. This means you must consider your audience's perspectives carefully and frame your persuasive attempts around issues that your audience will be open to considering. If you know your audience believes something quite strongly and is not open to change (views on religion often fall into this category), you probably will not be successful in convincing its members to change that view no matter how well reasoned or researched your speech is. However, if the audience is open to considering an alternative perspective (for example, that there is a place in our society for different religious practices), your persuasive efforts are more likely to be successful.

This means you must think carefully about the positions your audience members hold and choose a realistic argument before you attempt to change their views. It is often tempting to ask audience members to change their views completely, especially if you do not agree with those views. However, successful persuasion involves advocating a position, or some *aspect* of a position, that your audience can be open about. For example, it may be unrealistic to think you can change audience members' views on legalizing certain drugs if they have had bad experiences with drugs or people who use drugs. But you may be able to persuade them to see the benefits that some of these drugs offer in medical treatments. In other words, you might persuade them to reconsider some part of their position rather than undertake a radical change (Miller & Roloff, 1980; Reardon, 1991; Stiff, 1994). Your attempts at persuasion will likely be more successful if you take a realistic, audience-centered approach to changing others. Rather than asking for radical changes, approach your speech goals and your audience with some restraint.

Remember, audiences hold particular beliefs and positions because of their experiences and worldviews. If you respect those positions and experiences as you ask your audience to change, you will be more likely to give a successful speech.

Use Evidence Fairly and Strategically

Research on evidence and persuasion suggests that besides carefully researching, organizing, and delivering your speech, there are some strategies you can use to help construct effective persuasive arguments. These strategies involve two-sided messages, counterarguments, and fear appeals.

Because persuasive speakers advocate one position over others, they often frame an issue as two-sided, even if there are multiple perspectives on the issue (Chapter 15). A **two-sided message** *addresses two sides of an issue, refuting one side to prove the other is better*. Research suggests that when speakers discuss two sides of an issue, they are more persuasive if they actively refute the side they oppose rather than simply describe it without providing evidence for why the audience should share the speaker's views (Stiff, 1994).

Similarly, addressing **counterarguments**, *arguments against the speaker's own position*, enhances a speaker's credibility. For example, when Tony advocated a policy of controlled burns to prevent forest fires, he increased his believability when he also discussed the argument that controlled burns can get out of control and cause major damage. By acknowledging this counterargument, Tony illustrated why the concerns it raises are unfounded, strengthening his position that controlled burns prevent other fires from burning out of control.

Use two-sided messages and counterarguments with care. In persuasion, credibility is important, and you must take care that your opposing comments are not too judgmental or inflammatory. If you unfairly attack someone else's view or refute an opposing position too harshly, audiences may perceive you as less likable—and audiences find unlikable speakers less persuasive. In addition, audience members will focus their attention on assessing the merit of your judgmental claim rather than attending to your message (Whaley & Wagner, 2000). When Tony advocated for controlled burns, he avoided saying, "That's stupid. Anyone knows that the fear of out-of-control prescribed burns is as ridiculous as fearing you'll burn down your house by lighting your barbecue!" Instead, he clearly and directly illustrated why the fear is unfounded—but not stupid—and why his policy is preferable.

Speakers can also use fear appeals to persuade audiences to change or take action. A **fear appeal** is *the threat of something undesirable happening if change does not occur*. In political ads, politicians frequently employ fear appeals as a way to motivate voters. Research suggests that fear appeals may motivate audiences who are not initially invested in your topic to *become* invested (Roser & Thompson, 1995). A fear appeal causes audience members to take notice of an issue and see how it relates to them personally. When audiences already feel connected to the topic, fear appeals simply reinforce that connection. However, if a fear appeal is so extreme that audience members feel immobilized, imagining that there is nothing they can do to solve the problem, then they may simply avoid or deny the problem (Casey, Timmermann, Allen, Krahn,

two-sided message
message that addresses two sides of an issue, refuting one side to prove the other is better.

counterarguments
addressing the arguments against the speaker's own position.

fear appeal
threat of something undesirable happening if change does not occur.

& Turkiewicz, 2009; Jessop & Wade, 2008; Nabi, Roskos-Ewoldsen, & Carpentier, 2008; Rippetoe & Rogers, 1987: Roser & Thompson, 1995; Schmitt & Blass, 2008; Wong and Cappella, 2009). Thus, if you use fear appeals, temper them so your audience feels there is a solution to the problem that will actually work. For example, if your speech is about the risk of violent crime in your community, speak honestly about it but do not exaggerate it, and then offer practical steps that audience members can take to reduce their risk so they feel hopeful and empowered rather than defeated.

Use Language That Encourages an Audience to Change

Just as informative speaking relies on language that is clear and unbiased, persuasive speaking relies on language that will motivate an audience to think or act differently. The most obvious examples of persuasive language are words and phrases that indicate what an audience "should do," what the "best" solution would be, or how something is "better than" something else. Persuasive language often appeals to emotions as in "Wouldn't it be tragic if we failed to respond appropriately to this situation?" In addition, audiences should hear strong calls to action such as "I'm asking each one of you to attend the rally tonight" or appeals such as "Imagine what our national park would look like with power lines running through it." However, research indicates that the more invested people are in a position, the less effective are such phrases as "Today, I'll persuade you that" or "I'm here to convince you that" especially in your introduction (Chen, Reardon, Rea, & More, 1992). When you tell audience members you will persuade them, they tend to hold more firmly to their positions.

Research on persuasion in conversations suggests that speakers who use words and phrases that show they understand the feelings and motivations of others are generally more persuasive than speakers who do not (Waldron & Applegate, 1998). This means your language should reflect an appreciation for the positions audience members hold. Use language that helps you clarify your position and its merits without casting a negative light on the views of others. Although persuasive speeches are sometimes used to attack or argue, avoid this tactic when you enter the public dialogue by using respectful language, even if you and your audience disagree.

Using respectful language does not mean you should not try to motivate your audiences to change. On the contrary, the goal of persuasive speaking is to encourage an audience to think or act differently, and your language should reflect this challenge. Phrases like "Perhaps you've never thought about the impact of," "I encourage you to consider this evidence carefully," and "How can we let this kind of damage continue?" do not attack or demand but instead urge audiences to reevaluate their positions. Some of our best efforts at persuasion have resulted in speeches that respectfully challenge an audience to think in new ways.

Ethical Persuasive Speaking

Have you ever noticed that sometimes when you try to change someone, that person regularly resists your attempts (Brehm, 1996; Kearney, Plax, & Burroughs, 1991)? Can you recall when your parents tried to persuade you to do (or not do) something such as dress a certain way, date a certain kind of person, or attend a certain function? For many people, as soon as the persuasion began, so does the resistance. Why did this happen when your parents likely had your best interests at heart?

Research and personal experience tell us that when others try to persuade us, we feel our freedom to choose our own path is threatened. In the United States especially, the freedom to choose is often basic to our sense of self. When someone tries to convince us to think, feel, or do something new or different, many people dig in their heels and hold on to their positions even more firmly. The issues we try to persuade others about are often complicated, making the process of persuasion even more challenging. Questions of fact, value, and policy are rarely simple or clear-cut. When beliefs, preferences, experiences, and habits come into play, these questions can get clouded and emotional, and people often invest in particular outcomes.

Given these characteristics of persuasion, be sure you request change ethically. To persuade ethically is to persuade others without threatening or challenging their sense of freedom to choose what is best for them. Remember, when you persuade, you act as an advocate for a particular position, not as a bully who tries to force or threaten an audience to see things your way. Ethical persuasion also requires you to recognize the complexity of the issues you speak about and the possible effects of your proposed solutions on your audience. As you prepare your persuasive speech, keep the following four questions in mind. The first three address the complexity of audiences and issues, and the fourth helps you consider the effect of the changes you request.

Bono spoke during the 2011 World AIDS Day. Bono's successful advocacy for causes he believes in address the complexity of the issues. Other than his celebrity appeal, what is he doing right that makes him a powerful persuasive speaker?

1. What is my position on this topic, and why do I hold this position?

2. What are audience members' positions on this topic, and why do they hold these positions?

3. Why am I qualified to try to persuade my audience on this issue?

4. Is my request reasonable for my listeners, and how will they be affected by the change?

As an ethical persuasive speaker, you must understand your own position and the positions of your audience. Acknowledge your own master statuses, standpoints, and unique experiences as well as those of each member of your audience.

Kris Connor/Getty Images Entertainment/Getty Images

Similarly, ethical persuasive speaking requires you to present information in an ethical way. This means you must tell the truth, avoid distorting or manipulating evidence, and present information accurately and completely. Audiences dislike being manipulated and mislead. Even if a speaker gains support through the unethical manipulation of evidence or ideas, that support is usually lost when the audience discovers the deceit. Gaining support through ethical means will only increase your credibility.

PREPARATION OUTLINE with Commentary

No Child Left Behind: Addressing the School Dropout Rate among Latinos

by Dana Barker

Specific purpose: To persuade my audience that our nation must address the high dropout rate among Latinos

Thesis statement: The dropout rate among Latinos in high schools and colleges, caused by low economic status and lack of family support, is too high, and this problem must be addressed with increased funding and teacher training.

INTRODUCTION

I. I'll begin with a story from the Santa Fe New Mexican about Mabel Arellanes. (catch attention)
   A. After becoming pregnant and dropping out of school at sixteen, Mabel has reenrolled in high school and is the junior class president.
   B. Her change in attitude has led her to the hope of becoming a lawyer.
   C. But Mabel's story is not representative of the current trends among Latinos.
II. I have researched trends in Latino socioeconomic status, graduation rate, and population in the U.S. (establish credibility)
III. Today I will discuss the problem of a high Latino dropout rate and suggest a solution. (preview main points)

Transition: Let me begin by discussing the problem.

BODY

I. The dropout rate among Latinos in secondary schools and colleges is too high and must be addressed.
   A. The dropout rate is excessive.

Commentary

Dana created and gave this speech in 2008 to her public speaking class. She begins her speech by sharing an inspiring story about Mabel, a young Latina high school dropout. With this story, she reveals the topic and problem of her speech: Latino dropout rates.

She then establishes her credibility by explaining that she has conducted extensive research on her topic. She completes her introduction by previewing the main points of her speech.

Dana begins the body of her speech by clearly stating her argument: The dropout rate for

1. Statistics and firsthand accounts attest to the high dropout rate.
   a. According to the *News & Observer,* one in twelve Latino students dropped out of high school in North Carolina during the 2003–2004 school year.
   b. This statistic does not account for the 47.5 percent of Latino students who have not graduated in four years since the beginning of the 1999–2000 academic year.
   c. Gamaliel Fuentes, who dropped out of school at fifteen, said, "We have no money; that's why I dropped out of school. [My father] asked me, but I decided. Now, if I could go back in time, I would stay still in school."
2. The tendency for Latinos to drop out is triggered by low socioeconomic status and a lack of family support.
   a. The *Hispanic Outlook in Higher Education* explains that students coming from families of lower socioeconomic status are less likely to succeed in college because high schools do not prepare them well.
   b. Latino families expect their young people to contribute economically, and work schedules often conflict with studies.

Transition: Next, I will discuss the importance of addressing the Latino dropout rate.

B. Addressing the dropout rate will keep Latinos from remaining at a generally low economic status.
   1. Income is heavily dependent on education level.
      a. According to the *Daily Evergreen* newspaper, a person with a bachelor's degree can earn almost one million dollars more over the course of their lifetime than someone with no college education.
      b. A census report in the *San Antonio Express-News* found that Latinos earned merely 6.2 percent of the bachelor's degrees awarded in 2001.
      c. Yet, the U.S. Census Bureau found that Latinos made up 12 percent of the national population in 2000 and 13.3 percent in 2002.
      d. In her essay "Canto, Locura, y Poesia," Olivia Castellano of California State University, Sacramento, writes, "They [Latinos] carry a deeply ingrained sense of inferiority, a firm conviction that they are not worthy of success."
   2. Ultimately, all who hold the belief that our country is the "land of opportunity" are affected by the Latino dropout rate.
      a. The U.S. Census Bureau states that in 2001 two out of ten Hispanics lived below the poverty line, while only one out of four earned a yearly salary of $35,000 or more.
      b. Comparatively, around 50 percent of non-Hispanic whites earned $35,000 or more that year.
      c. These figures are far from exemplifying opportunity for Latinos.

Latinos in secondary schools must be addressed.

She supports her proposition by citing recent statistics about the North Carolina school system. In addition, she uses peer testimony to explain why Latino students are dropping out of high school and to establish pathos.

To support her point that dropout rates contribute to the generally low economic status of U.S. Latinos, Dana provides a source that describes the discrepancy of income levels between high school dropouts and university graduates. Again, the sources reflect the most current statistics she could find in 2008. She also provides statistics to highlight the low number of Latinos graduating from college.

Next, Dana uses expert testimony to explain why such low graduation rates exist for the Latino population.

Dana also provides statistics from a highly credible source to illustrate the typical disparity between the income level of Hispanics and non-Hispanic whites.

Dana's transition between her points I.B and I.C tells her audience that she is about to explain the consequences of not addressing the problem of Latino dropout rates.

Before moving to her solution, Dana draws her audience in personally by asking them to consider the urgency of the problem. Then Dana presents her solution, explaining that teacher training and educational success programs will help Latinos succeed in school and will help change the Latino mind-set about education.

She uses an example of a successful program, AVID, to support her claim. Note how with this example Dana uses analogical reasoning (Chapter 7) to convince her audience that her solution will be successful, suggesting that the success of this program could be repeated with similar programs. In addition, in point II. B, she succinctly states how her solution could be implemented.

Dana explains the potential results of implementing her plan. She informs her audience that the results will take time, but the plan could produce a newfound sense of accomplishment and pride among the U.S. Latino community.

Transition: But what will happen if the problem is not solved?

C. Since the percentage of Latinos in our population is still climbing, ignoring this issue will lead to a greater gap between the life of the typical American and the life of the Latino American.

Transition: As I proceed to discuss the solutions for this problem, are you beginning to sense the urgency of this situation?

II. To solve the problem of a high dropout rate, we must fund teacher sensitivity training and programs that help Latinos succeed in education, and Latinos must change their perspective on the importance of education and their ability to succeed.
   A. Programs that educate teachers about Latino culture and beliefs and that help Latino students succeed in education will have the most impact on the dropout rate.
      1. Properly educated teachers will become aware of how they are able to meet the needs of Latino students.
      2. The Santa Fe New Mexican reported on the success of a program called AVID, which boasts a 95 percent college entrance rate among its Latino students.

Transition: What can we expect from this solution?

   B. This solution, which can be implemented at the national, state, and local levels, is dependent on increased funding and the efforts of educators with experience in Latino culture.
      1. Increased funding will help reform educational budgets for Latino communities and fund college success programs like AVID.
      2. This solution also requires the collective efforts of highly knowledgeable professionals with experience in education and Latino culture who can train other educators.
   C. Given proper attention and execution, the plan to address the Latino dropout rate will help the dropout rate begin to fall and will instill pride in the Latino community.
      1. Although it will take at least a decade before results are fully apparent, perhaps even a generation, ideally the plan will result in an increase in Latinos earning bachelor's, master's, and doctoral degrees.
      2. The sense of accomplishment gained by furthering education will change the typical Latino mind-set regarding education and instill an overall sense of pride in the U.S. Latino community.

CONCLUSION

   I. I have discussed the problem of high dropout rate among Latinos, and I have discussed a possible solution for addressing the issue. (summarize main points)
   II. Hopefully, you can clearly see that the high Latino dropout rate is an issue of great concern, one that requires prompt and thorough attention. (reinforce thesis)

WORKS CITED

Castellano, Olivia. "Canto, Locura, y Poesia." *Race, Class, and Gender: An Anthology.* Compiled by Margaret L. Andersen. Edited by Patricia Hill Collins. Belmont, CA: Wadsworth, 1997.

Economics and Statistics Administration. The Hispanic Population in the United States, 2002. United States Department of Commerce. Accessed March 14, 2005. http://www.census.gov/population/

Ferry, Barbara. "High School Program Gives Students a Fighting Chance." *Santa Fe New Mexican.* February 15, 2005: p. B-1.

Hannah-Jones, Nikole. "School an Elusive Dream: For Latino Students, Desire for Diploma Often Clashes with Needs of Families." *News & Observer.* February 18, 2005: p. A1.

McGlynn, Angela Provitera. "Improving Completion Rates for Hispanic Students: 'Best Practices' for Community Colleges." *Hispanic Outlook in Higher Education* 14.4 (2003): pp. 21–25.

Silva, Elda. "Latino Grad Rate Still Lags across U.S.: Finances Often Hinder Earning a Four-Year Degree." *San Antonio Express-News.* June 6, 2004: p. 1K.

Turner, Drew. "Four Year Degree Worth the Wait." *Daily Evergreen.* January 10, 2005.

Dana completes her speech with a brief conclusion that summarizes her main points and reinforces her thesis.

Dana's bibliography of the specific research she references in her speech shows the currency of her sources. (She created the speech in 2008.) She relies on a variety of sources, including books, newspapers, and the Internet.

Chapter Summary

Persuasive Speaking Often Addresses Questions That Are Complex and Not Easily Resolved

- The goal of a persuasive speech is to alter or influence an audience's thoughts, feelings, or actions about issues that are not easily resolved.

Persuasive Speeches Generally Fall into Three Categories

- Questions of fact address the verifiable truth of an issue.
- Questions of value refer to the merit or morality of an action or belief.
- Questions of policy focus on the best solution to a problem.

Several Organizational Patterns Can Be Used for Persuasive Speeches

- Persuasive speeches on questions of fact and value can be organized with the chronological, spatial, and topical patterns.

- Persuasive speeches on questions of policy can be organized with the problem–solution, problem–cause–solution, causal, narrative, comparative advantages, and Monroe's motivated sequence patterns.
- All of these organizational patterns provide different ways to present information about a problem and proposed solutions. Which pattern you select depends on your audience and your speech goals.

Policy Speeches Request Immediate Action or Passive Agreement

- When you seek to gain immediate action, you attempt to encourage an audience to engage in a specific behavior or take a specific action.
- When you seek to gain passive agreement, you try to persuade audience members to adopt a new position without asking them to act in support of that position.

Remember Three Important Tips for an Effective Persuasive Speech

- Use persuasion realistically. Do not ask for radical changes if an audience is not likely to support your proposals. Adapt your request for change to your audience's ability to change.
- Use evidence fairly and strategically to strengthen your arguments and increase your chances for audience support. Address complex issues with two-sided messages and counterarguments so you can refute opposing positions and appear more credible to your audience.
- Similarly, use fear appeals to motivate your audience to change, but do not overuse this strategy to the point of immobilizing your audience with fear.
- Use language that will motivate your audience to change but will not threaten or insult it.

Elements of Ethical Persuasive Speeches Include the Following Actions:

- Request change without threatening or manipulating your audience.
- Make an effort to understand your audience members' positions on an issue as well as you understand it.
- Present information that is honest, accurate, and fair.

Key Concepts

bar graph (371)

call to action (359)

causal organization (365)

comparative advantages organization (367)

counterarguments (375)

elaboration likelihood model (ELM) (369)

fear appeal (375)

flow chart (370)

graph (371)

immediate action (359)

line graph (371)

Monroe's motivated sequence (368)

narrative organization (366)

organizational chart (370)

passive agreement (359)

picture graph (371)

pie graph (371)

persuasive speech (354)

problem–cause–solution organization (364)

problem–solution organization (362)

question of fact (354)

question of policy (356)

question of value (355)

two-sided message (375)

 ## Invitation to Human Communication Online

Speech Communication CourseMate includes an interactive eBook and interactive learning tools including National Geographic Explorer videos, student videos, quizzes, flash cards, and more. Speech Builder Express 3.0 and Speech Studio 2.0 are also available. Go to cengagebrain.com to access your CourseMate for *Invitation to Human Communication* where these resources can be found.

Further Reflection and Discussion

1. With other members of your class, develop a speech to persuade lawmakers to lower the voting age to sixteen. As you develop this speech, consider the implications of the requested change for as many constituencies as possible: sixteen-year-olds, parents, lawmakers, voter-registration workers, voting sites, mail ballots, candidates, teachers, the structure of education, and the like. What are the implications of this persuasive request?

2. You have just been informed you have only five minutes of the legislator's time to present your persuasive appeal developed in question 1. How will you revise your speech to account for this time frame? How will you determine what information to keep in and what to leave out?

3. Consider the speeches you have heard that changed your mind or actions regarding an issue. How were you persuaded to change? Can you incorporate any techniques from these speeches into your own persuasive speeches?

4. Your topic is public transportation. Develop a specific purpose statement, thesis statement, and main points for the following three types of persuasive speeches: a question of fact, a question of value, and a question of policy. Use the discussion of organizational patterns in this chapter to help organize your speech.

5. Write an outline for a persuasive speech on the subject of physical education in schools. Organize this speech according to Monroe's motivated sequence. Pay careful attention to each step in this organizational pattern. What are the advantages of this pattern over, say, a comparative advantages pattern or a problem–solution pattern? What are the disadvantages?

6. Search for a graphic antismoking ad online. Are the fear appeals used in antismoking campaigns legitimate? Do they motivate an audience to action, or are they so strong that they immobilize an audience? Why?

Activities and Web Links

Visit cengagebrain.com to access the CourseMate for Invitation to *Human Communication* where these activities and web links can be found.

1. Read this article on fear appeals. Write down three ideas or pieces of information that interested you in this article. Share this with the class and discuss how this affects whether you would use a fear appeal in a persuasive speech. Go to *Web link 14.1*.

2. Read this speech given by then President Ronald Reagan in Berlin, asking for the German government to tear down the wall that divided city. Write down the sentences that you find most persuasive. Identify any of the tips for persuasive speaking that are covered in this chapter. What makes this speech effective persuasion? What would have made it less effective? Go to *Web link 14.2*.

INVITATIONAL SPEAKING

IN THIS CHAPTER YOU WILL LEARN TO:

- Identify the three conditions for an invitational speaking environment.
- Describe the two types of invitational speeches.
- Apply the four most common patterns of organization for invitational speeches.

- Identify three tips for giving effective invitational speeches.
- Identify two principles for giving ethical invitational speeches.

15

Michael Nichols/National Geographic

Invitational speeches are designed to help you explore complex issues that have no easy answers. People like Jane Goodall, and her team, have spent their lives sorting out issues affecting chimpanzees. What environmental, social, political, or religious issues do you wish you could explore more fully?

Only if we understand, can we care. Only if we care, we will help. Only if we help, we shall be saved.

—*Jane Goodall, primatologist, National Geographic Explorer-in Residence*

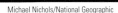

We all have encountered people whose positions on social and political issues are not at all like our own. In such cases, we are not likely to change their views nor are they likely to change ours, no matter how hard both parties try. In fact, in many situations, such as business meetings or community forums, trying to persuade someone that our view is the best is not only unrealistic but also can be inappropriate, especially in a situation in which mutual problem solving is the goal. Trying to persuade other people to change their views on a subject can also be inappropriate when we do not have enough information to know what is best for them or when their positions are so personal that it is not our place to ask them to change. For example, issues such as the death penalty, animal rights, and stem-cell research are tied to deeply held personal beliefs about politics, economics, and religion that are far beyond any one speaker's area of expertise.

As public speakers, what should we do in these types of situations? Do we simply give up when our audience sees things differently than we do? Or do we forge ahead with our attempts to persuade them even though we do not really understand their perspectives? In this chapter, you will learn a different approach, one that encourages us to explore the many sides of an issue.

You will learn that even though you may not be able to change the attitudes of your audience, or even want to change them, you can still enter the public dialogue. You will learn to engage in **invitational speaking**, *a type of public speaking in which a speaker enters into a dialogue with an audience to clarify positions, explore issues and ideas, or articulate beliefs and values.* To speak invitationally is to do something other than inform or persuade. To speak invitationally is to continue the public dialogue and seek mutual recognition despite firm differences in opinions, values, and beliefs (Bone, Griffin, & Scholz, 2008; Foss & Griffin, 1995).

Consider the following example that illustrates the difference between informative, invitational, and persuasive speaking. In a speech proposing that a school district change its school week from five days to four days, an informative speaker might describe the proposal and stop there. In a persuasive speech, the speaker might ask the audience to support the

invitational speaking

type of public speaking in which a speaker enters into a dialogue with an audience to clarify positions, explore issues and ideas, or articulate beliefs and values.

switch to a four-day school week and possibly take a course of action such as supporting a local initiative to make the change. However, recognizing that this issue is complex and contentious, Courtney chose to give an invitational speech on the four-day school week. In her speech, she explored the implications of schools changing to a four-day week and then invited her audience to discuss the topic with her. In her invitational speech, Courtney engaged her audience in a civil and open investigation of a topic and explored its complexities without trying to persuade her audience of the "right" decision.

invitational environment
environment in which the speaker's highest priorities are to understand, respect, and appreciate the range of possible positions on an issue, even if those positions are quite different from his or her own.

 ## The Invitational Speaking Environment

How does a speaker move away from persuading and go beyond informing in a speech? To speak invitationally, you must create an **invitational environment**. In this environment, your highest priorities are to

- understand the issue fully;

- respect diverse views;

- appreciate the range of possible positions on an issue, even if those positions are quite different from your own;

- engage in a dialogue with your audience; and

- create a space in which your audience can express its views just as you can express your own.

Although all speakers want to create an environment of respect, doing so is especially important in invitational speaking because the speaker and the audience members engage in a dialogue. Because invitational speaking allows for a dialogue, it is best suited for situations in which speakers have enough time with an audience to allow the full expression of a variety of positions on the subject.

A Real-World Example of an Invitational Environment

The events of September 11, 2001, created an atmosphere of chaos and conflict. The attacks on New York City and Washington,

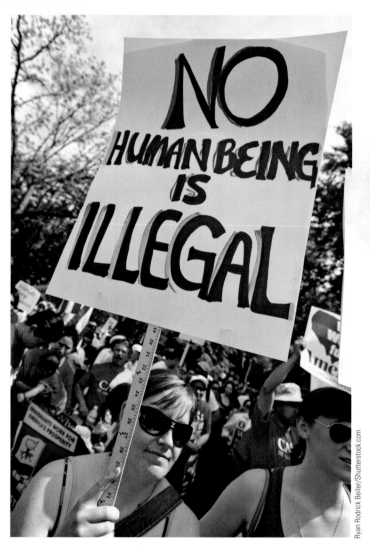

Ryan Rodrick Beiler/Shutterstock.com

Some of our most hotly debated issues are perfect topics for an invitational approach. Rather than persuade your audience of the "right" view, how might you create an invitational environment around immigration, such that your audience members feel comfortable and open not only to express their views but also to hear views they might disagree with or have not heard before?

D.C., and the failed attack leading to the plane crash in Pennsylvania seemed unimaginable to many people in the United States. Similarly, when talk began about replacing the fallen World Trade Center buildings and providing a memorial to the victims of the attacks, many people could not imagine what the new site would look like. The organizations responsible for rebuilding the site, the Lower Manhattan Development Corporation (LMDC) and the Port Authority of New York and New Jersey, recognized the public's need to provide input about the project, and they created an invitational environment in which people could do so. The LMDC twice held public meetings linking Long Island and New York City's five boroughs through videoconferencing to explore the issue of redeveloping the World Trade Center and Lower Manhattan. Furthermore, an LMDC Web site gave the public the opportunity to observe and participate in additional meetings. This unprecedented move invited thousands of citizens to participate in a dialogue (Lower Manhattan Development Corporation, 2004).

Onlookers view the World Trade Center building under construction on April 29, 2011, in New York City. Using an invitational approach, how might you build a speech related to the attacks, the U.S response to them, or even our views of different religions?

When the first round of designs for the memorial failed to inspire the citizens of New York, officials initiated a second design competition, receiving a record 5,201 entries from forty-nine U.S. states and sixty-three nations. Further public forums solicited input from the community, and a thirteen-member jury reviewed the submissions. When the jury—which included, among others, a family member of one of the attacks victims, architects, public officials, and a historian—finally reached its decision, its statement illustrated the invitational approach taken to select the finalists: "We understand the obligation we have to the victims, to their families, to society—indeed, to history—to serve the mission given to us; to remember and honor those who died, to recognize the endurance of those who survived, the courage of those who risked their lives to save the lives of others, and the compassion of all those who supported the victims' families in their darkest hours" ("World Trade Center Site Memorial Competition Jury Statement," 2003).

The jury admitted the task was not easy. Coming to a consensus "entailed hours of frank discussions, agreements, and disagreements, always with the goal of arriving at common ground." When selecting the finalists, the jury consulted with many members of the community, including New York City Mayor Michael Bloomberg, New York Governor George Pataki, people who live and work in Lower Manhattan, and representatives of the victims' families. In a final invitational move, the jury exhibited all 5,201 submissions, allowing the public to consider the meaning of each submission. When the final design, *Reflecting Absence,* was displayed, the jury avoided suggesting how the audience should think, feel, and react to the memorial. Instead, the jury acknowledged "that memory belongs primarily to the individual."

As the jury noted, "*Reflecting Absence* . . . evolved through months of conversation between the jury and its creators" (Lower Manhattan Development Corporation, 2003), making the process of selecting a memorial to the victims of the September 11 attacks on the World Trade Center a truly invitational one. As Port Authority Executive Director Joseph J. Seymour stated, "The rebuilding of Lower Manhattan has been the most open and accessible process in history" (Lower Manhattan Development Corporation, 2003).

This example illustrates one of the keys to creating a successful invitational environment: A speaker must alter the traditional roles of the speaker and the audience. Rather than taking on the role of the "expert" and assigning the role of the "listener" to the audience, invitational speakers consider themselves and the audience as both the experts and the listeners. They not only express their views but also listen carefully to their audience's views. They then facilitate a discussion of ideas, and the speaking environment becomes more than a speech given by one person to an audience. As the example about the World Trade Center memorial shows, the traditional relationship between the speaker and the audience is replaced with one that encourages the exchange of views without risk of attack or ridicule.

To build this invitational environment, you must create three conditions: equality, value, and self-determination. These conditions allow you and your audience to see one another as knowledgeable and capable, although perhaps in different ways. These three conditions are interrelated, but they are presented separately here to clarify each condition and its goal. However, all of these conditions help you create an atmosphere of mutual respect, understanding, and exploration. They help you communicate effectively with people who hold positions quite different from your own (Barrett, 1991; Benhabib, 1992; Ellinor & Gerard, 1998; Isaacs, 1999; Loeb, 2010; Peck, 1987; Rogers, 1962; Walker, 1989).

The Condition of Equality

When you create the **condition of equality**, you acknowledge that *all audience members hold valid perspectives worthy of exploration.* Your language, delivery, and presentation of ideas let audience members know that you recognize them as people whose knowledge, experiences, and perspectives are as valid for them as yours are for you. Because you and your audience are equal participants in a dialogue (although you still give the speech and lead the discussion), your audience members are able to offer their perspectives, share their experiences, and even question you—in the same way you do with them. A condition of equality creates a sense of safety and welcome that encourages audience members to share their perspectives. The jury who selected the World Trade Center memorial created the condition of equality by making every effort to recognize all community members as equals and to solicit their input.

The Condition of Value

When you create the **condition of value**, you recognize the *inherent value of your audience's views, although those views might be different from your views* as a speaker. In creating the condition of value, you let your audience know that when members express differing views and opinions, those differences will be explored in a spirit of mutual understanding and without judgment or any effort to change them. In fact, in creating the condition of value, you communicate that you will step outside your own standpoint (Chapter 2) to understand another perspective and see the world as your audience sees it. So when disagreement on an issue arises, you and the other participants in the dialogue try to understand the opposing positions and the reasons that people hold their views. The fact that jury members reopened the process after their first attempt is a reflection of the condition of value and their willingness to step outside their own standpoints.

The Condition of Self-Determination

As a speaker, you can create a **condition of self-determination** by *recognizing that the members of your audience are experts in their* *own lives*—that they know what is best for them and have the right to make choices about their lives based on this knowledge. Although their choices may not be the ones you would make, the members of your audience are free to decide for themselves how to think, feel, and act. The condition of self-determination means you will not close off conversation or try to persuade your audience to do something its members may not feel inclined to do. Rather, you create an atmosphere in which the people in your audience feel in control of their choices and are respected for their ability to make them. Once again, in the previous example, the jury displayed all 5,201 entries, allowed people to view each submission as well as the final selection, and determine for themselves the meaning of each.

In our increasingly diverse and complicated world, invitational speaking is a useful tool in some of the most difficult public conversations and exchanges. When you choose to speak invitationally, you are seeking a full and open exchange of ideas and positions. Creating these three conditions—equality, value, and self-determination—helps you succeed in this exchange. Remember, the goal of invitational speaking is to go beyond informing and to avoid any effort to persuade. Instead, when you speak invitationally, you try to explore issues in a spirit of acceptance and openness.

 ## Types of Invitational Speeches

The two types of invitational speaking are to explore an issue and to articulate a position. We will look closer now at each type of invitational speaking.

Speeches to Explore an Issue

When you give an invitational **speech to explore an issue**, you *attempt to engage your audience in a discussion about an idea, concern, topic, or plan of action.* Your goal is to present an overview of the issue and to gather different perspectives from your audience so you can understand the subject more fully. Quite often, you use what you have learned from your audience to solve problems or plan courses of action that appeal to a broad range of perspectives.

Begin this type of speech by stating your intention to explore the issue. Then lay out the positions on an issue, trying to go beyond presenting two sides of an issue. If you can present three or more perspectives on an issue, then you help your audience understand the complexity and the reasons why making a decision may be so difficult. You might also share your opinions about the issue, even if they are tentative, but only to help the dialogue and not for the intent of persuading your audience to agree with you. As a speaker, you are laying the groundwork for an open dialogue, one rooted in equality, value, and self-determination and one in which people feel heard and respected by one another.

speech to explore an issue
a speaker attempts to engage an audience in a discussion about an idea, concern, topic, or plan of action.

The following example illustrates an invitational speech to explore an issue. David spoke invitationally about the issue of the federal minimum wage. His goal was to get his audience thinking about the amount of money someone earning the minimum wage actually makes, the way of life of the working poor, and possible ways to address this issue.

Specific purpose:	To invite my audience to explore along with me the federal minimum wage and whether there are better approaches to assisting the working poor.
Thesis statement:	A federal minimum wage of $7.25 per hour leaves many working people dependent on public assistance agencies like our county's food bank, but raising the minimum wage creates many problems and may not be the best approach to helping the working poor.
Main points:	I. The minimum wage of 25 cents per hour set in 1938 has risen to $7.25 per hour, providing a full-time worker a little over $16,200 annually.
	II. In recent years, food banks and other public assistance agencies have seen huge growth in the number of working families seeking their aid.
	III. Experts suggest that raising the minimum wage may decrease employment opportunities for entry-level employees.
	IV. Other options exist, but all have their own limitations.
	V. An open discussion about the minimum wage can help us gain more insight into this complex issue.

In this speech, David provides some history regarding the federal minimum wage, debunks some of the myths surrounding the working poor, and presents a few of the existing approaches to this issue. He then opens the discussion, knowing that his audience will have strong views. However, throughout his speech, he set the stage for an invitational discussion so that audience members felt free to share their views.

Speeches to Articulate a Position

When issues are quite contentious, and when you and your audience hold fairly well-developed perspectives on those issues, you may want to give an invitational speech to

Today's new technologies are quickly leading to advances in a number of fields. However, the ethical implications raised by some advances, such as cloning and stem-cell therapies, are not always clear. Invitational speeches are well suited to exploring the pros and cons of issues such as these. As an audience member, how might you express your concerns about an issue such as stem-cell research in an invitational way?

Yuri Arcurs/Shutterstock.com

NATIONAL GEOGRAPHIC EXPLORER TIP ↗

Alexandra Cousteau
Emerging Explorer and Social Environment Advocate

Please share a situation in which you spoke to an audience of peers and they held positions of equal merit to you but different than yours. What specific approaches did you use to invite expression of a variety of perspectives?

Because we drink clean water, we can all agree we want the water resources in our own backyard to be unpolluted; we can all agree on certain number of things no matter who we are. And that aspect of water transcends both politics and religion. I had an experience working with groups in the Middle East made up of Israelis and Arabs, where students from both sides of the conflict would get together and study together and work together and talk together and tell each other their stories. And they realized through this process that they have the same stories. They had a story of conflict, a story of lost loved ones, and a story of fear of others. And because they told each other these stories from their own perspectives, when there was conflict in Gaza, they protested that conflict together and they grieved for each others' losses even though the other was traditionally considered the enemy. So I think we can overcome a lot of those barriers to mutual understanding through effective communication in an unbiased and open way that focuses on our own experiences rather than what we've been taught to believe.

articulate a position. When you deliver a **speech to articulate a position**, you *invite an audience to explore an issue from your perspective.* This type of invitational speaking is less common, and it is similar to informative speaking in that you share information with an audience. However, rather than simply giving people information, you are setting the stage for a conversation with audience members not only about your views but also about *their* views on the topic. The result is that both you and your audience leave the exchange with a richer understanding of a complex issue.

Consider the following example of an invitational speech to articulate a position. Martin chose the topic of guns and gun control. Rather than taking a persuasive tack to persuade his audience that the United States does not need stricter gun control laws, he chose an invitational approach. He knew that many in his audience strongly supported stricter regulations. Martin knew that changing their minds was not only unrealistic but could lead to angry interactions. So he chose to invite the audience into his world to see the issue of guns from another perspective. In doing so, he created an atmosphere of openness so people could voice their concerns, frustrations, and even their anger without judgment. Martin's specific purpose, thesis statement, and main points looked like the following:

speech to articulate a position
a speaker invites an audience to explore an issue from the speaker's perspective.

Specific purpose:	To invite my audience to consider some of the positive lessons that can be taught with the ethical use of guns.
Thesis statement:	Although many people fear guns, two hunting experiences in my childhood taught me to use guns responsibly and ethically, and I believe the lessons I learned have been invaluable in my life.
Main points:	I. People fear guns for a number of reasons.
	II. I had two memorable hunting experiences during my childhood, one positive and the other negative.
	III. Those experiences have proved to be invaluable in my life and shaped my current views on the responsible and ethical use of guns.
	IV. I'd like to explore with my audience members their views and the ways in which the ethical use of guns might possibly be a healthy part of our lives.

In a persuasive speech, Martin would try to convince the audience that guns actually are not as bad as some people think. In an informative speech, he would give his audience information about current gun-control laws. However, in this invitational speech, he was more interested in sharing positions than changing minds. His goal was to facilitate understanding and the exchange of ideas on gun control, an extremely controversial topic.

How necessary and effective are random searches at airport security checkpoints? This is a frequently debated topic. What are some of the benefits and drawbacks of these types of searches? How would you articulate your position about this topic in an invitational speech to your classmates?

Carolina K. Smith, M.D./Shutterstock.com

When you articulate a position, you develop that position as fully and openly as possible. You invite your audience to see the issue from your perspective and return the gesture by asking to see the issue from the perspective of your audience. Your goal is not to provide information or persuade anyone to change, although both of these things might happen. Instead, you seek to promote a deeper understanding of the issue by exploring different views on it so that both you and your audience will be able to frame it in more complete, inclusive ways in the future.

Trespassers Welcome

The life story of Australian aboriginal philosopher and educator Jack Beetson reads like a rags-to-riches story. The son of a Wongaibon mother and an Ngemba father, he was kicked out of school at age thirteen and got into trouble with the police. After spending a few years working in various unfulfilling jobs, he became a street kid in Sydney, Australia. As he neared thirty, he decided to continue his education and started attending Tranby Aboriginal College, an alternative learning environment for adult aboriginal students. He stuck around and several years later became the school's executive director. In 2001, the Year of Dialogue among Civilizations, he was awarded the Unsung Hero Award by the United Nations, one of only twelve people in the world to receive this award.

Today Beetson lives on his farm, the Linga Longa Philosophy Farm,

Courtesy of University of New England (Australia)

in New South Wales, Australia. A product of Beetson's lifelong efforts to bring indigenous and nonindigenous people together, the farm's workshops and forums provide a rare opportunity for people of all cultures to come together to explore their identities and differences in a friendly, informal environment. He and his wife, Shani, began the farm "so that nonindigenous Australia wouldn't have the excuse that 'there is no-where we can go to find out'" about indigenous culture. Beetson is so welcoming that he has said he'd like to put up a "Trespassers Welcome" sign on the front gate in the hopes that people will feel free to stop by for a conversation.

Beetson is a well-respected community leader who also travels extensively, speaking out about compassion, justice, and self-determination for aboriginal and indigenous peoples. He encourages other aboriginal people to share their culture and experiences with others in an effort to come to a mutual understanding. One of his latest endeavors is to use aboriginal culture, philosophy, and ceremony to help at-risk young people embrace their indigenous heritage and reconcile with nonindigenous people. Summing up his philosophy and approach, he says, "I share this particularly with young people who come out here who are living on the street . . . There's not a person on the planet who's better than you are, but always remember you're no better than anybody else either. That's how I've tried to live my life." ("Jack Beetson Spoke with Tony Jones," n.d.; "The Unsung Heroes of Dialogue," n.d).

What Do You Think?

1. Beetson suggests that no one is better than any other person. How might you engage your classmates invitationally on this claim?

2. Beetson suggests that we need to share our cultural backgrounds and experiences with others to increase our understanding of our differences. What cultural backgrounds or experiences might you share in an invitational speech, and how would you listen respectfully and openly to the background and experiences of others?

Speaking invitationally, like any form of speaking, has its challenges and rewards. Remember, people are more likely to feel free to share their positions when the conditions of equality, value, and self-determination are met, and these conditions can take time to develop, especially among strangers or when issues are hotly contested. You can create the conditions from the very beginning of a speech and through your delivery. You also create them through the organizational patterns you choose for your invitational speech, which are discussed next.

Organizational Patterns for Invitational Speeches

Many organizational patterns are suitable for invitational speaking. The easiest for beginning speakers are the familiar chronological, spatial, and topical, as well as a new pattern called *multiple perspectives*. As your skill

PRACTICING HUMAN COMMUNICATION

Select an Invitational Speech Type

In class, identify some of the most controversial issues we face today as a society. List these issues on the board. How many of these issues do you have strong feelings about? Which issues do you wish you could learn more about in an invitational way? Select two topics from the list and, with a partner, discuss the ways you could frame speeches about these topics invitationally. For each topic, would you want to give a speech to articulate a position or to explore an issue? How would you use equality, value, and self-determination to create an invitational speaking environment? Save this list for the next Practicing Human Communication activity.

at invitational speaking develops, you can modify these patterns and adapt to your audiences and speaking situations as needed.

Chronological Pattern

A chronological pattern of organization allows you to trace a sequence of events or ideas. This pattern works well for speeches to articulate a position and speeches to explore an issue. In the next example, Jenni uses this pattern to explore an issue. She develops the issue and explores how various thoughts on that issue have changed over time.

Specific purpose:	To invite my audience to explore the issues involved in implementing bilingual education in public schools across the United States.
Thesis statement:	Bilingual education has a long and controversial history in the United States, and understanding the complexity of this history helps us understand today's framing of the issue.
Main points:	I. Historically, bilingual education was designed to provide a better education for children who immigrated from a variety of countries.
	II. After World War I, legislation changed in many states, reducing the support for bilingual education.
	III. Today's debates over bilingual education reflect the cost of this kind of education as well as the right for children whose first language is not English to a quality education.
	IV. Now that we see the complex history, changing views, benefits, and costs of bilingual education, I'd like to explore this issue with my audience.

Jenni used the chronological pattern and traced the evolution of bilingual education to help her audience understand the issue more fully. In the discussion with her audience, she explored this history, listened to members' personal experiences and views, and raised questions of her own. Jenni's audience learned about the complexity of the issue and went beyond the "for" and "against" perspectives so commonly offered. Together, they explored issues and solutions that could work for a whole school rather than just one group of individuals.

A chronological pattern allows you to share history and offer background information that may help audience members enter a discussion. By tracing your perspective on an issue over time, you establish common ground and openness for seeing how the perspective or issue might continue to evolve.

Spatial Pattern

The spatial pattern of organization can help you organize your ideas according to location or geography. You can use this pattern to articulate your position or explore an issue. This pattern is helpful when you want to discuss what a topic has in common or how it differs across countries, nations, states, or cities. Riley used a spatial pattern to describe the ways communities have responded to hate crimes and to explore how his community might begin to heal from such a crime.

Specific purpose:	To invite my audience to visit the scene of several hate crimes committed across the country so we might know how to begin to heal from what happened in our own town.
Thesis statement:	Trying to understand the response to the many hate crimes that have been committed in other communities across the United States might help my own community heal from our recent tragedy.
Main points:	I. The response of a Texas community to the hate crime against James Byrd Jr. involved both public and private actions.
	II. Similarly, the response of a Wyoming community to the hate crime against Matthew Shepard was both private and public, bringing in the surrounding areas as well.
	III. The response of a California community to the hate crime against a church with a largely Middle Eastern congregation was far more public in nature.
	IV. With these responses in mind, I'd like to invite the audience to discuss ways in which we might respond to our own recent tragedy.

By describing how other communities responded to hate crimes, Riley stimulated and encouraged discussion with his audience about the needs of the community and how listeners felt they might respond to their own tragedy. By exploring this issue, both he and his audience began to formulate a plan of action that helped the community come to terms with a painful event.

You can use a spatial pattern to invite your audience to see how other localities have dealt with many types of public issues, such as transportation, health, poverty, crime, education, and pollution. You can also use this pattern in business speeches to compare how other businesses have approached a problem. This pattern allows you to connect your position to others or help your audience explore an issue using information from other places.

Topical Pattern

When you articulate a position, the topical pattern is effective. This pattern allows you to discuss the aspects of your topic point by point. Martin's speech on gun control previously discussed used the topical pattern. In that speech, Martin addressed audience fears about guns, his own experiences with guns, and the lessons he learned from those experiences. He then initiated a discussion with the audience about his position. Here is an example of the topical pattern from Phillip's speech articulating his position about sentencing people who commit serious crimes to death or to life in prison.

Specific purpose:	To invite my audience to consider that the death penalty may not be as just and efficient as keeping an inmate in prison for life.
Thesis statement:	Although the death penalty is commonly accepted as a just form of punishment, keeping inmates in prison without the possibility of parole may be a better solution, but both approaches present ethical dilemmas.
Main points:	I. Life sentences may be a better option than the death penalty, primarily because there have been cases of innocent people being placed on death row and subsequently executed.
	II. The death penalty does not seem to deter people from committing murder—the United States is one of the few industrialized countries to practice corporal punishment, yet it still has the highest rate of murder.
	III. Surprisingly, a life sentence is cheaper for taxpayers than an execution.
	IV. The suffering caused by a lifetime spent in prison cannot be overlooked.
	V. Because each approach presents moral dilemmas, I'd like to invite my audience to discuss what they think about sentencing people who commit serious crimes to life in prison compared with sentencing them to death.

Using the topical pattern, Phillip shared what he learned from his research about corporal punishment and life sentencing. However, he did more than inform his audience; he shared the ethical dilemmas of each and remained open to alternatives, new information, and concerns from his audience.

Multiple Perspectives Pattern

Although you can use this organizational pattern in other types of speeches, it is particularly well suited for invitational speeches. The **multiple perspectives pattern** allows you to *systematically address the many*

multiple perspectives pattern
pattern that allows the speaker to systematically address the many sides and positions of an issue before opening up the speech for dialogue with the audience.

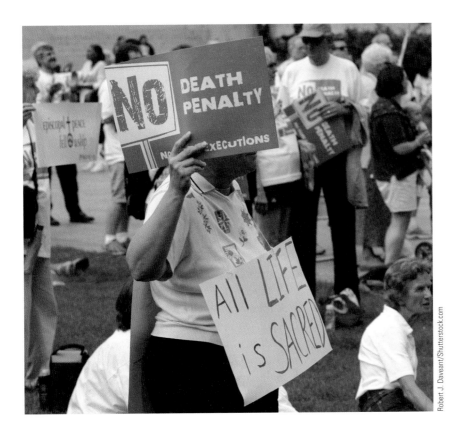

If you were in the audience for an invitational speech on the death penalty, what concerns or points might you bring up for discussion? How would you communicate your ideas to keep the discussion open and nonjudgmental?

sides and positions of an issue before opening up the speech for dialogue with the audience. You go beyond dividing an issue into only two opposing sides and illustrate multiple perspectives. This approach respects a diversity of opinions and also invites your audience to consider even more views than those you covered and makes room for additional perspectives from your audience.

This organizational pattern works well when you want to speak to explore an issue with an audience. In the next example, Cara invited her audience to explore what to teach in U.S. schools about the creation of the universe. She used the multiple perspectives pattern for her speech, inviting her audience to consider how views from different cultures might fit into an elementary or high school education. The following is the basic outline of her speech.

Specific purpose:	To invite my audience to explore the many theories of creation and their role in U.S. education.
Thesis statement:	Schools in the United States could consider teaching some of the many theories throughout time and across cultures that explain how the universe was created—particularly creationism, the Big Bang theory, intelligent design, ancient Egyptian and African theories, and Native American theories.

Main points:

I. One of the modern theories of how the universe was created, that God created the universe, comes from the Judeo-Christian tradition.

II. A second theory, proposed by the Greek philosopher Democritus in 400 B.C., set the stage for the Big Bang theory of creation proposed by most scientists today.

III. A third theory, known as the intelligent design theory, accounts for the origins of RNA and DNA.

IV. A fourth theory, offered by ancient Egyptian and African civilizations, presents a holistic view of existence in which many deities are worshiped as different aspects of God.

V. A theory advocated by many Native American peoples, suggests that the creator of all, sometimes known as Thought Woman, has both female and male aspects and "thinks" all things into being.

VI. I'd like to discuss with my audience the possibility that all of these creation theories be taught in U.S. schools to create a more inclusive curriculum.

To use a multiple perspectives organizational pattern, follow these three guidelines:

1. Do your research so you can explain the various perspectives on the topic to your audience.

2. Present each perspective fairly so audience members can make their own assessments.

3. Make room for even more points of view to be offered from the audience when you open your speech up for dialogue.

In this diverse world, invitational speaking is an option that allows you to continue the public dialogue, even about the most controversial issues. With effort and respect, you can establish the conditions of equality, value, and self-determination even when you disagree with someone. These three conditions become increasingly important because, as cultural critic bell hooks explains, if "a person makes a unilateral decision that does not account for me, then I feel exploited by that decision because my needs haven't been considered. But if that person is willing to pause, then at that moment of pause there is an opportunity for mutual recognition because they have at least listened to and considered, honestly, my position" (hooks, 1994, p. 241).

Visual Aids and Invitational Speeches

Because invitational speeches ask audiences to consider many sides of an issue, there are several reasons to consider using them. One of the best-known studies of visual aids in speeches assessed the amount of information the audience recalls because of visual aids (Figure 15.1)

In another study, researchers asked people to examine a series of photographs and identify those that were repeated. With as many as 200 photographs in a series, people still could pick out the repeat photographs (Nickerson, 1965). However, when recall was tested by listening to series of numbers, people begin to forget which numbers were repeated in series of only six or seven numbers. Although common sense tells us that it often is more difficult to remember numbers, this study reinforces the previous one: visual information greatly improves audience recall. So one of the goals of your visual aids is to help your audience remember information.

Research also suggests that visual aids can help you explain material and thus enhance the clarity of your information. Complex ideas and numbers can be hard to understand verbally but are much easier to sort out when displayed visually. Presenting an idea visually makes it more concrete. Using poster boards and flip charts and even putting lists on a whiteboard or smartboard, in addition to the visual aids mentioned in Chapter 13 and Chapter 14, are worth considering for your invitational speech.

Poster Boards, Flip Charts, and Whiteboards or Smartboards

Poster boards and flip charts can be a good choice for invitational speeches because they are durable and can be reused. Like smartboards and whiteboards, flip charts allow you to record information during

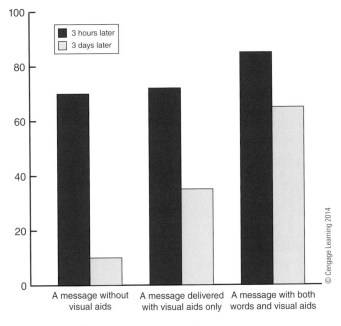

Figure 15.1 *Recollection of information based on visual aids*

Sources: Bohn and Jabusch (1982); Linkugel and Berg (1970); Zayas-Bazan (1977–1978).

list

series of words or phrases that organize ideas one after the other

your speech, which is convenient for speeches that involve discussion and brainstorming. Although many images can be shown to audiences electronically, a poster board allows a smaller audience to see the information up close.

Consider putting lists of ideas on any of these visual aids. A **list** is a *series of words or phrases that organize ideas one after the other*. Lists are text-based visual aids, meaning they rely on the written word rather than on images to convey meaning. Use lists when your material lends itself to itemizing a group or a series such as names, key features, or procedures. Lists help audiences keep track of material and identify the main points of a complex speech or discussion. Use the following principles to record ideas as you brainstorm with your audience, and discuss many aspects of an issue:

- Make your list brief and balanced.
- Use keywords or phrases.
- Avoid full sentences.
- Follow the six-word, six-line rule: a maximum of six words per line and a maximum of six items per list (Davidson & Klien, 1999).
- Include headings (Rabb, 1993).

Because of their size (about twenty-four by thirty-six inches), poster boards and flip charts are not suitable for large audiences. Use them for small groups where everyone will be sitting near enough to read them.

This invitational speaker is using a whiteboard to collect ideas from the audience in a small conference room. Different colors help him identify different ideas in his list of what his audience has shared.

Ian Lishman/Juice/Corbis

Use smartboards and whiteboards for larger audiences. If you choose these options as visual aids, consider the following guidelines.

Make the Design as Professional as Possible Take time to display your ideas neatly and professionally. Do not just throw something together. Instead, think carefully about what you want to include. Use color and images to attract interest and attention. Use rulers and guides to ensure straight lines for words and sentences. Print neatly and clearly so that you present a professional look.

Make sure you will have a stand for the poster board or flip chart. If you plan to hang your visual aids, bring pins or tape with you and think ahead about where you will display the poster board or flip chart so everyone can see it. If you are in a classroom, placing poster boards on the tray of the whiteboard is tempting but can cause problems. The boards tend to fall over, and because the chalk trays are usually behind you, you may block the audience's view of your posters. So consider where you will place them and perhaps ask a member of your audience to display them for you. Finally, think about where you will put poster boards when you have finished discussing them.

Speak to the Audience, Not to the Visual Aid As with whiteboards and smartboards, you may sometimes find yourself speaking to the poster board or flip chart rather than to the audience. To avoid this problem, practice your speech with the visual aid so you are able to glance at or point to it but talk to the audience.

 ## Tips for Giving Effective Invitational Speeches

Like informative and persuasive speaking, invitational speaking has specific guidelines to follow so you can give a more effective speech. Three tips will help you give effective invitational speeches and create a speaking environment of equality, value, and self-determination: (1) use invitational language, (2) allow time for discussion, and (3) know your position.

Use Invitational Language
One way you can create an effective invitational speaking environment is to use invitational language. Phrases such as "You should," "The correct position is," "Anyone can see," which advocate your position over others, only reduce your chances of creating the condition of equality. Equality means that all positions have merit; they are viable for the people who

Select an Organizational Pattern and Visual Aids for Your Invitational Speech

Return to the list of possible invitational speech topics you prepared in Practicing Human Communication earlier in the chapter. In groups, select a single topic and see if you can create a rough thesis statement and main points for four different invitational speeches on this topic, using each of the organizational patterns you read about. As a class, discuss which of these speeches you would find most interesting and why. Now identify several visual aids you might use effectively and discuss how you would incorporate them into the speech. As you discuss your favorite topic, organizational pattern, and visual aids, consider the tips for giving effective invitational speeches in the next section.

hold them, even if they may not be for you. Invitational language offers your view as one possible view but not as "the best" view.

Phrases such as "I came to this view because," "For me, this position makes sense because," "Because of that experience, I began to see this issue as," and "Although this may not work for all of you, this is the position I hold" communicate to your listeners that you value them and only are trying to explain your view and not impose it on others. Try to use phrases that display respect for and openness to other positions throughout your speech.

Invitational language is also important during discussions with your audience. In discussions, people may offer views different from yours or even the opposite of yours. Encourage those views and dialogue about those differences and disagreements rather than silencing or censoring them. Offer positive reinforcement to the ideas of others so the dialogue can develop openly and freely. Respond with questions such as "Can you elaborate on that idea?" "How might that work?" "Why do you think so?" "Can you explain why you prefer that solution?" and "What benefits do you see with that position?" As you engage audience members in an exploration of an issue, draw them out and get them to elaborate on their views. If the discussion becomes heated, keep track of ideas you want to return to later by writing notes on a whiteboard or flip chart. In an invitational setting, you are asking your audience to articulate their position as fully as you do your own. Your language can help you open up the dialogue rather than limit it.

Finally, if you encounter a hostile audience member, your language can help manage and even reduce some of that hostility. When audience members respond with anger, it is usually because the speaker has touched a sensitive nerve. But your language can defuse the situation and reestablish value. Use words and phrases that acknowledge your audience member's position, express your desire to understand that position more fully, and even apologize for upsetting that person. Rather than responding with angry words or denying that the person has reason to be angry, use language that communicates your respect for him or her as someone with views that may be different from yours.

Allow Time for Discussion

Exploring ideas and articulating positions with an audience take time. This means you must be patient and not rush through your presentation or hurry the discussion with your audience. If we are to create the conditions of equality, value, and self-determination and make a space for others in the public dialogue, then we must be willing to take the time necessary to do so. Sometimes this can seem inefficient. Western culture encourages us to get things done quickly and to make decisions without delay. Efficient presentations are often seen as brief, to the point, and tightly organized. However, in invitational speaking, brevity and efficiency may work against you if you become controlling and unwilling to explore someone's position. Invitational speakers must allow time for the dialogue about ideas.

When the time is limited, finding the time for invitational speeches can be challenging. If you are required or choose to speak invitationally, there is a solution to these time constraints. Begin by considering your time frame carefully. If you have only a small amount of time, reduce the scope of your presentation. Decide what you can address in a shorter amount of time and restructure your invitation. For example, instead of covering five different cultural views of creation, Cara could have named as many different theories of creation as she had been able to discover and then explained two of those views in detail. With this reduced scope, Cara still could have offered an invitation but with less detail than the presentation she first chose. By reducing the scope of your presentation, you respect the opinions of the audience and make it possible to engage in a discussion of the larger issue.

Know Your Position

One of the most important aspects of invitational speaking, especially when articulating a position, is to take time before you begin to put your speech together to figure out how you feel about the issue and why you feel as you do. This means you must research an invitational speech as thoroughly as you would any other type of speech. You must support your main ideas with evidence as well as personal opinion. To articulate your position fully and with respect for others, you cannot just ramble on about an issue that you have not given much thought to. You must take time to determine what your position is, why you hold it, and why it is correct for you. You will discover that your attempts to create conditions of value and self-determination will be enhanced if you speak with accuracy, clarity, and detail about your views and their place in your life. Similarly, when you explore an issue with an audience, you must be thoughtful about where you stand on that issue and make sure you are not presenting your view as the right one. Rather, be sure to present your views, if you do, as one option among many.

 ## Ethical Invitational Speaking

Ethical invitational speakers must be sure their purpose is mutual understanding and that they are speaking on a topic that they are open to discussing. Let's look at these two components of ethical invitational speaking.

Stay True to Your Purpose

It is tempting to try to invite an audience to consider your perspective with the underlying goal of persuading them that your view really is best. To speak ethically, you truly must have invitation as your goal.

Although you can create the three conditions of equality, value, and self-determination in other types of speaking, in invitational speaking, you create these conditions because your fundamental goal is the exchange and appreciation of perspectives, not persuasion. If you really want to change your audience, do not pretend you are offering an invitational approach. Give a persuasive speech instead.

Share Your Perspective and Listen Fully to the Perspectives of Others
If you are not able to listen to perspectives that are incompatible with your own or to grant them value, then it would be unethical for you to give an invitational speech. Ethical speakers stay true to their beliefs and values, and they do not pretend they are open to views when they are not. Thus, your topic in an invitational speech must be one about which you truly are open. This does not mean you have to be willing to change your view, but it does mean you have to be willing to listen with respect to other views. If you cannot grant value and self-determination to someone who disagrees with you on a topic, then give an informative or a persuasive speech on that topic. Religion, sexuality, and instances of oppression are three topics that may be especially difficult for invitational speeches because people have such strong beliefs about them.

STUDENT SPEECH with Commentary

Four-Day School Week: An Invitational Dialogue

by Courtney Felton

Are you ready to give an invitational speech? You can use the following speech as a model. Courtney Felton gave this speech in an introductory public speaking class. The assignment was to give a five- to seven-minute invitational speech, manage a five- to seven-minute dialogue with the audience, and wrap up with a one-minute conclusion. Courtney was also asked to provide at least four sources, meet the objectives of an effective introduction and conclusion, and provide relevant information. Notice how she created the conditions of equality, value, and self-determination and remained invitational throughout her dialogue with the audience. Access your CourseMate for Invitation to Human Communication to watch a video clip of this speech, see the accompanying outline, and read the discussion that followed the speech. (In the video, Eric Rollins delivered Courtney's speech.) Remember that you can use your CourseMate to access videos of other invitational speeches, including David Barworth's "Federal Minimum Wage" and Cara Buckley-Ott's "Creationism versus the Big Bang Theory."

Specific Purpose: To explore with my audience the idea of changing the five-day high school week to a four-day week.

Thesis Statement: Today I want to explore with you the idea of high schools changing from a regular five-day-week schedule to a four-day schedule with longer days.

Seven hours! That's almost enough sleep for a night. Or perhaps a solid day's worth of skiing. Or the time it takes to travel by plane across the country. Seven hours is also roughly the amount of time high school students spend in school in one school day. Take a second to imagine what it would have been like not having school on Fridays when you were in high school. This would have you with an extra seven hours you hadn't had before! That would have been seven hours to do countless activities.

The National Conference of State Legislatures states, "Supporters of the shortened week also boast of improved morale and increased attendance (by both students and teachers), open Fridays for sporting events and doctor appointments, and more time to spend with loved ones."

This idea of having a shorter high school week has been a topic of interest for me. Since all of us go to school—even though now it's college—I have a feeling it may be a topic that you might want to explore as well. Today I want to explore with you the idea of schools changing from the normal schedule of a five-day week to a four-day week with longer school days. Since I don't have a solid opinion on whether or not this would be beneficial to all schools, I'd like to share two of the many perspectives on this issue, one for and one against. I'd also like to hear your feedback on the issue.

I'd like to start by addressing the pros of a four-day school week. Perhaps the most significant issue right now in education is the idea of budget cuts. Cutting back on one day of school per week saves on expenses such as transportation, utilities such as heat for the school, food expenses, and the other costs to keep a school open.

Another advantage to having only four days of school is the option to hold sporting events on Fridays. And if students are free on Fridays, the attendance at games could increase. A March 12, 2009, Associated Press article from FoxNews.com, accessed on March 9, 2010, explains that "about 85 percent of the district's athletic events are scheduled on Fridays, so a Monday-to-Thursday school week means fewer Friday absences as students and teachers prepare for or travel to games."

A third advantage to the shortened schedule is the idea of having more time to spend with family or friends, taking care of doctor appointments, or being able to schedule any other weekday activity that one may not have time for on a five-day school schedule.

Exactly how many schools are actually doing this, though? An article from the *Wall Street Journal*, accessed on March 9, 2010, states, "Of the nearly 15,000-plus districts nationwide, more than 100 in at least 17 states currently use the four-day system, according to data culled from the Education Commission of the States."

While, in my opinion, all of these aspects seem appealing, I want to address another side of the issue and consider the views of those

Commentary

Courtney begins her speech with two simple words and a series of intriguing possibilities for what might take seven hours to do. In this way, she draws her audience into her topic and relates it to their lives.

Courtney cites a credible source (National Conference of State Legislatures) and uses a quotation that begins to introduce her topic. She then shares her own interest in the topic, relates her topic to her audience again, and reveals her specific purpose.

Courtney openly shares that she has no firm position and that she is interested in her audience's feedback. Although she offers only two positions on her subject, she is clear that there are many more. In doing so, she begins to establish an invitational environment for her audience.

Courtney shares the advantages and disadvantages of the shorter week in a fair and unbiased way. She cites her sources, is open about the pros and cons, and uses statistics and examples to explain some of the advantages of the shorter week.

Courtney continues to establish an invitational environment by clearly pointing out the exact number of schools that are adopting this plan.

Because she is exploring the issue with her audience, she then shares the disadvantages of the four-day week, presenting her evidence clearly and fairly.

She presents the cons of the four-day week invitationally, being open and nonjudgmental so that her audience can hear the evidence and make their own decisions about it. Notice that her language is unbiased.

Using a signpost ("Finally, it is important to consider"), Courtney addresses one final point before she opens the speech up to dialogue with her audience. In this point, she cites experts to enhance her credibility and to illustrate that she has done her research. She then closes with an invitation to her audience to explore the issue with her openly.

Just in case her audience was hesitant to participate, she prepared a list of questions she could use to encourage dialogue. Preparing like this helped her feel more confident and gave her a wide platform from which to begin the invitational dialogue.

Although she didn't need the questions, they reminded her to remain neutral during the discussion and address the many aspects of her topic.

opposing the change. Each of the articles I looked at on FoxNews.com as well as the NCSL site discussed the following issues.

While the shorter week appears to be helpful in saving money, it may cause parents to take on the cost burden. With their children home during a normal workday, parents have to find extra child care.

Another important problem opponents of the four-day schedule discuss is the increased length of the school day. As current students, some of us may feel like the school day is already long enough. Adding to the length may make high school students even more tired, less able to concentrate, and could hinder their learning time while at school. And extending school further into the day cuts into students' time for extracurricular activities on days other than Friday.

In addition, while an extra day off leaves time for family time and other activities, some parents—and even students—are afraid of how students will actually use this time off.

Finally, it is important to consider the current school reform movement. A research brief prepared by The Principles Partnership of the Union Pacific Foundation explains, "Some educators are concerned that the four-day week may appear to be inconsistent with the new emphasis for more time in school."

Now that we have explored both sides of the issue, as well as opinions of students, teachers, and parents, I think it is important to hear your opinions as well as ideas that I may not have addressed yet.

Courtney and her audience discussed the issues related to moving from a five-day to a four-day week in high schools. To encourage audience members to share their views, she prepared the following questions in advance:

- To begin, by a show of hands, who would like the keep the current school schedule?

- And who would want to change the high school week to four longer days rather than five?

- For those of you who want to change, what aspect of changing is most appealing to you?

- For those of you who think the current schedule should stay, what isn't appealing about changing for you?

- For those of you who were athletes in high school, how do you think changing this schedule would have affected your athletic schedule? Practice time, game time, et cetera?

- As a high school student, would you personally have been able to concentrate and work at the level you did on a five-day week for a longer amount of time at school?

- If you had had one extra free day, do you feel like you would have worked better as a student?

- What types of things would you have done with an extra day?

- What aspects of the four days of the week would have been hindered by your longer day at school?

- Are there any other drawbacks or benefits you want to share that I didn't cover?

When the discussion was over, Courtney concluded her speech.

Thanks for sharing your ideas and opinions. I think that really helped shed some more light on the situation and how students really feel about the issue.

We've heard today some of the views in favor of and some against changing the current five-day high school week to a four-day week with longer days. For students, perhaps a shorter week would allow for more time outside school, but it could also cut into sports practice time and extracurricular activities. For parents, finding day care could be an issue, but for the schools, it could be a way to save money.

On the whole, though, I think there are multiple perspectives to consider, and I've enjoyed being able to talk about some of them with you.

— From GRIFFIN, *Invitation to Public Speaking, Fourth Edition* © 2012 Cengage Learning.

Courtney closes her invitational speech by expressing her appreciation to her audience members for sharing their views. She summarizes the dialogue in a fair and neutral way, restates that there are many ways to think about her topic, and ends in a respectful tone.

Chapter Summary

To Speak Invitationally Is to Articulate Your Position or Explore an Issue with Your Audience

- To speak invitationally is to engage in a dialogue about differences and to offer and seek mutual recognition of the variety of positions possible on an issue.

In an Invitational Speaking Environment, the Speaker Develops Conditions of Equality, Value, and Self-Determination

- The condition of equality entails recognizing that both you and your audience hold valid perspectives that are important to explore.
- The condition of value involves recognizing that audience members' positions have merit, even if they differ from your own.
- The condition of self-determination involves recognizing that your audience members have the right to choose what is best for them, even if those choices are not the ones you would make.

There Are Two Types of Invitational Speeches: Speeches to Explore an Issue and Speeches to Articulate a Position

- When you give a speech to explore an issue, you want to gather different perspectives and engage

your audience in a discussion about an issue or plan of action.
- When you give a speech to articulate a position, you want to invite an audience to see the world as you do and to understand issues from your perspective.

The Four Most Common Organizational Patterns for Invitational Speeches Are the Chronological, Spatial, Topical, and Multiple Perspectives Patterns. Three Tips Are Useful for Invitational Speakers

- Research your topic to understand your own position and why you hold it so you can give the fullest expression of your views possible.
- Use invitational language that encourages the respect and expression of different views and that helps you have an open discussion of those views.
- Allow time for dialogue and discussion in your speeches.

Remember, Invitational Speakers Must Be Ethical and Choose Topics About Which They Truly Want to Invite an Exchange of Perspectives Rather Than Inform or Persuade Their Audience

Key Concepts

condition of equality (390)	**invitational environment** (387)	**multiple perspectives pattern** (398)
condition of self-determination (390)	**invitational speaking** (386)	**speech to articulate a position** (393)
condition of value (390)	**list** (402)	**speech to explore an issue** (391)

Invitation to Human Communication Online

Speech Communication CourseMate includes an interactive eBook and interactive learning tools including National Geographic Explorer videos, student videos, quizzes, flash cards, and more. Speech Builder Express 3.0 and Speech Studio 2.0 are also available. Go to cengagebrain.com to access your CourseMate for *Invitation to Human Communication* where these resources can be found.

Further Reflection and Discussion

1. Can you identify situations in which you might have preferred giving an invitational speech but gave another type instead? What might have been different if you had given an invitational speech rather than the type of speech you did give?

2. Imagine you are giving an invitational speech on the subject of gays and lesbians serving in the military. How might you create conditions of equality, value, and self-determination in this speech?

3. Identify a person or a group with whom you strongly disagree. Consider whether you might speak invitationally with that person or group and what benefits or disadvantages might result from such an interaction.

4. Develop an invitational speech to give to the person or group you identified in question three. Would you prefer to articulate a position or explore an issue with them? What is it about your position that you would like the person or group to understand, and what aspect of the other position would you like to explore? Did you allow time for these types of interactions in your speech?

5. Suppose that while you are giving the speech you developed in question four, a member of your audience strongly disagrees with the position you articulate. What kind of language could you use to acknowledge his anger and frustration but also continue to have a productive dialogue with him and other members of the audience? (You might role-play this scenario with members of your class.)

Activities and Web Links

Visit cengagebrain.com to access the CourseMate for *Invitation to Human Communication* where these activities and web links can be found.

1. Read this speech on animal rights. The speaker is presenting to a group that already holds the same opinion as he does. What position does the speaker take on the issue? Research additional viewpoints that you would need to add for this to be an invitational speech. What are the views on using animals for research testing? Are there

words or phrases in this speech that you might not use in an invitational speech? *Go to Web link 15.1.*

2. Create an outline for a chronological invitational speech on the issue of equal pay for equal work. What did women get paid for their work during World War II? What do they get paid now in comparison to men's wages? What are the laws about equal pay, and where do those laws fit into the chronology? Do women receive equal pay for work equal to men's? What should be done? Is current legislation effective? Should the government introduce more legislation? If so, what should the legislation require? These Web sites will provide information for you to use. *Go to Web link 15.2.*

Chapter 1

Bieri, J. (1955). Cognitive complexity–simplicity and predictive behavior. *Journal of Abnormal Psychology, 51*, 263–268.

Burke, K. (1973). *The philosophy of literary form: Studies in symbolic action* (3rd ed., pp. 110–111). Berkeley: University of California Press. (Original work published 1941)

Carter, S. L. (1998). *Civility: Manners, morals, and the etiquette of democracy* (pp. 15, 23). New York: Basic Books.

Culhane, T. T. R. (2011a). *The great conversation: Solar CITIES.* Speech prepared for Abu Dhabi Media Company, March 2011). Retrieved December 27, 2011, from http://solarcities.blogspot.com/2011/03/great-conversation-solar-cities.html.

Culhane, T. T . R. (2011b). Urban planner [December]. Retrieved December 27, 2011, from http://www.nationalgeographic.com/explorers/bios/culhane-thomas/.

Domangue, B. B. (1978). Decoding effects of cognitive complexity, tolerance of ambiguity, and verbal-nonverbal consistency. *Journal of Personality, 46*, 519–535.

Ehrlich, T. (Ed.). (2000). *Civic responsibility and higher education.* Westport, CT: Oryx Press.

Emanuel, R., Adams, J., Baer, K., Daufin, E. K., Ellington, C., Fitts, E., et al. (2008). How college students spend their time communicating. *International Journal of Listening, 22*, 13–28.

Ferreira da Cruz, M. R. D. (2008). Intercultural cybercommunication: Negotiation of representations of languages and cultures in multilingual chat rooms. *Journal of Multicultural Discourses, 3*, 98–113.

hooks, b. (1994). *Outlaw culture: Resisting representations* (pp. 241–242). New York: Routledge.

Khodarahmi, S. (2008, September–October). The end of language: LOL. *Communication World*, pp. 16–17.

Klemmer, E. T., & Snyder, F. W. (1972). Measurement of time spent communicating. *Journal of Communication, 22*, 142–158.

Kline, S., & Clinton, B. (1998). Development in children's persuasive message practices. *Communication Education, 47*, 120–126.

Martin, J., & Nakayama, T. (2008). *Experiencing intercultural communication: An introduction* (2nd ed., pp. 27, 28).

Martin, M. M., & Anderson, C. M. (1998). The cognitive flexibility scale: Three validity studies. *Communication Reports, 11*(1), 1–9.

Mill, J. (1984). High and low self-monitoring individuals: Their decoding skills and empathic expression. *Journal of Personality, 52*, 372–388.

Ogden, C. K., & Richards, I. A. (1923). *The meaning of meaning: A study of the influence of language upon thought and of the science of symbolism.* New York: Harcourt, Brace.

Reiss, J. (Director). (2007). *Bomb It* [Documentary film]. New York: Antidote Films (http://www.bombit-themovie.com).

Snyder, M. (1974). Self-monitoring of expressive behavior. *Journal of Personality and Social Psychology, 30*, 526–537.

Spitzberg, B. H., & Cupach, W. R. (Eds.). (2007). *The dark side of interpersonal communication* (2nd ed.). Hillsdale, NJ: Erlbaum.

Tannen, D. (1998). *The argument culture: Stopping America's war of words.* New York: Ballantine Books.

Tutu, D. M. (1994). Agents of transformation. In J. Allen (Ed.), *Rainbow people of God: The making of a peaceful revolution* (p. 125). New York: Doubleday.

Urban Dictionary. Retrieved January 8, 2009, from http://www.urbandictionary.com.

Chapter 2

ACLU. (2011, September 28). Federal court ruling on Alabama's anti-immigrant law undermines American values. Retrieved October 21, 2011, from http://www.aclu.org/immigrants-rights/federal-court-ruling-alabamas-anti-immigrant-law-undermines-fundamental-american.

Attree, P., French, B., Milton, B., Poval, S., Whitehead, M., & Popay, J. (2011, May). The experience of community engagement for individuals: A rapid review of evidence, heath, and social care in the community. *Health in and Social Care in the Community, 19*(3), 250–260.

Barlett, C. P., Christopher, L. Vowels, & Saucier, D. A. (2008). Meta-analysis of the effects of media images on 11 men's body-image concerns. *Journal of Social and Clinical Psychology, 27*(3), 279–310. Retrieved March 6, 2012, from http://www.public.iastate.edu/~cpb6666/pubs/Barlett%20Vowels%20%26%20Saucier.pdf.

Barton, J., & Pretty, J. (2010, May 15) What is the best dose of Nature and green exercise for increasing mental health? A multistudy analysis. *Environmental Science and Technology, 10*, 3947–3955.

BBC News. (2007). Defying the odds of medicine. Retrieved January 12, 2007, from http://www.bbc.co.uk/news/mobile/health-16137007.

Bechtoldt, M. N., Carsten, K. W., Dreu, D., Nijstad, B. A., & Zapf, D. (April 2010). Self-concept clarity and the management of social conflict. *Journal of Personality*, *78*(2), 539–574.

Borzekowski, D., Schenk, S., Wilson, J. L., & Peebles, R. (2010). e-Ana and e-Mia: A content analysis of pro–eating disorder Web sites. *American Journal of Public Health*, *8*, 100 1526–1534.

Brand-Williams, O. (2011). CAIR says Muslin-Americans harassed when crossing borders. *Detroit News*. Retrieved March 16, 2011, from http://detnews.com/article/20110325/METRO/103250392/CAIR-says-Muslim-Americans-harassed-when-crossing-border.

Bulanda, R. E., & Majumdar, D. (2009). Perceived parent–child relations and adolescent self-esteem. *Journal of Child and Family Studies*, *18*, 203–212.

Caunt, J. (2003). *Boost your self-esteem*. London: Kogan Page.

Cooley, C. H. (1968). The social self: On the meanings of I. In C. Gordon & K. J. Gergen (Eds.), *The self in social interactions. Vol. 1: Classic and contemporary perspectives* (pp. 87–91). New York: Wiley.

Cousteau, A. (2012, January 18). Telephone communication.

DeVito, J. A. (1986). *The communication handbook: A dictionary*, p. 269. New York: Harper & Row.

France begins ban on niquab and burqa: Women wearing a face veil in public could now be fined or given lessons in French citizenship. (2011, April 11). *The Guardian*. Retrieved from http://www.guardian.co.uk/world/2011/apr/11/france-begins-burqa-niqab-ban.

Hartstock, N. (1999). *Feminist standpoint theory revisited and other essays*. New York: Basic Books.

Holland, A., & Andre, T. (1994). Athletic participation and the social status of adolescent males and females. *Youth and Society*, *25*, 388–407.

Hormouth, S. E. (1990). *The ecology of the self: Relocation and self-concept change*. New York: Cambridge University Press.

Jhally, S., & Kilbourne, J. (Directors). (2010). *Killing us softly IV: Advertising's image of women*. [Documentary film]. Northampton, MA: Media Education Foundation.

Kilbourne, J. (1999). *Deadly persuasion: Why women and girls must fight the addictive power of advertising*. New York: Free Press.

Kimmell, M. (2008). *Guyland: The perilous world where boys become men*. New York: Macmillan.

Kuhlberg, J. A., Peña, J. B., & Zayas, L. H. (2101, August). Familism, parent–adolescent conflict, self-esteem, internalizing behaviors, and suicide attempts among adolescent Latinas. *Child Psychiatry and Human Development*, *4*, 425–440.

Loden, M., & Rosener, J. B. (1991). *Workforce America: Managing workforce diversity as a vital resource*. Homewood, IL: Business One Irwin.

Lovett, I. (2011). UCLA student's video rant against Asians fuels firestorm. *The New York Times*. Retrieved January 21, 2012, from http://www.nytimes.com/2011/03/16/us/16ucla.html.

MacDonald, K., & Greggans, A. (2010, September). "Cool Friends": An evaluation of a community befriending program for young people with cystic fibrosis. *Journal of Clinical Nursing*, *17/18*, 2406–2414.

Mead, G. H. (1934). *Mind, self, and society*. Chicago: University of Chicago Press.

Mehra, A., Kilduff, M., & Brass, D. J. (2001, March). The social networks of high and low self-monitors: Implications for workplace performance. *Administrative Science Quarterly*, *1*, 121–146.

Mruk, C. (1999). *Self-esteem research, theory, and practice*. London: Free Association Books.

Muhindi, M. M., & Nyakato, K. (2002). Integration of the Sudanese Lost Boys in Boston, Massachusetts USA. Retrieved November 10, 2011, from http://web.mit.edu/cis/www/migration/pubs/Mahindi.pdf.

Nisbett, R. E. (2000). *The geography of thought*. London: Nicholas Brealey.

National Geographic Video. (n.d.). God grew tired of us: Cultural differences. Retrieved January 21, 2012, from http://education.nationalgeographic.com/education/multimedia/cultural-differences/.

Paterson, C. H., Buser, T. J., & Westburg, N. G. (2010). Effects of familial attachment, social support, involvement, and self-esteem on youth substance use and sexual risk taking. *Family Journal*, *18*(4), 369–376.

Phinney, J. S., Cantu, C. L., & Kurtz, D. A. (1997). Ethnic and American identity as predictors of self-esteem among African American, Latino, and White adolescents. *Journal of Youth and Adolescence*, *2*, 165–185.

Piers, E. V., & Harris, D. B. (1996). *Piers-Harris Children's Self-Concept Scale, 2*. Los Angeles: Western Psychological Services.

Popper, B. (2011). Intel's Museum of Me features dead friends and ex-lovers. Retrieved May 31, 2011, from http://www.betabeat.com/2011/05/31/intel-museum-of-me-facebook-freaks-me-out-2011-05-31/?show=print.

Rau, A. B. (2011, February 23). Arizona immigration bills aim for bigger crackdown. *Arizona Republic*. Retrieved October

21, 2011, from http://www.azcentral.com/arizonarepublic/news/articles/2011/02/23/20110223arizona-immigration-bills-controversy.html.

Robins, R. W., Tracy, J. L., Trzesniewski, K. H., Gosling, S. D., & Potter, J. (2001). Personality correlates of self-esteem. *Journal of Research in Personality, 35,* 463–482.

Rose, B. (2004). Lost boys of Sudan in Chicago. Retrieved November 10, 2011, from http://www.lostboyschicago.com/Writings/JacobDing.htm.

Salamon, M. (2011). For college students, praise may trump sex and money, *Bloomberg BusinessWeek.* Retrieved January 11, 2011, from http://www.businessweek.com/lifestyle/content/healthday/648705.html.

Singer, M. R. (1982). Culture: A perceptual approach. In L. A. Samovar & R. E. Porter (Eds.), *Intercultural communication: A reader* (3rd ed., pp. 54–61). Belmont, CA: Wadsworth.

Skinner, C. (2010, October 3). Civil rights attorney assails Arizona's immigration law. *Desert News.* Retrieved May 10, 2011, from http://www.deseretnews.com/article/700070421/Civil-rights-attorney-assails-Arizonas-immigration-law.html?pg=1.

Snyder, M. (1979). Self-monitoring processes. In L. Berkowitz (Ed.), *Advances in experimental social psychology* (Vol. 12, pp. 85–128). New York: Academic Press.

Sterling, M. (2006). Do you make your first impression your best impression? Retrieved January 20, 2012, from http://entrepreneurs.about.com/cs/marketing/a/uc051603a.htm.

Story, L. (2007). Anywhere an eye can see, it's likely to see an ad. *The New York Times.* Retrieved January 15, 2007, from http://www.nytimes.com/2007/01/15/business/media/15everywhere.html.

Sunnafrank, M., & Ramirez, A., Jr. (2004, June). At first sight: Persistent relational effects of get-acquainted conversations. *Journal of Social and Personal Relationships, 3,* 361–379.

Tantleff-Dunn, S. (2001). Breast and chest size: Ideals and stereotypes through the 1990s. *Sex Roles, 3 & 4,* 231–242.

Taylor, D. L. (1995). A comparison of college athletic participants and nonparticipants on self esteem. *Journal of College Student Development, 36,* 444–451.

Thomas, J. J., & Daubman, K. A. (2001). The relationship between friendship quality and self-esteem in adolescent girls and boys. *Sex Roles, 1 & 2,* 53–65.

Ting-Toomey, S. (1999). *Communicating across cultures.* New York: Guilford.

Toegel, G., Anand, N., & Kilduff, M. (2007). Emotion helpers: The role of high positive affectivity and high self-monitoring managers. *Personnel Psychology, 2,* 337–365.

Trevino, J. (2003). *Goffman's legacy.* Oxford, UK: Rowman & Littlefield.

Umaña-Taylor, A. (2004, April). Ethnic identity and self-esteem: Examining the role of social context. *Journal of Youth and Adolescence, 2,* 139–146.

Wilkins, J. A., Boland, F. J., & Albinson, J. (1991). A comparison of male and female university athletes and nonathletes on eating disorder indices: Are athletes protected? *Sport Behavior, 14,* 129–143.

Willis, J., & Todorov, A. (2006). First impressions. *Psychological Science.* Retrieved January 20, 2012, http://www.psychologicalscience.org.

Wilson, G. A., Zeng, Q., & Blackburn, D. G. (2011, January–March). An examination of parental attachments, parental detachments and self-esteem across hetero-, bi-, and homosexual individuals. *Journal of Bisexuality, 1,* 85–96.

Zaslow, J. (2009, September 2). Girls dieting, then and now. *The Wall Street Journal Online.* Retrieved November 11, 2011, from http://online.wsj.com/article/SB10001424052970204731804574386822245731710.html.

Chapter 3

Andersen, P. A., & Guerrero, L. K. (1994). Patterns of matching and initiation: Tough behavior and touch avoidance across romantic relationship stages. *Journal of Nonverbal Behavior, 16,* 55–63.

Birdwhistell, R. (1970). *Kinesics and context.* Philadelphia: University of Pennsylvania Press.

Boone, R. T., & Sunningham, J. G. (1998). Children's decoding of emotion in expressive body movement: The development of cue attunement. *Developmental Psychology, 34,* 1007–1016.

Burgoon, J. K., Guerrero, L., & Floyd, K. (2010). *Nonverbal communication.* Boston: Allyn & Bacon.

Chartrand, T. L., & Bargh, J. A. (1999). The chameleon effect: The perception–behavior link and social interaction. *Journal of Personality and Social Psychology, 76,* 893–910.

Chua-Eoan, H. (2009, April 1). The Queen and Mrs. Obama: A breach in protocol. *Time.* Retrieved September 10, 2010, from http://www.time.com/time/world/article/0,8599,1888962,00.html.

Davitz, J. R., (1964). *The communication of emotional meaning.* New York: Macmillan.

Derks, D., Bos, A. E., & von Grumbkow, J. (2008). Emoticons and online message interpretation. *Social Science Computer Review, 26,* 379–388.

Derlega, V. J., Lewis, R. J., Harrison, S., Winstead, B. A., & Costanza, T. (1989). Gender differences in the initiation and attribution of tactile intimacy. *Journal of Nonverbal Behavior, 13*, 3–14.

DiNardo, M.L. (2011, October 21). If you're happy and you know it, must I know, too? Retrieved January 21, 2012, from http://www.nytimes.com/2011/10/23/fashion/emoticons -move-to-the-business-world-cultural-studies.html.

Don't touch: Michelle Obama abandons protocol with Queen. (2009, April 2). *The Times* [London]. Retrieved September 2010 from http://www.foxnews.com/politics/2009/04/02 /dont-touch-michelle-obama-abandons-protocol-queen/.

Dresser, N. (1996). *Multicultural manners*. New York: Wiley.

Eakins, B. W., & Eakins, R. G. (1988). Sex differences in nonverbal communication. In L. A. Samovar & R. Porter (Eds.), *Intercultural communication: A reader* (pp. 292–309). Belmont, CA: Wadsworth.

Ekman, P., & Friesen, W. (1967). Head and body cues in the judgment of emotion: A reformulation. *Perceptual and Motor Skills, 24*, 711–724.

Ekman, P., & Friesen, W. (1969). The repertoire of nonverbal behavior: Categories, origins, usage, and coding. *Semoitica, 1*, 49–98.

Ekman, P., Sorenson, E. R., & Friesen, W. V. (1969). Pan-cultural elements in facial displays of emotions. *Science, 164*, 86–88.

Field, T. (2002). Infants need for touch. *Human Development, 45*, 100–104.

Fox, K. (2010, November 20). *The smell report*. Social Issues Research Centre. Retrieved September 20, 2010, from http://www.sirc.org/publik/smell.pdf.

Givens, D. B. (2005). *The nonverbal dictionary of gestures, signs, and body language cues*. Spokane, WA: Center for Nonverbal Studies Press.

Goldberg, E. (2010, September 2). Nut ball AZ Governor Jan Brewer flees press conference and sits in silence. Retrieved September 3, 2010, from http://estergoldberg.typepad.com /views_from_a_broad/2010/09/nut-ball-az-governor -jan-brewer-flees-press-conference-and-sits-in-silence.html.

Graham, J. A., & Jauhar, A. J. (1982). *The effects of cosmetics on self perception: How we see ourselves*. Unpublished manuscript, University of Pennsylvania.

Halberstadt, A. G., & Saitta, M. B. (1987). Gender, nonverbal behavior, and perceived dominance: A test of the theory. *Journal of Personality and Social Psychology, 53*, 257–272.

Hall, E. T. (1959). *The silent language*. New York: Doubleday.

Hall, E. (1969). *The hidden dimension*. Garden City, NY: Anchor Books.

Hall, J. A. (1984). *Nonverbal sex differences: Communication accuracy and expressive style*. Baltimore: The John Hopkins University Press.

Harrigan, J. A. (1984). The effects of task order on children's identification of facial expression. *Motivation and Emotion, 8*, 157–169.

Heslin, R., & Alper, T. (1983). Tough: The bonding gesture. In J. M. Wiemann & R. P Harrison (Eds.), *Nonverbal interaction*. Beverly Hills, CA: Sage.

Hummert, M. L., Mazloff, D., & Henry, C. (1999). Vocal characteristics of older adults and stereotyping. *Journal of Nonverbal Behavior, 23*, 111–132.

Keeley, M. P., & Hart, A. J. (1994). Nonverbal behavior in dyadic interaction. In S. W. Duck (Ed.), *Understanding relationship processes. Vol. 4. Dynamics of relationships* (pp. 135–162). Thousand Oaks, CA: Sage.

Kido, M. (2000). Bio-psychological effect of color. *Journal of International Society of Life Information Science, 1*, 254–62.

Kramer, E. (1963). The judgment of personal characteristics and emotions from nonverbal properties of speech. *Psychological Bulletin, 60*, 408–420.

Lacey, M. (2010, September 2). The sound of silence. *The New York Times*. Retrieved September 10, 2010 from http://thecaucus .blogs.nytimes.com/2010/09/02/the-sound-of-silence/.

Lawrence, E. D. (2010, January 6). Hundreds attend Dearborn meeting about Twin Towers shirts. *Detroit Free Press*. Retrieved September 10, 2010, from http://www.pocketfives.com/.

Leathers, D. G. (1986). *Successful nonverbal communication: Principles and applications*. New York: Macmillan.

Leathers, D. (1997). *Successful nonverbal communication: Principles and applications* (3rd ed.). Boston: Allyn & Bacon.

Lieberman, D. A., Rigo, T. G., & Campain, R. F. (1988). Age-related differences in nonverbal decoding ability. *Communication Quarterly, 36*, 290–297.

Markhan, R., & Adams, K. (1992). The effect of type of task on children's identification of facial expressions. *Journal of Nonverbal Behavior, 16*, 21–39.

Maslow, A., & Mintz, N. L. (1956). Effects of esthetic surroundings. I: Initial effects of three esthetic conditions upon perceiving "energy" and "well-being" in faces. *Journal of Psychology, 41*, 247–254.

Matsumoto, D. (1989). Cultural influences of the perception of emotion. *Journal of Cross-Cultural Psychology, 20*, 92–105.

McClure, E. B. (2000). A meta-analytic review of sex differences in facial expression processing and their development in infants, children, and adolescents. *Psychological Bulletin, 126*, 424–453.

Mehrabian, A. (1971). *Silent messages*. Belmont, CA: Wadsworth.

Niedenthal, P., Halberstadt, J. B., Margolin, J., & Innes-Ker, A. H. (2000). Emotional state and the detection of change in facial expression of emotion. *European Journal of Social Psychology*, *30*, 211–222.

Nowicki, S., Jr., & Duke, M. P (1994). Individual differences in the nonverbal communication of affect: The diagnostic analysis of nonverbal accuracy scale. *Journal of Nonverbal Behavior*, *18*, 9–35.

Pittman, J., & Scherer, K. S. (1993). Vocal expression and communication of emotion. In M. Lewis & J. M. Haviland (Eds.), *Handbook of emotions*. New York: Guilford.

Prochnik, G. (2010). *In pursuit of silence: Listening for meaning in a world of noise*. New York: Anchor Books.

Reid, A., Lancuba, V., & Murrow, B. (1997). Clothing style and formation of first impressions. *Perceptual and Motor Skills*, *84*, 237–238.

Safdar, S., Friedlmeier, W., Matsumoto, D., Yoo, S. H., Kwantes, C. T., Kakai, H., et al. (2009). Variations of emotional display rules within and across cultures: A comparison between Canada, USA, and Japan. *Canadian Journal of Behaviour Science*, *41*, 1–10.

Singh, S. (2006). The impact of color on marketing, management decisions. *Management Decision*, *44*, 783–789.

Smith, P. B., & Bond, M. H. (1994). *Social psychology across cultures: Analysis and perspectives*. Boston: Allyn and Bacon.

Van Lancker, D., Kreiman, J., & Emmorey, K. (1985). Familiar voice recognition: Patterns and parameters—Precognition of backward voices. *Journal of Phonetics*, *13*, 19–38.

Villaros, L. (1994, January). Dangerous eating. *Essence*, pp.12–21.

Wood. J. (2013). *Gendered lives: communication, gender, and culture*. Boston: Cengage Learning.

Yarrow, L. J. (1963). Research in dimension of early maternal care. *Merrill-Palmer Quarterly*, *9*, 101–122.

Chapter 4

Austin, I., & Robins, L. (2009, December 23). BlackBerry breakdown puts users in uproar. *The New York Times*. Retrieved on September 7, 2010, from http://www.nytimes .com/2009/12/24/technology/companies/24blackberry .html.

Boyle, C. (2010). Hot 97 DJ suspended indefinitely after on-air Haiti HIV crack that sparked protests among listeners. *Daily News*. Retrieved January 12, 2011, from http://www.nydailynews.com /ny_local/bronx/2010/12/26/2010-12-6_hot_97_dj_suspended _for_haiti_slur.html.

Burke, D. (2010, November 2). Supreme Court torn over speech rights, private rites. *Christian Century*, p. 17.

Canary, D. J., & Hause, K. S. (1993). Is there any reason to research sex difference in communication? *Communication Quarterly*, *41*, 129–144.

Congressional Digest Corp. (2010, November). Does the Constitution protect the right of protestors to demonstrate during a private citizen's military funeral? *Supreme Court Debates: A Pro & Con Monthly*, *13*(8), 17–27.

Goleman, D. (2010). E-mail is easy to write (and to misread). *The New York Times*. Retrieved December 10, 2010, from http://www.nytimes.com/2007/10/07/jobs/07pre.html.

Harper, J. (2006, March 24). Riders shield mourners: Patriot Guard offers "corridor of honor" for troops. *Washington Times*, p. A9.

Harris, F. (2006, March 9). Bikers on guard at war funerals; Volunteer army of patriots shields grieving relatives from anti-gay pickets. *Daily Telegraph* (London), p. 8. Retrieved November 11, 2011 from www.patriotguard.org.

Holmes, J. (2006). *Gendered talk at work: Constructing gender identity through workplace discourse*. New York: Blackwell.

Howard, R. (2010, October 29). "The Dilemma's" gay joke: It stays in the movie. Los Angeles Times [online]. Retrieved November 11, 2011, from http://latimesblogs .latimes.com/the_big_picture/2010/10/ron-howard-on-the -dilemmas-gay-joke-it-stays-in-the-movie.html.

Hughes, S. A. (2011, October 10). Tracy Morgan on homophobic comments: It was all a misunderstanding. *Washington Post* [online]. Retrieved October 30, 2011, from http://www.washingtonpost.com/blogs/celebritology/post /tracy-morgan-on-homophobic-comments-it-was-a -misunderstanding-video/2011/10/11/gIQAsmkVcL_blog.html.

Johnson, S. K., Bettenhausen, K., & Gibbons, E. (2009). Realities of working in virtual teams: Affective and attitudinal outcomes of using computer-mediated communication, *Small Group Research*, *6*, 623–649.

Kanawattanachai, P., & Yoo, T. (2002). Dynamic nature of trust in virtual teams. *Journal of Strategic Information Systems*, *11*, 187–213.

Krulwich, R. (2009, April 6). Shakespeare has roses all wrong. National Public Radio. Retrieved November 29, 2010, from http://www.npr.org/templates/story/story .php?storyId=102518565.

Leaper, C. (1996). The relationship of play activity and gender to parent and child sex-typed communication. *International Journal of Behavioral Development*, *19*, 689–703.

Leaper, C., & Ayres, M. M. (2007). A meta-analytic review of gender variations in adults' language use: Talkativeness, affiliative speech, and assertive speech. *Personality and Social Psychology Review, 4*, 328–363.

Lee, M. J. (2011, October 11). Scott Brown accused of plagiarism. Politico.com. Retrieved October 30, 2011, from http://www.politico.com/news/stories/1011/65838.html.

Maltz, D. C., & Borker, R. (1982). A cultural approach to male–female miscommunication. In J. J. Gumperz (Ed.), *Language and social identity* (pp. 196–216). Cambridge, UK: Cambridge University Press.

Martin, C., Fabes, R., Evans, S., & Wyman, H. (2000). Social cognition on the playground: Children's beliefs about playing with girls versus boys and their relationship to sex segregated play. *Journal of Social and Personal Relationships, 17*, 751–771.

Mayor, M. (2011). *Pink boots and a machete: My journey from NFL cheerleader to National Geographic explorer* (pp. 297, 298). Washington, DC: National Geographic Society.

Merolla, A. J. (2010). Relational maintenance during military deployment: Perspectives of wives of deployed U.S. Soldiers. *Journal of Applied Communication Research, 1*, 4–26.

Mulac, A., Bradac, J. J., & Gibbons, P. (2001). Empirical support for the gender-as-culture hypothesis: An intercultural analysis of male/female language differences. *Human Communication Research, 27*, 121–152.

Mulac, A. J., Wiemann, J. M., Widenmann, S. J., & Gibson, T. W. (1988). Male/female language differences and effects in same-sex and mixed-sex dyads: The gender-linked language effect. *Communication Monographs, 55*, 315–335.

New words in the ODE. (n.d.). Retrieved October 27, 2010, from http://newsfeed.time.com/new-words-in-the-ode/.

Offers Briton his talks "without attribution": Biden meets Kinnock, but he's not speechless. (1998, January 12). Retrieved September 7, 2010, from http://articles.latimes.com/1988-01-12/news/mn-35246_1_joe-biden.

Ogden, C. K., & Richards, I. A. (1923). *The meaning of meaning: A study of the influence of language upon thought and of the science of symbolism*. New York: Harcourt Brace & World.

pearanalytics. (2009, August). Twitter study. Retrieved October 27, 2010, from http://www.pearanalytics.com/blog/wp-content/uploads/2010/05/Twitter-Study-August-2009.pdf.

Pennebaker, J. W., Mehl, M. R., & Niederhoffer, K. G. (2003). Psychological aspects of natural language use: Our words, our selves. *Annual Review of Psychology, 54*, 547–577.

Perpetua, M. (2011, September 22). Usher accused of plagiarism. Retrieved October 30, 2011, from http://www.rollingstone.com/music/news/usher-accused-of-plagiarism- 20110922.

Petrow, S. (2009, February 9). "That's so gay" is not so funny. Huffington Post. Retrieved November 16, 2010, from http://www.huffingtonpost.com/steven-petrow/thats-so-gay-is-not-so-fu_b_165109.html.

Roth Walsh, M. (Ed.) (1997). *Women, men, and gender: Ongoing debates* (p. 87). Rensselaer, NY: Hamilton.

Shepard, J. (2010, October 2). Judy Shepard on Gay Suicides. *Advocate* [online].Retrieved November 11, 2011, from http://www.advocate.com/News/Daily_News/2010/10/02/Judy_Shepard_on_Gay_Suicides/.

Simmons, A. M. (2007, October 1). Biker groups escorts fallen troops; Patriot Guard riders, an informal organization of motorcyclists, attends funerals to pay tribute to military personnel. *Los Angeles Times*, p. 1B. Retrieved November 11, 2011 from http://articles.latimes.com/2007/oct/01/local/me-bikers1.

Sisters reunite after 18 years in checkout line. (1983, September 29). Retrieved January 21, 2012 from http://news.google.com/newspapers?nid=1876&dat=19830928&id=iWEsAAAAIBAJ&sjid=2c4EAAAAIBAJ&pg=6778,6962937

Spurgeon, T. (2011, October 26). David Simpson accused of plagiarizing Jeff MacNelly cartoon [blog]. Retrieved October 30, 2011, from http://www.comicsreporter.com/index.php/david_simpson_accused_of_plagiarizing_jeff_macnelly_cartoon/.

Tannen, D. (2001). *You just don't understand: Women and men in conversation*. New York: Morrow.

Tannen, D. (2007, July 15). Who does the talking here? *Washington Post*. Retrieved September 7, 2010, from http://www.washingtonpost.com/wp-dyn/content/article/2007/07/13/AR2007071301815_pf.html.

"That's so gay" prompts a lawsuit. (2007, February 28). Retrieved November 16, 2010, from http://www.msnbc.msn.com/id/17388702/.

Watzlawick, P., Beavin, J. H., & Jackson, D. D. (1967). Some tentative axioms of communication. In P. Watzlawick, J. H. Beavin, & D. D. Jackson (Eds.), *Pragmatics of human communication: A study of interactional patterns, pathologies, and paradoxes* (pp. 48–71). New York: W. W. Norton.

Westboro Baptist Church. (2010, December 8). News release. Retrieved November 11, 2011, from http://www.godhatesfags.com/fliers/20101220_God-Hates-The-Media-Launch.pdf.

Wood, J. T. (2000). He says/she says: Misunderstandings in communication between women and men. In D. O. Bairthwaite & J. T. Wood (Eds.), *Case studies in interpersonal communication* (pp. 93–100). Belmont, CA: Wadsworth.

Wood, J. T. (2011). *Gendered lives: Communication, gender, and culture*. (9th ed.). Boston: Wadsworth Cengage Learning.

Chapter 5

Armour, S. (2005, November 6). Generation Y: They've arrived at work with a new attitude. *USA Today*. Retrieved November 3, 2011, from http://www.usatoday.com/money /workplace/2005-11-06-gen-y_x.htm.

Belkin, L. (2007, July 26). Life's work: When whippersnappers and geezers collide. *New York Times*. Retrieved November 3, 2011, from https://www.marycrane.com/press/26-07-26-07 _NYT_When%20Whippersnappers%20and%20Geezers%20 Collide%20-%20New%20York%20Times.pdf.

Brookfield, S. (1995). *Becoming a critically reflective teacher* (p. 115). San Francisco: Jossey-Bass.

Burns, S. M., & Lohenry, K. (2010, September). Cellular phone use in class: Implications for teaching and learning a pilot study. *College Student Journal*, , 44, 805–810.

Chesebro, J. L. (1999). The relationship between listening styles and conversational sensitivity. *Communication Research Reports*, 16, 223–238.

Emanuel, R., Adams, J., Baker, K., Daufin, E. K., Ellington, C., Fitts, E., et al. (2008). How college students spend their time communicating, *International Journal of Listening*, 22, 13–28.

Hibbard, L. G. (2011). Communicating with the net generation. Retrieved November 3, 2011, from http://www.dtic.mil /cgi-bin/GetTRDoc?AD=ADA543101.

Johnson, M. K., Weaver, J. B., III, Watson, K. W., & Barker, L. B. (2000). Listening styles: Biological or psychological differences? *International Journal of Listening*, 14, 32–46.

Johnstone, A. H., & Percival, F. (1976). Attention breaks in lectures. *Education in Chemistry*, 13, 49–50.

Klemmer, E. T., & Snyder, F. W. (1972), Measurement of time spent communicating. *Journal of Communication*, 22, 142–158.

Kolb, D.A. (1984). *Experiential learning: Experience as the source of learning and development*. Englewood Cliffs, NJ: Prentice Hall.

Lee Hecht Harrison. (n.d.). *Managing today's multigenerational workforce*. Retrieved November 3, 2011, from http://www.lhh.com/knowledgecenter/Pages /Managingtodaysmultigenerationalworkforce.aspx.

Middendork, J., & Kalish, A. (1996). The "change-up" lectures. *The National Teaching and Learning Forum*, pp. 1–7.

Nichols, M. P. (1995). *The lost art of listening*. New York: Guilford Press.

Reavy, P. (2008, May 27). Cell phone use is creating new problems in schools. *Salt Lake City Deseret News*. Retrieved November 11, 2011 , from http://www.deseretnews.com /article/700229338/Cell-phone-use-is-creating-new-problems -in-schools.html.

Sargent, S. L., Weaver, J. B., III, & Kiewitz, C. (1997). Correlates between communication apprehension and listening style preferences. *Communication Research Reports*, 14, 74–78.

Sims, R. R., & Sims, S. J. (1995). *The importance of learning styles: Understanding the implications for learning, course design, and education*. Westport, CT: Greenwood.

Steil, L. K., Barker, L. L., & Watson, K. W. (1993). *Effective listening: Key to your success* (p. 51). New York: McGraw-Hill.

Understanding scientific jargon. (n.d.). Retrieved from http://science.discovery.com/quizzes/science-jargon /science-jargon-quiz.html.

Villeneuve, M. (2012, April 17). Report: Men still out-earning women. *Burlington Free Press* [online]. Retrieved April 18, 2012, from http://www.9to5.org/media/press/report -men-still-out-earning-women.

White House. (2012, April) Equal pay task force accomplishments: Fighting for fair pay in the workplace [online]. Retrieved April 18, 2012, from http://www.whitehouse.gov /sites/default/files/equal_pay_task_force.pdf.

Wolvin, A., & Coakly, C. G. (1996). *Listening* (5th ed., p. 232). Madison, WI: Brown & Benchmark.

Chapter 6

Alberts, J. K., Yoshimura, C., Rabby, M., & Loschiavo, R. (2005). Mapping the topography of couples' conversation. *Journal of Social and Personal Relationships*, 22, 299–322.

Allen, K. R., & Walker, A. J. (2000). Constructing gender in families. In R. M. Milardo & S. Duck (Eds.), *Families as relationships* (pp. 1–17). Chichester, UK: Wiley & Sons.

Altman, I., & Taylor, D. (1973). *Social penetration: The development of interpersonal relationships*. New York: Holt, Rinehart & Winston.

Biblarz, T. K., & Savci, E. (2010, June). Lesbian, gay, bisexual, and transgender families. *Journal of Marriage and Family*, 72, 480–497.

Canary, D., & Wahba, J. (2006). Do women work harder than men at maintaining relationships? In K. Dindia & D. Canary (Eds.), *Sex differences and similarities in communication* (2nd ed., pp. 359–377). Mahwah, NJ: Erlbaum.

Canary, D. J., & Stafford, L. (1994). Maintaining relationships through strategic and routine interaction. In D. Canary & L. Stafford (Eds.), *Communication and relational maintenance* (pp. 3–22). San Diego: Academic Press.

Cancian, F. M., & Oliker, S. J. (2000). *Caring and gender*. Thousand Oaks, CA: Pine Forge Press.

Collins, H. (2010, August 19) "Teacher quits after Facebook post, diss parents, kids" Retrieved April 23, 2012 from http://www.aolnews.com/2010/08/19/teacher-quits-after-facebook-posts-diss-parents-kids/.

DeFrancisco, V. P., & Palczewski, C. H. (2007). *Communicating gender diversity*. Thousand Oaks, CA: Sage.

Downing, J. B., & Goldberg, A. E. (2010). Lesbian mothers' constructions of the division of paid and unpaid labor. *Feminism & Psychology*, *21*, 100–120.

Eiler, S. (2010, July 30). Content management: Does an age divide exist? *PRWeb*. Retrieved from http://www.prweb.com/releases/Eiler-Communications/social-media.

Ellison, N. B., Steinfield, C., & Lampe, C. (2007). The benefits of Facebook friends: Social capital and college students' use of online social network sites. *Journal of Computer-Mediated Communication*, *12*, 1143–1168.

Facebook post prompts prison probe. (2010, February 25). KETV 7 [television broadcast]. Omaha, NE. Retrieved November 16, 2011, from http://www.ketv.com/r/22675556/detail.html.

Finholt, T., & Sproull, L. (1990). A social influence model of technology use. In J. Fulk & C. Steinfield (Eds.), *Organizations and communication technology* (pp. 117–140). Newbury Park, CA: Sage.

Fitzpatrick, M. A. (2003). *Between husbands and wives: Communication in marriage*. Newbury Park, CA: Sage.

Fry, R., & Cohn, D'V. (2010, July 19). *New economics of marriage: The rise of wives. Pew Research Center Publications.* Retrieved July 28, 2010, from http://pewresearch.org/pubs/1466/economics-marriage-rise-of-wives.

Galvin, K. M., Bylund, C. L., & Brommel, B. J. (2003). *Family communication: Cohesion and change* (6th ed., p. 5). Boston: Allyn & Bacon.

Gershon, I. (2010). *The breakup 2.0: Disconnecting over new media*. Ithaca, NY: Cornell University Press.

Goldberg, A. E., & Perry-Jenkins, M. (2007). The division of labor and perceptions of parental roles: Lesbian couples across the transition to parenthood. *Journal of Social and Personal Relationships*, *24*, 297–318.

Haas, S. M., & Stafford, L. (1998). An initial examination of relationships maintenance behaviors in gay and lesbian relationships. *Journal of Social and Personal Relationships*, *15*, 846–855.

Hinduja, S., & Patchin, J. W. (2010). Cyberbullying: Identification, prevention, and response. Cyberbullying Research Center. Retrieved January 27, 2011, from http://www.cyberbullying.us/Cyberbullying_Identification_Prevention_Response_Fact_Sheet.pdf.

H.S. teacher loses job over Facebook posting (2010, August 18). Retrieved from http://www.thebostonchannel.com/r/24670937/detail .html.

Knapp, M. L. (1978). *Social intercourse: From greeting to goodbye*. Boston: Allyn & Bacon.

Knapp, M. L. (1984). *Interpersonal communication and human relationships*. Boston: Allyn & Bacon.

Knapp, M. L., & Daly, J. A. (2010). *Interpersonal communication* (4 vols.). Sage Benchmarks in Communication. London: Sage.

Laner, R., & Ventrone, N. A. (2000). Dating scripts revisited. *Journal of Family Issues*, *21*, 488–500.

Martin, J., & Nakayama, T. (2004). *Experiencing intercultural communication: An introduction* (2nd ed., pp. 27–28).

Military life. (n.d.). National Geographic [Online]. Retrieved from http://video.nationalgeographic.com/video/national-geographic-channel/specials-1/bin-laden-1/ngc-military-life/.

Mondello, B. (2010, July 14). *We are family: Two moms, a baster and a baddie*. National Public Radio. Retrieved July 14, 2010, from http://www.npr.org/templates/story/story.php?storyId=128407987.

Monsour, M. (2002). *Women and men as friends: Relationships across the lifespan in the twenty-first century*. Mahwah, NJ: Lawrence Erlbaum Associates.

National Public Radio. (2009, November 25). 2010 census will count same-sex couples. Retrieved July 10, 2010, from http://www.npr.org/templates/story/story.php?storyId=120816467&sc=emaf.

Nie, N., & Hillygus, D. S. (2002). The impact of Internet use on sociability: Time-diary findings. *IT & Society*, *1*, 1–20.

Peplau, L. A., & Beals, K. P. (2004). The family lives of lesbians and gay men. In A. L. Vangelisti (Ed.), *Handbook of family communication* (pp. 233–248). Mahwah, NJ: Erlbaum.

Petronio, S. (2002). *Boundaries of privacy: Dialectics of disclosure*. Albany: SUNY Press.

Pettigrew, J. (2009). Text messaging and connectedness within close interpersonal relationships. *Marriage & Family Review*, *45*(6–8), 697–716.

Putnam, R. D. (1995). Bowling alone: America's declining social capital. *Journal of Democracy*, *6*(1), 65–78.

Rainie, J. L. (2010, January 5). Report: Internet, broadband, and cell phone statistics. Pew Research Center Internet and American Life Project. Retrieved July 22, 2010, from http://www.pewinternet.org/Reports/2010/Internet-broadband-and-cell-phone-statistics/Report.aspx?r=1.

Rawlins, W. K. (1981). *Friendship as a communicative achievement: A theory and an interpretive analysis of verbal reports.* Unpublished doctoral dissertation. Temple University, Philadelphia.

Schwartz, M. J. (2010, June 22). Teens engage in risky online behavior. *InformationWeek.* Retrieved July 22, 2010 from http://www.informationweek.com/news/.

Shah, D. V., McLeod, J. M., & Yoon, S. (2001). Communication, context, and community: An exploration of print, broadcast, and Internet influences. *Communication Research, 28,* 464–506.

Spence, J. T., & Buckner, C. E. (2000). Instrumental and expressive traits, trait stereotypes, and sexist attitudes: What do they signify? *Psychology of Women Quarterly, 24,* 44–63.

Sproull, L., & Kiesler, S. (1986). Reducing social context cues: Electronic mail in organizational communication. *Management Science, 32,* 1492–1512.

Stevens, B. (2011, June 21). Social media and divorces: Examining the impact of Facebook and Twitter on relationships. Retrieved November 16, 2011, from http://www.scfamilylaw.com/2011/06/articles/divorce/guest-post-social-media-and-divorces-examining-the-impact-of-facebook-and-twitter-on-relationships/.

STOP cyberbullying. (n.d.). Retrieved January 27, 2011, from http://www.stopcyberbullying.org/what_is_cyberbullying_exactly.html.

Tom Tong, S., Van Der Heide, B., Langwell, L., & Walther, J. B. (2008). Too much of a good thing? The relationship between number of friends and interpersonal impressions on Facebook. *Journal of Computer-Mediated Communication, 13,* 531–549.

U.S. Census Bureau. (2009, November). Custodial mothers and fathers and their child support: 2007. Retrieved August 7, 2010, from http://www.census.gov/prod/2009pubs/p60-237.pdf.

U.S. Census Bureau. (2011, September 27). Census Bureau releases estimates of same-sex married couples. Retrieved November 16, 2011, from http://www.census.gov/newsroom/releases/archives/2010_census/cb11-cn181.html.

USC Annenberg School for Communication and Journalism, Center for the Digital Future.. (2011, June 3). 2010 digital future report. Retrieved November 16, 2011, from http://www.digitalcenter.org/pdf/2011_digital_future_final_release.pdf.

Vlahakis, G. (2010, July 22). "The breakup 2.0": A look at how new media is used to end relationships. Retrieved November 16, 2011, from http://www.eurekalert.org/pub_releases/2010-07/iu-b2072110.php.

Wood, J. (2013). *Gendered lives: Communication, gender, and culture* (10th ed., pp. 20–21). Boston: Cengage Learning.

Wright, P. H. (1982). Men's friendships, women's friendships, and the alleged inferiority of the latter. *Sex Roles, 8,* 1–20.

Chapter 7

Al-Ani, B., Mark, G., & Semaan, B. (2010). Blogging in a region of conflict: Supporting transition to recovery. In *Proceedings of the 28th International Conference on Human Factors in Computing Systems* (CHI 2010) (pp. 1069–1078). Atlanta: ACM Press. Retrieved November 29, 2011 from http://dmrussell.net/CHI2010/docs/p1069.pdf.

Aylor, B. (2003). Maintaining long-distance relationships. In D. J. Canary & M. Dainton (Eds.), *Maintaining relationships through communication: Relational, contextual, and cultural variations* (pp. 127–140). Mahwah, NJ: Lawrence Erlbaum Associates.

Bern, S. L., & Lenney, E. (1976). Sex-typing and the avoidance of psychological androgyny. *Journal of Personality and Social Psychological*: *International Journal of Conflict Management, 31,* 634–643.

Bone, J. E., Griffin, C. L., & Scholz, T. M. L. (2008). Beyond traditional conceptualizations of rhetoric: Invitational rhetoric and a move toward civility. *Western Journal of Communication, 72*(4), 434–462.

Brower, N., Mitchell, P., & Weber, N. (2002). Gender role, organizational status, and conflict management styles. *International Journal of Conflict Management, 13*(4), 78–94.

Carter, S. L. (1998). *Civility: Manners, morals and the etiquette of democracy.* New York: Basic.

Clark, L. S. (2009, April). Digital media and the generation gap: Qualitative research on U.S. teens and their parents. *Information, Communication & Society, 12*(3), 388–407, 403.

Dainton, M., & Aylor, B. (2001). A relational uncertainty analysis of jealousy, trust, and maintenance in long-distance versus geographically close relationships. *Communication Quarterly, 49,* 172–188.

Domestic Violence Statistics. (n.d.). Retrieved June 7, 2011, from http://domesticviolencestatistics.org/domestic-violence-statistics//.

Ferber, A., Jimenez, C.M., Herrera, A. O., & Samuels, D. R. (2008). *The matrix reader: Examining the dynamics of oppression and privilege.* Boston: McGraw-Hill Higher Education.

Gerstel, N., & Gross, H. (1984). *Commuter marriage: A study of work and family.* New York: Guilford.

Hall, E. T., & Hall, M. R. (1989). *Understanding cultural differences.* Yarmouth, ME: Intercultural Press.

Hofstede, G. (1986). Cultural differences in teaching and learning. *International Journal of Intercultural Relations, 10,* 301–320.

Holstrom, A. J. (2009). Sex and gender similarities and differences in communication values in same-sex and cross-sex friendships. *Communication Quarterly, 57*(2), 224–238.

Holt, J. L., & DeVore, C. J. (2005). Culture, gender, organizational role, and styles of conflict resolution: A meta-analysis. *International Journal of Intercultural Relations, 29*, 165–196.

hooks, b. (2004). *The will to change: Men, masculinity, and love.* New York: Washington Square Press.

Johnson, A. J., Becker, J., Craig, E. A., Gilchrist, E. S., & Haigh, M. M. (2009). Changes in Friendship commitment: Comparing geographically close and long-distance young-adult friendships. *Communication Quarterly, 57*(4), 395–415.

Johnson, A. J., Wittenberg, E., Haigh, M., Wigley, S., Becker, J, Brown, K., et al. (2004). The process of relationship development and deterioration: Turning points in friendships that have terminated. *Communication Quarterly, 52*, 54–67.

Kaushal, R., & Kwantes, C. T. (2006). The role and personality in choice of conflict management strategy. *International Journal of Intercultural Relations, 30*, 580, 581.

Kayany, J. M. (1998). Contexts of uninhibited online behavior: Flaming in social newsgroups on Usenet. *Journal of the American Society for Information Science, 49*(12), 1135–1141.

Kimmel, M. (2011). *The gendered society* (4th ed.). London: Oxford University Press.

Kunkel, A. W., & Burleson, B. R. (1998). Social support and the emotional lives of men and women: An assessment of the different cultures perspective. In D. Canary & K. Dindia (Eds.), *Sex differences and similarities in communication: Critical essays and empirical investigations of sex and gender in interaction* (pp. 101–125). Mahwah, NJ: Lawrence Erlbaum Associates.

Leung, K., & Lind, E. A. (1986). Procedural justice and culture: Effects of culture, gender, and investigator status on procedural preferences. *Journal of Personality and Social Psychology, 50*(6), 1134–1140.

Lloyd, S. A., & Cate, R. M. (1985). The developmental course of conflict in dissolution or premarital relationships. *Journal of Social and Personal Relationships, 2*, 179–194.

Merolla, A. J. (2010). Relational maintenance and noncopresence reconsidered: Conceptualizing geographic separation in close relationships. *Communication Theory, 20* (2), 169–193.

National Coalition Against Domestic Violence. (n.d.). Domestic violence facts. Retrieved November 16, 2011, from http://www.ncadv.org/files/DomesticViolenceFactSheet (National).pdf.

Putnam, L. (2010). Communication as changing the negotiation game. *Journal of Applied Communication Research, 38*(4), 325–335.

Ratcliff, K. (2005). *Rhetorical listening: Identification, gender, whiteness.* Carbondale: Southern Illinois University Press.

Rohlfing, M. E. (1995). Doesn't anybody stay in one place anymore? An exploration of the understudied phenomenon of long-distance relationships. In J. T. Wood & S. Duck (Eds.), *Understudied relationships: Off the beaten track* (pp. 173–196). Thousand Oaks, CA: Sage.

Sarah, A. A. (2009, May 6). A conflict close to home. Retrieved November 29, 2011 from http://azizabusarah.wordpress .com/2009/05/06/a-conflict-close-to-home/.

Seo, K. K., Miller, P. C., Schmidt, C., & Sowa, P. C. (2008). Patience, creating synergy between collectivism and individualism in cyberspace: A comparison of online communication patterns between Hong Kong and U.S. students. *Journal of Intercultural Communication*, no. 18. Retrieved November 29, 2011 from http://www.immi.se/jicc/index .php/jicc/article/view/55/28.

Stafford, L., & Merolla, A. J. (2007). Idealization, reunions, and stability in long-distance dating relationships. *Journal of Social and Personal Relationships, 24*, 37–54.

Stafford, L., Merolla, A. J., & Castle, J. D. (2006). When long-distance dating partners become geographically close. *Journal of Social and Personal Relationships, 23*(6), 901–919.

Taylor, M., & Segrin, C. (2010). Perceptions of parental gender roles and conflict style and their association with young adults' relational and psychological well-being. *Communication Research Reports, 27*(3), 230–242.

Thomas, K. W., & Kilmann, R. H. (2007). Thomas-Kilmann conflict mode instrument: Profile and interpretative report. Retrieved April 24, 2012, from http://www.opp.eu.com /SiteCollectionDocuments/pdfs/reports/tki_profile_and _interpretive_sample_report_sample.pdf.

Thornton, S. (2010). Spreading the message: FrontlineSMS uses mobile technology to help people help themselves. Retrieved November 29, 2011, from http://education .nationalgeographic.com/education/news/spreading -message/?ar_a=1&ar_r=3#page=2

Warech, M. A., Smither, J. W., Reilly, R. R., Millsap, R. E., & Reilly, S. P. (1998). Self-monitoring and 360-degree ratings. *Leadership Quarterly, 9*, 449–473.

White Ribbon Campaign. (2011). Retrieved April 24, 2012 from http://www.whiteribbon.com/about_us/.

Wood, J. (2013). *Gendered lives: Communication, gender, and culture* (10th ed.). Boston: Cengage Learning.

Zhang, S., Merolla, A., & Lin, S.-F. 2009, November. *The nature and consequences of topic avoidance in Chinese and Taiwanese close relationships*. Paper presented at annual meeting of National Communication Association, 95th Annual Convention, Chicago. Available at http://www.allacademic.com/meta/p367288_index.html.

Chapter 8

Albrecht, L. B., & Brewer, R. M. (1990). *Bridges of power: Women's multicultural alliances*. Philadelphia: New Society.

Ashcraft, K. (2001). Feminist organizing and the construction of "alternative" community. In G. J. Shepherd & E. W. Rothenbuhler (Eds.), *Communication and community* (pp. 79–110). Mahwah, NJ: Lawrence Erlbaum.

Bakhtin, M. M. (1993). *Toward a philosophy of the act* (V. Liapunov & M. Holquist, Eds.; V, Liapunov, Trans.). Austin: University of Texas Press. (Original work published 1979)

Batra, N. D. (2008). *Digital freedom: How much can you handle?* New York: Rowman & Littlefield.

Boyes, S. (2011). Crossing the Okavango Delta for world heritage status: Celebrating Botswana's wetland wilderness. Retrieved December 27, 2011 from http://newswatch.nationalgeographic.com/2011/12/22/crossing-the-okavango-delta-for-world-heritage-status-celebrating-botswanas-wetland-wilderness.

Bulletin Community Forum FAQ. (n.d.). Retrieved November 2011 from https://www.vbulletin.com/forum/faq.php?faq=vb3_board_usage#faq_vb3_forums_threads_posts.

Castells, M. (2009). *Communication power*. London: Oxford University Press.

Cong, G., Wang, L., Lin, C.-Y., Song, Y.-I., & Sun, Y. (2008). Finding question-answer pairs from online forums. In T.-S. Chua & M.-K. Leong (General Chairs), *Proceedings of the 31st Annual International ACM SIGIR Conference on Research and Development in Information Retrieval* (pp. 467–474). New York: Association for Computer Machinery.

Corbett, P. (2010, January 4). Facebook demographics and statistics report 2010: 145% Growth in 1 year. Retrieved July 2010 from http://www.istrategylabs.com/2010/01/facebook-demographics-and-statistics-report-2010-145-growth-in-1-year/.

Cousteau, A. (2009). Alexandra Cousteau's Blue Planet. Retrieved December 27, 2011 from http://newswatch.nationalgeographic.com/tag/blue-planet/.

Cousteau, A. (2011). Blue legacy. Retrieved December 27, 2011 from http://www.alexandracousteau.org/blue-legacy-overview.

Cousteau, A. (2012, January 18). Telephone communication.

Darlington, P. S. E., & Mulvaney, B. M. (2002). Gender, rhetoric, and power: Toward a model of reciprocal empowerment. *Women's Studies in Communication*, 25, 139–172.

Davison, K. P., Pennebaker, J. W., & Dickerson, S. S. (2000). Who talks? The social psychology of illness support groups. *American Psychologist*, 55(2), 205–217.

Dewey, J. (1910). *How we think*. Boston: D.C. Heath.

Everest Peace Project. (2009). Retrieved November 11, 2011 from www.everestpeaceproject.com/about/everest-peace-climbers/everest-peace-climbers.html.

Fahmy, M. (2010, May 11). Face-to-face time makes us happier than Facebook. Retrieved November 11, 2011 from www.reuters.com.

Foucault, M. (1972). *The archaeology of knowledge and the discourse on language*. (A. M. S. Smith, Trans.). New York: Pantheon.

French, J. R., & Raven, B. (1968). The basis of social power. In D. Cartright & A. Zander (Eds.), *Group dynamics*. New York: Harper & Row.

Frey, L. R. (Ed.). (1999). *The handbook of group communication theory and research*. Thousand Oaks, CA: Sage.

Frey, L. R. (Ed.). (2003). *Group communication in context: Studies of bona fide groups* (2nd ed.). Mahwah, NJ: Lawrence Erlbaum.

Goodwin, P. J., Leszcz, M., Ennis, M., Koopmans, J., Vincent, L., Guther, H., et al. (2001). The effect of group psychosocial support on survival in metastatic breast cancer. *New England Journal of Medicine*, 345, 1719–1726.

Green, D. A. (2011, March). Twitter is more than just a fad, so don't miss the boat. The Lawyer. Retrieved November 8, 2011, from www.thelawyer.com.

Hofstede, G. (2010). *Cultures and organizations: Software of the mind* (p. 158). New York: McGraw-Hill.

Internet and Environmental Education. (2010, June 23). Environmental panel. YouTube Harvard Extension. Retrieved December 27, 2011 from http://www.youtube.com/watch?v=lekNrH9edaM.

Janis, I. L. (1972). *Victims of groupthink* (p. 9). Boston: Houghton Mifflin.

Jansenn, D., & Kies, R. (2005, September). Online forums and deliberative democracy. *Acta Politica*, 40(3), 317–335.

Johnson, C. E. (2009). *Meeting the ethical of leadership: Casting light or shadow* (p. 8). Newbury Park, CA: Sage, 2009.

Kelly, J. A., Murphy, D. A., Bahr, G. R., Kalichman, S. C., Morgan, M. G., Stevenson, L. Y., Koob, J. J., Brasfield, T. L., & Bernstein,

B. M. (1993). Outcome of cognitive-behavioral and support group brief therapies for depressed, HIV-infected persons. *American Journal of Psychiatry*, *150*, 1679–1686.

Kets de Vires, M. F. R. (2001). *Struggling with the demon: Perspectives on individual and organizational irrationality* (p. 189). Madison: Psychosocial Press.

Kiesler, S., & Sproull, L. (1992). Group decision making and communication technology. *Organizational Behavior and Human Decision Processes*, *52*, 96–123.

Littlejohn, S. W., & Foss, K. A. (2007). *Theories of human communication* (8th ed., p. 232). Boston: Wadsworth/Cengage.

Mesterhazy, L. (2008, September 23). Two Israelis and a Palestinian: Conquering Everest together. Retrieved November 17, 2011 from http://www.haaretz.com/news/two-israelis-and-a-palestinian-conquering-everest-together-1.254383.

Minors, Z. (2010, August 16). Twitter goes to college, Retrieved November 8, 2011 from http://www.usnews.com.

O'Sullivan, P. B., & Flanagin, A. J. (n.d.). An interactional reconceptualization of "flaming" and other problematic messages. Retrieved November 17, 2011 from http://my.ilstu.edu/~posull/flaming.htm.

Putnam, L. L., & Stohl, C. (1990). Bona fide groups: A reconceptualization of groups in context. *Communication Studies*, *41*, 248–265.

Reid, M., & Hammersley, R. (2000). *Communicating successfully in groups: A practical guide for the workplace* (pp. 82–92, 92–99). Philadelphia: Routledge.

Starhawk. (1990). *Truth or dare: Encounters with power, authority, and mystery*. San Francisco: Harper & Row.

Stohl, C. (2001). Globalizing organizational communication. In F. M. Jablin & L. L. Putnam (Eds.), *The new handbook of organizational communication: Advances in theory, research, and methods* (pp. 323–375). Thousand Oaks, CA: Sage.

What Is an "Internet Forum"? (n.d.). Videojug Corporation Limited. Retrieved November 17, 2011 from http://www.videojug.com/expertanswer/internet-communities-and-forums-2/what-is-an-internet-forum.

Wilson, G., & Hanna, M. (1986). *Groups in context: Leadership and participation in decision making groups*. New York: McGraw-Hill.

Chapter 9

Alderton, S. M., & Frey, L. R. (1986). Argumentation in small group decision-making. In R. Y. Hirokawa & M. S. Poole (Eds.), *Communication and group decision making* (pp. 157–173). Beverly Hills, CA: Sage.

Alsever, J. (2008, October 20). How to handle a workplace bully. Retrieved from www.cbsnews.com/8301- 505125 _162-51242687/how-to-handle-a-workplace-bully/.

Barbuto, J. E. , Fritz, S. M., Matkin, G. S., & Marx, D. B. (2007). Effects of gender, education, and age upon leaders' use of influence tactics and full range leadership behaviors. *Sex Roles*, *56*, 71–83.

Bass, B. M. (1985). *Leadership and performance*. New York: Free Press.

Burns, J. M. (1978). *Leadership*. New York: Harper & Row.

Cherry, K. (n.d.). What is laissez-faire leadership? Retrieved June 9, 2011, from http://psychology.about.com/od /leadership/f/laissez-faire-leadership.html.

Cohen, A. (2010, July 21). New laws target workplace bullying. *Time*. Retrieved June 9, 2011, from http://www.time .com/time/nation/article/0,8599,2005358,00.html.

Davenport, N., Schwartz, R. D., & Elliott, G. P. (2005). *Mobbing: Emotional abuse in the American workplace*. Collins, IA: Civil Society Publishing.

Druskat, V. U. (1994). Gender and leadership style: Transformational and transactional leadership in the Roman Catholic Church. *Leadership Quarterly*, *5*, 99–119.

Eagly, A. H., Johannesen-Schmidt, M. C., & van Engen, M. L. (2003, July). Transformational, transactional, and laissez-faire leadership styles: A meta-analysis comparing women and men. *Psychological Bulletin*, *129*(4), 569–591.

Fairhurst, G. T. (2001). Dualisms in leadership research. In F. M. Jablin & L. L. Putnam (Eds.), *The new handbook of organizational communication: Advances in theory, research, and methods* (pp. 379–439). Thousand Oaks, CA: Sage.

Fisher, B. A. (1970). Decision emergence: Phases in group decision making. *Speech Monographs*, *37*, 53–66.

Food Not Bombs. (n.d.). The story of Food Not Bombs. Retrieved January 15, 2012, from http://www.foodnotbombs .net/story.html.

Forsyth, D. R. (1990). *Group dynamics* (2nd ed., p. 369). Pacific Grove, CA: Brooks/Cole Publishing.

Frey, L. R. (Ed.). (2003). *Group communication in context: Studies of bona fide groups* (2nd ed.). Mahwah, NJ: Lawrence Erlbaum.

Gastil, J. (1994). A definition and illustration of democratic leadership. *Human Relations*, *47*, 953–975.

Halverson, S., Murphy, S. E., & Riggio, R. E. (2004). Charismatic leadership in crisis situations: A laboratory investigation of stress and crisis. *Small Group Research*, *35*, 495–514.

Hirokawa, R. Y., & Salazar, A. J. (1999). Task group communication and decision making performance. In L. R. Frey, D. S. Gouran, &

M. S. Poole (Eds.), *The handbook of group communication theory and research* (pp. 167–191). Thousand Oaks, CA: Sage.

House, R. J. (2004). Illustrative examples of GLOBE findings. In *Culture, leadership, and organizations: The GLOBE study of 62 societies* (p. 4). Thousand Oaks, CA: Sage.

House, R.J., Hanges, P. J., Javidan, M., Drofman, P. W., & Gupta, V. (Eds.). (2004). Culture, leadership, and organizations: The GLOBE study of 62 societies (p.4). Thousand Oaks, CA: Sage.

House, R. J. , Hanges, P. J., Ruiz-Quintanilla, S. A., Dorfman, P. W., Javidan, M., Dickson, M., et al. (n.d.). Cultural influences on leadership and organizations: Project GLOBE (p. 2). Retrieved June 9, 2011 from http://www.thunderbird.edu/wwwfiles/sites/globe/pdf/process.pdf.

Jamieson, K. H. (1995). *Beyond the double bind: Women and leadership*. London: Oxford University Press.

Keyton, J., & Stallworth, V. (2003). On the verge of collaboration: Interaction processes versus group outcomes. In L. R. Frey (Ed.), *Group communication in context: Studies of bona fide groups* (2nd ed., pp. 235–260). Mahwah, NJ: Lawrence Erlbaum.

Lewin, K., Lippitt, R., & White, R. (1939). Patterns of aggressive behavior in experimentally created "social climates." *Journal of Social Psychology, 10*, 271–299.

Miller, K. (2006). *Organizational communication: Approaches and processes* (4th ed., p. 184). Belmont, CA: Thomson/Wadsworth.

Namie, G., & Namie, R. (2011). *The bully-free workplace: Stop jerks, weasels, and snakes from killing your organization*. New York: Wiley.

National Coalition for Dialogue and Deliberation. (n.d.). Retrieved February 11, 2012 from http://www.ncdd.org.

National Geographic. (n.d.). Lessons from the field. Retrieved November 2011, from http://environment.nationalgeographic.com/environment/water-lessons-from-the-field/.

Oetzel, J. G., & Ting-Toomey, S. (Eds.). (2006). *The Sage handbook of conflict communication: Integrating theory, research, and practice*. Thousand Oaks, CA: Sage.

Poole, M. S., & Garner, J. T. (2006). Perspectives on workgroup conflict and communication. In J. G. Oetzel & S. Ting-Toomey (Eds.), *The Sage handbook of conflict communication: Integrating theory, research, and practice* (pp. 267–292). Thousand Oaks, CA: Sage.

Popper, M. (2005). *Leaders who transform society: What drives them and why we are attracted to them* (pp. 18–21, 27–28). Westport, CT: Praeger.

Reid, M., & Hammersley, R. (2000). *Communicating successfully in groups: A practical guide for the workplace* (pp. 36–37). Philadelphia: Routledge.

Salazar, A. J. , Hirokawa, R. Y., Propp, K. M., Julian, K. M., & Leatham, G. B. (1994, June). In search of true causes: Examination of the effect of group potential and group interaction on decision performance. *Human Communication Research, 20*(4), 529–599.

Sargent, C. (2006). *From buddy to boss: Effective fire service leadership*. Tulsa, OK: PennWell Corp.

Seibold, D. R., & Meyers, R. A. (1986). Communication and influence in group decision-making. In R. Y. Hirokawa & M. S. Poole (Eds.), *Communication and group decision making* (pp. 133–156). Beverly Hills, CA: Sage.

Skogstad, A., Ståle, E., Torsheim, T., Aasland, M. S., & Hetland, H. (2007, January). The destructiveness of laissez-faire leadership behavior. *Journal of Occupational Health Psychology, 12*(1), 80–92.

Washington State Department of Labor. (2011, April). *Workplace bullying and disruptive behavior: What everyone needs to know*. Report no. 87-2-2011. Olympia: Washington State Department of Labor & Industries. Retrieved June 9, 2011, from http://www.lni.wa.gov/safety/research/files/bullying.pdf.

Western, S. (2008). *Leadership: A critical text* (pp. 23, 35). Thousand Oaks, CA: Sage.

Workplace Bullying Institute. (2011). Work shouldn't hurt. Retrieved June 9, 2011, from http://www.workplacebullying.org/targets/starthere.html.

Chapter 10

Andeweg, B. A., de Jong, J. C., & Hoeken, H. (1998). "May I have your attention?" Exordial techniques in informative oral presentations. *Technical Communication Quarterly, 7*(3), 281.

Bennett, J., & Ellison, J. (2010, April 10). Tracking the wage gap: In honor of equal pay day, 12 sobering figures about men, women, and work. *Newsweek*. Retrieved from http://www.newsweek.com/2010/04/19/tracking-the-wage-gap.html.

Braun, D. (2009, June 18). Angelina Jolie has a heartfelt message for World Refugee Day. National Geographic. Retrieved from http://newswatch.nationalgeographic.com/2009/06/18/angelina_jolie_world_refugee_day.

Browne, A., & Williams, K. R. (1993). Gender, intimacy, and lethal violence: Trends from 1976–1987. *Gender & Society, 7*(1), 78–98.

Buzawa, E., Austin, T. L., & Buzawa, G. G. (1995). Responding to crimes of violence against women: Gender differences versus organizational imperatives. *Crime and Delinquency, 41*(4), 443–466.

Dobash, R. P., Dobash, R. E., Cavanagh, K., & Lewis, R. (1998). Separate and intersecting realities: A comparison of men's and women's accounts of violence against women. *Violence Against Women*, 4(4), 382–414.

Eagly, A. H., & Chaiken, S. (1998). Attitude structure and function. In *Handbook of Social Psychology*, 4th ed. Eds. Gilbert, D. T., Fiske, S. T., & Lindzey, G. Boston: McGraw-Hill. 1, 323–390.

Earle, S. (2009). *The world is blue: How our fate and the ocean's are one*. Washington, DC: National Geographic Books.

Facts about violence. (2010). Retrieved January 7, 2012, from http://feminist.com/antiviolence/facts.html.

Federal Bureau of Investigation. (1989). *Crime in the United States. Uniform crime reports*. Washington, DC: U.S. Department of Justice.

Federal Bureau of Investigation. (1995, August). Violence against women: Estimates from the redesigned survey. Available from http://www.ojp.usdoj.gov.

Fenske, M. (2004). Movement and resistance (tattooed) bodies and performance. *Text and Performance Quarterly*, 4(1), 51–73.

Kidder, R. M. (1994). *Shared values for a troubled world*. San Francisco: Jossey-Bass.

Knapp, M. L., Hart, R. P., Friedrick, G. W., & Shulman, G. M. (1973). The rhetoric of goodbye: Verbal and nonverbal correlates of human leave-taking. *Speech Monographs*, 40(3), 182–198.

Lackie, L., & de Man, A. F. (1997). Correlates of sexual aggression among male university students. *Sex Roles*, 37(5–6), 451–457.

Lineberry, C. (2007a). Tattoos: The ancient and mysterious history. Retrieved June 24, 2010, from http://www.smithsonianmag.com/history-archaeology/1002306.html#ixzz0pX08ZUVx.

Lineberry, C. (2007b). Today's tattoos. Retrieved from http://www.smithsonianmag.com/people-places/tattoo_modern.html.

Marshall, G. (Ed.). (1994). *The concise Oxford dictionary of sociology* (p. 315). New York: Oxford University Press.

National Coalition Against Domestic Violence. (n.d.). Domestic violence facts. Retrieved January 7, 2012, from http://www.ncadv.org/files/DomesticViolenceFactSheet(National).pdf.

National Geographic.com. (n.d.). Ocean hero: Sylvia Earle. Retrieved December 27, 2011, from http://ocean.nationalgeographic.com/ocean/take-action/ocean-hero-sylvia-earle/.

National Geographic.com. (2009, October 10). National Geographic explorer-in-residence Sylvia Earle spots crisis facing our seas. Retrieved December 27, 2011, from http://www.thecre.com/zoning-news/?p=382.

National Organization for Women. (n.d.). Violence against women in the United States: Statistics. Retrieved January 7, 2012, from http://www.now.org/issues/violence/stats.html.

Olson, J. M., & Zanna, M. P. (1993). Attitudes and attitude change. *Annual Review of Psychology*, 44, 117–154.

Pew Research Center for People and the Press. (2007, January 9). A portrait of "Generation Next": How young people view their lives, futures, and politics. Retrieved May 24, 2011, from http://people-press.org/report/300/a-portrait-of-generation-next.

Rokeach, M. (1970). *Beliefs, attitudes, and values: A theory of organization and change*. San Francisco: Jossey-Bass.

Rokeach, M. (1973). *The nature of human values*. New York: Free Press.

Rosa, A., & Escholz, P. (1996). *The writer's brief handbook* (2nd ed., p. 7). Scarborough, Ontario, Canada: Allyn & Bacon.

Schwartz, S. H., & Blisky, W. (1990). Toward a theory of the universal content and structure of values: Extensions and cross-cultural replications. *Journal of Personality and Social Psychology*, 58(5), 878–891.

UNHCR. (n.d.). Goodwill ambassadors. Retrieved Feburary 17, 2012, from http://www.unhcr.org/pages/49c3646c3e.html.

U.S. Bureau of Labor Statistics. (2010). Labor force statistics from the current population survey 2010. Retrieved January 7, 2012, from http://www.bls.gov/cps/demographisc.hem#women.

Wood, J. T. (2013). *Gendered lives: Communication, gender, and culture* (10th ed.). Boston: Wadsworth/Cengage.

Chapter 11

Alder, J., & Carmichael, M. (2005, January 20). The tsunami threat. *Newsweek*, p. 42.

Best, J. (2001). *Damned lies and statistics: Untangling numbers from the media, politicians, and activists*. Berkeley: University of California Press.

Best, J. (2008). *Stat-spotting: A field guide to identifying dubious data*. Berkeley: University of California Press.

Bolner, M. S., & Poirier, G. A. (2002). *The research process: Books and beyond* (2nd ed., pp. 144–145, 168, 248). Dubuque, IA: Kendall/Hunt.

Buddy T. (2009, October 15). White House launches anti-meth campaign. Retrieved from http://alcoholism.about.com/b/2009/10/15/white-house-launches-anti-meth-campaign.htm.

Campbell, K. K. (Ed.). (1989). *Man cannot speak for her: Key texts of the early feminists*. New York: Praeger.

Casey, M. K., Timmermann, L., Allen, M., Krahn, S., & Turkiewicz, K. L. (2009). Response and self-efficacy of condom use: A meta-analysis of this important element of AIDS education and prevention. *Southern Communication Journal, 74*(1), 57–78.

Crossen, C. (1994). *Tainted truth: The manipulation of fact in America* (p. 42). New York: Simon & Schuster.

Fadei, R. (Ed.). (2000). *Applied algebra and statistics* (pp. 544, 545). Needham Heights, MA: Simon & Schuster.

Faigley, L., & Selzer, J. (2000). *Good reasons*. Needham Heights, MA: Allyn & Bacon.

Fisher, W. R. (1987). *Human communication as narration: Toward a philosophy of reason, value, and action* (p. 58). Columbia: University of South Carolina Press.

Fitch, S. P., & Mandziuk, R. M. (1997). *Sojourner Truth as orator: Wit, story, and song*. Westport, CT: Greenwood Press.

Gleason, M. M. (1999). The role of evidence in argumentative writing. *Reading & Writing Quarterly, 14*, 81–106.

Hult, C. A. (1996). *Researching and writing across the curriculum* (pp. 28–29). Boston: Allyn & Bacon.

Inch, E. S., & Warnick, B. (1998). *Critical thinking and communication: The use of reason in argument* (3rd ed., pp. 194–197). Boston: Allyn & Bacon.

Jamieson, K. H. (1988). *Eloquence in the electronic age: The transformation of political speechmaking* (p. 140). New York: Oxford University Press.

Jessop, D. C., & Wade, J. (2008, November). Fear appeals and binge drinking: A terror management theory perspective. *British Journal of Health Psychology* [serial online], *13*(4), 773–788. Retrieved May 27, 2010, from Academic Search Premier, Ipswich, MA.

Kahane, H., & Cavender, N. (1998). *Logic and contemporary rhetoric: The use of reason in everyday life* (8th ed.). Belmont, CA: Wadsworth.

Kalb, C. (2010, March 22). Culture of corpulence: American innovations in food, transportation, and technology are threatening to supersize us all. *Newsweek*, pp. 42-48.

Kennedy, G. (1991). *On rhetoric: A theory of civic discourse* (p. 37). New York: Oxford: Oxford University Press.

Kennedy, S. D. (1998). *Best bet Internet: Reference and research when you don't have time to mess around* (pp. 144–145). Chicago: American Library Association.

Killenberg, G., & Anderson, R. (1989). *Before the story: Interviewing and communication skills for journalists*. New York: St. Martin's Press.

King, L. (1995). *The best of Larry King Live: The greatest interviews*. Atlanta: Times.

Life or Meth. (2002). Australia's Life or Meth organization reports a 45 percent reduction of meth use in teens and a 75 percent reduction in adults. Retrieved May, 27, 2010, from http://www.lifeormeth.com/.

Lin, A. Y-M. (2012a). "Albert Yu-Min Lin, Research Scientist and Engineer" http://www.nationalgeographic.com/explorers/bios/albert-lin/ accessed January 31, 2012.

Lin, A. Y-M. (2012b). "In search of Genghis Kahn's Tomb" http://www.nationalgeographic.com/explorers/bios/albert-lin/ accessed January 31, 2012.

Lin, A. Y-M. (2012c). "The Missing Tomb" http://www.nationalgeographic.com/explorers/bios/albert-lin/ accessed January 31, 2012.

Limbaugh to NYTimes environment reporter Revkin: "Why don't you just go kill yourself." (2009, October 20). MediaMatters for America. Retrieved May 27, 2010, from http://mediamatters.org/mmtv/200910200020.

Maathai, W. (n.d.). Wangari Maathai quotes. Retrieved March 7, 2012, from http://womenshistory.about.com/od/quotes/a/wangari_maathai.htm.

Maathai, W. (2003). *The Green Belt movement: Sharing the approach and the experience*. (New York: Lantern Books, 2003).

Maathai, W. M. *Unbowed*. New York: Knopf, 2006.

Methresources.gov. (2009). Anti-meth ad campaign. Retrieved May 27, 2010, from http://www.methresources.gov/2009antimeth.html.

Nabi, R. L., Roskos-Ewoldsen, D., & Carpentier, F. D. (2008). Subjective knowledge and fear appeal effectiveness: Implications for message design. *Health Communication, 23*(2), 191–201. Retrieved May 27, 2010, from Academic Search Premier, EBSCOhost.

Obama, M. (2010, March 22). Michelle on a mission: How we can empower parents, schools, and the community to battle childhood obesity. *Newsweek*, pp. 40–41.

Perelman, C., & Tyteca, L. O. (1969). *The new rhetoric: A treatise on argumentation* (J. Wilkinson & P. Weaver, Trans.) (pp. 31–35). South Bend, IN: University of Notre Dame Press.

Perloff, R. M. (1993). *The dynamics of persuasion* (pp. 136–155, 170–179). Hillsdale NJ: Erlbaum.

Revkin, A. (2009a) (September 15). Are condoms the ultimate green technology? *The New York Times*. Retrieved May 27, 2010, from http://dotearth.blogs.nytimes.com/2009/09/15/the-ultimate-green-technology-condoms/.

Revkin, A. (2009b) (October 20). Thought experiments on birth and death. *The New York Times*. Retrieved May 27, 2010, from http://dotearth.blogs.nytimes.com/2009/10/20/thought-experiments-on-sex-and-death/.

Rippetoe, P. A., & Rogers, R. W. (1987). Effects of components of protection-motivation theory on adaptive and maladaptive coping with a health threat. *Journal of Personality and Social Psychology*, *52*(3), 596–604.

Rogat Loeb, P. (1999). *Soul of a citizen: Living with conviction in a cynical time* (pp. 68–69). New York: St. Martin's Griffin.

Roser, C., & Thompson, M. (1995). Fear appeals and the formation of active publics. *Journal of Communication*, *45*, 103–121.

Schmnitt, C. L., & Blass, T. (2008). Fear appeals revisited: Testing a unique antismoking film. *Current Psychology*, *27*(2), 145–151. Retrieved May 27, 2010, from Academic Search Premier, EBSCOhost.

Steward, C. J., & Cash, W. B., Jr. (2006). *Interviewing: Principles and practices* (11th ed., p. 1). Boston: McGraw-Hill, 2006.

Stiff, J. B. (1994). *Persuasive communication* (pp. 89–106, 102–104), New York: Guilford Press.

Taylor, P. H., Rice, P. F., & Williams, R. H. (2000). *Basic statistics* (chap. 2, pp. 1–4). Cincinnati: Thompson Learning.

Toulmin, S. (1950). *The place of reason in ethics* (p. 72). Chicago: University of Chicago Press.

Toulmin, S. (1969). *The uses of argument.* London: Cambridge University Press.

Toulmin, S., Rieke, R., & Janik, A. (1979). *An introduction to reasoning*. New York: Macmillan.

Vancil, D. (1993). *Rhetoric and argumentation* (p. 134). Boston: Allyn & Bacon.

Van Eemeren, F. H., & Gootendorst, R. (1992). *Argumentation, communication, and fallacies: A pragma-dialectical perspective*. Hillsdale, NJ: Erlbaum.

Walton, D. N. (1996). *Argumentation schemes for presumptive reasoning*. Mahwah, NJ: Erlbaum.

Wong, N. C. H., & Cappella. J. N. (2009, February). Antismoking threat and efficacy appeals: Effects on smoking cessation intentions for smokers with low and high readiness to quit. *Journal of Applied Communication Research* [serial online], *37*(1), 1–20. Retried May 27, 2010, from Academic Search Premier, Ipswich, MA.

Zarefskyk, D. (2002). *Public speaking: Strategies for success* (pp. 153–154). Needham Heights, MA: Allyn & Bacon.

Chapter 12

Andersen, P. A., Hecht, M. L., & Hoebler, G. D. (2002). The cultural dimension of nonverbal communication. In W. B. Gudykunst & B. Moody (Eds.), *Handbook of international and intercultural communication* (pp. 89–106). Thousand Oaks, CA: Sage.

Aucion, D. (2010, March 5). For young activists, video is their voice. *Boston Globe*, pp. A1–A12.

Austin, G. (1966). In M. M. Robb & L. Thonssen (Eds.), *Chironomia or a treatise on rhetorical delivery*. Carbondale: Southern Illinois University Press. (Original work published 1806)

Ayres, J. (1988, October). Coping with speech anxiety: The power of positive thinking. *Communication Education, 37*(4), 289–296.

Ayres, J., & Hopf, T. S. (1985). Visualization: A means of reducing speech anxiety. *Communication Education, 34*(4) 318–323.

Ayres, J., & Hopf, T. S. (1989). Visualization: Is it more than extra attention? *Communication Education, 38*(1), 1–5.

Ayres , J., & Hopf, T. S. (1990). The long-term effect of visualization in the classroom: A brief research report. *Communication Education, 39*(1), 75–78.

Ayres, J., Hopf, T., & Ayres, D. M. (1994). An examination of whether imaging ability enhances the effectiveness of an intervention designed to reduce speech anxiety. *Communication Education, 43*(3), 252–258.

Beatty, M. J. (1988, January). Situational and predispositional correlates of public speaking anxiety. *Communication Education, 37*(1), 29–30.

Beebe, S. A. (1974). Eye contact: A nonverbal determinant of speaker credibility. *Speech Teacher, 23*(1), 21–25.

Beebe, S. A. (1979–1980). Effects of eye contact, posture, and vocal inflection upon credibility and comprehension. *Australian Scan Journal of Nonverbal Communication, 7–8*, 57–70.

Behnke, R. R., & Sawyer, C. R. (1999). Milestones of anticipatory public speaking anxiety. *Communication Education, 48*(2), 164–172.

Bippus, A. M., & Daly, J. A. (1999). What do people think causes stage fright? Naïve attributions about the reasons for public speaking anxiety. *Communication Education, 48*(1), 63–72.

Birdwhistell, R. (1970). Kinesics and context. Philadelphia: University of Pennsylvania Press.

Bode, N. (2007, April 24). Zip un-hip lyrics: Rap bigs say industry should "bleep" out three dirty words. *Daily News* (New York), p. 4.

Branham, R. J., & Pearce, W. B. (1996). The conversational frame in public address. *Communication Quarterly, 44*(4), 423.

Bull, P. E. (1987). *Posture and gesture.* New York: Pergamon.

Bulwer, J. (1974). *Chirologia: Or the natural language of the hand, and chiromomia: Or the art of manual rhetoric* (J. W. Cleary, Ed.). Carbondale: Southern Illinois University Press, (Original work published 1644)

Christenfeld, N. (1995, Fall). Does it hurt to say um? *Journal of Nonverbal Behavior, 19*(3), 171–186.

Cobin, M. (1963). Response to eye contact. *Quarterly Journal of Speech, 48*(4), 415–419.

Cousteau, A. (2012, January 18). Telephone communication.

Daly, J. A., Vangelisti, A. L., & Weber, D. J. (1995, December). Speech anxiety affects how people prepare speeches: A protocol analysis of the preparation processes of speakers. *Communication Monographs, 62*(4), 383–397.

Dowis, R. (2000). *The lost art of the great speech: How to write one, how to deliver it.* New York: American Management Association.

Finn, A. N., Sawyer, C. R., & Schrodt, P. (2009, January). Speech anxiety affects how people prepare speeches: *Communication Education, 58*(1), 92–109.

Fremouw, W. J., & Scott, M. D. (1979). Cognitive restructuring: An alternative method for the treatment of communication apprehension. *Communication Education, 28*(2), 129–133.

Gamboa, G. (2007, April 25). Industry insiders call for limits on rap lyrics: Group seeks voluntary standards for language. *Houston Chronicle,* p. 2.

Gates, L. (2000). *Voice for performance.* New York: Applause.

Geier, T., Jensen, J., Jordan, T., Lyons, M., & Markovitz, A. (2009, December 11). The 100 greatest movies, TV shows, albums, books, characters, scenes, episodes songs, dresses, music videos, and trends that entertained us over the past 10 years. *Entertainment Weekly, 1079/1080,* 74–84.

Gudykunst, W. B., & Moody, B. (Eds.). (2002). *Handbook of International and Intercultural Communication.* Thousand Oaks, CA: Sage.

Hartz, A. J. (1996). Psycho-socionomics: Attractiveness research from a societal perspective. *Journal of Social Behavior and Personality, 11,* 683.

Herman, C. P., Zanna, M. P., & Higgins, E. T. (1986). *Physical appearance, stigma, and social behavior: The Ontario Symposium, Vol. 3.* Hillsdale, NJ: Erlbaum.

Hildebrandt, H. W., & Stevens, W. W. (1963). Manuscript and extemporaneous delivery in communicating information. *Speech Monographs, 30*(4), 369–372.

Hip-hop setting the beat in first: Black artists hold billboard's top 10." (2003, October 4). Boston Globe. Retrieved from http://www.hsan.org.

Kangas Dwyer, K. (1998). *Conquer your speechfright: Learn how to overcome the nervousness of public speaking.* Fort Worth, TX: Harcourt.

Kangas Dwyer, K. (2000). The multidimensional model: Teaching students to self-manage high communication apprehension by self-selecting treatments. *Communication Education, 49*(1), 72–81.

Lucas, S. E. (2001). *The art of public speaking* (7th ed., p. 290). New York: McGraw-Hill.

Martin, S., & Darnley, L. (1996). *The teaching voice* (p. 60). San Diego: Singular Publishing Group.

McCroskey, J. C. (1972). The implementation of a large scale program of systematic desensitization for communication apprehension. *Speech Teacher 21*(4), 255–264.

McCroskey, J. C. (1977). Oral communication apprehension: A summary of recent theory and research. *Human Communication Research, 4*(1), 78.

McCroskey, J. C., Sallinen, A., Fayer, J. M., Richmond, V. P., & Barraclough, R. A. (1996). Nonverbal immediacy and cognitive learning: A cross-cultural investigation. *Communication Education, 45*(3), 200–211.

McCullough, S. C., Russell, S. G., Behnke, R. R., Sawyer, C. R., & Witt, P. L. (2006, February). Anticipatory public speaking state anxiety as a function of body sensations and state of mind. *Communication Quarterly, 54*(1), 101–109.

McGarvey, R. (1990, January–February). Rehearsing for success: Tap the power of the mind through visualization. *Executive Female,* pp. 34–37.

Mehrabian, A. (1981). *Silent messages: Implicit communication of emotion and attitudes* (2nd ed.). Belmont, CA: Wadsworth.

Mino, M. (1996). The relative effects of content and vocal delivery during a simulated employment interview. *Communication Research Reports, 13*(2), 225–238.

Morris, T. L., Gorham, J., Cohen, S. H., & Huffman, D. (1996). Fashion in the classroom: Effects of attire on student perceptions of instructors in college classes. *Communication Education, 45*(2), 135–148.

Morrow, P. (1990). Physical attractiveness and selection decision making. *Journal of Management, 16*(1), 45–60.

Palmer, M. T., & Simmons, K. B. (1995). Communicating intentions through nonverbal behaviors. *Human Communication Research, 22*(1), 128–160.

Robinson, T. E., II. (1997). Communication apprehension and the basic public speaking course: A national survey of in-class treatment techniques. *Communication Education, 46*(3), 190–197.

Rodenburg, P. (2001). *The need for words: Voice and the text.* New York: Routledge.

Rozell, P., Kennedy, D., & Grabb, E. (1989). Physical attractiveness and income attainment among Canadians. *Journal of Psychology, 123*(6), 547–559.

Rubinstein, R. P. (2001). Dress codes: *Meanings and messages in American culture* (2nd ed.). Boulder, CO: Westview.

Samovar, L. A., & Porter, R. E. (1991). *Communication between cultures* (pp. 205–206). Belmont, CA: Wadsworth.

Smiley Group. (2006). *The covenant with black America.* Chicago: Third World Press.

Smith, T. E., & Frymier, A. B. (2006, February). Get "real": Does practicing speeches before an audience improve performance? *Communication Quarterly, 54*(1), 111–125.

Soper, P. L. (1956). *Basic public speaking* (2nd ed., pp. 143, 150, 151). New York: Oxford University Press.

Stein, M. B. , Walker, J. R., & Forde, D. R. (1996). Public-Speaking Fears in a Community Sample: Prevalence, Impact on Functioning, and Diagnostic Classification. *Archives of General Psychiatry, 53*(2), 169–174.

Trees, A. R., & Manusov, V. (1998). Managing face concerns in critics: Integrating nonverbal behaviors as a dimension of politeness in female friendship dyads. *Human Communication Research, 24*(4), 564–583.

Weiss, C. D. (2008, January 2). Good-looking lawyers make more money, researcher says. *ABA Journal.* Retrieved from www.abajournal.com/news/article/good_looking_lawyers_make_more_money_researcher_says.

Winters, J. J., Horvath, N. R., Moss, M., Yarhouse, K., Sawyer, C. R., & Behnke, R. R. (2007, Winter). Affect intensity of student speakers as a predictor of anticipatory public speaking anxiety. *Texas Speech Communication Journal, 31*, 44–48.

Witt, P. L., & Behnke, R. R. (2006, April). Anticipatory speech anxiety as a function of public speaking assignment type. *Communication Education, 55*(2), 167–177.

Witt, P. L. , Roberts, M. L., & Behnke, R. R. (2008, Summer). Comparative patterns of anxiety and depression in a public speaking context. *Human Communication, 11*(1), 219–230.

Wood, J. T. (1999). *Interpersonal communication: Everyday encounters* (2nd ed., p. 148). Belmont, CA: Wadsworth.

YouTube Fact Sheet. (2010). Retrieved from http://frameconcepts.com/youtube-fact-sheet/

Chapter 13

Dannels, D. P. (2001). Time to speak up: A theoretical framework of situated pedagogy and practice for communication across the curriculum. *Communication Education, 50*(2), 144–158.

Johnson, J. R., & Szczupakiewicz, N. (1987). The public speaking course: Is it preparing students with work-related public speaking skills? *Communication Education, 36*(2), 131–137.

LeBeau, D. (2008). Saving America's dog. Retrieved June 10, 2010 from http://network.bestfriends.org/groups/conferences/news/archive/2008/10/29/saving-americas-dog-aspx.

Martinez , M., & Simon, D. (2011, December 16). Barry Bonds gets probation, house arrest for obstruction of justice. Retrieved January 9, 2012 from http://www.cnn.com/2011/12/16/justice/barry-bonds-sentencing/index.html?iref=allsearch.

Meet Shorty Rossi. (2010). *Pit boss* [Television series]. Animal Planet. Retrieved October 28, 2010, from http://animal.discovery.com/tv/pit-boss/bios/shorty-rossi.html.

Morreal, S., Osborn, M., & Pearson, J. (2000). Why communication is important: Rationale for the centrality of the study of communication. *Journal of the Association for Communication Administration, 29*(2), 1–25.

National Association of Colleges and Employers. (2012). Job outlook 2012 survey. Retrieved March 7, 2012, from http://www.naceweb.org/Research/Job_Outlook/Job_Outlook.aspx accessed.

Quinn, T. J. (2007, July 21). Jury's in on Bonds: Feds eye fall indictment. *New York Daily News.* Retrieved June 10, 2010 from http://www.nydailynews.com/sprots/baseball/2007/07.

Rosynsky, P. T. (2007, August 13). Bonds threatens to sue detractors. *Mercury News* (San Jose, CA). Retrieved August 22, 2007, from http://www.mercurynews.com.

Rowlands, T. (2006, April 14). Sources: Grand jury looking at whether Bonds lied about steroid use. CNN Justice. Retrieved June 10, 2010 from http://articles.cnn.com/2006-04-14/justice/bonds_1_grand-jury-bay-area-laboratory-bonds-and-other-athletes?_s=PM:LAW.

Weise, L. (2009). Downtown dog rescue needs your support—letter writing camp. Retrieved December 27, 2009, from Ashleyandhobie.com, Animal Rescue for Southern California Message Boards. Available at http://ashleyandhobie.com/board/viewtopic.php?f=26&t=15481&p=66869

Williams, L., & Fainaru-Wada, M. (2004, December 3). What Bonds told BALCO grand jury. *San Francisco Chronicle.* Retrieved June 10, 2010 from http://sfgate.com/chi-bin/article.cgi?file.

Wolvin, A. D. (1989). The basic course and the future of the workplace. *Basic Communication Course Annual, 10*, 1–6.

Chapter 14

Brehm, J. W. (1996). *A theory of psychological reactance*. New York: Academic Press.

Cannizaro, S. (2003, December 5). Group plans to file suit against refinery: They allege pollution violations. *Times-Picayune* (New Orleans), p. 1.

Cannizzaro, S. (2004, February 13). Two groups suing refinery: They claim plant violates Clean Air Act. *Times-Picayune* (New Orleans), p. 1.

Casey, M. K., Timmermann, L., Allen, M., Krahn, S., & Turkiewicz, K. L. (1990, January). Response and self-efficacy of condom use: A meta-analysis of this important element of AIDS education and prevention. *Southern Communication Journal* [serial online], *74*(1), 57–78.

Chen, H. C., Reardon, R., Rea, C., & More, D. J. (1992). Forewarning of content and involvement: Consequences for persuasion and resistance to persuasion. *Journal of Experimental Social Psychology, 28*(6), 523–541.

Gargaro, C. C. (n.d.). Ribbon campaigns: The most comprehensive ribbon list on the "net." Retrieved March 7, 2012, from http://www.gargaro.com/ribbons.html.

Gronbeck, B. E., McKerrow, R. E., Ehninger, D., & Monroe, A. H. (1990). *Principles and types of speech communication* (11th ed., pp. 180–205). Glenview, IL: Scott, Foresman/Little, Brown Higher Education.

Jessop, D. C., & Wade, J. (2008, November). Fear appeals and binge drinking: A terror management theory perspective. British *Journal of Health Psychology* [serial online], *13*(4), 773–788.

Kearney, P., Plax, T. G., & Burroughs, N. F. (1991). An attributional analysis of college students' resistance decisions. *Communication Education, 40*(4), 325–342.

Lester, P. M. (2004). *Visual communication: Images with messages* (4th ed., pp. 111–118), Boston: Wadsworth/Cengage.

Livestrong. (n.d.). Retrieved March 21, 2012 from www.livestrong.org.

Louisiana Bucket Brigade. (n.d.). Clean air. Justice. Sustainability. Campaigns/Programs. Retrieved March 7, 2012, from http://www.labucketbrigade.org.

Martins, D. Explorer Bios. http://www.nationalgeographic.com/explorers/bios/dino-martins. Retreived February 23, 2012.

Martell, A. (n.d.). Call for Canadian government to hold Rituximab clinical trials for ME/CFS patients. Retrieved March 7, 2012, from http://www.blueribboncampaignforme.org/.

Miller, G. R., & Roloff, M. E. (Eds.). (1980). *Persuasion: New directions in theory and research*. Beverly Hills, CA: Sage.

Nabi, R. L., Roskos-Ewoldsen, D., & Carpentier, F. D. (2008). Subjective knowledge and fear appeal effectiveness: Implications for message design. *Health Communication, 23*(2), 191–201.

Petty, R. E., & Cacioppo, J. T. (1986). *Communication and persuasion: Central and peripheral routes to attitude change*. New York: Springer-Verlag.

Reardon, K. K. (1991). *Persuasion in practice*. Newbury Park, CA: Sage.

Rippetoe, P. A., & Rogers, R. W. (1987). Effects of components of protection-motivation theory on adaptive and maladaptive coping with a health threat. *Journal of Personality and Social Psychology, 52*(3), 596–604.

Roser, C., & Thompson, M. (1995). Fear appeals and the formation of active publics. *Journal of Communication, 45*(1), 103–121.

Schmitt, C. L., & Blass, T. (2008). Fear appeals revisited: Testing a unique anti-smoking film. *Current Psychology, 27*(2), 145–151.

Seiler, W. J. (1971). The effects of visual materials on attitudes, credibility, and retention. *Speech Monographs, 38*(4), 331–334.

Sine, R. (2000, July 20). Neighbors seeking proof of pollution. *Times-Picayune* (New Orleans), p. 1.

Smiley, T. (Ed.). (2006). *The covenant with Black America*. Chicago: Third World Press.

Stiff, J. B. (1994). *Persuasive communication* (pp. 117–119). New York: Guilford Press.

Swerczek, M. (2002, October 18). Residents to learn to test air quality: Devices to check for chemicals on display. *Times-Picayune* (New Orleans), p. 1.

TeenHelp.com. (n.d.). Jelly bracelets and their meaning. Retrieved March 7, 2012, from http://www.teenhelp.com/teen-sexuality/jelly-bracelets.html.

Waldron, V. R., & Applegate, J. L. (1998). Person-centered tactics during verbal disagreements: Effects on student perceptions of persuasiveness and social attraction. *Communication Education, 47*(1), 55–56.

Watchdog group to protest refinery: Activists to mix with Exxon stockholders. (2005, May 24). *Times-Picayune* (New Orleans), p. 1.

Whaley, B. B., & Wagner, L. S. (2000). Rebuttal analogy in persuasive messages: Communicator likability and cognitive responses. *Journal of Language and Social Psychology, 19*(1), 66–84.

Wong, N. C. H., & Cappella, J. N. (2009, February). Antismoking threat and efficacy appeals: Effects on smoking cessation intentions for smokers with low and high readiness to quit. *Journal of Applied Communication Research* [serial online], *37*(1), 1–20.

Yellow Ribbon America. (n.d.). Helping our nation's military and their families in their local communities. Retrieved March 7, 2012, from http://www.yellowribbonamerica.org/

Chapter 15

Barrett, H. (1991). *Rhetoric and civility: Human development, narcissism, and the good audience*. Albany: State University of New York Press.

Benhabib, S. (1992). *Situating the self: Gender, community, and postmodernism in contemporary ethics*. New York: Routledge.

Bohn, E., & Jabusch, D. (1982, Summer). The effect of four methods of instruction on the use of visual aids in speeches. *Western Journal of Speech Communication, 46*, 253–265.

Bone, J. E., Griffin, C. L., & Scholz, T.M. L. (2008). Beyond traditional conceptualizations of rhetoric: Invitational rhetoric and a move toward civility. *Western Journal of Communication, 72(4)*, 434–462.

Davidson, W., & Klien, S. J. (1999, March). Ace your presentation. *Journal of Accountancy, 187*, 61–63.

Ellinor, L., & Gerard, G. (1998). *Dialogue: Creating and sustaining collaborative partnerships at work*. New York: Wiley.

Foss, S. K., & Griffin, C. L. (1995). Beyond persuasion: A proposal for an invitational rhetoric. *Communication Monographs, 62*(1), 1–18.

hooks, b. (1994). *Outlaw culture: Resisting representations*. New York: Routledge.

Isaacs, W. (1999). *Dialogue and the art of thinking together*. New York: Currency.

Jack Beetson spoke with Tony Jones. (n.d.). Television program transcript, Australian Broadcasting Corporation. Retrieved May 22, 2006, from http://www.abc.net/au /lateling/content/2006/s1644688.htm

Linkugel, W., & Berg, D. (1970). *A time to speak* (pp. 68–96). Belmont, CA: Wadsworth.

Loeb, P. R. (2010). *Soul of a citizen*. New York: St. Martins's Griffin.

Lower Manhattan Development Corporation. (2003, January 2). Renew NYC. [Online]. Retrieved June 16, 2004, from http://www.renewnyc.com.

Lower Manhattan Development Corporation. (2004, January 13). Memorial-reflecting absence: WTC memorial jury statement for winning design. [Online]. Retrieved June 16, 2004, from http://www.renewnyc.com.

Nickerson, R. S. (1965). Short-term memory for complex meaningful visual configurations: A demonstration of capacity. *Canadian Journal of Psychology, 19*(2), 155–160.

Peck,. M. S. (1987). The different drum: *Community—making and peace*. New York: Simon & Schuster.

Rabb, M. Y. (1993). *The presentation design book: Tips, techniques and advice for creating effective, attractive slides, overheads, multimedia presentations, screen shows, and more.* Chapel Hill, NC: Ventana.

Rogers, C. R. (1962). The interpersonal relationship: The core of guidance. *Harvard Educational Review, 32*(4), 416–429.

The Unsung Heroes of Dialogue. (n.d.). Retrieved March 7, 2012, from http://www.un.org/Dialogue/heroes.htm.

Walker, M. U. (1989). Moral understandings: Alternative "epistemology" for a feminist ethics. *Hypatia, 4*(2), 15–28.

World Trade Center Site Memorial Competition Jury Statement. (2003, November 19). *The New York Times*. Retrieved June 16, 2004, from http://www.nytimes.com/2003/11/19 /nyregion/19WTC-JURY-TEXT.html.

Zayas-Bazan, E. P. (1977–1978). Instructional media in the total language picture. *International Journal of Instructional Media, 5*, 145–150.

Michael J. Harte

Cindy L. Griffin

is professor of communication studies at Colorado State University. She received her PhD from Indiana University and has taught public speaking; civility; gender and communication; communication, language and thought; contemporary theories of rhetoric; history of rhetorical theories; feminist theories of discourse; identity, voice and agency; and graduate seminars in women's studies. A proponent of civic engagement and civility in our communication and our lives, her research interests include developing the theory of invitational rhetoric, advancing theories that help communication scholars and students understand our complex identities, and exploring the relationships between civility, power, and rhetoric. She is the author of *Invitation to Public Speaking* (Cengage, 2012) and *Invitation to Public Speaking Handbook* (Cengage, 2011); co-editor of *Standing in the Intersections: Feminist Voices, Feminist Practices in Communication Studies* (with Karma Chávez, SUNY Press, 2013); coauthor of *Feminist Rhetorical Theories* (with Sonja Foss and Karen Foss; Waveland, 2006), and has published articles and book chapters that address identities, civility, feminisms and rhetorical and communication theories. She also served as the editor of *Women's Studies in Communication* from 2006 to 2010.

Elizabeth Emerling

Jennifer Emerling Bone

is a special assistant professor of communication studies at Colorado State University. She received her PhD from the University of Colorado at Boulder and has taught introduction to human communication; public speaking; gender and communication; theories of persuasion; argumentation; contemporary rhetorical criticism; rhetoric and social movements; contemporary public address; and evolution of rhetoric. Seeking to understand how marginalized voices create public arguments, through her research, she examines how historical women used narratives and storytelling to change social and political attitudes about birth control. She has published in *Women's Studies in Communication* and *Western Journal of Communication* (with Cindy Griffin and T. M. Linda Scholz), has a coauthored chapter in *Contemplating Maternity in the Era of Choice: Explorations into Discourses of Reproduction* (edited by Sara Hayden and D. Lynn O'Brien Hallstein), and instructor's manuals and supplements for *Invitation to Public Speaking* (by Cindy Griffin). She also served as the basic course director at Colorado State University from 2010–2012.

KEENPRESS Productions

Alexandra Cousteau

Her legendary grandfather, Jacques, and father, Philippe, explored the world's ocean wonders, but today Alexandra Cousteau explores new ways to save them. "I believe water will be the defining crisis of our century—from droughts, storms, and floods to degrading water quality. We'll see major conflicts over water and the proliferation of water refugees. We inhabit a water planet, and unless we protect, manage, and restore that resource, the future will be a very different place from the one we imagine today."

"People," Cousteau says, "have created the problem, so it's critical to get the public excited and eager to participate in a solution. A sustainable society will only come about through the accumulated actions of billions of individuals, and that's an enormous challenge." Cousteau's latest initiative, Blue Legacy, was created to tell the story of our Water Planet to the world, to inspire people to take meaningful action on critical water issues, and to help shape society's dialogue to include water as one of the defining issues of the century and a critical component of climate change.

Courtesy of Chris Rainier

Thomas Taha Rassam Culhane

Culhane's nongovernmental organization, Solar C.³I.T.I.E.S., works with residents of Cairo's poorest neighborhoods to install rooftop solar water heaters. "They generate 200 liters of hot water and 200 liters of cold water for each household every day," Culhane explains. "And since the technology is completely CO_2 free, it contributes nothing to global warming. If people don't have access to enough water, it becomes a serious health issue. And when women spend all their time tending stoves to heat water, then how can they go to school or get ahead?" Culhane's grasp of these daily challenges is personal; he and his wife moved to a slum apartment themselves to gain firsthand experience.

With Culhane's help, more than 30 solar tanks now dot the rooftops of the Zabaleen's primarily Coptic Christian community, as well as Darb Al-Ahmar, an Islamic Cairo neighborhood. "I divide my time between the two, working to bring them together," Culhane notes (hence the name Solar C.³I.T.I.E.S: Connecting Community Catalysts Integrating Technologies for Industrial Ecology Systems). "I knew if they could actually meet one another and connect on a project to solve common problems, they would overcome their differences. They immediately began sharing and building on each other's expertise. Now we're using the strengths of both Christianity and Islam to fight a common enemy: environmental degradation."

Sylvia Earle

Sylvia Earle, called "Her Deepness" by the *New Yorker* and the *New York Times*, "Living Legend" by the Library of Congress, and the first "Hero for the Planet," is an oceanographer, explorer, author, and lecturer with experience as a field research scientist. She also is executive director for corporate and nonprofit organizations, including the Aspen Institute, the Conservation Fund, American Rivers, Mote Marine Laboratory, Duke University Marine Laboratory, Rutgers Institute for Marine Science, the Woods Hole Oceanographic Institution, National Marine Sanctuary Foundation, and Ocean Conservancy.

Former chief scientist of NOAA, Earle is founder of the Mission Blue Foundation and chair of the Advisory Council for the Harte Research Institute for Gulf of Mexico Studies. She has a BS from Florida State University, an MS and a PhD from Duke University, and 15 honorary degrees. She has authored more than 150 scientific, technical, and popular publications, lectured in more than 60 countries, and appeared in hundreds of television productions. Earle has led more than 60 expeditions and logged more than 6,000 hours underwater, including leading the first team of women aquanauts during the Tektite Project in 1970 and setting a record for solo diving to a depth of 1,000 meters.

Albert Yu-Min Lin

Albert Yu-Min Lin's explorations are groundbreaking, because they never break ground. He uses noninvasive computer based technologies to gather, synthesize, and visualize data without disturbing a blade of grass. "Exploration has always been about going where we haven't been able to go before," Lin notes. "Environmental, cultural, or political obstacles may have prevented us from exploring certain places. Today technology helps us navigate past those old barriers." For Lin, cutting-edge tools such as satellite imagery, ground-penetrating radar, and remote sensors permit him to make archaeological discoveries while respecting the traditional beliefs of indigenous people.

Today Lin and other researchers from a cross section of fields have at their fingertips a veritable high-tech toy store. It's called the California Institute for Telecommunications and Information Technology and it fosters interdisciplinary collaboration. It allows Lin to access an unparalleled array of digital 3-D immersive technologies and then link his efforts to those of other scientists. A case in point is Lin's search for the tomb of Genghis Khan, a quest that has eluded scientists and historians for centuries.

Cecilia Lewis

Dino Martins

The threatened habitats that support pollinating insects may often be out of sight and out of mind, but Dino Martins brings their importance home. "Pollinators are one of the strongest connections between conservation and something everyone needs—food." With his infectious enthusiasm and practical solutions, Martins acts as a pollinator himself, carrying crucial information to Kenya's isolated farmers, schoolchildren, and a larger world of travelers and scientists.

Growing up in rural Kenya, Martins saw the most basic interface between farms, food, and nature every day. "In the developing world, subsistence farmers are on the front lines of poverty, hunger, and either saving or destroying forests. Africa is especially vulnerable since so many of the crops that provide nutrition are 100 percent dependent on wild insects." All across East Africa, Martins works to identify the most useful plants and pollinators, return them to their habitats, and help both ecosystems and local communities thrive. He stresses that "farmers need to understand why leaving a little space for nature isn't a luxury, but a necessity for productive, sustainable agriculture."

MARK THIESSEN/National Geographic

Mireya Mayor

It all started when Mireya Mayor's college anthropology class began studying primates. "It's true that I was a cheerleader who had grown up taking ballet and piano lessons," Mayor says. "But I was seized by the fact that some of these incredible animals on the verge of extinction had never been studied, and that in some cases, not even a mere photograph existed to show their existence. The more questions I asked the more it became clear to me that much about our natural world still remained a mystery."

Mayor has dedicated her life to solving that mystery, studying rare primates in the wild throughout the world and working closely with local populations. Today, Mayor is a Fulbright scholar and National Science Foundation Fellow, dividing her time between research in Madagascar, appearing as a correspondent on the National Geographic *Ultimate Explorer* television series, and completing a PhD in anthropology. Mayor's discovery of a new species of mouse lemur in Madagascar put her own work in the spotlight. "It was one of those things you never thought could happen in the 21st century," she recalls.

Aydogan Ozcan

Aydogan Ozcan has the PhD, the expertise, and the engineering acumen to perfect the world's most complex medical diagnostic technology. Instead, he's solving global health issues—with a cell phone. His UCLA research team has invented a way to turn common cell phones, already in the hands of four billion people worldwide, into imaging tools that will bring accurate medical diagnoses to the most remote, resource-poor corners of the planet.

Courtesy of the Ozcan Research Group at UCLA

In many rural villages, patients remain untreated until mobile units reach them. Even then, tools are woefully inadequate. "Many diseases remain entirely missed; people are dying from simple infections that could be easily treated if only they were diagnosed." Heavy yet powerful conventional microscopes, the mainstay of diagnosis for centuries, are impractical on a global level. Ozcan's invention solves the dilemma of poorly trained technicians by arming the phones with sophisticated algorithms that do the interpreting of blood samples. To tackle the most expensive part of microscopes—lenses—his team simply eliminated them.

Aziz Abu Sarah

In a place where struggles over land have fueled hatred and distrust for centuries, Aziz Abu Sarah is finding common ground. His effort to build relationships, not walls, amid the Israeli-Palestinian conflict is especially amazing in light of his own past.

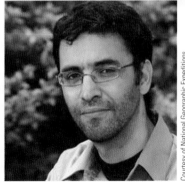

Courtesy of National Geographic Expeditions

Abu Sarah's childhood as a Palestinian boy in Jerusalem was shattered when his brother was imprisoned, tortured, and killed. Necessity brought him into a Hebrew class for Jewish newcomers to Israel. He learned that they were ordinary human beings just like himself and overcame his hatred. Based on his own transformative experience, Abu Sarah dedicates his life to using personal stories and cross-cultural learning to forge unprecedented understanding and positive social change at a people-to-people level. A walking embodiment of the reconciliation he strives to achieve, Abu Sarah is a Muslim who works closely with rabbis and Christian groups and speaks Arabic, Hebrew, and English. In the United States, he is co-executive director of George Mason University's Center for World Religions, Diplomacy and Conflict Resolution (the oldest conflict resolution school in the world).

GLOSSARY

accommodation: a conflict style in which individuals do what they are asked in order to resolve the conflict (9)

acronyms: the first letters of initials of terms that form a word (4)

action-oriented listener: listener who wants speakers to provide clear, detailed, and straight-to-the-point information (5)

adaptors: gestures we use to manage our emotions (3)

ad hominem fallacy: an argument in which a speaker attacks a person rather than challenge that person's arguments (11)

affect displays: nonverbal movements that indicate how we feel (3)

affective questions: questions that acknowledge that people have feelings as well as ideas that are important to share (9)

affirmation: positive statements that assert that what we wish to be true is already happening (12)

agenda: formal and organized outline of items to address in order to meet the goals of the meeting (9)

ambushing: listening carefully to information in order to attack what the speaker has to say (5)

analogical reasoning: reasoning by way of comparison and similarity (11)

androgynous: displaying both masculine and feminine traits or behaviors (7)

androgynous communicators: individuals who are adept at using different speech styles, depending on the situation (4)

anomalies: exceptions to a rule and unique instances that do not represent the norm (11)

articulation: physical process of producing specific speech sounds to make language intelligible to our audiences (12)

artifacts: the personal objects we use to communicate something about ourselves (3)

asynchronous: message that is sent but not received at the same time (6)

attitude: general positive or negative feeling a person has about something (10)

audience-centered speaker: speaker who considers the positions, beliefs, values, and needs of an audience (10)

auditory communication system: paralanguage (3)

auditory listener: listener who needs to hear verbal descriptions and explanations (5)

authoritarian leader: leader who tells others what to do, gives orders, and makes the final decisions regarding how to act or what to do next (9)

authority rule: allowing the leader or head of a group to make the final choice (9)

avoidance: a conflict style in which individuals will not address or acknowledge the conflict (9)

avoiding: when couples attempt to stay away from each other (6)

bandwagon fallacy: a suggestion that something is correct or good because everyone else agrees with it or is doing it (11)

bar graph: a graph that shows quantities at a specific moment in time (14)

behavioral objectives: actions a speaker wants an audience to take at the end of a speech (10)

belief: a person's idea of what is real or true or not (10)

blind window: information that others know about you but that you are not aware of (6)

bonding step: step that occurs when a couple commits to their relationship (6)

brainstorming: process of generating ideas randomly and uncritically without attention to logic, connections, or relevance (8, 10)

breadth: the range of topics discussed in self-disclosure (6)

bullying: repeated unreasonable actions of individuals (or a group) directed toward an employee (or group of employees) that are intended to intimidate, degrade, humiliate, or undermine; actions that create a risk to the health or safety of the employee(s) (9)

call to action: an explicit request that an audience engage in some clearly stated behavior (14)

careful listener: listener who overcomes listening interference in order to listen effectively to another person's message (5)

causal pattern: a pattern of organization that highlights cause-and-effect relationships; pattern of organization used when a problem is based on a cause-and-effect relationship (13, 14)

causal reasoning: a process of reasoning that supports a claim by establishing a cause-and-effect relationship (11)

channel: means by which ideas are communicated (1)

chronemics: how humans organize and structure time and the messages conveyed as a result of this organization (3)

chronological pattern: a pattern of organization in which you illustrate how a topic has developed over time or what sequential steps an audience must take to complete a task (13)

circumscribing: when couples begin communicating less frequently, share less personal information, and spend shorter amounts of time together (6)

civic engagement: individual and collective actions designed to identify and address issues of public concern (1)

civility: expressing care and concern for others, the thoughtful use of words and language, and the flexibility to see the many sides of an issue (1)

civil listener: listener who is open to hearing different views and perspectives, even when there is disagreement (5)

closed questions: yes-or-no questions that limit the kind of answers a person can give (9)

coercive power: ability to punish those who do not meet demands or follow the rules set by the group (8)

cognitive complexity: capacity to make sense of social behavior in a multidimensional way (1)

cognitive restructuring: process that builds confidence because it replaces negative thoughts with positive thoughts called *affirmations* (12)

cohesiveness: degree of mutual interest among members of a group (8)

collectivist culture: culture that values relationships and harmony with others (6)

collectivism: the degree to which organizational, societal, and family practices encourage and reward collective distribution of resources and collective action as well as the degree to which they express pride and loyalty (9)

colloquialisms: words and phrases used in relaxed, informal conversations (4)

communication: use of symbols by humans to create messages for other humans (1)

communication apprehension: anxiety about speaking in any number of situations (interviews, speeches, etc.); the level of fear or anxiety associated with either real or anticipated communication with another person or persons (1, 12)

communication climates: climates that set the tone for interpersonal relationships (7)

communicating civilly: making a decision to be open to hearing different views and perspectives, even though we may not agree with them (1)

communicating ethically: considering the moral impact of our words, ideas, and views on other people when we communicate (1)

comparative advantages organization: this type of organization illustrates the advantages of one solution over others (14)

competition: a style of managing conflict in which one individual makes sure her or his needs are met with disregard for the needs of others

complementation: when the nonverbal signal elaborates or expands the meaning of the verbal message (3)

compromise: a style of managing conflict in which the needs of every member of the group are considered and met; commonly referred to as a win-win approach (9)

computer mediated communication: the exchange of messages transmitted between two or more people using a digital electronic device (6)

consensus: general or widespread agreement among all the members of a group (9)

concern for others: when individuals attempt to get along with and satisfy another's needs using cooperative communication (7)

concern for self: when individuals seek to satisfy their own desires and needs through direct and assertive communication (7)

conclusion: the claim you are attempting to prove as true (11)

condition of equality: acknowledging that all audience members hold valid perspectives worthy of exploration (15)

condition of self-determination: recognizing that the members of your audience are experts in their own lives (15)

condition of value: realizing the inherent value of your audience's views, although those views might be different from yours (15)

confirming: listening in order to recognize, acknowledge, and express value for another person (5)

confirming statements: statements that validate other people by recognizing them, acknowledging their ideas and feelings, and approving or supporting their ideas (7)

connectives: words and phrases used to link ideas in a speech (10)

connotative definition: subjective meaning of a word or a phrase based on personal experiences and beliefs (11)

connotative meanings: the meanings we associate with particular words based on our experiences, understanding, or opinions of the word (4)

content messages: the actual things we say (1)

content-oriented listener: listener who pays close attention to the facts and details of a message (5)

contradiction: when verbal and nonverbal forms of communication conflict with one another (3)

conversational style: a speaking style that is more formal than everyday conversation but also remains spontaneous and relaxed (12)

counterarguments: addressing the arguments against the speaker's own position (14)

credible: to gain the trust of your audience and to communicate that you have considerable knowledge of your topic (10)

critical listener: listener who listens for accuracy of content and the implications of a message (5)

cultural competence: the ability to relate appropriately to members from a different culture (4)

culture: learned patterns of perception, values, and behaviors shared by a group of people (1, 6)

decode: interpreting or trying to understand what the sender is communicating (1)

deductive reasoning: a process of reasoning that uses a familiar and commonly accepted claim to establish the truth of a very specific claim (11)

defensive listener: listener who perceives a message as a personal attack or a form of criticism (5)

definition: statement of the exact meaning of a word or phrase (11)

democratic leaders: leadership type characterized by the distribution of responsibility among the group members, a desire to empower all members of the group, and a willingness to assist in decision making (9)

denotative meanings: the literal or commonly accepted meaning of a word (4)

denotative definition: objective meaning of a word found in a dictionary (11)

depth: how personal the information is in self-disclosure (6)

dialect: pattern of speech shared by an ethnic group or people from specific geographical locations (12)

dialogue: civil exchange of ideas and opinions between two people or a small group of people (10)

differentiating: when individuals in a couple begin to spend time on their own interests in order to express their individuality and separate from their partners (6)

direct quotation: an exact word-for-word presentation of another's testimony (11)

disconfirming statement: statement that rejects or invalidates another person's statements (7)

doublespeak: language used to purposefully disguise the actual meaning of something (4)

either-or fallacy (false dilemma): an argument in which a speaker claims our options are "either A or B," when actually more than two options exist (11)

elaboration likelihood model (ELM): model that explains an audience's motivation for processing persuasive messages in either a central processing or a peripheral processing route (14)

emblems: gestures that can be translated into words (3)

emoticons: typed characters used to convey feelings (3)

emotions: internal mental states that focus primarily on feelings (11)

empathy: ability to see the world through another person's eyes and to understand their feelings and perspectives (1)

emphasis: using nonverbal cues that strengthen what is stated verbally (3)

encode: putting ideas, thoughts, and meanings into a message (1)

environment: cultural backgrounds and experiences that people bring to the exchange (1)

environmental factors: surroundings that influence how we think, feel, and behave as we communicate with others (3)

equivocal words: words that have more than one meaning (4)

ethics: moral standards behind the decisions and how they affect others (8)

ethnocentrism: belief that our own cultural perspectives, norms, and ways of organizing society are superior to other cultures (1, 10)

euphemisms: polite terms or more socially acceptable ways to describe something that someone may find unpleasant (4)

evidence: information speakers use to develop and support their ideas (11)

examples: specific instances used to illustrate a concept, experience, issue or problem (11)

experiential listener: listener who learns best by touching, exploring, and participating in what is being described (5)

experimenting step: step when small talk is used to learn more about the other person and to help present a likable self-image (6)

expert power: ability to influence others because of some skill, knowledge base, or set of experiences (8)

expert testimony: the testimony of someone considered an authority in a particular field (11)

extemporaneous speech: carefully prepared and practiced speech from brief notes rather than from memory or a written manuscript (12)

external noises: things that keep you from sending or receiving a message clearly (1)

eye contact: visual contact with another person's eyes (12)

facework: verbal and nonverbal strategies used to present different faces to others (2)

facial expression: movement of eyes, eyebrows, and mouth to convey reactions and emotions (12)

fallacy: an argument that seems valid but is flawed because of unsound evidence or reasoning (11)

false cause: an error in reasoning in which a speaker assumes that one event caused another simply because the first event happened before the second (11)

false cause fallacy: an argument mistaking a chronological relationship with a causal relationship (11)

family: network of people who live together over long periods of time bound by ties of marriage, blood, or commitment, legal or otherwise, who consider themselves as family and share a significant history and anticipated future of functioning in a family relationship (6)

fear appeal: threat of something undesirable happening if change does not occur (14)

feedback: verbal and nonverbal signals we give to one another while we communicate (1)

flaming: uninhibited expression of hostility such as swearing, name-calling, ridicule, and insults directed toward another person, his or her character, religion, race, intelligence, and physical or mental ability (7)

flow chart: chart that shows direction or motion (14)

formal role: role that is clearly defined and assigned (8)

forums: when messages or topics are posted online and individuals have an opportunity to post their individual responses and ideas to those original messages (8)

framing: the way people use language to define the conflict situation (7)

friendly relations: situation that allows each person to determine whether common interests exist (6)

friendship or warmth touch: conveys a sense of closeness and caring between individuals (3)

functional or professional touch: the least intimate touch, including touch by others according to their professional position (3)

gender egalitarianism: the extent to which an organization or society minimizes gender-role differences (9)

gender: society's use of verbal and nonverbal symbols to express masculinity and femininity (6)

gender roles: feminine and masculine social expectations in a family based on a person's sex; the social expectations for how males and females should behave (6, 7)

general purpose: the broad goal of a speech—to inform, invite, or persuade (10)

gestures: movements, usually of the hands but sometimes of the entire body, that express meaning and emotion or offer clarity to a message (12)

globalization: processes through which local and regional ideas, products, and practices are transformed into worldwide ideas, products, and practices (1)

graph: a visual comparison of amounts or quantities (14)

group: small number of people who belong together, share something in common, or are assigned to a similar task (8)

group communication: interacting with a small but organized collection of people (1)

groupthink: mode of thinking that people engage in when they are deeply involved in a cohesive in-group when the members' striving for unanimity override their motivation to realistically appraise alternative courses of action (8)

growth/therapy group: group whose goals are to help individuals cope with issues, recover from a crisis or trauma, or resolve personal concerns (8)

haptics: the study of communicating via touch (3)

hasty generalization: reaching a conclusion without enough evidence to support it (11)

hasty generalization fallacy: an argument based on too few cases or examples to support a conclusion (11)

hearing: vibrations of sound waves on our eardrums; the impulses are then sent to the brain (5)

hidden agendas: unspoken goals and visions for the group that can get in the way of progress or take a group in a direction other than the one it has explicitly stated (8)

hidden window: information that you understand about yourself but are not willing to share with others (6)

high-context culture: culture in which people emphasize direct and literal communication (6)

high self-monitors: individuals who are acutely aware of their self-expressions and identity management behavior (2)

humane orientation: the degree to which individuals in organizations or societies encourage and reward individuals for being fair, altruistic, friendly, generous, caring, and kind to others (9)

hyperpersonal communication: communication that occurs when individuals express themselves more freely in a mediated channel than in a face-to-face interaction (6)

hypothetical example: an instance that did not take place but could have (11)

identity: social categories that we and others identify as important characteristics of who we are (2)

identity management: process of altering our own behaviors in order to shape others' impressions of who we are (2)

illustrator: nonverbal behavior that reinforces spoken words (3)

immediate action: when our goal as a speaker is to encourage an audience to engage in a specific behavior or take a specific action (14)

impromptu speech: speech that you have not planned or prepared in advance (12)

independent couple: couple who holds less traditional views of family roles and expectations (6)

individualistic culture: culture in which individuals make their own decisions, take responsibility for their actions, and are self-sufficient (6)

inductive reasoning: a process of reasoning that uses specific instances, or examples, to make a claim about a general conclusion (11)

inflection: manipulation of pitch to create certain meanings or moods (12)

informal role: role that is not formally assigned to individuals in the group (8)

initiation step: step involving the first set of interactions made between people (6)

informative speech: speech that communicates knowledge and understanding about a process, an event, a place or person, an object, or a concept (13)

informative speaking environments: environments in which a speaker has expertise or knowledge that an audience needs but does not already have (13)

insensitive listener: listener who pays attention to the content or literal meaning of the message without attending to the relationship level of the meaning (5)

insulated listener: listener who purposefully avoids listening to specific pieces of information (5)

internal preview: statement in the body of your speech that details what you plan to discuss next (10)

internal summary: statement in the body of your speech that summarizes a point you have already discussed (10)

integrating step: step consisting of two individuals merging their social circles and organizing their daily activities around each other (6)

intensifying step: step when there is an increase in communication, intimacy, and connectedness (6)

interdependent couple: couple who shares traditional views or marriage and family life, activities, and interests (6)

interpersonal communication: communication with other people that ranges from highly personal to highly impersonal (1)

interpersonal conflict: when two interdependent parties express different opinions, goals, or interests (7)

interpersonal relationship: relationship that involves the establishment of a personal connection with another person through the intentional use of communication (6)

interview: planned interaction with another person that is organized around inquiry and response, with one person asking questions while the other person answers them (11)

intimate partner violence: willful intimidation, physical assault, battery, sexual assault, or other abusive behavior perpetrated by an intimate partner against another (7)

intrapersonal communication: when people communicate internally with their own selves (1)

invisible communication: chronemics, olfactics, and haptics (3)

invitational environment: environment in which the speaker's highest priorities are to understand, respect, and appreciate the range of possible positions on an issue, even if those positions are quite different from his or her own (15)

invitational speaking: type of public speaking in which a speaker enters into a dialogue with an audience to clarify positions, explore issues and ideas, or articulate beliefs and values (15)

jargon: technical language used by professional groups (4)

kinesics: the study of bodily movements such a gestures, posture, eye contact, and facial expressions (3)

labels: words used to describe ourselves and others (2)

laissez-faire leader: leader who offers little or no guidance and allows individuals to make all decisions themselves, giving them as much freedom as possible (9)

language: a collection of symbols or words used to communicate with others (4)

leader: someone who guides or directs a group or activity with vision, charisma, and care (9)

leading questions: questions that urge people to respond in a particular way (9)

learning groups: groups that offer members a new skill or provide members with new information (8)

legitimate power: ability to control or influence others because of the formal position one holds in the group (8)

liking: determined by our body orientation, facial expression, use of touch, and proximity (3)

line graph: a graph that shows trends over time (14)

list: series of words or phrases that organize ideas one after the other (15)

listening: process of giving thoughtful attention to another person's words and understanding what you hear (5)

listening interference: anything that stops or hinders a listener from receiving a message (5)

listening style: preferred approach to understanding a message (5)

logic: system, principles, and arguments that make up a person's worldview (1)

looking-glass self: the way other people's perceptions of us define our own perceptions of ourselves (2)

love or intimacy touch: touch between family members or romantic partners (3)

low-context culture: culture in which people emphasize direct and literal communication (6)

low self-monitors: people who communicate without paying much attention to how others are responding to their messages (2)

main points: most important and comprehensive ideas you address in your speech (10)

major premise: the general principle that states a familiar and commonly accepted belief (11)

manuscript speech: speech that is read to an audience from a written text (12)

mass communication: communication designed and generated by media organizations to reach large audiences (1)

master statuses: significant positions a person occupies within society that affect that person's identity in almost all social situations (10)

mean: the average of a group of numbers (11)

median: the middle number in a series or set of numbers arranged in a ranked order (11)

minor premise: specific instance that helps establish the truth of the conclusion (11)

mode: the number that occurs most often in a set of numbers (11)

monochronic cultures: cultures in which people carefully schedule tasks, complete them one by one, and follow strict agendas (3)

monotone: a lack of variation in a speaker's rate, pitch, and volume; speaking without any change in pitch (3, 12)

Monroe's motivated sequence: step-by-step process used to persuade audiences by gaining attention, demonstrating a need, satisfying that need, visualizing beneficial results, and calling for action (14)

moves toward friendship: when people begin to self-disclose in small amounts (6)

multiple perspectives pattern: pattern of organization that allows the speaker to systematically address the many sides and positions of an issue before opening up the speech for dialogue with an audience (15)

narrative: a story that recounts or foretells real or hypothetical events (11)

narrative organization: organizational pattern that uses one or more stories to construct an argument; narratives can be brief or extended (14)

nascent friendship: time when people interact on a personal level, choose to participate in a range of activities with another, and let down their guard in communication (6)

noise: things that interfere with the transmission and reception of a message (1)

nonverbal communication: the process of conveying meaning without using the spoken word (3)

norms: patterns of behavior that are expected of individuals and seen as correct or even necessary in specific situations (8)

olfactics: the use of our sense of smell to gather information (3)

open questions: questions that give people freedom to answer in a range of ways (9)

open window: information about yourself that is already known by you and others (6)

oral reports: presentations given by one or two of the group members who present a group's findings, conclusions, or proposals to other members of the group or to a larger audience (8)

organizational chart: chart that illustrates the structure of groups (14)

panel discussion: structured discussion among group members and facilitated by a moderator that takes place in front of an audience (8)

paralinguistics: the vocal aspects of nonverbal communication, such as rate, volume, pitch, and emphasis (3)

paraphrase: to provide a summary of another's testimony in the speaker's own words (11)

passive agreement: when the speaker's goal is to ask audience members to adopt a new position without asking them to act in support of that position (14)

pauses: hesitations and brief silences in speech or conversation (12)

peer testimony (lay testimony): testimony of someone who has firsthand knowledge of a topic (11)

people-oriented listener: listener who is concerned about the feelings and emotions of other people as well as the quality of interpersonal relationships (5)

perception: process of acquiring and interpreting information from sensory data (2)

perception checking: we consider a series of statements or questions to confirm (or challenge) our perceptions of others and their behaviors (2)

personal appearance: specific aspects of our appearance including facial features; skin color; hair color, length, and style; and body type; the way someone dresses, grooms, and presents her- or himself physically (3, 12)

personal testimony: one's own testimony used to convey a point (11)

persuasive speech: speech whose message attempts to change or reinforce an audience's thoughts, feelings, or actions (14)

phonology: the study of how sounds are used to communicate meaning (4)

physiological noises: things that are going on in our bodies (1)

picture graph: a graph that shows information in pictures or images (14)

pie graph: a graph that shows the relative proportions of parts of a whole (14)

pitch: highness or lowness of a speaker's voice (12)

polychronic cultures: cultures in which people take on several tasks at once and view time as flexible (3)

posture: how speakers position and carry their bodies (12)

power and assertiveness: measure the degree to which members of an organization or society expect and agree that power should be unequally shared or that individual assertiveness is valued (9)

power over: ability to control others and dictate the course of events (8)

power with: power of a strong individual in a group of equals, the power not to command, but to suggest and be listened to, to begin something and see it happen (8)

preview: brief overview of each of the main points in your speech (10)

primary dimensions: identity traits that we are born with and that are significant parts of who we are (2)

probing questions: questions that help people talk more about an issue or feeling (9)

problem-cause-solution organization: a pattern of organization that focuses on identifying a specific problem, the causes of that problem, and a solution to the problem (14)

problem-solution organization: an organizational pattern that focuses on persuading an audience that a specific problem exists and can be solved or minimized by a specific solution (14)

pronunciation: act of saying words correctly according to the accepted standards of a language (12)

proxemics: the use of space; use of space during communication (3, 12)

public or presentational communication: when one person gives a speech to other people, most often in a public setting (1)

pseudolistening: when listeners act like they are listening or pretend to be paying close attention to the message (5)

public dialogue: ethical and civil exchange of ideas and opinions among communities about topics that affect the public (10)

question of fact: question that addresses whether something is verifiably true or not (14)

questions of policy: question that addresses the best course of action or solution to a problem (14)

question of value: question that addresses the merit or morality of an object, action, or belief (14)

rate: speed at which we speak (12)

real example: an instance that has actually taken place (11)

real time: when people in a room together can speak and hear one another in the moment without needing computers, phones, or the like (9)

reciprocity: the mutual exchange of symbols and meanings; actions of interdependence or mutual respect; when people who help you later need help, you return the favor (1, 9)

red herring fallacy: irrelevant information inserted into an argument to distract an audience from the real issue (11)

referent: concept or thing the symbol represents (1)

referent power: ability to influence others because of an association with or respect for the people who hold power in the group (8)

reflected appraisal: the process of developing an image of who we are based on the way others describe us (2)

reflective-thinking method: six-step method for structuring a problem-solving and decision-making discussion (8)

regionalism: words or phrases common to particular geographical regions (4)

regulation: the process of controlling conversations and interactions with others (3)

relational messages: the parts of the communication that give us information about how we are or are not connected to another person (1)

relational stress: stress that occurs when there are interpersonal incompatibilities among group members based on differences in their personalities, communication styles, attitudes, and preferences (9)

relationship maintenance: process of keeping a relationship together through the use of mundane activities (6)

repetition: using the nonverbal signals that reproduce what is said verbally (3)

responsiveness: displaying positive facial expressions, posture, and gestures (3)

reward power: ability to give others what they seek or will benefit from for meeting the demands of the group or following the rules set by the group (8)

rhetorical question: question used for effect that audience members are not supposed to answer out loud but rather in their own minds (10)

role: expected and defined pattern of behavior carried out by an individual or individuals (8)

role-limited interaction: engaging in small talk and sharing only minimal amounts of information (6)

secondary dimensions: identities that we acquire, develop, or discard throughout our lives (2)

selective attention: process of consciously or unconsciously selecting sensory data to maintain our focus (2)

selective listening: when listeners only pay attention to particular parts or sections of a message (5)

self-concept: perception of who we are and what makes us unique as well as similar to others (2)

self-disclosure: intentional sharing of personal information that would not otherwise be known to others (6)

self-efficacy: person's belief that she or he can be flexible (1)

self-esteem: how we feel about ourselves based on perceptions of our own strengths and weaknesses (2)

self-fulfilling prophecy: to act in accordance to expectations (2)

self-monitoring: ability to observe one's own behaviors and communication and to see how they are affecting others (1)

semantics: the meaning of specific words (4)

semantic triangle of meaning: illustrates the ways people use or hear a symbol of word and attach a meaning to it (1)

separate couple: couple who is extremely autonomous (6)

sex: biological and genetic characteristics (6)

sexual arousal touch: the type of touching that conveys sexual meaning and stimulation (3)

sign: something that represents something else (11)

signpost: simple word or statement that indicates where you are in your speech or highlights an important idea (10)

silence: the lack of vocal sound (3)

single cause fallacy: when speakers assume a particular effect only has one cause (11)

slang: informal nonstandard vocabulary used by members of a co-culture or group who have similar interests, goals, or life experiences (4)

slippery slope fallacy: an argument in which a speaker claims that taking a first step in one direction will inevitably lead to undesirable further steps (11)

social comparison: comparing ourselves with others in order to determine our value or worth in relationship to those others (2)

social groups: formal or informal groups of individuals who gather to meet the personal, communal, and collective needs of people (8)

social or polite touch: part of an initial interaction, greeting, or informal ritual (3)

social-penetration theory: describes the variation in breadth and depth of self-disclosure in a relationship (6)

spatial pattern: a pattern of organization that allows you to address topics logically in terms of location or direction (13)

specific purpose: focused statement that identifies exactly what a speaker wants to accomplish with a speech (10)

speech about concepts: a speech about abstractions, things you cannot perceive with your senses—such as ideas, theories, principles, worldviews, or beliefs (13)

speech about events: a speech that describes or explains significant, interesting, or unusual occurrences (13)

speech about objects: a speech about anything that is tangible—that is, can be perceived by the senses (13)

speech about places and people: a speech that describes significant, interesting, or unusual places or people (13)

speech about processes: a speech that describes how something is done, how something comes to be what it is, or how something works (13)

speech to articulate a position: a speech in which a speaker invites an audience to explore an issue from the speaker's perspective (15)

speech to explore an issue: a speech in which a speaker attempts to engage an audience in a discussion about an idea, concern, topic, or plan of action (15)

speech topic: subject of your speech (10)

spotlighting: practice of highlighting a person's race, ethnicity, sex, sexual orientation, or physical disability (5)

stabilized friendship: when trust has been established, allowing friends to communicate fully, share private information, and establish additional relationship rules (6)

stage hogging: when people make the conversation about themselves instead of showing interest in the person who is talking (5)

stagnating: when couples have minimal interaction or shared activities (6)

standpoint: the perspectives from which a person views and evaluates society (2)

state or situational anxiety: apprehension about communicating with others in particular situations

statistics: numerical summaries of facts, figures, and research findings (11)

stereotype: broad generalization about a group of people based on limited exposure to an individual or members of that particular group (2)

substitution: when we rely on nonverbal codes instead of verbal ones (3)

summary: concise restatement of your main points at the end of your speech (10)

symbol: word, gesture, sound, image, or object that stands in for or represents something else (1)

symbolic interactionism: process of understanding our sense of self based on other's observations, judgments, and evaluations of our behavior (2)

sympathy: feeling sorry or pity for another (1)

symposium: public discussion in which several people each give speeches on different aspects of the same topic (8)

synchronous: message that is received in real time (6)

systematic desensitization: technique for reducing anxiety that involves teaching your body to feel calm and relaxed rather than fearful during your speeches (12)

syntax: the rules that govern word order (4)

task groups: problem-solving groups formed when individuals want to take on a job or solve an issue that is affecting them or those around them (8)

task stress: stress that consists of contrasting views and opinions among group members regarding the tasks at hand (9)

team: collections of individuals who come together to attempt to win something, to set a record, or be the best at some task or event (8)

team presentation: when several individual members of a group each present a different speech on a single topic (8)

terminating: when individuals in a couple make their separation final (6)

testimony: opinions or observations of others (11)

thesis statement: single declarative sentence that summarizes the main ideas, assumptions, or arguments you want to express in your speech (10)

thought (or reference): memory or past experiences people have with the words being communicated (1)

time-oriented listener: listener who views time as a commodity, does not want to have it wasted, and wants speakers to be clear, succinct, and to the point (5)

topical pattern: a pattern of organization that allows a speaker to address different aspects of a topic (13)

trait anxiety: apprehension about communicating with others in any situation (12)

transformative leader: leader who creates significant change in the life of people and organizations (9)

transitions: phrases that indicate you are finished with one idea and are moving to a new one (10)

two-sided message: message that addresses two sides of an issue, refuting one side to prove the other is better (14)

uncertainty avoidance: the extent to which members of an organization or society strive to avoid uncertainty by relying on social norms, rituals, and bureaucratic practices to alleviate the unpredictability of future events (9)

understand: to gain knowledge of a view or an idea (1)

unknown window: information about yourself that is yet to be discovered by you and others (6)

value: a person's idea of what is good, worthy, or important (10)

verbal clutter: extra words in sentences that do not add meaning (5)

virtual group: group of individuals who have never met one another in person, but communicate regularly through electronic means (8)

virtual meetings: meetings that take place via electronic means such as Skype or teleconferencing or other electronic media that can bring people together across distances (9)

visual communication system: includes the codes of kinesics, proxemics, and artifacts (3)

visualization: a process in which you construct a mental image of yourself giving a successful speech (12)

visual listener: listener who needs to see something in order to understand it (5)

vocal cues: aspects of the human voice that create rhythm or musical flow (3)

vocalized pauses: the use of filler words or sounds such as *er, um,* and *uh* (3, 12)

vocal variety: changes in the volume, rate, and pitch of a speaker's voice that affect the meaning of the words delivered (12)

volume: loudness of a speaker's voice (12)

waning friendship: friendship that experiences a breach in trust, less quality or quantity of time spent together, or a violation in relational expectations (6)

workplace democracy: system of governance that truly values individuals' goals and feelings (9)

emotional, 10, 56
ethical, 5, 181
evolutionary nature of, 24
family and, 25
flexibility in, 19
hyperpersonal, 136
interactive model of, 13–14
interpersonal, 9, 89–81
intrapersonal, 9
invisible systems, 59, 66–71
irreversibility of, 24
linear model of, 11
mass, 11
models of, 11–17
nonverbal. *See* Nonverbal communication
one-way, 13–14
online mobility and, 24
open, 181
as process, 7
reasons to study, 21–26
relational, 14–15
self and, 25
self-concept and, 37
style and gender, 84
as symbolic, 6
temporal, 66–67
topics and, 85
transactional model of, 14
types of, 9–11
virtual, 91
visual systems of, 59
communication apprehension, 25, 319
communication climates, 160
communication style, 84
communication topics, 85
comparative advantages organization, 367–368
competence in communication, 18–21
competing conflict style, 148
competition, 218
complementation, 58
completeness, 344
compromise, 219
compromising conflict style, 148, 158
computer charts and graphs, 372
computer-mediated communication (CMC), 135–137, 155
concept speeches, 337–338
concern for others, 147
concern for self, 147
conclusions, 281
conclusions, speech, 258–259
condition of equality, 390
condition of self-determination, 390–391
condition of value, 390
confidence, 319–320
confirming others, 100
confirming statements, 160
conflict, 146
    accommodating style, 148
    avoiding style, 148
    civil approach to, 161–162

collaborating style, 148
competing style, 148
culture and, 152–153
gender and, 148–149, 153
gender roles and, 149
groups and teams and, 214, 218–219
international, 155–156
interpersonal relationships and, 146–147, 161–162
managing, 157–160
nature of, 147–160
resolution styles, 157–160
responses to, 147
styles of, 148
technology and, 153–156
conflict stage, 214
connectives, 250–251
connotative definitions, 7, 279
connotative meanings, 78
consensus, 220
Conte, Victor, 345
content messages, 25
content-oriented listeners, 107
contradiction, 59
contrast, 32
conversational style, 298
conversation and gender, 85, 88
"Cool Friends" (MacDonald and Greggans), 41
counterarguments, 375
couples, 123
Cousteau, Alexandra, 46, 171, 178, 304, 317, 393
Cousteau, Jacques, 178
Cousteau, Jan, 178
Cousteau, Philippe, 178
credibility, 254
critical listening, 114
Crossen, Cynthia, 275
Culhane, Thomas Taha Rassam, 22, 79, 135, 235
cultural competence, 83
culture
    backgrounds and experience, 13
    collectivism and individualism in, 192
    communication and, 8
    communication in groups and teams and, 191–193
    conflict and, 152–153
    definition of, 9
    dynamic patterns of, 9
    equality and inequality in, 192
    interpersonal relationships and, 140–141
    language and, 81–83
    leadership and, 207–208
    nonverbal communication and, 55
    perception and, 33
    self and, 33
    self-concept and, 37
    short- and long-term orientation, 193
    task and social orientation and, 192–193
    technology and, 154–155
    uncertainty and change in, 192
Cupach, William, 17

cyberbullying, 137–138
Cyberbullying Research Center, 137
cyberharassment, 138
cyberstalking, 138

D

Dalai Lama, 174, 312
databases, 267
Datta, Aparajita, 229, 353
Daubman, Kimberly, 41
debriefing talk, 90
decision making
    by consensus, 221
    in groups and teams, 188–191
decoding, 12
deductive reasoning, 281–282
defensive listening, 104
definitions, 279
deliberation, 219
democratic leadership, 202–203, 205
demonstrations, 256
denotative definitions, 6, 279
denotative meanings, 78
Department of Homeland Security (DHS), 49
depth of self-disclosure, 132
de Rothschild, David, 329
devil's advocate, 191
Dewey, John, 188
dialect, 307–308
dialogue, 230
Diaz, Luis (DJ Cipha Sounds), 92
Dickey, Derrick, 122
Digital Freedom: How Much Can You Handle? (Batra), 184
digital generation gap, 153
Dilemma, the, 95
Ding, Jacob Deng, 30
direct quotations, 279
disagreements, 17
disconfirming statements, 160
dissolution stage, 214
distance, 162–163
Dole, Elizabeth, 92
domestic violence. *See* intimate partner violence
Domestic Violence Awareness Project, 167
"Don't Touch" (2009), 69
dos Santos, Feliciano, 75
doublespeak, 81
Downey, Raymond, 202
Downtown Dog Rescue, 335
Druskat, Vanessa Urch, 206–207
dyads, 9
dynamic patterns of culture, 9
dysfunctional roles, 187

E

Earle, Sylvia, 244
Edwards, Elizabeth, 93
Edwards, John, 93